OUT NOW!

# OUT NOW!

## A Participant's Account
## of the American Movement
## Against the Vietnam War

**FRED HALSTEAD**

MONAD PRESS / NEW YORK

Library of Congress Catalog Card Number 78-059265
ISBN: 0-913460-47-8 (cloth); 0-913460-48-6 (paper)
Manufactured in the United States of America

First Edition, 1978


Published by Monad Press for the Anchor Foundation


Distributed by:
Pathfinder Press
410 West Street
New York, N.Y. 10014

# Contents

# Preface

President Lyndon Baines Johnson characterized the fighting in Vietnam as "real war" in midsummer 1965.* However, the beginning of the Second Indochina War, in which the United States was a central protagonist, is usually set at 1960. This book is an account of the resistance that grew up among the American people against that war. It covers events from 1960 to 1975.

I was not a detached observer of these events but an active opponent of the government's intervention in Southeast Asia from the beginning, a partisan of the antiwar movement, centrally involved in its activities. What is more, I was a spokesperson for one of the distinct political tendencies within the movement and took part in the various disputes over policy that shaped it.

In writing this book I do not pretend to have been neutral in these controversies. But I have tried to get the facts straight—even when they didn't serve my preconceptions—and present as accurately as possible the views of those with whom I did not necessarily agree. The contest of ideas was an important factor in the birth and growth of the antiwar movement and will no doubt be an indispensable part of sorting out its lessons.

This book is a contribution to the history of the antiwar movement by a participant, not a definitive or all-inclusive account. That would take many volumes, and scholarship and resources far beyond my command. It is an inside story based on the vantage point I enjoyed in the successive national antiwar coalitions, the major mass demonstrations, and many of the decisive polemics. At the same time it should be remembered that the movement involved millions of Americans, thousands of dedicated activists, hundreds of organizations, and a multitude of local, national, and international events. Only a small portion of all that could be related in this narrative.

*New York Times, July 29, 1965.

When this work was begun in 1974 the events seemed fresh in mind and I thought I could rely largely on memory. I soon found, however, that memory plays tricks and has to be checked against harder sources and refreshed as to context. What is more, as I began to do this, different vantage points than my own came into play, and I began to realize that there was more to the story than met my eye at the time.

In telling the story I made use of some books, but there was very little such secondary source material available. The story had to be largely reconstructed from primary sources, including personal interviews and letters from participants to the author, but mainly from documents of the time, including minutes of meetings, position papers, letters circulated among activists, leaflets, movement manuals, and inner organizational memos and reports.

Fortunately it was common within this very open movement for such documents to be copied and distributed to leading activists. I therefore had access to much of this material as it was produced, and early, at the insistent urging of Pat Quinn of the staff of the State Historical Society of Wisconsin, began saving some and sending more to the society at Madison, which was also collecting from other sources.

So in writing this book I was able to make use of extensive files at Madison as well as my own collection. Other participants kindly made available copies of documents from their own files. In addition I made use of the smaller collections on this movement at the Library of Social History in New York, the Tamiment Collection of the New York University Library, and the Bancroft Library at the University of California at Berkeley.

The author's collection has been donated to the State Historical Society of Wisconsin. Part of the collection is organized by chapters of this book and contains copies of unpublished documents cited in the footnotes and designated "copy in author's files." Since the library prefers not to deal with tape recordings, the taped interviews remain in my possession.

As a general rule in this book sources are cited in footnotes only for direct quotation. The rest is my own responsibility, as are any errors.

Fred Halstead
Los Angeles
March 1978

# A Note on the History
## of the Indochina Wars

The area of Southeast Asia now organized as the independent states of Vietnam, Cambodia, and Laos was a colony known as French Indochina when the Second World War began in Europe in 1939. With the fall of France in 1940 the French colonial regime in Indochina declared allegiance to Vichy, the government the Nazis set up in southern France. The colonial administration was therefore affiliated through World War II with a power friendly to the German-Japanese Axis.

Japan occupied Indochina in 1940 and ruled through the French administration for most of the Second World War. In March 1945, following the ouster of the German armies from France and the fall of the Vichy regime, the Japanese occupation overthrew the French officials in Indochina and declared Vietnam independent under Emperor Bao Dai, who cooperated with the Japanese. The formal independence of Vietnam dates from that time, although the country was held by Japanese troops until their surrender in August 1945.

Since 1940 there had been an indigenous guerrilla resistance in Vietnam to both the Vichy French colonialists and the Japanese invaders. It had been supplied in part by the Anglo-American Allies. Its name was the Viet Minh (League for the Independence of Vietnam) and its leader was Ho Chi Minh, head of the underground Indochinese Communist Party. In retrospect, it is ironic that the first American troops in Indochina were a handful sent there along with U.S. supplies to aid Ho Chi Minh in connection with the Allied efforts against the Japanese.

By August 1945 the Viet Minh forces were in control of much of the countryside; then, with the Japanese surrender to the Allies, a spontaneous popular revolution swept Vietnam's cities on August 19, 1945, which brought the Viet Minh to power. The new government, a coalition between the Indochinese Communist Party and various nationalist capitalist parties, proclaimed the Democratic Republic of Vietnam (DRV) and issued a declaration of independence modeled in part on the one drafted in the American Revolution in 1776.

Pledging itself to uphold the Potsdam agreements drafted by the Allied chieftains at the end of the war, the DRV welcomed British troops into Saigon at the beginning of September. Important sections of the mass movement in the south opposed this decision. In particular the Vietnamese Trotskyists, who had been part of the resistance and were strong in the Saigon area, warned that the British would come as conquerors and not as friends. The Communist Party on September 14 ordered the disarming and arrest of the Trotskyists, many of whom were then shot without trial. The British, once established in Saigon, attacked the independence forces and restored power in that area of the country to the French colonial regime, now controlled by the de Gaulle government in Paris.

Throughout most of 1946 an uneasy truce was maintained between the Ho Chi Minh government in the north and the French forces in the south. In March 1946 the Viet Minh signed an agreement with France which recognized the DRV—in the north only—as a semiautonomous part of the French Union. But this agreement authorized the landing of French troops in Hanoi. In November 1946 the French commander in Hanoi ordered a massive bombardment of Haiphong harbor and by the end of the year the Viet Minh had been driven into the countryside. There they began a prolonged guerrilla war against the French.

According to the Pentagon Papers, the decision by the administration of President Harry S Truman to give military aid to France in her colonial war against the Viet Minh "directly involved" the United States in Vietnam and "set" the course of American policy.[1]

The United States supported and supplied the French counter-revolutionists in Indochina, with particularly heavy aid following the victory of the Chinese revolution in 1949. Nevertheless, the

1. Cited in Neil Sheehan's introduction to *The Pentagon Papers as Published by the New York Times* (New York: Bantam, 1971), p. xi.

French were decisively defeated by the Viet Minh in 1954 at the famous battle of Dienbienphu.

The First Indochina War—that between the Viet Minh and the French—ended with a compromise negotiated in 1954 at Geneva. Under its terms the French quit the northern half of the country, above the seventeenth parallel, leaving it to the Democratic Republic of Vietnam. The southern part of the country was to be administered by an interim government under Bao Dai for two years, during which time, according to the Geneva Accords, the French would depart. Then elections were to be held to reunify the country. This surprising concession of territory to foreign influence, after the crushing defeat administered to the French forces at Dienbienphu, came—as the Pentagon Papers later confirmed—as the result of heavy pressure on the Vietnamese delegation at Geneva from Molotov and Chou En-lai, the representatives respectively of the Soviet Union and China.[2]

The French did depart on schedule, but their place was taken by the United States government, which moved in with massive military support to the South Vietnamese regime. Bao Dai was replaced by a pro-American puppet, Ngo Dinh Diem, who established a ruthless and corrupt dictatorship and refused to hold the elections promised for 1956.

Diem launched expeditions into the South Vietnamese countryside to reimpose the landlords who had been ousted by the guerrillas for siding with the Japanese or French during the resistance and the First Indochina War. The land-hungry peasants, many of them veterans of the Viet Minh, rose up and new guerrilla fighting broke out and spread.

By 1959 the United States had escalated its aid to Diem to the point where American combat personnel were being dispatched to South Vietnam under the guise of "advisers" to the South Vietnamese army. At this juncture the Democratic Republic of Vietnam, or North Vietnam, began to aid the resistance in the South. The first American servicemen were killed in July 1959. In 1960 the resistance formed the National Liberation Front (NLF), which its enemies dubbed the "Viet Cong."

The Second Indochina War was on. It lasted fifteen years. Here is how the opposition to it in the United States unfolded.

2. *United States-Vietnam Relations, 1945-1967* (Washington: U.S. Government Printing Office, 1971) (a more extensive version of the Pentagon Papers), Book 1, Part III, C., pp. C-1, C-2.

# 1

# The Old Peace Movement

A peace movement of sorts existed in the United States in 1960 but it had nothing to do with the war in Vietnam. It is necessary to recall that in the early 1960s the war was not a central issue in American life. It was something reported only occasionally and, as far as the general population was concerned, opposed only by the more consistent pacifists and the more conscious radicals.[1] Even within the peace movement, however, the weight of the anticommunist hysteria was so heavy that it was hard to see how serious resistance to the Vietnam venture could develop.

The word "hysteria" is used here advisedly and not as an epithet. What was involved was not criticism of policies of the Soviet government, or revulsion at the crimes of Stalinism, or honest differences of opinion or ideology. It was a question of reading the "communists" out of the human race. You could drop bombs on them and feel no regret. In this country "communists" were refused the elementary right to participate equally with others in social and political life. By "communists" was meant anyone belonging to the so-called totalitarian left, a term coined in Social Democratic circles and applied to any tendency that considered the Bolshevik revolution of 1917 a good thing.

The old peace movement was mainly concerned with nuclear disarmament. Its central demand was to stop nuclear tests, which

---

1. In some countries the word "pacifist" is applied to anyone involved in a peace movement. In the United States the usage is generally much narrower, applying only to those who renounce all wars and who refuse to bear arms even in self-defense. In this book the word is used in the latter sense throughout.

were poisoning the atmosphere. Common in the early 1960s were demonstrations of women, often organized by Women Strike for Peace. These were small demonstrations, usually numbering only a few dozen participants—the movement did not have tens of thousands then. They would carry signs depicting milk bottles showing how much strontium 90 was getting into the milk.

The coalition of liberals and pacifists that organized the larger actions demanding nuclear disarmament and an end to testing excluded "communists" as such. It also excluded other peace issues such as the war in Vietnam, which were embarrassing to the liberal Democrats and others within the Establishment that the movement was trying to influence.

The organizations that dominated the movement were the Committee for a SANE Nuclear Policy and Turn Toward Peace.[2] They insisted on excluding the embarrassing radicals and the embarrassing issues. By threatening to pull out of the coalition they generally forced others into line.

Other groups in this coalition were the traditional religious pacifist organizations like the American Friends Service Committee and the Fellowship of Reconciliation, Women Strike for Peace, the much older Women's International League for Peace and Freedom, the Student Peace Union, the War Resisters League, and the newer, radical, civil-disobedience-oriented Committee for Nonviolent Action.

Generally the only radical political groups accepted as part of this coalition were those in the Social Democratic milieu. These included the Socialist Party–Social Democratic Federation and its youth group, the Young People's Socialist League (YPSL), as well as Students for a Democratic Society. SDS was then the youth affiliate of a very respectable Social Democratic foundation, the League for Industrial Democracy.

The more consistent pacifists and some of the more militant participants in this coalition—as well as the excluded radical groups—opposed the war in Vietnam in their own names. But they were each too small to do much more than make the record. A united front of all these groups might have done something more effective, but such unity was virtually forbidden at the time.

---

2. Turn Toward Peace was founded in 1961 ostensibly as a coordinating center for joint activities of some sixty-six groups, including SANE. In actuality it functioned as just one more peace group with policies very close to SANE's.

The youth radicalization of the 1960s did not begin around Vietnam or within the old peace movement. Nevertheless, the change in mood was reflected in some of the activities of groups which were a part of the old coalition. One of these occurred May 3, 1960, in New York City, during the annual air-raid drill. Once a year in those days in major cities like New York everybody had to get off the streets and go into subways or "shelter" buildings to practice an air-raid drill. It was against the law not to take cover, and the law was enforced. The radical pacifists had organized resistance to these drills by standing outside after the alarm sounded. They would be arrested. At first these demonstrations involved handfuls, but in 1960 the demonstrations grew far beyond the number of people who organized them. That year, in New York's City Hall Park, a thousand people, myself among them, gathered to express solidarity with the demonstrators. When the alarm sounded, the whole crowd stayed in place. So the police picked up the few who more or less got in line to be arrested—their vans would hold no more—and the rest of us defied the drill and got away with it. The great bulk of this crowd had come with no intention of committing civil disobedience but found a strength in their numbers and in the mood that prevailed. This mood was not connected with any particular war—no doubt some of the people there had never heard of Vietnam. It was a mood of opposition to the repressive and hysterical atmosphere of the cold war. The crowd was overwhelmingly young.

A few days later, on May 13, the famous outburst took place at the San Francisco hearings of the House Un-American Activities Committee (HUAC—later changed to the House Committee on Internal Security). This event also had nothing directly to do with the Vietnam War. It was a hearing to which a number of academic figures had been subpoenaed, a routine occurrence during the time of Senator Joseph McCarthy and for some years after he was censured. But on this occasion the hearing was jammed with hundreds of students protesting the thought-control atmosphere the hearing was designed to promote. Many radicals were pleasantly surprised at this news that young people were defying the norms of the "silent generation."

Just a week later, on May 19, 1960, the Committee for a SANE Nuclear Policy held a rally at Madison Square Garden in New York. The meeting was entitled "A Salute to the Summit," and had been planned to support a positive outcome of a meeting between the U.S. and the USSR to work out an agreement to stop atmospheric nuclear testing.

A few days before the Garden event the summit meeting collapsed. An American U-2 spy plane had been shot down spying over the Soviet Union. So the name of SANE's rally was not very appropriate, but the determination of the audience was all the greater.

Speakers included Eleanor Roosevelt, Governor G. Mennen Williams of Michigan, United Auto Workers President Walter Reuther, and Alf Landon, the 1936 Republican presidential candidate. The rhetoric was distinctly moderate. Norman Thomas, the seventy-six-year-old leader of the Socialist Party–Social Democratic Federation, advocated a unilateral U.S. ban on testing, but most of the other speakers insisted on "adequate inspection" guarantees. Since this was the very point the U.S. State Department used to excuse the continuation of tests, these speakers were heckled by a large part of the audience. The rank and file, it turned out, was angrier and further to the left on this issue than those on the platform.

The head of SANE at that time—formally one of its cochairmen—was Norman Cousins, editor of the *Saturday Review* and the leading figure in the right wing of the old peace movement. But the person who had organized the promotional work on the rally was a SANE staff member, Henry Abrams, who was a veteran radical. In his fifties at the time of the rally, he was familiar with and respected by many people in left-wing circles, including the Communist Party. There was no secret about this. It was one reason a man like Abrams could be an effective organizer in the New York City of the time.

The members of SANE's governing board did not really object to getting work for building a rally, or other activities, out of radicals of various sorts, so long as they didn't fight for a position different from that of those in control of the organization and so long as no one made an issue of it. Actually, Abrams, who by all accounts had done a remarkable job on promotion, had no say in the political line or choice of speakers at the rally.

As preparations for the Garden event were under way, Abrams was subpoenaed by the Senate Internal Security Subcommittee, the upper house counterpart of HUAC. Senator Thomas J. Dodd (Democrat—Connecticut), an all-out advocate of the continuation of nuclear tests, was the subcommittee's acting chairman. Clearly Dodd was not trying to increase SANE's effectiveness in its campaign against nuclear testing.

Abrams took the Fifth Amendment in answer to questions about his political views and associations at a so-called closed hearing of the subcommittee May 13. In those days to exercise the constitutional right to refuse to testify against oneself in hearings of this kind was still, in the minds of many, tantamount to a confession of treason. Nevertheless, it was common to take the Fifth Amendment because, among other reasons, once you answered political questions about yourself you could be jailed for contempt of Congress if you then refused to answer questions about anyone else, even associates from the distant past. The committee would get more names, issue more subpoenas, and so on. That's why the analogy with the Salem witch-hunts was applied.

SANE cochairman Cousins tried to mollify Dodd by cooperating with him. By coincidence Cousins was a neighbor and personal friend of Dodd in Connecticut. He went to Washington to talk to the senator. Two days before the rally Cousins fired Abrams.

On May 25, just six days after the rally, Dodd made a Senate speech in which he took credit for the firing of Abrams, disclosing that he had told Cousins: "I don't want to release this material twenty-four hours before your meeting." Dodd also claimed that Cousins had "offered to open the books of the organization to the Subcommittee and to cooperate with it in every way."[3]

In the same speech Dodd pressed hard on the opening yielded by Cousins, declaring: "On the basis of the evidence that has come to me I do not believe the Committee for a Sane Nuclear Policy has taken the necessary measures to create a climate that is inhospitable to Communist infiltration." He said SANE would be acceptable only "if they would purge their ranks ruthlessly of Communist infiltration, and if they would clearly demarcate their own position from that of the Communists. First by stressing the need for adequate inspection."

Actually, SANE's official position could not be clearly demarcated from that of the U.S. government any more than from that of the Soviet government. The leaders of SANE tied their program to summit dealings, bringing pressure for a mutually agreed test ban. The Soviet government had already agreed to

3. *Congressional Record*, Senate, May 25, 1960.

halt atmospheric tests if the U.S. would do likewise. The argument Washington gave for refusing this offer was a demand for "adequate inspection" guarantees. Just what "adequate" meant was anybody's guess, since in any case atmospheric tests could not be hidden. SANE specifically avoided a demand for unilateral halting of the tests. It was reduced to calling for a more reasonable attitude by U.S. negotiators.

In this context Dodd's ultimatum in effect was that SANE could win acceptability only by becoming an apologist for the very position it was organized to change.

SANE did not go that far, but its board upheld the firing of Abrams. It was later revealed that members of the board had held an informal meeting at which a staff member of the Senate subcommittee was present and a purge of SANE was discussed.

This didn't satisfy the subcommittee, which publicly attacked SANE, released the Abrams testimony from the "closed" hearing, and announced the subpoenaing of thirty-eight additional persons associated with SANE.

In the course of this controversy a number of other SANE staff members quit in protest over the collusion with the subcommittee. When Youth SANE demanded Abrams's reinstatement the group was suspended by the adult organization's leadership. SANE survived, but it was badly compromised, particularly with young people beginning to become active in the peace movement.

Two articles analyzing this crisis in SANE were written that year by A. J. Muste, sometimes called the dean of American pacifists. In the second, published in the November 1960 issue of the pacifist magazine *Liberation,* he said:

> We feel that what has happened in SANE is tragic, partly because we cannot shake off the conviction that it need not have happened. Everything in our political life shows that we are at a turning point and that Americans sense it.

Muste was not given to overstatement, and he was no superficial commentator. His long career—he was then seventy-four—had substantially contributed to all the major movements for social change on the American scene since the First World War, including labor, civil rights, and antiwar. He had himself been instrumental—together with Cousins and Norman Thomas—in launching SANE in 1957, although in 1960 he was not part of its leadership.

If SANE had stood up against the Dodd attack, defending Abrams and the movement generally against cold-war congressional inquisitions, said Muste, it

might have called forth a tremendous response; might have put new heart and courage into many people, especially young people, fed up with conformism and apathy; and might have led to the development of a more radical movement against nuclear war and war preparations. Such a movement would be invulnerable to attempts at Communist control, if such were made.

The very fact that Muste—a consistent civil libertarian—felt constrained to put the argument in those terms shows the heavy weight of the atmosphere of anticommunism that still existed. But although Muste was here appealing to the milieu of the SANE leaders, red-baiting was not his point. He was warning them that they had missed an opportunity to inspire the radicalizing youth and that they were leaving a vacuum.

He had stated this in so many words in his first article on the SANE crisis, published in the July-August 1960 *Liberation:*

The problem of the thirties and forties was that the CP was relatively powerful and *it* was setting up peace fronts which *it* controlled. It drew people into them on false pretenses. I combatted this policy. As I have already said, I am opposed to any united front with the CP now. But the peace movement in this country today is not being built by the CP. SANE, for example, is in the hands of American liberals and pacifists. People who in any genuine sense want to work for peace have to accept this fact, and be governed by it. The fact may draw, among others, people who formerly belonged to CP fronts. It also means that they have "nowhere else to go." This is to say, the moment they try to establish "control" over such a movement or to divert it from the line of firm opposition to nuclear war preparation and war-like moves by *any* nation, they render themselves impotent, for the movement will simply evaporate.

They are impotent, provided that there is a vigorous, militant peace movement, which is clearly against U.S. nuclear war policy and therefore combats the Congressional political-inquisition agencies. In the absence of such a movement there would be a vacuum. I am not sure that such a vacuum could be filled, but if it were it would be by elements which profited by the default of American liberals, non-Stalinist radicals and pacifists.

In his second SANE-crisis article, Muste emphasized his own

across-the-board pacifist approach, one reason he was at the time opposed to a united front including the CP, which was uncritical of Soviet nuclear tests. In the process he touched on the essential reason for the liberal default:

> In large measure, the liberals on whom SANE seeks to build still think in nationalistic terms and cling to the "deterrence" concept with all that this implies. They have not arrived at the stage of radical criticism of the U.S. politico-economic regime and realization of the profound changes that will have to take place in it, if nuclear war is in fact to be averted. . . . In other words for them the "enemy" is still over there. Even if they agree intellectually, they are in a sense incapable of "feeling" that the "enemy" is *equally* in the Congressional committees, the Pentagon, the Atomic Energy Commission, and other agencies of the Cold War and nuclear politics over here.

With regard to the Vietnam War, the default by the liberals—including many of those leading the old peace movement—would continue to the point where Muste himself would become a vigorous supporter of a nonexclusive united front. But that was later.

*          *          *

Between 1960 and 1965 a radicalization of some of the youth in the U.S. began to appear, not around Vietnam at first, but around two other issues: the Cuban revolution and the civil rights struggle in the South. Cuban dictator Fulgencio Batista was overthrown by Castro's guerrillas on New Year's Day, 1959. The first Black student sit-in occurred at a Woolworth dime store lunch counter in Greensboro, North Carolina, on February 1, 1960.

From the time the Cubans nationalized their major industries in 1960 through the Cuban missile crisis of 1962, the U.S. perspective for military attack on Cuba was hardly a secret. The opening gambit in such an attack was launched by CIA-organized Cuban counterrevolutionaries in April 1961. It was crushed at the Bay of Pigs before the beachhead could be established. Adlai Stevenson, perhaps the country's most widely respected liberal Democratic figure, besmirched his own reputation in the eyes of many admirers by repeating in the United Nations the cover story for that affair, later revealed by the administration itself to have been pure invention. What hurt young liberals the most was that this lie obviously had nothing to do with keeping information from "the enemy"—which knew all too well exactly what was really going on—but was designed to fool the American people. (One Stevenson admirer who was shocked by this development was a young cub reporter for the Cincinnati *Post & Times-Star* named Jerry Rubin.)

In the U.S. a series of educational meetings and demonstrations were held opposing intervention in Cuba. These were organized mainly by the Fair Play for Cuba Committee. This was, in a very real sense, an antiwar movement, but one which the old peace movement refused to endorse. Radical pacifist Dave Dellinger, however, played a prominent role in these activities.

At first the Cuban revolution received widespread sympathy in the U.S., particularly among the youth, but after U.S. holdings were nationalized in 1960 and the full force of the anticommunist campaign was unleashed against the Castro regime, support by adult liberals tended to fall away. The Fair Play for Cuba Committee became a united front of American radicals and prorevolutionary Cuban residents of the U.S. (The political complexion of the Cuban-American community reversed itself over the next few years as many of those favoring the revolution returned to their homeland and many of those against it emigrated to the U.S.)

The Fair Play committee established a precedent for united activity of several sectors of the American left that had not been on speaking terms for many years. For example, at a demonstration of 5,000 in New York's Union Square protesting the Bay of Pigs invasion in 1961, two of the main speakers were Peter Camejo of the Trotskyist Young Socialist Alliance and Mike Stein of Advance, a youth group associated with the Communist Party. It was the presence on the scene of a new and broader force—in this case the Cuban Americans—that impelled this unity. (Both Camejo and Stein would later play significant roles in the anti-Vietnam War movement.)

The Southern civil rights struggle was sparked by college students and gave birth to the Student Nonviolent Coordinating Committee (SNCC), originally affiliated with Martin Luther King, Jr.'s Southern Christian Leadership Conference, and based mainly on Black campuses in the South. There was widespread support by Northern students, including picketing of stores in the Woolworth chain. In addition some Northern students and sympathizers went South on such activities as Freedom Rides, SNCC community organizing projects, and the Mississippi summer voter registration campaigns.

A central issue in the Berkeley Free Speech Movement (FSM), which burst forth in the fall 1964 semester, was the right of students to carry out support activities on the Berkeley campus of the University of California for the Southern civil rights struggle. Jack Weinberg, later a member of the Independent Socialist Club, was arrested for setting up a table for the Congress of Racial Equality (CORE). Several thousand students surrounded the police car in which Weinberg was under arrest and for two days used its roof as a stage for speeches while Weinberg sat inside. (Weinberg was the author of the famous comment, "Don't trust anyone over thirty," and later played a part in the Berkeley Vietnam Day Committee.)

By the end of 1964, then, there existed a few thousand young people who had already begun to consider and adopt radical ideas and who had become activists to one degree or another around the Southern civil rights struggle and/or the Cuban revolution. These youth were ready, willing, and able to enter a struggle against the Vietnam War, but they could not do so through the old peace movement coalition, which was still dominated by the shibboleths of the cold war.

*          *          *

The rebellion of Youth SANE in 1960 was another sign of a different mood among young people. The direct witch-hunt attack had the effect of making a significant number of people stand up against it rather than run for cover, which had been the pattern of the 1950s. The youth turned off by SANE's attitude—this involved dozens, not thousands—gravitated toward the activities of the Fair Play for Cuba Committee, the Student Peace Union, or SDS. A not insignificant percentage of these youth were themselves children of "old left" radicals—"red diaper babies" they were sometimes called in movement circles. While they didn't necessarily agree with their parents they did have an edge on the general population in recognizing the hysterical nature of the witch-hunt.

They knew their parents were all-too-ordinary people, not the sinister conspirators painted by such sterling characters as Senator Dodd (later proven to have been embezzling money at the very time of his anticommunist crusade). What is more they did not share their parents' terror of the witch-hunt, and in this they were more typical of their generation. Within the peace movement itself Youth SANE tended to be replaced by the Student Peace Union. SPU was founded in 1959 by pacifists, but in the early 1960s its national office was dominated by members of the Young People's Socialist League, who held what is known in radical circles as the "Third Camp" position.

According to this theory there are not one but two imperialist "camps" dividing the world between them. The first was composed of the advanced capitalist countries of the United States, Western Europe, and Japan. The second, according to this view, was the bloc of postcapitalist countries represented by the Soviet Union and China, which these people held equally to blame for the cold war. A "Third Camp" was supposed to be formed in opposition to the other two. In practice most of those who held this theory were neutral on the side of the capitalist world.

The SPU was very small in 1960, but grew rapidly until 1962. It was formally nonsectarian; members did not have to belong to any particular political tendency. It also had some orientation toward action, holding demonstrations from time to time. Students who wanted some peace activity on a campus could constitute themselves an SPU chapter without much formality.

SPU reached its peak in 1962 when it took the lead in organizing a demonstration of some 5,000 in Washington protesting atmospheric testing. Control of this event had, however, been taken over by Turn Toward Peace, which was concerned lest the youth raise embarrassing issues. The demonstration was held near the White House, and President Kennedy sent hot coffee outside for some of the participants, a gesture of goodwill that would have been inconceivable had the issues of U.S. intervention in Cuba or Vietnam been raised.

At its height SPU went into a crisis over the attempt of its national office to impose the "Third Camp" position on the activities of the chapters. The SPU leaders insisted that demonstrations on the issue of Cuba or Vietnam blame Russia and China equally with the U.S. Virtually all the newly radicalizing youth would agree that the Soviet Union had been wrong in crushing the revolt in Hungary in 1956, but that it was the U.S. that was at fault in trying to put down revolutions in Cuba and

Vietnam. The SPU position made no sense to them.

During the Cuban missile crisis in October 1962 an emergency ad hoc meeting was held at the Living Theatre in New York in which members of the traditional peace coalition sat in the same room with the excluded radicals and others to discuss a response. I was there and I remember that Bayard Rustin—who came with Muste—spoke with considerable effect against common action. The issue was not organizational rivalry, but a political position: The crisis, he argued, had been caused at least as much by Cuba, which had obtained missiles from the Soviet Union capable of reaching the U.S., as it was by President Kennedy, who threatened to bomb them and interdict Soviet ships on the way to Cuba unless Russia removed the missiles.

To Rustin, and some other pacifists, the question of Cuba's sovereign right to defend itself against U.S. invasion was irrelevant. The missiles were the essence of the matter.

My own position—and frankly, as a resident of the U.S. I was none too comfortable about the missiles—was that the cause of the crisis was the obvious U.S. intention to crush the Cuban revolution by force, that Cuban sovereignty had to be respected, and that it was the duty of Americans to center their protest on their own government. I reminded people that U.S. missiles had been pointed at Cuba all along. In addition, those of us who held this position were willing to agree that the others should express their own views in the coming demonstration through speakers and signs. But for Rustin and others, no association whatever with our "Hands Off Cuba" position was tolerable. The meeting failed.

Some of those present, however, adjourned to Hamish Sinclair's apartment and formed an ad hoc Committee to Halt World War Three. It sounds tendentious now, but considering what the Cuban missile crisis involved, it was not meant to be funny. It was an indication of the frustration in radical circles at the time.

This group, together with the Fair Play for Cuba Committee, called an emergency demonstration at the UN Plaza for Saturday, October 21. The old peace movement coalition meanwhile called a demonstration for Sunday. Then the Student Peace Union, even though it was accepted as a full participant in the Sunday event, also organized its own demonstration for the same place as the Saturday affair, insisting that the thrust had to be equal blame. Their slogan was: "U.S.-USSR, No War Over Cuba."

On Saturday the SPU leaders got there first. As the other group arrived—many of our signs said "Hands Off Cuba"—the SPU leaders insisted on separating the demonstrations. We set up a picket line with a chant, "One Line Against the War." Virtually all the 2,000 persons present joined a united demonstration. The SPU leaders were left alone on the sidelines. In essence, this is what happened to SPU nationally during this period.

The Sunday demonstration, which the radicals decided to join as well, was the largest ever held at the UN up to that time—10,000. But the radicals were strictly second-class citizens, excluded from the speakers' list and prohibited from carrying their own signs.

In 1963 the SPU national office further alienated the radicalizing youth by attacking Dagmar Wilson of Women Strike for Peace for defending nonexclusion. Subpoenaed by HUAC, Wilson had refused to take the road of the SANE leaders in 1960. She stood up to the committee, proudly declaring that WSP accepted the support and activity of anyone who shared its aims.

For a time members of the Young Socialist Alliance participated in SPU, where they advocated a different policy. In the March 1963 *Young Socialist*, YSA official Barry Sheppard wrote:

SPU will be able to get out of its present stagnation and crisis only if it again reaches out, to really begin to build SPU. SPU must remain as broad as possible. Red-baiting, exclusion, internal witch-hunts: they are the death of SPU. A healthy SPU will look for new members from all political groups and recruit rather than exclude. It will not insist that any members adopt any particular political position as long as they are for peace.

The then-very-small YSA had little effect on SPU at the time, but the same approach was later to carry the YSA to a central role in the anti–Vietnam War movement.

The Vietnam intervention became a public issue within the old peace movement coalition in 1963. The radical pacifists were themselves recruiting youth who reflected the new mood. These people were appalled at what the U.S. was doing in Vietnam and chafed under the agreements made with groups like SANE to keep the issue out of coalition actions. Symbolically, relations between two protégés of A. J. Muste—Bayard Rustin, who defended the old position, and Dave Dellinger, who sided with the youth—became increasingly strained.⁴

In the spring of 1963 a crack in the situation appeared at the traditional Easter Peace Walks sponsored by the old coalition in solidarity with the British Aldermaston "ban the bomb" marches. Shortly before Easter, Bertrand Russell, a key figure in the British Campaign for Nuclear Disarmament, issued a statement declaring that the U.S. was conducting a war of annihilation in Vietnam. The question of Vietnam was once again excluded from these Easter walks in the U.S., but many of the marchers—there were 6,000 this time in New York City—appeared wearing buttons that said, "I like Bertrand Russell." The rank and file was forced to express itself in this indirect manner. Some of the youth, however, took a different way.

The SPU was a part of the coalition and its officers were part of the exclusion agreement, but they didn't bother to take a vote in the chapters. The New York City off-campus chapter—it wasn't based at a university but took in high school students and a few college-age youth who were not students—decided to take up the Vietnam issue. Its members appeared in the Easter Peace Walk with signs against the Vietnam War.

These youth were halted and told to remove their signs as they entered the UN Plaza where the rally was held. Two of them, Bonnie and Debbie Weinstein, high school students and members of the YSA whom I knew, called me over and asked me what they should do. Although I had nothing to do with the organization of the event—indeed if I had tried to attend the organizing meetings I would probably have been excluded as a member of the "totalitarian left"—I waved the group on past the marshals.

There was no physical intimidation involved. (I was even carrying one of my children in my arm at the time.) But there was a moral effect. At first the marshals were furious, but when I asked them if they opposed the war in Vietnam they said yes. When I told them that a peace movement that doesn't speak out

---

4. It is important to note a distinction here between the Third Camp position and that of the pacifists. For the consistent pacifist like Muste, opposition to the use of violence by any nation or side in a struggle is a moral imperative. But this does not necessarily mean that pacifists do not take sides. The real difference between Rustin and Dellinger was not that either changed his position on violence, but that Rustin sided with the U.S. in Vietnam and Dellinger with the revolution.

against a war in which its own country is the aggressor is not much good, they agreed.

Those with the Vietnam signs proceeded to the wall at the back of the demonstration in full view of the crowd and speakers' stand, and held the signs high. Bayard Rustin was the chairman. He stopped the rally and insisted those signs be removed. The crowd sided with the signs, however, and Rustin's pleas went for naught. Similar incidents occurred in Chicago and Minneapolis where Easter Peace Walks were also held that year.

A. J. Muste was a speaker at the New York event. He devoted his speech to an effective denunciation of the U.S. intervention in Vietnam. I was often asked later if I thought Muste had changed his speech because of what happened in the crowd, or if he had planned to make that speech beforehand. I never asked him, but I'm reasonably sure he didn't change his speech.

Muste was a person of principle who would not hide his views on such an important question out of expediency. But he avoided faction fights like the plague, not out of lack of character, but because they offended his philosophy of reconciliation. In my opinion it was one of his few weaknesses. When there are real differences over fundamental questions it is not possible to reconcile everybody all the time. Muste knew that, of course, but he always seemed to try.

It was perfectly in character for him to have avoided an organized fight within the coalition and to have planned such a speech on that occasion, acting as an individual. He could get away with it because no one in the movement—not even Rustin, who did not lack gall—would presume to tell Muste what he should or should not say.

The fact that both Muste and the off-campus chapter of SPU chose the Easter Peace Walk of 1963 as the occasion to interject the Vietnam issue into the old peace coalition was in one sense purely coincidental. But in a more profound sense it was not. The old peace movement was already pregnant with the new, and Vietnam was a subject of sharp discussion within it from then on.

\*　　　　\*　　　　\*

The first wave of campus demonstrations against the war in Vietnam occurred in the fall of 1963 during a tour of the U.S. by Mme. Ngo Dinh Nhu, wife of the head of the South Vietnamese secret police and sister-in-law of President Diem. The Buddhist demonstrations against the regime in South Vietnam earlier that year had affected the American population. Mme. Nhu was notorious for—among other things—using the term "barbeque" to refer to the self-immolation of Buddhist monks protesting religious persecution by the ruling Catholic family.

The campus demonstrations on the occasion of her visit took place when she appeared at universities as a guest speaker. It is a gauge of the times—and of the influence of Francis Cardinal Spellman, who was one of Diem's sponsors—that no opposition appeared to Mme. Nhu's visit at Fordham University. At Columbia, however, a group of 300 jeered her.

The number of demonstrators at other campuses—several organized by SPU chapters—varied from a dozen at Chapel Hill, North Carolina, to several hundred at Madison, Wisconsin, and Ann Arbor, Michigan. At that time there were 14,000 U.S. military personnel acknowledged to be in Vietnam.

*          *          *

In the spring of 1964, when the number of U.S. troops in Vietnam had passed the 20,000 mark, one significant attempt was made by radical groups to mount a united-front protest against the Vietnam intervention. On March 13-15 a symposium on "Socialism in America" was held in New Haven sponsored by the Yale Socialist Union, the first group of its kind to appear on that campus in many years. Some 400 students from East Coast colleges attended and the program included spokespersons from all the major groups in the U.S. calling themselves socialist.

When it became clear that a majority of those present were anxious to protest the war in Vietnam, the conference set up a steering committee to fix a date and organize demonstrations. The time was set for May 2, 1964. The coordinators of the protest, which was to take place in several cities, were Russell Stetler, a Haverford College student who had recently joined SDS; Levi Laub of the Progressive Labor Movement (later Progressive Labor Party); and Peter Camejo of the Young Socialist Alliance. The demonstrations attracted some 600 participants in New York City, 800 in San Francisco, and lesser numbers in several other places.

Following these demonstrations, Laub and other PL members who were on the original steering committee initiated a new organization called the May Second Movement (M-2-M). Its stated purpose was to oppose imperialism and in particular the war in Vietnam.

In the summer of 1964, M-2-M and another small radical group, Youth Against War and Fascism, sponsored two demonstrations in New York City against the war in Vietnam. On both occasions the demonstrations were scheduled for Times Square in the face of an arbitrary police ban on marches or rallies there. Seventeen were arrested the first time, and a week later, on August 15, the 200 marchers were attacked by police as they attempted to enter the square. More than forty persons were arrested and several brutally clubbed.

Through M-2-M, PL was the first of the radical tendencies to focus on the Vietnam issue as a key to organizing the radicalizing youth. PL's quick eye for a hot issue—a talent its leaders exhibited on more than one occasion—was not sufficient, however, to compensate for the organizational methods they applied in M-2-M, methods taken—by their own acknowledgment—from Stalinist tradition.

While the May 2, 1964, demonstrations had been set up on a united-front basis—including all tendencies that wished to participate—M-2-M was strictly a PL front. It soon became clear that PL deliberately excluded all other organized tendencies from M-2-M, which they nevertheless advertised as a broad movement. There is a world of difference between a united front in which anyone who claims agreement with the matter at hand can participate while maintaining their own political identity, and a front in which one tendency attempts to impose its own particular multi-issue program on a whole movement which has no such homogeneity.

Parties with relatively overwhelming resources and hegemony in the radical movement—like the CP had in the 1930s—can get away with that for a time. (Even then the "success" is ephemeral and generally plays havoc with the cause the front is supposed to promote.) But PL had no such raw power. It attempted to build M-2-M as *the* student antiwar movement and remained largely isolated from the real mass movement as it actually developed. PL finally dissolved M-2-M early in 1966 when as a central orientation it sent the younger PL members into SDS.

As the saying goes, "There's no sucker like one with a little larceny in his heart." PL had more than a little as SDS was destined to learn. But that was later.

# 2

# The SDS March on Washington

At the end of 1964 SDS was still formally a part of the Social Democratic wing of American liberalism, still affiliated with and in part financed by the League for Industrial Democracy. But significant strains in this relationship had developed in the early 1960s.

The nearly moribund Student League for Industrial Democracy—thirteen students attended its 1958 national convention—changed its name to Students for a Democratic Society in January 1960. This was partly to take some distance from the adult leadership of the League for Industrial Democracy which had no appeal to, and indeed little sympathy for, the new activism beginning to arise on campuses. Thus began the process of differentiation from the "old left."[1]

1. As used in SDS circles of the time, the term "old left" generally referred to the left of Marxist origin that had emerged from the 1930s. It was divided into three main tendencies: the Stalinists, the Trotskyists, and the Social Democrats. In the United States in 1960 the parties of these tendencies were respectively the Communist Party (CP), the Socialist Workers Party (SWP), and the Socialist Party-Social Democratic Federation (SP-SDF).

From the 1930s to 1956 the CP was by far the largest, most influential radical party in the U.S. In 1956, however, the CP lost most of its members in a crisis precipitated by the Khrushchev revelations of Stalin's crimes and the Soviet suppression of the subsequent Hungarian revolt. Since then, no party has had hegemony on the American left.

There were groups other than these three which considered themselves socialist, but almost all of them were either splinters from, or in the milieu of, one of the three main historic tendencies. (An exception is the Socialist

In 1961 SDS National Secretary Al Haber convinced the LID leaders that SDS needed a certain organizational independence, particularly the right to join in united action with other student groups like the Southern-based Student Nonviolent Coordinating Committee, if it was to stay abreast of its generation. But Haber succeeded only after a bitter fight in which LID first fired and then rehired him.

The tensions developed nearly to the breaking point immediately following the SDS convention held at the United Auto Workers FDR Camp at Port Huron, Michigan, in June 1962. That convention, attended by a total of fifty-nine persons, forty-three of whom had voting power, did three things that infuriated the LID leaders. It modified a clause in the old SLID constitution aimed at excluding communists, it seated as an observer a member of the Progressive Youth Organizing Committee, which was associated with the Communist Party, and it adopted the famous Port Huron statement.

---

Labor Party, which predates all the others. The SLP, however, had consistently abstained from the existing trade unions, civil rights, or antiwar organizations. It played no role in the organized anti-Vietnam War movement.)

With the advent of the Sino-Soviet dispute, the Stalinists split into Moscow-oriented and Peking-oriented varieties. In the mid-1960s, the main Maoist group in the U.S. was the Progressive Labor Party (PL).

In Western Europe, Britain, Japan, Australia, etc., there are mass labor and Social Democratic parties based on the trade unions. The lack of this phenomenon in the United States of the period under discussion made the miniscule SP-SDF and its youth group YPSL appear almost irrelevant. The appearance, however, was superficial, for there existed a larger milieu of trade union officials and intellectuals calling themselves either liberals or socialists who had a common Social Democratic origin and ideology and were loosely associated through periodicals, foundations, and social service organizations such as the League for Industrial Democracy.

In the U.S. by the 1960s the Social Democracy by and large no longer held socialist pretensions, but constituted a more or less distinct wing of liberalism operating mainly within the Democratic Party. It included elements of the leadership of several important trade unions, including the United Auto Workers, the United Federation of Teachers in New York, and especially the International Ladies Garment Workers Union. The Social Democracy also had a certain overlap with the pacifist movement through such figures as Bayard Rustin and Dave McReynolds, both members of SP-SDF and protégés of A. J. Muste.

The Port Huron statement proclaimed the method of "participatory democracy" and the strategy of building a "new left" of "socialists and liberals" in America. The document, the first draft of which was written by Tom Hayden, was designed to stimulate discussion and was basically liberal in content. It even contained a version of the theory of "realignment" of progressive forces within the Democratic Party, so dear to the hearts of SP-SDF figures like Bayard Rustin and Michael Harrington.[2]

But the statement captured some of the revulsion of the newly radicalizing youth against the stultifying atmosphere of cold-war liberalism. It said:

Americans are in withdrawal from public life, from any collective effort at directing their own affairs. . . . The American political system is not the democratic model of which its glorifiers speak. In actuality it frustrates democracy by confusing the individual citizen, paralyzing policy discussion, and consolidating the irresponsible power of military and business interests.[3]

It should be recalled that this was written during the administration of John F. Kennedy. It expressed a critical attitude toward the White House "Camelot" not shared by other Social Democratic circles.

What is more, the statement contained an explicit criticism of the anticommunism that preoccupied the Social Democratic milieu in the U.S.:

An unreasoning anti-communism has become a major social problem for those who want to construct a more democratic America. . . . Even many liberals and socialists share static and repetitious participation in

---

2. The "realignment" theory was a variation of coalition politics, the idea of seeking progressive change through a coalition of liberals, labor, and civil rights forces within the Democratic Party. According to "realignment," the most conservative sectors should be forced out of the Democratic Party and into the Republican Party, thus producing a meaningful two-party system with liberals dominating one party, conservatives the other. The overtly racist Southern Democrats were seen as the major obstacle to this development. The Port Huron statement called for the development of "two genuine parties" by "shuttling of the Southern Democrats out of the Democratic Party."

3. *The Port Huron Statement* (Chicago: SDS, 1966), pp. 11-12.

the anti-communist crusade and often discourage tentative, inquiring discussion about "the Russian question" within their ranks.

To top off its dissidence, the Port Huron statement implied the U.S. was to blame for the continuation of the cold war:

> Our paranoia about the Soviet Union has made us incapable of achieving agreements absolutely necessary for disarmament and the preservation of peace.

This was too much for the LID leaders, who called Haber and new SDS president Tom Hayden to a hearing at which they were grilled by Harrington and others. LID changed the lock on the SDS national office and cut off funds to the youth group.

In his scholarly study *SDS*, Kirkpatrick Sale quotes SDS National Executive Committee member Bob Ross's comment on this attack:

> All of us felt our careers were going to be ruined, and America's best liberals were on the lip of red-baiting us out of existence. We knew we weren't communists, but the idea that our parent organization thought we were, was Kafkaesque.[4]

After lengthy maneuvers and negotiations during which Haber was replaced as national secretary, the near split was provisionally patched up. But the SDS leaders had had a lesson in the "democratic" morality of the Social Democratic leaders, and shed some illusions. From then on SDS tended more and more to practice nonexclusion—if not proclaim it. The pressures in this direction were particularly strong because of the SDS interest in SNCC, which had adopted nonexclusion in the heat of the Southern civil rights struggle, where heavy red-baiting attacks by racists were frequent.

SDS was also deeply influenced by the unsuccessful attempt of the Mississippi Freedom Democratic Party to unseat the Dixiecrat state delegation at the Democratic Party convention in 1964. SDSers were particularly angered by the role played by Bayard Rustin in opposing the challenge. The anger was all the deeper because the attempt was not revolutionary, but essentially fell

4. Kirkpatrick Sale, *SDS* (New York: Vintage, 1974), p. 65.

within the "realignment" strategy, so often pushed by Rustin. During the 1964 presidential campaign, virtually the entire old peace movement threw itself behind Lyndon Johnson against Barry Goldwater. Johnson's campaign statements were carefully designed to leave the mistaken impression that he would not escalate the U.S. intervention in Vietnam. Goldwater was more candid. Most of the radicals followed suit in backing Johnson, including the Communist Party. The major exception was the Trotskyists of the Socialist Workers Party and the Young Socialist Alliance, who ran their own candidate, Clifton DeBerry. He denounced the "illegal undeclared war" being fought "because the corporations and billionaires who really run the U.S. believe that it is their divine, imperialist, white-supremacist right to control Southeast Asia" and warned that both "Johnson and Goldwater wholeheartedly carry out this dirty policy."[5]

The depth of the illusion in Johnson within the old peace movement, and the moral outrage that followed when the reelected president began the major escalation, was perhaps best expressed by Dr. Benjamin Spock, who had joined SANE in 1962 and became its most prominent and effective spokesman. Spock campaigned for Johnson and two days after the election the president made a personal phone call to thank him. Spock quotes Johnson as saying, "I hope I will be worthy of your trust."

> I was so embarrassed, [continues Spock] to have the President of the U.S. hoping to be worthy of *my* trust that I cried, "Oh, President Johnson, I'm sure you will," little knowing that within three months he would have betrayed me and the millions of other Americans who voted for him because he said he was the peace candidate.[6]

SDS's Political Education Project (PEP), under the leadership of Steve Max and Jim Williams of the "realignment" faction, also threw itself behind the pro-Johnson effort. They rallied around the president heedless of the Gulf of Tonkin affair that took place in the midst of his campaign. In August two American destroyers, under orders to patrol as close as eleven miles to the North Vietnamese shore, were allegedly fired upon by North Vietnamese torpedo boats on patrol against Saigon commandos who

5. *Militant*, August 10, 1964.
6. Lynn Z. Bloom, *Dr. Spock: Biography of a Conservative Radical* (Indianapolis: Bobbs-Merrill, 1972), p. 253.

had repeatedly raided that area of the North Vietnamese coast. Johnson used this staged incident as the pretext to launch the first U.S. bombing raid on North Vietnam and to press through Congress the infamous Tonkin Gulf resolution that was subsequently used as the authority for the massive escalations of the next three years.

The resolution was adopted with virtual unanimity, only two senators, Wayne Morse and Ernest Gruening, voting against. In the House only Adam Clayton Powell of Harlem registered a weak dissent by abstaining.

Support for Johnson was by no means unanimous within SDS. To differentiate from the official Democratic campaign slogan, "All the Way with LBJ," SDS National Secretary C. Clark Kissinger put out a button that said, "Part of the Way with LBJ." This was widely assumed to have been the official SDS electoral stand. Kissinger says he put out the button on his own and that SDS as a whole had no position on the election, since a majority of the leadership by that time did not consider electoral activity a fruitful method of building a radical base. And it is true that the Political Education Project itself did not long survive the election campaign.

Nevertheless the general impression was left that SDS had supported Johnson as a lesser evil chiefly because of his advertised differences with Goldwater on the war.

For the duration of the election campaign this tended to obscure somewhat the depth of the alienation among SDS ranks from the older Social Democratic milieu.

This divergence is pointed up by an incident that took place within another sector of the Social Democracy. The Young People's Socialist League held a convention over Labor Day weekend—not long after the Gulf of Tonkin affair. The convention adopted a resolution opposing both of the capitalist parties in the elections. The national office of SP-SDF thereupon suspended YPSL for taking a position "outside the basic framework of democratic socialism."

The theory behind this was apparently that if YPSL members didn't support the Democratic Party candidate some of them might vote for the SWP candidate DeBerry, who was calling for immediate withdrawal from Vietnam. The SP-SDF considered it sufficient grounds for expulsion for any member to support SWP candidates.

The action was the more galling in that the SP-SDF convention itself had not fielded a candidate and the pro-Johnson wing at the adult convention did not have a majority. Nevertheless prominent SP-SDF members, including Norman Thomas and Michael Harrington, were campaigning for Johnson. The right to publicly express viewpoints different from party policy was in essence limited to the right wing. This violation of the professed democratic principles of the self-styled democratic socialists was a bit thick, and YPSL ceased to function as a viable organization just as the new antiwar movement was about to be born.

Relations between LID and SDS, on the other hand, went smoothly during the election campaign. This proved to be temporary, however.

Not long after the November election it became clear to any careful observer that the U.S. was preparing an escalation of the war. The November 18 *Wall Street Journal,* for example, reported:

"The decision on whether or when to 'escalate' warfare in Southeast Asia hasn't yet been made. But Governmental activity which one lofty participant calls 'feverish' suggests the decision point is close at hand."

The essential reason for this was the near collapse of the Saigon regime. Mass desertions to the rebel side were occurring in major battles. It was obvious Saigon would not be able to hold out without a drastic change in the situation. General Maxwell Taylor, President Kennedy's favorite counterinsurgency expert and in 1964 U.S. ambassador to Saigon, requested U.S. air strikes against North Vietnam and Laos. The request was not kept secret, plainly as a test of public reaction.

Still the old peace coalition as a whole would not respond. An ad hoc formation, under the leadership of the pacifists, called emergency demonstrations for December 19. The one in New York drew a thousand people to Washington Square. Chaired by Dave McReynolds of the War Resisters League, the speakers included A. J. Muste, Norman Thomas, and A. Philip Randolph, the septuagenarian president of the Brotherhood of Sleeping Car Porters.

In this atmosphere the SDS National Council meeting was held in New York during the Christmas–New Year school holiday. This meeting marks the birth of the new antiwar movement because it initiated the first national march on Washington against the Vietnam War. Those present at the meeting, however, didn't see the decision as particularly historic. Other matters taken up by the meeting seemed more important to them at the time. The Berkeley Free Speech Movement, which had dominated the fall semester, was a major preoccupation of the NC members. So were SDS's several ERAP (Economic Research and Action Project) community organizing efforts. Rennie Davis in Chicago, Paul Potter in Cleveland, and Tom Hayden in Newark were key figures in this work.

Even the SDS Peace Research and Education Project (PREP) was concerned centrally not with Vietnam but with plans for a civil disobedience protest against the Chase Manhattan Bank over loans to South Africa. But PREP leaders Todd Gitlin and Paul Booth did invite I. F. Stone to the meeting for a talk on U.S. involvement in Vietnam. It deeply affected those present. The next day, December 30, 1964, a long session took place at which various proposals for action on Vietnam were discussed and the march on Washington for April 17, 1965, finally decided upon. Clark Kissinger recalls:

It was at the Cloakmakers' [an International Ladies Garment Workers Union affiliate] Hall in Manhattan. I think it was the last time the Social Democrats provided a meeting hall for us. When we got into the room there was a giant, about ten-feet-high, portrait of Lyndon Johnson, which we turned around and faced against the wall.[7]

The idea for the march was actually a compromise proposed by Jim Brook, an associate of Steve Max's, as a counter to Todd Gitlin's idea of a draft-refusal campaign that Brook thought too radical. Sale describes the climax of the debate as follows:

Many ERAPers and the more alienated of the younger members oppose a march as too tame; others argue that the whole thing has too much of a single-issue focus to it and is not radical enough; while Kissinger and a number of campus-oriented people join with the PEP types in support of it because they see it as an effective way to organize among students and build up the organization on the campus level. Then, during a lull, a number of ERAPers leave the room. Kissinger, in the chair, calls for a vote on the march. It passes, with strong support from the chapter delegates, less enthusiasm from the NC members.[8]

7. Author's taped interview with Clark Kissinger, October 16, 1973.
8. Sale, *SDS*, p. 171.

Kissinger recalls that the meeting specifically decided that the march would be organized on a basis of nonexclusion. "There was no opposition to this that I can remember," he says. The meeting adjourned after midnight. SDS had just kicked over the traces.

Certainly no one there anticipated that the issue of the Vietnam War would assume such consuming importance for the U.S. and the world, or that the action they had just taken would catapult SDS into national prominence by next April 17. But to some extent the break with LID policy was deliberate. The SDS national office leaders were aware that a refreshing breeze of youthful radicalism was stirring. They wanted to get that wind in their sails and what they considered the irrelevant baggage of the "old left," including the exclusionism of the Social Democrats, just got in the way. SDS was to be master in its own house.

SDS was still not significantly larger than the other radical youth groups, but it considered itself the main group of the "new left." In a modest way—they expected perhaps two or three thousand—a nonexclusive march on Washington organized by SDS would allow it to take center stage for an action with some appeal on campuses nationally.

As far as the war itself was concerned, it was one of many equally vital issues and the march itself was viewed as just one of several projects to occupy SDS in the spring semester. SDS was not unique in this low-key approach to Vietnam at the time. None of the other radical groups considered it an overriding preoccupation either.

PL had founded M-2-M with Vietnam as a central concern but the M-2-M actions in the summer had failed to draw large numbers, while the Berkeley Free Speech Movement had captured national attention. In January, M-2-M leaders decided the group would become involved in student protest generally rather than emphasize Vietnam. When Clark Kissinger contacted the various radical groups early in January to invite them to join in building the march on a nonexclusive basis, M-2-M at first hesitated, endorsing only after support for the action grew beyond original expectations.

Observers from the W.E.B. Du Bois Clubs, the new youth group associated with the Communist Party, had been present at the SDS National Executive Council meeting which called the action and had indicated interest, but once again with no special emphasis.

Even the Trotskyists, who would later be the most consistent advocates of mass anti-Vietnam War demonstrations, were blessed with no special talent for prophecy. The YSA convention, which took place in Chicago at the same time the SDS council was meeting in New York, paid no special attention to Vietnam.

We made a cold-blooded decision [recalls Jack Barnes, then YSA national chairman] that we would not press any special, central campaign from the convention. We decided we'd have to let the incoming leadership see what pops, and go from there. We rejected initiating something ourselves, trying to suck it out of our thumb. And shortly after we got back to New York, Kissinger contacted us for a meeting. He told us about the march and said he wanted to show us the draft of the call to see what we thought about it. We said OK and he said, "I'll meet you at the Jeff" [the Jefferson Book Shop, a radical bookstore in Manhattan].

The main thing we raised with him was to make it clear in the call that the U.S. had no right in Vietnam, the call should be clear on Vietnamese self-determination. He agreed. Later he asked us not to carry our own signs. We didn't much like that. We wanted to advocate immediate withdrawal. He said SDS would make up sets of signs with different slogans and at least one of them would satisfy us. We could carry that. We decided to acquiesce. As soon as we heard about the march, we knew that it could be a breakthrough. Our approach was not to form a special caucus or something like that but to throw the whole YSA into building committees to get people to go to Washington for the march.[9]

In January SDS sent letters to all student political organizations and adult peace groups asking endorsement and inviting each group to appoint a liaison. The invitation was ignored by most of the peace groups. I. F. Stone, however, got Senator Gruening to agree to speak, and the American Friends Service Committee endorsed. SDS, then, was reasonably assured of a modestly successful action as it readied its call for release to the public early in February.

On February 7, 1965, Johnson announced a major escalation of the war, beginning with sustained bombing of North Vietnam. The U.S. would try to save the Saigon regime by massive increase of U.S. forces, including ground forces. The military manpower needs would be supplied by the draft rather than calling up the reserves.

Overnight, demonstrations were spontaneously organized, par-

9. Author's taped interview with Jack Barnes, April 27, 1974.

ticularly at campuses, across the country. There were literally
hundreds of them. In some places SDS chapters took the initiative, but there weren't very many SDS chapters then. Most were
organized by ad hoc committees called together by individuals
with some radical experience, or experience in the civil rights,
free speech, Fair Play for Cuba, or old peace movement activities.
On February 8, SDS issued its call for the April 17 march on
Washington, urging "the participation of all students who agree
with us that the war in Vietnam injures both Vietnamese and
Americans and should be stopped." The call said:

> The current war in Vietnam is being waged on behalf of a succession of
> unpopular South Vietnamese dictatorships, not in behalf of freedom. No
> American-supported South Vietnamese regime in the past few years has
> gained the support of its people, for the simple reason that the people
> overwhelmingly want peace, self-determination, and the opportunity for
> development. American prosecution of the war has deprived them of all
> three.
> The war is fundamentally a *civil* war, waged by South Vietnamese
> against their government; it is not a "war of aggression." Military
> assistance from North Vietnam and China has been minimal; most
> guerrilla weapons are homemade or captured American arms. The areas
> of strongest guerrilla control are not the areas adjacent to North
> Vietnam. And the people could not and cannot be isolated from the
> guerrillas by forced settlement in "strategic hamlets"; again and again,
> Government military attacks fail because the people tip off the guerrillas;
> the people and the guerrillas are inseparable. . . .
> Well over half of the area of South Vietnam is already governed by the
> National Liberation Front. . . . Thousands of Government troops have
> defected—the traditional signal of a losing counter-guerrilla war. . . .[10]

These facts were accurate at the time. But the next sentence in
the call, set in capital letters in the original, indicates some
illusion as to the war's duration: "HOW MANY MORE LIVES
MUST BE LOST BEFORE THE JOHNSON ADMINISTRA-
TION ACCEPTS THE FOREGONE CONCLUSIONS?"
The SDS authors were not the only ones who did not know then
that the answer to that question would preoccupy the country for
the next ten years and create a crisis in confidence in the
government so profound that its effects are still reverberating.
The concluding sentences of the call caught the mood of youth

10. SDS archives, State Historical Society of Wisconsin.

who had become politically aware largely during the Southern civil rights struggle and had closely followed the community organizing done by SNCC.

We are outraged that $2 million a day is expended for a war on the poor in Vietnam, while government financing is so desperately needed to abolish poverty at home. WHAT KIND OF AMERICA IS IT WHOSE RESPONSE TO POVERTY AND OPPRESSION IN VIETNAM IS NAPALM AND DEFOLIATION? WHOSE RESPONSE TO POVERTY AND OPPRESSION IN MISSISSIPPI IS—SILENCE? It is a hideously *immoral* war. America is committing pointless murder.

\*     \*     \*

The quick demonstrations in response to the February escalation proved the existence of a reservoir of radicalized youth larger than had been previously manifest, but the outrage was still largely confined to radicals. The great bulk of the population was still confused on the war, still not ready to see their own government as being involved in shameful and immoral deeds.

Here and there, those in favor of the war—or rather those against the protesters—mustered more than the demonstrators. For example, at one university set in a conservative Ohio community, the YSA organized a handful of students to protest the war on February 9. They were set upon by some 150 right-wing-instigated students who burned their picket signs and kicked and shoved them. Campus police stood by, refusing to intervene, though one demonstrator, Barbara Brock, was kicked in the face. The campus was Kent State University.

\*     \*     \*

Following these early demonstrations, the SDS march became the national focus for the entire protest movement. Endorsements came in from many figures prominent in other causes, even from persons only SANE had previously been able to approach with success.

One delicate problem facing SDS was the fact that the old peace movement traditionally scheduled peace walks on Easter weekend and April 17 was the day before Easter. There was a certain resentment, even among those traditional peace movement leaders now anxious to join a united protest against the

Vietnam War, because SDS had preempted the period for a demonstration under its exclusive sponsorship.

Early in March, Ralph DiGia, the gentle, soft-spoken executive secretary of the War Resisters League, who had spent years in prison for his pacifist principles, arranged a meeting with SDS and the traditional peace groups to iron out this problem. It was agreed to cancel the Easter walks and support the Washington march as the national focus of spring activity against the war. SANE had scheduled a "Walk with Dr. Spock" for New York on Saturday, April 17, and this was shifted to April 10, largely through the good offices of Women Strike for Peace.

The traditional groups proposed, however, that SDS give over direction of the march to an ad hoc committee of leaders from the several peace organizations. It was by no means certain that this group would resist demands from SANE and Turn Toward Peace to exclude the unrespectable radicals and ban the idea of "immediate withdrawal" from the march.

The SDS negotiators, Kissinger and Paul Booth, did yield to the extent of agreeing to ban "immediate withdrawal" signs, provided placards for all other specific solutions were also banned. This was later changed to the arrangement where SDS printed up a variety of signs and asked other groups not to bring their own. (As it turned out, the promised "immediate withdrawal" placards never materialized and the Trotskyists had to be satisfied with placards proclaiming, "Self-Determination, Not U.S.-Imposed Dictatorship.")

Kissinger and Booth agreed to the joint sponsorship deal but explained they couldn't make the decision on their own. In mid-March the SDS national office sent out a mail ballot to the National Council on the sponsorship question. The results were: twenty-four for the ad-hoc sponsorship, nineteen against, two abstentions.

The whole matter was about to be thrown back to what amounted to the old peace movement coalition. But several members of the majority then changed their vote, including Kissinger, who explained in a communication:

Since, however, there were violent opinions on both sides, a number of votes were conditional, and the margin so close, a number of National Officers changed their vote from For to Against to avoid embarking on a radical change in plans without a clear organizational consensus.[11]

Sale characterizes this as "in the best democratic traditions of the organization." The LID leaders had other words for it, but their reputation for strict adherence to majority votes was tarnished in SDS circles from the Port Huron incident. What was in all probability involved here was not a complicated and cynical maneuver—that would have been out of character for both Kissinger and Booth—but a series of reactions to different pressures from different parts of the movement. It left bad feelings, however, which contributed to pressures against the march.

During the final weeks of preparations SDS put up some subway posters in New York City showing a Vietnamese burned by napalm and the caption: "WHY ARE WE BURNING, TOR-TURING, KILLING THE PEOPLE OF VIETNAM? . . . TO PREVENT FREE ELECTIONS." This angered many people in LID and the old peace groups who said it implied that if the U.S. pulled out of Vietnam free elections would follow.

In San Francisco, where a march was being organized to coincide with the Washington affair, Western Area Turn Toward Peace Director Robert Pickus issued a press release denouncing it. "It is time that someone within the peace movement challenged activity which is in fact more hostile to America than to war," said Pickus. Getting out of Vietnam, he continued, "is not the way to end the war in Southeast Asia" and such slogans are not the way "to help change America's mind about the use of national military power there. . . . America is involved in Vietnam. It should stay involved. The question is how. . . ."[12]

On Thursday before the Washington march, some fifteen prominent pacifist, peace movement, and Social Democratic figures, called together by Bayard Rustin, met at Turn Toward Peace Executive Director Robert Gilmore's house to discuss the upcoming event. Muste, who was present, later gave some of the details in an interview with Jack Newfield published in the May 7, 1965, *Village Voice.* As quoted by Newfield, Muste said Rustin "wanted to torpedo the march because he thought communists

11. SDS worklist mailing, March 21, 1965. SDS archives, State Historical Society of Wisconsin.
12. Cited by Dave Dellinger, "The March on Washington and its Critics," *Liberation,* May 1965.

had taken over in some places."
Most of those at this meeting, however, were supporters of the march. In a debate lasting many hours they watered down Rustin's original proposal to a statement welcoming the march but dissociating from some of its participants and features. The statement referred to exclusion in the following terms:

> We welcome the cooperation of all those groups and individuals who, like ourselves, believe in the need for an independent peace movement, not committed to any form of totalitarianism or drawing inspiration from the foreign policy of any government.[13]

This part of the statement was downright laughable to radicals familiar with the Social Democratic milieu, which contained "State Department socialists" who drew material support as well as inspiration from the foreign policy of the U.S. government, but who were not considered outside the pale.

The statement also characterized President Johnson's April 7 Johns Hopkins speech as suggesting "a healthy shift in American foreign policy." In this speech Johnson declared for "unconditional negotiations" on condition they took place from a position of U.S. strength in Vietnam, and pointedly did not include the NLF as a party to the negotiations. It was also the speech where Johnson offered vast sums in American "aid" to North Vietnam if only they would settle on terms agreeable to the U.S.

Nevertheless, the statement had been changed from one attacking the march to what appeared to some of those who agreed to sign it late that tired night as one of critical support. Dave McReynolds and Ralph DiGia refused to sign. Dave Dellinger had not even been invited to the meeting. Those who signed included Rustin, Gilmore, Norman Thomas, H. Stuart Hughes, and even Muste. The last three later apologized for the way it was used.

Actually, if Rustin had called the meeting to cripple the march itself he acted much too late, since the statement didn't make the papers until the day of the event. More likely Rustin simply wanted the traditional peace movement to be clearly dissociated from an event he felt would be a fiasco from the point of view of appealing to the liberal Establishment.

As it turned out, the march was unprecedented in size and

---

13. Cited by Dellinger, *Liberation,* May 1965.

completely orderly. What little hostile press it got was directly due to the statement Rustin had initiated.

This included an April 17 editorial in the liberal *New York Post* which began:

> On the eve of this weekend's "peace march" on Washington, several leaders of the peace movement have taken clear note of attempts to convert the event into a frenzied, one-sided anti-American show. Some of the banners advertised in advance are being carried to the wrong place at the wrong time.

The effects of this incident were minimal on the march itself, but its repercussions were a stunning blow to the Social Democracy and its chances to influence a new generation.

After the march Yale Professor Staughton Lynd, a pacifist friend of Rustin who had been director of the Mississippi Freedom Schools during SNCC's 1964 summer campaign, wrote an open letter in which he berated Rustin:

> The lesson of your apostacy on Vietnam appears to be that the gains for American Negroes you advise them to seek through coalition politics within the Democratic Party come only at a price. The price is to become a "national civil rights leader" who delivers his constituency. The price is to urge "jobs and freedom" for Americans only. The price, at a time when we desperately need to stand together and transcend old bitterness, is to set the stage for a government witch-hunt. The price is to make our brothers in Vietnam a burnt offering on the altar of political expedience.[14]

The spring 1965 issue of *Studies on the Left* carried a long editorial based on a taped interview with Clark Kissinger, though this was not acknowledged at the time, detailing the internal struggle within the old peace movement over the march on Washington. It concluded:

> The attempts to gain control of the March on Washington, and later to discredit it, like the attempts to force the MFDP to compromise at Atlantic City, illuminate the growing divergence between the new radicals and those still caught up in the ideological concerns of the old left and the strategies of realignment and coalitions at the top. The continued refusal of sections of the peace movement to work with overt Communist and left-wing groups, even within a protest activity spon-

14. *Studies on the Left,* Spring 1965.

sored and controlled by a non-Communist organization whose principles and activity all respected, indicates a steadily growing isolation of the traditional peace groups from the new student movements. The difficulty these organizations found in functioning as supporters rather than as sponsors of the March grew out of this isolation and a concomitant ignorance of the extent and spirit of student alienation from the concerns of the Cold War.

*        *        *

The crowd of 20,000[15] that bright Saturday in Washington, April 17, 1965, was double the number expected. Demonstrations much larger than that were later to be routine for the antiwar movement but at the time it was unparalleled. Considering the character of the march it was even more impressive. This was no innocuous "propeace" affair but a demonstration by Americans in their own capital against a specific war being prosecuted by their own government. Nothing like that had ever happened before in Washington on anything like this scale.

The demonstrators gathered on Pennsylvania Avenue to picket the White House,[16] then marched to the hill where the Washington Monument stands, for a rally at the Sylvan Theater on the South Slope. The cherry trees were still in bloom and the flags circling the monument were held full by a spring breeze. The holidaylike setting was in contrast to the seriousness of the crowd, which felt not only a sense of great purpose, but, as I remember it, almost a sense of danger. Not the immediate, physical kind, but something impending.

15. The figures cited in this work for the number of participants at demonstrations are my own responsibility except where otherwise stated. Disinterested objectivity hardly existed in connection with this very controversial movement and there is always a certain amount of guesswork in estimating the larger crowds. The figures cited by government agencies are particularly suspect, since it was the specific policy of two presidents to deny that the movement had any appreciable following. My own estimates are based on personal observation and, where I was not present, on an average of the available estimates. In any case the figures used here give a good idea of the relative size of the various demonstrations.

16. The president himself was not in Washington, but in Texas where local SDSers from the University of Texas in Austin sponsored a picket line of several hundred at the gate of Johnson's ranch.

Those present were trying to show that Johnson didn't have the consensus he claimed on the war. The turnout was exciting, but they knew they represented a minority of Americans who were ready and willing to challenge their own government on such an issue. This was Pentagon-FBI-big-money-lobby territory, inhospitable to radicals and steeped in superpatriotic pork-barrel politics, capital of the American behemoth at the height of its American Century, self-righteous and thoroughly convinced of its own invincibility. This crowd of hounded radicals, betrayed liberals, questioning youth, and a few busloads of Black Mississippi civil rights fighters was sitting in the middle of all that power and, however gently, telling it to go to hell.

"Don't you know there's a war on?" a man shouted from a passing car bearing a Confederate flag, as the last of the march crossed Constitution Avenue into the monument grounds.

At one point in his speech that day, I. F. Stone, that wistful little liberal with the steely dedication to journalistic truth, warned the crowd that this town was not going to be easy to change.

Staughton Lynd presided, invoking the spirit of Jean-Paul Sartre and the French intellectuals who had opposed the French war in Algeria. Other speakers included Senator Gruening and Robert Parris (formerly Bob Moses) of SNCC. In line with the SDS emphasis on community work, Iva Pierce, a member of the Cleveland ERAP Welfare Mothers Project, was scheduled, but couldn't attend because of an accident. Her speech was read to the audience. There were songs by the SNCC Freedom Voices, Phil Ochs, Judy Collins, and Joan Baez.

SDS President Paul Potter, tall, thin, close-cropped hair, wearing jacket and tie, spoke last, and it was his speech that most remained with those who heard it:

Most of us grew up thinking that the United States was a strong but humble nation that . . . respected the integrity of other nations and other systems; and that engaged in wars only as a last resort. . . . If at some point we began to hear vague and disturbing things about what this country had done in Latin America, China, Spain, and other places, we remained somehow confident about the basic integrity of this nation's foreign policy. . . . The withdrawal from the hysteria of the Cold War era and the development of a more aggressive, activist foreign policy has done much to force many of us to rethink attitudes that were deep and basic sentiments about our country.

And now the incredible war in Vietnam has provided the razor, the terrifying sharp cutting edge that has finally severed the last vestiges of illusions that morality and democracy are the guiding principles of American foreign policy. . . . The further we explore the reality of what this country is doing . . . in Vietnam, the more we are driven toward the conclusion of Senator [Wayne] Morse that the United States may well be the greatest threat to peace in the world today. That is a terrible and bitter insight . . . our refusal to accept it as inevitable or necessary is one of the reasons that so many people have come here today. . . .

And it is only the kind of terror we see now in Vietnam that awakens conscience and reminds us that there is something deep in us that cries out against dictatorial suppression. The pattern of repression and destruction that we have developed and justified in the war is so thorough that it can only be called cultural genocide. . . .

What kind of system is it that justifies the United States or any country seizing the destinies of the Vietnamese people and using them callously for our own purposes . . . that consistently puts material values before human values—and still persists in calling itself free and still persists in finding itself fit to police the world? . . .

We must name that system. We must name it, describe it, analyze it, understand it and change it. For it is only when that system is changed and brought under control that there can be any hope for stopping the forces that create a war in Vietnam today. . . .[17]

In his book *The War at Home,* Thomas Powers notes:

many of those in the crowd listening to Potter were old Socialists, Trotskyists, Marxists, and they all felt the answer to his question bursting from their lips: *Say the word!* they wanted to shout. *Say the word! Capitalism!*[18]

The observation is, as I recall, accurate.

Potter later explained:

I did not fail to call the system capitalism because I was a coward or an opportunist. I refused to call it capitalism because capitalism was for me and my generation an inadequate description of the evils of America—a

17. SDS press release, "Text of Speech by Paul Potter, President of Students for a Democratic Society, March on Washington, April 17, 1965." (Copy in author's files.)

18. Thomas Powers, *The War at Home: Vietnam and the American People, 1964-1968* (New York: Grossman, 1973), p. 77.

hollow, dead word tied to the thirties and a movement that had used it freely but apparently without comprehending it.[19]

SDS at that time did not call itself socialist. Powers describes the attitude then prevalent in leading SDS circles:

> When the New Left attacked the system, they were referring to cold, elitist bureaucracies and the powerlessness of ordinary people, not just private property. They were collectivist almost by instinct but at the same time feared that the old, sterile disputes of the left were simply waiting to be revived.[20]

Potter ended the rally with a stirring appeal to build a new movement:

> that understands Vietnam in all its horror as but a symptom of a deeper malaise, that we build a movement that makes possible the implementation of values that would have prevented Vietnam, a movement based on the integrity of man and a belief in man's capacity . . . to tolerate all the weird formulations of society that men may choose to strive for . . . a movement that will wrench the country into a confrontation with the issues of the war; a movement that must of necessity reach out to all these people in Vietnam or elsewhere who are struggling to find decency and control for their lives.

The crowd stood and applauded, then moved down the wide, grassy mall between the monument and the capitol.[21] Those at the front of the march, looking over their shoulders, viewed a spectacular sight of the throng making their way, banners and placards aloft with the low afternoon sun streaming through them, down the long slope toward the steps of the capitol. There the march stopped as a petition to Congress was delivered. Then the crowd dispersed.

The text of the petition accurately summed up the politics of the first national demonstration of the new antiwar movement:

> We, the participants in the March on Washington to End the War in

---

19. Paul Potter, *A Name for Ourselves* (Boston: Little, Brown & Co., 1971), p. 101.
20. Powers, *The War at Home*, p. 77.
21. Subsequent major demonstrations in Washington were unable to take this route because of prolonged construction across the Mall.

Vietnam, petition Congress to act immediately to end the war. You currently have at your disposal many schemes, including reconvening the Geneva Conference, negotiation with the National Liberation Front and North Vietnam, immediate withdrawal, and UN-supervised elections. Although those among us might differ as to which of these is most desirable, we are unanimously of the opinion that the war must be brought to a halt.

This war is inflicting untold harm on the people of Vietnam. It is being fought in behalf of a succession of unpopular regimes, not for the ideals you proclaim. Our military are obviously being defeated; yet we persist in extending the war. The problems of America cry out for attention, and our entanglement in South Vietnam postpones the confrontation of these issues while prolonging the misery of the people of that war-torn land.

You must act now to reverse this sorry state of affairs. We call on you to end, not extend, the war in Vietnam.[22]

\*          \*          \*

On the same day as the SDS March on Washington and the *New York Post* editorial red-baiting it, the reactionary New York *Daily News* carried an editorial dealing with the report that antiaircraft missiles were being installed around Hanoi:

The sensible thing for our side to do is to make certain that these missile sites are being built, then give two hours warning to everybody in the area to get out of the way, then blow the whole layout to Kingdom Come with hydrogen or conventional bombs. . . .

*Daily News* editorials were not noted for moderation, but the very fact that the largest circulation daily in the U.S. could make such a statement is an indication of the immense task that lay before the new antiwar movement.

22. *Militant,* April 26, 1965, full text.

# 3

# The Teach-ins:
# Ann Arbor, Washington, Berkeley

While preparations were under way for the march on Washington, another important part of the new antiwar movement was initiated at the University of Michigan at Ann Arbor. A meeting of some two dozen faculty members—most of them on the young side and without tenure—took place March 11 to discuss a response to the Vietnam situation, possibly through an ad in a newspaper signed by a large number of faculty. Marc Pilisuk, a professor on the staff of the Mental Health Research Institute, was present and later observed: "Meetings of this type were not new in Ann Arbor. Many of the same faces were present again, veterans of a string of advertisements for the test ban, for a fair housing ordinance, for the election of Lyndon Johnson."[1]

This time the sense of anger and frustration led to discussion about more serious action. William Gamson, a sociologist, pro posed a one-day faculty strike during which a special school would be held to teach the hidden truth about American intervention in Vietnam. There was considerable hesitation over such a bold move but it was agreed that an attempt would be made to obtain signatures from faculty pledging such action. If the number of signers was large enough, the strike would be called. The university administration and even the state legislature got wind of the proposal and began to threaten reprisals. The faculty senate considered taking action against those who signed the first call, only three of whom out of forty-nine had tenure.

1. *Teach-Ins: U.S.A.* Edited by Louis Menashe and Ronald Radosh (New York: Praeger, 1967), p. 8.

On March 16 a group of these met to reconsider. Their main motives were not worry about their own jobs—though that was a legitimate concern—but the fear that the issue of Vietnam would get lost in a dispute over faculty responsibility and the chance to make a broad impact would be dissipated in an isolated action by a handful. A teacher of anthropology, Marshall Sahlins, came up with the idea of staying in regular classes but holding the school on Vietnam at night—all night long if interest were great enough.

This proposal was put to a meeting of signers of the strike call held Wednesday, March 17, 1965, and finally adopted after an all-night discussion. The protest was scheduled for March 24-25 beginning at eight o'clock at night and running to eight in the morning. In addition, faculty pledged themselves to spread the idea to other campuses. By analogy with the sit-in tactic of the Southern civil rights movement, the action was called a "teach-in."

Some of the angrier faculty and students considered the decision a copout under pressure. But those who were serious students of the subject knew the U.S. government's public rationale for intervention in Vietnam was a tissue of inaccuracies and that the country badly needed to learn the facts. What better way could the academic community use its expertise at this stage of the struggle? "Be true to yourself" is always a good rule in movement struggle, as in other areas of life.

The strike threat itself, coming as it did in the aftermath of the traumatic events of the Berkeley Free Speech Movement, was not without its positive results. The university administration was so relieved at the change in plans that it offered cooperation in providing facilities. It even suspended the rules regarding women students to allow them to stay out of the dorms past curfew to attend the teach-in. (The women's liberation movement was yet to come.)

Faculty and students threw themselves into preparations. Long-distance calls were made to colleges across the country. Teachers visited the student dorms and fraternity and sorority houses to spread the word and ask for help organizing. A new relationship with the students was born. The response was beyond expectations. By the night of March 24 dozens of other campuses had scheduled teach-ins, and by eight o'clock that night over 3,000 students showed up for the event in Ann Arbor.

The lectures were held in four halls. At one point the building had to be temporarily evacuated because of a bomb threat. A midnight demonstration was held outdoors in below-freezing weather. At that rally, Frithjof Bergmann of the philosophy department declared: "The Viet Cong is a popular movement in the classic sense." He called on the U.S. government to allow "the Vietnamese to be governed by the government they have chosen themselves."[2]

The teach-in was picketed by some seventy-five students organized by right-wing groups, but they made no dent. An organized attempt to break up the midnight rally was overcome when students attending the teach-in formed a line to prevent the right-wingers from breaking into the ranks of the demonstration.

Above all the teach-in was an educational experience. The arguments of the State Department were analyzed, in some cases by experts in the field, including some who had worked for the government and knew parts of the story from the inside. The students were not passive participants. They asked questions, argued, probed, challenged assumptions. In addition to the lectures, over a dozen smaller discussion groups were formed which, in Pilisuk's words,

reached a depth of concern and an intensity of argument rarely seen at universities. One honors student later told me that this was her first educational experience provided by the university during four years' attendance. . . . On that night, people who really cared talked of things that really mattered.[3]

Professor Robert S. Browne, an economist who had spent six years as a State Department adviser in Vietnam, spoke at Ann Arbor and then flew to New York, where he lectured and reported on the Ann Arbor event to a similar teach-in the next night at Columbia University attended by 2,500.

Many of the speakers publicized the April 17 march on Washington and on the single night of the first Ann Arbor teach-in over a hundred students signed up for the long bus ride to the Washington demonstration.

During the next month the teach-ins spread to hundreds of campuses across the country and were to become a feature of campus life for the next year, often being the first antiwar activity on a particular campus, especially in conservative areas.

2. *Militant,* April 5, 1965.
3. *Teach-Ins: U.S.A.,* p. 11.

In the course of this period, the government position on Vietnam lost its moral authority in the academic community. This in turn had profound—if not so immediate—effects in many other areas of American life.

The impact of the teach-ins went far beyond the issue of the war itself in the narrow sense. The teach-in tactic together with the nonexclusive stance of the new antiwar movement generally shattered the norms of "the silent generation" and helped break down the stultifying effects of the anticommunist hysteria. For the first time in years, and on a level previously unknown in the modern United States, the academic world was alive with the discussion of controversial ideas.

In a sense, the Free Speech Movement had spread across the country. Even the previously excluded radicals found it possible to set up literature tables, sell their books, distribute their leaflets, get their spokespersons on campuses to talk to significant numbers of students willing to seriously consider all ideas.

What A. J. Muste had sensed in his admonition to SANE during the Dodd attack back in 1960 became clearly manifest in the period of the teach-ins: the resurgence of a reservoir of "young people, fed up with conformism and apathy."

The Ann Arbor teach-in was organized as a protest against the war, not simply as an even-handed debate with proponents of U.S. policy in Vietnam, though the government position was voiced there. But in many places the format was one of debate and the State Department was besieged with requests for speakers to present the government point of view. As it turned out it didn't really matter too much either way, for with few exceptions such debates ended in defeat for the government side. Their experts could point to occasional errors of assumption which were widespread among opponents of the war—the fact that neither the U.S. nor Saigon representatives at Geneva had signed the part of the accords calling for elections in 1956, for example—but these were really just quibbles. What the government spokesmen couldn't sell was a convincing and compelling reason for the U.S. being involved in the war in any case.

In the course of the teach-ins tens of thousands of persons became serious students of the available literature on U.S. intervention in Vietnam. The essential outline of the developments later exposed from a government source itself in the Pentagon Papers actually became common knowledge in teach-in circles from 1965 on. In this process two pieces of literature

played a particularly important role. One was the analysis by
I. F. Stone of the State Department's *White Paper on Vietnam*
published in April 1965. The other was a report written by Robert
Scheer on a grant from the Center for the Study of Democratic
Institutions, called *How the United States Got Involved in
Vietnam*. If the American antiwar movement can be said to have
had a work which played a role analogous to that of Tom Paine's
*Common Sense* in the American Revolution, Scheer's little
pamphlet was it.

On April 23, 1965, Secretary of State Dean Rusk made a speech
in which he referred to the wave of teach-ins with the following
comment: "I sometimes wonder at the gullibility of educated men
and the stubborn disregard of plain facts by men who are
supposed to be helping our young to learn—especially to learn
how to think."[4]

The next day an uprising began in the Dominican Republic
with the aim of restoring the popular reform constitution overthrown by a military coup in 1963. Within three days the
Constitutionalists had defeated the old regime in a decisive battle
on the outskirts of the capital. The dictatorship, however, was
saved by an invasion of 24,000 U.S. troops sent on the initial
pretext of rescuing a handful of U.S. citizens (none of whom were
in any case threatened by the Constitutionalists).

From the point of view of imperialist policy the Dominican
invasion was a success, since the Constitutionalists were eventually defeated and a regime headed by Joaquin Balaguer, a former
appointee of the old Trujillo dictatorship, was imposed on the
island nation. But the Dominican events in 1965 contributed to
the "credibility gap" already widening over the question of
Vietnam.

During May an Inter-Departmental Speaking Team on Vietnam Policy, composed of three U.S. officials who had recently
served in Vietnam, was sent to a number of Midwest campuses.
The team had no success in stemming the tide of opposition,
though in most places it was politely received. At the University
of Wisconsin at Madison, a large part of the audience of some 700
wore black armbands, stood during the talks, and besieged the
lecturers with hostile questions. One such exchange went like
this:

4. From a speech before the American Society of International Law,
quoted in *Facts On File: World News Digest,* April 22-28, 1965, p. 145.

Student: "Why do prisoners we take confess to infiltration only after a month of interrogation?"

Thomas F. Conlon, of the State Department: "Have you ever had anything to do with interrogation?"

Student: "No, and I don't want to."

Conlon: "Sometimes it takes a long time before a prisoner wants to talk."

Another student shouts: "Torture!"

Conlon: "Do you also charge the North Vietnamese with torture?"

The second student: "I condemn torture whoever does it."

Conlon: "The Americans do not torture."

"But we run the show," shouts someone in the audience.

Conlon: "We do not run it."

Shouts from all over the hall: "Aw come on, let's be honest."[5]

An article on the team's tour by Barry Sheppard in the May 17, 1965, *Militant* concludes:

We can only hope that the administration does go ahead and send out other teams all over the country, because there apparently is nothing like these direct confrontations with the administration's spokesmen to further expose the lies and hypocrisy of the government and build up the university opposition to the Vietnam war.

The first government "truth team" on Vietnam, however, proved to be the last.

\*        \*        \*

The same Ann Arbor faculty meeting which had changed the original strike idea to the teach-in also agreed that if the first event were successful a national teach-in in Washington would be initiated. Later on it was decided that for the national event "the overweighing consideration was the prospect of confronting Administration spokesmen," according to Professor Anatol Rapoport, one of the original organizers.[6] Therefore a debate, rather than a protest format, was agreed to.

A letter signed by 400 University of Michigan faculty members

5. *Teach-Ins: U.S.A.,* p. 134.
6. Ibid., p. 174.

was sent to McGeorge Bundy, one of Johnson's top foreign-policy advisers and a member of the group of Ivy League intellectuals originally recruited to the service of the John F. Kennedy administration. In reply Bundy invited representatives of the teach-in group to Washington to negotiate. According to Rapoport:

> Mr. Bundy's first objection to our proposed format was based on the fact that we did not represent a whole spectrum of the community. In this he was undoubtedly right, although to our way of thinking, this was irrelevant to what we thought the country needed—namely, a confrontation between the Administration and a responsible opposition. We felt that such an encounter was made necessary by the fact that a meaningful debate on foreign policy had been effectively prevented in Congress, where it should normally take place if the democratic process were not to become a dead letter.[7]

The agreement arrived at with Bundy was for the main event of the national teach-in to be a debate between Bundy and an academic figure critical of government Vietnam policy, with each side being supported by a panel of other academics. Thus, said Rapoport, "the impression would be avoided—as Mr. Bundy insisted it should be—that the academic community was unanimously opposed to the present policy on Vietnam."

Bundy's acceptance was announced and the Inter-University Committee for a Public Hearing on Vietnam began building the national teach-in from a headquarters in Ann Arbor. The event was scheduled for May 15, 1965, in Washington.

A telephone network connected with local radio stations and campus public-address systems was set up to carry the proceedings to 122 university areas. In addition National Educational Television broadcast the event in full and live, as well as later repeats of the highlights.

The government side insisted on having a say about who the opposition debater would be, as well as bringing other pressures. The final result was a format which bore little resemblance to the teach-ins around the country. Nevertheless the event had a powerful effect in further undermining the authority of the government's position.

One reason was that Bundy canceled out at the last minute, on the excuse that, of all things, he had to work on the crisis in the

7. Ibid., p. 175.

Dominican Republic. When this was announced to the generally polite live audience in Washington, the groans were audible. The audience then listened with subdued but rising anger to a classic of cold-war double-speak, contained in Bundy's brief statement of regret:

It has been argued that debate of this kind should be avoided because it can give encouragement to the adversaries of our country. There is some ground for this argument, since it is true that Communists have little understanding of the meaning of debate in a free society. The Chinese will continue to pretend that American policy is weaker because 700 faculty members have made a protest against our policy in Vietnam. The American people, whatever their opinion, know better. They know that those who are protesting are only a minority of American teachers and students. . . . They understand what Communists cannot understand at all, that open discussion between our citizens and their government is the central nervous system of our free society. We cannot let the propaganda of such totalitarians divert us from our necessary arguments with one another any more than we can let them be misled by such debates if we can help it.[8]

Seven hundred faculty members indeed! The audience looked around at itself. There were several thousand in the Washington hall alone—far more than 700 of them protesting faculty members—not to mention the 122 other audiences on the telephone hookup. Bundy's statement was absurd while its arrogance was frightening. Right then and there, the credibility gap began to widen into a chasm.

Bundy wasn't the only one that day to attempt to wrap himself—and U.S. Vietnam policy—in the cloak of defense of free speech while disparaging those who exercised it on a meaningful question. Arthur M. Schlesinger, Jr., another of Kennedy's academic brain trust—though not then still in the administration—spoke for the government side, with some criticisms. ("A limited increase in the American ground force commitment and a decreased emphasis on air power are indispensable to negotiations. Indeed if we took the Marines now in the Dominican Republic and sent them to South Vietnam, we would be a good deal better off in both countries."[9]) At one point he appealed to the audience to remember that one thing the U.S. was

8. Ibid., p. 154.
9. Ibid., p. 170.

defending in Vietnam was the right of the academic community to debate issues. A good part of the audience actually hissed. Schlesinger was visibly shaken. The best government brains simply couldn't understand that people don't like to be abused that way.

In the absence of Bundy the main government debater was Professor Robert Scalapino of the University of California at Berkeley. His opponent was Professor George M. Kahin of Cornell, backed up by Hans Morgenthau, professor of political science at the University of Chicago. Both Kahin's and Morgenthau's presentations shot gaping holes through the government position, though neither challenged the right of the U.S. to be in Vietnam. In general, the opposition spokespersons at the national teach-in did not advocate immediate withdrawal, but stayed within the framework of how to make U.S. foreign policy more effective and realistic. As William Appleman Williams later commented, it had aspects of a seminar on "finding even better ways of doing what we [the U.S.] are already doing too well."[10] Nevertheless it was the first time in their lives that a mass audience of Americans had witnessed a real debate on U.S. foreign policy, and recognized the simple fact that the government position appeared very weak. Another important feature of the affair was the appearance—for a special lecture on the origins of the cold war—of Isaac Deutscher, the Marxist biographer of Trotsky.

The very fact that Deutscher was invited by the organizers was an indication of the depth of questioning going on in the academic community. For many years it had been virtually impossible to hear a Marxist at any but a very few American universities, and most American students—not to mention the general public—had never heard the notion challenged that Russia and China were to blame for the cold war. But here was Isaac Deutscher, short, bald, grey goatee, with impeccable credentials as a historian, Western Europe's most renowned expert on Soviet affairs, telling a mass audience of Americans across the country that it was the Western capitalist world, not the noncapitalist countries, which was the source of the cold war. And what is more, doing it with convincing logic in terms not only academicians could understand.

I was sitting in the press section at the time and some of the

10. *York Gazette and Daily* (York, Pennsylvania), June 19, 1965.

Washington reporters, who had been grinding out the State Department line so long they didn't know anything else existed, had difficulty catching the tenor of Deutscher's speech, though it would have been crystal clear to any average high school student. They reacted with crude jokes at the old man's appearance. But Deutscher's lecture was not the least of the contributions to a change in attitudes which the national teach-in helped stimulate.

*          *          *

The greatest of the local teach-ins occurred at Berkeley May 21-22, 1965. Organized as Vietnam Day at the University of California, it attracted spokespersons for virtually the entire spectrum of opposition to U.S. policy in Vietnam and a few who defended the State Department position. In the course of the thirty-six-hour affair some 30,000 persons particpated, with crowds for some speeches reaching 12,000.

This event gave rise to the Vietnam Day Committee (VDC) as well as to the next major national and international initiatives of the new antiwar movement.

Berkeley's Vietnam Day was quite different from the national teach-in. It was not that its organizers did not want to debate government spokesmen. They offered Professor Scalapino whatever time he wanted on the program, and even invited the government team of speakers on Vietnam.

But the Berkeley organizers refused to allow the government or the university, or even the more Establishment-oriented movement figures, to set the terms of the debate. To a certain extent the government had succeeded in this at the national teach-in. In general the position of the liberal Establishment was that certain ideas were simply not open to challenge—anticommunism, for example, or the very right of the U.S. to be in Vietnam.

The attitude of the Berkeley organizers is summed up in this comment written by James Petras after the event on the attempt by Robert Pickus of Turn Toward Peace to set the terms of the program:

> He sought to impose an organizational apparatus to check the credentials of all participants, in order to insure that they agreed with his general views. He agreed to join if all others submitted to his particular form of "democracy." His method of operation seemed to us a "rule or ruin" approach.

Nevertheless, Pickus did have the chance to speak at Vietnam Day. His line was the most absurd heard that day: he said that he was opposed to U.S. violence in Vietnam, but he declined to support the withdrawal of U.S. soldiers. To oppose American intervention in Vietnam, as Hal Draper [of the International Socialist Club] pointed out in his debate with Pickus, is to call for the *immediate* withdrawal of U.S. troops. To call for it "later" (under whatever pretense) is to legitimatize violence in the here and now—since one cannot impose utopian dreams on what the U.S. army does in fighting a war of conquest. One would not be too irreverent to refer to this type of "peace" approach as "War now—Peace later."[11]

The idea for Vietnam Day originated with a small group of unaffiliated "new left" students, Barbara Gullahorn, Bob Fitch, and Jerry Rubin, a graduate student originally from Cincinnati.

During preparations for the April 17 San Francisco demonstration (which coincided with the SDS march on Washington) these students had met Stephen Smale, a young professor in the mathematics department at Berkeley who was active in the local American Federation of Teachers. They proposed the idea of a giant town meeting on Vietnam at the Berkeley campus. Smale, in cooperation with another professor, Morris Hirsch, approached the university administration with demands for facilities. Smale recalls:

The Free Speech Movement was fresh in mind in those days and had quite a threat on the administration, which was worried about precipitating another free-speech issue. This was important. We made big demands. A super teach-in, with outdoor loudspeakers and everything. They opposed it at first, but timidly. We got the essentials.[12]

The impish, iconoclastic Rubin had found a kindred soul in Smale, and, what is more, one who had some influence and a feel for a mass movement. After a sharp struggle with some of the local union officials, Smale got the local AFT to join in sponsorship of Vietnam Day. People started paying attention.

The event was organized in open, nonexclusive meetings where ideas for speakers were discussed and committees formed to do

11. *We Accuse* (Berkeley: Diablo Press, 1965), p. 3. (This book was a transcript of the major speeches at Vietnam Day. Petras supplied an editors' preface on behalf of the VDC.)

12. Author's taped interview with Smale, October 6, 1973. Library of Social History, New York.

the work. Much of this was done out of Rubin's apartment by volunteers. One of these was Paul Montauk, a chef in his forties then teaching culinary arts for a Job Corps program, who became secretary-treasurer for Vietnam Day. Montauk was a longtime member of the Socialist Workers Party. Hanging on the phone in Rubin's apartment, tying up practical details—never Rubin's strong point—Montauk became enthusiastic and he convinced the Trotskyists, including the Young Socialist Alliance, to throw themselves into the project. After similar initial hesitation, the other organized radical tendencies participated as well, and a significant unity was forged—with the "independents" taking the lead—which carried beyond the event and into the first period of the VDC.

Both Rubin and Smale tended to be contemptuous of the existing radical groups, considering them "old left" and almost irrelevant. But they were not exclusionists and welcomed the participation of everyone willing to help. Rubin made no secret of the fact that he viewed his role as helping to build an entirely new type of radical movement. Just what the program of this new movement would be was never very clearly articulated by Rubin. But its methods would be pragmatic, cultural as well as political, and aimed first of all at challenging the stifling norms of the cold-war liberal Establishment. For Rubin, style was as important as program in politics. Later it would *be* politics in the sense of Marshall McLuhan's "the medium is the message."

Rubin's overall approach wasn't worth much in the long-term task of constructing a movement. But for building a relatively simple operation like a big teach-in it had its positive sides. The object of the teach-in, after all, was not to hammer out a particular program or organization, but to challenge previously unchallenged ideas before the widest possible audience. Its thrust was to feed the awakening desire to consider new or previously proscribed ideas, to break down the xenophobia of the cold war, and to awaken a morality of human solidarity within an America long dominated by the ethic—and the style—of the corporation ledger. All this Rubin understood. In addition it was Rubin who first of all pushed for Vietnam Day—and afterward the Vietnam Day Committee—to have an international character. He was deliberate in his attempts to bring to bear on the United States the weight of the rest of the world's thinking about Vietnam.

Smale and Rubin pressed for the dramatic and the colorful. Though they were often in the minority, their stamp was left on the affair, which had a cultural quality in the broad sense. In part because of this it produced an effective moral statement on the quality of American life under the liberal Establishment. As Hirsch, Smale, and Rubin put it in a reply to an attack on the event by Professor Scalapino, "the problem of Vietnam is the problem of the soul of America."[13]

Scalapino's attack came in a statement issued before the teach-in explaining his refusal to speak. Said Scalapino:

> A few individuals, most of whom would not dream of treating their own disciplines in this cavalier fashion, have sponsored a rigged meeting in which various ideologies and entertainers are going to enlighten us on Vietnam.
>
> Only a handful of the performers have ever been to Vietnam or made any serious study of its problems. The objective is propaganda, not knowledge. . . . This travesty should be repudiated by all true scholars irrespective of their views on Vietnam. . . .[14]

At the teach-in itself this was answered in kind by Paul Krassner, the editor of *The Realist* and an expert in the cavalier treatment of pomposity. Quipped Krassner: "I noticed at the lunch wagon back there that there was a change in the menu, and veal scalapino has now been changed to 'chicken scalapino.'"

The reply to Scalapino by Hirsch, Smale, and Rubin, released a few days before the event, was more political:

> The purpose of Vietnam Day is to present to the Bay Area community alternatives to current U.S. policy. The information and ideas that will be related on these days cannot be found in the mass media, the State Department *White Paper,* or even in university classrooms. We are contributing to democratic dialogue by expressing views which, although widespread in Asia and Europe, are rarely presented to the American people. . . .
>
> Professor Scalapino has implied that the only people who are qualified to discuss Vietnam in public are academic or State Department experts on Vietnam. We do have such technical experts on the program: Professor Stanley Scheinbaum, who designed the strategic hamlet program for the Government, but who now regrets it, is one example. But to restrict public discussion to "experts" leads to a dangerous elitism because, in the end,

---

13. *Teach-Ins: U.S.A.,* pp. 30-31.
14 *Ibid.,* pp. 29-30.

decisions on foreign policy are based on value judgments, not just on a simple recording of facts. The issues in Vietnam are too important to be settled by Cold War gamesmanship or academic hair splitting. One of the purposes of Vietnam Day is to transfer the discussion from the Rand Corporation to the streets.[15]

This remarkable statement would work out in real life for the next eight years, even literally with the Pentagon Papers exposé in 1970. None of the Vietnam Day organizers in 1965 had ever heard of Daniel Ellsberg or Anthony Russo, the two Rand Corporation experts who would make those papers public. At the time Ellsberg was just aother JFK intellectual dedicated to winning the war in Vietnam. But the moral offensive of which Vietnam Day was an important part would work its way into the most unlikely places.

\*        \*        \*

Isaac Deutscher also appeared at Vietnam Day, where he delivered an eighty-minute lecture after midnight, outdoors, to one of the largest audiences at the affair. It covered the same ground as his Washington speech, but in addition he took on the essence of the argument in McGeorge Bundy's letter to the national teach-in on free speech under Communist governments. Said Deutscher:

I still believe that class struggle is the motive force of history, but in this last period, class struggle has all too often sunk into a bloody morass of power politics. On both sides of the great divide, a few ruthless and half-witted oligarchies—capitalist oligarchies here, bureaucratic oligarchies there—hold all the power and make all the decisions, obfuscate the minds and throttle the wills of nations. They even reserve for themselves the roles of the chief protagonists and expound for us the great conflicting ideas of our time. The social struggles of our time have degenerated into the unscrupulous contests of the oligarchies. Official Washington speaks for the world's freedom, while official Moscow speaks for the world's socialism. All too long the peoples have failed to contradict these false friends, either of freedom or of socialism. On both sides of the great divide the peoples have been silent too long and thus willy-nilly have identified themselves with the policies of their governments. The world has thus come very close, dangerously close, to a division between revolutionary and counter-revolutionary nations. . . .
Fortunately, things have begun to change. The Russian people have

15. Ibid., p. 30.

been shaking off the 'old conformism and have been regaining their critical attitude towards their rulers. . . . I am sure that without the Russian de-Stalinization there would not have been this amount of freedom and critical thinking that there is in America today. And I am also sure that your continued exercise of freedom and continued voicing of criticism and of critical political action will encourage the further progress of freedom in the communist part of the world. . . . The more you exercise your freedom, the more will the Russians feel encouraged to speak up critically against the mistakes and blunders of their government.[16]

Deutscher concluded with a peroration, the more remarkable for the standing ovation it evoked from an audience of not-so-out-of-the-ordinary American youth. He said:

The division may perhaps once again run within nations rather than between nations. And once the divisions begin to run within nations, progress begins anew, the progress toward the *only* solution of our problem, not of all our problems, but of the critical political problems and social problems, the *only* solution, which is a socialist world, one socialist world. We must, we can and we must, give back to class struggle its old dignity. We may and we must restore meaning to the great ideas, partly conflicting ideas, by which mankind is still living; the ideas of liberalism, democracy, and communism—yes, the idea of communism.[17]

*      *      *

One international figure the organizers of Vietnam Day sought to get, without success, was Jean-Paul Sartre. The great French existentialist philosopher and novelist, whose courage in speaking out against inhumane policies of his own government in Algeria had been an inspiration to many intellectuals in America, refused all invitations to speak in the U.S., even cancelling a scheduled appearance at Cornell after Johnson's February escalation of the war. In explaining his reasons Sartre said the U.S. would change only slowly, "and more, I think, if one resists it, than if one preaches to it."

Regarding those Americans opposed to the war, Sartre said:

The problem is not whether or not I would have helped such Americans

16. *We Accuse*, pp. 51-52.
17. Ibid., p. 52.

more or less by going there. The fact is that I cannot help them at all. Because their political weight unhappily, is nil. . . . These people are totally impotent. One of them wrote me: "If you do not come to us, if you break off all communication with us, it must be that you regard us as the accursed of this earth!" I do think, in fact, that a man of the American Left who has a clear view of the situation, and who sees himself isolated in a land entirely conditioned by the myths of imperialism and anticommunism, such a man, I say, and with all respect, is indeed one of the accursed of this earth. He totally disapproves of the politics carried on in his name and his action is totally ineffective—in any case, for the present. . . .

American opinion can become sensitive on this subject only as a result of a deep crisis; a military disaster or the threat of world war. The only way we have of contributing to this awareness is by making a brutal and global condemnation of American policy in Vietnam and by trying to provoke wherever possible—that is to say, in Europe—protests against that policy.[18]

Norman Mailer was as close to an existential-minded novelist as Vietnam Day was able to provide. In his speech, which drew perhaps the largest crowd of the event and a standing ovation, he expressed a feel of the situation in the United States in one way similar and in another in striking contrast to that of Sartre. Said Mailer:

If we wish to take a strange country away from strangers, let us at least be strong enough and brave enough to defeat them on the ground. Our marines, some would say, are the best soldiers in the world. The counterargument is that native guerrillas can defeat any force of a major power man-to-man. Let us then fight on fair grounds. Let us say to Lyndon Johnson, to monstrous [Secretary of Defense] McNamara, and to the generals on the scene, "Fight like men. Go in man-to-man against the Vietcong. Call off the Air Force. They prove nothing except that America is coterminous with the Mafia. Let us win man-to-man or lose man-to-man, but let us stop pulverizing people whose faces we have never seen." But, of course, we will not stop, nor will we ever fight man-to-man against poor peasants. Their vision of existence might be more ferocious and more determined than our own. No, we would rather go on as the most advanced monsters of civilization, pulverizing instinct with our detonations, our State Department experts in their little bow ties, and our bombs.

Only listen, Lyndon Johnson, you've gone too far this time. You are a

18. Jean-Paul Sartre, "Why I Will Not Go to the United States," *Nation*, April 19, 1965.

bully with an Air Force, and since you will not call off your Air Force, there are young people who will persecute you back. It is a little thing, but it will hound you into nightmares and endless corridors of night without sleep. It will hound you. . . . They will go on marches and they will make demonstrations, and they will begin a war of public protest against you which will never cease. It will go on and on and it will get stronger and stronger.[19]

19. *We Accuse*, pp. 21-22.

# 4

# The First International Days of Protest

The new antiwar movement was barely born when it faced a
crisis of leadership on a national level. At first this emerged as a
crisis within SDS. The practical significance of the SDS call for a
march on Washington against the war in Vietnam was precisely
that it came from an organization viewed at the time as an
accepted part of the old peace movement. This made possible a
broad unity in action none of the small radical and pacifist
groups could inspire on their own.[1]

The success of the march on Washington placed SDS on center
stage nationally. Not only were all the radical groups that
wanted to be part of the new movement willing to follow its lead,
reluctantly or not, but so were tens of thousands of unaffiliated
youth, disaffected liberals, and most of the older peace groups.

1. In the San Francisco Bay Area the local SDS was too small and
weak to take the lead on the April 17 march held in solidarity with the
one in Washington. The ad hoc committee which organized it proved
unable to maintain the unity characteristic of the Washington affair. The
committee split shortly before the demonstration after a Du Bois Club
motion was passed excluding certain radical slogans and speakers.
Interestingly the immediate withdrawal slogan was not among those
excluded.

Leslie Evans, then YSA chairman in San Francisco, recalls: "A big
meeting was held at a house in Berkeley. . . . Agreement had been
reached on some points and others were still under debate when one of
the Du Bois leaders announced that it was impossible to come to any
agreement with PL and the YSA and that the minority at the meeting
should get out of the house, which was private property (it belonged to

For the moment SANE had lost hegemony even within the moderate wing of the movement—first because of its failure to take the initiative on the Vietnam issue and then for its failure to support the march on Washington. SDS had the authority, but it needed to use it. Unfortunately, both for SDS and for the new antiwar movement, the moment was lost. It is one of the ironies of the 1960s that though SDS helped give birth to the new antiwar movement with its call for the march on Washington, and this more than any other activity built SDS nationally, nevertheless after the April 17 event SDS never again took a major national antiwar initiative, nor did it ever again play an important national role in the new antiwar movement. This was its default in spite of the fact that most SDS chapters were involved in local antiwar activity and responded positively to national initiatives from elsewhere, initiatives either downplayed or actually opposed by the SDS national office.

In part this was due to a general crisis in which the SDS national office found itself in the summer of 1965. It didn't initiate much of anything else either.

Signs of this were present in the SDS National Council meeting which took place in Washington April 18, the day following the march. Clark Kissinger reported this meeting as "one of the most pleasant and productive in recent SDS history."[2] Indeed, following the march, the atmosphere was euphoric and there were ideas aplenty proposed on what to do next. But almost nothing specific was done, except to decide to move the national office to Chicago. Carl Oglesby, who had been in SDS only a few months but who had spoken well at the Ann Arbor teach-in, was hired to head up a Research, Information and Publications project to provide

---

someone supporting the Du Bois side in the debate)." (Letter to the author, May 16, 1975.)

PL, the YSA, and the Afro-American Committee for African and Asian Solidarity held a separate and smaller march. Shortly thereafter the local YSA concluded that the split had been a mistake. According to Syd Stapleton, then a YSA leader in Berkeley, "We didn't understand what they understood back East, that this could be the beginning of a big, ongoing movement against the war, that the important thing was to remain inside it, building a left wing inside it. The Du Bois Clubs one-upped us at a meeting, so we organized a competing march. It was a piece of sectarian idiocy." (Letter to the author, May 19, 1975.)

2. Kirkpatrick Sale, *SDS* (New York: Vintage Books, 1974), pp. 193-94.

literature on Vietnam and other questions. It was also agreed to cooperate with the professors then organizing the national teach-in. But there was no decision for any plan for a new national initiative or focus for Vietnam activity.

Kissinger proposed a campaign of leafletting military bases and induction centers, urging young men not to register for the draft, not to report if already registered, or to refuse to continue to serve if already drafted. The object was to court arrest and then have the SDSers defend themselves on the grounds of the Nuremberg Doctrine flowing from the trials of Nazi war criminals at the end of World War II.

The suggestion was promptly labeled "Kissinger's Kamikaze plan" and was referred to a committee for further study with the admonition that before any such thing could be implemented the membership would have to be polled. The general idea of an SDS draft-resistance campaign was kicked around for the next six months, greatly modified in various statements put out by SDS spokesmen, but never implemented. It received widespread publicity in the media and as a result of attacks on SDS by congressmen and government officials. But when the referendum was finally held in the fall the proposal was defeated by a vote of 279 to 234 with 35 abstentions, approximately one-fourth of the paid-up membership having voted, according to Paul Booth.[3] The defeat of the proposal received very little media coverage, however, and the general impression was left that SDS was in the leadership of a draft-resistance movement. But that just wasn't so.

At the April 18 meeting Hayden suggested a call for a new Continental Congress to meet in the summer. This wasn't even referred to a committee but simply dropped.

The SDS convention that summer, held June 9-13 in Kewadin, Michigan, decided that SDS would not take a leading role in the new antiwar movement. In part this was due to the influence of the "new guard" of SDSers for whom resistance to any kind of centralized structure or initiative was becoming a matter of principle. (An example of this was the fact that the post of national secretary, which when occupied by Kissinger played a crucial role in launching the march on Washington, was not filled at this convention.)

3. *National Secretary's Report* (SDS) by Paul Booth, November 1965. (Copy in author's files.)

But the "old guard" also opposed an antiwar focus on the grounds that the demonstrations and similar activity could not stop the war, that they were a diversion from the more important community work such as the ERAP projects, and that the key strategy was to build a grass-roots radical base over an extended period of time which could eventually "stop the seventh war from now," as the phrase current in SDS circles put it.

Years later, many SDSers of 1965 would look back on this decision as perhaps SDS's biggest mistake. Kissinger recalls that at the time the leading figures in SDS were preoccupied with the experience of the Student Nonviolent Coordinating Committee in its community projects in the South, and had the idea that SDS could reproduce something like that in the North and among white as well as Black poor.[4]

Sale quotes Todd Gitlin on the SDS default as follows:

Our failure of leadership—which was undeniable—was a reflection of the fact that our hearts were not on the campuses. . . . We were just plain stupid. . . . The leadership was already a closed elite, we didn't *understand* what an antiwar movement would be, we didn't have any *feel* for it. My own feeling then was that it was a big abstraction . . . because that kind of movement is so big, because I couldn't see what it would be, day to day. What we surrendered then was the chance for an anti-imperialist peace movement.[5]

In this vacuum, SANE itself, now under great pressure from its own ranks to do something on Vietnam,[6] would attempt to reestablish hegemony in the antiwar movement by at last mounting a campaign on the issue, though within the confines of the old

4. Author's taped interview with Clark Kissinger, October 16, 1973.
5. Sale, *SDS*, p. 214, emphasis in original.
6. For example, an April 18 letter to the national SANE office from Abe Bloom, vice-chairman of Washington SANE, said: "This is being written the day after the great demonstration in Washington. Twenty thousand students and others demonstrated for peace in Vietnam. It was very sad to those of us in SANE, that every publicity release mentioning names of organizations sponsoring and supporting the demonstration had a big blank where SANE should have been. It was the most significant peace action that ever took place in Washington, and National SANE was not part of it. Whatever reasons or policies led to our abstention must be wrong and need reevaluation." (Copy in antiwar files, Library of Social History, New York.)

exclusionary policy and of a political line that specifically avoided outright opposition to U.S. involvement in Vietnam. Willy-nilly, forces to the left of SANE moved to provide a national focus for the new movement on a more radical and nonexclusive basis. But so great was the expectation that SDS would itself do this sooner or later that those who eventually filled this vacuum were not aware at first that this is what they were heading into.

The process can be traced to the Berkeley Vietnam Day at which several prominent militant pacifists including Dave Dellinger, Staughton Lynd, and Bob Parris spoke. Each advocated a campaign of nonviolent civil disobedience against the war, invoking the fresh experience of the campaign of Southern Blacks against de jure segregation. Lynd's talk received probably the greatest applause at the entire Berkeley event. In it he argued against the strategy of seeking social change through "coalition politics," that is, through the Democratic Party, and in favor of the development of an extraparliamentary opposition.

Referring to an article by Michael Harrington in which the Social Democratic leader had said that an escalation of the war in Vietnam would tend to bury the social reforms of Johnson's so-called Great Society and antipoverty programs, Lynd said:

> We need to say to Mr. Harrington, and Mr. Rustin, that escalation has now occurred and that coalition politics in this situation means coalition with the Marines. Is there an alternative? I think the alternative is nonviolent revolution. And for the benefit of the FBI men present, I would like to make it clear that what I mean is not the violent overthrow of the United States government, but the non-violent retirement from office of the present administration. And further, that the way to bring this about is the creation of civil disobedience so massive and so persistent that the Tuesday Lunch Club that is running this country—Johnson, McNamara, Bundy and Rusk—will forthwith resign.[7]

Lynd also raised a variation of the Continental Congress idea. He suggested

> that there might convene in Washington . . . a new Continental Congress drawn from the community unions, freedom parties, and campus protests . . . which would say to one another . . . : "This is a moment of crisis, our

7. *We Accuse* (Berkeley: Diablo Press, 1965), p. 156.

government does not represent us. Let us come together and consider what needs to be done."

A month after Lynd's speech, on June 20, a meeting was held in Washington, D.C., which initiated a call for an Assembly of Unrepresented People to be held in the capital August 6 to 9, the twentieth anniversary of the dropping of the atom bombs on Hiroshima and Nagasaki. The June 20 meeting was organized by the Washington Action Project (WAP), a summer-long program of opposition to the Vietnam War being coordinated by Bob Parris and Eric Weinberger. Weinberger was a member of CNVA and a veteran of many arrests in civil rights protests in Tennessee.

By the time the call to the Assembly of Unrepresented People was distributed in July the proposal had been greatly modified from the Continental Congress idea. At most this affair would be a preliminary to such a larger undertaking. The August event was designed not to be massive, but as a gathering of activists who would hold workshops on various issues in the overall movement for social change, and support or participate in some symbolic civil disobedience actions.

On August 6, representatives of the CNVA, the War Resisters League, the *Catholic Worker,* and the Student Peace Union were to attempt to present to the president a "Declaration of Conscience" committing some 6,000 signers to "conscientious refusal to cooperate with the United States Government in the prosecution of the war in Vietnam."[8]

On August 7-8 workshops were scheduled on the grass around the Washington Monument, and on August 9 a march to the capitol to read a Declaration of Peace in the halls of Congress, or as close as they could get, sitting down in nonviolent civil disobedience at the point where they were stopped.

The assembly went off more or less as planned, with some 2,000 persons participating at one point or another during the four days. It culminated in a march August 9 of some 750 persons toward the capitol, with 350 being arrested when they sat down after police stopped them. The sit-down served as the final

8. The same document had been presented at the White House April 28, 1965, when only 4,500 had signed. Signers included A. Philip Randolph, SNCC Chairman John Lewis, W. H. Ferry of the Center for the Study of Democratic Institutions, Rev. Philip Berrigan, Bayard Rustin, and A. J. Muste.

session of the assembly. It was conducted surrounded by police and their vans which took seven hours to haul everyone to jail. This was the largest mass arrest in Washington history up to that time. The event received considerable publicity, and angry denunciation in Congress, much of it misdirected at SDS. The cover of the next week's issue of *Life* magazine carried a photograph of Dellinger, Parris, and Lynd doused with red paint thrown by a heckler. A member of the American Nazi Party who had thrown the paint was released on $10 bail, while Dellinger drew forty-five days in jail for his part in the sit-down.

*          *          *

The most significant result of the assembly, however, grew out of the fact that it gathered together a number of leading antiwar activists from around the country and marked the point at which SDS was bypassed on the antiwar issue.

The call to the assembly was signed by some thirty movement activists including Dellinger, Lynd, Parris, Weinberger, and Donna Allen, who was prominent in the Washington area Women Strike for Peace. Also listed as signers of the call were several SDSers including Carl Oglesby, Dena Clamage, and Mel McDonald. Oglesby had taken off on a tour of Asia shortly after being elected SDS president in June and wasn't around the SDS national office during the six weeks prior to the assembly. Clamage and McDonald were volunteers in the SDS national office who more or less on their own and in spite of the Kewadin convention tried to provide some coordination of Vietnam activity from the Chicago SDS headquarters. But apparently they had minimal influence on this matter with those in charge of the national office. The SDS *Worklist* mailing of July 28, 1965, carried a statement dissociating SDS from the Washington assembly and discouraging attendance at it.

The SDS national office once again missed a chance to play a central role in the new antiwar movement, because, as it turned out, the Assembly of Unrepresented People gave birth to the first of the national coordinating bodies of the anti–Vietnam War movement, the National Coordinating Committee to End the War in Vietnam (NCC).

In this regard there is an interesting error in Sale's generally accurate account of the SDS role. Says Sale:

> After the failure of the Kewadin convention to push SDS into becoming the coordinating antiwar organization in the Movement, a group of independent antiwar activists (among them Staughton Lynd, David Dellinger, Robert Parris Moses, and Stanley Aronowitz) got together to establish a National Coordinating Committee to End the War in Vietnam—the organization that, in many guises over the years, became the coordinator of most of the major marches of the decade—and its first action was the August march.[9]

Aside from being so compressed as to conceal more than it reveals about the history of the antiwar movement, this statement implies that the National Coordinating Committee to End the War in Vietnam was formed and then it called the August event. The opposite is true. The call to the August assembly came first. The NCC was formed at a workshop at the assembly, a workshop which had not even been scheduled prior to the event. This workshop resulted from a separate line of development which also had its origin in the Berkeley Vietnam Day.

The success of that great teach-in inspired its organizers to set up the Vietnam Day Committee (VDC) cochaired by Jerry Rubin and Stephen Smale, which for the next year was the major antiwar group in the San Francisco Bay Area. In line with Rubin's emphasis on the importance of international opposition to the U.S. role in Vietnam, the VDC developed the idea of International Days of Protest to be held October 15 and 16 in as many countries and in as many U.S. cities as possible.

In late June the VDC set up an International Committee "to establish contacts with organizations and individuals abroad to publicize among them the forthcoming international protest."[10]

At this time the VDC activists still looked to SDS for national coordination within the United States. A VDC mailing of this period declares:

> The Vietnam Day Committee in Berkeley, California, has called October 15 and 16 to be International Days of Protest against American

9. Sale, *SDS*, p. 220.

10. VDC report on International Days of Protest, "The International Protest Movement Against American Intervention in Vietnam," p. 1. (Copy in author's files.)

Military Intervention. We plan a community protest meeting in Berkeley on October 15 to be followed by massive civil disobedience on October 16.

SDS (Students for a Democratic Society) has been invited by us to organize simultaneous regional meetings and to establish October 15 and 16 as days of national focus of Vietnam protest activity. The SDS Vietnam Committee [presumably Clamage and McDonald] has warmly accepted this idea and is recommending it to the National Council of SDS, which meets in midsummer. Their approval is expected to be a formality.[11]

But no such approval was forthcoming. By the beginning of August the VDC was still on its own in building the October 15-16 protests within the United States. In spite of the fact that the VDC was then in the midst of a series of demonstrations attempting to stop troop trains passing through the East Bay area—a project close to Rubin's heart—Rubin took off for Washington to attend the Assembly of Unrepresented People with the specific purpose of appealing to the movement activists who would be gathered there for support to the idea of spreading the October 15-16 actions across the United States.

The agenda for the assembly called for two sets of workshops: one dealt with different issues such as civil liberties, civil rights, poverty, free universities, etc.; another set dealt with Vietnam and was to be divided according to constituency—students, professional people, trade unionists, etc. There was no provision for a workshop on national coordination or national focus of antiwar activity.

In part this was due to the multi-issue approach of the initiators and organizers of the assembly. They viewed it as concerned with the whole gamut of social problems facing America, not simply the war. It would indeed have been presumptuous of them to attempt to set up a form for the national direction of the entire *Movement* in the broad sense of that term, especially since many of them at that time looked to SDS itself as the best channel for such a development.

At the opening general meeting of the assembly, before the workshops began, Parris cautioned: "This is only the beginning. It's entirely open. . . . Let's concentrate on what it is you want to do, and begin to learn about what others are doing. If this

11. "News from VDC on October 15-16," undated. (Bancroft Library, University of California at Berkeley.)

coordination happens, we'll feel justified."[12]

But the lack of provision for a discussion of a national antiwar focus was also due to the still widespread assumption that SDS would sooner or later take the initiative on this issue. The decision of the Kewadin convention to avoid this was not well understood at the time even among local SDS chapters, let alone outside the organization.

Rubin shared the general "new left" aversion to a single-issue, ad hoc approach to the Vietnam activity. At one point in the discussions he declared: "But the students are not 'single issue' oriented. They oppose the system." What was needed, he said, "is a permanent radical organization . . . based on the principle of nonexclusion."[13] But Rubin was not willing to wait for SDS, or anyone else, to take the initiative nationally on the burning issue of the war. He wasn't about to leave the field to the Establishment-oriented liberals of SANE either. The VDC had already taken the first step, as far as he was concerned, and everyone ought to get behind broadening the effort nationally.

The Socialist Workers Party and the Young Socialist Alliance were unique among the organized radical tendencies in their approach to this question. They were, of course, a multi-issue political tendency, but in their view the best way to build a massive movement against U.S. involvement in the Vietnam War was to focus on that issue and attempt to involve everyone opposed to the war, regardless of their views on other matters. You couldn't do that if people willing to oppose the war were also required to take positions they didn't necessarily agree with on other questions in order to participate in the antiwar formations. So they favored the development of a united front of all tendencies against the war, of single-issue antiwar committees locally, and of a single-issue national coordination of antiwar activity.

In spite of this difference with the initiators of August 6-9 the YSA caught the logic of the dynamic that had been set in motion by the calling of the assembly in the context of rapid development of antiwar sentiment. In a July 5 communication from the YSA national office to the membership, Doug Jenness, director of the YSA's antiwar activity at the time, declared:

12. *Militant,* August 23, 1965.
13. Ibid.

No matter how SDS, SNCC, Lynd and others characterize the [assembly] workshop sessions and no matter what they expect them to accomplish or not to accomplish, these workshops will likely take the form of a national conference of the leading people in the antiwar committees throughout the country. The coming together of the activists, organizers and leaders of the current antiwar movement in Washington to discuss, and hopefully decide where the antiwar movement should go, is an important event. A call for the next major mass action will most likely be issued from this gathering.[14]

But the YSAers also shared the illusion that SDS still had the initiative, could still be expected to move on the Vietnam issue, and should not or could not be bypassed. This contributed to a costly tactical error by the YSA. Shortly after sending off the July 5 letter, Doug Jenness recalls:

I attended a planning meeting of the assembly at 5 Beekman St. [the Manhattan address which housed the national offices of several radical pacifist groups as well as *Liberation* magazine] that gave me the impression that it was totally disorganized and wouldn't really come off. After giving an impressionistic report [to the YSA leadership] it was agreed that I should write a letter scaling down the participation we had projected on July 5.[15]

The letter, dated July 15, 1965, declared:

The preparation for this event has been very poorly organized. No arrangements for transportation have been made, very little publicity has gone out, and many other organizational details have not been carried out. SDS, which supports the action and is planning to participate, is not willing to carry organizational burdens. Therefore it is likely that the Assembly will not be very large.[16]

It recommended that YSAers from the West Coast not attend because of the cost, those from the Midwest should go only if their antiwar committees could pay the fare (which insured almost no attendance, since such committees rarely had much money), and that East Coast YSAers who could make it inexpensively should

14. Letter from YSA national office to membership by Doug Jenness, July 5, 1965. (Copy in author's files.)
15. Letter to the author from Doug Jenness, October 4, 1973.
16. Letter from YSA national office by Doug Jenness, July 15, 1965. (Copy in author's files.)

concentrate on selling literature with only token attendance at workshops.

The night of August 6, however, before the workshops scheduled to begin the next day, one YSAer did meet with Rubin. He was Dick Roberts, then a reporter for the socialist weekly *Militant* and a former activist at the University of Wisconsin at Madison. Roberts recalls:

"I was tremendously enthusiastic about the idea of building a coordinating committee to nationally organize the antiwar movement. I had no trouble persuading Jerry Rubin of the value it would have."[17]

Rubin then succeeded in arranging a previously unscheduled workshop on national Vietnam action where he could raise the October 15-16 proposal. This workshop was attended by between 75 and 200 people, depending on the time of day, most of whom were student antiwar activists. Some SDSers were present, but, aside from McDonald, played no role. Lynd, Parris, and Dellinger, the main initiators of the assembly, likewise played no active role in this workshop. Stanley Aronowitz, one of the editors of *Studies on the Left* and a somewhat critical adult supporter of SDS, did take an active part, as did Irving Beinin, the business manager of the *National Guardian* and an activist in Manhattan's Lower East Side Mobilization for Peace Action. The Du Bois Club had a sizable presence. A handful of YSAers were there, only three of whom were delegates from antiwar committees.

Two central disputes took place in the workshop. Rubin's proposal to organize nationally the October 15-16 International Days of Protest was counterposed to a proposal by the Du Bois Clubs to simply support an action being planned for Washington, D.C., on October 15 by SANE and the Americans for Democratic Action (ADA). This was entirely consistent with the general approach of the CP tendency, which favored "coalition politics" in the Democratic Party and followed the lead of the liberals in general, and SANE in particular, in the peace movement. The CP tendency was, of course, opposed to its own exclusion, but aside from this it agreed essentially with SANE's strategy—to attempt to convince the liberal Establishment to negotiate rather than escalate. The Rubin proposal won handily.

The second dispute was over where the office of the new coordinating committee was to be located. Both Chicago and

17. Letter to the author from Dick Roberts, October 2, 1973.

Madison, Wisconsin, were proposed. This involved which political tendencies would have most influence in the national office, though the arguments were not put that bluntly. The Du Bois Clubs supported Madison, where they had strong influence in the local University of Wisconsin antiwar committee headed by Frank Emspak. Emspak's name was widely known because of his late father, Julius Emspak, a top official of the United Electrical Workers and one of the most prominent Stalinist trade union leaders of the 1940s.

Most of the others present, including Rubin, McDonald, and the YSAers, supported Chicago, in part for the obvious reason that it was a much more important and central city but also because the SDS national office was located there. At first the Chicago proposal carried when McDonald said he thought office space could be assured in the Illinois metropolis. But later, presumably after checking with the SDS national office, McDonald reported that he was unable to promise an office.

"At this point," Jenness recalls, "Emspak immediately piped up and said that there were facilities available in Madison. . . . We had no alternative to present, and we had no comrade from Chicago present to pipe up and say 'yes, there are facilities available in Chicago.' "[18]

Thus the National Coordinating Committee to End the War in Vietnam (NCC) was set up with its headquarters in Madison and Frank Emspak as national coordinator. A steering committee of thirty-four persons was designated, most of them simply the delegates from local committees who happened to be present at the workshop. Some nationally known figures like Dellinger were co-opted to the steering committee by acclamation. It was understood that at this point the committee was a more or less accidental body so it was agreed that its tasks would not be to set policy, but merely to put out a national call for October 15-16 and coordinate activities, that newly formed antiwar groups or those not present at the founding workshop could add representatives, and that a national convention would be held in November on Thanksgiving weekend. A meeting of the steering committee, open to observers from all groups opposed to the war, was scheduled for September 18 in Ann Arbor to prepare for the convention.

As far as the Vietnam issue was concerned, SDS had been

18. Jenness, October 4, 1973, letter to author.

bypassed, though it took some time for this fact to sink in.

What is more, the older ideological tendencies, particularly the Communist Party and the Socialist Workers Party—and the youth groups allied with them—were beginning to play a more central role in the new movement. And for want of someone to volunteer office space in Chicago, the CP tendency now had dominant influence in the national office of the NCC.

The report on the assembly by Jenness to the YSA National Executive Committee declared:

This first step toward organizing the antiwar movement on a national basis points to the necessity for the YSA to become as involved as possible in the antiwar movement. The norm should be that every member of the YSA should belong to an antiwar committee and the main thrust of local work should be antiwar work.

The report ended with this wistful comment: "As long as the antiwar movement is ascending, it is better to err on the side of over involvement if we must err at all."[19]

\*                     \*                     \*

The NCC did a modest job of coordinating and publicity in building the October 15-16 International Days of Protest. Far more was done by the Berkeley VDC and by other local committees and coalitions that organized the activities in particular cities. The VDC was chiefly responsible for spreading the word internationally. But the success of these demonstrations in the United States depended not so much on the activity of the NCC as on its very existence, which signified a unity behind the initiative of the Berkeley VDC. The important thing is that a national call went out. The mounting escalation of the war and the spreading antiwar sentiment assured a significant response to a unified call, particularly since no major force within the antiwar movement challenged it.

In this regard the attitude of SANE was important. To its credit, SANE proved it had learned a lesson from the fiasco of the earlier attacks by the right wing of the movement on the SDS march on Washington. SANE changed the date of its not widely publicized plans for an October 15 event in Washington "in order to avoid a conflict with events sponsored by other organiza-

19. Report from Jenness to YSA NEC, August 15, 1965.

tions."[20] This gave its chapters an opening to participate in the October 15-16 events locally, though not without registering a certain discomfort with the situation. Referring to the NCC, SANE declared:

> While the Coordinating Committee, an outgrowth of the "Assembly of the Unrepresented," is itself an unrepresentative group of the Left and those radical pacifists with a penchant for civil disobedience, SANE believes its chapters and members should indeed help to promote community-centered activities at that time—as long as they involve a cross-section of groups in your city. And while activities of a protest nature are wholly inadequate to the present intricate and fast-changing situation, there is a gamut of useful community activities which might be undertaken."[21]

There followed a list of suggested activities of an educational nature which did not include, yet did not exclude, demonstrations.

This was a concession of no small import because it meant that the building of October 15-16 could proceed without open attacks from the right wing of the movement and where local sponsors chose to do so, they had a good chance to involve the more moderate forces. That's the way it worked out in New York City.

There Dave Dellinger and Norma Becker, a teacher in the New York school system and chairperson of a citywide teachers' antiwar committee, called some meetings to gather forces interested in organizing a New York response to the call for October 15-16. Nonexclusion was the rule, but as more groups became involved some balked at public association with others. A compromise was worked out whereby formally a committee was established as a group of individuals, but each was understood to be a prominent member of an antiwar committee, or of a community, trade union, political, or pacifist group. In effect the committee became the most broadly representative united-front-type coalition on the left to develop in New York City in decades. Abner Grunauer, a retired professional who was a member of New York SANE, participated actively, though SANE would not allow him to have his name listed on the committee's literature for October 15-16. This was a formality, however, since New York SANE contributed its share both to the committee's discussions

20. *SANE Action,* September 7, 1965.
21. Ibid.

and to the building of its activities, as well as to its finances through the purchase of leaflets, and sending out its own mailings.

The New York plans called for a speakout, possibly involving civil disobedience, to be held at the Whitehall Street military induction center on October 15, and a mass march and rally on Saturday, October 16. The October 15 affair was organized by the pacifists and sponsored by anyone else who wished, while the Saturday event was sponsored by the entire committee. This was necessary because some of the groups involved with the full committee did not wish to be associated with civil disobedience.[22]

At Grunauer's suggestion it was agreed that the mass march would be on Fifth Avenue. For some reason Grunauer insisted it be called a parade, so the group was dubbed the Fifth Avenue Vietnam Peace Parade Committee. Thus the rather incongruous name of what developed into the largest and most important local antiwar coalition in the United States in the late 1960s.

At first the Parade Committee had no staff, no money, and no office. Constituent groups were asked to donate whatever they could. The office was set up in a cubbyhole occupied by the Teachers Committee at 5 Beekman Street where the top two floors were largely devoted to a complex of pacifist groups including the War Resisters League, the Committee for Nonviolent Action, the Catholic Peace Fellowship, *Liberation* magazine, and the offices of Dellinger and A. J. Muste. From the start Muste took a keen interest in the project. (After the October events he became the Parade Committee's chairman.) Dellinger and Becker were the coordinators, and for the October 16 event a staff of four was loaned by constituent organizations. Eric Weinberger of CNVA; Dave McReynolds of the WRL; Linda Dannenberg (later Morse), a pacifist from Philadelphia; and myself from the Socialist Workers Party. Al Urie, also of CNVA, staffed the October 15 affair.

I recall this telling incident during one of the first staff meetings where Muste was present. He reported that a man "of some experience in this type of organizing" had volunteered his services and that though the offer was for only part time, Muste

---

22. David Miller, a Catholic pacifist, burned his draft card in front of the TV cameras at the October 15 Whitehall speakout, in defiance of a law passed by Congress earlier in the year outlawing this particular form of symbolic protest.

thought it might be important to add him to the staff and list it that way in the committee's literature. The man was Henry Abrams, who had been fired by SANE back in 1960 because of Senator Thomas Dodd's red-baiting attack. Muste made this proposal in the tentative way he had of throwing out a suggestion to see what the reaction would be. It was clear he took a certain pleasure in seeing it accepted, and later adopted by the entire committee, including the representative of SANE. It was a new day.

The first leaflet advertising the New York march not only contained the name of Henry Abrams at the top of the staff list (it worked out that way alphabetically) but also the names of many of the committee members, each of whom  was recognizable as prominent in one of the various groups supporting the march, though none of the organizations was listed.

The list included Al Evanoff of District 65, Retail, Wholesale and Department Store Workers, AFL-CIO; Moe Foner of Hospital Workers Local 1199; Elizabeth Sutherland of SNCC; Margery Haring of the American Friends Service Committee; Dixie Bayo of the Movement for Puerto Rican Independence (MPI); Lila Hoffman of Women Strike for Peace; Levi Laub of the Progressive Labor Party; Clifton DeBerry of the Socialist Workers Party; Robert Thompson of the Communist Party (who died the day of the march); John Fuerst of SDS; Dave McReynolds, who in addition to his WRL position was also a member of SP-SDF; Stanley Aronowitz of *Studies on the Left*; Irving Beinin of the *National Guardian,* and many others.[23]

To the sizable and sophisticated New York radical milieu the appearance of such a list backing the same action in itself contained a certain magical appeal. Partly this was due to the attractiveness of unity, partly because the unaffiliated could feel assured that this was not just another "front" controlled by one group for its own narrow purposes, but also because it represented a refreshing challenge to the cold-war, witch-hunt atmosphere.

The unity was not easily come by and at times the committee seemed on the verge of breaking up. It might have, if it hadn't been for the deep respect virtually everyone involved had for

23. "Call for the Ocotober 16, 1965, Fifth Avenue Vietnam Peace Parade and Mass Rally," undated. (Copy in author's files.)

A. J. Muste, and for his skill as a conciliator. This respect stemmed from Muste's long involvement with the pacifist, labor, radical, and civil rights movements,[24] and from his habit over the years of helping out anyone who was suffering discrimination, harassment, or imprisonment because of activities on behalf of unpopular social causes. It was not a question of asking him for money, though if the case were desperate enough, A. J. could usually find a source for bail or aid in providing personal items for prisoners and things of that sort. Often it was just the use of his name on a letterhead, his appearance at a picket line, or his intervention—as an ordained minister—on behalf of some radical, like as not an atheist, forced to deal with a prejudiced agency where a word from a religious source would ease the way.

Muste, it must be said, had about him a certain aura of respectability, not entirely uncultivated, which he never hesitated to use on behalf of the unrespectable. There were never any political strings, certainly not general political agreement, attached to his aid. If he didn't think something was right in and of itself, Muste wouldn't do it. And if he did think so, that was enough for him. There was hardly a person on the Parade Committee, except the very youngest, whose life—either personally or through friends and political associates—had not been touched at one time or another by these unstinting efforts of A. J.

Nor did his effectiveness at conciliation depend on his bending his own views to the middle. Occasionally he did straddle issues under dispute, but as a rule Muste was a person of sharply defined, often quite radical, views. In the Parade Committee discussions he would state his own position and seek to convince others of it, but he never cut off relations or expressed anger with anyone because they didn't agree with him. He would listen carefully to the other side's argument, find the logic in it, then try to find a point where there was agreement and work together on that, biding his time for movement in his direction on other matters. So it was with the main bone of contention within the Parade Committee in preparing for October 16—the question of what the demands of the demonstration would be.

Some of the smaller groups such as the Spartacist League, which originated in a split from the SWP, wanted slogans like

24. See Nat Hentoff's biography, *Peace Agitator: The Story of A. J. Muste* (New York: Macmillan, 1963).

"Victory to the Vietnamese Revolution." Needless to say, such suggestions were anathema to groups like SANE.

I spoke against excluding such slogans, but saw no useful purpose for them in a demonstration appealing to Americans with demands directed at the U.S. government. We were, after all, not speaking to Vietnamese. Both from the point of view of those simply opposed to the war, and those who, like myself, were partisans of the Vietnamese revolution, our central task as Americans was to put maximum pressure on the U.S. to get out of Vietnam. That would help the Vietnamese revolution more than anything else we could possibly do. And we would be far more effective in that respect with activities and slogans designed to mobilize the maximum number of Americans around the key point of getting out of Vietnam than with revolutionary-sounding but, from the point of view of mobilizing the mass of Americans, essentially empty rhetoric.

The main debate centered around "negotiations" versus "immediate withdrawal," or some form of it like "Bring the Troops Home Now." SANE, backed by other liberal-oriented forces including the CP, insisted on adopting the demand for "negotiations." Most of the radical pacifists, including Dellinger and Muste; the Trotskyists; and the representatives of the campus committees supported "immediate withdrawal."

The former group presented themselves as concerned with the practicalities: All wars end with some type of negotiations. This one will too. The U.S. is not about to just pack up and leave unilaterally (not everyone in SANE was convinced that it should). The problem, then, was to get the negotiations started, to have a cease-fire while they proceeded, get the U.S. to negotiate with those they were fighting, including the National Liberation Front. What is more, the argument went, it is clear there are differences within the Establishment in the U.S., reflected in Congress. We must back the "doves" in this debate and raise demands which can convince the powers-that-be that there was a way to end the fighting.

Most of the other groups were concerned with the principles in the case: Of course there will eventually be negotiations. But our problem is not to advise U.S. statesmen, or even congressmen, but to put maximum pressure on the U.S. government to stop its invasion of Vietnam. The U.S. simply has no right whatever to be militarily involved in Vietnam, and only a demand for getting out immediately can clearly and unequivocally express this moral imperative. The "negotiations" demand does not clearly differentiate between our outrage and Johnson's maneuvers. Johnson also claims to favor negotiations. What is more, the "negotiations" demand when directed by Americans at the American government implies some right of the U.S. in Vietnam, something over which to negotiate, and implicitly violates the sovereignty of the Vietnamese.

Once, when the argument reached this point, one of the "negotiations" supporters shouted: "Bullshit. How do you even withdraw without negotiations?"

To which several on the other side shouted in unison: "On ships and planes, the same way you got in."

When it became clear there was no meeting of minds, it was agreed to disagree. SANE, however, objected to the proposals that everyone simply carry whatever slogan they wished, or that the committee adopt several slogans, including one on "negotiations" and another on "withdrawal." SANE insisted that "immediate withdrawal" could not even appear, that if it did they would have to dissociate themselves from the affair. To this the others replied, then "negotiations" can't appear either. It was finally agreed that the committee would adopt only one slogan: "Stop the War in Vietnam Now," with which both sides could agree.

SANE then insisted that only the single official Parade Committee slogan be permitted. I and others balked at this on the grounds that we had had enough of the attempts to remove signs from the hands of movement people and that we would not be a part of any such thing.

Muste listened to this heated debate and then said directly to me: "But will *you* and *your people* agree not to organize flooding the parade with other slogans?" Under the circumstances it was a reasonable point.

So it was finally resolved that the sponsoring groups would each refrain from making signs with slogans other than the one agreed to, that we would ask our members to carry the Parade Committee signs, that if any individual or small group that was not party to the agreement brought their own, the Parade Committee would not attempt to physically remove them. It was also resolved that all the groups would be welcome to distribute their own literature. This agreement was honored by all the major groups.

As part of the agreement, the call to the demonstration contained this statement:

A variety of groups have programs and platforms for ending the war. We urge you to consider them seriously and to make up your own mind which activities and groups you should work through. We all agree that any solution must include the removal of all foreign troops from Vietnam and the right of the Vietnamese people to determine their own future, free from external interference. . . .

Many groups and individuals are cooperating in organizing this parade. They have agreed upon a single slogan which will appear on the hundreds and hundreds of posters and banners which will be carried—a massive sea of posters and banners each with the slogan STOP THE WAR IN VIETNAM NOW. Posters will be supplied to the marchers—if you wish to make your own, please use the slogan STOP THE WAR IN VIETNAM NOW.[25]

The Spartacist League walked out of the committee over this question, carried their own slogans the day of the march, and chastised the SWP for being party to the one-slogan agreement.[26] It is true that this was an uncomfortable compromise for those of us in the SWP, particularly since virtually every member of the Parade Committee with the exception of the SANE representative professed to be personally in favor of immediate withdrawal from Vietnam, and those who supported the "negotiations" slogan claimed to do so only because they thought it was a better way to appeal to broader forces. This concession went against our grain because we were thoroughly convinced—and remained so—that SANE's equivocal position on the war was not only morally unacceptable but not nearly as popular an approach to the mass of the American people as the immediate withdrawal position. But we made the agreement for October 16, lived up to it scrupulously, and never regretted having done so.

For us this was a way to remain in the best possible position to continue the fight for a mass movement with the principled program of unequivocal opposition to the U.S. military presence in Vietnam. To have split the committee over slogans would either have greatly reduced the size of the demonstration or isolated the left wing from the rank and file of the liberal-oriented groups, probably both, precisely at a time when thousands of people were opening their minds to new ideas.

25. "Call for the October 16, 1965, Fifth Avenue Vietnam Peace Parade and Mass Rally."
26. Spartacist leaflet. (Copy in author's files.)

If the compromise had meant subsuming the left wing under the program of the right wing, we would not have agreed to it. But the agreed-upon slogan did not exclude the immediate withdrawal solution. Also the Parade Committee was nonexclusive. We all had a chance to participate in working out common agreements. And what is crucial, each group maintained its right, within the committee and publicly, to press its own point of view in discussions and literature. Under those conditions the compromise was both principled and tactically wise, in my opinion. It gave us a chance to patiently explain to a receptive audience, and to await a change in the relationship of forces which would make possible a new step forward in our strategic goal of developing a mass movement to force the unconditional withdrawal of U.S. forces from Vietnam.

The Parade Committee printed up several thousand placards to be carried by marchers October 16, and because only the single slogan was used, variety was provided by artwork—such as a detail from Picasso's *Guernica,* and big photographs of Vietnamese to give the observers a look at the "enemy." Different effects were also provided by different contingents. One of the most effective that day was the Bread and Puppet Theater, directed by Peter Schumann, which was led by a huge puppet of President Johnson followed by depictions of Vietnamese victims of the bombing and relatives in mourning.

In addition the slogan was printed on balloons filled with helium which were distributed to the children in the march. The object of all this was not just color and variety, but to set a tone which would make it as easy as possible for onlookers to open their minds to the demonstrators, and as hard as possible for hostile forces to attack the march. We were all well aware of the bitterness with which prowar forces viewed what we were doing. Antiwar demonstrators in those days were consistently labeled traitors who were stabbing "our boys" in the back.

The New York demonstration was prepared in the context of a generally hostile atmosphere from the major news media and the city officials, not to mention the federal government. The event got almost no favorable publicity beforehand in the daily press and had to be publicized mainly by leaflets distributed by volunteers, by word of mouth, and a few hundred dollars worth of ads, mainly in the alternate press.

After considerable haggling, a permit was obtained from the city authorities for a march in the street on Fifth Avenue from

Ninety-first to Sixty-eighth streets, but Parks Commissioner Newbold Morris refused to allow the rally at the Mall in Central Park, so it had to be held in the street. This was a headache both for the organizers and for the traffic, which was blocked for an extended period. There was no good technical reason for this. It was just bureaucratic hostility to the new movement. But the demonstration probably had a greater impact as a result. It was the last time the parks were refused to the Parade Committee.

Along the route of march there were several organized bands of prowar hecklers. Some of them tried to rush the march and start fights. The marchers kept themselves in general good order, however, flowing past the hecklers, isolating them, and refusing to be provoked. What made this possible was the size of the demonstration—some 30,000—and the fact that the great bulk of the onlookers were either friendly or simply curious in a nonhostile manner. The organized groups of hecklers and provocateurs found themselves isolated and, to their surprise, unable to get support for attacks on the march from bystanders on the street.

This in itself made the marchers feel they had won a significant victory, for in truth no one really knew beforehand what the reaction of the general public would be. Two weeks later, on October 30, a march to support the U.S. role in Vietnam was held, also on Fifth Avenue. In spite of front-page publicity for a week ahead of time in a major New York daily, the *Journal American*; backing by the city council, American Legion, and the Veterans of Foreign Wars; the presence in the reviewing stand of Senator Jacob Javits; and the use of twenty-five marching bands, the prowar parade was smaller than the October 16 affair, and far smaller than its backers had predicted.

\*     \*     \*

Meanwhile in Berkeley the discussions within the VDC in preparation for the International Days of Protest assumed a different character from those in the New York Parade Committee. At that time the question of "immediate withdrawal"— essentially that the U.S. had no right whatever in Vietnam—was a settled issue within the radical, student-dominated VDC. The more moderate groups in the Bay Area peace movement—like Turn Toward Peace—were simply not involved. The discussions in the loosely structured, "participatory democracy"-type meetings of the VDC tended to center around style and tactics, and the decisions were made less by vote than by experiment. Those who liked an action participated and those who didn't simply abstained from that particular activity.

This period of VDC activity was characterized by imaginative and nettlesome forms of protest. For example, a VDC activist discovered that dogs were being trained for possible use in Vietnam at a small army facility in Tilden Park, not far from Berkeley. Soon, official-looking signs appeared all over the park warning that military dogs were being trained in the area, were vicious, and would attack people. A signature in small type said the sign was posted as a public service by the Vietnam Day Committee.[27] The army was thereafter plagued by protests and was soon forced to close the facility.

When it became known that napalm bombs were being manufactured in Redwood City, about thirty miles south of San Francisco, and transported on the highways to Port Chicago, about twenty miles north of Berkeley, VDC activists painted a pickup truck an official-looking gray and mounted a large, yellow sign with flashing lights on the back that said: "Danger, Napalm Bombs Ahead." They would then follow the trucks carrying the napalm through the heavily populated Bay Area. This contributed to the furor about napalm which was growing in the country.[28]

The VDC organized well-publicized picket lines against President Johnson in June when he appeared at a United Nations anniversary ceremony in San Francisco, and in August against General Maxwell Taylor when he returned from Vietnam. At Taylor's hotel, demonstrators blocked an elevator while Taylor was on it and distributed a flyer with the general's picture and the caption: "Wanted for war crimes."

Always sensitive to the international implication of the Vietnam issue, the VDC organized picket lines to cheer the crews of a Mexican and a Greek ship after they refused to accept U.S. war cargoes for Vietnam.

In August the VDC organized several attempts to stop trains carrying troops and materiel bound for Vietnam. Students as far away as Utah informed the VDC beforehand when the trains

27. One of these posters was made available to the author by Paul Montauk of Berkeley.
28. Letter to the author from Syd Stapleton, June 17, 1965.

were coming through. These demonstrations varied from a few dozen to a few hundred. They succeeded only in slowing down the trains briefly, but they got wide publicity. They also provided the first concerted experience in reaching GIs with the antiwar message. The results of this aspect of the troop-train demonstrations were not entirely positive. Some of the demonstrators carried signs and shouted slogans that were hostile to the GIs.

The YSAers raised some sharp discussion within the VDC on this question, but it would take many months and a lot of experience before the movement as a whole would come to see GIs as an important element of the antiwar constituency.[29]

One by-product of these discussions, however, was the plan for leafletting GIs at the Oakland Army Terminal as part of the October 15-16 demonstrations. The VDC printed up a special leaflet for the purpose, written by Jerry Rubin and heavily edited by Asher Harer, a San Francisco longshoreman, a Trotskyist, and a longtime activist in labor and radical causes in the Bay Area. It was headlined: "Attention All Military Personnel" and it began:

You may soon be sent to Vietnam. You have heard about the war in the news; your officers will give you pep talks about it. But you probably feel as confused and uncertain as most Americans do. Many people will tell you to just follow orders and leave the thinking to others. But you have the right to know as much about this war as anyone. After all, it's you— not your congressman—who might get killed.[30]

As it turned out, the demonstrators never got to the Oakland Army Terminal so these leaflets had to be distributed elsewhere. Originally the Berkeley VDC plan for October 15-16 had been announced as a teach-in at the UC campus followed by "massive civil disobedience," something that always proved easier to talk about than to actually organize. In July the *VDC News* carried an article on October 15-16 signed by Rubin, Gullahorn, and Smale which said:

If on October 16 in Berkeley, for example, thousands of students and others block the gates of the Oakland Army Terminal where munitions are shipped to Vietnam, and are arrested, attention will be focused

29. Ibid.
30. VDC leaflet dated October 16, 1965. (Copy in author's files.)

dramatically on the issues in Vietnam to an extent that no atrocity in Vietnam can match. The issue will be opened. Scenes of thousands of middle-class youth being carried away by military police will be in every American living room. . . .[31]

As the demonstration approached, the plan was modified as follows: After the teach-in October 15, demonstrators would march through the streets of Berkeley and Oakland to the terminal at Maritime Street, where army barracks lay on one side and ships loading for Vietnam on the other. There, according to the VDC announcement,

we intend to continue our teach-in in an empty lot opposite the barracks and to beam it to the soldiers, asking them to consider seriously the implications of their participating in an immoral war. . . . If the police try to interfere with the march or try to disperse the teach-in, we will be arrested rather than submit to this infringement of our civil liberties. . . . Of course even in this case there will be an opportunity to avoid arrest for those who wish to.[32]

The teach-in went off as planned. That evening some 15,000 demonstrators left the campus marching toward Oakland. The Oakland authorities had refused a parade permit. As the marchers approached the Oakland city limit they could see some 400 Oakland police wearing riot helmets, brandishing special riot weapons, blocking the way. The march stopped less than a hundred yards from the police line. As spectators and a group of about 100 right-wing counterdemonstrators filled the gap between the march and the police, a previously agreed-to subcommittee of the VDC held a swirling, confused discussion on what to do. Smale says he favored asking the whole crowd to sit down on the spot but Steve Weissman and Jack Weinberg favored turning the march to a nearby park in Berkeley. They convinced the majority of the subcommittee and the march proceeded to the park, where the teach-in was continued and another march called for the next day.[33]

On Saturday, October 16, only 5,000 marchers returned to the Oakland city limits where they were again stopped by police.

31. *VDC News,* July 1965. (Copy in author's files.)
32. VDC leaflet, undated. (Bancroft Library, University of California at Berkeley.)
33. Author's taped interview with Stephen Smale, October 6, 1973.

Actually there were two lines of police, one directly in front of the march, made up of Berkeley cops, and the other just across the city line, made up of Oakland cops. At this point, members of the Hell's Angels motorcycle gang, rushing from the Oakland side, tried to attack the front of the march, shouting "America for the Americans!" To do this, however, they had to pass through the two lines of cops. The Oakland cops let them through, and the Berkeley cops tried to stop them at the border. A fight ensued in which a Berkeley policeman's leg was broken, whereupon the Hell's Angels were hauled off to the Berkeley jail. The antiwar demonstrators held a sit-down, but were not arrested. They dispersed peacefully.[34]

The VDC managed a comeuppance against both the Hell's Angels and the Oakland authorities. On October 20 the VDC received a call from the Central Labor Council of Richmond, a city just north of Berkeley, seeking support for a strike in which the Hell's Angels and another motorcycle gang, called Hitler's American Sons, were acting as strikebreakers.[35]

The VDC responded with pleasure, sending 150 pickets to the plant to join various unionists who had also been called. The Richmond police then cordoned off the area and the strikebreakers couldn't get in. Union business agent Clyde L. Johnson of Millmen's Local 550 of the United Brotherhood of Carpenters publicly thanked the VDC saying, "This is the best picket line I've seen since the 1930s."[36]

The VDC also announced another march through Oakland. Oakland Mayor John C. Houlihan appealed to Governor Edmund G. Brown to declare illegal the use of the Berkeley campus for organizing the march. A general uproar ensued in civil liberties circles, and even the liberal Republican *San Francisco Chronicle* ran a biting editorial, declaring:

Last weekend there was introduced into the free and great society of the East Bay the concept of the Oakland Wall. Here at checkpoint Houlihan, foreigners were held up by the city's defense forces, impregnable against all comers except the Hell's Angels.[37]

34. Author's taped interviews with Stephen Smale and Paul Montauk, October 6, 1973, and with Syd Stapleton, October 28, 1973.
35. VDC defense guard leaflet. (Copy in author's files.)
36. *Militant,* November 1, 1965.
37. *San Francisco Chronicle,* October 21, 1965.

On behalf of the VDC, attorney Vincent Hallinan obtained a court order allowing the march through Oakland, though not to the Army Terminal, and enjoining the Oakland authorities from interfering with it.

On November 20 the VDC finally made it past the Oakland border, this time with 20,000 antiwar marchers en route to a rally at De Fremery Park. Speakers at the rally included two state assemblymen, as well as Nathaniel Walker, a Black student who headed a delegation of civil rights fighters from Selma, Alabama, and Donald Duncan, a retired master sergeant of the U.S. Special Forces who had turned against the war during eighteen months in Vietnam.

\*     \*     \*

The October 15-16 demonstrations were the largest up to that time. In addition to Berkeley and New York, they took place in some sixty cities across the United States, mainly where campus-based Committees to End the War in Vietnam (CEWVs) had been formed. All told, perhaps some 100,000 Americans demonstrated on those days. The movement was still relatively small, but October 15-16 put it on the map as not just a flurry, and provided a visibility proving that Johnson's claimed "consensus" on the war did not really exist.

In addition, the VDC's international call was responded to by hundreds of organizations around the world in one way or another. There were demonstrations in twelve European countries and in Canada, Australia, Mexico, Chile, and many other places. The effect of the American antiwar movement overseas was perhaps best expressed by a letter to the VDC from the National Anti-Atomic March Committee in Brussels (where 3,000 demonstrated October 16):

"We admit that we did not dare believe . . . that the students of the United States would express so widely and with such energy, their criticism of a policy which causes such great anger in our country. . . ."[38]

38. Report by International Committee of VDC, undated. (Copy in author's files.)

# 5

# The SANE March on Washington and the NCC Convention

The October 15-16 demonstrations touched a sore nerve in government circles, and a rash of statements attacking the antiwar movement issued from congressmen and administration officials. Senator Thomas J. Dodd, still on his anticommunist crusade, declared: "We have to draw a line, and draw it soon, and draw it hard, between the right of free speech and assembly and the right to perpetrate treason."[1]

The day of the New York and Berkeley marches, Attorney General Nicholas Katzenbach declared at a press conference in Chicago that the Justice Department was watching the movement and that "there are some Communists involved in it and we may have to investigate."[2]

On November 1, FBI director J. Edgar Hoover expressed the official Johnson administration contempt for the movement in these words:

Anti-Vietnam demonstrators in the U.S. represent a minority for the most part composed of halfway citizens who are neither morally, mentally nor emotionally mature. This is true whether the demonstrators be the college professor or the beatnik.[3]

An editorial in the October 29 *Time* magazine entitled "Vietniks—Self Defeating Dissent" summed up the administration's stance:

1. *Time*, October 29, 1965.
2. *National Guardian*, October 23, 1965.
3. *New York Times*, November 3, 1965.

90

The Vietniks are not going to be able to talk the U.S. out of Vietnam. They made their best try last spring, with a tide of so-called teach-ins, at a time when the approaching monsoon season in Vietnam was supposed to guarantee Communist victories; rather than submitting to defeat-by-weather, President Johnson simply stepped up the U.S. effort. For a while, the Vietnik decibel count dropped, only to soar up again when it became evident that the course of the war in Vietnam had turned and that, assuming only the will to stick it out, the U.S. and its South Vietnam ally were on the way to winning. . . . This being the case, it seems just a bit improbable that President Johnson and his national constituency will suddenly succumb to the revived outcry of a thumbnail minority. . . .

The fact is the Vietniks, by encouraging the Communist hope and expectation that the U.S. does not have the stomach to fight it out in Vietnam, are probably achieving what they would least like: prolonging the war and adding to the casualty lists on both sides.

The assertion that "the course of the war in Vietnam had turned" was based on the massive intervention of U.S. troops and bombers into the war, which, according to the administration, was designed to "drive the North Vietnamese to the conference table,"[4] and actually had saved the Saigon regime from the imminent collapse it faced at the beginning of the year. By September the authoritative Paris daily *Le Monde* was reporting that U.S. saturation bombing of NLF-controlled areas in South Vietnam had reached a level surpassing the heaviest bombings in World War II. By November the Pentagon admitted there were 160,000 troops in Vietnam with stated plans for 200,000 by the end of the year.

A central feature of Johnson's escalation policy during the spring and summer had been that official reports of increased U.S. involvement were downplayed, released only piecemeal,[5] and accompanied by a propaganda offensive designed to undercut critics on grounds that the U.S. was seeking an end of the war

---

4. Ibid., May 1, 1975.

5. For example: officially the first U.S. regular combat troops, 3,500 marines, were ordered to Danang on March 7, 1965. The announced purpose was to protect the air base there. They soon found themselves deployed far in the field in areas previously controlled for years by the guerrillas. This was called "dynamic defense," one of the many euphemisms with which Pentagon press agents enriched the language in the course of the war.

through negotiations. By October the "negotiations" offensive launched in the president's Johns Hopkins speech back in April had worn thin. A candid appraisal of the situation was presented by William Beecher in the October 14 *Wall Street Journal:*

All around Washington are high level planners who predict that the war is to be settled, not around the conference table, but more likely by the unilateral disengagement of Communist forces from the battle. It is this infinitely more desirable prospect that has made the talk of negotiations subside. . . .

The negotiations chant served the administration designs quite well. It helped quiet criticism, both domestic and foreign, about our "militaristic" policy in Vietnam. And at a time when we were launching a mammoth buildup of combat forces, constant talk of negotiations also served to allay the fears of Hanoi, Peking and Moscow about an ultimate invasion of the North. . . .

Beecher advised: "For such benefits as these, some lip service to negotiations ought to continue. . . ."

Nevertheless, the administration statements about the "consensus" behind its war policy and the insignificance of its critics had a certain whistling-in-the-wind character about them. It had already become apparent that, aside from the largely student-led opposition to the war, there were doubts and divisions in many areas of the population, including within the American ruling class itself where some forces were not at all sure this was the right war at the right time.

The reason for these doubts in high circles was pointed to by columnist Walter Lippmann:

The essential fact which is beginning to seep through dispatches of some of the American correspondents, is that while the Americans can seize almost any place they choose to attack, the Viet Cong will almost surely come back once the Americans leave. . . . The war in Vietnam is like punching a tub full of water. We can make a hole with our powerful fists wherever we punch the water. But once we pull back our hand, possibly to punch another hole in the water, the first hole disappears.[6]

What is more, the weeks immediately following the International Days of Protest saw the first major ground combat by large American units. The results were inconclusive and the casualties

6. *Washington Post*, September 30, 1965.

high. The number of U.S. combat deaths was reported in the November 14 *New York Times* as over 1,000. The December draft call had been set at 40,200, the largest since the Korean War, and draft boards across the country began to sink their levies into students, married men, and young doctors.

*New York Times* editorial writer James Reston, who had echoed the administration line in criticizing the October 15-16 protesters immediately after those demonstrations, conceded in his November 14 column that

> there is a quiet uneasiness in this country about the war in Vietnam—far more widespread and probably more important than the noisy demonstrations in the universities. . . . Officials go on talking as if one more summer or one more winter of American action will bring the desired result, but in private they concede that this kind of war could go on for years.

In this situation the antiwar movement prepared for its next major national activities. These were a "March on Washington for Peace in Vietnam" on November 27, initiated by forces around SANE,[7] and the first convention of the National Coordinating Committee to End the War in Vietnam (NCC), Thanksgiving weekend, November 25-28.

Around these events the dispute within the movement over "negotiations" or "immediate withdrawal" reached a sharp struggle. The struggle involved basic strategy: whether the movement should orient toward those forces within the ruling class which were beginning to criticize the escalation policy, and develop a constituency behind them, or whether the movement should build itself as an independent power in the streets. Also involved in this struggle was an estimate—enunciated most clearly by SDS—that challenged the very character of the new antiwar movement as such, holding that the radicals and student youth could not really affect the war and ought to concentrate on other issues.

SANE was the group most clearly identified with the first perspective—orienting toward critics within the Establishment.

---

7. The November 27 affair was commonly referred to as the SANE march. Technically, however, it was not sponsored by SANE but by a list of prominent individuals, including leaders of SANE. Sanford Gottlieb, the march coordinator, was a SANE staff member.

Under pressure of events—including the new antiwar movement as well as the escalation—national SANE had begun as early as June to take up the Vietnam issue and to consider organizing a demonstration on the question. It insisted, however, on maintaining its old exclusionary policy.

Two days after the International Days of Protest a press conference was held in Washington to publicly announce the November 27 SANE march. The event was noteworthy in that a member of the U.S. House of Representatives, George Brown, Jr. (Democrat-California), appeared as a sponsor of the march. By the standards of Congress at the time, it must in fairness be said that Brown's appearance required some courage. But it wasn't too clear whether he was against the war or for it. He declared: "I'm not calling for withdrawal of American troops . . . and I'm not calling for a surrender to the Viet Cong. We are trying to improve the understanding of the American people of the situation in Vietnam."[8]

March director Sanford Gottlieb decried the government attacks on the movement, but he told the conference: "I hope the Communists would not participate. We will not welcome them, but we can't control the Communists. There will be no attempt to screen the participants."

There would, however, be an attempt to screen the signs and to prohibit organizational literature.[9]

The left wing of the movement, then, could come to the demonstration, but it was not allowed to express its own views on the war. And SANE's line for the march was to express its concern over, rather than outright opposition to, the U.S. involvement in the war.

All this was in line with SANE's strategic perspective. It saw itself as working within the Establishment—particularly among liberal Democratic politicians—to convince them that negotiations should begin in Vietnam, and to strengthen the hand of those who did adopt this "dove" position. In this respect the "immediate withdrawal" slogans were a liability. They would shut off the friendly ears of Establishment figures, all of whom accepted the basic premises of the cold war.

This perspective was clearly stated by the march organizers:

8. Quoted in "Report No. 2" by the coordinator, October 20, 1965. (Copy in antiwar files, Library of Social History, New York.)
9. Ibid.

The March on Washington has a detailed, carefully elaborated set of proposals designed to encourage a negotiated settlement. This statement makes clear the distinct difference in approach between the Administration and its critics. The former assumes that increased military pressure will bring the North Vietnamese to the conference table while the critics suggest that deescalation is the proper path.[10]

This was accurate as far as critics within Congress were concerned. But the new antiwar movement had been having an entirely different experience in reaching out to ordinary people beginning to have doubts on the war.

The ad hoc Committees to End the War in Vietnam and Vietnam Day Committees had spread across the country ever since the sustained bombings of North Vietnam had begun in February. With the withdrawal of national SDS from a leadership role, these independent committees became the backbone of the new movement—that is, the movement that grew up outside the exclusionary policies of the old peace movement coalitions.

These committees were nonexclusionary, almost always for immediate withdrawal, and action-oriented. They found through experience that it was easier to appeal to the ordinary people they were reaching at the campuses and on the streets with a demand for getting the U.S. out of Vietnam lock, stock, and barrel, than with the complicated and equivocal appeals that preoccupied the negotiations wing of the movement. These CEWVs and VDCs were generally referred to within the movement as "independent committees" because they were not affiliated with any national multi-issue political party or youth group such as SDS, M-2-M, YSA, Du Bois Clubs, etc. This made it possible for them to include members of all such groups as well as unaffiliated independents. They accepted anyone who wanted to work against the war, including members of various radical tendencies, Democrats, Republicans, independents, or anyone else. They were actually local united fronts.

With one exception the multi issue radical youth groups, including SDS and the Du Bois Clubs, tended to look upon the CEWVs and VDCs as rivals to their own local chapters. The exception was the YSA, which threw itself into building the independent committees and fought within them to maintain their focus on antiwar activity and their nonexclusive character.

10. Ibid.

This necessarily meant opposing any moves to have the committees adopt any particular multi-issue political program, including that of the YSA, or to endorse political candidates.

This difference in approach led to a clash between the SWP-YSA tendency and SDS within the New York Committee to End the War in Vietnam (NYCEWV). This presaged in part the struggle which was to break out at the NCC convention.

The New York CEWV had been formed originally by SDS as a citywide coordinating group for an SDS summer project of community organizing on the war issue.

The campus and neighborhood groups which proliferated during the summer and which affiliated to the NYCEWV were, however, not local SDS chapters, but independent committees carrying out antiwar activity. When SDS pressed its multi-issue approach within the steering committee of the NYCEWV, the SWP and YSA members, who were delegated from independent committees, argued for maintaining the focus on antiwar work. A general assembly of the local groups in the CEWV was scheduled for November 4 at which this issue was to be resolved. But at a November 1 steering committee meeting, a bloc of forces led by Stanley Aronowitz, a supporter of SDS, and Carl Griffler, a supporter of the CP-Du Bois Club tendency, carried a vote to dissolve the NYCEWV. (Griffler chaired, though to my knowledge this was the first NYCEWV meeting he'd ever attended.) It was then announced that henceforth the office would operate as a regional SDS group with SDS's multi-issue program.

"This rather surprising move," commented YSAer Jon Britton, "apparently reflected fear on their part, not entirely unjustified, that our line (promoting independent Vietnam committees not officially tied to any radical organization including SDS) would carry" at the November 4 general assembly.[11]

The SWP and YSA were sharply denounced by some within the movement for having resisted this SDS move. The *National Guardian*, a strong supporter of SDS in this period, reported that the former NYCEWV leadership said it had failed as a coordinating body for the independent CEWVs because "groups such as the Socialist Workers Party would not accept a non-sectarian

11. Letter from Jon Britton to YSA membership, November 12, 1965. (Copy in author's files.)

policy,"[12] i.e., that of SDS. This put the matter exactly on its head.

SDS National Secretary Paul Booth declared:

> The Trotskyites are so new to the coalition that they don't know how to act. . . . Within the new left, you know, we work for consensus, but how can you get consensus if there is an already committed bloc? The self-destructive forces within the coalition really shouldn't be underestimated.[13]

The fact that the New York Committee to End the War in Vietnam had just self-destructed was certainly not in line with the perspective of the SWP and YSA for the antiwar movement. The same fact was, however, quite in line with the kind of thinking going on at that time in the SDS national office. Although there was some confusion about what SDS's multi-issue program *was* at that time, the national office attitude toward antiwar activity was becoming increasingly clear to those who studied its statements, if not to the general public.

For example, an article by Lee Webb and Paul Booth entitled "The Anti-War Movement: From Protest to Radical Politics" was published by SDS in preparation for the NCC convention. It declared:

> Essentially, we think that the movement against the war in Vietnam is working on the wrong issue. And that issue is Vietnam. We feel that American foreign policy, and thus the war in Vietnam, is impervious to pressure placed directly on it. Secondly, we feel that the issue of the war in Vietnam cannot involve masses of people here in the United States. Finally, we look with extreme concern on the single-issue orientation of the anti-war protest. We think that this single issue politics, perhaps valid in another time, is simply an obstacle at this time. We are concerned about all of the issues of America and think that the only way to deal with them is together.[14]

YSA Chairman Jack Barnes characterized the multi-issue/single-issue argument as "largely a sham battle that

12. *National Guardian*, November 13, 1965.

13. Quoted by Thomas Brooks, *New York Times Magazine*, November 7, 1965.

14. Original mimeographed edition distributed at NCC convention. (Copy in author's files.) Reprinted in *Our Generation*, May 1966.

covered up rather than elucidated the issues at stake." Said Barnes:

> All the radical organizations are multi-issue and none believe that society can be changed (either to socialism or some form of participatory democracy) nor war in general abolished by a program or pattern of activity around a single issue. Thus any member of SDS, YSA, Du Bois, M-2-M, has a multi-issue approach to the war.
>
> However, the Committees to End the War in Vietnam, one of the components of the anti-war movement, were formed around the single issue End the War in Vietnam; U.S. get out. Any attempt to add further planks to *their* program would destroy them. Those who make them up agree on this basic point and no other. To make other conditions for membership in these organizations would *narrow* not broaden them. This includes points like attitudes toward independent politics, class character of U.S. government, support for NLF, and what to do with your draft card.[15]

For the SDS leaders, the attempt to draw the maximum number of Americans into antiwar activity was doomed to frustration and only interfered with their work of developing a radical base in the population. For the SWP and the YSA, however, the movement to get the U.S. out of Vietnam was an imperative central objective which ought not be abandoned. What is more, the YSA viewed the growing antiwar sentiment as a key factor in building a radical base.

> Actually the radical groups have been outstripped by a radicalization of a special type [I wrote in one of three articles published by the socialist weekly *Militant,* in preparation for the NCC convention]. It is a radicalization which has other roots besides antiwar activity to be sure— such as civil rights, free speech, etc.—but the great majority of the youth are not committed to any particular multi-issue radical approach. No radical tendency is dominant in the movement. Many of these youth are not even radicals in their general political approach. Some of them are simply Democrats or even Republicans. But they are ready, willing and able to be flatly opposed to U.S. intervention in Vietnam and to work with all tendencies opposed to the war. . . .
>
> This situation imposes a certain responsibility on the radical groups which they should be careful not to abuse. In the natural course of events—with the professional liberals and the Democratic and Republi-

---

15. Letter to YSA membership, November 12, 1965. (Copy in author's files.)

can politicians almost universally supporting the war or at least refusing
to organize against it—the radicals find themselves initiating, playing
key roles in and leading a growing mass movement. But it is a movement
in which the great majority of the participants are not committed to any
particular radical program on general social questions, but only on the
issue of getting the U.S. out of Vietnam. . . . The worst abuse of this
situation would be for any tendency to attempt to turn these independent
committees into a front for its particular multi-issue program, a front
which draws people in on the Vietnam war issue and then uses them to
support other issues which they did not bargain for when they joined.
Such things have occurred in the past and the results have always been
disastrous.[16]

In the second of the three articles, which were not simply my
own view but were based on SWP and YSA positions adopted
after extensive discussion, I said:

It is well within possibility that not just a few hundred thousand, but
millions of Americans can be actively involved in the struggle against the
Vietnam war. A movement of that scope, even though centered around
the single issue of the war, would have the most profound effects on every
social structure in the country, including the trade unions and the soldiers
in the army.

It would very probably also result in a general rise in radical consciousness on many other questions, just as it has already had an impact
against red-baiting. But above all, it could be the key factor in forcing an
end to the Pentagon's genocidal war in Vietnam. The lives of untold
thousands of Vietnamese men, women and children, and U.S. G.I.'s may
depend upon it. That alone is reason enough to put aside sectarian
differences to unite and help build a national organization which can
encompass anyone willing to oppose U.S. involvement in Vietnam,
regardless of their commitment, or lack of it, on other questions.[17]

That, then, was the view of the Trotskyist organizations on the
potentialities of the antiwar movement. And I admit that when
we heard statements such as those by Gitlin and Booth and had
experiences such as that with the NYCEWV, we prepared to
argue very strongly at the NCC convention. An additional factor
that gave urgency to this struggle, in our way of thinking, was
that the exclusionary, right wing of the movement, led by SANE,

16. *Militant,* November 15, 1965.
17. Ibid., November 22, 1965.

was moving to center stage once again with the march on Washington. In our view it was good that national SANE was finally becoming actively involved on the Vietnam issue. But if the nonexclusionary, immediate-withdrawal wing of the movement were to be left without national focus, the leadership would inevitably revert to SANE, which still couldn't bring itself to break with the anticommunist hysteria or to flatly oppose the U.S. involvement in the war. (SANE had even excluded Staughton Lynd, Robert Parris of SNCC, and Nobel Prize winner Linus Pauling, a major figure of the movement to stop nuclear testing, from sponsorship of the SANE march, "for tactical reasons" as Gottlieb later explained, because their past activities had apparently been too militant in the minds of some of the sponsors SANE was seeking.[18])

This was the practical implication in the SDS abstentionist position—leave the organization of antiwar activity *as such* to the right wing, while the left wing concerns itself with other matters. We were not about to sit through a "participatory democracy" bull session which was going in that direction without forcing a discussion on this matter. Not even if it meant resurrecting Robert's Rules of Order.

The exact nature of the NCC had been left ambiguous by the founding workshop in August. Whether it was to be a coordinating committee for the whole antiwar movement or the national organization of the independent committees was anybody's guess. The Du Bois Clubs favored the former perspective. SDS, and a number of its older supporters who considered themselves in tune with the "new left"—though many were not without a certain "old left" experience themselves—favored the development of a multi-issue formation for general radical social change. Some supporters of this view proposed transforming the antiwar movement into a new political party, running candidates in its own right.

Stanley Aronowitz and Irving Beinin were spokespersons for this general view. While they did not agree with the SDS national office in its downplaying of the Vietnam issue, they wanted SDS to lead antiwar activity and use this to build a multi-issue radical formation. The SDS abdication of antiwar leadership was a

18. "NCC Workshop Reports and Plenary Decisions. Evaluation of the SANE March: Discussion with Gottlieb." NCC mailing, December 18, 1965. (Copy in author's files.)

source of some pain to them. (For his part, Beinin remained consistently active in antiwar formations.) The YSA favored the establishment of a national organization of the independent committees which could adopt the position of immediate withdrawal and be the cutting edge of the broad antiwar movement. If the NCC chose to be a broad umbrella group, then the YSA hoped the NCC convention would provide an opportunity for the independent committees to establish their national organization which would affiliate with the NCC.

A meeting of the NCC steering committee that took place in Ann Arbor September 18-19 to prepare for the convention continued the ambiguity. It decided on a delegated convention including representatives of campus and community committees against the war as well as representatives of national groups. A number of individuals were added to the steering committee at this meeting and in subsequent weeks. At this meeting Emspak expressed some irritation at the fact that SANE had not sent a representative. He was anxious that the NCC be an umbrella group, including groups like SANE. The meeting voted to change the location of the NCC convention from Madison, Wisconsin, to Washington, D.C., to allow participants to attend the SANE march, already scheduled for the Saturday of the same weekend.

Interestingly, the YSAers at this meeting first opposed this change on the grounds that it might contribute to a taming of the left. They abstained on the vote. They agreed later, however, that the change was for the best. For the nonexclusionary wing of the movement to have held its convention in direct competition with the SANE march would have weakened the movement, not strengthened it. It would have created division around an *action*, something generally to be avoided. For all its equivocation, the SANE march did call for a halt to the bombing of North Vietnam and was generally seen by the public as an action against the administration's war.

A competing convention would have tended to isolate the radicals from the moderates, force even radical activists to choose between a well-publicized action and a meeting, and tend toward giving the right-wing leaders hegemony. In a mass movement, the problem of revolutionaries is not how to avoid contact with reformist forces, but how to relate to them in a principled, effective way. This was particularly important in this case because the rank and file of SANE itself was already considerably to the left of its national leadership on the war in Vietnam.

Emspak's reasons for desiring a relationship with SANE were quite different from these considerations, however. It was simply that he and other supporters of the general line of the CP-Du Bois tendency had a strategic perspective for the antiwar movement which was similar to SANE's. Their central concern was promoting détente between the United States and the Soviet Union to end the cold war, and they saw the antiwar movement as building a constituency for those politicians who might be convinced to negotiate over Vietnam as the major powers had done at Geneva in 1954.[19]

This meant a concentration on electoral activity—mainly within the Democratic Party—during election periods. But the congressional elections weren't scheduled until November 1966. The campaigning wouldn't begin in earnest until early summer. In the meantime, single-issue antiwar activity could gather forces. Later, these might be channeled into Democratic Party

---

19. In this regard it is interesting to compare the demands listed in the SANE march call with those listed in a CP leaflet distributed at the NCC convention. Said the SANE call: "We ask that our government call for a cease-fire, and to this end: Halt the bombing of North Vietnam; Halt the introduction of additional men and material, and ask the other side to do the same. We ask that our government state the conditions under which it will accept peace in Vietnam, and to this end: Reiterate U.S. support for the principles of the 1954 Geneva Accords—the eventual withdrawal of all foreign military forces, a prohibition against military alliances, the peaceful reunification of Vietnam, and self-determination for the Vietnamese people. . . ."

The CP leaflet said: "*We demand* that President Johnson acknowledge the right of the people of South Vietnam to choose for themselves the government they want—free of all military or political interference. *We demand* an end to the brutal slaughter of Americans and Vietnamese and an end to the drafting and shipping of additional thousands of American youth to South Vietnam. *We demand* an immediate halt to the bombing of North Vietnam and withdrawal from the South in accordance with the Geneva Agreement. *We demand* that our government meet immediately with the National Liberation Front to assure an *end to the war—Now!*" (Copy of this leaflet in author's files.)

The CP wording sounds more militant, but the demands are the same. Immediate withdrawal is studiously avoided in both and withdrawal is qualified as contingent on the Geneva Agreement, which each side in the war interpreted differently and which would obviously have to be renegotiated since it predated the U.S. invasion of Vietnam.

politics. The CP–Du Bois position on the NCC was, then, simply to sit tight.

A memo from the Du Bois Clubs national office to the NCC outlining their suggestions for the convention said:

> There is, for example, some talk of making the NCC into an organization unto itself, taking up other issues, and such; other talk is of running candidates. We believe that all of this is premature at best. We recommend that the National Coordinating Committee remain a coordinating committee, that it limit its scope to the issue of Vietnam where the broadest support and greatest unity can be built, and that discussion and decisions regarding peace candidates can be done for now on a local basis.[20]

Between the Ann Arbor meeting and the convention a number of additions were made to the steering committee of persons opposed to the idea of a national organization of the independent committees. These included Carl Griffler, Ed Greer of New Haven, and Arnold Johnson, an old-time national leader of the Communist Party.

During the same period a series of meetings were held in New York of an "advisory" subcommittee of the steering committee to discuss preparations for the convention. It included Beinin, Aronowitz, and Johnson, and was generally unresponsive to suggestions that the question of a national organization of the independent committees be placed on the convention agenda.

On November 4 a position paper outlining such a perspective, which had been passed by the Washington Heights (an area of Manhattan) CEWV, was circulated by members of eight New York area CEWVs, some of whom were also members of the YSA. The paper said:

> The independent committees must stress again and again that they stand on the principle of every people's right to self-determination, a principle upon which this country was founded. This is important because a great majority of the American people still believe in this principle. This is the reason the Johnson Administration tries to justify its intervention in Vietnam by claiming that the U.S. is really there to support self-determination against aggression from the North. We must therefore convince the American people that it is our government and not North

20. Memo to members of the NCC from W.E.B. Du Bois Clubs of America, November 1, 1965. (Copy in author's files.)

Vietnam or China that is violating the Vietnamese people's right of self-determination. Consequently, we must sharply differentiate ourselves from Johnson and his demagogic appeals for "unconditional negotiations" and demand that our government end its intervention. . . . Because of the danger of escalation of the war to all of Asia and even world nuclear war, we must be dead serious about ending U.S. intervention in Vietnam. We can be optimistic too. The potential exists for organizing millions of Americans, including those in the army, around this program. . .

We hope that out of the Washington Convention will come both a national co-ordinating structure for the entire anti-war movement and a national organization of the independent committees to end the war in Vietnam.[21]

But, when the Madison office released the agenda, there was no provision for discussing the latter point.[22] There were twelve workshops, including everything from "Ideology's Relation to American Foreign Policy" to "Civil Disobedience," but none where representatives from independent committees could meet to discuss the possibility of forming a national organization.

From discussions with those on the "advisory committee" in New York we knew the reason for this omission: some of them didn't want this question discussed. They held that the NCC was already sufficient national organization for the independent committees. They wanted it both ways: The NCC was to be considered the national organization of the independent committees and also the umbrella group for the whole movement. Therefore it couldn't adopt the immediate withdrawal position.

That would leave the immediate withdrawal wing without national focus. A number of YSAers, including Kipp Dawson, a delegate from the San Francisco State College VDC, caucused in Washington, as delegates were arriving the day before the convention. They came up with the idea of a thirteenth workshop for members of independent committees to discuss this question. When I arrived in town late that night and heard of this, I thought nothing much about it. It seemed perfectly logical and

21. "A Draft Perspective for the Anti-War Movement." Submitted by individual members of the Queens, New York University, Tompkins Square, Chelsea, Village View, Columbia, and City College of New York antiwar committees; passed by the Washington Heights CEWV. November 4, 1965. (Copy in author's files.)

22. *Peace and Freedom News,* no. 10, November 12, 1965. (Copy in author's files.)

was certainly within the tradition of the new movement, where at the various gatherings anyone could have a workshop on anything they wanted to discuss. Indeed, the NCC itself had come out of a previously unscheduled workshop at the August assembly.

The YSA representatives talked the idea over with other arriving delegates, including Jack Weinberg and Jerry Rubin of the Berkeley VDC, who agreed. A call for such a workshop was drawn up, signed by thirty-three delegates from various CEWVs and VDCs, and distributed to the delegates as they entered the Lincoln Memorial Congregational Temple on Eleventh Street for the first session of the convention.

The first plenary session was scheduled to be brief: announcements on workshops and an opening address by Emspak.

Lew Jones, a member of the convention staff from the Washington CEWV, and a YSAer, began with announcements. He simply listed each workshop and the room where it would be held. When he got to the thirteenth workshop, Emspak grabbed the microphone and tried to take it out of Jones's hand. The audience looked on bewildered as the two of them did a little dance wrestling with the mike. To everyone's astonishment this was the beginning of a swirling, three-day fight—which would dominate the entire convention—over whether the independent committee workshop would be held or not.

Jones succeeded in completing the announcement and handed the mike over to Emspak, who set aside his opening remarks and sharply attacked those who had called the thirteenth workshop. He said it was an attempt to split the NCC, that the NCC itself was all the national organization the independent committees needed, and that anyone interested in a national organization should attend the workshop on "Structure of the NCC" which, along with three others, was scheduled at the same time as the thirteenth.

The rest of the first plenary session was characterized by points of order, unclear procedural motions, and attacks directed at the YSA as attempting either a "take-over" or a split. Robin Maisel, a delegate from the Philadelphia Area CEWV, stated that the purpose of the workshop was not to leave the NCC, that even if a national organization of independent committees were set up, they and the national organization would still be in the NCC. He said half the convention delegates were not from independent committees, that over thirty delegates had registered as from local SDS chapters, and that *they* had a national organization. The session adjourned to the workshops with Emspak insisting that the thirteenth dissolve itself and come to the meeting on NCC structure.

Meanwhile Marilyn Milligan, Jack Weinberg, and Jerry Rubin, all delegates from the Berkeley VDC and all signers of the controversial workshop call, gathered around fellow VDCer Steve Weissman to caucus. Weissman, a Berkeley leader of SDS, was against the workshop. Milligan reportedly said: "I knew we shouldn't have signed. Those so-called members of independent committees aren't independents at all. They're Y.S.A. The Trots seem to be trying to steal the movement."[23]

Actually all thirty-three of the workshop sponsors were prominent activists in, and all but two, elected delegates of, legitimate independent committees. Slightly less than half of them were also members of the YSA, a fact of which they made no secret. Nevertheless such accusations became a veritable campaign throughout the convention.

As the independent committee workshop convened, the room was jammed, not only with independent committee delegates who came to discuss, but with people determined that the workshop should not take place. The atmosphere was ugly and there were some threats to break it up physically. The workshop was in the church cellar. I came running down one of two symmetrical staircases which led from the floor above, when I noticed a big CPer I'd worked with in a rent strike in New York a year or so before, bounding down the other staircase. We almost had it out right there. It was only then that I became aware of the forces we were up against. We were prepared for an argument with SDS, but breaking up a workshop was not their style in those days. This was going to be a fight with the CP.

Jack Weinberg, who was chairing the meeting, was obviously none too comfortable with the situation in which he found himself. What had seemed in normal conversation to be a reasonable and logical idea, now appeared in the face of the concerted attack as a dangerous move to be associated with. A motion was put to dissolve the workshop. It failed, but an orderly meeting was obviously impossible. Another motion, to adjourn temporarily into the NCC structure workshop and meet again that evening, passed.

23. Renata Adler, *New Yorker*, December 11, 1965.

The NCC structure workshop was uneventful, though it did become obvious that the question of a national organization of independent committees could not be discussed there because the chairman, Carl Griffler, insisted it was out of order. I admit taking an immediate dislike to Griffler's chairmanship when he allowed Beinin and Aronowitz to speak for fifteen minutes on the nature of the NCC and tried to cut me off in three, on the same subject. I took ten, which was all I needed anyway. Aronowitz, incidentally, was a delegate from the West Side (New York) Committee for Independent Political Action (CIPA), a multi-issue radical group involved in electoral politics. He considered it an "independent committee."

Griffler had been appointed to chair this workshop by the steering committee, which by this time had so many additions— by what standard or method was never explained—that no one was quite sure just who was on it.[24] I was convinced then, and still am, that it was artificially packed with supporters of the Madison office.

That evening the thirteenth workshop reconvened at the Hotel Harrington, where several others were also being held as well as a meeting of the steering committee, and where many of the 1,500 persons in attendance at the convention were housed. The thirteenth workshop room would only hold about 200 people, standing. Since I was not a delegate from an independent committee, I didn't try to get in, but stood at the edge of the crowd which was pressing at the door. Danny Rosenshine, a delegate from the Cleveland CEWV, was delivering a report on the history of the new movement and the role so far played in it by the various political youth groups and the independent committees. Suddenly Irving Beinin pushed past me into the room. He was built a bit like a bulldog anyway, and had that kind of look on his face. Though I knew he was going to try to get the meeting to disband, I couldn't help but admire his energy and fight—he was

24. A report on the NCC convention from the National Executive of the Du Bois Clubs states: "68 out of 73 steering committee seats were controlled by independent committees. There were 5 votes for national organizations, while the independents had 68." (Copy in author's files.) No source is cited for these figures, which in any case are suspect on the face of it because they do not account for the committee seats held by prominent individuals, who were not placed on the committee as representatives of organizations.

no youth—as he plowed through the crowd to the microphone. He demanded to speak on behalf of the steering committee. Lew Jones, in the chair, made him wait until Rosenshine was finished, and by then Beinin was livid. He declared the meeting out of order and an attempt to "split." For Beinin, the explanations that even if a national organization of independent committees were formed, it and the committees would still be part of the NCC umbrella was beside the point. He viewed this convention as the first national gathering of the "new left" which should contribute to the formation of a new mass multi-issue radical or broadly inclusive socialist party, of the type of the time of Debs. In this view, to organize independent committees into a national organization centered on the war issue would tend to reduce the NCC itself to being a single-issue coordinating group.

But the arguments he used in this meeting were not that subtle. He simply declared the meeting at war with the steering committee and the prominent people on it and out of order. Those involved in calling this workshop were either dupes of or members of "a small group" trying to split the independent committees away from the rest of the movement and take them over for its own purposes. In the debate that followed, Weinberg threw in the towel. He said he still favored a national organization of independent committees, but didn't want to cause trouble with the steering committee, so he favored adjourning. Jerry Rubin stood up on a chair, declared he had been duped by the YSA, and, waving the workshop call, said it was "beyond my comprehension" how he had ever put his name on it.

The motion to adjourn was defeated and Rubin led a walkout, including most of the Berkeley delegation. The workshop did not collapse, but from then on the YSA was the only organized force leading the fight for it. The meeting prepared some working papers for distribution to the convention, and, in a compromise, voted to adjourn for the next day—Friday—to see what developed in the NCC structure workshop and whether the NCC itself could adopt an "immediate withdrawal" position.

The next day a workshop on future national action decided to propose national days of protest for March 25-26, 1966, under the theme: "Bring the Troops Home Now!"

But in the Friday night and Saturday morning plenary sessions, the convention proved incapable of adopting the immediate withdrawal position for the NCC.

Friday night, the question of participation in the next day's

SANE march was being discussed in a wild session when a delegation of Southern civil rights activists moved that the convention support the SANE march by attending it under the slogan: "Freedom Now—Withdraw Now!" There was much cheering, but a countermotion was quickly made by Aronowitz that the SANE march be supported but no recommendation be made on slogans. He declared that personally he would carry the withdrawal slogan, but that the NCC was a broad body, coordinating for many groups, some of which would not accept the withdrawal slogan, and that therefore it would be incorrect for the convention to adopt it.

Bob Heisler, a delegate from the New York Du Bois Club, opposed the motion of the Southern delegation on the simple basis of opposition to the withdrawal slogan.[25] He said the movement "should not let Johnson steal the 'negotiate' slogan." The Aronowitz motion passed.

Aronowitz, however, remained one of the leading opponents of the idea of a national organization of the independent committees which *could* adopt the withdrawal slogan, in spite of his clear statement as to the umbrella perspective for the NCC. This was not his only contradiction. Like Beinin, he also envisaged the NCC developing into a new multi-issue radical group, something the moderate forces such as SANE certainly wouldn't involve themselves with. The inevitable logic of a multi-issue umbrella including such groups as SANE would have to be a coalition of radical-liberal forces subordinated to the multi-issue program of the liberal politicians, to a wing of the Democratic Party, in the practicalities of the situation. In Marxist terminology, the technical name for such a coalition is a "popular front." (This is one

25. A peculiarity of the Du Bois Clubs' own brand of participatory democracy must be noted here. The group's founding convention in 1964 had adopted a statement on Vietnam including the following: "This convention demands the immediate withdrawal of all U.S. troops and war material from South Vietnam and a return to the Geneva Agreement of 1954." The resolution made no mention of negotiations as such (copy in author's files). Formally the "negotiations" demand was not added, and the "immediate" dropped, until the Du Bois National Committee meeting in Philadelphia December 2-4, immediately *after* the NCC convention. The Du Bois Club spokespersons operated on the negotiations line, however, at the NCC convention and for some time beforehand. (*Dimensions,* Discussion Journal of the W.E.B. Du Bois Clubs, vol. 1, no. 1, January 1966. Copy in author's files.)

reason the SWP and the YSA wanted no part of it. We were willing to work with liberal politicians on a point of agreement— that is, in a single-issue coalition—but not to support the rest of their program or to vote for them.) This held out no contradiction for the CP or the Du Bois Clubs, however. It was part of their strategic perspective for the movement.

The Saturday morning plenary was calm and orderly, chaired by Dave Dellinger. It took up the proposed March 25-26 national action. It was here that Paul Booth, in a quiet, almost apologetic tone, outlined the SDS position, including the point that the antiwar movement couldn't affect this war, that it was necessary to build a grass-roots radical movement that would grow and eventually "stop the seventh war from now." He made a motion against another national antiwar demonstration. "It's defeated unanimously," announced Dellinger as the vote was taken, "including Paul Booth." In the interest of not hurting the action, Booth said he would not vote for his own negative motion.

The theme of the national action was voted separately. Not only Trotskyists, but many others, including Staughton Lynd, a consistent supporter of "immediate withdrawal," though not of the thirteenth workshop, spoke for "Bring the Troops Home Now!" Hugh Fowler, national chairman of the Du Bois Clubs, spoke against it, and for specifying no theme. Once again the motion not to specify carried. It was clear that the NCC itself could not adopt immediate withdrawal.

The convention adjourned to attend the SANE march. Meanwhile the rest of the convention—including most of the other workshops—had not been going well by anybody's standards. In part this was due to the atmosphere created by the fight over the independent committee workshop. The corridors were full of accusations and counterarguments. The great bulk of those present had not attended the disputed workshop and had only the vaguest idea of what was going on in that respect, which only added to the confusion.

Most workshops had accomplished little, for the simple reason that the forces at this convention did not, and could not, agree on much more than what had brought them together in the first place—opposition to the war in Vietnam. The "multi-issue" discussions were confused and frustrating, as they would inevitably have been whether the fight over the thirteenth workshop had occurred or not. In addition, the steering committee had been in almost continuous session, trying to agree on what to do, and failing for the same inexorable reason.

Even some ardent supporters of the "immediate withdrawal" position, like Staughton Lynd and Dave Dellinger, appalled by the heat of the dispute, blamed the shambles on the YSA, not for the YSA's position, with which they had much agreement, but for fighting for it on the level of parliamentary debate and maneuver. The whole atmosphere reminded me of a line from Kipling: "If you can keep your head when all about you are losing theirs and blaming it on you. . . ."

By this time the supporters of the Madison office had convinced themselves that if the independent committee workshop—which was scheduled to reconvene after the march—actually succeeded in meeting for a full session, it would mean the capture of the convention by the YSA. The only grain of truth to this was that the YSA was the only national youth group that supported the independent committee workshop and that workshop was the only place where a specific realizable proposal—aside from March 25-26 and a February 12 demonstration in the South—was being considered. The steering committee itself had not come up with one.

After briefly checking out the SANE march, I came back to the hotel and sat in on the steering committee meeting, just listening. Someone tapped me on the shoulder and handed me a note asking me and Jack Barnes, national YSA chairman, to go to a certain room in the hotel. We left quietly and went there.

It was the proverbial smoke-filled room—a small one—crowded with a number of prominent members of the steering committee who I now noticed had not been at the meeting downstairs. These included Dellinger, Lynd, Beinin, Aronowitz, and several others. We asked what was wanted of us and one of them replied: Isn't there some way we can work this thing out? So we told them our views, which was nothing we hadn't already stated in front of the convention delegates. They seemed to have difficulty grasping our point that what happened with the independent committee workshop was not up to us but to the delegates from the independent committees.

Two astounding facts struck me—and Jack—after only a little of the conversation. First, there was no one present from the CP or the Du Bois Clubs or the Madison office. Second, these people—and apparently those in the meeting downstairs as well—did not know that the independent committee workshop was scheduled to try to meet once again, when the delegates returned from the march. They would have been able to find this out if they had simply milled about among the ordinary delegates where it had been announced.

Jack and I felt no obligation to tell them, either, so some of them could run down and try to break up the workshop again. So we just sat there, passing the time of day, as long as we could. Suddenly there was loud knocking at the door. It was Adam Schesch of the NCC staff in Madison, who had finally noticed who was missing from the meeting downstairs. He had put two and two together and gone searching for the culprits. He demanded the meeting disband and return to the steering committee. "Is this participatory democracy?" he shouted. (Indeed it *was* a logical outcome of the "new left" affectation of contempt for the rules of give-and-take debate. In themselves these are no guarantee of democracy, but without them decision by a self-appointed clique is impossible to avoid.) With Schesch riding herd, we all returned to the steering committee meeting where Jack and I continued to pass the time of day, until the independent committee workshop was well under way.

When word of this finally reached the steering committee, it broke up immediately, some of its members running down the hall yelling, "The Trots have taken over." This time, however, the workshop had placed guards at the door who wouldn't let anyone in who wasn't a member of an independent committee. An exception was Lynd, who spoke before the group. The meeting proceeded without disruption, with about 170 present. The steering committee waited dejectedly for the outcome. In light of their fears, the outcome was anticlimactic.

The workshop decided that the formation of a national organization of independent committees would be premature at this point. Instead it formed a caucus of individuals to advocate the idea. It adopted some working papers describing what such a national organization might look like, and it drew up a proposal for the structure of the NCC to present to the final session of the convention on Sunday morning.

With this news, the steering committee reconvened for another night-long session in which it tried to agree on a different proposal for NCC structure.

Meanwhile, the SANE march had drawn some 35,000 participants, the biggest antiwar action so far. Signs carried by the marchers expressed a variety of views on ending the war, including "immediate withdrawal." Since the issuance of the call, the march organizers had modified their position on this score to one of asking "courteously" those with such "unauthorized" signs to put them down, but letting them participate anyway if they didn't. Dierdre Griswold, of Youth Against War and Fascism, had announced at the NCC convention that YAWF had printed a large number of such signs which were available for those who wanted them.

The platform, however, was so moderate that it was difficult to tell whether some of the speakers were against the war. Norman Thomas, Coretta King, and Dr. Spock were distinguished exceptions, but still quite mild. SANE had, however, invited Carl Oglesby, then president of SDS, to be a sponsor and to speak at the affair. He was to represent the radicals. He was shunted to nearly the end of the long rally and the crowd was beginning to leave around the edges. The edges hesitated as he began to speak, then stayed, enraptured, and the crowd gave him an ovation when he finished. The chairman, Sanford Gottlieb, walked over to him and raised Oglesby's arm like a prize fighter who'd just won a bout.

Oglesby's speech was a work of art. It was, at one and the same time, a moving indictment of the U.S. involvement in the war, and a summary of the current thinking of the best of the SDS "old guard." With a kind of equivocal anger, it captured the mood of the liberals betrayed by their own kind in government, which is one reason it was so deeply felt by so many of those who heard it. Said Oglesby:

> The original commitment in Vietnam was made by President Truman, a mainstream liberal. It was seconded by President Eisenhower, a moderate liberal. It was intensified by the late President Kennedy, a flaming liberal. Think of the men who now engineer that war—those who study the maps, give the commands, push the buttons, and tally the dead: Bundy, McNamara, Rusk, Lodge, Goldberg, the President himself.
> They are not moral monsters.
> They are all honorable men.
> They are all liberals. . . . Maybe we have here two quite different liberalisms: one authentically humanist; the other not so human at all.

He conjured up a conversation between the revolutionaries of 1776 and the liberals who now ran the country:

Our dead revolutionaries would soon wonder why their country was fighting against what appeared to be a revolution. The living liberals would hotly deny that it is one: there are troops coming in from outside, the rebels get arms from other countries, most of the people are not on their side, and they practice terror against their own. Therefore: *not* a revolution.

What would our dead revolutionaries answer? They might say: "What fools and bandits, sirs, you make then of us. Outside help? Do you remember Lafayette? . . . And what's this about terror? Did you never hear what we did to our own Loyalists? Or about the thousands of rich American Tories who fled for their lives to Canada? And as for popular support, do you not know that we had less than one-third of our people with us? That, in fact, the colony of New York recruited more troops for the British than for the revolution? Should we give it all back?"

Revolutions do not take place in velvet boxes [continued Oglesby], they never have. It is only the poets who make them lovely. What the National Liberation Front is fighting in Vietnam is a complex and vicious war. This war is also a revolution, as honest a revolution as you can find anywhere in history. And this is a fact which all our intricate official denials will never change.

But it doesn't make any difference to our leaders anyway. . . . There is simply no such thing, now, for us as a just revolution. . . . Never mind the melting poverty and hopelessness that are the basic facts of life for most modern men; and never mind that for these millions there is now an increasingly perceptible relationship between their sorrow and our contentment.

Can we understand why the Negroes of Watts rebelled [in August 1965]? Then why do we need a devil theory to explain the rebellion of the South Vietnamese? Can we understand the oppression in Mississippi, or the anguish that our Northern ghettoes make epidemic? Then why can't we see that our proper human struggle is not with Communism or revolutionaries, but with the social desperation that drives good men to violence, both here and abroad?

There followed a summary of American foreign policy, and its pursuit of counterrevolution with "6,000 military bases on foreign soil." Then he continued:

We have lost that mysterious social desire for human equity that from time to time has given us genuine moral drive. We have become a nation of young, bright-eyed, hard hearted, slim-waisted, bullet-headed make-out artists. A nation—may I say it?—of beardless liberals. . . .

Some will make of it that I overdraw the matter. Many will ask: What about the other side? To be sure, there is the bitter ugliness of Czechoslovakia, Poland, those infamous Russian tanks in the streets of Budapest.

But my anger only rises to hear some say that sorrow cancels sorrow, or that *this* one's shame deposits in *that* one's account the right to shamefulness. And others will make of it that I sound mighty anti-American. To these, I say: Don't blame *me* for *that!* Blame those who mouthed my liberal values and broke my American heart. . . .[26]

\* \* \*

Back at the convention, the full steering committee failed to agree on a proposal for the structure of the NCC. A hurried meeting Sunday morning, attended by less than half the members, finally agreed to present a draft originally submitted by the Madison CEWV and revised by Weinberg and others. As revised, it was similar to that proposed by the thirteenth workshop, with only two significant points of difference: The workshop proposal contained a specific nonexclusion clause: "No group shall be excluded from participating because of its political views." The steering committee proposal did not. The workshop proposal limited national political organizations to one vote, the steering committee proposal gave a vote to any local chapter of a national political organization that was the sole antiwar group in its area.[27]

Because of Sunday services, the final session of the convention could not be held in the church. Unfortunately the alternate hall held only 400 people, not much more than the voting delegates. The fact that so many of the 1,500 persons who had attended the convention did not attend this last session also contributed to the confusion that so many carried away with them.

The session consisted of some workshop reports and a debate on structure. The steering committee proposal was adopted by a vote of 110 to 45. Most of the delegates simply didn't vote. (There were 378 delegates registered, exactly half of whom were registered from independent committees.[28]) The significance of the

26. Quoted from *Biweekly Information/Action Report*, early December 1965. Ann Arbor. (Copy in author's files.)

27. "Convention Resolutions on NCC Structure," *Bring the Troops Home Now Newsletter*, December 4, 1965. (Library of Social History, New York.)

28. "Reflections on the NCC Convention's Credentials" by Jens Jensen, *Bring the Troops Home Now Newsletter*, December 25, 1965. Jensen was a member of the credentials committee.

116    *Out Now!*

session was not the adopted structure document—which was never implemented anyway—but the fact that the session took place at all, and was orderly with Dellinger in the chair. This indicated that the convention had ended without a split, and that there would at least be unity around the calls to the next scheduled demonstrations—a February 12 day of antiwar actions in the South and March 25-26 nationally.

Immediately following the convention the caucus from the thirteenth workshop held a meeting attended by 140 members of independent committees. A motion to form a national organization of independent committees then and there got only a handful of votes. A motion to continue as a grouping of individuals in the "Caucus to Constitute a National Organization of Local Independent Committees for the Withdrawal of U.S. Troops Now" was passed. A caucus steering committee of three was elected: Kipp Dawson, Danny Rosenshine, and Jens Jensen, chairman of the Cambridge, Massachusetts, CEWV. It was also decided that the caucus would put out a "Bring the Troops Home Now Newsletter." A motion to support the NCC was passed unanimously.

*          *          *

The reports on the convention often credited—or blamed—the YSA for leading the fight for immediate withdrawal and the thirteenth workshop. Very few, however, mentioned the leading role played by the CP and the Du Bois Clubs, which had blocked with the older "supporters of SDS" to lead the fight on the other side.

A report on the convention from the National Executive of the Du Bois Clubs, however, took credit as follows:

In the steering committee, the DBC played a decisive role. We were able to take many of the [Du Bois] caucus conclusions into these discussions, to contribute ably to the deliberations, to build close working relations with key independents, and to gain the respect of most of the delegates present. We provided a strong backstop to the independents who finally exposed the maneuvers of the minority faction without becoming the sole source of that exposure. . . .

Though we did not play a dominant role in providing programmatic suggestions, we contributed greatly in finally bringing the issues of program to the plenum, and far outshined all others in the overall contribution we made.[29]

SDS itself, it was generally recognized, played no role at all beyond Booth's "seventh war from now" speech.

A remark by Jack Weinberg during the structure debate indicated the discomfort of many self-styled "new lefters" at finding themselves in a struggle essentially led—on opposite sides—by the two main ideological tendencies of the "old left." Weinberg was explaining why he and others had modified the Madison proposal in an attempt to reach a compromise when he said: "We didn't want to come out of here . . . with a Third and Fourth International of the peace movement." The response of the audience indicated he wasn't the only one who knew what the lineup really was.[30]

Following the convention the YSA was roundly denounced for its role there. Some of this was simply traditional vilification of Trotskyists by Stalinists. Some of it came from moderates who resented the unequivocal character of the immediate withdrawal demand. But much of it came from movement figures not particularly prejudiced against the YSA as such who blamed it for the fact that so sharp a dispute had occurred. The fact that the steering committee had not put a key point on the agenda in spite of repeated requests was ignored. The other fact that the YSAers and other delegates from independent committees had maneuvered around the steering committee to make sure it would be on the agenda was considered the major crime. To Staughton Lynd, for example, the problem was one of "trust" and "feeling." An article by Lynd and Bill Tabb in the NCC newsletter declared:

> Although we resented the attempt to form a new organization based on the position "Bring the Troops Home," we think many if not most of the delegates agreed with the position and that the group obliged us to face the key question of the difference between demanding negotiations and demanding troop withdrawal. . . . Although the steering committee and the NCC generally are not dominated by Stalinists, the Du Bois Clubs, or a conspiracy of persons favoring a popular front, in making this false charge, the YSA did bare the critical failure of the NCC: the absence of

29. "Report on the Convention of the National Coordinating Committee to End the War in Vietnam. From the National Executive of the W.E.B. Du Bois Clubs of America." (Copy in author's files.)

30. This incident is also described in *New America*, December 18, 1965.

trust and communication—and of "being in touch"—between the coordinating committee office and the local groups. . . . The problem involves structure and requires structural changes, but is essentially a problem of feeling.[31]

James P. Cannon, the seventy-five-year-old national chairman of the SWP, took a different view of the matter of trust.

If I would criticize our comrades who were in charge of the fight in Washington, it would perhaps be for a fault that is hard to avoid in the absence of experience of this sort. That is, the underestimation of political opponents; an assumption that everything is going to be on the level, which is a very bad assumption when you have Stalinists and Social Democrats to deal with. They may possibly have been caught by surprise. I didn't doubt for one minute about the ambush being prepared after I heard that several weeks before the conference was held the *Daily Worker* and the *People's World* suddenly began to promote the conference in high gear. I know what that means. I don't have the slightest doubt that they stacked the convention with every kind of delegate from every kind of paper organization they could mobilize. I don't doubt that they stacked the steering committee, that they rigged the agenda, in such a way that the delegates of many independent committees and our own people ran into a prepared fight in which there was room for everything except the one thing they were most interested in. That was promoting the real slogan of the movement. . . . And of the right and necessity of the independent committees organized under that slogan to unite themselves nationally. . . .

I think our comrades were correct to adopt that slogan [Bring the Troops Home Now!] and their militancy at the conference and their refusal to be bluffed or bulldozed is quite admirable. All the more so that they were perhaps taken by surprise and hadn't had previous experience with what the perfidy of Stalinism and the Social Democracy is really like. I will guarantee you that they will never be taken by surprise again.[32]

It is now known, from documents released through the SWP's lawsuit against government harassment, that the Federal Bureau of Investigation tried to add fuel to the fires roasting the YSA

31. *Peace and Freedom News,* no. 12, December 13, 1965. (Copy in author's files.)

32. "Revolutionary Policies in the Antiwar Movement," by James P. Cannon, in *Revolutionary Strategy in the Fight Against the Vietnam War* (New York: Education for Socialists Bulletin, April 1975), pp. 15-16.

after the NCC convention. This was part of the FBI's COINTEL-PRO efforts to disrupt various radical, Black, and antiwar groups. One of these FBI-authored documents, entitled "An Open Letter to Trotskyites" and purporting to come from within the radical movement, was mailed anonymously to members of the SWP as well as to antiwar committees and other radical groups. It said in part:

Presently, you've been struggling with your party in its efforts to become part of the greatest ground swell of opposition to this country's imperialist policies that has ever existed. To this end, you had high hopes as the party's youth arm, the Young Socialist Alliance, was dispatched to Washington, D.C. last Thanksgiving to participate in anti-war conferences and a massive demonstration of protest to U.S. intervention in Vietnam. Surely, this was an unprecedented opportunity to militate against Washington and Wall Street. But, true to the SWP's history of sectarianism, you witnessed the young "trots" promote a divisionary and undermining line of "immediate withdrawal" at these conferences.

Prophetically, you saw your party and its youth soundly defeated at this conference in yet another attempt to recruit through division and domination. Your attempt to "save face", following this debacle, was the promotion of a Caucus of "independent" anti-war committees based solely on immediate withdrawal of U.S. forces in Vietnam. And you justly suspect now that this tactic is viewed by radicals and independents alike as a "paper front" composed of committees hastily formed and led by YSA members throughout the country. . . . Your humiliation in the public and radical press is now complete. . . .[33]

But this was a police provocateur's pipe dream. Actually, the morale of the YSA and its influence within the antiwar movement were greatly enhanced by the fight it helped lead around the issues at the NCC convention. This was one of the convention's few lasting results. Before the convention the YSA was generally considered the smallest and least influential of the three major radical youth groups (SDS, Du Bois Clubs, and YSA). After the convention it was recognized as a leading force in the immediate-withdrawal wing of the antiwar movement. That wing had as yet no national organization, but it was clear that it would not be buried and it did retain a national voice in the *Bring the Troops Home Now Newsletter,* within the broader movement.

One report on the convention, by Renata Adler in the *New Yorker,* was entitled "The Price of Peace Is Confusion." This pretty much summed up the impression gained by the media as well as some of the delegates. Many observers at that time viewed the dispute at the convention as a sign of sectarian madness as well as a tempest in a teapot—an apparent power struggle in a movement with little power and certainly no emoluments for those who were fighting so desperately over what seemed a minor organizational issue. And at times the fight did assume grotesque forms. But the issue at stake was not really that simple, any more than the battle of Gettysburg was really over possession of some Pennsylvania wheat fields, all proportions guarded.

The calling of the thirteenth workshop was the point on which those with two fundamentally different perspectives for the antiwar movement happened willy-nilly to find themselves locked in struggle to decide which program would prevail.

Oglesby's speech at the SANE march was generally considered to have been the high point of the Thanksgiving antiwar events. It was reprinted again and again as an effective and moving piece of antiwar literature. But so far as direction for the movement was concerned, Oglesby was ambivalent. Toward the end of the speech, he said:

> Those allies of ours in the government—are they really our allies? If they *are,* then they don't need advice, they need constituencies; they don't need study groups, they need a *movement.* And if they are *not,* then all the more reason for building that movement with a most relentless conviction.

Should the movement become a constituency for the liberal politicians, or should it be built as an independent movement in the streets? Oglesby raised the question, but he didn't answer it. Neither did SDS at the time. The Du Bois Clubs and the YSA did, each in their own way. The two opposite answers they gave to that question underlay the outwardly confusing fight at the NCC convention.

# 6

## The Second International Days of Protest and the Reactions to the Buddhist Demonstrations

Reverend A. J. Muste was respectable enough to receive an invitation to sponsor the SANE march, but he turned it down because the call was too equivocal. SANE insisted on a multilateral approach, blaming both sides for the war and calling on both sides to take initiatives for peace. As a pacifist, Muste was prepared to appeal to both sides to stop the killing. But he also felt it was important for Americans to demand a unilateral ceasefire by the U.S. The call did not reflect his view, he said, that the U.S. "has no business—and never had—in Vietnam and should withdraw."[1] At the same time he urged people to attend the march because he felt a small turnout would be a setback for the cause of peace.

Muste attended at least part of the NCC convention. The white-haired old man even sat through one of the late night sessions of the steering committee. As I recall, it was crowded and the table and chairs had been removed to make more room. People, including Muste, sat on the floor. He was tall, but lean, and looked more comfortable than I with his legs folded under him, his well-worn suit and tie unruffled. But he did not speak.

A. J.—everybody called him that—was not exactly close-mouthed, but he wasn't given to aimless talk either. He had long since decided who he was and where he was going and he didn't do his thinking out loud. He would sometimes offer an apparently offhand remark, often a bit of whimsy, but it seemed to me these always made a point. At the convention proceedings, however, he said nothing.

1. *National Guardian,* December 4, 1965.

121

Yet that gathering of antiwar radicals must have had a certain importance for him. Nearly half a century of his life had been spent opposing wars—not simply in the abstract, but in particular, while they were being prepared *and* while they were being prosecuted. After the advent of atomic weapons he viewed his work with even greater urgency, not simply as a spiritual need for individual moral witness, or a struggle for desirable social change—both of which motivated Muste—but as a necessity of human survival. Moreover, Muste was not a passive pacifist. For him nonviolence was a method of affecting events.

He was also very practical. Unlike most of the pacifists, Muste had a background of personal experience in the rise of industrial unionism in the United States, having spent sixteen years, from 1919 to 1935, deeply involved in working class struggles and contributing in no small measure to the victory of several important strikes. He understood mass movements, had no fear of them, and well knew the key role played in the birth of such developments by handfuls of persecuted organizers.

What is more, he had often cast his lot with the unrespectable radicals—ever since he had to leave his Congregationalist pulpit in Newtonville, Massachusetts, for remaining a pacifist *after* the country entered World War I. Now a movement against a war in progress presented the possibility of involving popular masses. Muste took it seriously, if anyone did.

This is not to say that Muste agreed with what the Trotskyists did at the convention. His well-established aversion to faction fighting would have inclined him to be critical. But he did not join the chorus denouncing the YSA. His published comment was rich in content and evenhanded, and typical of his approach to reconciliation. Significantly, it came in the context of a defense of the new antiwar activity against some of the criticisms raised by a group of Social Democrats in the right wing of the old peace movement.[2] Said Muste:

It was to be expected that in the midst of this upsurge of anti-war sentiment and of such a war as the Vietnamese war, proposals for an end-the-war "movement" should emerge and efforts to build such a

2. Muste answered an article in the November 25, 1965, *New York Review of Books* signed by Irving Howe, Michael Harrington, Bayard Rustin, Lewis Coser, and Penn Kimble. Howe and Coser wrote for the magazine *Dissent* and Kimble was a member of New York SDS.

"movement"—*the* movement which would do the job—should be undertaken. It was also inevitable that the question whether the end-the-war "movement" might not be made the starting point for a new political alignment, a new "revolutionary" line-up, and what have you, should be broached and that various groups should think they have *the* answer to that broader question and proceed to act upon it. All this is obviously too vast a matter to go into in detail here.

I am not at the moment sanguine that *the* "movement" is about to come into existence. I must in all honesty confess my distress over the fact that, e.g. at the Convention of the National Coordinating Committee in Washington, November 25-28, and on other occasions there have been displays of sectarianism and embittered ideological controversy, which will not facilitate the emergence of a movement of radical opposition to the war, if they persist. But I am convinced that movement, revolt [against the war], cannot be suppressed and that this is in itself a "revolutionary" development. If the revolt is to express itself in various ways and not in a single "movement," then it is my hope that the adherents of each tendency or program will work very hard at their job as they see it and while not abandoning political dialogue, will not dissipate energy in personal or organizational attacks on each other. The issue will in any event be decided largely by forces and developments over which none of us exercise a substantial measure of control.[3]

On December 3, a few days after the NCC convention, I was invited to a meeting at 5 Beekman Street, where Muste had his office. Those present included Muste, Dellinger, Beinin, Eric Weinberger, Beverly Sterner, who was Muste's secretary, and Jerry Rubin.

The meeting opened with Beinin raking me over the coals. He said the real question was whether the SWP and YSA were going to remain part of the movement. He did not say we ought to be excluded, but suspected we were intent on a split. There were similar thrusts from around the room. Bev Sterner was particularly incensed, saying something like: Fred, how could you *do* that? Muste spoke last, directly to me, asking where I thought we should go from here. I told them we were certainly not contemplating any kind of split, and that I thought the Parade Committee was a good model of how the various groups could work together. Muste replied simply, we can start from there. That ended the roasting.

The rest of the meeting was devoted to a proposal by Rubin for

3. *Liberation,* January 1966.

reorganizing the NCC office. For the time it was a grandiose plan. It involved a $100,000 budget for one year, a fifteen-member full-time staff, including regional desks, traveling organizers, fund-raisers, and even a printer. The plan called for the NCC office to be moved from Madison to Chicago. Rubin said he would go there and bring five full-timers from Berkeley with him. Rubin would present the plan at the first standing committee[4] meeting of the NCC projected for January 8-9 in Milwaukee.

Rubin made no bones about the fact that a major motivation for his proposal was to avoid domination of the NCC office by one ideological tendency, at least one from the "old left." In the printed version of his proposal he said:

The healthiest aspect of the current movement is the involvement within [it] of large numbers of people not previously organized. They are new to politics. They examine matters empirically and they are developing a perspective. Many of their friends still believe in the American Dream. The Stalin-Trotsky conflict as applied to 1965 America and the world seems like an ecclesiastical debate.

It is these independent radicals who have formed the basis of the Berkeley VDC. The national organizations, with their ideological world views, and their pattern tactical approaches, are active in the VDC. But they are far outnumbered by the independents. This is the strength of the VDC. This has kept the friction of Du Bois, YSA, Third Camp, and SDS to a minimum. . . . This should also be the model for the NCC. Concerning two points: The NCC should be located in an area of heterogeneous political tendencies, which offset one another and in which

---

4. As used here the term "standing committee" refers to the body composed of representatives of the constituent groups. The structural document adopted at the NCC convention contains that usage, and the term "administrative subcommittee" for a much smaller body of seven members which the standing committee was empowered to elect. It uses the term "steering committee" to refer to the larger body as it existed before and during the convention.

There is some confusion in other documents over these terms. According to one version, the "steering committee" was the larger body of some seventy members and the "standing committee" was the smaller body of eight members. In another version these terms appear to be reversed. As I recall it, the "administrative subcommittee" was never elected—though it may have existed informally—and the term "steering committee" was used throughout to refer to the larger body. In this book, however, the usage is the same as in the most authoritative document available to me, the structural document adopted at the convention (copy in author's files).

the opportunity for independent point of view is greatest. Most of the staff members of the NCC should be independents. Leadership should be diffused and balanced between various points of view, representing individuals of various sized groups, various regions, and of various perspectives.

Close control on the office should be exercised by a representative administrative body representing the independent committees throughout the country, a group small enough so that it can maintain democratic control of the staff.[5]

This obviously implied a certain criticism of the current NCC office under Emspak's direction.

Rubin returned to Berkeley, met with the VDC, and on December 9 held a press conference together with VDCers Windy Smith and Larry Laughlin in which they announced the plan, as well as the March 25-26 "international days of protest." They also announced they would be joining the NCC staff. All this, apparently, without consulting Emspak, who, when he read it in the December 10 *New York Times,* was not pleased.

By phone Rubin apologized for not emphasizing to the press that the plan was simply a proposal to the January 8-9 meeting. It was then printed with that explanation in the NCC newsletter along with statements supporting its main points by Dellinger, Lynd, Beinin, Weinberg, and others.

For my part, I was ambivalent toward the Rubin proposal. I was willing to vote for it, but if Emspak resisted, it would take a fight to implement it. Frankly, I was not eager for another experience with Rubin as an ally in a faction fight. In a letter to YSAers recommending support for the Rubin plan, Doug Jenness said:

Rubin's proposal is actually the same proposals we were making before the convention when we thought it would be possible for the NCC to become a national organization based on and responsible to the independent committees. The major difficulty with Rubin's proposal is that more likely than not the centrists who support it will not wage a determined fight for it. It is impossible for us to fight for this proposal which would place Rubin in the staff unless Rubin himself is willing to fight for it. We are not sure at this point how hard Rubin and Co. will fight.[6]

5. *Peace and Freedom News,* no. 13, December 31, 1965.
6. Letter to YSAers from Doug Jenness, YSA national office, December 20, 1965.

Meantime, events in the war itself set the stage for a substantive political debate at the January 8-9 meeting. Two weeks before Christmas the NLF proposed a twelve-hour truce for the Christian holiday. On December 22 the U.S. announced it would observe a thirty-hour truce beginning Christmas Eve. Senators Mike Mansfield and Robert F. Kennedy proposed extensions. Fighting resumed the day after Christmas, but the U.S. bombing of North Vietnam did not.

On December 30 the White House announced that a major probe for negotiations was under way. Johnson played the "peace offensive" for all it was worth, ostentatiously sending prominent personal emissaries around the world—including to Warsaw, where in those days U.S. diplomatic messages were passed to the Chinese—to look for signals that Hanoi was willing to talk terms. The pause lasted thirty-seven days and ended after Johnson piously declared on TV January 31, "Now the world knows more clearly than ever who insists on aggression and who works for peace."[7]

There was never any real secret about Johnson's purpose in the bombing pause. It was twofold: first, to once again tell Hanoi to abandon the revolution in the South or face destruction of its own cities, and second, to prepare the political atmosphere for continued massive escalation of the war. Johnson still refused to have anything to do with negotiations with the NLF.

No matter how the Hanoi regime responds to the U.S. pause in the bombing of North Vietnamese targets [William Beecher commented in the *Wall Street Journal* December 30] the Johnson administration plans to go to Congress next month with double-barrelled requests for more money so the war can be pressed harder if necessary. . . . If Hanoi fails to rise to the opportunity for a peaceful dialogue then the President will have gone a long way to disarming his critics at home and abroad who have raised doubts about the sincerity of his interest in a negotiated settlement.

Hanoi gave its answer January 4:

The United States is thousands of miles away from Vietnam. The Vietnamese people has never laid hands on the United States. The United States Government has no right to send troops to invade south Vietnam and to launch air attacks on the Democratic Republic of Vietnam. It has no right to impose on the Government of the Democratic Republic of

7. *Washington Post*, February 1, 1966.

Vietnam any condition whatsoever in exchange for stopping its air raids on north Vietnam.

United States aggression is the deep root and the immediate cause of the serious situation now prevailing in Vietnam. With the ending of this aggression peace will be immediately restored in this country.[8]

Seventy-seven congressmen and some twenty senators, including Senator J. William Fulbright, chairman of the Senate Foreign Relations Committee, appealed for an extension of the bombing pause and more serious attempts to negotiate, but studiously avoided any threat to vote against the increased war funding. After all, the argument went, you can't expect the president to negotiate from weakness.

The "peace offensive" was accompanied by the first full-scale U.S. attack on the Mekong River Delta region of South Vietnam, with U.S. forces burning out villages that had for years been under NLF control. It was prepared by massive air strikes, including B-52 bombers shifted from Northern targets. By January 9 it had become the largest ground operation of the war.

The "peace offensive" presented the antiwar movement with a crisis around the problem of how to cut through Johnson's duplicity. The negotiations wing of the movement concentrated its efforts on Congress, but its arguments were easily parried by the administration. It came down to a matter of trust, of whether the president was sincere or not. What is more, the hawks replied with an argument designed to appeal to the war weariness itself: strike hard and get it over with.

Fulbright himself would later refer to this in one of a series of lectures at Johns Hopkins University in which he described some of the dangers inherent in the situation:

. . . as the war goes on, as the casualty lists grow larger and affect more and more American homes, the fever will rise and the patience of the American people will give way to mounting demands for an expanded war, for a lightning blow that will get it over with at a stroke. The first demand might be for a blockade of Haiphong; then, if that doesn't work, a strike against China and then we will have global war.[9]

In line with the hawk arguments, various prowar groups began

8. *Militant,* January 17, 1966.
9. *New York Times,* April 20, 1066.

organizing rallies to "support our boys," by which they meant support the war. This was also a central argument used to keep the doves in Congress in line on votes for military appropriations. It was one thing to criticize, but it was another to actually use congressional power to block the war effort. That was characterized as stabbing "our boys" in the back.

In the face of these developments the immediate-withdrawal wing of the movement had a clear, popular response: If you want to get it over with, get out of Vietnam now! If you want to support our boys, bring them home now! What had seemed to many merely a moral position now assumed greater practical significance, and the pressure for the immediate withdrawal demand increased within the movement.

Emspak, however, stuck to the negotiations position. Declaring "the peace movement has been disarmed by the peace offensive," he said: "We in the peace movement can either ignore the ploy as a 'hoax' or we can respond in such a way as to attempt a change in the nature of the offensive itself." He emphasized a demand "that the U.S. agree that the inclusion of the NLF is necessary in any government in South Vietnam."

"To this end," he continued, "we must support the Senators, etc., who are more or less in agreement with this position."[10]

The National Executive of the Du Bois Clubs commented as follows on the "peace offensive":

> Many Americans have been heartened by this move, as they welcome any serious attempt to end this brutal war. President Johnson tells us he wants a negotiated peace in Vietnam; so does the whole world. But the only basis for peace in Vietnam is that there be free elections in Vietnam, and that the Vietnamese people are guaranteed self-determination under the Geneva Accords.[11]

The Geneva Accords called for internationally supervised elections.

This was a common formula with the congressional doves and was often presented by SANE. I had commented on this position as follows in an article analyzing the NCC convention debate:

10. *Peace and Freedom News,* no. 14, January 21, 1966.
11. "To: All Du Bois Clubs, Key Contacts, and Peace Groups. From: National Exec. W.E.B. Du Bois Clubs," January 4, 1966. (Copy in author's files.)

Right off the bat, this whole business of calling for self-determination for the Vietnamese through internationally supervised elections is a contradiction in terms. If a people has self-determination it determines things for itself, including how its elections shall be run or whether it shall have them or not.

To make the point sharp, put it this way: "Self-determination for the Soviet people, internationally supervised elections in the Soviet Union." Or: "Internationally supervised elections in the United States." Neither the Soviet Union nor the U.S. would brook any such nonsense, and the Vietnamese should not be asked to accept it either. . . .

It is true, of course, that Hanoi did accept the Geneva Accords in 1954 to end the fighting with the French. It is also true that the Vietnamese might once again feel they have to negotiate and accept something short of full sovereignty as the price of ending the fighting. That is their right. It is they, after all, who are under the gun.

But it is a different matter for U.S. citizens to ask the U.S. government to negotiate anything in Vietnam. Such demands implicitly recognize some sort of U.S. rights in Vietnam. But it has none, and the only correct thing for it to do is get out. . . . The Johnson administration already claims that it respects the Geneva Accords. Demands to end the war which are couched in these terms give the administration a way out, a way to equivocate, a way to claim they are meeting the demand while they proceed with the war.[12]

The NCC standing committee meeting, which took place in Milwaukee January 8-9, featured a lengthy discussion of the "peace offensive." Almost everyone present agreed with an analysis presented by Ed Greer of New Haven, who characterized the Johnson move as a hoax designed to cut the ground out from under critics of the war. It was decided to put out a press statement on the "peace offensive." A draft drawn by Robin Maisel of the Philadelphia CEWV was hotly debated. It declared:

It has become evident over the past two weeks that President Johnson's "Peace Offensive" is not aimed at producing a peaceful settlement of the Vietnam war which will guarantee the right of self-determination for the Vietnamese people. The purpose of the President's recent foray in diplomacy is to disarm his critics at home and abroad.

The NCC Standing Committee meeting in Milwaukee, Wisconsin, January 8 and 9, demands that the President immediately withdraw American forces from Vietnam and leave Vietnam for the Vietnamese. The alternative is a further escalation of the war, the loss of tens of

12. *Militant*, December 13, 1965.

thousands of American lives, and an ever-increasing economic and social burden on the American people.[13]

Opponents of the statement, including Emspak, argued that the meeting was too sparsely attended to make policy for the NCC. Someone—as I recall it was Dellinger, who favored the immediate withdrawal statement—then proposed that it be released simply in the name of those present. Maisel accepted the amendment and the debate proceeded on the substance of the matter. Greer opposed the statement on the grounds that the movement should advocate negotiations. He said that though "the overwhelming majority here is for withdrawal now," including himself, he was against saying so publicly because the moderates and "peace candidates" he wanted to appeal to would be alienated by such a move. He said he was also opposed to characterizing the Johnson maneuvers as a hoax for the same reasons, though he had done so in so many words in his own analysis earlier in the meeting.

Jerry Rubin, fresh from a jail sentence in San Francisco for his part in the Maxwell Taylor demonstration the previous summer, was outraged at this. The job of the movement, he declared, is to convince the American people of the truth about the Vietnam War and American society and it can't do that with "tricks or mirrors." The movement can't maneuver with the American people, he said, and fairly shouted: "Tell the truth!"[14]

Mary Walters, a longtime peace activist from Denver with the powerful hands and torso of one who has had to use canes to walk, declared this was no time for the antiwar movement to be diverted into a "liberal swamp."[15]

When the hand vote was taken it was 19 for releasing the statement and 18 opposed. Emspak and Greer then demanded a vote on the basis of proxies and weighted votes. Each committee was entitled to one vote for each 100 members or fraction thereof, and some committees which could not send representatives had given proxies to other delegates. In any case, it was all on the honor system, since no one could really check what a committee's membership was. Rubin and Weinberg cast four votes for the

13. *Bring the Troops Home Now Newsletter*, no. 4, February 1, 1966.
14. Ibid.
15. From the author's handwritten notes taken at the January 8-9, 1966, NCC standing committee meeting.

Berkeley VDC—a modest enough claim for a group that had called events attended by tens of thousands. They both groaned, and Rubin did a little dance of the absurd near the stage, as Greer cast seven votes, five of them proxies from a single high school group. When the proxies and weighted votes were counted, the result was 38-25 against releasing the statement.[16]

The media reported this outcome as a victory for the "moderates" in the antiwar movement. In truth it was the beginning of the end for the NCC. There are some things you just can't get away with unless you've got a lot of crude power, and Emspak and company certainly didn't have that.

The rest of the Milwaukee meeting was desultory, since it was evident nothing could really be decided there. The Rubin proposal for enlarging and moving the national office was set aside to be discussed at another meeting projected for April. Rubin went back to Berkeley, leaving Weinberg on the NCC staff in Madison. He was uncomfortable there—the NCC newsletter listed him as a "guest member" of the staff. He lasted a short time and gave it up. Lynd, Dellinger, and Beinin gradually lost interest in the NCC.

The April meeting was never held. In March, Emspak wrote a letter to Henry Abrams in New York, copies of which were sent to several people in the movement. It was not generally well received. It said:

Re: The Meeting—we have two basic questions: should we have it? and then, if we do, would we win? At first I felt that we should have it. In other words, take the bull by the horns, walk in well organized, win all the votes, and walk out after having accomplished something. . . .

If this plan is to work, then we have to have overwhelming majorities there. If we do not, then we will be stymied at the outset. The object of this whole plan is to get the idiocy out of the way beforehand and spend 90% of our time on the summer project. . . .

The other alternative is not to have the meeting at all and then risk a battle over that. I do not think too many people give a good God damn whether or not we have a meeting. If we propose a good summer project and organize regional meetings in April to discuss it, I think most people would agree to it. We are going to find out with a special poll to be taken this week.[17]

16. *Bring the Troops Home Now Newsletter*, no. 4, February 1, 1966.
17. Letter from Frank Emspak to Henry Abrams, March 10, 1966. (Copy in author's files.)

Though no poll had been mentioned at the standing committee, a ballot was sent out containing three choices: to have an April meeting, to have regional meetings which would then "submit reports to the NCC office," to have no meeting. The covering letter contained the following statement: "Failure to respond will have to be regarded as a disinterest in having a meeting."[18]

Just to keep things on the up and up, Emspak invited YSAer Lew Jones to Madison to help count the ballots after they were returned in the mail. Jones didn't bother.

Emspak was right about one thing. Not too many people in the know gave "a good God damn" whether the NCC had another meeting or not.

The NCC staff continued to work hard—at no small personal sacrifice for some of them—doing some useful research and turning out a newsletter which helped spread the word about the March 25-26 demonstrations and other activities before and afterwards. But the one factor which had made the NCC more than just another information center—on a very modest scale at that—was gone. It could no longer be a form for unification of the new antiwar movement or provide a national focus for action. In part this was due to the awareness—which spread more or less slowly through the movement after the Milwaukee meeting and more rapidly after the March demonstrations were over—that as far as policy was concerned Emspak was running a one-man show, which in his case meant a one-tendency show. He lacked both the political and human sensitivity to other points of view and their spokespersons to be an effective central figure in a coalition of heterogeneous forces.

Emspak was only twenty-two, and lacked experience, but in a movement largely composed of rebellious youth this in itself was no drawback. But Emspak was no rebel. He had an ideology of sorts, it is true, though even there he was fuzzy, unsure of himself, and dependent on others for ideas. But politics above all involves people and their relations with one another. And radical politics is, above all, people and their dreams. For Emspak, politics was a post. His main initial advantage over others was his name and his connections—which he had inherited from his father, Julius, along with the name's prominence. But the antiwar movement of 1966 was not the half-million-dues-paying-member United Electrical Workers Union of the 1940s. Frank

18. Copy of the ballot and covering letter in author's files.

Emspak was essentially an officeholder—some would say a bureaucrat—in a movement whose only power was a dream.

The second reason for the demise of the NCC as a national unifier of the new movement was the particular perspective that Emspak represented. He had little further interest in keeping the movement in the streets beyond the March demonstrations, but looked toward the fall congressional elections, and campaigning on behalf of "peace candidates," mostly within the Democratic Party. The NCC summer project never amounted to much except for a few sparsely attended "regional conferences" and reports in the newsletter on activities carried out by local groups on their own without initiative from the NCC.

Material from the Madison office increasingly focused on the elections, with long lists of "peace candidates" being mailed out. Technically, the NCC did not endorse particular candidates and the lists were just "for information," but the general thrust was clear enough. It caused dissension among antiwar activists who opposed these particular candidates, or who were backing rival candidates who were not listed.

On June 4, 1966, the *New York Times* carried a report of an NCC press conference in New York at which it said Emspak had endorsed Ted Weiss, a candidate in the Democratic Party primary from the nineteenth congressional district, as well as Herbert Aptheker, the historian, who was a prominent member of the Communist Party running as an independent in Brooklyn. This report caused disaffection from the NCC from both the right and left. (Muste also endorsed Aptheker, as well as Judy White, the SWP candidate for governor, as a personal demonstration against the anticommunist hysteria, but he made it clear these were personal endorsements, not connected with organizations of which he was an officer.)

James Weinstein, who also ran in the nineteenth district and was the chairman of the West Side Committee for Independent Political Action, an NCC affiliate, wrote Emspak as follows:

I was shocked to see that the NCC has endorsed Ted Weiss without consulting those organizations which it supposedly coordinates that are located within his congressional district. . . .

If you are a coordinating committee, I suggest you stick to coordinating. If you are a policy making body, I suggest you inform your affiliates of how that policy is made so that they may then consider whether to remain affiliated. If you think that under cover of participatory democracy you can do whatever you please and then deny responsibility for it, I suggest you think again.[19]

In a letter to Jack Smith of the editorial staff of the *National Guardian,* Emspak complained that Smith had reportedly referred to the NCC as "Emspak's NCC," and explained:

I personally cannot publicly endorse any campaign, or candidate, nor can anyone else in the employ of the NCC. This was the staff vote after all the confusion over Weiss began. Furthermore, the NCC did not endorse specific political candidates at the press conference on summer projects. We simply listed them, the list coming from the American Friends Service Committee National Legislative Committee, as we listed all other peace activity that was going on this summer. Hence, we did not endorse Weiss, nor did we take a position that political action is the only way to end the war or anything else like that.

I hope you will pass the above on to people and read this to Irving [Beinin], since apparently he believes that we endorsed political candidates.[20]

Emspak's claim to have listed "all other peace activity going on this summer" was an exaggeration, to say the least. That would have taken a book. The listing, including that of candidates claiming to favor peace, was highly selective. In any case, the circulation of the *New York Times* was considerably greater than the NCC staff's letters of denial, and the movement as a whole was left with the same general impression that the *Times* reporter carried away from the press conference.

The difficulty posed by Emspak's general approach was not limited simply to the disaffection it created among those not wishing to be associated with specific candidacies—though this was enough to destroy the NCC as a coordinating group of electorally diverse forces. But it came precisely at a time when the tendency toward dilution of the new movement's antiwar thrust was greatest, that is, during the months preceding an election. It was inevitable that during such a period, the leaders of the right wing of the movement—such as SANE—would devote themselves largely to electoral activity behind Establishment candidates,

19. Letter from James Weinstein to Frank Emspak, June 8, 1966. (Copy in author's files.)

20. Letter from Frank Emspak to Jack Smith, June 27, 1966. (Copy in author's files.)

and the various individuals and multi-issue groups in the left wing would divide on which candidates to support, or whether to support any. (Dellinger, for example, was something of an anarchist, averse to electoral activity, as well as a pacifist, and didn't endorse any candidates for office.)

Equally important, no candidate for Congress really ran on only one issue. To support them for *election* meant supporting their whole program, including their support to the capitalist system and to the rule by the capitalist class. The electoral thrust meant turning the antiwar movement into a constituency behind the program of liberal politicians, which was an entirely different thing from getting politicians, liberal or otherwise, to support the antiwar movement.

After the March actions, Emspak flatly refused to take the one initiative that a national coordinating group could do well. That is, provide a national focus for demonstrations which could unify in action those opposed to the war regardless of what electoral position they had. This left a vacuum which was not easy to fill, especially since Emspak resisted anyone else doing so.

In a comment on the NCC convention written in January, Dave Dellinger had stated: "If some group captures the NCC, it will capture a shell, because at that moment most of the people will go elsewhere to continue their anti-war activity undistracted."[21]

In the long run this would prove to be true. But it was easier said than done. It didn't happen in a moment and it didn't happen automatically. Old formations sometimes die hard, particularly when they are backed by even one significant tendency in a movement. In the heat of events not everyone is in a position to follow every significant detail. An understanding of what has transpired works its way more or less slowly through the body of the movement, accompanied by much hesitation and confusion, until some more or less dramatic development dispels the illusion which sticks to the form long after its content has been lost.

So it was with the NCC. After the January 8-9 Milwaukee gathering it never held another standing committee meeting, never held another convention, never called another demonstration, never initiated another activity of national significance. But

21. *Liberation,* January 1966. Contained in the introduction to an article by Steve Weissman.

it continued to enjoy a certain authority within the movement until events passed it by.

The supporters of the *Bring the Troops Home Now Newsletter* campaigned effectively both before and after the March demonstrations to build the independent committees, to keep them focused on antiwar activity, and to educate for the immediate-withdrawal position. But the *Newsletter* (the term "caucus" was dropped after the Milwaukee meeting in favor of "supporters of the *Newsletter*") was not a national organization, much less one with the authority to initiate a national focus for antiwar action.

Fortunately, there existed in the movement a figure who was everything Emspak was not, and who would throw his immense personal authority behind any reasonable move to reconstitute a national focus for action. His purpose was not to bypass the NCC—although that proved to be necessary—but to keep the antiwar movement visible and in the streets, putting maximum pressure on all the politicians. That figure was A. J. Muste, and the initial instrument he used in this process was the Fifth Avenue Vietnam Peace Parade Committee.

\*          \*          \*

The Fifth Avenue Vietnam Peace Parade Committee had originally been formed for one action only, the October 16, 1965, New York march. It did not reconstitute itself formally until after the NCC convention, and its first activity after that was a meeting January 16 at Manhattan Center at which 4,500 persons heard reports from Staughton Lynd, Tom Hayden, and Herbert Aptheker, who had just returned from a trip to North Vietnam. A. J. Muste chaired the meeting.

In those days for an American to travel to Hanoi was akin to an act of civil disobedience, and there was some danger the three men might be prosecuted on one charge or another. To organize a meeting for them was in itself an act of defiance of the administration's attempts to create prowar fever. The meeting also served to launch the Parade Committee's plans for the Second International Days of Protest, which is the way the March 25-26 demonstrations came to be advertised after Rubin's December 9 press conference in San Francisco.

During the "peace offensive," members of the Parade Committee organized an ad hoc Times Square Demonstration Committee to respond quickly if the bombing of the North resumed. The ad hoc form was used because some participants planned civil disobedience and the Parade Committee itself contained some groups which didn't wish to be associated with that type of action. The Parade Committee staff and office, however, was made available to the ad hoc group. When the bombing resumption was announced, some of the pacifist groups immediately began a twenty-four-hour vigil at the United Nations, while the staff got on the phones. The next evening, February 1, a thousand people marched from the UN to Times Square, where they ringed the Allied Chemical building and the armed forces recruiting station in the center of the square. Thirty-two persons were arrested for sitting down in the slushy snow on Broadway and snarling rush-hour traffic for ten blocks.

Significantly, the police were careful in their handling of those arrested. This was in marked contrast to previous incidents in Times Square, where since 1963 the authorities had banned large demonstrations, and police had clubbed those who disobeyed the edict. The difference this time was due in part to the influence of A. J. Muste, who had made careful preparations for the civil disobedience, and whose presence seemed to have a certain calming effect on the police; but it also signified an awareness by the city authorities that they were dealing now with a movement that had far wider sympathy than before.

Although New York SANE did not participate in this action, a committee of Veterans for Peace, originally formed to support the SANE march in November, did. These were mainly veterans of World War II, older and on the moderate side in politics. One of these, Ed Bloch, led the march wearing a faded Marine Corps uniform with a bronze star and a purple heart pinned to his chest.

Vets for Peace was one of some eighty groups that participated in Parade Committee activities in this period. The number would grow to 150 before the year was out. Another was Veterans and Reservists to End the War in Vietnam, composed largely of veterans and current reservists. Its membership was more radical. The Vets for Peace would frequently carry American flags. Vets and Reservists would carry only the thirteen-star version, from the period of the American Revolution.

The presence of these groups made it morally much more difficult for certain pseudopatriotic groups of right-wing veterans to heckle or attack Parade Committee activities, and they were frequently used to lead demonstrations or marches in areas where attacks might be expected.

Shortly after the Times Square demonstration, Muste showed the Parade Committee staff an invitation some friend of his had received in the mail to attend a banquet February 23 at the Waldorf Astoria Hotel sponsored by the Freedom House foundation. It stated that President Johnson would appear and be presented with an award inscribed: "Freedom at home was never more widely shared nor aggression more wisely resisted than under his leadership."[22]

The night of the banquet, February 23, the Parade Committee held a demonstration of 5,000 outside the hotel and Muste presented our own "Freedom Award" to Elizabeth Sutherland of the Student Nonviolent Coordinating Committee, who took it on behalf of Julian Bond, the former SNCC activist who had been elected to the Georgia state legislature but had been deprived of his seat because he refused to dissociate himself from a SNCC statement opposing the war and the draft.

From then on demonstrations plagued President Johnson almost every time he ventured out for a previously announced public appearance in the United States. Outside the Waldorf Astoria, and on many subsequent demonstrations, there arose spontaneously a biting chant: "Hey, hey, LBJ—How many kids did you kill today?"

Meanwhile, James Peck, who was a sort of one-person institution among the pacifists át 5 Beekman Street, had entered the banquet hall inside the Waldorf with antiwar slogans painted on the shirt under his jacket. He got in by simply buying a ticket for the banquet beforehand from Freedom House. He waited until the president was introduced and then stood on his chair, started to take off his jacket and shouted: "Mr. President, peace in Vietnam!" He shouted it three times before plainclothes police hauled him off, trying to stuff a napkin in his mouth. (Peck got sixty days in jail.)[23]

22. *Bring the Troops Home Now Newsletter,* no. 6, March 7, 1966.
23. The issue had a certain additional impact because of Jim Peck's long record in the civil rights movement. In 1947 he had taken part in the first Freedom Ride, an attempt to integrate bus travel through the South, which was broken up by racists. Peck was also on the second Freedom Ride when it was halted by racists who burned the bus in Alabama in 1961. Peck was badly beaten, but the second Freedom Ride became the focus for a worldwide uproar which scandalized the Kennedy administration for inaction on Southern civil rights. It is also interesting to note how

At the February 23 event the police allowed the pickets only on the opposite side of Park Avenue from the hotel, while the bulk of the crowd had to picket further down the street or stand in a side street where the Parade Committee had set up a sound truck for its award ceremonies. This left the end of the picket line closest to the hotel isolated from the main crowd—a dangerous situation since the police were thickest precisely where the crowd was small and packed into a cul de sac. At one point it looked like the police might attack this exposed end of the line where some angry pickets had concentrated and were taunting the cops in provocative terms. When I saw this I ran back toward the sound truck to get a bullhorn to use to tell the pickets to get out of there before they got hit.

Then I saw Muste coming in the other direction, toward the trouble. "You're going in the wrong direction," he said, and I turned. The cops were already swinging when we got there. Muste talked to the cops and I to the demonstrators and the situation calmed down without serious injuries.

I cite this incident not to show that Muste had personal courage—that was an altogether common trait in the movement—but that he was deliberate. He took his own principles seriously and he took responsibility for what went on.

\*       \*       \*

The night before the Waldorf Astoria demonstration the Parade Committee held a meeting at which the threat of a split occurred. The dispute had nothing to do with the next day's activity but concerned the slogans for the March 26 demonstration which was being planned as the committee's part in the Second International Days of Protest.

A subcommittee proposed "Stop the War in Vietnam Now" as the central slogan everyone could agree upon. It also recommended six additional slogans to be printed officially by the

---

this was another movement whose threads touched A. J. Muste. CORE, which sponsored both Freedom Rides and which was catapulted by the second one into national prominence and a place as one of the major civil rights organizations of the 1960s, originated as a project of the Fellowship of Reconciliation when Muste was its chairman, and James Farmer was a Muste protégé.

Parade Committee and listed in the call with the statement that these represented different approaches and not all the sponsoring groups agreed with all of them. These included "Negotiate with the NLF" and "Support the GIs, Bring Them Home Alive." A motion was put to change the latter to "Bring Them Home Now." This would make it an immediate withdrawal slogan. Abner Grunauer, the representative of New York SANE, objected, saying his group couldn't accept that and wouldn't participate if it were adopted.

After extended discussion the committee divided down the middle on the vote, $17\frac{1}{2}$ to $17\frac{1}{2}$.[24] (Two representatives from one group were unable to agree and divided their single vote.)

The lineup was New York SANE, New York Women Strike for Peace, the CP, the Du Bois Clubs, and the more moderate professional and neighborhood groups against "now"; the radical pacifists, the SWP, the YSA, the campus committees, and the more radical neighborhood groups in favor. But with the exception of SANE and a few others, those who voted against "now" said they did so to keep the coalition together, not because they really opposed the slogan.

Dave Dellinger, who as chairman of the meeting had not voted, broke the tie with a vote for "now." The radicals cheered. It was the first time immediate withdrawal was to be included in a major coalition not limited to the radical or student forces. But Grunauer announced he couldn't accept this and would have to leave the committee. Others declared that if he went, they would too. A bitter argument over procedure ensued with Grunauer and others denouncing Dellinger as reckless, saying he had no right to decide the issue with the committee so evenly divided. A motion was put to reconsider.

Dellinger opposed reconsideration, saying times had changed and he didn't think SANE would really drop out. It would be morally indefensible, he said, not to include an immediate withdrawal slogan among the six. The vote was against reconsideration, 17 to 16. Grunauer announced he was leaving the committee. Others, including Mike Stein of the CP and Jose Ristorucci of the Du Bois Clubs, followed him toward the door.

In an instant the following thought crossed my mind: How are we going to explain to all those thousands of people in the

24. Minutes, February 22, 1966, Parade Committee file, State Historical Society of Wisconsin, Madison.

movement outside this room why the Parade Committee split over one word in a list of seven slogans? I shouted: "Hold it Abner, I'm changing my vote to an abstention." Several others followed suit and the motion to reconsider passed. Dellinger and some of the other radicals, including the YSAers, looked at me like I'd just stabbed them in the back. I even had some explaining to do in the next meeting of the New York branch of the Socialist Workers Party, whom I represented at the meeting.

I was stalling for time, it is true, hoping some shift would occur in the other side during the rest of the meeting. But that's not all there was to my maneuver. Convincing the movement of the immediate withdrawal position was a process. As long as we had the right to continue that educational process there was nothing to gain and a lot to lose from a split. Exactly when we won a formal vote on the point was less important than maintaining unity in action and staying in the best position to reach the ranks of the moderate groups. I would have favored reconsideration rather than a split even if reconsideration took six months. As luck would have it, it took only until the next meeting.

Muste, who favored the "now" slogan, said he would meet with New York SANE and Women Strike for Peace to see if they wouldn't agree to having it included along with the statement that not all groups agreed with all the slogans. He did so, and at the next Parade Committee meeting, March 9, the SANE and WSP representatives reported that their organizations had so agreed. That still left the CP and the Du Bois Clubs, but since they had said they took the position they did only to keep the others from leaving, they now had to accept it too. Immediate withdrawal had become one of several official slogans in the major local coalition in the country.

*             *             *

The March 26 parade in New York drew some 50,000 demonstrators, double the size of the October 16 event. In general, the Second International Days of Protest was twice the size of the first, though in Berkeley there was no march this time, due in part to a crisis in the VDC there. A march sponsored by several Bay Area campus VDCs drew 7,000 in San Francisco.

On a world scale the Second International Days of Protest was, according to the NCC newsletter, the largest and most extensive peace demonstration in history. Activities took place in a third of the world's countries and on every continent during a three-day period. In West Germany and France, where fear of the U.S. giving atomic weapons to the German military in return for West German support to U.S. policy in Vietnam was also an issue, demonstrations occurred in most major cities. Carl Oglesby of SDS spoke to a crowd of thousands in a cold rain in Rome, while a few blocks away a smaller group of neofascists demonstrated in support of the U.S. war effort.

New Zealand and Australia, which had troops on the U.S. side in Vietnam, also had significant antiwar demonstrations. The largest actions occurred in Japan, where the massive anti-A-H-bomb organizations and radical student groups participated. Brussels saw a big demonstration in which even the Catholic church was a sponsor. In Manila a demonstration protested plans to send a corps of Filipino engineers to South Vietnam to back up the American effort.

Demonstrations also occurred in all the Scandinavian countries, in Guinea, Kenya, Egypt, Syria, Algeria, Cyprus, Israel, Uruguay, Chile, Argentina, Peru, Mexico, Canada, and England. Significantly, some of the largest demonstrations occurred in countries whose governments were most supportive of the U.S. role in Indochina.

On the Berkeley campus itself, U.S. Ambassador to the United Nations Arthur Goldberg received an honorary degree from the university administration at ceremonies March 25 in the Greek Theater attended by 14,000. In his acceptance speech, Goldberg—a liberal who had once been general counsel for the United Steelworkers union—delivered a defense of the administration's Vietnam policy. But he faced a sea of placards held up by members of the audience bearing such slogans as "I Oppose This War," "Arthur Goldberg, Doctor of War," and "U.S. Get Out of Vietnam."

After the ceremony Goldberg and half the audience moved to Harmon Gymnasium where Goldberg had agreed to "discuss" the issue with the Faculty Peace Committee. Professor Reginald Zelnik cautioned that this was not a debate and appealed to the audience to refrain from heckling or cheering. In a remarkable display of restraint the audience listened quietly while the discussion proceeded.

Then at the end Professor Zelnik called for a standing vote for approval or disapproval of administration policy on Vietnam. About 100 stood for approval, 7,000 stood for disapproval. It was a devastating defeat for Goldberg and the administration, and the vote was shown on TV news that night.

The movement was wider on the Second International Days of Protest, with significant demonstrations taking place in over 100 cities in the U.S. as well as elsewhere in the world. In several cities outside New York the events were organized by coalitions similar to the Parade Committee. In Chicago, Jack Spiegel, a local official of the Shoeworkers Union, and Sid Lens, director emeritus of Local 329 of the United Service Employees Union, who was also a pacifist and a contributor to *Liberation,* worked to bring together a broad coalition starting with the Chicago CEWV and the Chicago Peace Council. The local SANE chapter and the local American Friends Service Committee, however, pulled out a few days before the event. Nevertheless, the Chicago turnout was 5,000, compared to 700 in October.

But the New York parade represented the broadest unity. "The protest," commented the generally unsympathetic New York *Herald Tribune,* "had a different complexion from the one last October 16. . . . Although most of the sponsors were the same, the marchers this time seemed to represent much more of a cross section of Americans."[25]

Many of the participating groups organized special contingents and brought their own specific concerns into the march. For the first time there appeared a contingent from Harlem, organized by the Afro-Americans Against the War in Vietnam under the banner: "Bring Our Black GIs Back Home." Some of these marchers carried placards saying: "The Vietcong Never Called Me a Nigger."

Women Strike for Peace passed out shopping bags printed with antiwar slogans. The Teachers Committee had a large contingent carrying black placards with white lettering, like blackboards. By far the largest contingent was students.

The Parade Committee had an argument about flags, finally voting to have none except those carried by the veterans groups, but some vendors showed up and did a brisk sale in American flags, something that would change over the years as even the moderate antiwar activists became more alienated from the government. Walter Teague, who headed a small group called the U.S. Committee to Aid the National Liberation Front, made up a bunch of NLF flags and passed them out to a contingent of

25. New York *Herald Tribune,* March 27, 1966.

radical youth. This angered the moderate groups, but the main problem with this as far as I was concerned was that the rightist hecklers generally chose that spot to attack the parade, and special precautions had to be taken by the marshals.

In general, however, there was a markedly more friendly attitude by bystanders toward this demonstration. Maris Cakers of the Workshop in Nonviolence (WIN), however, drew the unenviable assignment of lining up a group of marshals between the march and a group of hecklers who were trying to provoke a fight by spitting. Poor Maris was covered with it while the cops stood by ready to arrest the marshals if they lost their tempers.

But all in all it was a great day, something of what they used to call a "happening," with people on the sidelines waving from windows and some even joining in. Speakers at the rally, which this time was held at the Mall in Central Park, included the ex-Green Beret Donald Duncan, Jerry Rubin, Juan Mari Bras of the Movement for Puerto Rican Independence, and Cleveland Robinson, chairman of the Negro American Labor Council and a vice-president of the Retail, Wholesale, and Department Store Union. "You are the true continuers of the revolutionary tradition started in this country in the eighteenth century," said Bras. "You are the people that are saving the respect and honor of the American nation in this moment of history."[26] And, in good part, that's the way the American antiwar movement thought of itself.

Norman Mailer, who was not a scheduled speaker, just showed up and was given the mike for brief comments. In those days a certain song was being plugged by the media on every possible occasion. Said Mailer:

Lyndon Johnson runs the most consummate public relations machine in the history of Christendom. And he knows how good that machine is. He had a song—a hit song—called "The Green Berets" which was written by computers. And it drew on some fine Scotch airs, let me tell you. But Lyndon Johnson knows that when 60,000 people, as reported in the *Daily News,* will go out and march down Fifth Avenue being heckled, there is an incredible potential resistance to the war and an incredible tacit resistance.[27]

26. *In the Teeth of War,* edited by Donna Gould and Dave Dellinger (New York: Fifth Avenue Vietnam Peace Parade Committee, 1966), p. 40. This book was a photographic essay on the March 26, 1966, demonstration.

27. Ibid., p. 59.

Mailer's reference to the *Daily News* came from having over-heard the *News* reporter—using the phone in the bandshell—report a crowd of 60,000. By the time it got into print, however, it was 30,000. The *News* commented editorially:

> The Saturday shenanigans gave aid and comfort to the enemy in time of war, and thereby fitted the U.S. Constitution's definition of treason. So why not a prompt declaration of war to Congress, to spur the Justice Department to get busy with some Treason prosecutions.[28]

Muste's remarks at the rally were in contrast to Senator Fulbright's fears, expressed elsewhere, that escalation would produce a war hysteria. Said Muste:

> This demonstration and those going on all over the country signify that we are not going to be intimidated by the escalation of the war. I believe that the response of the people of New York and the people of the United States to the escalation of the war is going to be the escalation of the protest against the war and the demand that the war end.
>
> I believe this not only because of the number of people involved, but also because of the unity that has been achieved, and is constantly growing, among the forces that are opposed to this war. Our Vietnam Peace Parade here in the city and the response to it today is evidence of the power of unity. I hope that all of us who are partaking in this demonstration and thousands upon thousands more in this city will take the lesson of what happens when there is unity among the forces opposed to this war, whatever their differences.[29]

\*             \*             \*

The unity in New York was not merely formal. It was organized around specific actions. This would generally prove to be the key to unity in the antiwar movement for the duration of the war. The movement as a whole was composed of such diverse forces that it could not unify on any sort of extensive program but only around some specific action against the war. The various programs found expression in speakers, literature, and even in different contingents all involved in the same action.

The problem of effecting unity then came down to the calling of actions around which the various forces could unify. But after the

28. New York *Daily News*, March 29, 1966.
29. *In the Teeth of War*, p. 23.

Second International Days of Protest the NCC refused to do this. The SDS national office was no less remiss, though SDS was still growing and its local chapters were still often mainly devoted to antiwar activity on their own.

SDS had long since ceased to lead in national antiwar initiatives. If anything, it catered to the moods of frustration and impotence that from time to time would take over much of the organized movement. These were strongly manifest in the late spring and early summer of 1966 and continued through the elections. Even before the Second International Days of Protest, for example, SDS President Carl Oglesby characterized the antiwar activity as a "wilderness of warmed-over speeches and increasingly irrelevant demonstrations."[30]

The reasons for the periodic ebbs were not always due to the objective conditions, such as events in the war itself, or the centrifugal pressures of an election period. There were also significant subjective factors which would repeat themselves with remarkable regularity.

From 1965 to 1973, the antiwar sentiment was the main—but by no means the only—engine for a broader radicalization. People would challenge the war and many would find themselves looking for the causes, questioning other features of American life, and beginning to develop one or another general radical perspective. There was a tendency to assume that everyone else opposed to the war had come to the same conclusions as themselves and to try to use the antiwar committees or coalitions for other purposes. This tendency existed not only with the liberals seeking to reform the Democratic Party and with certain of the multi-issue radical groups, such as SDS, the Du Bois Clubs, and Progressive Labor, but was a strong sentiment among some of those who were not affiliated with a multi-issue radical group. The particular antiwar committee or coalition to which they belonged seemed the logical form to use for the implementation of their general radical program.

A feeling of frustration with antiwar activity intensified this attitude. "We're tired of marching" was a common complaint, by which was meant not physical exhaustion, but boredom and a sense of futility. This mood would often take over immediately after a successful activity—successful in the sense that it in-

30. *Studies on the Left*, January-February 1966, p. 54.

volved relatively large numbers and included many people who had not been involved before. Then the escalation of the war would continue. Without a clear historical perspective—something the "new left" in general and SDS in particular disparaged—it appeared that the antiwar movement was powerless to change policy on the war itself.

In the March 1966 issue of *Liberation*, Muste commented:

> One hears it said by some that groups like Students for a Democratic Society should not concentrate on anti-Vietnam war activity as S.D.S. did in 1965 leading up to the April 17 demonstration in Washington. The reason often given is that the U.S. course in the war is only a symptom of a deeper trouble, that the real problem is to build a democratic society from the ground up. This, the reasoning continues, should lead to community projects in which people are helped in a "participatory democracy" pattern to deal with their own problems. From a very different quarter I have heard people criticize the peace and pacifist movements as "crisis oriented" and hence ineffective.

Referring to the "seventh war from now" argument, Muste said:

> It seems to me that the idea of accepting one's impotence in relation to the present war but getting ready to prevent or stop a later one is, on reflection, sophistry. . . . The war which in one way or another we support or acquiesce in or, on the other hand, oppose is always the going one.

Muste then touched upon what could prove to be the truly historic role—in the long-term sense—of the American movement against the Vietnam War. That is to break the traditional pattern of domestic reform movements concerning themselves solely with national or local issues while going along with the foreign policy of American capitalism including its imperialist wars. This pattern even involved the expectation among many union officials and some civil rights leaders that concessions for their constituencies would be paid for out of the profits resulting from successful prosecution of imperialist wars abroad. At the very least it involved tacit agreement by such reformist leaders not to rock the boat on foreign policy, in return for a more sympathetic ear within the government. Such considerations underlay the approach of the bulk of American labor leaders, and of the leaders of the NAACP and the Urban League toward the war. They were a factor in the hesitancy of even such pacifist figures as James Farmer of CORE and Martin Luther King to campaign against the war.

Said Muste:

There is what seems to me an even more basic reason why all true democrats and revolutionaries have to face up to the Vietnam issue. The prevailing pattern of American development and of the reaction of liberals, progressives and radicals to that development since about 1910 has been that of attempts, more or less successful, to deal with domestic economic and social problems, accompanied by what basically amounted to drifting into an international course which led to war, to uncontrolled military-technological escalation, to "hardening into bitter empire." . . . [B]y that fatalistic process we moved as a sleep-walker might to the devastation of Europe and Japan, to the production of A- and H-bombs, to the unspeakable atrocities of Hiroshima and Nagasaki, to Santo Domingo and Vietnam. It seems to me it will be a fatal mistake if we lose this perspective now. It is true that there are poor here, but the problem of poverty is most acutely one of the poor in Asia, Africa and Latin America. . . . The Great Society has yet to be built here and not by appropriations from above. But the Great Society, if there is to be one, will be a world phenomenon, not an American.

In the same article Muste declared:

So this is a call to escalate the protests. I have in mind demonstrations, parades, picketing, vigils, sit-ins, fasts, mass rallies, street-corner meetings, draft-card burnings, nonviolent invasions of missile bases, arms factories, the White House and the Pentagon, "unauthorized" journeys of Americans to Vietnam, anything and everything of this kind anyone can think of.

Muste himself made a trip to Vietnam in April, not to the North, but to South Vietnam. According to Bradford Lyttle of CNVA, the idea for the trip had first occurred some months previously

when Premier Ky passed a law in South Vietnam saying that anyone publicly advocating peace would be liable to summary execution. A number of us noted this in the New York *Times* and it seemed to us that this created a situation in which one could carry out a very effective nonviolent action project for peace in Saigon. The Ky law was somewhat like the law which Congress passed recently against draft-card mutilation. [Johnson signed that measure into law August 30, 1965.] As soon as a law like this is passed, there is something inside pacifists which says that this law must be publicly and openly violated in order to show that such laws cannot terrify or terrorize the people.[31]

While the CNVA members were getting passports and making preparations for such a trip, a wave of demonstrations swept South Vietnam. Initiated by Buddhists on March 10 when Ky ousted Buddhist sympathizer General Nguyen Canh Thi from the ruling group, the protests soon spread to soldiers and students and assumed an antiwar character, calling for peace and American withdrawal. These demonstrations and the attempts by Ky to crush them had been going on for over a month when Muste led a delegation of six CNVA members on a flight to Saigon.

At the same time the Parade Committee held a demonstration in Times Square April 16 in solidarity with the Vietnamese demonstrators. This Parade Committee action did not involve civil disobedience, but for the time it was a bold plan. The idea was to ring the six-block Square area with marchers walking single file on the sidewalks. No permit was necessary for this. Such a strung-out demonstration, however, would mingle with the regular Times Square crowds and could not be defended against concerted attacks if the bystanders were hostile. The object was to prove that the antiwar sentiment was not really confined to the relatively small numbers who had demonstrated, but that such demonstrators would not meet with serious hostility from the ordinary American in the street, not even in Times Square, an area frequented by GIs on leave.

Some 4,500 demonstrators showed up and there was remarkably little heckling and no violence. Such hecklers as appeared were isolated by the ordinary bystanders who, if they were not outright friendly to the demonstrators, at least respected the right of the demonstrators to dissent on this war. Such an atmosphere had never previously existed in the U.S. during a war in modern times.

We did not attempt this kind of demonstration blindly. We knew that the atmosphere was changing rapidly in spite of the frustration and discouragement felt in some movement circles. The war was being questioned ever more widely in the population as a whole. In part this was due to the cumulative effect of antiwar activity in face of the escalation, in part to the effect on

31. *Liberation*, May-June 1966, p. 11.

the American population of the Buddhist demonstrations in South Vietnam, and in part to the recent hearings of the Senate Foreign Relations Committee, which were widely publicized. The hearings had effectively exposed as ridiculously weak many of the administration arguments in support of its war policy, though the committee members, including Fulbright, continued to vote for the war appropriations. They invoked the "support our boys" problem—or excuse.

We had an interesting experience in this regard with the GIs who happened to be visiting Times Square the day of the demonstration. When they first saw us they would tend to be hostile. They had probably never seen antiwar demonstrators face to face before, and from the major news media or their orientation officers could only have obtained the impression that we were unsympathetic to their situation. But when we showed them our signs that said: "Support Our Boys—Bring Them Home Now," they were taken aback. A little face-to-face conversation soon revealed that some of them were as opposed to this war as we were—even more angry about it. And the rest were full of doubts and for the most part willing to listen to our arguments.

The six pacifists who went to Saigon were Muste, Lyttle, Karl Meyer of the *Catholic Worker*, Professor William Davidon of Haverford College, Barbara Deming, an editor of *Liberation*, and Sherry Thurber, a student who had been active in civil rights. They discovered a visa wasn't necessary for Americans traveling to Saigon for a week or less, so they bought tickets in their own names, stopped in Tokyo to make contact with pacifists in Saigon through the Japanese peace movement, and got into Saigon without incident.

On April 20 they held a press conference in a Saigon hotel which was broken up by plainclothes agents of the Saigon regime. On April 21 they attempted a vigil outside the American embassy, were immediately arrested by the South Vietnamese authorities, and put on a plane for Hong Kong. An American reporter was beaten by Saigon police in the process and the whole affair received considerable publicity worldwide. Muste returned to the U.S. more convinced than ever that the American antiwar movement had to stay in the streets during the summer regardless of the election campaign.

But in spite of repeated suggestions the NCC declined to act. On May 4 the Parade Committee held a meeting at which it decided to call a major mass action during the August 6-9 period, the anniversary of the atom bombing of Hiroshima and Naga-saki. In a separate vote it decided to call on other groups and countries to do likewise, that is, to call another International Days of Protest August 6-9. A motion was made that the theme of the New York demonstration be "Bring the Troops Home Now." It passed with only one dissenting vote.[32]

The meeting also set a Manhattan Center rally for May 23, at which Muste would speak on his Saigon trip and the call for August 6-9 would be released publicly. In the meantime, Muste agreed to send a letter appealing for the August 6-9 actions to committees around the country.

On May 10 Muste sent the letter on Parade Committee station-ery, also signed by committee coordinators Norma Becker and Dave Dellinger. Anticipating some of the arguments against the action, the letter declared:

Despite the traditional summer lull, the Committee feels that the urgency of the Vietnam situation requires large-scale protests that cannot be postponed till the fall without the danger of cruel insensitivity to heart-rending appeals of the Vietnamese people. The main anti-Ky, anti-U.S. demonstrations took place *after* the March 26 International Days of Protest, further exposing the hypocrisy of U.S. pretensions and creating new reservoirs of persons who are disillusioned with the war and ready to take part in public protests. Intensive community organizing campaigns have been planned for many areas of the country, as part of a determined effort to broaden the base of the movement. These campaigns should activate new people, and major demonstrations, in turn, will add drama, color and concreteness to these crucial organizing efforts. . . . Let multitudes rally in all parts of the world on those days. Let peace-minded persons and organizations in every state of the United States and in every country of the world devise ways to call for an end to military intervention in Vietnam as a first imperative step to ending the threat of nuclear war and bringing justice, freedom and peace to mankind.[33]

During this period the Parade Committee staff called both the NCC Madison office and the office of the *Bring the Troops Home Now Newsletter*, then published in Cambridge, Massachusetts, to

32. Parade Committee minutes, May 4, 1966. Parade Committee file, State Historical Society of Wisconsin, Madison.
33. Parade Committee mailing, May 10, 1966. "A Call for International Days of Protest Against the War in Vietnam on August 6 to 9." Parade Committee file, State Historical Society of Wisconsin.

ask for their support for August 6-9.

On May 11, the *Newsletter* sent a letter to all supporters informing them of the Parade Committee plans and saying: "We urge you to take this up with your committee and get the ball rolling. Even though many campuses have no summer session, the potential still exists to build a large and effective Days of Protest."[34]

The May 9 issue of *Peace and Freedom News*, the NCC newsletter, made no mention of August 6-9 and devoted its front page to an article on the various candidates who would be speaking at a SANE convention, and a "voters pledge" presentation outside the White House scheduled for May 15 by SANE.

On May 15, Emspak wrote to Dellinger as follows:

I received the call from the NY Parade Committee on Friday. It sounds very final. I was under the impression from my conversation with you that you intended this to be a sort of a poll of opinion, not a statement of fact. It seems that you are going to call a press conference no matter what people say.[35]

Emspak said he did not object to the International Days of Protest, only to the timing. With schools out, a summer demonstration would be smaller than those the previous fall and spring, inviting unfavorable comparison. Certain international groups had decided to commemorate July 20, the anniversary of the 1954 Geneva Accords, and couldn't move again by August 6.

Furthermore [said Emspak], a demonstration provides an excuse not to think about tactics and strategy carefully. People have something that is easy to do and which does not require real long term commitment. It seems to me that we should allow enough time to elapse to develop both thinking and projects for long term aims. Also, I think that summer projects will have a tendency to be turned into campaigns to organize for another demonstration which will not be as useful as the long term work they can be doing.

In this letter Emspak also indicated that he knew the NCC was being bypassed and didn't like it.

34. "To All Newsletter Supporters." From Gus Horowitz for the *Newsletter,* May 11, 1966. (Copy in author's files.)
35. Letter from Emspak to Dellinger, May 15, 1966. Parade Committee file, State Historical Society of Wisconsin.

if national action is called now, we have the means in the NCC to hold polls and try to get a national feeling about it. It seems to me that the actions of the Parade Committee in this light do great harm to the idea of national coordination and democracy within the movement.

The last point was not well received by the Parade Committee staff. We knew Emspak was avoiding a meeting of the NCC standing committee, and we were not willing to wait while the decision to *act* was submitted to the tender mercies of one of Emspak's polls.

At the May 18 Parade Committee meeting the whole question was opened again in light of the NCC opposition. After long discussion, it was voted to proceed with August 6-9 in New York, to invite other groups around the country to join in, but, in a compromise suggested by Muste, to hold off announcing it as an International Days of Protest.

It was also agreed that speakers at the May 23 meeting would include I. F. Stone and Isaac Deutscher, who would be in the country, having been invited to Berkeley for the first anniversary of the Vietnam Day teach-in there.

In a sense the May 23 meeting was in itself a test of strength. Partisans of the NCC national office were afraid of it. At best the CP and the Du Bois Clubs took an ambivalent attitude toward it. They couldn't denounce the gathering openly, but they didn't build it either, partly because of the problem with Emspak and partly because they were not too eager to build a meeting featuring Deutscher, the biographer of Trotsky and a well-known critic of Soviet policies from a Marxist point of view.

Some 1,500 showed up, however, which made it a modest success. There Dellinger made the public announcement about August 6-9, reporting that groups in twenty-five cities across the country had indicated plans for demonstrations on those days, as well as groups in a number of other countries. The meeting was chaired by Dr. Otto Nathan, the executor of Albert Einstein's estate and a Parade Committee stalwart. Nathan opened the rally with a statement that the committee had a clear-cut reply to President Johnson's recent demand that his critics should state an alternative policy. To loud applause Nathan declared: "Mr. President, bring our boys home now!"

Muste charged that the Johnson administration was fanning a dangerous anticommunist hysteria in the country. (On March 4, Attorney General Nicholas Katzenbach had petitioned for the registration of the Du Bois Clubs with the Subversive Activities Control Board, a remnant of the McCarthy witch-hunt period.) Muste referred to recent incidents such as the bombings of the San Francisco Du Bois Club headquarters and the Berkeley VDC office and the murder of Leo Bernard—a YSAer and an activist in the Detroit CEWV—by an anticommunist fanatic. Said Muste: "I hope none of us will slow down our opposition because of such incidents." Referring to the growing questioning of the war policies in Congress, he said the administration may be trying to find a way to "save face" in Vietnam, but that is not the responsibility of the antiwar movement which must keep up the pressure. "If we yield in any way," he concluded, "or slow down our intransigent opposition to the war, we shall be traitors to everything human. But if we continue, we shall have the undying gratitude of the overwhelming majority of the people of the earth."[36]

Deutscher delivered a stirring defense of the Vietnamese revolution, and concluded with a tribute to the American antiwar movement, declaring its emergence a momentous development in U.S. and world history and a great source of optimism for the future. "I hope you won't permit your voice to be stifled," he said. "See yourself in the historical perspective. See the weight of what you are doing!"[37]

After the meeting Deutscher spoke with Muste and a few others of us in a nearby restaurant. He and Dellinger had just returned from the Berkeley event and had been disappointed that it was much smaller than the previous year. Clearly, the movement on the West Coast was in crisis, and in an ebb for the moment. But Deutscher was sure the movement nationally would find its resurgence and was pleasantly surprised that the ebb had not affected New York to the same degree.

\*       \*       \*

The same frustrations and centrifugal tendencies that affected the movement nationally also affected the Berkeley Vietnam Day Committee—even more drastically. Berkeley had long been a peculiar sort of island unto itself. It was a lovely little city

36. *Militant*, May 30, 1966.
37. Ibid.

occupying a geographically distinct and favored spot. It lay between the water on the west and high rolling hills on the east, free of the summer heat on the other side of the hills, of the chill fog of San Francisco across the bay, and of the factories and urban sprawl of Oakland to the south with its large working class Black ghetto. Berkeley was near enough to be acutely aware, but not really a part, of the urban, industrial, military, agribusiness, and transportation complexes surrounding it.

Both the city and the university had always been comfortably controlled by California's richest families, largely through an appointed board of regents in which all power over the university was—and still is—vested. But certain material privileges were consciously cultivated for the community and a superficial freedom in philosophical matters was tolerated, if not encouraged.

These factors—not the least of which was the relatively cheap and easy living for those who could maintain some connection with the huge university—had long attracted a radical-intellectual-bohemian milieu which included perpetual students in their late twenties or early thirties and nonstudent hangers-on. Because of this, Berkeley in a small measure escaped the total impact of the witch-hunt of the 1950s when the "silent generation" dominated America's campuses and none of the major radical tendencies were able to maintain viable student groups. Berkeley was one of the very few universities in the country—if not the only one—where an avowedly socialist organization existed throughout that decade.[38]

Beginning in 1960 and for some years following the breakthrough of the Free Speech Movement in 1964, the Berkeley milieu was like a hothouse in which every sort of experimental idea, mood, and fad could take root and even flourish until it was tested in the real world outside the rarefied atmosphere of the street and coffeehouse culture of Telegraph Avenue. As with many ephemeral offshoots of bohemia, much of this would not pass the test, though something of lasting value would occasion-

---

38. It was the Third Camp–oriented Independent Socialist League of which Hal Draper was a leader. Michael Harrington was also a member of the ISL until it entered the SP-SDF in 1958. Some of its members founded the Independent Socialist Club, which later became the International Socialists (IS).

ally emerge that would not have had the chance to get started elsewhere.

But the very factors that allowed Berkeley to act as a vanguard—a high degree of sensitivity to changing trends in the general population combined with a separation from the often conservative concerns of the workaday world—made the Berkeley milieu even more subject to moods of frustration and impotence as the antiwar movement faced the ebb following its first exciting year. The Berkeley milieu was also quicker to grasp at straws and seek solutions, not in persistent groundwork for the next upsurge, but in grandiose schemes and shortcuts.

All of this was personified in the figure of Jerry Rubin. Some of his strongest qualities now became his weakest. Rubin returned from the Milwaukee NCC meeting in a determined mood, but it quickly shifted from one focus to another. Following his report on the NCC to a VDC general membership meeting, he supported a motion to put the VDC formally on record as standing for immediate withdrawal. It passed unanimously. The pressure in Berkeley on this issue was so strong that the Du Bois Club members simply didn't fight for this aspect of their own organization's national policy. But Rubin soon gave up his plans to breathe new life into the NCC. Instead, he threw himself into an election campaign in the seventh congressional district, which included Berkeley and part of Oakland's Black ghetto.

Robert Scheer, the author of the by-then-famous pamphlet *How the United States Got Involved in Vietnam,* an editor of *Ramparts,* and a well-known Berkeley radical-liberal, was planning to run in the Democratic Party primary against Congressman Jeffrey Cohelan, a moderate liberal who was then still a down-the-line supporter of Johnson's Vietnam policy.

Rubin, Steve Weissman of SDS, and most of the leaders of the VDC had already supported a motion at a VDC meeting November 19 to endorse the Scheer candidacy. That was before the campaign was officially announced. It was, however, understood that those who didn't choose to back Scheer could remain in the VDC and build its antiwar activity. The motion passed by a two-thirds majority in a meeting of 150 activists, with the YSAers, Weinberg, and some of the other radicals opposed, the CP and the Du Bois Clubs in favor. At that time the question of how much the VDC itself would be involved in Scheer's campaign was left open.

Scheer had the support of the Berkeley liberals, and even of

part of the left wing of the Democratic Party machine, including
Simon Casady, head of the California Democratic Council (CDC).
(The orthodox Johnson forces punished Casady by removing him
from this post.) But Scheer also appealed for support and direct
participation from the radicals. He declared he would campaign
for immediate withdrawal from Vietnam and emphasize other
radical issues.

In mid-January, Rubin declared:

> I decided to stay in Berkeley at this time instead of going to work for
> the NCC because I believe that we here in this area are about to launch
> the most exciting political development in the left in the country. . . .
> The Bay Area is a radical's dream. Oakland is a city teeming with
> unrest, exploitation and potential new social forces. The potential coali-
> tion includes a mass radical student base, a liberal middle class, and the
> large Negro ghettos. These forces must now combine issues—ranging
> from poverty, slums and racial discrimination to the war in Vietnam, to
> the *quality* of life in America—and offer new politics in the Bay Area.[39]

Rubin retained what he regarded as his radical perspective but
exhibited a certain naiveté with regard to its chances inside the
Democratic primary:

> The Berkeley VDC has not yet decided whether or not to make this
> move. Certainly if it does it will maintain its own identity within the new
> alliance and continue direct action protests. But I am going to argue that
> we put much of our energy into the new direction of a political candidate
> in this district against liberal-fink Congressman Jeffrey Cohelan. The
> goal of this campaign will be quite simply, the beginning of a long-range
> change from radical protest to radical protest-politics.
> I reject the notion of electoral politics which argues that we must get
> the best we can in a liberal-labor coalition today. I am talking about a
> radical alternative, and probably a 20-year struggle. The question for me
> is whether or not our beautiful movement is ready now to begin the task
> of constructing nonviolent revolution.
> The experiment to be launched very shortly in the Bay Area with the
> campaign against Cohelan . . . will be, along with the political experi-
> mentation in the South,[40] the seeds of a third-party radical new left in
> America.
> I am very excited at these possibilities.

39. *VDC News*, January 28, 1966.
40. Rubin's reference to the South was to the Mississippi Freedom
Democratic Party—a move by civil rights forces to reform the state

Earlier in a debate with Steve Weissman, Duncan Stewart, assistant editor of the *VDC News*, declared that socialist candidates could make a better case for VDC endorsement, since they were running for office under a political party that was against the war and not for it. But he opposed the VDC endorsing them either, in order to avoid forcing nonsocialists out. Stewart continued:

> To turn the VDC into the "campus arm" of the forces in the Democratic Party that are supporting Scheer would be a very serious blow to the Berkeley VDC. It will make Berkeley the first independent committee against the war to fall prey to coalition politics. Let those who want to join the . . . Democratic Party do so—but let them not try to drag the Vietnam Day Committee with them.[41]

On January 19 the VDC held a meeting to decide whether or not to work with the Scheer campaign. A statement was presented in support of this proposition signed by Barbara Gullahorn, Marilyn Milligan, Steve Weissman, and Jerry Rubin. It said in part:

> We believe that the building of a new America—a radical and human America—based on independent power at the grass roots is the most pressing need in our society. At present, however, because of California election law, there is no effective forum other than the Democratic primary in which to advocate the creation of this independent power. Thus our participation in the Democratic primary is purely tactical: We do not believe that the Democratic Party can be reformed. We believe that the Democratic Party is a barrier to the social changes which the people of this country so desperately need.[42]

Stewart's position was supported by the YSA, as well as by the ISC of which Weinberg was now a member. For Rubin, the fact that Scheer was running in the Democratic primary was just a

---

Democratic Party—and to the Lowndes County (Alabama) Freedom Organization, an independent Black-dominated electoral party whose symbol was a black panther and which advocated self-defense. The symbol would soon be taken by a group of Black radical youth in Oakland who would found the Black Panther Party.

41. *VDC News,* November 15, 1965.
42. Statement on the Scheer Campaign by Rubin, et al. (Copy in author's files.)

detour through which he hoped to maneuver. For the Du Bois Clubs, however, as well as for the liberals, it was directly in line with their settled perspective.

The YSAers knew they were at a distinct disadvantage in this discussion. Their own electoral stand, while quite straightforward and clear—under no conditions would they support a Democrat or Republican in an election—was simply rejected out of hand by almost everyone else. For almost all other Americans—including 90 percent of the radicals—the SWP and YSA position on elections was and still is, in great measure, the most difficult of concepts to grasp, or at least to agree with.

Unlike many countries where masses of workers—not to mention radicals—would no more think of voting for a capitalist party than they would think of voting for their boss as president of their union, in the United States the two major parties have had such a total monopoly on the electoral process that the tradition of independent working class political action that flourished before the First World War has been largely wiped out. In 1966 it had been half a century since any candidate on a socialist ticket had been elected to Congress. A vote for a socialist candidate was generally considered a wasted vote.

The Socialist Workers Party enjoyed a certain grudging respect for keeping alive the dim embers of independent socialist electoral action, and the other radicals would often speak of the need to resurrect the tradition. But when it came down to an actual election in which there appeared to be some difference on an important issue between the candidates in the two major parties, the rest of the radicals would generally react in shocked disbelief when the SWP and YSA stood by their anticapitalist electoral principle.

During the debate at the January 19 meeting, YSAer Syd Stapleton drew an ovation when he declared: "You shouldn't be burning your draft cards, you should be burning your Democratic Party cards."[43] But the great majority nevertheless endorsed the Scheer campaign.

For the Trotskyists the fundamental issue involved was very simple: An election poses the question of state power. As socialist revolutionaries they would never support the right of a capitalist party to hold state power. But the simplicity of this idea didn't

---

43. Taped interview with Lew Jones, September 2, 1975.

make it any easier for the others to accept, and Rubin's tortured arguments about maneuvers inside the Democratic primary appeared far more relevant and realistic to the average Berkeley radical than the electoral stand of the YSA.

The YSAers had no chance to convince the majority of the VDC activists—not to mention the mass of students who had responded to VDC calls for action—not to vote for Scheer because he was running in the Democratic primary. Nor did they consider this necessary so far as their work in the VDC was concerned. Their strongest argument was that the VDC as such should not endorse candidates, but should concentrate on antiwar activity directly, while VDC members could, as individuals or members of political groups, take whatever electoral stand they wished. But in January 1966 the YSAers could not yet carry this point.

The January 19 meeting resulted in effect in a cold split, with Rubin, Steve Weissman of SDS, the Du Bois Clubs, and the liberals concentrating their time and energies on Scheer's campaign, and the YSA, Weinberg, and some of the independents trying to keep the VDC alive in direct antiwar activity. The latter group included independents such as Bill Miller and Mike Delacour, who personally endorsed Scheer, but who wanted the VDC to concentrate on antiwar activity.

Scheer kept his promise to make opposition to the American presence in Vietnam a central feature of his campaign, and the primary in the seventh district came to be widely regarded as a referendum on the war. But this very fact increased the tendency—pushed hard by the liberals and professional Democratic politicians backing Scheer—to water down any general radical thrust in the interest of getting out the maximum vote and winning the election.

Those who had expected this campaign to be the beginning of a new multi-issue radical formation became increasingly disillusioned. What is more, in order to vote in the primary it was necessary to be registered as a member of the Democratic Party. Pressure on the radicals to do so and to join the CDC was an early feature of the Scheer effort. The roughly one thousand students who worked actively on Scheer's campaign found themselves building the Democratic Party apparatus, not an apparatus for a new radical politics, and some of them didn't like it.

For a short time Rubin was Scheer's campaign manager. But Rubin was neither a careerist nor a liar. He actually tried to do what he said he was going to do—use the campaign to build a base for his conception of a new radical politics. The liberals and hard-nosed politicians were appalled at Rubin's approach—proposing a "Jefferson-Marx" fund-raising affair, for example—and he was soon forced out.

At the election in June, Scheer got 45 percent of the vote, a remarkable showing, especially considering the money and muscle the national Democratic Party machine had marshaled against him. The shaken Cohelan soon began slipping over to the ranks of the congressional doves, along with many others taking their distance from Johnson's reputation on the war. (By 1968, Cohelan would lose to Ron Dellums, an outright supporter of the antiwar movement.) Scheer did not go on—as Rubin had first hoped he would—to run an independent campaign in the 1966 general election as part of the "seeds of a third-party radical new left in America."

Most of the students who had thrown themselves into the Scheer campaign simply dropped out of antiwar activity for the next period, and some of the radicals among them renounced all electoral activity as an effective means of building a multi-issue radical movement. Scheer himself would later embrace this position, for a time, at least.

Meanwhile the VDC faced an uphill battle to maintain antiwar activity. In February the VDC began pressing for a campus-wide referendum on the war. In preparation for this they organized a move to turn the classrooms into discussions on the war. Four hundred teaching assistants voted to endorse this plan and these discussions were actually held in more than one-third of the classes. On February 9, between four and five thousand students walked out of classes to attend a rally against the war. The administration granted the referendum. When it was finally held in May as part of the student elections, there were six positions on the ballot: Immediate withdrawal, UN-supervised elections, negotiations and cease-fire, stay in but maintain a defensive posture, endorse Johnson's current position, all-out escalation. The eight groups on campus considered radical, including the YSA, the ISC, the Scheer campaign, the Du Bois Clubs, and the Faculty Peace Committee, issued a joint statement calling for a vote for immediate withdrawal. It won, with the other positions gaining a descending number of votes in the order listed above. It was clear the antiwar sentiment was still spreading, but many antiwar activists were nevertheless becoming discouraged.

In early March, while the leading YSAers were out of town attending the YSA convention, a group of former activists in the VDC, including Du Bois Club members, but not Rubin, declared the VDC moribund and set up a new, multi-issue radical organization called the Peace/Rights Organizing Committee. It carried out only one significant activity. It produced most of the signs distributed to the audience at the March 25 ceremonies where Ambassador Goldberg spoke. It broke up and disappeared soon afterward. Once again, its founders simply couldn't agree on what the multi-issue program should be.

In early April, the remaining VDC activists called a demonstration for Telegraph Avenue on April 12 in solidarity with the South Vietnamese protests then in full swing. The liberals in the Scheer campaign were afraid the VDC action would reflect badly on the campaign, and tried to get it called off.

The VDC persisted. The VDC tried but failed to obtain a permit for Telegraph Avenue where the rally was scheduled. Four days before the demonstration, the VDC headquarters was bombed, injuring four persons and destroying the office. The VDC announced it would proceed with the demonstration on Telegraph Avenue anyway.

On April 12 about 4,000 persons gathered on the avenue near Moe's Book Store, where the demonstration had been scheduled. The committee's sound truck was quickly approached by police to halt the rally, but it turned out the main sound equipment was set up in a second-story apartment above the bookstore. The speakers, including the writer Paul Goodman and Peter Camejo, were barricaded inside and started speaking from the fire escape outside the window. The police started breaking down the barricade. They tried to arrest everyone in the room but somehow Camejo and Syd Stapleton slipped out—they were later indicted—to join the crowd. After some difficulty, they got about half of it to march on city hall, with Patti Iiyama leading a group of about 100 women to get it started. There the police charged again and the crowd dispersed.

The liberals among the Scheer forces were furious lest the campaign be connected in the public mind with such goings on. Scheer denounced the demonstration. That made the VDC activists furious.

A week later a general membership meeting was held to refurbish the VDC and elect a steering committee. (Before that, the steering committee had been voluntary, which sometimes meant anyone who could catch Rubin's ear.) Three YSAers, Jaimey Allen, Pete Camejo, and Syd Stapleton, presented a position paper which declared:

> We cannot let the problems and difficulties of sustaining the VDC lead us to simply throw it aside as though it were a passing phenomenon of Berkeley radicalism. The Berkeley VDC has simply been an expression of the protest against the Vietnam war and as such it is part of the general phenomenon throughout the country. The VDC is not an answer to all problems. It cannot be the organizational form for protest on many issues precisely because it has succeeded in uniting us around the question of Vietnam and provided a working basis for people with many different approaches to unite in support of self-determination for Vietnam.[44]

Some 120 activists attended the meeting, but except for Rubin, who had already had his falling out with the Scheer campaign committee, the Scheer forces, including Steve Weissman and the Du Bois Club members, stayed away. The tenor of the meeting was captured in a letter written at the time by Lew Jones, who described the election of the steering committee:

> Syd [Stapleton] received a near unanimous vote—by far the largest anyone else received. Weinberg was second. Three independents were next, followed by Peter [Camejo], who got a majority of votes of those present, followed by Jaimey [Allen] and another independent. . . . Rubin was nominated, but didn't receive a majority of votes and so was not elected. The meeting was very spirited—during the nominations people like Bettina [Aptheker, a leading Du Bois Club member] and Weissman were nominated, but that just resulted in riotous laughter and their names were not even put on the blackboard. Rumors were afloat that Scheer would show and "expose the VDC" as he had threatened. So at one point in the meeting a coed got up and moved that they send a message to Scheer telling him, "to go fuck himself." This was not voted on, but would have passed.[45]

All of this might have seemed a victory for the YSA's line, but, according to Jones, "it was too much of a victory. It is important that Bettina and Rubin, and maybe a couple of others be on that

---

44. "Preliminary Suggestions for Reactivating the VDC," by Stapleton, Allen, Camejo, undated. (Copy in author's files.)
45. Letter from Lew Jones to Gus Horowitz and Peter Buch, April 22, 1966. (Copy in author's files.)

steering committee. . . . Hopefully that will be taken care of at the next meeting."

Since the steering committee was to have fifteen members, and only eight received a majority vote at the first meeting, the next meeting had a runoff election for seven more. But in spite of Jones's admonition, Rubin didn't make it then either, and Aptheker and Weissman refused to attend.

These meetings also decided that the next major action would be another teach-in on May 21, 1966, the first anniversary of the massive first Vietnam Day.

In those days the YSA was still quite small, and its members were far outnumbered by others in the VDC; but it and the ISC were the only organized radical groups still trying to build the VDC. Though only three YSAers—Stapleton, Allen, and Camejo—sat on the fifteen-member steering committee, they were among the most active and they were all strong characters. Those opposed to the existence of a single-issue antiwar formation—which included the Scheer campaign and the Du Bois Clubs—simply dismissed the VDC as a "Trot front," and actually campaigned against it.

In part because of this, in part because of the general ebb then manifest, there was no chance that May 21 could repeat the success of the previous year. The organizers hoped for perhaps 3,000. But the event was rained out, and only about 1,000 showed up.

The crowd contributed some $2,400, enough to cover expenses and pay off a small part of the enormous debt left over from the Rubin regime, but the event was otherwise considered a failure.

At the initiative of the YSAers, the Berkeley VDC called a broad meeting of the various antiwar groups in the Bay Area in an attempt to heal the split and lay plans for the August 6-9 protests called by the New York Parade Committee. The meeting, on June 23, was well attended. It agreed—with the CP and the Du Bois Clubs abstaining on the vote—to set up a Bay Area-wide committee to organize the August event. It was first called the August 6-9 Committee and later the United Committee to End the War in Vietnam and was structured more like the Parade Committee than the old student-radical-dominated VDC. The VDC became the "campus VDC" with the more modest task of organizing the UC contingent for the broader action. The days of the old Berkeley VDC acting as the main focus for Bay Area antiwar work and playing a key role in initiating national and international activities were over.

For his part, Rubin swung from the Scheer campaign to pushing for a new mode of propaganda. The last issue of the *VDC News*, published a week before the May 21 event, carried the plaintive headline: "Do You Still Care?" On the back page appeared an article by Rubin about the film "Days of Protest," a documentary on the October 1965 Berkeley demonstrations. Said Rubin:

> To reach people we are going to have to develop a new political expression. Our puppet shows are a small start in this direction. We cannot rely on the printed word. People don't like to read; we are an ear and eye culture. We need to develop the following tools of expression to develop new political communication: the film, music, rock-and-roll, comic strips. . . . The problem of the left is that so often when it talks it sounds so much like the Left, so sectarian. Few speakers can overcome this barrier. Mario Savio [a prominent figure in the 1964 Free Speech Movement] and Bob Scheer are rare exceptions. This film is a rare exception. It may be the best left progaganda made in recent history, and it may be our most important tool in rebuilding our movement.[46]

The film wasn't bad, but it could not possibly play the role Rubin hoped for it. Like many other Berkeley radicals—and not only in Berkeley—Rubin simply faded from the antiwar scene into the psychedelic street culture, then heavily influenced by the still legal drug LSD.

He showed up in August in Washington, exhibiting some of the old flair, wearing the costume of an American revolutionary of 1776 at a hearing of the House Un-American Activities Committee to which he had been subpoenaed. He was among a group arrested on the Berkeley campus in November in a demonstration against navy recruiters. In the spring of 1967 he ran his own impish campaign for mayor of Berkeley, emphasizing cultural radicalism. But it would be a full year after the Scheer campaign before he would once again step center stage in the antiwar movement.

For six weeks following the Parade Committee's call for demonstrations August 6-9, 1966, the NCC Madison office continued to resist the idea. An example of the strained relations

46. *VDC News*, May 14, 1966.

between the NCC and the Parade Committee was a June 6 letter signed by Muste, Becker, and Dellinger and sent to committees across the country. It said:

> Through a misunderstanding, an inaccurate report on the Parade Committee's action in relation to the suggested August 6-9 days of protest appeared attached to the May 19 issue of the *Peace and Freedom News*, published by the National Coordinating Committee to End the War in Vietnam in Madison, Wisconsin.
>
> The letter stated: "Recently, many committees received a letter from the New York Parade Committee suggesting another International Days of Protest for the August 6-9 weekend. Originally, the letter stated that the Days would be announced at a meeting May 23. Subsequently, the Parade Committee voted to reconsider its program."
>
> It is the last sentence which is inaccurate. Actually, the Parade Committee, at its May 18 meeting, voted to proceed with its plans for action in New York on the August 6-9 days, and to ask other groups nationally and internationally to have actions on the same dates. This was announced as planned, at the Manhattan Center rally May 23. The Parade Committee did, however, decide not to use the phrase "International Days of Protest" pending further discussion and contact with groups overseas.[47]

Within the Parade Committee itself the centrifugal tendencies of the elections, the lack of unity on a national level, and the general ebb were being felt. The committee set June 18 for a city-wide Peace Action Conference to develop plans for August 6-9. But as the meeting approached it appeared some of the affiliated groups were having second thoughts. There was little chance the action would be called off, but another sharp dispute was shaping up and the success of the August actions was in doubt.

A few days before the conference, however, a new development appeared which unified the Parade Committee, involved even broader forces, and laid out a new area of activity. A group of soldiers walked into Dellinger's office and asked the Parade Committee for help in publicizing an action some of them were about to take. Thus began the case of the Fort Hood Three.

---

47. Parade Committee file, State Historical Society of Wisconsin.

# 7

## The Fort Hood Three
## and August 6-9, 1966

The antiwar movement periodically grappled with a sense of powerlessness because it seemed incapable of affecting the war itself in any direct material way. From time to time, different strategies were proposed in an attempt to overcome this problem. Many of these ideas revolved around the draft.

As early as May 1964 the May Second Movement (M-2-M) began a campaign to get signatures on a pledge of refusal to fight in Vietnam. At their founding conference in the summer of 1964, the Du Bois Clubs adopted a motion to endorse this pledge. By February 1965, M-2-M had collected some 1,000 signatures. These were almost entirely from students, however, who at the time enjoyed the automatic 2-S student deferment, so the project had no practical significance except for organizing purposes. It eventually faded away.

In October 1965, M-2-M announced a plan for the formation of antidraft unions. A few were formed in local areas and engaged in some propaganda activity but organized no actual draft resistance. They, too, faded from the scene.

As part of the First International Days of Protest in October 1965, the SDS affiliate at Ann Arbor, VOICE, led a sit-in at the local draft board and thirty-eight persons were arrested. This incident got wide publicity because afterward the draft board—with the approval of Selective Service director General Lewis B. Hershey—changed the status of some of the student demonstrators from 2-S to 1-A, as a punitive measure. The case became a cause célèbre and gained wide support on the civil liberties issue. It also made Hershey a pet object of derision among students and helped put SDS in the limelight, though it had no direct effect on the draft itself.

The SDS national office several times in 1965 and early 1966 announced antidraft programs, some of which received wide publicity, but with one exception these were not carried out. The exception was not really a draft resistance program, but an activity against procedures of the Selective Service System which had begun to cut into the 2-S deferment for students.

In February 1966, General Hershey announced that local draft boards could henceforth induct college students in the lower levels of academic achievement. Two methods were devised to determine this ranking. First: the universities were asked to rank their male students according to grades and give the government this information. Second: a national examination would be given to all male students periodically to test their general intelligence and academic achievement and the results would be used by local draft boards.

At its National Council meeting in May, SDS adopted an idea suggested by Lee Webb for a counterdraft examination. SDS printed half a million of these exams, containing questions and answers on Vietnam and American foreign policy. The idea was to pass them out at the regular draft exam centers on May 14 when the first such test was scheduled. But the council declined to accept a corollary proposal by Paul Booth that the SDSers refuse to take the regular exam as a show of seriousness.

On May 14, SDSers handed out the counterdraft exam at most of the 1,200 test centers. The students took it, read it, and many agreed that it was an effective piece of antiwar literature, but they also took the draft exam in an attempt to protect their own 2-S deferment.

It would not be until the end of December 1966 that SDS would adopt a position of draft refusal. In the earlier period it was the pacifists—those who opposed military service in principle—who organized this kind of activity, though many others talked about it. In the long run also it would be the pacifists who would organize it most effectively.

Their participation in this work did not depend on statistics, which in 1965 were not at all encouraging from the point of view of draft resistance. That year 180,000 men were drafted and there were only 341 cases of draft law violation.[1]

---

1. For number drafted: Department of Defense, Selected Manpower Statistics, May 1974, P27.61. For Selective Service Act violations: *Statistical Abstract of the U.S.,* 1973, table 445, p. 274.

For the pacifists draft refusal or at least legal conscientious objection was a philosophical or spiritual imperative and they'd have done it regardless of any broader effect. Some of them did, however, hope it would assume proportions great enough to interfere directly with the ability of the Pentagon to fill its manpower needs. This hope was never realized for the simple reason that the actual draft call—however large in absolute terms—was always only a small part of the available manpower pool. Advocates of draft resistance also hoped that it would help create a political atmosphere which would make the war unworkable, and this hope was realized to some degree. But that came later.

An entirely different approach was advocated by the SWP and the YSA. To some extent this *was* based on statistics, but also on a traditional Leninist view long held by the SWP and known as the proletarian military policy.

According to this approach, revolutionaries should not purposely isolate themselves from the working class youth being drafted, enlisting under the hot breath of the draft, or already in the armed services. In fiscal 1965-66 for example, there were an average of some 28,000 men a month being drafted, additional thousands enlisting—often simply to have a choice of services rather than wait to be drafted and have no choice—and some 3 million youths of draft age (18½ to 26) were already in the military service.[2]

Since deferment was much easier for upper- and middle-class youth to obtain, those being drafted or already in the service were heavily weighted to the side of lower income working class youth including disproportionate numbers of Blacks, Chicanos, Puerto Ricans, and Native Americans.

In the view of the SWP and the YSA the draft was a secondary issue in any case, subordinate to the political issue of the war itself. This contrasted sharply with the early Du Bois Club approach which leaned toward the idea that a movement against the draft could be broader than the movement against the war. In the fall of 1965 the National Peace Committee of the Du Bois Clubs issued a document which said:

The Vietnam war and the increased draft quotas that accompany the

2. For number drafted: same as in note 1. For number in service: *Statistical Abstract of the U.S.*, 1973, table 441, p. 272.

war bring more profound focus onto the question of the draft itself. But if there is to be a successful anti-draft movement, that is, one that encompasses the broadest anti-draft feeling, the question of the Vietnam war per se will be an incidental question. That is to say, we will have to organize people where they are. We will have to include in such a movement even those young persons who may support the Vietnam war but are not willing to give their lives for it.[3]

Doug Jenness, one of the YSA leaders, expressed a different gut feeling on the matter in a letter to Chicago SDSer Earl Silbar when the latter made a proposal for action against draft boards. According to Jenness,

a fight against a draft board does not help organize or inspire other sections of the population. It tries to organize the sentiments of scared students who want to stay out of the army rather than build a movement directed squarely against the Johnson administration. The majority of people who come into opposition against the war are not looking for a way out of the draft—they are looking for effective ways to expose and oppose the war. . . . The ordinary American is not a pacifist and sees nothing wrong with the Selective Service System or with the army; when he opposes the war, his response is simply to get the troops out—not to dismantle the Selective Service System.[4]

While this letter was indicative of an attitude among YSAers it actually overstated the YSA position somewhat. The YSA did adopt a position of political opposition to the existing draft. It supported the defense cases of draft resisters and was often involved in support demonstrations on their behalf. But YSAers did not advocate or engage in draft refusal. This was not out of legalistic considerations but because they didn't think it the most effective thing to do.

To them it seemed that, in a choice between spending two years or so in jail or an indefinite time in exile as opposed to spending two years in the army talking to fellow GIs against the war, the army was politically the more effective choice. This decision was left up to the individual, but with few exceptions YSAers who were drafted chose to enter the military.

Later, when antiwar activity among GIs became widespread

3. *End the Draft!* Published by the Du Bois Clubs National Peace Committee, Michael Myerson, director. Fall 1965. (Copy in author's files.)
4. Letter from Doug Jenness to Earl Silbar, March 15, 1966. (Copy in author's files.)

and a number of soldiers who had been active YSAers in civilian life were prominently involved, it was assumed by many within the movement that the YSA had deliberately sent people into the army. This was never the case. They were drafted. Nor did the YSAers quietly allow themselves to be drafted. As a general rule, YSAers called by the draft would notify the authorities in writing of their antiwar position and declare their intention to maintain these views and express them within the army. When a YSAer showed up for induction, it was often with a bundle of antiwar literature under his arm and accompanied by a demonstration of friends and supporters. In the early period they were drafted anyway. After the army had some experience with these organizers, however, the letter was usually enough to ensure a reconsideration of the induction.

The YSA and SWP preferred to keep their members in civilian life if possible, where they could organize freely and spend far more time on antiwar activity—not to mention socialist political work—than was possible in the army. They had no illusion that their own small forces could make a critical difference—except by occasional example—in activities within the army, which were tenuous and difficult at best.

The proletarian military policy was a political approach, not an adventure, not a fad, and certainly not a gimmick. It advocated pointing the antiwar movement toward the great mass of ordinary working class Americans, including those in the military, and including the 99 percent who were not opposed on principle to all military service.

Nor did those of us in the YSA and SWP view GI antiwar activity as a substitute for building the antiwar movement in the civilian population. On the contrary, it was our view that the civilians were the key force. Without a mass antiwar movement in the civilian population the GI movement could never get beyond occasional isolated individual acts. There was, however, an important reciprocal factor. Any antiwar stand by GIs carried great weight with the civilian population and cut, like nothing else could, through the "support our boys" demagogy of the hawks. Conversely, the more massive the civilian movement, the easier it was for the GIs to express their own opposition to the war.

In addition, we in the SWP also had our hopes that a GI movement could develop which would have a direct effect on the war machine. We knew this was at least theoretically possible.

because it had happened before. Not only in extreme situations of social collapse like Russia of 1917, but within the U.S. military itself in what was called the "going home movement" following World War II.

In late 1945 and early 1946 the huge U.S. overseas military machine had to be hastily demobilized, contrary to plan, because of a massive campaign by GIs which had broad support in the civilian population at home. This movement involved contact with trade union and other groups within the U.S., petitions to Congress, distribution of literature by the GIs themselves on military facilities, and even large demonstrations by men in uniform. These activities took place both in Europe and the Pacific.[5]

Although this movement had been virtually ignored in history books, a dim memory of it remained and had been kept alive in particular in the SWP, which considered it an important historical development. As an eighteen-year-old sailor in the U.S. Seventh Fleet in China waters, I had seen a part of this movement personally, though I had nothing to do with organizing it.

At the time the part of the fleet I was with was actually involved in the Chinese civil war—another fact rarely mentioned in the history books—ferrying Chiang Kai-shek's troops to Northern China to fight the Communists. The GIs I was acquainted with had by and large accepted the Second World War as some kind of necessity. But we knew nothing about the Chinese civil war until we found ourselves involved, and we wanted no part of it. It was not so much a political mood as a simple desire to go home, though I remember some of the GI orators using words like "imperialism" in their agitation. As I recall, the organizers were older than I was, usually noncommissioned officers with some sort of specialized skills and a background of trade union experience.

I remember that at the time it was considered no big thing for GIs to be painting banners or turning out leaflets on military

5. For accounts of this movement see: *GIs and the Fight Against War* by Mary-Alice Waters (New York: Young Socialist Pamphlet, 1967); "The Army Mutiny of 1946," by R. Alton Lee, *Journal of American History,* December 3, 1966, pp. 555-71; and *Soldiers in Revolt* by David Cortright (Garden City, New York: Anchor/Doubleday, 1975), pp. 149-51.

mimeograph machines, or even requisitioning space on military airplanes to attend distant meetings. I observed one of these meetings at the Red Cross building in Shanghai, which was a gathering place for GIs in the area. The lobby had a big banner in it: "GIs Unite—We Want to Go Home!"

If the officers didn't like these goings-on, there was not much they could do about it. The sentiment was too widespread and they were too dependent in day-to-day life on the noncommissioned officers who were participating. The movement was finally halted by decree, but this was possible only because the rapid demobilization had already begun and was irreversible, at least as far as that body of men was concerned.

In 1965 and 1966 we in the SWP thought a lot about that earlier experience and described it on every possible occasion to other antiwar activists. Could anything like that develop among American GIs in Vietnam? We weren't sure, but we didn't exclude it. And we did what we could to press the point that GIs had a right—if anyone did—to express their opinions on the war in Vietnam, and to organize and demonstrate against it.

In the first years of the antiwar movement the YSA was the only major radical youth group to consistently advocate work among GIs. (The much smaller Youth Against War and Fascism also saw GIs as an important constituency.)

The other groups considering themselves Marxist did not, in principle, oppose all military service, and when drafted their members usually entered the army. But these groups had no orientation toward GIs. On the contrary, like SDS and the pacifists, they viewed antidraft work as central. The idea of looking to GIs as part of the antiwar constituency was considered bizarre at that time by most of the movement.

Peculiarly enough, it was some of the pacifists—including Muste and Dellinger—who were among the earliest to seriously consider the idea of reaching GIs. They did not counsel entering the army, even when forced by the draft. And they tended to consider antidraft activity more important in general, but they did not exclude the possibility of reaching GIs with the antiwar message, or even with their own pacifist message.

One thing the radical pacifists had in common with the Trotskyists was a strong faith in the capacity of ordinary people to learn and change. In each case, this faith had a different philosophical basis, and, regarding Dellinger and myself, this would later be reflected in serious tactical disputes as the movement matured.

\*        \*        \*

The first widely publicized case of GI antiwar activity was that of Lieutenant Henry Howe, Jr., who had gained his army commission through the Reserve Officer Training Corps (ROTC) program at the University of Colorado. Howe was not a radical and had expressed pride at being able to serve in the military. But Johnson's escalation of the war in spite of the election promises of 1964 shocked Howe. He became bitter at President Johnson. While stationed at a base near El Paso he decided to join an antiwar demonstration there on November 6, 1965.

The demonstration was small, about a dozen students and faculty from Texas Western College, who had to brave a large crowd of hecklers. Nevertheless Howe, who was off-duty at the time, joined the picket line wearing civilian clothes. He carried a sign which contained two slogans: "End Johnson's fascist aggression in Vietnam" and "Let's have more than a choice between petty, ignorant fascists in 1968."

Though the demonstration was peaceful and orderly, Howe was pointed out to local police as an army officer and arrested on a subterfuge "vagrancy" charge, then turned over to military police and court-martialed. Actually, he had broken no laws. Regulations which had been outlined by Secretary of Defense Robert McNamara during the civil rights demonstrations of 1963 had recognized the rights of GIs to demonstrate while off duty and in civilian clothes.

But Howe was convicted by the court-martial of conduct unbecoming an officer and using contemptuous words toward the president. He was sentenced to two years in prison. The Denver antiwar movement and Howe's family in Boulder set up a "Freedom Now for Lieutenant Howe Committee" and mounted an effective campaign of publicity while the American Civil Liberties Union appealed the case. The campaign succeeded in winning Howe's release on parole after he had served three months.

The next GI case to attract wide attention was the Fort Hood Three. At the time it was not publicly known, but the story of the Fort Hood Three is not complete without reference to a fourth GI who was not directly involved in the case but played a key role in connecting it with the organized antiwar movement. He was Pfc. Carl Edelman, a cook at Fort Gordon, Georgia. I had known Edelman slightly on the Lower East Side of New York City before he was drafted. He was a big, burly youth from a radical working class background, tough, gutsy, and generally well liked by his associates.

In the army Edelman became convinced on his own that the antiwar movement could reach GIs. In February 1966 he wrote a letter to this effect to the Southern Coordinating Committee to End the War in Vietnam, an NCC affiliate in Atlanta. It began: "To the U.S. Peace Movement: The soldier is not the enemy." Edelman continued:

The other evening a few of us were watching the news on television, Huntley-Brinkley. They showed a couple of shots of an antiwar demonstration in New York City. The immediate reaction was an outburst of nasty epithets: "Send those bastards to Vietnam," "All of those beatniks should be sent to the front lines," etc. Not a few seconds later, the pictures of dead and wounded American soldiers were shown. The result of "operation masher". Out of the mouths of the same soldiers who only a few moments before were condemning anti-war demonstrators, came "Why in hell are those boys dying", "They should get rid of McNamara", "If Johnson wants to fight, he should go over there". These are some of the contradictions. . . .[6]

Edelman met the other soldiers while they were in signal school at Fort Gordon before being assigned to the 142nd Signal Battalion at Fort Hood. There they were given a thirty-day leave and orders to report to the Oakland Army Terminal on July 13, 1966, for shipment to Vietnam. They decided to take a stand and refuse to go, and they contacted Edelman at Fort Gordon to talk it over.

There had been previous incidents, reported briefly in the press, of GIs refusing—or attempting to refuse—duty in Vietnam. But these had been quickly buried by the army, which either shipped the GIs off to Vietnam or arrested them immediately and held them virtually incommunicado. The antiwar movement heard about these cases only after the fact and had no way to reach the GIs and mount a defense.

Edelman advised the Fort Hood GIs to contact antiwar organi-

6. *SCC Newsletter,* February 23, 1966. (Copy in author's files.)

zations and prepare for maximum publicity and backing from the civilian movement before making a move. This could be done during their thirty-day leave. Edelman had a leave of his own coming, so he took it and went North with the other GIs.

One of them, Dennis Mora, was a member of the Du Bois Clubs, which was the first group they contacted. They were referred to Vets for Peace, which in turn referred them to the Parade Committee. That's how they happened to walk into Dellinger's office in mid-June.

I was on the Parade Committee staff then and Dellinger called me in to talk it over with the GIs. Dellinger and I made sure they knew what they were doing and that they knew they would probably spend a few years in jail if they went through with it. Dellinger was in favor of the move they proposed—to refuse to go to Vietnam. I told them frankly that in their place I wouldn't do the same, that I would go to Vietnam, which would only be a year, and spread the antiwar message as best I could over there.

But we both assured them that if they went ahead with their plan we were sure the Parade Committee would back them. It was clear they knew the consequences and had their minds made up, so we consulted with Muste and worked out a procedure to make it impossible for the army to keep the case quiet. What is more, with the agreement of the GIs, we decided to use the case to encourage the movement to approach soldiers and to begin to develop that area of activity.

The three Fort Hood GIs in consultation with Edelman had figured out their own strategy in basic outline, and even contacted a lawyer, before coming to the Parade Committee. Their plan was to hold a press conference to announce their stand, to allow time for the civilian movement to mobilize behind them, then to report to the Oakland base as scheduled, but to refuse to embark for Vietnam.

We invited them to present their case before the June 18 conference of antiwar activists which had been previously scheduled by the Parade Committee to make plans for the August 6-9 demonstration. They did so, and got the support they asked for.

A press conference for the GIs was arranged where they would publicly announce their stand. Careful preparations were made to assure that prominent figures in the movement would be present, as well as the members of the GIs' families who could make it. A public meeting was set for a week later at which the GIs were scheduled to speak. Antiwar groups on the West Coast were contacted to prepare to meet the GIs at the airport near Oakland on July 9 and to hold additional press conferences and meetings with them in the Bay Area before they reported at the Army Terminal on July 13.[7] In addition, a legal defense committee was set up to go into operation immediately after the GIs made their public announcement, with Muste and Staughton Lynd as cochairmen and Dellinger as secretary.

On June 30 in New York's Community Church the press conference went off as planned. Present were SNCC Chairman Stokely Carmichael and CORE Public Relations Director Lincoln Lynch as well as Muste, Dellinger, Lynd, members of the GIs' families, and a large number of Parade Committee members. As the three GIs faced the TV cameras one of them, Dennis Mora, read the following joint statement:

We are Pfc. James Johnson, Pvt. David Samas, and Pvt. Dennis Mora, three soldiers formerly stationed at Fort Hood, Texas in the same company of the 142 Signal Battalion, 2nd Armored Division. We have received orders to report on the 13th of July at Oakland Army Terminal in California for final processing and shipment to Vietnam.

We have decided to take a stand against this war, which we consider immoral, illegal and unjust. We are initiating today, through our attorneys, Stanley Faulkner of New York and Mrs. Selma Samols of Washington, D.C. an action in the courts to enjoin the Secretary of Defense and the Secretary of the Army from sending us to Vietnam. We intend to report as ordered to the Oakland Army Terminal, but under no circum-

7. The early communications mention four Fort Hood GIs planning to refuse orders to Vietnam. One of them dropped out before the press conference. The circumstances are interesting. This GI considered himself a libertarian conservative and a follower of the ideas of novelist Ayn Rand. The GIs were invited to a regular Parade Committee meeting at which the custom was to go around the room with each person making a self-introduction, including name and organization, for the benefit of newcomers. When it came Mike Stein's turn he said as usual: "Mike Stein, New York Communist Party." After the meeting the fourth GI told us he would have to drop out because his philosophy would not permit him to associate with a member of the Communist Party. He said he considered the Parade Committee honest and would not do anything to jeopardize the other GIs. As far as I know he kept this promise though he was detained and questioned by army authorities after the others made their public announcement. He was sent to Vietnam. Later he wrote from there saying he still opposed the war.

stances will we board ship for Vietnam. We are prepared to face Court Martial if necessary.

We represent in our backgrounds a cross section of the Army and of America. James Johnson is a Negro, David Samas is of Lithuanian and Italian parents, Dennis Mora is a Puerto Rican. We speak as American soldiers.

We have been in the army long enough to know that we are not the only G.I.'s who feel as we do. Large numbers of men in the service either do not understand this war or are against it. . . .

The Viet Cong obviously had the moral and physical support of most of the peasantry who were fighting for their independence. We were told [in army training] that you couldn't tell them apart—that they looked like any other skinny peasant.

Our man or our men in Saigon has and have always been brutal dictators, since Diem first violated the Geneva promise of free elections in 1956.

The Buddhist and military revolt in all the major cities proves that the people of the cities also want an end to Ky and U.S. support for him.

The Saigon Army has become the advisor to American G.I.'s who have to take over the fighting.

No one used the word "winning" anymore because in Vietnam it has no meaning. Our officers just talk about five and ten more years of war with at least a half million of our boys thrown into the grinder. We have been told that many times we may face a Vietnamese woman or child and that we will have to kill them. We will never go there—to do that—for Ky!

We know that Negroes and Puerto Ricans are being drafted and end up in the worst of the fighting all out of proportion to their numbers in the population; and we have first hand knowledge that these are the ones who have been deprived of decent education and jobs at home. . . .

We have made our decision. We will not be a part of this unjust, immoral, and illegal war. We want no part of a war of extermination. We oppose the criminal waste of American lives and resources. We refuse to go to Vietnam![8]

The announcement was front-page news in the major media. The Fort Hood Three Defense Committee immediately sent out to antiwar groups across the country fact sheets on the case including statements by the three GIs. Dozens of antiwar groups began reproducing and distributing these, concentrating on areas where GIs could be found, such as bus stations and airports near major bases.

8. *The Fort Hood Three.* Pamphlet published by the Fort Hood Three Defense Committee (New York: 1966), pp. 9-11. Fort Hood Three file, State Historical Society of Wisconsin, Madison.

The army's first reaction was to try to divide the three GIs. A few days after the press conference, Samas received a telegram from his parents in Modesto, California, asking him to call home immediately. The Modesto police had contacted them, told them their son was being used as a "tool of the Communists," and on behalf of the army offered Samas a deal. Said Samas: "They had told my father that if I would retract my statement and withdraw completely from the civil action now in progress that I would receive a discharge from the army and no serious repercussions would result."[9]

Samas's parents were upset but after talking it over with their son decided to back him in his stand. The three GIs were followed around New York by plainclothes agents, and, according to a statement by Samas written at the time:

> They have attempted to intimidate the three of us in one way or another and have approached all of our parents in different ways. But we have not been scared. We have not been in the least shaken from our paths. And we will not be, even if physical violence is used. We are not pacifists. We are not non-violent, and if the need arises we will fight back.[10]

On the morning of July 7, a telegram signed by Muste, Dellinger, and Becker for the Parade Committee was sent to Attorney General Nicholas De B. Katzenbach and Secretary of Defense Robert McNamara, and released to the press. This telegram was the result of serious deliberation and was carefully written. It outlined the response of the antiwar movement to the initial army attack against the Fort Hood Three and took the offensive by projecting an ongoing campaign toward GIs. It declared:

> We strongly condemn harassment by Federal agents of servicemen such as Pfc. James Johnson, Pvt. Dennis Mora and Pvt. David Samas, who have filed injunction in Federal Court against shipment to Vietnam on grounds of immorality and illegality of that war.
>
> We are reliably informed that on July 4 an officer of the Modesto, California, police force visited the parents of Pvt. Samas. The officer said he had been contacted by "higher authorities" and that if Pvt. Samas would rescind his action and his statement against the war, and in effect

9. Ibid., p. 16.
10. Loc. cit.

abandon his fellows, he would not be prosecuted and would receive an Army discharge. The officer obviously acted under instruction of Federal agents in proposing such a bribe.

Such acts show desperation in attempting to stem growing opposition to the war among young men facing the draft or already in military service. The peace movement will continue to aid in every possible lawful way anyone, civilian, soldier, sailor or Marine, who opposes this illegal and immoral war. The young men in the armed services are entitled to know the truth about the war and to engage in discussions about it. Citizens are likewise entitled to communicate the truth about the war to servicemen and the peace movement is determined to exercise that right.[11]

Later that month in a report on the case to the New York branch of the Socialist Workers Party, I commented on that telegram:

There are many ways something like that could be said, and most of them would be wrong. But this isn't wrong. It is just right. And it ought to be given a lot of attention—a lot of thought. What could be more reasonable than that the young men in the armed services are entitled to know the truth about the war, and to engage in discussions about it? Anything else is pure and simple thought control, brainwashing, and everything else evil and outrageous. Can anybody reasonably challenge that proposition? Isn't it completely in accord with what almost every American considers reasonable? . . .

This is not a fascist country, in spite of what some people who are very loose with words say. And it is extremely important to know that it isn't a fascist country. Extremely important. For one thing, regardless of how the liberties we are supposed to enjoy are abused by this or that authority, the traditions of free thought, free speech, freedom of discussion, and so on, run extremely deep in the American people. They haven't been burned out. They remain deep among the people, all of them, including those in the army.

We know that in effect many of these liberties have been sham and mockery because it has been almost impossible to put them to effective use. You can vote, but you vote for peace candidate Johnson and he gives you war. You can demonstrate, but the government pays no attention. You can talk but nobody in power listens. But now these freedoms can be used to greater effect. Now the movement is going to use. . . . them. It is entitled to use them, and it is going to use them up to the hilt. It is not asking anybody to do anything wild or anything strange, or anything illegal—just to exercise these rights.

11. Ibid., p. 26.

The question is, does an ordinary American youth have the right to form his own opinion on being used, and maybe killed, in a war some place half-way around the world. A war which millions of his fellow citizens consider to be immoral and illegal. Does he or doesn't he? Obviously he does! . . .
Now we don't want to imply that automatically this is going to be the big thing; that a point is going to be reached in a few months where thousands of GIs will be reached, and the word will get to Vietnam and there will be a big "going home movement" and the war will be over because of this case. But it may be the beginning of that process.[12]

On the evening of July 7 some 800 antiwar activists gathered in the public meeting at the Community Church to hear the three GIs tell their own story. On their way to the church the three men were abducted by the federal agents following them and spirited off to the stockade at Fort Dix, New Jersey. The men were still on leave and had not yet broken any laws. The abduction—the men were not formally arrested until they refused orders to go to Vietnam—was an obvious attempt to prevent them from speaking and to cut off the demonstrations scheduled for their arrival in the Oakland area.

The meeting proceeded anyway, with members of the GIs' families speaking on their behalf. Volunteers hastily painted signs in the back of the hall and the meeting closed with the audience marching to Times Square for an emergency demonstration on behalf of the GIs. This too got good coverage in the media.

At the meeting itself, Grace Mora Newman spoke on behalf of her brother Dennis. The other two GIs had managed to get copies of their speeches to relatives before they were hauled away. James Johnson's speech was read by his brother Darwin.

After basic training I began to seriously consider the prospect of Vietnam. I devoted much of my free time to reading, listening, and discussing America's role in Vietnam. I felt that I had been following blindly too long in the Army. A soldier is taught not to question, not to think, just to do what he is told. Are your convictions and your conscience supposed to be left at home, or on the block? I had to take a stand.

I once told a Colonel about my opposition to the war. I was told that I was being paid to be a soldier not a politician. Should I let the Pentagon decide whether I should live or die? After studying the situation in

12. This verbal report was transcribed and distributed to other SWP branches, July 21, 1966. (Copy in author's files.)

Vietnam, I learned that the government was not being honest with the American people. The government tells us that the United States is in Vietnam at the request of the Vietnamese government in Saigon. They fail to tell us, though, that the Saigon government was not elected by the people. There have never been free elections there. In fact, the U.S. government installed a regime of its own choosing, headed by Diem, in 1954. Since then there has been a succession of military dictators. All supported at our expense. Not one of these governments was worth the support of the people. They were supported by our army.

The government also tells us that we are spending our men and money to preserve freedom in Vietnam. Yet the current dictator, General Ky, declared that Adolf Hitler was his hero. Like Hitler, he uses extreme brutality to crush any opposition that may arise. President Johnson tells us that he is trying to bring about discussions for peace in Vietnam. Yet peace offers were made by North Vietnam last spring. But they were rejected by our government and the American people were not told about them. . . .

Now there is a direct relationship between the peace movement and the civil rights movement. The South Vietnamese are fighting for representation like we ourselves. . . . Therefore the Negro in Vietnam is just helping to defeat what his black brother is fighting for in the United States. When the Negro soldier returns, he still will not be able to ride in Mississippi or walk down a certain street in Alabama. There will still be proportionately twice as many Negroes as whites in Vietnam. . . .

It is time that the Negro realizes that his strength can be put to much better use right here at home. This is where his strength lies. We can gain absolutely nothing in Vietnam. All this is leading to the decision I have made. I know it is my right to make this decision.[13]

Samas's speech was read by his seventeen-year-old wife, Marlene. It contained the following advice to the peace movement:

I have never been involved with any of the peace groups until a few weeks ago when we approached the Parade Committee for help. As a civilian I was interested and extremely concerned, but I neglected to show my concern. In a great way I too am responsible for the boys who already are in Vietnam.

But even as an unaffiliated civilian, I was closer to the peace movement than most soldiers are now. To me the peace movement always looked like concerned students and citizens trying to protect their country from war and nuclear devastation. To a soldier the movement appears very differently. The soldier is very far indeed from the outside world and the

13. *The Fort Hood Three,* pp. 19-20.

normal news media do not usually reach him. News of the free world reaches him through letters from home, or through his buddies. It often seems that the peace groups are united against the soldier, and that forces the soldiers to cling together and ignore the real issues made public by the peace movement. The stories that reach the soldiers usually show that the peace movement is backing their enemies, and is against the Army, and against the individual soldiers. Upon too many occasions groups have offered aid to the Viet Cong and too few times have they approached the G.I.'s with help.

The G.I. should be reached somehow. He doesn't want to fight. He has no reasons to risk his life. Yet he doesn't realize that the peace movement is dedicated to his safety. Give the G.I. something to believe in and he will fight for that belief. Let them know in Vietnam that you want them home, let them know that you are concerned about their lives also. Tell them you want them to live, not die. Bring home our men in Vietnam! . . .

In the end we depend entirely upon the public. We have placed ourselves in the hands of the people of the United States, and all of our hopes lie with them. . . .[14]

Two days later the Parade Committee took several busloads of demonstrators to Fort Dix to demonstrate on behalf of the three GIs. Before the buses arrived the base authorities sent military police through the little village of Wrightstown, which lies just outside the main gate, chasing GIs off the street so they wouldn't mix with the demonstrators. A number of them retreated inside bars and restaurants, however, and watched through the windows. A line of MPs prevented the demonstrators from entering the base so they set up a picket line outside while Muste and members of the families argued with the officers in charge. Distributors ran around putting leaflets anywhere GIs might get them. It was the first large demonstration at an army base. Over the years to come there would be countless others.

When it came time to leave, my assignment was to walk the few blocks of the town making sure all the demonstrators made it back to the buses. It was a hot day and when this was done I stopped in a bar for a beer. I hadn't thought to remove my Parade Committee marshal's armband and I suddenly realized I was alone in a bar filled with soldiers. A half dozen of them, well along in their cups, surrounded me at the bar and started baiting. I tried to be friendly but they were looking for a fight. I was about resigned to getting some lumps when one of them, a wiry white

14. Ibid., p. 17.

Southerner with narrow-set eyes, poked at my armband. "Gimme that," he said. "I want to take it with me to Vietnam." I took off the armband, handed it to him, and said the first thing that came to mind: "OK, but don't kill any peasants." He backed away with shock on his face. "I wouldn't do that," he said quietly. The group dissolved and I finished my beer and left. It wasn't going to be easy, but the discussion, at least, had begun.

*           *           *

The courts turned down the injunction requested by the Fort Hood Three on the ground that they didn't have jurisdiction, and in spite of appeals they consistently refused to hear the substantial issues in the case. The court-martial also refused to consider these issues, so the three GIs were convicted and sentenced. The conviction was upheld through the military appeals and the three men spent two years in prison. For some time after they were first confined, the defense committee organized demonstrations and widespread publicity campaigns to protest harsh treatment the men received at the first stockades where they were held. These were effective and their conditions did improve. The men never faltered, and when they were released returned to civilian life as supporters of the antiwar movement. By that time, the movement as a whole had become acutely aware of the importance of antiwar activity by GIs.

*           *           *

A by-product of the Fort Hood Three case was a spirit of unity in New York behind the Parade Committee in preparations for the August 6-9 protests, as well as increased standing of the Parade Committee in the movement nationally.

In addition, the war continued to escalate. Hours before the June 30 Fort Hood Three press conference, the U.S. bombed oil storage depots in Hanoi and Haiphong, the first time those population centers had been attacked by U.S. forces. As a result, demonstrations previously called for July 4 in several cities were larger than expected, including one of 5,000 in Los Angeles sponsored by the Peace Action Council there.

The August 6-9 demonstrations were not expected to be as large as those in the spring because of the traditional summer lull with vacations and schools being out. Nevertheless, in several cities, including Cleveland, Atlanta, and San Diego, the August protests were the largest antiwar actions yet held, though the turnout in such cities was still in the hundreds. Significantly, in many cities the activities were sponsored by new, broader coalitions, in some cases patterned after the Parade Committee.

In Washington, D.C., President Johnson's daughter, Lucy Baines, was married August 6. The timing of this event—which was played up in the media like a celebration of royalty—displayed a certain lack of sensitivity to the human tragedy of Hiroshima Day. Some 500 antiwar demonstrators marched in front of the White House in spite of police attempts to keep them away on the excuse that the wedding reception was being held there.

The San Francisco demonstration drew 10,000, with Vincent Hallinan, Peter Camejo, Robert Scheer, and Ann Samas, mother of one of the Fort Hood Three, among the speakers. In general, defense of the Fort Hood Three was a feature of the August actions and in many places leafletting of GIs was stressed. In Madison, Wisconsin, the university was used to feed some 2,000 reserve troops passing through on summer training and the antiwar movement there leafletted them heavily, finding an unexpectedly friendly response.

These demonstrations also featured another aspect of antiwar activity in which interest was growing. This was the exposure of the use by the U.S. in Vietnam of the terror weapon napalm, jellied gasoline which sticks to the flesh and consumes it with flames.

Demonstrations against napalm had previously taken place at factories producing it in Redwood City and in Torrance, California, where a Dow Chemical plant was located. In April 1966 two Brooklyn women, Denzil Longton and Terry Radinsky, had organized a demonstration at a stockholders meeting of the Witco Chemical Company, one of the producers of napalm. They then formed the Citizens Campaign Against Napalm and launched a nationwide consumers' boycott against Saran Wrap, one of the products of Dow, a chief producer of napalm.

Longton was a member of the Parade Committee and convinced it to make the Dow Chemical offices in Rockefeller Plaza a target of the August 6 New York demonstration.

Participants gathered in various parts of the city, including the different boroughs, and started feeder marches featuring a variety of effects. There were thirteen feeder marches in all, including one from Harlem and a Latin American contingent starting from the East Side. Three of them were led by units organized by the Bread and Puppet Theater. The marches converged in Times Square, circled the area, and then marched past the Rockefeller Plaza Dow offices to a rally in the streets nearby. The crowd was 20,000, a remarkable turnout for midsummer.

The families of Johnson and Mora, two of the Fort Hood Three, sat on the speakers' stand and Grace Mora Newman was a featured speaker as were Lincoln Lynch of CORE and Ivanhoe Donaldson of SNCC. Dave Dellinger introduced John Morgan, a marine from Camp Lejeune who while in the service had become a pacifist and was refusing to bear arms. (He was later jailed for his stand.)

While the president's daughter celebrated her wedding in Washington, another young woman, Kamiko Kosaka, her arm badly scarred from the effects of the Hiroshima bombing she had experienced as a child, was introduced to the New York demonstration as a guest of honor, representing the Japanese peace movement.

With the feeder marches the New York demonstration lasted all day and large parts of the city became aware of it. This time, there were few organized hecklers, though the feeder marchers were occasionally engaged in heated discussions along the way. (This was the demonstration from which David Loeb Weiss, using a crew of volunteer filmmakers, produced the prize-winning documentary *Anatomy of a Peace Parade.*)

As the demonstration came to a close and the crowd was dispersing, Muste sat on the edge of the stage with the wind blowing his hair, sporting a Parade Committee button and looking pleased as Punch. In his speech earlier he had said:

> That we should have, increasingly, opposition to the war among the armed forces themselves is a tremendously significant development which the Johnson administration is going to have to take account of. And I am here to tell you and urge you to join in backing up the right of all the men in the armed services today to have their right of free thought, free speech and free discussion inside the armed forces, as well as outside, in opposition to the war.[15]

15. *Militant,* August 22, 1966.

# 8

# The Cleveland Conferences of 1966

Two weeks before the August 6-9 Days of Protest, Muste attended a meeting hosted by the University Circle Teach-In Committee in Cleveland, Ohio. It was the first of three conferences in Cleveland in the latter half of 1966. These would at last draw together the various threads of the antiwar movement into a national coalition which could initiate unified action on a far broader scale than SDS, the Berkeley VDC, the NCC, or the New York Parade Committee had been able to do.

University Circle is an area where the campuses of Western Reserve University and Case Institute of Technology, then separate and later merged, are located. The University Circle Teach-In Committee had originated shortly after the first Ann Arbor teach-in in March of 1965, to organize a similar event at Case Western Reserve. It continued afterward, carried out a number of educational projects, and developed an impressive list of academic and community figures associated with the group. Included were national SANE cochairman Dr. Benjamin Spock, whose home was in Cleveland, as well as Paul Olynyk of the local SANE chapter.

The teach-in committee had generally confined itself to educational activities and had not been directly involved in the demonstrations against the war organized by the local SDS chapter and the Cleveland CEWV. But one of the leading figures in the teach-in committee, Western Reserve sociology professor Sidney Peck, was helpful to the youth in these groups and generally paid close attention to developments in the movement as a whole.

The professors around the teach-in committee were also involved in electoral activity. Like their counterparts in Ann Arbor, most of them, including Peck, had campaigned for Johnson-Humphrey in 1964 as a peace ticket.

The Cleveland group was associated with a national organization, the Inter-University Committee for Debate on Foreign Policy. The latter stemmed from the original Inter-University Committee for a Public Hearing on Vietnam which had organized the national teach-in at Washington, D.C., in May of 1965.

In 1966 it was headquartered in Ithaca, New York, where Cornell professor Douglas Dowd, the president of its executive council, lived. It too had not been involved in demonstrations, but had organized teach-ins, provided speakers and materials for various conferences and educational activities, and had also been involved in electoral politics. Its approach was summed up in a statement which appeared in the March 6, 1966, *New York Times* when the congressional primary campaigns were in full swing. On political action the statement declared:

Reasoned dissent seeks power, and finds expression, in the normal contests for political office. Primaries and general elections make the case against present Administration policies. All must try to promote the candidacy of opponents to this war, in the political party of their choice. The Inter-University Committee will send documents to help candidates organize effective campaigns and assist the reasoned presentation of dissenting views in any way that is consistent with our basic functions.

By mid-1966, however, when the primaries were over, a number of those associated with the Cleveland and Ithaca organizations had become acutely aware of a practical political problem. In spite of the fact that the teach-ins and the antiwar movement had succeeded in making the war an issue of debate, even in Congress, very few of the so-called peace candidates had survived the primaries to run in the general elections. Even more important, President Johnson ignored the criticism, continued to escalate the war, and was in firm control of the Democratic Party nationally. Unless some unforeseen development occurred, he would be the party's candidate for president in 1968.

The previous perspective of the moderate teach-in professors, more or less confined to educational activity and electoral politics within the Democratic Party, was at an impasse as far as the war was concerned. In the course of discussions around this problem within the Cleveland committee, Western Reserve professor Richard Recknagel suggested the idea of the first Cleveland conference, and Peck picked up on the idea. Perhaps it was time for the moderate, electorally oriented forces to move into additional activity in combination with the more radical street-oriented forces, and develop a mass breadth that the new antiwar movement lacked. As part of the moderate spectrum, the teach-in professors might be in a good position to encourage this development. Another consideration involved was that on the other hand perhaps this would contribute somewhere down the line to the development of a "new politics"—more radical and aware that the war was not a mistake on the part of administration officials but a symptom of a more general problem in the United States.

The University Circle Teach-In Committee invited representatives of some fifteen organizations—either national in scope or local groups with national impact—to discuss the possibility of a mobilization of antiwar forces for the fall.

These included the American Friends Service Committee, CORE, the Universities Committee on the Problems of War and Peace, the Fellowship of Reconciliation, the New York Parade Committee, the NCC, SDS, SANE, SNCC, the National Emergency Committee of Clergy Concerned about Vietnam (later Clergy and Laymen Concerned), Massachusetts Pax, Women Strike for Peace, the Women's International League for Peace and Freedom, and the Inter-University Committee for Debate on Foreign Policy.

On July 22 some thirty people from these organizations met in a downtown hotel in Cleveland. Muste represented the Committee for Nonviolent Action and the Parade Committee. According to the record:

Dr. Sidney Peck explained the rationale for convening this meeting. The peace movement has so far been highly fragmented and energy wasted by duplications. We here in Cleveland, after extended discussions, felt that we could act as a catalytic agent to bring together a number of groups who oppose the war in Vietnam and who might consider ways and means for coordinated activities.[1]

The first few hours of the meeting were consumed in a discussion of which groups ought to be included in whatever combined effort was decided upon. Hugh Fowler, national chair-

---

1. Report on the Cleveland meeting of July 22, 1966. (Copy in author's files.)

man of the Du Bois Clubs, was in Cleveland and had indicated a desire to attend the meeting. A position of nonexclusion was finally adopted unanimously.

Paul Potter, representing SDS, proposed Fowler be invited. At Peck's suggestion this was approved on condition that a representative of the YSA also be called. So Fowler and Cleveland YSAer Paul Lodico joined the rest of the meeting.

Douglas Dowd presented an analysis of the war: the previous attitude of the teach-in professors and the moderate peace movement—that the U.S. had blundered into the war in Vietnam and that this "blunder" could be reversed by pressing for negotiations—was no longer tenable. It was now clear the administration wanted military victory and permanent bases in Southeast Asia. This would require obliteration of the Vietnamese and possible war with China. What is more, this spelled the end of the promised domestic reforms of Johnson's Great Society and an erosion of democracy.

There was general agreement on this, but little agreement on what to do about it. The meeting was rambling—over fourteen hours in all—and most of the speakers were not optimistic. Dowd, however, spoke strongly in favor of regional demonstrations in the fall, combining the war with other issues, and he raised the possibility of getting a million people involved. Muste spoke for a mobilization in the fall, for immediate withdrawal, and nonexclusion.

The meeting finally agreed to another, larger conference a month later, with the Inter-University Committee for Debate on Foreign Policy taking responsibility for calling it and the Cleveland teach-in group again acting as host. Many of the participants left with the impression that the first meeting had been of questionable success but because of the urgency of the situation were not opposed to trying it again.

According to a letter from Lodico at the time, describing the July 22 gathering:

Pessimism and futility were the pervasive moods of the conference. The people there generally spoke of whatever mobilization there would be in the fall as just the first step in "building an anti-fascist coalition." Recknagel of the Teach-In Committee said several times that that was what this country needed.[2]

2. Letter from Paul Lodico to the author, July 26, 1966.

The invitation to the second conference, signed by Dowd, declared the purpose to be:

> to work toward a mobilization late in October that will have at least the following characteristics: a) it will occur a week or two before the November elections; b) it will take place in many locations—how many, and where, to be decided—rather than in, say, only Washington; c) it will be sponsored by all groups represented in a particular locality, rather than by one organization; d) speakers and issues at the various meetings will not emerge in a unitary pattern, but will be determined by the multiplicity of groups and issues most relevant in a given locality; e) participation by one group will not be taken to imply let alone require approval of the specific stand of any of the other groups participating; f) such participation on a multi-group multi-issue basis would be allowed to suggest that all groups recognize the need to stand together for at least one day, and in some cases to begin to work together toward something more, to express concern for those things being done and left undone by national, state and local governments and the people they represent. . . . It is our hope that a mass mobilization of more than a million people all over the nation can be achieved—a mobilization of clergy, students, the poor, the discriminated against, those, in sum, who see the hope for peace, decency, progress, and democracy ebbing away.[3]

I was not present at the first Cleveland conference but Muste reported on it to the Parade Committee. He considered the fact that the Inter-University Committee was ready to participate in demonstrations an important development. He was anxious that the second conference—in spite of hesitations being expressed by some of those involved in the first meeting—take place and be attended by more antiwar groups. When he received a copy of Dowd's invitation to the second meeting—which included a summary of the first—Muste mimeographed it and sent it out, with his own covering letter, to antiwar committees and groups across the country. Said Muste:

> I think those who receive this material will recognize that it is of considerable interest and significance and that there was a fairly wide participation in the meeting. It seems to me to follow that the meeting being planned . . . is of great importance and that there should be a very broad response to this meeting.[4]

3. Letter to "Dear Friend" from Douglas Dowd, August 3, 1966. (Copy in author's files.)
4. Letter from A. J. Muste, August 9, 1966. (Copy in author's files.)

Nevertheless the second conference was almost canceled. On August 16 the Inter-University Committee sent the following two-sentence letter:

> Response to the call for the August 20-21 Cleveland planning meeting was very weak for several reasons—some political, some (we hope most) practical. The meeting has therefore been cancelled and whether or not it will be recalled will be decided at a later date.[5]

The response to the invitations—including those circulated by Muste—continued to arrive, however, and on August 26, Dowd sent another letter declaring:

> After much consultation we have planned another *planning* meeting in Cleveland, for the weekend of September 10-11, again with the hope that we can arrange a nationwide multi-issue, multi-group mobilization *before the November elections.*[6]

By the time the meeting took place it was being billed as a "National Leadership Conference." It was held in the Baker building at Western Reserve University with about 140 persons registered, from the groups which had attended the first conference as well as many more, including a number of local independent antiwar committees and area coordinating groups. National SANE, however, did not send a representative. Hugh Fowler of the Du Bois Clubs and Jack Barnes of the YSA were there, as were the editors of the *Bring the Troops Home Now Newsletter* and representatives of the NCC, including Emspak. Significantly, there was no one present from the national office of SDS, though a few local chapters were represented.

Dowd couldn't make the meeting, so it was opened by the Inter-University Committee's executive vice-president, Robert Greenblatt, a Cornell assistant professor of mathematics still in his twenties. The conference was chaired by Muste.

Sidney Peck, who opened the discussion on the proposed mobilization, said he hoped that "when we leave this conference we will have come to some agreement on what we can do on a national level in terms of a unified effort to express the full

5. Letter to "Dear Friend" from Cynthia Richardson, August 16, 1966. (Copy in author's files.)

6. Letter to "Dear Friend" from Douglas Dowd, August 26, 1966. Emphasis in original. (Copy in author's files.)

potential of the sentiment against this war."[7]

Then he laid out a proposal and a method of approach which, to those familiar with the difficulties facing the movement, was bold indeed, and at the same time deliberately rooted in the nature of the problem. "A cardinal point," said Peck, "which we probably will emphasize over and over again is the unified character of this mobilization—its non-exclusionary outlook, its effort to involve and to include all those—each and every one— who are in any way, for whatever reasons, opposed to this war."

It now seemed clear, said Peck, that it would not be possible to mount a major mass mobilization by the time of the November elections, but that certain groundwork could be laid for unified activity in that period upon which a major effort later could be built.

He outlined certain immediate objectives: First, to take the initiative, instead of waiting to respond to administration attacks or dramatic escalations in the war. Second,

We are going to show the American people, and the world, that regardless of the profound and real difficulties of an ideological, political, and other sort that separate us and divide us, and that reflect genuine differences in the constituencies we represent—that nevertheless we have come to a realization we can no longer allow these difficulties to loom as obstacles in the *development of a unified effort.*

Third,

to make sure that, in every way, the issue of this war remains a basic fundamental issue in the election period itself; that the administration, politicians, those who want to hide this issue under the rug, are confronted with it.

Fourth, to

inject this question of the war into the electoral scene in a multitude of forms . . . which in fact represent the full spectrum of outlook in the anti-war and peace movement.

Fifth, the development of

---

7. Peck's remarks were stenographically recorded and later reproduced. (Copy in author's files.)

acceptance of the principle of diversity. . . . That is to say, the development of *a mutual respect for differences of approach,* so that all movements in the whole opposition to the war are included irrespective of the particular disagreement over this tactic or that tactic, this activity or that activity, this particular form or that particular form.

Finally, *"to develop a kind of mechanism, a kind of ad hoc means"* for a continuation of this thrust toward unity, *"to provide the essential groundwork and the basis for a mobilization of truly massive proportions in the near future"* (emphasis in original).

All of this was rather abstract, but it touched a responsive chord, for in truth most of those present knew in their bones that the antiwar sentiment was far broader than any of them had been able to tap, and that if only they could all pull together, they might be able to bring it to the surface in spite of the hostility of the administration and the major news media.

As to the specifics of the fall activity, Peck had little to suggest, and left it open for proposals from the different groups. But, he said, "One thing that we can agree on is that no matter what we do in the pre-election period, *let us do it pretty much at the same time.* Let us set aside *a time when we can do it together, however differently may be the activities that we carry on"* (emphasis in original).

On the basis of this fall experience, then, said Peck, in the spring the movement could "mobilize the most massive opposition to the war that has ever been undertaken as yet." He suggested concentrating the spring effort on two centers, New York City and San Francisco.

His stated reason was that New York and San Francisco were, respectively, the seat and the founding place of the United Nations, and that the mobilization should have an international thrust to it, an appeal over the government's head to the people of the world.

We can bring to bear a world leverage, a world responsibility, a truly universal concern that this war must end. . . . It would demonstrate and show to the people of the world that the American people, while they have not been able to express their true sentiments in the form of a change in political decision-making, nevertheless are fully conscious of *their responsibility not to allow this war to be carried on in their name, and not to allow established power to legitimize what it does in the name of the American people.* [Emphasis in original.]

But a technical calculation was also clearly involved. In those days Washington, D.C.—where the government was the biggest employer and where the atmosphere was heavily dominated by administration policy regarding the war—was still not a good place for a large local turnout for antiwar activities. From the point of view of maximum involvement of local people New York and San Francisco were the best cities. In addition, the previous marches on Washington had attracted only token numbers from the West Coast because of the transportation costs. Having a concentrated mobilization on each coast would maximize the overall turnout. "The assumption would be," said Peck, "that at least half a million people could be mobilized for such an effort in the New York area where you could draw from the whole Eastern seaboard."

During a long discussion some thirty specific proposals for fall activities were made which ranged from lobbying congressmen to a general strike the day before the election. Many of these were considered unrealistic by most of the people present, and there was little agreement on the others.

It was finally decided simply to call for four days of activity preceding the elections: November 5 through 8, around the themes, for peace in Vietnam, for economic justice, and for human rights.

A steering committee composed of those members of the Inter-University group's executive committee who were present, Muste, and a few others he appointed from the chair, met and made an effort to draw up a proposal for an organizational structure and a mandate as to what action this structure should call.

It was presented to the larger body by Sid Lens and modified by him on the spot. Lens had a habit of doing this, though there was never any malice involved. Ideas jumped from the top of his mind, and he had an obsession for trying to get peace groups to work together on new projects. It was almost part of his character. At times these traits led him to propose the fuzziest compromises on the flimsiest bases, and this was a source of irritation to those who worked with him, including me. A saving grace is that Lens was not stubborn about it. If his idea didn't sell, or was changed, he didn't seem to be threatened or to take it personally. What is more, there were moments when no one else would give it a try and when the objective situation so strongly dictated a unified effort that almost any try was better than none. So it was on this occasion.

As presented by Lens, the proposal was as follows: On the authority of the conference a call would be issued for four days of "noncompliance" with the war, November 5 through 8, just before the elections. The themes would be opposition to the Vietnam War, for human rights, and for economic justice. Local groups would be completely autonomous in deciding tactics and program for the days. In each area, local groups would be urged to join together to plan the four days of activities. The conference would set up a letterhead committee including a representative group of those present plus additional prominent people who would be asked to serve. In addition a smaller administrative committee would be formed. The chairman, A. J. Muste, would act as liaison with the press.

The committee would be ad hoc and temporary.[8] The last point was necessary so people would not feel obligated to some ongoing organization which might compete with or replace their own. This was a matter of some sensitivity to Frank Emspak and the NCC.

After considerable additional discussion it was decided that the newly formed group, to be called the November 5-8 Mobilization Committee, would not recommend particular activities for the four days of mobilization, but simply send out a list of the suggestions made at the conference plus others submitted to it later, which local groups would use or not as they saw fit. The formation of the administrative committee was left up to Muste, who was also authorized to add people to the letterhead as new constituencies became involved.

In truth the decisions of the conference except for the date of the mobilization were vague, the unity flimsy. In effect, the implementation rested on Muste, on his great personal authority, and on the confidence that most of the people present had in him as a fair arbiter. No one else could have carried it off.

There remained one knotty problem. Frank Emspak objected to any implication that the NCC was being bypassed, and he insisted that it be assigned some special role in the new formation, possibly that the office be located in Madison. The reaction to that suggestion need not be described. In some painful negotiations it was finally decided that the November 5-8 Mobilization Committee would have three officers: Muste as chairman,

8. "Proceedings, National Leadership Conference, Cleveland, September 10-11, 1966." (Copy in author's files.)

Patricia Griffith of the Inter-University Committee for Debate on Foreign Policy as administrative secretary, and Frank Emspak as field secretary. It would have two offices, one in Ithaca under Pat Griffith and the other in New York under Muste. Emspak would travel, organizing in the field.

It was agreed that the committee would call another conference after the elections to evaluate the results of the fall experience "and to consider future action." The logic of all this was that the conference had begun to implement Peck's proposal pointing toward a much larger mobilization in the spring.

In his original presentation Peck had suggested the possibility of one action being a strike in which people might call their workplaces saying they were "sick of the war" and weren't coming to work that day. The strike idea had been set aside as far beyond the capacity of this group to organize, but Peck continued to suggest using the phrase "sick of the war."

In a meeting held in Muste's office a few days after the conference, a follow-up meeting of about twenty persons came to an impasse on writing the call. The problem was how to get in a variety of issues as they related to the war. It was finally agreed that, as decided by the conference, the document would be "A Call for a Mobilization November 5 through 8 for Peace in Vietnam, for Economic Justice and for Human Rights." But this would be preceded by a section headlined "Sick of the War in Vietnam?" followed by a number of reasons such as: "because: The U.S. has intervened in a civil war of the Vietnamese nation and has transformed it into an American war on mainland Asia"; and "it diverts billions of dollars away from efforts that should be made to create economic justice for all of our people."[9]

The call contained no mention of negotiations, and did not contradict immediate withdrawal, but it didn't spell it out either. In my opinion this was another reason for the "Sick of the War" format. Peck was anxious to avoid a fight. In any case most of those in favor of the withdrawal demand thought there was no chance to have the November 5-8 Committee adopt it without blowing the fragile unity apart, so we didn't press it to a vote. In this situation there was no question of the withdrawal wing being buried without a national voice. The main thing was a call for unity in action against the war. Different groups could express their own ideas on how to end it.

9. Copy of the call in author's files.

So the call went out bearing "Sick of the War in Vietnam?" across the top. Like a lot of other things about the November 5-8 Mobilization Committee, it wasn't exactly inspiring, but it was better than nothing.

The signers of the call did, however, represent a significantly broader spectrum than had sponsored any previous national antiwar activity. All were listed as individuals, without organizational identification. They included Mrs. Coretta (Martin Luther) King, Jr., who was listed that way, and Rev. Richard Fernandez of Clergy Concerned, who acted as the mobilization committee's treasurer. No one from national SANE was listed though Paul Olynyk from Cleveland SANE was.

The list also reflected stirrings within the Catholic milieu in the United States and included the Reverend Philip Berrigan and Edward Keating, the San Francisco lawyer who had founded *Ramparts* in 1962 as a liberal Catholic lay magazine and in 1966 was still its publisher.

The follow-up meeting in New York put Emspak on full-time staff, though he had not ingratiated himself in the Parade Committee office with some remarkably insensitive cracks about Muste's advanced age behind the old man's back. The question of what tasks the field secretary would undertake was left to discussions between Muste and Emspak. In the meantime the *Bring the Troops Home Now Newsletter* had volunteered two traveling organizers, Peter Buch, the *Newsletter*'s coeditor, and Robin Maisel of the Philadelphia Area CEWV.

After a private meeting between Muste and Emspak, the latter emerged with the assignment of touring the "Northwestern and Southwestern area of the country." Buch got the Midwest and the South and Maisel got the Eastern seaboard. Actually the West Coast was left to fend for itself. In these tours Emspak covered a total of five cities: Denver, Boulder, Phoenix, Tucson, and Albuquerque, all in the mountain and desert West. Buch covered eighteen cities and Maisel fourteen, both in the much more heavily populated Eastern half of the country.

It was the only time I ever saw Muste pull a maneuver like that. Or perhaps Emspak wanted it that way. In any case, it was Emspak's last fling as a national antiwar leader.

Ordinarily in a year like 1966, when there were elections for Congress but not for president, the president of the United States would make frequent public appearances in the weeks before the election, the purpose being to campaign on behalf of his party's congressional candidates who needed an extra boost. This time, however, the congressional candidates were less than enthusiastic about this tradition. The reason was Johnson's identification with the escalating war. (The number of U.S. troops in Vietnam reached 340,000 by November 1966.)[10]

The pattern was already well established that virtually any preannounced public appearance by Lyndon B. Johnson would be the occasion for an antiwar demonstration. Most Democratic Party candidates were not denouncing the war, they were just trying to avoid the issue. The Republicans, while no more opposed, were not above trying to put the onus on the Democrats.

So the administration strategists cooked up a different plan. In October, Johnson made a seventeen-day tour of the Far East which captured headlines in the preelection period and featured a conference in Manila with representatives of other governments involved on the U.S. side in the Vietnam War, including the Saigon regime, South Korea, Australia, New Zealand, and the Philippines. The Manila conference was supposed to produce a new "peace offer" and the whole trip was aptly characterized in the U.S. press as a "barnstorming" tour designed to show how popular the president and his Vietnam policies were in the "free" Far East.

The large entourage of White House correspondents that accompanied the president's party generally did their best to report "huge and enthusiastic" crowds greeting Johnson. But in Wellington, New Zealand, demonstrators appeared in the crowds carrying signs such as "Lyndon B. God" and "Lyndon B. Johnwater," a play on Goldwater, the hawk against whom Johnson had run as a peace candidate in 1964.[11]

In Canberra, Australia, 3,000 pickets waited in vain for Johnson's appearance at the Rex Hotel, which was canceled at the last minute. According to the *New York Post* the crowd was "drinking beer and singing songs and exchanging good-natured banter with the cops and asking the milling reporters what the hell had happened to the bloody cowboy." Their slogans included: "None

10. Thomas Powers, *The War at Home* (New York: Grossman, 1973), p. 132.
11. *World Outlook* (later *Intercontinental Press*), October 28, 1966.

of the Way with LBJ" and "We're Not Cattle and This Is Not Your Ranch."[12]

In Melbourne, October 21, Johnson's special limousine was stopped as it drove past two blocks of demonstrators, and doused with red and green paint which also covered three Secret Service men. The Aussies were sporting about it though. The paint was water-based and washed off much more easily than the affront to the president's policies.

In Sydney on October 22, Johnson's motorcade was rerouted because of the massive antiwar demonstrations along the preannounced route.

William Askin, the Premier of New South Wales [according to an October 23, 1966, dispatch from Sydney printed on a back page of the *New York Times*], said here tonight that the over-anxiety of American security men had ruined President Johnson's visit to Sydney yesterday. . . . Although Mr. Johnson had wanted to get out of his car to talk with people even at points where the demonstrations were most violent, his security men had persuaded him not to do so and had speeded the motorcade and altered its route.

The Premier also said that Mr. Johnson had left a reception given him at the Sydney Art Gallery earlier than planned, at the insistence of his security men who were worried by clamorous demonstrations outside the building against the President and U.S. policy in Vietnam.

CBS-TV reported to the American audience that the pickets and their slogans were so familiar to the newsmen accompanying the president that they seemed to be "Made in America."

In Manila, Johnson was haunted by the most American slogan of all. Reuters reported October 24:

Bloody fighting broke out tonight on the steps of the Hotel Manila where President Johnson and other leaders . . . are staying. Helmeted armed police and troops swinging rifle butts charged 3,000 anti-American student demonstrators who retaliated with stones and other missiles.

A roaring chant of "Hey, Hey, LBJ, How Many Kids Did You Kill Today" changed to screams of panic and anger as police clubs and army rifle butts slammed into the banner-waving students.[13]

From Manila, Johnson made a previously unannounced stop at Camranh Bay in South Vietnam. As part of the precautions,

12. Ibid.
13. *Militant,* October 31, 1966.

Vietnamese were kept off base during the visit, and as part of the show, troops "were ordered in from the field, with full packs, because their presence would make better photographs."[14] Otherwise there would have been no combat troops in the area the president visited, which was in the middle of the most secure U.S. base in Vietnam.

It was here, in a speech at an officers' club, that Johnson let slip a remark that belied the highly touted peace-seeking mission of his tour. Said Johnson: "I thank you, I salute you, may the Good Lord look over you and keep you until you come home with the coonskin on the wall."[15] That's as clear a statement for uncompromising military victory as can be made in the American vernacular. Back home, the advocates of negotiations were duly flustered.

The finishing touch was put on Johnson's tour by the Malaysian Security Police, who opened fire on an antiwar demonstration of 500 in Kuala Lumpur and killed a twenty-one-year-old demonstrator, Ong Chong. Johnson was guarded by 4,000 policemen and an undisclosed number of troops while in Malaysia. Hundreds of radical and student leaders had been arrested throughout the country just before his arrival. Nevertheless demonstrations took place in at least three Malaysian cities.

In Manila, while Johnson, under the name of seeking peace, was selling the next escalation to his allies at the conference, one of the American reporters accompanying the tour, Pete Hamill, went around the city getting reactions to the president's visit.

In four hours of prowling around Manila last night [he wrote], I could not locate a single person who thought this carnival will accomplish anything. . . . It might be the final judgment of the historians that Lyndon Johnson was the man who finally broke down a country's capacity to believe anything. There isn't much left of words like freedom, liberty and compassion when they are debased so viciously as they are being debased here.[16]

Hamill's reports of the trip were not typical of the general run of stories which emanated from the president's entourage. Never-

14. *New York Post*, October 26, 1966.
15. A. Hugh Sidey, *A Very Personal Presidency* (New York: Atheneum, 1968), p. 150.
16. *New York Post*, October 24, 1966.

theless the feel of this circuslike-tour-turned-sour did get over to much of the American public. Johnson's highly touted Far East trip tended to have exactly the opposite effect domestically of what its organizers had planned. In addition, the Far East demonstrations—particularly those in Australia, which got the widest coverage in the United States—were a much needed boost to the morale of the American antiwar movement.

\*        \*        \*

The November 5-8 activities were fairly widespread—including some areas not previously involved—but with a few exceptions quite diffuse. In many places they did not involve street demonstrations at all, but a variety of other activities like teach-ins, indoor meetings, fund-raising affairs, leafletting of everything from army bases to polling places, confrontations with candidates, and door-to-door canvassing. The November 5-8 Committee did not endorse candidates, but it did consider electoral activity as part of the mobilization. In some cases this meant including antiwar material along with boosting of candidates supported by a particular participating group. In others it involved passing out leaflets at the polls asking voters not to vote for candidates who favored the war; in others encouraging candidates to endorse or participate in various antiwar activities.

Where street demonstrations did occur, they were generally of modest size. In a few places, however, they were larger than ever before. In Cleveland, for example, in spite of a cold rain, 1,200 people marched behind Dr. Spock, Lincoln Lynch, Marshall Windmiller, Reverend Gregg Taylor, and Darwin Johnson, brother of one of the Fort Hood Three.

In Detroit, actions were carried out in the face of threatened violence by an ultraright group called Breakthrough, which had made previous physical attacks on antiwar demonstrators, and which apparently operated with a certain immunity from the police. Before the November 5-8 events, Donald Lobsinger, a leader of Breakthrough, sent a message to the Detroit Common Council threatening "bloodshed" if "inflammatory" signs were displayed by the antiwar people. Nevertheless a thousand antiwar demonstrators marched on November 5 in an unseasonable snowstorm. The march was led by a group of Blacks from the Afro-American Unity Movement and a contingent of Veterans

Against the War. Breakthrough heckled, but did not attack, and the four days of activities were peaceful.

Also in the Detroit area, an old-time trade unionist, John W. Anderson, initiated one of the most interesting developments to emerge from the November 1966 elections.

The elections themselves, which took place November 9, were generally considered a defeat for the Democrats, who lost forty-seven seats in the House, far more than previous off-year losses for the party controlling the presidency, and exactly the same as the number gained in the Democratic sweep in 1964. No doubt the stigma of the war had much to do with this, but the results were open to various interpretations, since congressional elections always involve many issues, and such things as local patronage can be more decisive in particular cases than policy matters. In any case, obscuring, burying, and dodging issues—particularly in regard to foreign policy—was such a high art in the American two-party system that in many ways elections were virtually meaningless in that respect.

In only one small city in the entire country did the voters have a chance for a clear vote on the war. That was Dearborn, Michigan, a suburb of Detroit and home of the giant Ford River Rouge plant. Johnny Anderson lived there. He was a retired auto worker and former president of Fleetwood Local 15 of the United Auto Workers union. He succeeded in getting the backing of Dearborn Mayor Orville Hubbard and the city administration to have a referendum on the war included in the November ballot.

I had met Anderson in Detroit in 1954 when I worked in an auto plant there. He was a veteran left socialist, a builder of the union in its heroic days, who had never abandoned the ideals of his youth, though he had grown a little tired and frustrated by then. The 1950s were not an easy time for such as he. But in the mid-1960s he recaptured a bit of his youth and at one point was chairman of the Detroit area antiwar coalition. In 1951—in the teeth of the witch-hunt—Johnny Anderson had stood up in the national UAW convention to oppose a resolution backing Harry S Truman's undeclared war in Korea. Anderson called for the withdrawal of U.S. troops, but only a handful of the delegates dared to vote with him.

Fifteen years later he wrote the Dearborn referendum on Vietnam. It asked:

"Are you in favor of an immediate cease-fire and withdrawal of

U.S. troops from Vietnam so the Vietnamese people can settle
their own affairs?"[17]

The Dearborn vote was 20,667 against and 14,124 in favor. Just
over 40 percent had rejected the war policy of both major political
parties and voted for immediate withdrawal. And Dearborn was
no Berkeley. It was an all-white, largely middle-income, working
class, Midwest suburb, with nary a hippie in sight. The results
were an important straw in the wind.

*    *    *

In New York the Parade Committee kicked off the mobilization
with a demonstration of 20,000 converging from feeder marches
to a rally in the streets at Sixth Avenue between Fortieth and
Forty-second streets. Candidates for public office had been
invited to appear and be introduced to the crowd, but none of the
Democrats or Republicans came, only independents and socialists. Those introduced were Herbert Aptheker, Leslie Silberman,
and James Weinstein, all running for Congress, and Judy White,
Socialist Workers Party candidate for governor.

Tables were set up where the crowd got bundles of leaflets for
later distribution. These included special leaflets aimed at GIs
and others warning of a postelection escalation in the war.

Speakers included Ruth Turner of CORE; Hospital Workers
Union Local 1199 President Leon Davis; Sue Eanet, the New
York coordinator of SDS; David Mitchell, the first "illegal" draft
card burner, who had been convicted of resisting the draft but
who was still out on bail (he later went to prison); Edward
Keating, publisher of *Ramparts*; and Allen Ginsberg, the poet.

The speech by Ginsberg still sticks in my mind. Essentially, it
went something like this: This war is evil. We don't want it. We
can get rid of it within ourselves. I declare the war ended. The
war is over. It does not exist. Live in peace.

Ginsberg was such a mystic I wasn't really sure whether he
meant that literally or not. But it wasn't delivered as a poem, and
it made me angry at the time because what we all needed in those
days was some inspiration to hold on and reach out, not advice
on how to put the problem out of mind. There was already too
much of that in a variety of forms.

17. *Bring the Troops Home Now Newsletter,* November 23, 1966.

In general the November 5-8 mobilization did not have the impact the International Days of Protest did. But it did have an effect in preventing the issue of the war from being buried during the elections, which is what most of the candidates were trying to do. The election period had weakened the antiwar movement, but not destroyed it. Organizationally perhaps the most important effect of this mobilization was that in many areas groups which had not worked together previously did meet in response to the call, plan some sort of cooperative activity, and agree to meet again. That had been the first part of Sidney Peck's proposal and in a modest way it worked.

Following the fall actions Emspak, Buch, and Maisel wrote brief reports on their tours which were distributed at the evaluation conference. But Maisel wrote an additional report which he sent to me containing some opinions he apparently did not want to present as a spokesperson for the rather delicate coalition. It didn't contradict his other report, but it was less diplomatic, more critical, opinionated, and therefore more revealing of the real state of affairs in the student movement. Said Maisel:

> The general attitude on the campus seems to be heavily loaded with pessimism and a trend towards multi-issue or at least multiple issueism. There is also a wave of anti-demonstration fever running around. I can't tell if this is recent or just one of the periodic dips in the anti-war movement. The fight over withdrawal openly appears to be over but as multi-issueism creeps in there is a tendency to compromise on this point so as to get the "broadest" group together.
>
> On a number of campuses the anti-war committees, after being single-issue organizations for a bit more than a year, have affiliated in one way or another with SDS. The only justification for it is that SDS will provide them with literature, speakers, and a name which is known nationally so that the organization can use it to attract new people. It is not the program of SDS which attracts these kids, for they are going out and writing their own ticket, without regard for what SDS is doing nationally. . . . What seems to be looked for here is a nationally organized group which is so broad that there will be no interference and no absolute responsibilities to it. The SDS affiliations are also a sign of the single-issue vs. multi-issue confusion.
>
> The pessimism manifests itself in the following argument: "We can't end this war. Perhaps we can end the war 10 wars from now. So let's organize for that and prepare." This leads to multi-issueism. This is not entirely unhealthy or wrong. . . . Their confusion stems from their desire to involve the "people" and at the same time attempting to do so by petit-bourgeois programmatical and organizational methods, rejecting the

power of the American working class as hopelessly stymied by the bureaucracy, rejecting the soldiers as utopian (and incidentally confusion over the Ft. Hood Three as just another 3 guys who refused to go and not seeing the significance of the fact that they are *in* the army and the effect such actions can have upon the army). Therefore I found . . . a multi-issue approach rampant. I don't know what effect the elections will have, but there are already signs that a good number of these people are looking to Bobby Kennedy as their savior in '68.[18]

Maisel had made the entire tour driving an old car and sleeping on couches. Yet, when I had seen him a time or two in the course of it he looked as if he'd just stepped out from behind a desk in a bank. He had one of those small, neat bodies that seem to go together with efficient personalities, and was sometimes slightly disturbing to those of us not so inclined. On the organization of November 5-8 his remarks were blunt:

A note on organization. The last set of demonstrations [November 5-8] was very very poorly organized. The publicity was too "busy" and very poor. The next set should really go to town on the printing job including posters, simple calls with plenty of white space for local groups to fill in their own bit of information. In general the chaos of the last set of demos must be eliminated to be really successful for the future. A single national office, rather than two or three or more must be established. A clear chain of command is necessary. Some full-time staffers are needed, not that the last set was poor, but Griffith, Muste et al. are involved in so many things that they cannot and will not put in full time. The Ithaca office has nine (9) organizations running out of it. Griffith is the staffer for almost all of them. . . .

The distribution of antiwar paraphernalia must be better organized and things like "sick of the war" buttons dropped. They were universally despised everywhere I went. Bring the Troops Home Now buttons were much preferred. In addition such slogans as "sick of the war" are very demoralizing and only serve to aid the anti-demonstration fever and the multi-issue approach without providing a slogan or an issue to organize around. It doesn't say a thing to anyone outside of the anti-war movement, is misunderstood by students, and again organizationally, the color and quality looked shoddy.

The last point, except perhaps for the technical aspect of the criticism, was of course at variance with the views of such figures

18. "Report on East Coast antiwar tour" by Robin Maisel, undated. (Copy in author's files.)

as Sid Peck, who had made it clear when he motivated his proposal that he favored a multi-issue approach.

In summary Maisel said:

Because of the lack of success of the anti-war movement in ending the war with a demonstration or two the weakest forces have taken to defeatism, pot smoking, LSD and the like. A lot, surprising numbers in fact, of the anti-war people of the last two years have dropped out of activity and are actually trying to hold back those who do want to go forward and build.

Now that this doleful note has been inserted it would be well to indicate that I think there is a tremendous untapped potential on the campuses among freshmen and sophomores who just need some simple action to get them in motion, such as a national march on D.C. This is easy to organize for them, by comparison with the IDPs [International Days of Protest], and they would come out of the woodwork.

In his report to the committee, Maisel put it this way:

There is a tremendous potential yet to be tapped by the anti-war movement. The "anti-demonstration fever" that I encountered is, I believe, a temporary condition which will occur cyclically for a while to come. We have seen, however, that large national actions tend to break people out of the doldrums and give the movement a shot in the arm by enlarging our base, adding new forces and new ideas. Large visible manifestations have the effect of not only encouraging new people to join the anti-war movement, but also of showing that the anti-war movement is growing. The fact is the anti-war movement is larger than ever, not smaller, and a massive display will prove it to the rest of the country.[19]

With this point Peck was not in basic disagreement. For his part, he entered the evaluation conference prepared to press for the second part of his original proposal—which he mimeographed for distribution to the delegates—that is, a mass mobilization in New York and San Francisco in the spring.

The invitation to the conference was sent out from Ithaca by Robert Greenblatt, who was sensitive to the mood of the campus milieu, and it contained language that implied a somewhat different approach. This presaged the main tension at the conference.

19. Field Reports, undated. (Copy in author's files.)

Over and over again [wrote Greenblatt], our experience indicates a disenchantment with symbolic mass "protest action" (e.g. marches, rallies, etc.) and a greater readiness for building solid political foundations. While the number of people willing to "march" is on the decline, more people are ready to go into the community to do leafleting, door-to-door canvassing and similar actions limited only by the ingenuity of the leadership. . . .

The mobilization can be termed a success if only on the grounds that it made us aware of this new mood in the peace movement. But the partial successes created an even greater responsibility; the responsibility of responding to the need for community organization.[20]

Of course nobody was opposed to community organizing. But the term had different meanings, and as used by SDS in those days it was specifically counterposed to antiwar activity as such, especially to mass demonstrations. The SDS national office considered these a waste of time, or worse, a diversion which drew energies away from their concept of community organizing, which was none too clear itself. This in spite of the fact that local SDS chapters often found their most successful activities to be antiwar demonstrations around such things as the appearance on campus of a Johnson administration official, or a military recruiter, or an instance of university complicity with the war.

To many liberals, community organizing meant pushing doorbells for Democratic Party politicians, or between elections building a local reform Democratic Party base in preparation for the next election. In spite of their voting habits this was anathema to most radicals outside the CP milieu, and even there it was not attractive when the elections were far away. In SDS, community organizing in its positive sense meant building a radical base (the adjective "revolutionary" was also increasingly being used now that the new guard had taken over from the old). But that was an abstraction. When it came to putting it into practice the experiments were rarely inspiring, and often sifted down to a handful of SDSers sitting in a room escalating their rhetoric.

To the SWP and the YSA, community work meant building the *socialist* movement in as many places as possible and participating in whatever living struggles they could on a local level, including union, civil rights, civil liberties, antiwar, and other

20. Letter to "Dear Friend" from Robert Greenblatt for the November 5-8 Mobilization Committee, undated. (Copy in author's files.)

activities. There was nothing new or glamorous about it for them. It was vital, but generally painstaking, tedious work, and certainly no panacea.

Except for election periods, and with a different political thrust, the CP's activities were similar. The Du Bois Clubs, however, while their ideology was close to that of the CP, were not nearly so homogeneous or so tightly organized. They tended to see themselves in direct competition with SDS for influence in the same milieu and just at this time had a strong tendency to adapt in the same direction as SDS, though with a somewhat more defined program.

All of this would be reflected in the dispute at the third Cleveland conference. And something more. The pacifists also were divided into liberals and radicals and would tend to adapt to the moods of those wings. But a stabilizing factor for the pacifists—at least those involved in the antiwar movement—was the simple fact that they could not in any case ignore the war. Opposition to war was supposed to be what they were all about. This simple fact was not really so simple at all. It was one of the striking features of the American movement against the Vietnam War, and it had not been so in previous wars, with a few exceptions like A. J. Muste and Dellinger.

James P. Cannon had commented on this in 1965 in a speech to the Los Angeles SWP branch:

The classic pacifism we know, which Lenin denounced as worse than useless, was a pacifism that denounced war until it started and then rallied around the flag. I don't know whether many of you present here have seen that characteristic of the old pacifism, as I recall it, especially from the First World War. At that time there was a tremendous movement of opposition to America's entry into the war. So strong was the popular sentiment that Woodrow Wilson was reelected to the presidency primarily on the slogan "He kept us out of war."

Many public speakers, politicians and, of course, preachers, spoke against entry into the war. I can't forget the effect it had upon us militants. We thought we had the population with us in our opposition— until the declaration of war. Then everything went out of the movement and the loudest pacifists became the loudest patriots, right away. They said you don't fight the government when it is at war. So the pacifists had simply led the people up to the expectation of opposition and then led them down immediately.

We have a sort of pacifism today that is still operative after the shooting has started. We have an active war in Vietnam, rapidly escalating since last February when they began bombing right and left, but there is still a considerable segment of the pacifist movement that does not cease to protest. That's new.[21]

What accounted for this phenomenon could be the subject for another book. No doubt it includes such factors as the lurking danger of nuclear war, but in any case it reflected and contributed to a sense of human urgency which underlay the entire third Cleveland conference and without which the meeting could not have succeeded and probably would have torn itself apart.

The conference itself took place November 26, once again in the Baker building at Western Reserve University. It was not much larger than the previous one, 180 participants this time, with about 150 of them registered from some seventy local and national groups. There were more youth this time and fewer older people. One reason for this was touched upon in a letter to Sidney Peck from Peter Weiss, a New York attorney involved in reform Democratic Party politics and husband of prominent Women's Strike for Peace activist Cora Weiss. "I mean, after all," wrote Peter Weiss, "don't you think two weekends in Cleveland are enough for a New Yorker to contribute to the provinces in one year? In other words, I cannot possibly be there this weekend."[22]

The letter indicated, however, that both Peter and Cora Weiss were not unsupportive of the Cleveland effort, and was an example of the fact that Peck and others were in touch with a number of representative personalities who, while not present at the Cleveland conference, could be expected to cooperate if they considered the result to be constructive.

The meeting was addressed by Dr. Spock, at the urging of Sid Peck. Spock was cochairman of national SANE. He made no commitments on SANE's behalf and did not participate in the deliberations, but his speech was friendly and designed to encourage the effort. His very appearance was a boost to morale and lent authority to the conference among those of its more hesitant participants.

Dave Dellinger, who had not been a part of the November 5-8 Committee because of an extended trip to Asia, gave an eyewit-

21. "Revolutionary Policies in the Antiwar Movement," by James P. Cannon in *Revolutionary Strategy in the Fight Against the Vietnam War* (New York: Education for Socialists Bulletin, 1975), p. 13.

22. Letter from Peter Weiss to Dr. Sidney Peck, undated. (Copy in author's files.)

ness report on the situation in Vietnam. He had stopped briefly in Saigon and later spent three weeks in North Vietnam, where he saw the effects of the U.S. bombers.

At that time the Johnson administration was demanding a quid pro quo from North Vietnam before considering any deescalation of the war. Dellinger commented: "If we stop sending our bombers over their country, they will stop shooting at them."

He said there was no mood in Hanoi or the NLF to conciliate with the U.S. Their terms for settlement were simple, said Dellinger: recognition of Vietnamese independence and withdrawal of U.S. forces. He also described the civilian areas he had personally seen which were destroyed by U.S. bombs. It was a moving report and increased the sense of urgency.[23]

Pat Griffith reported on the November 5-8 demonstrations and these were evaluated in discussion. Here the differences appeared. Some people thought the lesson to be drawn was more community organizing and less demonstrations. Others thought there was no contradiction.

Then came the discussion about future action, and here there were many attempts to reconcile the differences, assorted suggestions for how the mobilization committee could assist, or provide leadership, in community organizing. In my view these were not very realistic. The different forces involved had different multi-issue approaches to community work. A concentrated mobilization would help us all, regardless of what other things the committee was able to agree to do. In any case if this committee did not call a mobilization, it wouldn't hold together to do anything else anyway.

I made a speech there I was to repeat at many subsequent conferences. The essence was this: "There are only three forces in the United States which have the power to stop this war: the American ruling class which started it, the working class which makes and transports the war materiel, and the GIs who fight it. The first will react only if we reach the other two. Because if we reach the other two and the rulers don't stop the war, it will be more than Vietnam they'll be in danger of losing. So we should use whatever base we've got now to reach out to and involve the unions, the workers, and the GIs. Anything that helps that is

23. Spring Mobilization Committee press release. (Copy in author's files.)

good. Anything that hurts that is bad. A mass mobilization will help."[24]

Peck was for reconciling the two approaches, which meant he favored setting a date for the mobilization in addition to other plans. I found myself supporting his side of the discussion against those opposed to setting any date at all. It had finally come down to this as the meat of the matter.

In essence we were discussing the SDS position for community organizing *as opposed to* mass demonstrations. This was peculiar because SDS itself had boycotted the meeting, or at least had not considered it relevant enough to send a significant number of people. Only Earl Silbar was there from Chicago SDS. The record shows only three others registered from SDS chapters, and two of these were YSAers who belonged to their local SDS chapter because it was *the* antiwar committee on campus. (Paul Booth was there, but he was registered from the National Conference on New Politics and was no longer a part of the SDS national office.)

So how did the argument turn around the SDS view? To explain this anomaly it is necessary to recall that SDS was at this time far and away the largest radical youth group. It was still growing. It was still considered respectable by many moderate groups, and at the same time it had a reputation for antiwar activity that exceeded its deeds.

It was often in the news and like Jesse James was blamed for all sorts of things, only some of which it did. It was, in a sense, a legend in its own time. And like all legends it was in good measure illusion. It was above all a name, and a reputation, synonymous with "new left," which any group of students could adopt for the asking, without the foggiest notion of what the SDS national office was doing, and often caring little.

Among many older liberals and radicals it was also a hope. They looked to it as the beginning of a major new political movement and they filled in its blanks with their own conceptions and identified with it. All this is one part of the reason why the conference debated the SDS position on demonstrations. While SDS wasn't bodily present in the room, it was present in everybody's mind.

The other part of the reason was that the view of the SDS national office just happened at this time to coincide with the current mood on campus—as noted by Maisel and Greenblatt

24. Handwritten notes. (Copy in author's files.)

from different vantage points. That same mood existed off campus as well and was fairly well represented at the conference.

For the YSA it was a mood to be overcome. For Hugh Fowler, national chairman of the Du Bois Clubs, it was a mood to be accommodated to, and he adopted it as his political position. Fowler led the discussion from the side opposed to setting the date.

It was clear the majority present favored setting the date, but the issue could not be settled by mere majority vote. The coalition was too fragile for that to work. If vote there was to be, it had to be overwhelming. An additional problem in this respect was that the attendance at the conference was not really representative of the ideological composition of the movement outside the room. Almost half the registered delegates were members or sympathizers of the YSA. This was neither an accident nor the result of purposeful packing. They were all legitimate representatives of active antiwar groups.

In part this reflected the simple fact that the YSAers took this conference more seriously than members of the other radical youth groups. In part it reflected a change in the relationship of forces within the student antiwar movement. The YSA was beginning to grow rapidly, and its members were far more consistent in antiwar activity than others, so more of them played leading roles in the various local groups.

In that sense the conference *was* representative of the existing state of the active prodemonstration wing of the student antiwar movement which had shrunk to the sectors influenced by the YSA, and not a great deal more. The YSA near-majority was due mainly to an ebb in the student antiwar movement, coupled with the fact that the YSA had resisted the liquidationist mood.[25]

This placed a responsibility on the YSA not to act as if it owned the movement. Because it didn't. It could have jammed through a motion setting a date, or for immediate withdrawal, or for the socialist revolution for that matter. But none of that would have solved the problem of unifying the different ideological forces in calling an action. Only a unified call could begin to reverse the mood.

25. This conference, and one other in Chicago in December 1968, when a snowstorm and another political ebb kept attendance down, were the only national antiwar gatherings where the YSA had such a disproportionate presence.

And that would never happen if the new coalition were locked up from the beginning by one ideological tendency or if the other tendencies even thought that were the case. The major opponents of the spring mobilization had to be convinced or neutralized, not voted down.

So the YSAers simply argued the point, a few of them on the floor, but most of them in the corridors, with anyone who would listen. This created a certain bandwagon atmosphere to be sure, and there were some who resented it, but not those who really favored the action.

In a sense, the people at this conference had the responsibility to act as if they represented the movement not as it was in the room at the moment, but as it would be when the far broader forces waiting to be tapped became involved in the period immediately ahead.

The break in the discussion came from an unexpected source— at least I didn't expect it. Up to this point it wasn't clear how the CP stood. Then Arnold Johnson took the floor. He was the CP's peace activities director, sometimes active on the Parade Committee in New York, and incidentally, an associate of Muste's in the early 1930s. Muste had headed the Conference for Progressive Labor Action then, and Johnson had been one of its more effective young organizers. I don't know if that had anything to do with his stand on this occasion. In any case he made a demonstrative speech in favor of setting the date for a mass mobilization in New York and San Francisco.

Hugh Fowler did not look pleased. But it was downhill for his view from then on. Arnold Johnson's speech was a convincing presentation of the need and the opportunity. There were other speeches along similar lines. The vote was decisively in favor of setting the date for the spring mobilization. If the Du Bois Clubs national office was not enthusiastic, it was at least not about to denounce the result as a "Trot plot."

\*            \*            \*

The conference established the Spring Mobilization Committee to End the War in Vietnam, with Muste as chairman and Dellinger, Greenblatt, Ed Keating of San Francisco, and Sidney Peck as vice-chairmen. The committee consisted of those members of the November 5-8 Committee who wished to serve as well as others to be added as the support broadened. It was charged with "organizing a national action April 15, 1967, in the San Francisco Bay Area and New York City, which shall be international in scope, with the details to be worked out by the Committee at its executive meetings."[26]

The founding document also declared that the committee

shall be charged with suggesting, stimulating, and/or organizing such actions of a more limited and more localized nature as may be feasible, with the aim of broadening the influence of the peace movement as much as possible, as long as these actions clearly fall within the consensus reached by the diverse viewpoints at this conference.

The Spring Mobilization Committee shall also seek to widen the movement into such localities and professional milieux, including but not limited to, labor, literary, military, civil rights, traditional peace groups, religious, electoral, as are not presently organized or which need organizational assistance.

Referred favorably to the executive committee were the following themes for the mobilization: "End the war in Vietnam—Bring our GIs home; Stop the bombing; Abolish the draft; For economic justice and human rights."

The committee was also charged with promoting a silent vigil at Christmas in as many localities as possible.

The location of the central office was referred to the executive committee. The Madison staff of the NCC had proposed Cleveland, but it was clear that New York was the logical choice, since the mobilization would be there, and that another office would have to be set up in the Bay Area for the San Francisco event.

At the end of the conference Otto Nathan, himself an older man much beloved by the many who knew him, took the floor to pay tribute to Muste, and we all gave A. J. a big hand as he looked back at us from the stage with that bit of whimsy on his face.

\*       \*       \*

The second part of Sid Peck's proposal had been adopted. But it now remained to be implemented. Some people who had attended the conference, and a whole lot more who hadn't and who weren't even represented there, remained to be convinced. As part of this

---

26. "Motions Passed (as amended) at Evaluation Conference, Cleveland, November 26, 1966." (Copy in author's files.)

process, shortly after the conference, Peck sent out another document to various people around the country. It concluded:

> It would be good if one could state that the anti-war movement has had a significant impact on the policies of the Johnson Administration. Obviously, this is not the case! Therefore, all that we can do at present is to encourage a mood of popular opposition to the war and channel that opposition into visible political acts of dissent. That is why the mobilization is viewed as the most appropriate political tactic to advance in the immediate period ahead. It is directly expressive of an over-all strategic concern to end the war, in line with the principle of national self-determination for the Vietnamese people. If the war can be brought to an end on that basis, the American people will have made an important contribution to the cause of world peace. For, in essence, they will be rejecting the whole concept of imperial world rule under U.S. hegemony, known by any other name as Pax Americana.
>
> There is no doubt that this development would constitute a significant political achievement.[27]

No doubt indeed!

27. "Some Reasons for a Massive Mobilization to End the War in Vietnam," undated. Signed by Sidney M. Peck, coordinator, University Circle Teach-In Committee. (Copy in author's files.)

# 9

# The Birth of the
# Student Mobilization Committee

Robin Maisel had a bent toward attention to detail and this
had led him to play a key role in the first successful campaign
against germ warfare research on an American campus. He was
a student at the University of Pennsylvania in Philadelphia, the
oldest university in the country, which Benjamin Franklin had
helped to establish. In the mid-1960s it was heavily dependent on
government research grants for its financing.

In the summer of 1965 Maisel had a part-time job at the
university bookstore. His duties included delivering books ordered
by various departments on campus, including the Institute for
Cooperative Research (ICR) located on the second floor of a
building which served otherwise as a warehouse. His curiosity
was aroused, he said later, by "the rather peculiar setup at the
ICR. . . . There were locks and buzzers and peepholes and ID
badges and all the other rather obvious paraphernalia of a secret
operation, straight out of a class D spy movie. On reflecting on it
today it seems they were downright silly as well as deadly."[1]

Maisel started paying attention to the books he was delivering
to the ICR, which aroused his curiosity further. He looked
through the bookstore's records for the invoices for ICR orders for
the previous six months and copied down the titles. Separately
they were innocent enough, but together they showed that the
ICR had a central interest in rice, epidemic diseases of both
plants and animals, air turbulence, and Vietnam. It didn't take
too much imagination to guess that the ICR was doing research

1. Letter from Robin Maisel to the author, May 25, 1975.

on dropping something nasty on Vietnam.

Maisel attended the Assembly of Unrepresented People in Washington in August 1965 and there announced that the University of Pennsylvania Committee to End the War in Vietnam was onto something big in connection with war research at the university. With assistance from other antiwar activists he collected enough information to be sure that chemical and biological warfare research was being done by the ICR. Maisel wrote a paper detailing the facts for the Philadelphia Area Committee to End the War in Vietnam. In October 1965, when the fall semester was under way and a maximum number of students were on campus, and just ten days before the scheduled International Days of Protest activities, the CEWV sent the information to the president of the university, Gaylord P. Harnwell. Copies of the letter were sent to the United Nations Special Commission on Genocide, the International Red Cross, all the local press, and selected members of the U.S. Senate and House of Representatives.

The exposé created a furor on campus. Dr. Knut Krieger, director of the ICR's operations Spicerack and Summit, then admitted these projects were involved in chemical and biological warfare research for the U.S. military. Krieger saw nothing wrong in this. In its essence his position was backed by Harnwell, who was obviously embarrassed but who claimed his first duty was to assure adequate financing for the university.

At a rally at city hall October 15, which was part of the International Days of Protest, Maisel spoke on the ICR activities. Staughton Lynd was also a speaker and that night he told the story at the fiftieth anniversary dinner of the Women's International League for Peace and Freedom. The antiwar movement was well alerted. The campus and Philadelphia area CEWVs then began a concerted campaign that took over a year—assisted by further exposés in *Viet Report* and *Ramparts*—before the university was finally forced to terminate the projects.

The campaign was not an easy one. Maisel was fired and the CEWV had to repeatedly defend its pickets outside the ICR offices against organized physical attacks. It succeeded in winning the sympathy of most of the student body and faculty at first for its simple right to speak out on the secret project. It used that right in a careful and deliberate campaign during which it refused to be provoked—though a few fists did fly—and kept itself squarely on the side of academic freedom, free speech, and against the degrading manipulation of the university, until the majority of the academic community was won to the protest itself.

A pamphlet published by the Philadelphia Area Committee to End the War in Vietnam early in 1966, before the germ and chemical warfare projects had been forced off campus, declared:

It has been shown that the campus is a good place to look around for ways to expose the Johnson administration on the Vietnam war. The role of the university in military work can be shown successfully and the work done for the war effort can be seriously hampered and delayed by such costly things as having the operation move off campus and deeper underground. Exposure makes it harder for the university to get people to work on the "dirty" projects. The faculty can be reasoned with and discouraged from working on projects that might jeopardize their standing with their colleagues. Only the second-rate brains at the University of Pennsylvania will now be attracted to the ICR. The university community, its teachers, researchers and students, must refuse to permit their knowledge to be used as a tool of the government's new foreign policy. The businessmen, bureaucrats and Pentagon Strangeloves can be forced to go it alone, without the help of the "community of scholars."[2]

Later Maisel commented:

In my opinion the anti-ICR activity was a model of how the antiwar movement could turn public opinion and help to stop the war. We went on a nonstop campaign of publicity, demonstrations, protests, letter writing around the world, etc. We got professors of biology as far away as Australia to write the U. of P. to say they would never set foot on the campus as long as the ICR was there. We hounded them every minute. We had to have fist fights to defend our right to speak out. A small band of dedicated activists became a huge band of dedicated antiwar students who finally put the ICR to rest.[3]

This experience made Robin an unshakable optimist regarding

---

2. *Germ Warfare Research for Vietnam: Project Spicerack on the Pennsylvania Campus* by Joel Aber, Jules Benjamin, and Robin Martin (Philadelphia Area Committee to End the War in Vietnam, 1966), p. 27. Due to an editorial error Robin Maisel was listed as Robin Martin in this pamphlet. His original paper, slightly rewritten, is reproduced in part as section one of the pamphlet. The appendix contains the book list he discovered.

3. Letter from Maisel to author, May 25, 1975.

the ability of the antiwar movement to actually affect the war itself. He never appeared to tire or become discouraged. The Spicerack experience, he said, kept him going. Maisel was a member of the YSA and in the above sense he personified its political line on the perspective of the antiwar movement. This attitude was true of the YSA as an organization, though not of course, of every individual member all the time. But the fact that the YSA was a disciplined organization and, what is more, one in which the line was hammered out in discussions involving the entire membership, settled by majority vote, and acted upon in unison, greatly reinforced the staying power of its members.

The YSA also set for itself quite businesslike norms regarding technical organizational matters and for Maisel this was entirely in character. When decisive action was in the air these qualities were often appreciated by others, but to those whose mood or perspective was otherwise at any given moment, they were a source of irritation. So it was when in early December, 1966, Robin was given the assignment of going to Ithaca to help get out the first issue of the Spring Mobilization Committee's newsletter, the *Mobilizer*.

Following the November conference I drove from Cleveland to Ithaca with Patricia Griffith and Robert Greenblatt to check out the Glad Day Press. This was a printing cooperative that supplied material to teach-ins and was one of the several groups which shared offices—and Pat Griffith's talents—with the Inter-University Committee.

On the way Griffith expressed concern that the Spring Mobilization Committee had no staff as yet, and that she wouldn't be able to devote much time to it, since she had only been on temporary loan from the Inter-University Committee for the November 5-8 activities. She mentioned that Robin Maisel had stopped through Ithaca on his fall tour, had helped put out a big mailing, and she had been impressed by his efficiency. So it was agreed that I would ask Maisel to go to Ithaca.

Douglas Dowd was out of the country when Maisel arrived. By that time Greenblatt and Griffith had apparently had some second thoughts and were hesitant about the Spring Mobilization, or at least about having the Ithaca office used in connection with it. For one thing, Griffith was already overworked. Maisel recalls:

I waited all day at the Glad Day Press for him [Greenblatt], working away like a busy bee, but he never showed. Finally, about midnight, when they were closing up shop, I asked Pat Griffith if she could get someone to put me up for the night. She said no. So I rang the bell of the people who lived upstairs from Glad Day Press, woke them up and asked to sleep on their floor that night. They said I could, so I did, and reflected on the rather cool welcome I had gotten.[4]

The next morning Maisel returned to the office.

During the day they made it perfectly clear I was unwelcome but there was no way they could gracefully get rid of me. They suggested that I could not use the office equipment. . . .They suggested that I go rent my own office. I got a room in a boarding house, got a typewriter on loan from IBM's office in town and called you [Fred Halstead] at the Parade Committee. You said to keep plugging away and that A. J. Muste would look into fixing things up. Meanwhile I prepared the mailing list for the first issue of the *Mobilizer,* which as yet had no material.

By the third day Griffith and Greenblatt were talking to me again and I was eating one meal a day at their expense, for lunch, while they tried to explain to me why there could not be an issue of the *Mobilizer.* I listened and ate and waited until late evening to call you for instructions. As I recall your words, you said to get the *Mobilizer* out at all costs even if it just had pictures. The main problem was to get something out that said volume I, number 1. That would mean no. 2 and no. 3 would follow and eventually we would have the Spring Mobilization.

You sent an article by A. J. up to me which I proceeded to type out in full, justifying the lines, making it look as attractive as possible, while I tried to think of some way to convince Griffith and Greenblatt to go ahead with the *Mobilizer.*

After about a week, Greenblatt and Griffith flew to New York to attend a meeting on the Spring Mobilization at 5 Beekman Street. We discussed the *Mobilizer* there and it was my impression they agreed it should be put out immediately. A few days later Maisel called me and said he was still having difficulty. I told him to "Get that goddamn thing out!"

Finally, recalls Maisel,

I called the guy who ran the printing press about 6:00 in the morning and persuaded him to come right down and run off the *Mobilizer* . . . to the tune of 3,500 copies. He got it done before noon when the crew began to straggle in. [Maisel apparently could not resist this jibe at "new left"

4. Ibid.

office hours.] It had A. J.'s article, an announcement of the Student Strike meeting to take place in Chicago, a thing about Christmas vigils, a return address, and a couple of pictures. But most of all it had volume I, number 1 at the top.

Griffith and Greenblatt were furious; I had to put out the mailing alone, which I proceeded to do.

Maisel borrowed the stamps from one of the committees in the office, took the mailing to the post office, loaded the files of the Mobilization Committee in his car, and drove back to New York.

The next day [he continues], I took the files and stuff down to the Parade Committee loft. We had about 1,500 copies of the *Mobilizer* left over after the mailing (maybe a bit less). I had succeeded in antagonizing virtually everyone in Ithaca with my insistence on getting out the *Mobilizer*. I had become everyone's most unfavorite person, so I think that put the kibosh on any further work in the Spring Mobilization Committee for me.

And so it did, which was the committee's loss.

For my part I had hit it off well with both Griffith and Greenblatt and we enjoyed each other's company, in spite of differences, after as well as before this incident. Not so with Robin Maisel. The incident, however, was really my doing and to some extent Muste's, who was gently prodding me as well as others, though not in the stark terms I had used with Maisel. But Maisel got the blame for being too pushy. In truth he had only been a good soldier. It was one of those little injustices that people sometimes find themselves willy-nilly involved with, and which could have discouraged—or even worse, embittered—a young activist if he had taken it personally. Fortunately, Maisel was not inclined to do so, at least not so it showed. I shouldn't have let Maisel take all the heat, but I still don't think I was wrong to press the matter.

Among other things, what was involved here was an act of *will,* and there are moments when that's what leadership is all about. The Cleveland conferences had laid the groundwork for building the Spring Mobilization, but it was still a hesitant, tentative process. The inertia had to be overcome or the momentum would never develop. I had learned before—and Muste had enough experience with mass movements to know—that in such situations timing is of the essence, and he who hesitates is lost.

The working committee had agreed unanimously not to put out

the formal call to the Spring Mobilization until we had time to broaden the base and secure wide sponsorship. This was wise and necessary, but it also left a certain gap. For a time the only announcement was a press release that the conference had taken place. It emphasized the Christmas vigils, since the time was short for preparing this. It mentioned only in passing that the conference had planned a massive mobilization for the spring and gave no details at all.

Muste's article in the first *Mobilizer*—which also contained the motions adopted at Cleveland—was addressed centrally to this broadening process within the overall peace movement. It was vital that the movement itself—in the narrow sense of the few thousand activists of all varieties who would read the *Mobilizer*—be aware that this process was seriously under way and become involved in it as soon as possible.

In the article Muste said it had been agreed that "pending the issuing of the formal 'Call' for the April 15 Mobilization, there should be a prompt exploration of what forces, individual or collective, might be enlisted in support of this mobilization."[5] He analyzed what these various forces might be, and which could be realistically expected to be involved in the immediate future.

He then addressed an appeal to the most moderate elements critical of the war, as follows:

It seems to me that the question whether we should continue to do what we are doing to the Vietnamese people and thereby to ourselves—not to say escalate—is not something that is tolerable or debatable or negotiable. You seem essentially to agree. If so, what follows? A murder is being perpetrated on the public highway, on our own doorstep, as it were, in our name. Then, the time to stop it, to refrain at least from anything which somehow eases things for the murder, is NOW. If the several hundred thousand leading Americans who probably hold some such position as this would make that public and act upon it, a salutary change in American life would take place. It would mean the breaking of a spell, a new day for mankind. What are we waiting for?

Turning to the more radical elements, of which the Cleveland conference was more representative, he said:

5. *Mobilizer,* vol. I, no. 1, December 19, 1966. Published by the Spring Mobilization Committee to End the War in Vietnam. (Copy in author's files.)

Naturally, there were vigorous exchanges on the floor of the Conference between those who, to put it crudely, pleaded that the anti-war movement needed and could mount the greatest demonstration ever of Americans against the abomination being perpetrated in Vietnam by the government of this country, and those on the other hand who questioned this approach and emphasized the need of work on the local level, geared to the problems of people and thus developing a truly democratic "power base for radical action." My impression is that during the Conference itself and at the meeting of the provisional Working Committee the next day the participants agreed that, properly dealt with, these two approaches were not antithetical but go together. . . .

My own very strong conviction is that all the anti-war radical forces in this country should and must *concentrate* attention and efforts as the new year begins, rally forces, and that a Spring Mobilization is relevant, and indeed imperative in this context. There is—let us not lose sight of it for a moment—the elementary fact that atrocious murder is being perpetrated every day, every hour, in Vietnam.

The feeling of let-down, of hopelessness, which overcomes some at times because the Johnson war-machine grinds on is in the final analysis something to be ashamed of. Johnson and the war-machine are things to be faced, to stand up to, not to stand in awe of or cringe before. Our task is to disarm them, not to be morally and politically disarmed by them. Did we really think the job would be easy and to be attained at a modest price?

Muste finished his article with a reiteration of the Mobilization's stand on nonexclusion in which he touched on one of the profound political processes that the new antiwar movement had impelled:

We adhere to the policy of "non-exclusion," first and most of all, because it is right in principle, necessary to the political health of the nation. People of the Left (Communists with or without quotation marks) should be permitted and expected to function normally in the political life of the country.

The concept that Communist nations are *ipso facto* enemies, which expresses itself as we have already pointed out, in the strategy of supporting by arms any government provided it is anti-Communist, and the deep-rooted anti-Communist psychology in the American people— these are the factors that in the final analysis back the war in Vietnam and support the American military establishment. I do not think we can effectively combat these evils while at the same time practicing an exclusion or containment policy within the antiwar movement itself.

In practice a non-Communist coalition is in danger of becoming an anti-Communist one, though it may desire to avoid that. In any event, its program will in the long run tend to be moderate and its resistance to the war restrained in policy. It will tend to seek allies to its right. If by any chance its resistance to the war policy should be stiffened and become radical then it will find itself classified with the Left, the "enemy," anyway and in its actual withdrawal of support from the Administration and from the war actually will be in that revolutionary and noble position.

Muste's concluding words—in light of all that followed later their wisdom is more striking than appeared when I first read them—were as follows:

To maintain a radical anti-war coalition is a difficult and delicate task. It is not, be it noted, an attempt to merge parties or to build a political coalition but a cooperative effort of individuals covering a wide spread of opinion. It demands a high sense of responsibility on everyone's part. Nor does it require slurring over differences and avoiding genuine dialogue, but rather, in a notable phrase of Buber's, "bearing these differences in common."

What no doubt clinches the matter is that if we were to abandon the "non-exclusion" principle we would quickly disintegrate. Our advocacy and practice of it has obviously not, as some prophesied would happen, put an end to popular discontent with the war or other forms of opposition and criticism. "Non-exclusion" is, therefore, something to be proud of and to nail to the masthead of the Spring Mobilization, confident that an increasing number of Americans will come to understand its correctness and its potentialities.

The Mobilization, then, would start where it was, consolidate its own immediate potential base on the principles that had brought it this far, and reach out from there. One of the most important parts of this base was the student antiwar movement. As of the date of the first *Mobilizer,* December 19, 1966, it was largely in a state of disarray so far as national focus was concerned. The *Mobilizer,* however, carried the following brief announcement:

A meeting to plan a national student strike has been called for December 28th and 29th in Chicago. The call for the meeting was issued by a list of almost 200 individuals. The purpose of the strike, according to the issuers of the call, is to put the colleges on notice that students oppose the war in Vietnam and the use of the universities as an agent for the prosecution of the war.

The conference on the Student Strike is being hosted by the Chicago Peace Council. It will be held at the University of Chicago.

There followed addresses to contact for further information.

           \*          \*          \*

The student strike conference was initiated by Bettina Aptheker, a student at the University of California at Berkeley who had earlier been on the steering committee of the Free Speech Movement there. It is a measure of the prevailing depth of the anticommunist psychology in the United States that she made national news when she was elected to the student government after she had publicly announced her membership in the Communist Party in November 1965. Such an occurrence would have been unthinkable in the previous fifteen years or so. She was also a member of the Berkeley chapter of the Du Bois Clubs, the daughter of the Communist Party's best-known scholar, Herbert Aptheker, and a genuine student leader in her own right with a certain charisma.

In the spring of 1966 Bettina wrote an article for the Du Bois Clubs' discussion bulletin which indicates that her thinking on some matters was moving in a different direction from that of Hugh Fowler, the Du Bois Clubs' national chairman. In this article she defended the idea of supporting candidates within the Democratic Party, but she also took issue with the antidemonstration mood of SDS, and suggested a nationwide student-faculty strike and a march to "bring a million people to Washington" against the war and for a real war on poverty. "Let's propose such a demonstration," she wrote, "and bring together the entire movement to do it."[6]

Bettina Aptheker did not attend the Cleveland conferences, but at the one in September a mimeographed paper signed by her was distributed, entitled: "Proposal for a National Student Strike for Peace." It tentatively announced a meeting to plan such an action, declaring: "If, within the next few weeks a number of people from various sections of the academic community will sign the call for a meeting in Chicago during the *Christmas recess,* the call will be printed, with the signatures, and mailed and distributed as widely as possible." In motivating the idea, she wrote:

6. *Dimensions.* Discussion journal of the W.E.B. Du Bois Clubs, Spring 1966. (Copy in author's files.)

We need a nationally co-ordinated student action to give focus and direction to the movement, as well as making it possible for students who are organizing on campuses with a small movement to feel a part of a national action, and less isolated. The primary object is to develop a *militant, effective* and *broad united* demonstration against the war. . . . The strike is proposed for the Spring, 1967.[7]

By the time of the November Cleveland conference the Chicago student meeting had been set and it was agreed to include the announcement of it in the Spring Mobilization Committee material.

The SWP and the YSA were initially hesitant in their attitude toward this meeting. For one thing a national student strike was simply not realistic in the near future, in their view. For another they were not eager for a repeat of the NCC convention a year earlier, and it was clear that this conference was being promoted by the CP and to a certain extent by the Du Bois Clubs. Since Bettina was the central figure in calling the conference, and she was a member of both the CP and the Du Bois Clubs, there was some fear that the whole thing would simply be controlled by those groups and the YSA would not get fair treatment.

The conference, however, was getting broad sponsorship, including local SDS figures, and in talks Aptheker gave during this period she said she was flexible on the question of a strike and that the main thing was to call a national student action and to create a national center for the coordination of student antiwar activities. So the YSA decided to help build the conference. At the very least it would be a place to plug the Spring Mobilization.

Several Chicago YSAers, including Dan Styron, a student at Roosevelt University, volunteered their assistance to the group organizing the student conference out of an office in Chicago. They found the atmosphere cooperative. Styron was asked to serve on the preparations committee, which included youth from moderate organizations like the Young Christian Students, as well as some from the Du Bois Clubs, the CP, SDS, and a few unaffiliated activists.

The national office of the Du Bois Clubs had been moved to Chicago sometime earlier, and it soon became clear, according to

7. "Proposal for a national student strike for peace." Submitted by Bettina Aptheker, University of California, Berkeley. Emphasis in original. Undated. (Copy in author's files.)

Styron, that one thing the CP and the Du Bois Clubs had in mind was that out of the student conference would come a national student antiwar center in which they would play a significant role. But it also became clear that the difference between Hugh Fowler of the Du Bois Clubs and Arnold Johnson of the Communist Party which had appeared at the founding conference of the Spring Mobilization Committee existed among the people in Chicago building the student strike meeting.

Styron and the other YSAers found themselves blocking with Bettina Aptheker, Danny Friedlander, a student at the University of Chicago, and others who favored close cooperation with the Spring Mobilization Committee, against some of the Du Bois Club and SDS members who were not strong for the spring demonstration.

One of the problems Styron had anticipated was a fight over the negotiations versus immediate withdrawal demands. On December 20 in a letter to Lew Jones he wrote: "Yesterday, however, with no big push on my part, Bettina volunteered the information that she thinks the correct demands for the conference to adopt are (1) Immediate withdrawal of all American troops, and (2) Self-determination for Vietnam."[8]

Styron further observed: "The phrase, 'What we don't want is another NCC,' is repeated over and over again by the CPers."

Styron continued:

> The agenda, which we agreed to, implements this line. As it stands now
> . . . the conference will open with the delegates (everyone who comes) voting on the convention rules, agenda, who the chairman will be, etc. Then Bettina and [Sidney] Peck will make short statements. . . . In these statements they will emphasize (1) The purpose of this conference is to project a spring student action based on the campuses and for the purpose of building a student anti-war movement on the national level. (2) One of the main purposes of the student action will be to mobilize students to attend the national mobilization on April 15. (3) The conference looks on the Mobilization committee as a broad formation which the conference should collaborate with in the closest possible way. (4) A strike looks impossible at this time, and we should discuss what forms the spring student action should take.

Styron then listed the various proposed workshops, including

8. Letter from Dan Styron to Lew Jones, December 20, 1966. (Copy in author's files.)

opposition to war research, antidraft, defense of civil liberties, etc. "The general spirit of the conference," he wrote, "is supposed to be that of an active workers conference just prior to an organizing drive."

In conclusion Styron said: "Both Bettina and I have the keys to the office and are looked on as being in charge of the general operation, although she is the undisputed leader." Then he commented rhetorically: "Obviously, this can't happen. Tell us what the hell is going on?"

The conference opened December 28 in a building at the University of Chicago. This was not available beforehand, so housing assignments for delegates arriving the night before were given out at the SDS national office, which was conveniently located. An informal conference steering committee meeting was held there that night as well, which I sat in on as an observer. There is no record of this meeting but two things about it stand out in my memory.

First was the SDS national office itself. I had not seen it since the preparations for the SDS march on Washington in early 1965 when it was in New York and C. Clark Kissinger was the national secretary. Then it was maintained in a businesslike fashion. But in Chicago in December 1966 it was different. The national officers were not present at the time because of an SDS National Council meeting in Berkeley, but they had certainly left the office in a monumental mess.

Fastidiousness is not one of my strong points, but I could hardly believe my eyes when I saw it. There wasn't a desk in the place where you could find space to put down an ordinary piece of paper to take notes. Desks and tables were piled high with old leaflets, inky used stencils, filing folders with their contents spilling out, coffee cups, used food bags, and assorted other impedimenta. There was a large rack for trays of mail-address plates, but some of the trays had not been replaced. They were on the desks, stacked on top of typewriters, on the floor, some of them spilled out, and loose plates scattered around. Most painful of all were the disorganized heaps of unopened mail, some of it on the floor with footprints ground into it.

I leafed through some of the envelopes looking at the return addresses and postmarks. They were from small towns and big cities across the country including areas the radical movement had little or no contact with as yet. Some of them were weeks old. If that's the way they operated as a rule, and apparently it was, there must have been hundreds, perhaps thousands, of youth who had written in for literature, ideas, guidance, and inspiration and had simply never been answered.

I had some differences with SDS before that, of course, but from that night on I had a hard time taking that outfit seriously. No matter how bright or bold their projects might be they would never be effectively organized without a little respect for ordinary work and for the tools of the trade.

The second memory is of the meeting itself. Bettina opened it with a somewhat hesitant approach. The preparations committee had pretty much set aside the strike idea for the moment as unrealistic, but the people now present from out of town had not been part of those discussions. She began simply asking questions, trying to draw the others out in a sort of Socratic method. But no one answered for the longest time. Just to get it started I found myself answering along the lines of supporting the Spring Mobilization. I was ill at ease in this since I was not a delegate and certainly not a student or youth, but the others didn't speak. The first part of the meeting turned into a dialogue between Bettina and me in which I laid out the whole perspective outlined by Peck and Muste and urged the students to build the Spring Mobilization in addition to whatever else they might do. There was general agreement, or at least no contrary perspective presented, and the meeting then proceeded to go over a proposed agenda for the following day which made the spring action the first point after the routine procedural matters.

The conference was attended by some 250 youth from around the country as well as from Canada and Puerto Rico. There were a few older observers and guests like Jack Spiegel of the hosting Chicago Peace Council, Sid Peck, Brad Lyttle of CNVA, and myself. Paul Booth, while not sanguine about the proposed spring action, agreed to act as parliamentarian and help chair the conference. The Parade Committee delegate was Linda Morse Dannenberg, who was on the committee's full-time staff and of student age.

The ideological spread of those attending was broader and proportionately much more representative than had been the case among the youth at the November Cleveland conference. This in itself indicated that a certain momentum had already begun to develop.

The point on a spring action opened with remarks by Bettina Aptheker, Eugene Groves, representing the National Student

Association, Steve Kindred of SDS, and Sid Peck. Kindred, who had been a leader of the anti-draft-ranking demonstrations at the University of Chicago, said he saw good reasons for occasional mass actions. But he raised some questions he said were on the minds of SDSers present, including whether a demonstration would help the movement "go beyond protest" and whether it wouldn't "soak up resources and energy" and thereby detract from local actions. These questions were discussed extensively with points being made that national action can be complementary to local activity and was important for reaching other layers of the population.

Peck ended the discussion, saying the Spring Mobilization was not viewed as simply another International Days of Protest. "We think it is important," he said, "to keep the notion of 'mass' in front of us. . . . It is not merely a matter of making the record because we feel guilty about the war. . . . We hope to energize and consolidate opposition movements throughout the world."[9]

Workshops took place that night and the next morning. A committee from these then drew up a proposal for the spring, which was presented to the conference as a whole. It contained the following:

We, the Student Mobilization Committee, urge all those students who wish to oppose the criminal war in Vietnam to dedicate themselves anew to the task of ending the war. Specifically we propose that April 8 15th be designated as Vietnam Week. We urge national student action during Vietnam Week which will culminate in the transportation of as many students as possible to New York and San Francisco as part of the general Spring Mobilization of the antiwar movement on April 15. Finally, we propose that the focus of End the War in Vietnam Week be on: 1. Bringing the GIs home now; 2. Opposing the draft; 3. Ending campus complicity with the war effort.[10]

The University of Chicago had been the scene of another conference on December 4 attended by some 500 people to protest the university's complicity with the draft and to discuss draft resistance. Thirty-two of those present, including Paul Booth and

9. *Militant,* January 9, 1967.
10. Resolutions adopted by the national student conference in Chicago, December 28-30, 1966. (Copy in author's files.) Also reproduced in the *Student Mobilizer,* vol. I, no. 1, January 17, 1967.

SDSer Jeff Segal, had signed a "We Won't Go" pledge. (Segal was out on bail pending appeal, having already been convicted and sentenced to four years in jail for refusing induction.)

There was some discussion of this development and the resolution was amended to include after "opposing the draft," the words "and supporting the right of individuals to refuse to cooperate with the military system." This formula committed the new group to support draft resisters but did not limit it to those who advocated or engaged in draft resistance.

During the discussion Steve Kindred reported, somewhat regretfully, that the SDS National Council, then meeting in Berkeley, had by a narrow margin declined to endorse the Spring Mobilization. He said he hoped the position might be reversed, possibly by referendum, after discussion with those SDSers who took part in this conference.

The spring action proposal as amended was passed overwhelmingly.

There was only one sharp dispute at the conference. Significantly it was reminiscent of one that had taken place at the workshop at the Assembly of Unrepresented People in 1965, which had founded the NCC. The issue was where the national office of the new Student Mobilization Committee would be located. And on this point the marriage almost broke up before the honeymoon was over. The two proposals were Chicago and New York. (Some wit called out "Madison!" and was almost hooted out of the room.)

The CP and the Du Bois Clubs supported Chicago. The YSA and some radical pacifists supported New York. The SDSers by and large, as well as most of the rest of the delegates, were indifferent on the matter. The underlying question was, of course, what political atmosphere the new group would be influenced by. The Du Bois Clubs' national office was located in Chicago, the YSA's in New York. But much more important, Muste and the radical pacifists were strongest in New York. This last fact was decisive in the thinking of Jack Barnes and myself. In our opinion the new group would have by far the greatest chance of holding together if it were close to Muste's universally acknowledged influence and skill as a reconciler. What is more the Spring Mobilization in the Eastern half of the country was not to be focused on Chicago but New York.

The meeting soon divided into three sharply defined groups:

those adamant on Chicago, those adamant on New York, and those who didn't see the difference—or who did and wanted no part of *this* argument—and simply abstained from the discussion or voting. The relationship of forces was tested when a procedural matter—whether to adjourn for dinner—came up on which those favoring Chicago voted one way and those favoring New York the other. The vote was a tie, about one-third one way, exactly the same number the other way, and about a third not voting. Linda Dannenberg, who was chairing that session, took the vote again. Exactly the same result to the last digit. She tried a third time. Exactly the same. "That's discipline for you," she cracked, and used her prerogative as chairperson to move to another point on the agenda while caucusing proceeded in the rear of the hall.

There followed a painful period, with messages going back and forth between caucuses while those left on the floor of the conference stalled for time on the remaining pieces of relatively noncontroversial business. It finally came down to a worried discussion in the lobby between Jack Barnes, Bettina Aptheker, and Mike Zagarell, the CP's youth leader. Jack eventually convinced Bettina on New York, at least for the initial period, and Zagarell went along.

Overnight, Zagarell had second thoughts and the same tension occurred the next day. Aptheker, however, finally persuaded Zagarell to accept New York and the conference so voted.

The idea of a national student strike was not discussed but referred for further discussion, groundwork, and reconsideration at a later time. Strikes would be considered for the spring only at a few selected campuses where the situation might be favorable.

The conference also voted to send out a number of suggested proposals for ongoing local activity, for Vietnam Week, and for preparations for the April 15 mass mobilization. These were not simply a hodgepodge listing of every suggestion made during the workshops, but a set of well-defined, reasonably thought-out proposals including antidraft actions, opposing recruitment for the military and war industries on campus, campus tribunals for exposing university complicity with the war, etc. Most of them were actually implemented to one degree or another.

The conference also voted to publicize the War Crimes Tribunal which had been initiated by the Bertrand Russell Peace Foundation and was scheduled to begin in February 1967. In addition it resolved "to condemn the colonial imposition of the draft onto Puerto Ricans."[11]

A separate student call to the Spring Mobilization was adopted including the demands for immediate withdrawal, against the draft, and ending university complicity with the war. The adopted implementation document declared:

1. The groups involved in the conference are urged to send a staff person to the New York April Spring Mobilization office to immediately begin organization and mail out the proceedings of this conference.

2. That the immediate major task of this staff be to search out major figures in the academic community, the civil rights, peace, and student movements to be included as sponsors of the national call that emanates from this conference. That sponsors be initiated by local committees as well as the New York staff.

3. That upon accomplishment of this broadening, a Continuations Committee be composed of a representative from each organization that composed the steering committee of this conference, plus one from any organization or individuals who volunteer to participate in Vietnam Week and agree to the call. That this continuations committee make further plans.

4. That all this be done in cooperation with and consultation with the Spring Mobilization Committee officers, but that the continuations committee also maintain a separate identity oriented toward the involvement and organization of the campus and youth in the national student Vietnam Week and the April 15 Mobilization and other anti-war actions. That the question of whether or not the full student mobilization committee remain in New York or be located in some other place be decided by the student continuations committee on the basis of future development of the mobilization.

5. That this conference direct the continuations committee to encourage solidarity actions with the April 15 Mobilization particularly in the Midwest and South, and that they urge the Spring Mobilization Committee to join in encouraging those solidarity actions.

6. That this continuations committee convene a conference on as broad a basis as possible following the Spring Mobilization to evaluate the national student anti-war week and mobilization and consider plans for future action.[12]

It was understood that the CP, the YSA, and hopefully SDS would immediately each provide a staff person in New York, and

11. Ibid.
12. Ibid.

that Linda Dannenberg would be acting executive secretary. Thus the Student Mobilization Committee to End the War in Vietnam was born.

The antiwar movement, then, entered 1967 with two viable national coalitions, distinct but cooperating. One in a position to appeal to the broadest forces in the adult arena and the other, more radical, based on students and the immediate withdrawal demand. Both were founded on the principle of nonexclusion. A long detour had ended, at least for the time being. Now the big job of organizing could begin.

# 10

## April 15, 1967

In his article in the first *Mobilizer*, Muste pointed out that it had been agreed there should be "a prompt exploration of what forces, individual or collective, might be enlisted in support of this mobilization." Two of the areas he discussed in relation to this exploration were the labor and civil rights movements.

Regarding labor, Muste expected no immediate dramatic results, but he did consider it important and expressed a certain hope for the future.

There is [he said] no current evidence that millions could be brought into the streets at one time to demand an end to the U.S. role in the war. For that to happen, large numbers of labor unionists would have to be involved. This may some day happen, but not very likely by April 15, 1967. On the other hand, if it were to happen that tens or hundreds of thousands of labor unionists appeared on the streets in an anti-war demonstration, it would not be true, as some tend to think, that this would not make an appreciable impact on the Administration either. In such case, for example, strikes in war industries would become possible, even likely, and that would take the protest out of the "token" or symbolic category.[1]

This way of thinking was much closer to a traditional Marxist approach than that of many of the newly radicalizing youth who tended to view the organized labor movement as a pillar of "the Establishment" and among the last places to look for decisive aid to the antiwar cause. If one judged from the top leadership of the

1. *Mobilizer,* December 19, 1966.

American union movement, the pragmatic impression of these youth was entirely understandable. The AFL-CIO Executive Council was solidly in support of Johnson's war policies, while AFL-CIO President George Meany was, if anything, more of a hawk than Johnson himself. The AFL-CIO International Affairs Department—headed by Jay Lovestone, former head of the Communist Party turned professional anticommunist—hardly concealed the fact that it acted as an ex-officio arm of the U.S. State Department in the cold war.

An incident early in the antiwar movement, at the AFL-CIO convention in San Francisco in December 1965, had further reinforced the negative impression many student radicals had of the union movement. At that time a group of about fifty student antiwar demonstrators from Berkeley, Stanford, and San Francisco State College appeared in the gallery of the Civic Auditorium where the public was admitted to observe the convention proceedings. They went there not to demonstrate against the AFL-CIO but because Secretary of State Dean Rusk had been invited to speak. His talk was devoted to a defense of the war policy and an attack on its critics. The students were not disruptive and simply held antiwar signs as Rusk spoke. When Rusk concluded, Meany ordered the sergeants at arms to "clear the kookies out of the gallery," which was done none too gently. Meany commented:

"We were glad to have them while Secretary Rusk spoke, on the theory that it might add a little bit to their inadequate education, but now we want to go ahead with our business."[2]

The incident became notorious in student antiwar circles.

Two days later, San Francisco State student Kipp Dawson spoke at a Bay Area YSA conference. She gave a report on the NCC convention and her remarks did not deal directly with what happened at the AFL-CIO gathering, but in the course of her report she made the following observation:

We must keep in mind the fact that the antiwar movement was born

2. "Proceedings of the Sixth Constitutional Convention, AFL-CIO," December 10, 1965, p. 133. The next order of business, incidentally, was a report by Communications Workers of America President Joseph A. Beirne, an active collaborator with the Central Intelligence Agency, providing union cover for its operations in labor movements overseas. (See *CIA and CWA* by Cynthia Sweeney, a pamphlet published by CWA Local 11500 members, San Diego, 1975. [Copy in author's files.])

and is growing in a period of general economic prosperity and the corresponding high rate of living for the working class, which has bred temporary extreme conservatism in the trade union movement. This means that the movement has developed largely without the support or influence of the working class, and almost solely among one layer of the population: the students.[3]

The antiwar sentiment—and even the deeper radicalization among the youth—was not confined to students. It affected workers, especially young workers, as well. But it affected them as individuals or as members of doubly oppressed groups, such as Blacks, rather than as workers or as union members as such. And in most cases they could not express it through the unions.

With some exceptions the mid-1960s was not a time of sharp union struggles. When such did occur—as for example with the farm workers led by César Chávez, where the union's grape and lettuce boycotts received an important boost from the student movement—the workers involved and even the union leadership were much more inclined to be open to the antiwar cause. But as a general rule such alliances were not impelled by the prevailing economic situation. A change in that situation would provide the basis for a qualitative change in the antiwar movement. But as Muste observed, that was something over which "we in the radical anti-war movement have little or no control."[4]

Throughout this period there was a running dispute over whether or not the union movement—or even the working class— could be an ally in the antiwar struggle. As a matter of policy the YSA held that it could, and that everything possible ought to be done to involve workers and unionists in the movement. Similar hopes were held by the CP, the SWP, and a number of individuals such as Muste, Sid Peck, and Stewart Meacham of the American Friends Service Committee, all of whom had some experience with, or at least more than superficial knowledge of, the pre-1950s union movement.

SDS and most of the young self-styled new lefters, however, tended to take an entirely pragmatic view of the matter. What appeared before their eyes at the moment was the whole truth as far as they were concerned. They were influenced by such

3. Report to Bay Area YSA Conference, December 12, 1965, by Kipp Dawson. (Copy in author's files.)
4. *Mobilizer,* December 19, 1966.

theorists as Herbert Marcuse who held that the working class in advanced capitalist countries like the United States had been more or less permanently pacified by concessions and was no longer a major force for social progress. That role was assigned to students and intellectuals. It was even declared that students as such were *the* new revolutionary force.

In my view one error involved in this approach was the identification of the union movement as a whole—and even of the working class—with the union officialdom. The weight of the union bureaucracy in holding back membership involvement in the antiwar movement is clearly revealed in a comparison of the experience of the New York Parade Committee with two different unions. These were District 65 of the Retail, Wholesale and Department Store Workers on the one hand, and the International Ladies Garment Workers Union (ILGWU) on the other.

Both were affiliated with the AFL-CIO. To a significant extent they were involved in different aspects of the same industry in the same part of New York City. The ILGWU had jurisdiction over the production of women's garments, District 65 over the wholesale houses supplying cloth and other items to the factories, as well as over the major retail outlets in the city for the finished product.

The two unions therefore necessarily maintained certain cooperative relations. The membership of both these unions in New York City was largely Black and Puerto Rican; a lot of the white members were Jewish. In many cases they ate in the same luncheonettes, gathered on the same street corners, voted for the same liberal politicians, and occupied more or less the same rungs on the economic and social ladder.

The bulk of these respective memberships were no more or less inclined to be antiwar in the one case than in the other. But members of the ILGWU in New York who were opposed to the war could not express this within the union without fear of harassment, and in no case *through* the union. Members of District 65 who opposed the war could, if they chose, be active in a peace committee within the union. Al Evanoff, assistant vice-president of District 65 and a Parade Committee stalwart, was active in this group. The committee did not set policy for District 65, but it could use union facilities like other committees which involved a part of the membership. Such activists could wear union hats and carry banners identifying themselves as members of the union on antiwar demonstrations, post notices on union bulletin boards, etc.

James Johnson, Sr., father of the James Johnson of the Fort Hood Three, was a member of District 65 and one of its shop stewards. He was able to take up a substantial collection within the union for his son's defense, and to publicize the case to the entire union membership, with the sympathetic assistance of the union officials. If he had been a member of the ILGWU he would have had to keep his mouth shut on this matter inside the union.

At first only a small part of the District 65 membership was involved in these activities. The officials, who were generally sympathetic, did not impose their antiwar views on the union as a whole. But as the general antiwar sentiment increased, so it did among District 65 members, and they could express it in an organized form within the union. Eventually when the antiwar view became a majority, the union itself did adopt an antiwar position and participate officially in many important antiwar activities.

The ILGWU membership, however, remained totally immobilized on this question throughout the war. The difference was the leadership. The ILGWU was controlled by a hidebound, rightwing Social Democratic, virtually all-white bureaucracy that maintained unquestioning support of the Meany-Lovestone line throughout. District 65, which was more democratic, had a multiracial officialdom and a radical tradition that had not been entirely buried, at least as regards resistance to the anticommunist hysteria and to slavish support of government foreign policy.

It was not prowar sentiment on the part of the rank and file that kept the bulk of the unions out of the antiwar movement, it was the bureaucracy. And the objective conditions during the 1960s for a cracking of that bureaucratic hold were not favorable. There was, however, some important union involvement that developed from small beginnings and which by 1970 was growing much more rapidly.

It is a law of political life that changes often appear first on the edges, around the cracks and fissures, in the areas somehow not quite typical, rather than in the decisive central weight of a social organism. But such exceptional situations are not just exceptional. They contain within them elements that go through the heart of the whole, but are simply more hidden there, less able to be manifest in the early stages of change. If the process is real, and not illusory or artificial, changes around the edges are both indicators of and contributors to coming change in the more decisive sectors.

The special circumstances that made possible the beginnings of union involvement in the antiwar movement fell roughly into three categories, sometimes combined. These were (1) unions where the membership *and the leadership* included large percentages of oppressed national minorities, whose outlook had been affected by the civil rights movement; (2) unions with a radical history and a leadership that still retained certain features of this tradition and to that degree defied the general norm of the American union officialdom, at least as regards the anticommunist hysteria and foreign policy; (3) unions where much of the membership and leadership was fresh out of college and had themselves been part of the student radicalization. These last included unions of welfare workers and in certain areas teachers.

In addition the labor movement as a whole contained a heavy sprinkling of individual union leaders who had once been radicals. Not all of these had entirely rejected all their youthful ideas, though even those who hadn't were more than careful about expressing them. But here and there an occasional such figure who for one reason or another felt secure from reprisals by the AFL-CIO tops would take an antiwar stand. Muste's own personal history put him in a position to take advantage of this as well as anyone could.

\*        \*        \*

Muste started his activist life as a Christian pacifist preacher, but between 1919 and 1936 he had been deeply involved with the labor movement, part of the time as a Marxist.

In 1919 he went to Lawrence, Massachusetts, with a group of Quakers to aid a bitter strike of 30,000 textile workers there. Among other things he wanted to introduce some ideas of mass nonviolent struggle. The strike was in bad shape when they arrived and Muste soon found himself elected executive secretary of the strike committee. He was badly beaten by strikebreaking police when he led a march, but he stuck it out and the strike was won. It was one of the early victories for industrial unionism in a mass-production industry.

For a time Muste was general secretary of the Amalgamated Textile Workers Union. Between 1921 and 1933 he was director of

Brookwood Labor College, a school for union organizers for which some AFL unions provided scholarships, though the college was independent of the AFL.

During this period he became a vice-president of the American Federation of Teachers. More important, he helped train a significant number of the organizers who later built the industrial unions of the CIO.

Many of his students later moved to the right as they became comfortable in the union bureaucracy, while Muste had moved to the left, but he generally maintained cordial relations with them, at least on a personal level. In 1929 Muste helped found the Conference for Progressive Labor Action (CPLA), whose members came to be known as Musteites. Its strategy was to work within the AFL on a program of militant industrial unionism, including opposition to racial discrimination.

The great debate within the union movement of the time was whether to continue the dominant AFL policy of organizing only certain skilled crafts into separate unions for each craft, or whether to organize all the workers in an industry—including the unskilled or semiskilled mass-production workers—into one union. In opting for the second course, the CPLA laid some of the groundwork for the rise of the CIO.

The Musteites were also active in organizing unemployed leagues in the depths of the Great Depression. In 1934, through a strategy of unity between the unemployed and the strikers at the Auto-Lite plant in Toledo, Ohio, the CPLA led the first victorious strike in the auto industry. (Sam Pollock, one of the CPLA leaders of this strike, later became president of the Cleveland Meat Cutters. He was one of the very few union officials to attend the conference that gave birth to the 1967 Spring Mobilization.)

It was also in 1934 that the Trotskyists led the successful Minneapolis Teamster strikes. In part on the basis of these experiences the Musteites and the Trotskyists merged their organizations in December 1935 to form the Workers Party of the United States. By that time Muste considered himself a revolutionary Marxist and had in effect set aside both his religion and his pacifist philosophy, though he was still a practitioner of mass nonviolent direct action—at least, as nonviolent as possible.

In this period Muste participated in a number of important labor struggles. In early 1936 at the Goodyear rubber strike in

Akron, he was partly responsible for the successful introduction of the sit-down strike technique—borrowed from France—into the American labor scene.

But Muste was disturbed when a majority of the newly born Workers Party voted in early 1936 to dissolve the organization and seek membership in the Socialist Party of Norman Thomas. He was discouraged by the defeats of the revolution in Europe, and became convinced that the revolutionary movement could not stop the gathering world war. In this mood he reached back to the origins of his own character and in July 1936 underwent a religious reconversion that was to last the rest of his life.

Muste left the Trotskyist movement and returned to pacifism and the church; but he remained a socialist and, as usual, continued to regard his old comrades without rancor.

He became industrial secretary of the Fellowship of Reconciliation (FOR) and for a time director of the Presbyterian Labor Temple in New York City. In 1940 he became executive secretary of the FOR. In this capacity he assisted those who were jailed for opposition to the Second World War and contributed to the development of a host of organizations and causes, including the Congress of Racial Equality, originally an FOR staff project.

In 1953 he left the active staff of the FOR, becoming secretary emeritus. Muste had many profound differences with the Communist Party but he demonstratively defended their civil liberties during the witch-hunt and was attacked for this by FBI Director J. Edgar Hoover. In the 1950s he threw himself into the campaign against nuclear weapons and testing, personally participating in the early civil disobedience actions that called attention to the threat, and eventually helping to found both SANE and the Committee for Nonviolent Action.

Muste also had some influence with Martin Luther King, Jr., who had first come to national prominence as the leader of the Montgomery bus boycott of 1956. Bayard Rustin, then a Muste protégé who also worked in the national office of an all-Black union, the Brotherhood of Sleeping-Car Porters, had been the New York contact of E. D. Nixon, the working sleeping-car porter who originated the boycott and convinced King to be its spokesman. Through Rustin, Muste was consulted on many of the strategies that gave birth to the modern civil rights movement.

In 1963 King himself declared: "I would say unequivocally that the current emphasis on nonviolent direct action in the race relations field is due more to A. J. than to anyone else in the country."[5]

Developments as profound as the American antiwar movement do not just drop from the sky, and they are certainly not imported, as certain red-baiting congressmen would have had us believe, and as some high government officials even deluded themselves into believing. They are intimately connected with the whole history of social struggles in the country and A. J. Muste personified this.

\*    \*    \*

The Committee for a SANE Nuclear Policy held a rally against the Vietnam War at Madison Square Garden on December 8, 1966. A crowd of 20,000 jammed the Garden as hundreds stood outside listening to the proceedings on loudspeakers. The rally was an interesting contrast to the one on nuclear testing six years earlier that had figured in the red-baiting attack by Senator Thomas J. Dodd and the firing of SANE staffer Henry Abrams. In 1960 Norman Thomas had been the most militant speaker on the platform. This time he was the most conservative. It was not Thomas who had changed.

SANE still represented the more conservative wing of the antiwar movement, with most speakers voicing the "negotiate" position, but the demand to bring the troops home now was raised by at least two of the speakers, Floyd McKissick of CORE and Grace Mora Newman of the Fort Hood Three Defense Committee, and received the loudest applause. Most of the speakers bitterly attacked President Johnson. Rev. William Sloane Coffin, cochairman of the rally, presented a vigorous defense of the student antiwar movement.

One of the speakers was Joel R. Jacobson, president of the New Jersey Industrial Union Council, which was composed of unions that had belonged to the CIO before the 1955 merger with the AFL. Jacobson drew a big applause when he announced that there were 5,000 union members present. Jacobson spoke on behalf of a new formation, the Trade Union Division of SANE. This group was controlled completely by trade unionists and was

5. Nat Hentoff, *Peace Agitator: The Story of A. J. Muste* (New York: Macmillan, 1963), p. 18.

actually the device some union officials had chosen to begin a hesitant move to take their distance from the Meany policy on the war.

Before the formation of the Trade Union Division of SANE there existed another organization called Trade Unionists for Peace, which in New York was affiliated to the Parade Committee. It had been initiated in August 1965 by Aaron Wool, a rank-and-file New York printer who had first attempted to get a prominent union official to head up a committee of unionists opposed to the war. Failing this, he called together the rank-and-file unionists he knew who wanted to do something on the issue and launched the organization.

Similar groups were formed in several other cities. They carried out educational campaigns aimed at unionists and provided some sort of union presence on the early demonstrations. Their literature was widely distributed and even reproduced in various union publications. It played a role in encouraging such discussion as there was on the war in the union movement. But these groups remained small committees of rank-and-file members from different unions, with no official standing and few resources. The Trade Union Division of SANE, however, was largely composed of union officials with considerable authority and resources at their command.

On December 17 the Chicago Trade Union Division of SANE sponsored a conference on "The Labor Movement's Responsibility in the Search for Peace." It was attended by some 350 people, mostly secondary officers of unions in the Chicago area with a few from other parts of the country. The keynote address was given by Frank Rosenblum, general secretary-treasurer of the Amalgamated Clothing Workers, AFL-CIO, and an old friend of Muste's.

Rosenblum was largely responsible for the fact that the ACW, which in other political respects was not much different from the rest of the major AFL-CIO unions, did not go along with the Meany position on the war and that its officials were able to speak out on the question. Other unions with significant numbers of officials present included the Amalgamated Meat Cutters, the Packinghouse Workers (these two later merged), and the United Auto Workers.

The conference was not advertised as being against the war. The invitation simply posed certain questions: "What are the peaceful alternatives? Does Labor need peace for effective collective bargaining in 1967? Can the 'Great Society' be achieved and poverty eliminated in a wartime economy?"[6]

The conference adopted a statement of purpose for the new organization that was considerably more moderate than even SANE's recent positions. It said in part:

We believe it is increasingly clear that the simple solution to the Vietnam war offered again and again—"victory through escalation"— cannot succeed, and can only intensify the suffering of the people of Vietnam. It is clear also that negotiations must take place among all those involved in this conflict.

We shall therefore urge steps, such as a cessation to bombing, to help bring about such negotiations, rather than further escalation of the conflict. . . . And we plan to carry the discussion of these and other issues of peace and war to our trade-union brothers, to the members of our unions, and to all our fellow Americans.[7]

The teach-in professors had been bolder than that, almost two years previously. Nevertheless this conference represented a beginning of organized public dissent with the Meany position among the labor officialdom.

Muste attended the Chicago trade union conference, as did Jack Spiegel, who was one of the sponsors, Sid Lens, myself, and a few other antiwar activists who had some connection with or special interest in the union movement. One of the things we wanted to do was to solicit support for the Spring Mobilization. But the bulk of the union officials involved were not simply hesitant about this. They were downright frightened by the idea.

This did not stem from a lack of feeling on their part about the war. They knew it was wrong and doing no good for American labor. Other considerations were involved. First was fear of reprisals from the Meany forces and other top union leaders who supported the war (or more precisely, who supported government foreign policy no matter what it was). Second was fear of having the student radicalization or its spirit introduced into the ranks of organized labor. Not all of them were exactly opposed to the last possibility. They were just afraid of it. They sensed that such a development could mean a knockdown, drag-out fight with the

6. An invitation: "For a Trade Unionists' Conference to Seek Peaceful Alternatives," December 17, 1966. Issued by the Chicago Trade Union Division of SANE. (Copy in author's files.)

7. *Militant,* December 26, 1966.

Meany forces, would upset all sorts of arrangements the union officials had with Democratic and Republican politicians, and might well mean stirring up the rank and file.

Their whole way of existence had simply become too comfortable and routine for them to seriously contemplate entering into any such process voluntarily. And as union officials went, those at this conference were among the best. There were few social formations in the United States as profoundly conservative—in the sense of being frightened of change—as the union bureaucracy.

The best we could do was to approach individuals in the corridors with information about the mobilization. It was simply not to be mentioned in the proceedings themselves. But the organizers couldn't quite bring themselves to snub Muste. After all, he was who he was and he was there; not pushing, but there.

They finally invited A. J. onto the platform, not in his capacity as chairman of the Spring Mobilization, but as an ordained minister—to give the invocation. And they let us know they felt damned brave about it.

\*       \*       \*

The connection of the antiwar movement with labor was much more tenuous than that with the civil rights movement. One of the reasons was that the modern Southern civil rights movement had for the most part developed after the witch-hunt period known as McCarthyism had begun to ebb. The period of dramatic growth of the unions, on the other hand, had come before the shattering experience of the cold-war witch-hunt, which affected the unions more than any other social formation and which almost completely severed the historic continuity of radicalism in the labor movement.

It is necessary to recall that in the 1930s and 1940s the Communist Party had dominant influence among radicals. All the other groups were a small fraction of its size. It had far more people than the others to throw into the labor upsurge of the 1930s and the building of the CIO. By the mid-1940s its members and close collaborators controlled the national leadership of over a dozen CIO unions and were a major force in many others.

In those days there was always considerable faction fighting within the union movement in which the Stalinists—there were no varieties then, just one monolithic ideology—were a major factor, sometimes blocking with other forces in the power fights over policy matters and control of various unions.

Between the Stalin-Hitler pact of 1939 and June 1941, the Stalinists campaigned against the U.S. entry into the Second World War. Following the Nazi invasion of the USSR they campaigned for it. During the war they were superpatriotic, enforced the no-strike pledge, and campaigned for all-out production for the war. In this period they were tolerated by the government and even drew certain advantages from this relationship in the power fights within the union movement.

With the end of the war and the advent of the cold war, however, the government turned on them and began the anti-communist witch-hunt, first of all in the union movement. This became a central issue in the power fights within the unions. A number of top union leaders who had collaborated with the Stalinists for opportunist reasons suddenly switched for the same reasons, becoming the most virulent anticommunists.

In 1949, ten international unions[8] were expelled from the CIO on charges of being "Communist dominated." A period of jurisdictional warfare ensued that weakened the whole union movement. The largest of these unions, for example, the half-million-member United Electrical Workers (UE), was split into the UE and the anticommunist-led International Union of Electrical Workers (IUE). After several years of jurisdictional battles, the UE was down to less than a fourth its former size and the IUE and UE combined had less than two-thirds the number of members the UE had before the split.

By the late 1950s the CP was no longer a major factor even in the expelled unions, most of which finally merged with their AFL-CIO rivals, and some of which were simply wiped out. Only the West Coast International Longshoremen's and Warehousemen's Union (ILWU) survived relatively intact. It, and the much reduced UE, remained outside the AFL-CIO. These two were the first international unions to my knowledge to take a position against the Vietnam War.

In the course of this whole process not only the Stalinists but the bulk of all the active radicals in the union movement were

---

8. The term "international union" denotes the entire union, not a local or regional part of it. It derives from the fact that many of the unions have locals in Canada as well as the U.S.

purged, and those who weren't did not generally buck the tide. The right-wing union officials had the active support of the government and the congressional witch-hunt committees in this purge. In one industry alone, maritime, the government refused to renew the seaman's certification papers of thousands of radical unionists of all varieties on spurious "security" grounds.

By the late 1950s the radical yeast that had given the social consciousness to the union movement had been almost entirely wiped out. The "business unionists," the pure and simple bureaucrats in it for comfortable jobs, the opportunists—and here and there the gangsters—had free rein, unhampered by the criticism of the radicals, for whom the union movement was a sacred cause. Not all of these were forced out, but most of those who remained were pretty thoroughly intimidated. A top union officialdom, as slavish to the State Department's foreign policy as the Stalinists ever were to Moscow's, was firmly entrenched.

\*       \*       \*

Another figure whose life was intertwined in this process, in some ways similar and in others quite different from that of A. J. Muste, was the well-known Pittsburgh labor priest, Monsignor Charles O. Rice.[9]

As a young priest in the 1930s Father Rice was closely associated with Dorothy Day's Catholic Worker movement. He early campaigned against racial discrimination and anti-Semitism, which was not the norm for American priests in those days. He was one of the first, if not the first, priests to walk labor picket lines in the 1930s. He participated in many labor battles, including the Heinz strike of 1935 and the Little Steel strike of 1937 in which a number of strikers were killed. On the radio and in writings for the *Pittsburgh Catholic* and other publications he supported the organizing drives of the CIO. He became a

9. The term "labor priest" as used in the U.S. should not be confused with the term "worker-priest" as used in Europe. The American labor priests were active with the union movement from the outside, as educators, publicists, advisers, and supporters. They did not hold union office but were close to many union leaders. The European worker-priests lived as workers, worked in factories, etc., and endeavored to be part of the rank and file.

confidant of union leaders, particularly CIO President Philip Murray.

In the 1940s he figured prominently in the inner union faction fights on the anticommunist side. He was the leading figure connected with the Pittsburgh chapter of the Association of Catholic Trade Unionists (ACTU), which from time to time served as an ideological focus for anticommunist caucuses in the CIO. He played a particularly prominent role in the fights in and around the UE.

According to an article by Michael Harrington, Rice had some contact with the House Un-American Activities Committee and the FBI in their attacks on CP unionists.[10] Harrington's article was mainly about the role of ACTU in the anticommunist caucuses and was written in 1960, long after the events it describes. It was written from an anticommunist point of view, though a moderate Social Democratic one with some implied criticism of the violations of civil liberties involved in the witch-hunt. Interestingly, Rice now says it was this article that started him rethinking the issues in the anticommunist purges. Probably the situation within the unions by then, and more broadly in the world, also had something to do with it.

Of his earlier role Rice says:

In my anti-Stalinism I was very much influenced by the murder of Trotsky—that had a traumatic effect on me—and by all those trials. I remember listening and watching very carefully the news of the Moscow trials. The people pleading guilty when it was absurd. And later one of the trials when they got [Joseph Cardinal] Mindszenty, they forced him, got him to say what obviously he didn't want to say. That probably did more to make people fearful of communism than almost anything else. It was a coup so far as they were concerned over there, but it was terribly counterproductive in the United States. At the time I believed there was some chance of their taking over and messing things up for us in the United States. Foolishly, I think now, but that's hindsight.

But there was a feeling among many anticommunists that communism was irreversible. That when they took over that was it, and that as they took each little—or big—piece of territory, it moved under the monolith, the curtain shut down, freedom was ended. There was no variety, and they moved on to another piece and digested it. I really felt

---

10. "Catholics in the Labor Movement: A Case History" by Michael Harrington, *Labor History,* Fall 1960. Harrington was himself a former editor of the *Catholic Worker.*

Joseph Hansen

August 6, 1960, march of 2,500 in New York to commemorate bombing of Hiroshima. Sponsored by the Committee for a SANE Nuclear Policy and the American Friends Service Committee.

Harry Ring

A. J. Muste

Alan Mercer

Ruth Gage-Colby

Militant

Above, SDS march on Washington, April 17, 1965. Below, New York Fifth Avenue Peace Parade Committee demonstration in New York, October 10, 1965, during the First International Days of Protest.

Militant

Walter Lippmann        Brian Shannon        Bob Adelman

Above, left to right, Harry Ring, Cora Weiss, Dave Dellinger.
Below, Fred Halstead, Jerry Rubin, A. J. Muste.

Susan Muysenborg                        Eli Finer

Militant

Above, steering committee of the *Bring the Troops Home Now Newsletter*, elected at the thirteenth workshop at the NCC convention, Thanksgiving weekend, 1965. From left, Jens Jensen, Kipp Dawson, Dan Rosenshine. Below, the Fort Hood Three in June 1966; from left, Pvt. Dennis Mora, Pvt. David Samas, Pfc. James Johnson.

Fred Halstead

Maury Englander

Above, relatives of the Fort Hood Three in August 6, 1966, New York Parade Committee demonstration. Below, Rev. James Bevel at a meeting of the Spring Mobilization Committee, New York, February 4, 1967.

Flax Hermes

Harry Ring

Brian Shannon

Above, left, Syd Stapleton; right, Bettina Aptheker with Jerry Rubin. Below, part of April 15, 1967, San Francisco march.

Flax Hermes

Above, April 15, 1967, San Francisco. Below, from left, Dr. Benjamin Spock, Rev. Martin Luther King, Jr., and Msgr. Charles Owen Rice head up April 15, 1967, march in New York.

April 15, 1967, New York.

Joseph Hansen

Opposite page, part of crowd of 400,000 at UN building, New York, April 15, 1967. This page, top, Coretta Scott King speaking to 75,000 at Kezar stadium, San Francisco, the same day.

Press conference announcing October 1967 march on the Pentagon. Above, left to right, H. Rap Brown, unknown, Fred Halstead, Dave Dellinger. At left, Abbie Hoffman and Jerry Rubin.

March on the Pentagon, October 21, 1967. Above, front of the
march leaves rally site at Lincoln Memorial, crossing the Potomac toward the Pentagon on the Virginia side. Below, military
police confront demonstrators at the Pentagon face later in the
day.

Charles Lerrigo

Above, antiwar veterans leaflet military police at the Pentagon, October 21, 1967. Below, the following morning, MPs and U.S. marshals attack remaining demonstrators camped on the ground in front of the Pentagon.

United Press International

Stop the Draft Week, 1967. Above, Oakland police, using clubs and tear gas, advance on antiwar demonstrators at Northern California induction center, October 20, 1967. Below, right, New York antidraft demonstration, December 6, 1967, at Whitehall induction center; at left, plainclothes cops blackjack a Vietnam veteran during Stop the Draft Week in New York.

April 27, 1968. Above, part of crowd of 200,000 in New York's Sheep Meadow during decentralized nationwide protest demonstrations. Below, high school demonstrators in New York.

At right, Lew Jones of the YSA speaking at Chicago SMC conference, January 28, 1968. To his right is C. Clark Kissinger, former SDS national secretary.

Below, Peter Camejo (on stairs in dark sport coat) addressing Berkeley student meeting in summer of 1968.

Flax Hermes

Ron Alexander

At left, Linda Morse motivating walkout of Radical Organizing Committee at SMC split conference, Hotel Diplomat, New York, June 29, 1968.

that. I don't feel it now but I felt it then. And then, you see, there wasn't much evidence of variety in communism.

The Communists, the Stalinists, the CP, they played it pretty stupidly. They insisted for the longest while on these resolutions on behalf of whatever foreign policy the CP wanted at the moment. Whether the policies were right or wrong we could argue forever, but for the CP in the unions it was almost suicide. I think it was Matles [an official of the UE] who told me the Communists eventually pulled out and didn't care what the union leaders did, but by then it was too late. They had made themselves sitting ducks. There really wasn't much you could fault them on the way they handled their unions compared to the other CIO leaders. But the way they twisted and turned—at the time of the Molotov-von Ribbentrop pact[11] for example—and the way they shunted between [United Mine Workers President John L.] Lewis and [Philip] Murray depending on who was following the line that the Kremlin favored, *that* hurt them very badly. It made them vulnerable. It made them sitting ducks during the cold war because you could say, look here's what these people have done all the time.

Looking back on it from my point of view now, it really didn't make any difference what line they followed on foreign policy. They should have been judged in the union movement on the basis of their trade unionism. I think the purging of the left-wingers, the total purging of them, the cleaning out of them from the labor movement, was tragic. I think it would have been better, and it would have made a much healthier labor movement, if we were able to have people of whatever persuasion remain in the unions and fight back and forth, as they were doing, and watch each other.

But it is probably true that ACTU and the others didn't have that much of an effect on the general outcome. American labor tends to be idealistically monolithic. And it lends itself to a monolith of leadership. The trade union leaders are naturally intolerant. They insist as much as a company would insist that everyone march together and they have this business that you need unity in organization and that you have to rally around the leader and follow him. They have that feeling.[12]

In early 1965 Rice was disturbed by the U.S. invasion of the Dominican Republic. That is when, he says,

I began to straighten myself out and get a true antiwar view on

11. Also known as the Stalin-Hitler pact.

12. Taped interview with Msgr. Rice by Paul Le Blanc, October 27, 1975. (Copy in author's files.)

Vietnam and the Dominican invasion. The invasion was taking place when I was invited to speak to an American Legion Post in Mount Oliver. Prominent in that post were men like Tom Fagan, local head of the Teamsters, and other labor fellows, and I gave them a real old-time rabble-rousing antiwar speech. And they ate it up at the time. But two months later those same fellows had been brainwashed by the powers-that-be. The powers-that-be got together and through their various resources they influenced these people.[13]

In the spring of 1966 the Pittsburgh Coalition to End the War in Vietnam invited Rice to speak at a rally. Paul Le Blanc, who spoke for SDS on the same occasion, describes the circumstances:

The antiwar movement in Pittsburgh consisted primarily of independent radicals influenced by the "new left" and by such periodicals as the *National Guardian* (now the *Guardian*), a few members of SDS, some left-liberal college students, and members of the Communist Party and the W. E. B. Du Bois Club.

At the time we were particularly concerned about being red-baited because the Du Bois Club members in our coalition had proposed that Hugh Fowler be a speaker at the rally, and we had all agreed on that. All of us were very much opposed to the old anticommunist exclusionary policies, and we felt solidarity with the Du Bois Club, which was being attacked by the government. At the same time we were afraid that if the only "big shot" at our rally was the national leader of the Du Bois Clubs, the whole effort would be dismissed by the media as simply "the work of the Communists." Rice's participation, we felt, prevented that. We were astonished that he agreed. It seemed a turning point. The news coverage we received was quite good, although Rice was attacked quite angrily in at least one TV editorial and became a favorite target of local right-wingers. . . .

Rice's decision to speak at our rally at the Federal Building on the Second International Days of Protest [March 26, 1966] provided the first "big name" for our movement. It also helped prepare the groundwork for the broad coalition of liberals (of the ADA [Americans for Democratic Action] and reform-Democrat variety) with the radicals and student activists which formed later that year. At the rally at which Rice spoke, there were about 200 people; that autumn, we filled [Pittsburgh's] Carnegie Hall with about 900; and that was just the beginning.[14]

Rice recalls that Pittsburgh Bishop John J. Wright and the

13. Ibid.
14. Letter from Paul Le Blanc to the author, October 25, 1975.

pope were much more tolerant of his antiwar activities than his old associates in the labor movement. His invitations to speak at union gatherings, and his contacts with union officials fell off sharply. He chose to become a parish priest at a church in Pittsburgh's Black ghetto.

As part of the broadening process of the Spring Mobilization Committee, the Rt. Reverend Monsignor Charles O. Rice was asked to become a sponsor. He agreed. On April 15, 1967, he marched at the front of the New York demonstration.

\*       \*       \*

The civil rights movement of the late 1950s and early 1960s was centrally concerned with the elimination of de jure segregation in the South. Before it began, the "Jim Crow" laws passed after the Reconstruction period were still in force. Blacks in most areas of the South and in some border states could not attend the same schools as whites. In many areas they were required by local law to sit in the back of buses, to use separate and invariably unequal public facilities, such as waiting rooms, lunch counters, and so on. In many areas of the South they were barred from the polls by bureaucratic manipulation or by terror, usually combined.

This Southern system was recognized in federal law through Supreme Court decisions upholding the so-called separate but equal doctrine. In 1954 the Supreme Court reversed its previous stand and declared the "separate but equal" doctrine to be in violation of the U.S. Constitution. A crucial factor in forcing this ruling was the pressure of the colonial revolution—especially the Chinese revolution. The U.S. government was embarrassed in its relations with the nonwhite world by the judicially sanctioned segregation in its Southern states.

In the narrow sense the ruling dealt with a Kansas school district, but it laid the legal basis for a campaign to challenge the whole Southern system of de jure segregation. The original suit was brought by the National Association for the Advancement of Colored People, which emphasized proceeding with the campaign through the courts.

The movement assumed a mass direct-action form with the Montgomery, Alabama, boycott of segregated city buses which began in December 1955 and lasted through most of 1956. Its success made Rev. Martin Luther King, Jr., a national figure and led to the formation of the Southern Christian Leadership Conference (SCLC). This group, headed by King, was a coalition mainly of Black Southern preachers who called upon their church congregations to participate in or support the Gandhian nonviolent direct-action projects led by King.

The Southern student sit-ins against segregated public facilities that began in 1960 gave birth to the Student Nonviolent Coordinating Committee (SNCC), whose chapters were located on Black campuses in the South.

The Freedom Rides of 1961 against segregation on interstate buses traveling through the South catapulted the previously small Congress of Racial Equality (CORE) into becoming a major force in the movement.

These four were the major organizations of the civil rights movement. The Urban League, a middle-class-oriented Black group composed largely of business and professional people, was also sometimes involved.

Until 1966 none of these groups had adopted a formal position against the war. Individual SNCC leaders, including the group's chairman, John Lewis, had stated their opposition, but not in the name of their organization. Both Martin Luther King and James Farmer, head of CORE, were pacifists and had expressed opposition as individuals to the killing in Vietnam, but in the early years they avoided association with the antiwar movement. Whitney Young and Roy Wilkins, respective heads of the Urban League and the NAACP, simply supported U.S. foreign policy.

The stated reason why SNCC, CORE, and SCLC did not take a position from the first against the war was that foreign policy as such was not the concern of their organizations, and they felt that becoming involved with it would reduce their effectiveness in the struggle for equality for Blacks.

In the early period the most prominent Black leader to speak out strongly against U.S. policy in Vietnam was Malcolm X, whose base was in Harlem, not the South. He, too, was centrally concerned with the struggle for equality by Afro-Americans, rather than Vietnam or other questions. But he often spoke of the need to internationalize the Afro-American struggle so that American Blacks would not look upon themselves as a minority. For example, in November 1964 Malcolm said:

> [What] I would like to impress upon every Afro-American leader is that there is no kind of action in this country ever going to bear fruit unless

that action is tied in with the over-all international struggle. You waste your time when you talk to this man, just you and him. So when you talk to him, let him know your brother is behind you, and you've got some brothers behind that brother. That's the only way to talk to him, that's the only language he knows.[15]

The real reason behind the stands of Whitney Young, Roy Wilkins, and to a certain extent Martin Luther King, Jr., and James Farmer, was that if civil rights leaders didn't rock the boat on U.S. foreign policy, if they proved themselves supportive in that sense, or at least kept their mouths shut, it would be easier to gain domestic concessions. Malcolm's approach was different. In January 1965 he declared:

in 1964, the oppressed people of South Vietnam, and in that entire Southeast Asia area, were successful in fighting off the agents of imperialism. . . . Little rice farmers, peasants, with a rifle—up against all the highly-mechanized weapons of warfare—jets, napalm, battleships, everything else, and they can't put those rice farmers back where they want them. Somebody's waking up. . . .

Now, in speaking like this, it doesn't mean that I am anti-American. I am not. I'm not anti-American, or un-American. And I'm not saying that to defend myself. Because if I was that, I'd have a right to be that—after what America has done to us. This government should feel lucky that our people aren't anti-American. They should get down on their hands and knees every morning and thank God that 22 million black people have not become anti-American. You've given us every right to. The whole world would side with us, if we became anti-American. You know, that's something to think about.

But we aren't anti-American. We are anti or against what America is doing wrong in other parts of the world as well as here. And what she did in the Congo in 1964 is wrong. It's criminal, criminal. And what she did to the American public, to get the American public to go along with it, is criminal. What she's doing in South Vietnam is criminal. She's causing American soldiers to be murdered every day, killed every day, die every day, for no reason at all. That's wrong. Now, you're not supposed to be so blind with patriotism that you can't face reality. Wrong is wrong no matter who does it or who says it. . . .[16]

In a radio interview January 28, 1965, Malcolm pointed out a

---

15. Exchange with Jesse Gray at the Audubon Ballroom, November 29, 1964. *Malcolm X Speaks* (New York: Merit Publishers, 1965), p. 89.
16. Ibid., pp. 148-49.

weakness in the government's position on Vietnam which the civil rights leaders had declined to exploit:

> It's a problem anytime the United States can come up with so many alibis not to get involved in Mississippi and to get involved in the Congo and involved in Asia and in South Vietnam. Why that, right there, should show our people that the government is incapable of taking the kind of action necessary to solve the problem of black people in this country. But at the same time she has her nose stuck into the problems of others everywhere else.[17]

At this time a drive to register Black voters was in progress around Selma, Alabama. The local white authorities resisted with arrests and beatings. On one occasion Rev. James Bevel of the SCLC walked out of the Clark County courthouse in Selma after demanding that Blacks be registered to vote there, and was clubbed down by Sheriff James Clark himself.

SNCC workers invited Malcolm X to speak in Selma on February 5, 1965. He was well received by the young demonstrators and expressed a desire to cooperate with the civil rights groups. But Malcolm was assassinated two weeks later before anything more could come of it, and just as the new antiwar movement was being born. Had he lived he may well have played an important role in it.

In March 1965, when the Alabama drive reached a peak with a Selma-to-Montgomery march, aimed at forcing the federal government to intervene to protect the voting rights of Blacks, the question of Vietnam actually was interjected into the civil rights struggle.

On March 7, state troopers under orders from Governor George C. Wallace, and local possemen had stopped the march with a brutal assault, injuring at least eighty-six marchers.

SNCC Chairman John Lewis, who had been clubbed and was later hospitalized, spoke to an angry crowd of marchers taking sanctuary in a church:

"I don't see how President Johnson can send troops to Vietnam . . . to the Congo . . . to Africa and can't send troops to Selma, Alabama." The next day even NAACP Executive Director Roy Wilkins, referring to the landing of 3,500 U.S. marines in

Vietnam the previous week, burst out at a press conference with: "Dammit, they can send somebody to Alabama and defend the government right here!"[18]

Fannie Lou Hamer, a leader of the Mississippi Freedom Democratic Party, sent a telegram to President Johnson demanding that he pull U.S. troops out of Vietnam and send them to Alabama to protect the rights of Blacks. Lewis also announced SNCC support to the April 17, 1965, SDS march on Washington against the war in Vietnam.

The federal government was so embarrassed over the Selma events that President Johnson was forced to use the National Guard to protect the marchers and to announce a voting-rights bill, the details of which were stronger than anything he had previously promised. The introduction of the Vietnam issue was not, of course, the reason for this, but it certainly helped increase the pressure on the government.

With the exception of SNCC, however, the civil rights organizations deliberately abstained from the antiwar movement through 1965. At its convention that fall SCLC adopted a resolution declaring that "the primary function of our organization is to secure full leadership rights—for the Negro citizens of this country" and limited the efforts of SCLC in mass actions to the question of racial brotherhood. It did say that in the event of "perilous escalation of the Vietnam conflict we respect the right of Dr. King and the administrative committee to alter this course and turn the full resources of the organization to the cessation of bloodshed and war."[19] The door was open but King didn't walk through it for another year and a half.

On January 6, 1966, SNCC released a statement that made it the first of the major civil rights groups to make opposition to the government's Vietnam policies a part of its formal program as an organization. The incident that precipitated this statement was the murder of another SNCC worker, Samuel Younge, shot down while attempting to integrate a gas station restroom in Tuskegee, Alabama. The statement also declared, "We are in sympathy with and support the men in this country who are unwilling to respond to the military draft which would compel them to contribute their lives to U.S. aggression in the name of the

18. *Militant,* March 15, 1965.
19. *Liberation,* September 19, 1965.

'freedom' we find so false in this country."[20]

It was Julian Bond's refusal to dissociate from this statement that was used by the Georgia state legislature as grounds for depriving him of the seat in that body to which he had been elected.

In March 1966, James Farmer resigned as executive director of CORE to take a post as head of a social work foundation recently set up by the Johnson administration. Under his successor, Floyd McKissick, CORE moved to an antiwar position. In April the executive board of SCLC adopted a resolution asking President Johnson to consider withdrawing from Vietnam, but continued its reluctance to become involved directly in antiwar activity.

Martin Luther King did become a sponsor of Clergy and Laymen Concerned About Vietnam, but he continued to abstain from strong public criticism of the government's Vietnam policies through 1966. The reason was not a lack of personal opposition to the war. Nor was King ignorant of the connection between the colonial revolution and the struggle of American Blacks. King, like Malcolm X and A. J. Muste, was a person of considerable depth and not a superficial thinker. During the early days of the movement in Montgomery, the colonial revolution was one of the themes he used in his speeches to the mass meetings of the boycotting Blacks there. In March 1956 I heard one of these speeches, which I was told by others present was not atypical. In it King said:

You know whether we want to be or not, we are caught in a great moment of history. . . . It has reached the point where you are part of this movement or you are against it. . . . It is bigger than Montgomery. . . . the vast majority of the people of the world are colored. . . . Up until four or five years ago most of the one and one-quarter billion colored peoples were exploited by empires of the West. . . . India, China, Africa. Today many are free. . . . And the rest are on the road. . . . We are part of that great movement.[21]

But that had been before King was a national figure, before his speeches were widely reported, before every controversial statement he made was dissected by powerful "friends," and before U.S. troops were in Vietnam. In my opinion that early speech,

20. *Militant,* January 17, 1966.
21. *Militant,* March 19, 1956.

which had other themes as well, and whose central thrust was to raise the morale of the then-beleaguered ranks of the Montgomery protesters, was far richer in content and more beautiful in form than the widely heralded "I have a dream" speech at the 1963 March on Washington. King was always best when he was closest to the common people, rather than the liberal Establishment.

The reason for King's abstention from the antiwar movement in 1965 and 1966 was political expediency. He occupied the central—as well as the center—position in the civil rights movement. It was on him that the greatest pressures fell, and the greatest responsibility. His policies were not undisputed, but he was the only single figure with the authority to unify the whole movement—and its supporters—around particular campaigns.

While his strategy included mass actions, it was not aimed at building an independent power. King's approach was heavily dependent on the old idea of a labor-liberal-civil rights coalition within the Democratic Party. He had entrée to high government officials and liberal politicians, especially within the Democratic Party.

He was constantly besieged with advice and warnings that for him to campaign against the war would jeopardize these relations. And in truth King's standing in the country and in the world was so high—outside the U.S. no doubt higher than any other American—that for him to take up the antiwar cause would be a tremendous symbolic blow to the administration. Washington could not be expected to react kindly to it.

On one occasion in 1965 King actually tested this out, with due regard for the anticommunist posture then required by anyone wishing to remain "in" with the liberal Establishment. Speaking at Virginia State College in Petersburg on July 5, he said:

> I'm not going to sit by and see war escalated without saying anything about it. . . . It is worthless to talk about integration if there is no world to integrate in. I am certainly as concerned about seeing the defeat of Communism as anyone else, but we won't defeat Communism by guns or bombs or gases. We will do it by making democracy work. . . . The war in Vietnam must be stopped. There must be a negotiated settlement even with the Vietcong.[22]

22. William Robert Miller, *Martin Luther King* (New York: Weybright & Talley, 1968), p. 236.

King was promptly called by administration officials and vilified in political circles. "Friends of the movement" such as New York's Governor Nelson Rockefeller let him know they didn't like it. The antiwar movement at the time was still small and the favorable response seemed to come from sources with little influence. King backed off.

Through 1966 A. J. Muste would occasionally telephone King to inform him of some antiwar project and indicate there was a standing invitation if King could see his way clear to participate. As was his habit, Muste never used strong pressure but he was not above pointing out that the young people in the nonviolent movement were asking questions.

In truth King's authority with the youth in his own movement had been eroding for some time. The disputes between King and the militants, especially those in SNCC, did not turn around the war in Vietnam. More central were such questions as the strategy of the movement, Black nationalism—which King opposed and to which the Black youth were attracted—and philosophical nonviolence as opposed to a posture of self-defense. But King's moral authority in these arguments could not be separated from his abstention on the Vietnam question. As the militants saw it, King had put himself in the position of actively advocating nonviolence only to the Blacks in their struggle, while in effect remaining publicly silent on the government's policy of wholesale violence in Vietnam.

By mid-1966 the civil rights movement as King had shaped it was in deep crisis. The fight against de jure segregation had largely been won, and that for voting rights in the South was being won. But there was little celebrating. The spontaneous uprisings in the big city Black ghettos—which broke out on a small scale in Harlem in 1964 and then on a huge scale in Watts in 1965, hit several Northern cities in the summer of 1966. The focus of attention shifted from the rural South to the big cities, mostly in the North where there had never been Jim Crow laws and where Blacks could vote, but where de facto discrimination and segregation were as bad as in the South.

The slogan "Black Power" was being popularized by SNCC's new chairman, Stokely Carmichael. The Black Panther Party was beginning to organize on a program of independent Black political action and armed self-defense, and its rhetoric was getting less and less defensive.

There was an intimate connection between the war and the

arguments during this period in and around the civil rights movement over nonviolence. The war was not the origin of the dispute—that lay in the experiences of the movement itself, particularly with racist murders. But the war was a constant underlying theme. The fact that liberals who supported, or did not oppose, the Johnson war policy were constantly admonishing Blacks to stick to strict nonviolence in their own struggle, was enraging not only to the militants but to masses of ordinary Black people.

Strangely, Roy Wilkins of the NAACP was not as vulnerable on this point as King, because Wilkins was not a pacifist and the NAACP had always recognized the right of self-defense. While King was not usually attacked openly on this question, by implication he was constantly referred to.

For example, CORE Associate Director Lincoln Lynch, in explaining why CORE in spite of its pacifist origins had at its 1966 convention supported self-defense, declared:

> Let no one ask us to sit idly by, with hands in our pockets, knees on the ground, praying to some supreme being up there, while Ku Klux Klaners are murdering the Chaneys, the Goodmans, the Mrs. Liuzzos, the Evers and so on. Let *no man* ask us to sit by and see such things happen while we pray and say that we are nonviolent. Let the American public begin to talk to us about nonviolence when the President practices nonviolence in Vietnam.[23]

This contradiction was a factor in the rage of the Black youth of the 1960s. The government was advising them to be patient and strictly nonviolent in their own struggle for freedom at home, while threatening them with prison for not being violent in Vietnam. The majority of the Black population understood the issues in the war much earlier than the whites in part because of such contradictions.

All these pressures increased through 1966 and by the time the Spring Mobilization Committee started building for the April 1967 demonstration, we began to get signals that the Southern Christian Leadership Conference—and Martin Luther King himself—were preparing to move on the Vietnam question.

On January 13, 1967, Rev. James Bevel of the SCLC attended a

23. *Militant,* August 8, 1966.

meeting in New York of the working committee of the Spring Mobilization. In previous discussions between Bevel and Dellinger the suggestion had been made that Bevel become national director of the Spring Mobilization and the purpose of the meeting was to hear Bevel's ideas on the project.

Most of us on the committee were quite anxious to have Bevel aboard—especially since it meant a chance that King would speak at the April event.

We knew there had been some soul-searching over the war question going on in the leadership of the SCLC, but we were not prepared for Bevel's presentation. It was in fact one of the strangest meetings I have ever attended. Bevel began with what I could only assume was some sort of allegory that I was not equipped to understand. It was a long, rambling story involving someone he spoke to in his cellar during recent long periods of meditation. Perhaps he meant God, but I don't really know.

I looked around the room for some indication of what the others were thinking. It might as well have been a poker game in West Texas. Finally Cora Weiss caught my eye. She was one of those people who could say a great deal with a look. This one said something like "I don't get it either, but be careful, Fred."

Anyway, in the course of the process in Bevel's cellar, he had a revelation that the war could be stopped, and soon, but not by demonstrations in the United States. Instead we should get large numbers of people, including prominent figures, to go to both North and South Vietnam, perhaps on a special ship, and in some unexplained way they would interject themselves between the warring armies, forcing them to shoot the "peace brigade" or stop the killing entirely.

It was not really a new idea. Bevel himself had been known to suggest something similar as far back as 1965, long before his more recent meditations. And it wasn't new then either. As far as I was concerned it was a harebrained scheme at best, and politically wrong in any case. The last thing the Vietnamese needed was another large batch of uninvited foreigners messing around in their country, with or without guns.

But as per Weiss's admonition, I was careful in the discussion. It was clear no one else wanted to take the blame either, for shutting the door to the man who had the "in" with Martin Luther King. The discussion was long, and rather delicate. Two things did become clear in the course of it. First, the peace brigade idea was Bevel's alone, not SCLC's or King's. Second,

Bevel's participation in a leading capacity with the Mobilization had the approval of both King and the SCLC. The only thing to do was to make the best of it.

The minutes of this discussion are quite succinct and do not reveal its details or its flavor. They are, instead, a diplomatic summary of the result as far as the committee was concerned. They read in full:

> Discussion with James Bevel: (a) James Bevel outlined his views on non-violent approaches to a program of actually ending the war in Vietnam, including a campaign around a "Declaration of Civilization" and an international team of prominent figures to visit Vietnam.
>
> (b) Much discussion centered on the proposal of organizing a visit to Vietnam, north and south, by a team of world figures, Americans like Rev. Martin Luther King, Jr., and prominent people like Gunnar Myrdal from other countries, with a perspective of thousands of people eventually traveling to Vietnam from all countries and backgrounds. The April 15 mobilization was seen as a possible launching occasion for such a project. There was discussion pro and con on this proposal. Bevel said he was flexible on details, but thought strongly that the April 15 mobilization should be viewed not as an end in itself but as a beginning, the launching of a serious campaign for ending the war and that this would make the April 15 action more attractive.
>
> *Proposal on National Director:* Dave Dellinger proposed that James Bevel be National Director of the Spring Mobilization. This was supported with the general agreement and enthusiasm of the body. James Bevel agreed to accept the position.[24]

Bevel proved to be no mere figurehead director. He swept into the New York operation with all the energy he had displayed in the Southern civil rights campaigns, bringing with him a group of young Black preachers from SCLC. Some of them—like Bernard Lafayette—had been members of the old guard of SNCC.

Bevel spent little time on organizational details, concentrating instead on outreach to new forces and publicity. His colleagues from SCLC kept an eye out for anything that might reflect badly on Martin Luther King should he decide to associate himself with the activity. In this regard we had some discussion about the reasons for our policy on nonexclusion, and Bevel went along

24. Minutes of the Working Committee of the Spring Mobilization Committee, January 13, 1967. (Copy in author's files.)

with it. As time went on he spoke less and less about the peace brigade idea and it faded away. Overall he played a positive role in building April 15.

And he did succeed in getting Martin Luther King's agreement to speak at the New York demonstration.

*         *         *

Not long after Bevel joined the Mobilization it became clear that King had made up his mind to enter the fight against the war. He knew very well it meant a break with the Johnson administration, probably the loss of significant financial supporters to SCLC, and possibly even a rupture in relations with the NAACP and the Urban League. He made the move in a careful but deliberate way, covering his right flank as best he could. The April 15 mobilization was not to be his opening shot, but a culmination of a series of preparatory public statements. These were made in association with certain people inclined to be tolerant of the antiwar cause who were also a part of the groups he was most concerned about maintaining ties with, such as liberal politicians and clergymen.

The first such statement came on February 25, 1967, in Beverly Hills, California, at a conference on the war sponsored by *Nation* magazine. Also speaking at the conference were Democratic Senators Eugene McCarthy of Minnesota, George McGovern of South Dakota, and Ernest Gruening of Alaska as well as Senator Mark Hatfield of Oregon, a Republican. All were prominent doves. Said King:

The promises of the great society have been shot down on the battlefield of Vietnam. The pursuit of this widened war has narrowed domestic welfare programs, making the poor, white and Negro, bear the heaviest burdens both at the front and at home. The recently revealed ten billion dollar mis-estimate of the war budget alone is more than five times the amount committed to anti-poverty programs. The security we profess to seek in foreign adventures we will lose in our decaying cities.

We are willing to make the Negro 100 per cent of a citizen in warfare, but reduce him to 50 per cent of a citizen on American soil. Half of all the Negroes live in substandard housing and he has half the income of whites.

There is twice as much unemployment and infant mortality among Negroes. There were twice as many Negroes in combat in Vietnam at the beginning of 1967, and twice as many died in action—20.6 per cent—in proportion to their numbers in the population as whites.[25]

In the same speech he called the war immoral, a violation of the UN Charter and of the principle of self-determination, and declared: "We must demonstrate, teach and preach until the very foundations of our nation are shaken."[26]

In mid-March the Mobilization Committee got word that it could announce King as a speaker for April 15.

On April 4 in a major speech at Riverside Church in New York, King explained his dilemma during the previous period:

> As I have walked among the desperate, rejected and angry young men I have told them that Molotov cocktails and rifles would not solve their problems. . . . They asked me if our own nation wasn't using massive doses of violence to solve its problems, to bring about the changes it wanted. Their questions hit home, and I knew that I could never again raise my voice against the violence of the oppressed in the ghettos without having first spoken clearly to the greatest purveyor of violence in the world today—my own government . . .[27]

The reaction of the liberal Establishment was classically articulated by an editorial in the *Washington Post* of April 6:

> Dr. King has done a grave injury to those who are his natural allies in a great struggle to remove ancient abuses from our public life; and he has done an even graver injury to himself. Many who have listened to him with respect will never again accord him the same confidence. He has diminished his usefulness to his cause, to his country and to his people.

On April 15, 1967, Martin Luther King, Jr., joined Msgr. Charles Owen Rice at the head of the New York march. Later he stood together briefly on the platform with Floyd McKissick of CORE and Stokely Carmichael of SNCC, their arms around each other's shoulders, to greet the giant crowd.

During the building of the April 15 demonstrations the antiwar movement still operated by and large in an atmosphere of

25. *Militant,* March 13, 1967.
26. Miller, *Martin Luther King,* p. 266.
27. *New York Times,* April 5, 1967.

hostility on the part of the major news media in the United States. Statements by movement spokespersons challenging the official version of the conduct of the war were not taken seriously by the media, though they generally proved to be far more accurate than the official handouts. There was plenty of information of this kind in the foreign press, in reports by occasional critical visitors from various countries to Vietnam, and even in letters from GIs that would find their way into print, not infrequently in the *Congressional Record.* This material was picked up by movement publications like *Viet Report,* leaflets, and newsletters, and distributed as widely as resources permitted. But the major media were dominated by the official versions and denials. The circumlocutions, euphemisms, and double-talk of the Pentagon and State Department press agents were not as a rule seriously challenged in the major newspapers and on TV.

In December 1966, however, a series of dispatches was filed from Hanoi by *New York Times* Assistant Managing Editor Harrison E. Salisbury, which provided a major breakthrough in this regard and helped lay the basis for a more searching approach on the part of sections of the major media. The editors of the *New York Times* no doubt had their own journalistic and political reasons for sending Salisbury on this assignment. His dispatches, however, appeared in a changing political context in which the antiwar movement was a factor.

It was the standing position of the North Vietnamese that they would not enter negotiations while the North was being bombed by the U.S. As Christmas approached there was hope among critics of the escalation policy that the traditional holiday truce might once again be extended, the bombing of the North suspended, and that this might lead to negotiations. On December 13, however, reports appeared in the foreign press that the U.S. had escalated the bombing of the North by strikes on Hanoi proper, and civilian areas had been hit. The administration issued denials. The reports persisted and the Pentagon offered the explanation that military targets near Hanoi may have been hit, but that any damage to the city proper must have resulted from North Vietnamese antiaircraft ordnance falling back upon the city.

It was the kind of denial that would be taken seriously only by those who were willing to believe anything just because the government said it. In those days there were a lot more people with that attitude than there are now.

In New York City a number of antiwar figures had previously arranged an emergency demonstration to be set in motion on a few hours' notice should another major escalation of the war take place. The bombing of Hanoi was one of the several acts that it had previously been decided would trigger this demonstration. The idea, initiated by Norma Becker, was that leading activists in the New York City antiwar movement would pledge to commit civil disobedience at the Whitehall draft induction center near Wall Street in Manhattan in the event of such an escalation. A small committee headed by Muste was empowered to set the time for the action when it judged the escalation was indeed occurring.

This procedure was decided upon precisely because we anticipated that another escalation would be denied at first and obscured as much as possible by the administration. The fact that a number of leaders of the New York antiwar movement would be arrested protesting the escalation would, it was hoped, at least break into the major news media, whereas mere statements by movement spokespersons would have been ignored or given short shrift.

Civil disobedience by small groups was never my cup of tea. But I went along with this plan and signed the pledge, because the chances were that a mass demonstration could simply not be organized on such short notice and it was important that the country, and particularly the movement, should receive a clear signal about the escalation.

So on December 15, two days after the first reports of the Hanoi bombing and while the administration was still contemptuously denying them, fifty-two of us, led by Muste and supported by a much larger crowd of pickets, blocked the main entrance to the induction center and sang Christmas carols while the police loaded us into vans one by one. The movement, at least, got the message about protesting the escalation.

Incidentally, when they threw me into a cell in the Tombs, A. J. was already inside, sitting quietly on a bench. "Look what you got me into," I joked. "It's every man for himself," he replied, which like most of his offhand humor also contained a philosophical point. None of us knew it then, but that was to be A. J.'s last arrest.

Shortly thereafter a delegation of American women went to Hanoi at the invitation of the Vietnamese Women's Union. They were Barbara Deming, an editor of *Liberation*; Pat Griffith; Grace Mora Newman, sister of one of the Fort Hood Three; and Diane

Nash Bevel, one of the heroic figures of SNCC's early civil rights battles and the wife of James Bevel. A major reason for their trip was to see for themselves, and report back to the United States, what kind of bombing had actually been taking place in North Vietnam. These women were in Hanoi at the same time Harrison Salisbury was, and on one occasion even found themselves huddling together with the newsman in the same Hanoi hotel cellar during a U.S. bombing raid.

On December 24 Salisbury's first dispatch refuted the U.S. denials of the December 13-14 raids, declaring that "damage certainly occurred right in the center of town." Salisbury's reports confirmed that the U.S. had been bombing North Vietnamese population centers since 1965, that extensive damage had been caused to civilian areas where even U.S. military dispatches did not claim there were military targets, and that Hanoi proper was indeed being bombed.

The articles provoked a deep reaction in sections of the American news media. Salisbury's *New York Times* stories were reproduced in important papers across the country. The *Denver Post* of December 28 commented: "It is far from reassuring to have his on-the-spot reports conflict so sharply with the official pronouncements of the government of the United States." The same day the *Cleveland Plain Dealer* declared:

> The credibility gap yawns wider as one reads Salisbury's account from the capital, Hanoi. . . . The government is waging a war of steel and fire in Vietnam. It should not treat the American people as a second adversary, to be kept at bay with a smoke screen of distortion and soothing syrup.

Following the Salisbury articles, three major TV stations in the Pacific Northwest—KING-TV in Seattle, KREM-TV in Spokane, and KGW-TV in Portland—carried an editorial attacking Johnson's conduct of the war and demanding an immediate halt to the bombing of North Vietnam. Stimpson Bullitt, the president of King Broadcasting Company, which owned the stations, said the editorial was prompted by the failure of the networks to give adequate coverage to the critics of U.S. involvement in Vietnam.

"In their regular newscasts, which is what most people see," Bullitt said, "the networks are just showing us pictures from Vietnam on the sacrifices and misfortunes of war and talking about the enemy. They're not covering the real controversy over our policies."[28]

This was an important breakthrough in the all-important TV media. This attitude did not spread overnight, but little by little the reports from Vietnam became more revealing and the dissimulating handouts of government officials more and more subject to searching review.

Still, the attitude of the press toward the antiwar movement itself was not friendly. Characteristic was a New York press conference held by Deming, Newman, and Griffith on January 10 shortly after their return to the U.S. The reporters were generally hostile. One of them asked if the women didn't realize they were "being used" by the North Vietnamese. Deming replied:

"It is undeniable that what we are saying is useful to them. But it is a truthful report and we believe it will also prove useful to the American people."[29] Another reporter confronted the women with a Defense Department denial of one of their previous statements that "lazy dog" bombs were being dropped by the U.S. on North Vietnam. These were one variety of antipersonnel weapon in which a batch of small bombs contained in a larger one are scattered when the main receptacle hits, and which explode later spraying small pieces of metal over a wide area. They are completely useless against structures and only affect flesh. Griffith responded by displaying half of one of the small bombs which she had brought back with her in her purse. (Typically, the Defense Department denial had been a subterfuge based on a quibble over the formal name of the device.) Said Deming:

This attempt to terrorize the people into surrendering is just not going to work. Unlike our people, it is very clear to these people what they are fighting for—even the children. For them it is simply a matter of getting rid of foreign domination of their country. They will fight to the last child to win their independence. If they are bombed back into the jungle, they will fight from the jungle. They are quite prepared to do this. This is something the American people must look at. The only way to defeat these people is to exterminate them. Our government is moving in that direction. The American people must ask themselves if this is what they want.[30]

28. *New York Times,* January 1, 1967.
29. *Militant,* January 16, 1967.
30. Ibid.

A. J. Muste himself took a trip to North Vietnam with an international delegation of elder ministers, departing at the end of December and returning to the U.S. on January 25, 1967. He also reported that the Vietnamese "seem absolutely determined to see it through." He was pleased to find that the preparations for April 15 had progressed well during his absence. For the next two weeks he devoted himself to this work. On February 11, 1967, he died of a heart attack at the age of eighty-two.

There was much feeling and some tears among those who knew and worked with him, but little anguish because there was no sense of tragedy about A. J.'s life or death. He had lived long and done well by the tasks he set himself.

In terms of the particular role he played in the antiwar movement A. J. was irreplaceable. But when it came, his death did not shatter the coalition. To be sure, there were problems later that would have been easier and perhaps better resolved if he had still been around. But he was not a star or a guru or an organizational dynamo with all the reins in his own two hands. Like all good organizers he was a team worker who tried to bring out the best in those with whom he worked. He was indifferent to the limelight, had accumulated little fame, and few illusions were attached to him. So with his passing the movement simply carried on.

He had lived long enough to play a crucial role in unifying and broadening the antiwar movement while working to maintain its radical thrust, its ability to cut away at the root of the problem. If he had died six months earlier—before the Spring and Student Mobilization Committees were established and on their way— there might well have been some greater political cost.

"Some of A. J.'s friends and co-workers," commented Dellinger in *Liberation,* "have been saying that he would not have died when he did unless he felt that he could afford to." Elsewhere in the same article Dellinger made the following observation about Muste:

He managed to work creatively with those who shared only a part of his philosophy or strategy, without sacrificing the integrity of his own deepest beliefs or being prevented from engaging in the actions that stemmed from them. It was part of his greatness that he could feel that he was right without becoming self-righteous or demeaning those who could not share in all his activities or attitudes. It was enough for him that they walked part of the way with him and that while walking together he and they could probe and examine and analyze so that each might learn from the other.[31]

As one who "walked part of the way" with Muste I appreciated this tribute.

*       *       *

Bevel's approach to building April 15 was at least dramatic. He also had a way of shaking cobwebs from the mind. On one occasion he burst into the New York office with: "What this demonstration needs is some Indians." This time Bevel's argument was simple and clear enough: There were some 15,000 Native Americans in the U.S. forces in Vietnam, a proportion several times their weight in the population as a whole, and like Blacks, their casualties were out of proportion. What is more, Native Americans know what it is to be on the receiving end of genocidal war. Somewhere out there, said Bevel, are Indians who will want to participate in this demonstration.

After some initial inquiries, Paul Boutelle got the assignment of sending out some letters to Native American groups inviting them to participate. Boutelle then visited some Indian reservations. At the Onondaga reservation in upstate New York, he recalls:

I stopped near three Native Americans working on a car to ask directions to the longhouse where the meeting I was to speak to was being held. One of them—he was in his twenties—said: "What do you want, nigger? Did you come here to get us to sit-in, demonstrate, or riot?" I didn't get mad at him. I understood he had the white Establishment's interpretation from the TV or newspapers of what was going on in this country, or maybe that it was just whites and Blacks fighting each other over the Indians' land. Another thing too: Indians are the most oppressed and economically deprived people in North America. These three were fixing an old car and I was driving a new one. It wasn't mine, of course, just rented so I could get from the airport to the reservation. But there was no use trying to explain that.

I just told him he shouldn't use the white man's derogatory names toward me because I wasn't using any names like that toward him. I told

31. *Liberation,* January 1967. This issue was late, and some of the material in it was written in February.

them why I was there—I'd been invited by a friend, Mad Bear Anderson, to speak to a gathering of Iroquois chiefs about the antiwar movement. Eventually I found the longhouse and the council was interested, but there was a conflict of dates, and they couldn't make it April 15.[32]

Boutelle finally got a positive response from Robert Burnette, a Rosebud Sioux who lived on the reservation at Mission, South Dakota, and was director of the American Indian Civil Rights Council. Burnette wrote: "The more I see of our policy towards the Vietnam war, the more it reminds me of the way Indians ended up on reservations."[33]

Boutelle visited the Rosebud Sioux reservation and was well received. Burnette organized a busload of Rosebud Sioux to make the two thousand-mile trip to the East Coast. They planned to attend the mobilization in New York and then go on to Washington for a demonstration of their own at the Bureau of Indian Affairs. The Mobilization had little difficulty raising the money for the bus.

But Burnette had not counted on the government's crude response and its use of the FBI as an agency for political dirty tricks. Later Burnette wrote the following account in an affidavit to the Emergency Civil Liberties Committee:

Two FBI agents, a Bureau of Indian Affairs officer, and a City Marshal began questioning and intimidating those who were to take the trip and due to the intimidation and lies, only 7 out of the 35 chose to remain in the group to make the trip.

Such accusations as "the participants were to march with niggers" and that this was "nothing but a nigger march," and "had nothing to do with Indians" made these people choose to remain on the Reservation and not participate.

Those remaining went out on the Reservation and gathered others, and on the way picked up others in Winner, South Dakota; making a total of 19. These people proceeded to New York and did participate in the parade and rally, and two of them appeared on the speakers' platform in front of the United Nations headquarters.[34]

On April 16 the bus went to Washington while Burnette, who

32. Taped interview with Paul Boutelle by the author, August 20, 1975.

33. "Roundup of Nationwide Mobilization Activity," April 3, 1967. Spring Mobilization Committee mailing. (Copy in author's files.)

34. "No First Amendment for First Americans" by Robert Burnette, *Rights*, Spring 1967. Journal of the Emergency Civil Liberties Committee.

had some arrangements to make, followed by other means. According to the Sioux on the bus, FBI agents met them in Washington and told the driver not to wait at the agreed meeting place. The Indians on the bus, unfamiliar with the city, were unable to find Burnette, or he the bus, in spite of frantic appeals to the police and in spite of the fact that the police and FBI knew where both Burnette and the bus were.

The demonstration in Washington was therefore aborted. Burnette was worried sick and didn't know the others were safe until they arrived back in South Dakota, where he telephoned from Washington. His narrative continues:

Mr. Burnette immediately proceeded back to [South Dakota] by car and upon talking to the various people involved, learned just what took place in Washington, D.C., and the part the FBI and Federal Park Police had played in the separation of the chartered bus and Mr. Burnette. This separation was deliberately carried out.

Upon returning home, Mr. Burnette was advised by those who took part in the rally in New York, that all were to be arrested as soon as Mr. Burnette returned to the Reservation. This threat was made by Tribal officials, Office of Economic Opportunity officials, and Federal officials. But it was never carried out.

Up to this very day (May 11, 1967) we have been receiving continuous pressure from the FBI agents—even some people who had not participated. They too have been questioned simply because of the similarity of their names. These FBI agents have been using older models of automobiles in order to conceal their presence on the Reservation. . . . It is the opinion of Robert Burnette that these acts took place solely for the purpose of keeping the American Indian out of a very touchy international issue because of the impact the American Indian has internationally. . . .

But Burnette's intrepid band had already had an international impact. On April 13, Burnette and Chief Lame Deer of the Rosebud Sioux, and Mad Bear Anderson of the Tuscarora, spoke at a street corner meeting at 125th Street and Seventh Avenue in Harlem. Burnette said:

We are losing Indian boys by the hundreds. Last July 4th, when the white man was celebrating his independence, I lost a first cousin in Vietnam. We Indians are without any rights anyway. What are we fighting for? We are destroying little people. Our people are being forced to kill in Vietnam.

People have asked me "What are you doing in Harlem?" My answer is that I have come to the other reservation. . . . The government plays a game of divide and conquer. Some day we'll all get wise and not let them do this to us. This society is run by the dollar and by the landlords. This is not right. No man owns the land we stand on. It belongs to the people that use it. When you die it goes to somebody else.[35]

Mad Bear Anderson said:

They used germ warfare against us in 1870 when they drove my people across into Kansas. They promised us homes, land and tools. . . . Wagons came filled with clothes and blankets. They were infected with smallpox! My people took them and they died and died.

Anderson had been to Vietnam several times as a seaman. He said:

When I walk down the streets in Saigon, those people look like my brothers and sisters. They have a right to determine their own destiny. Many told me they detest American GIs being over there. In Vietnam the people should not be forced to accept a government at the point of a gun.[36]

On April 15 Native Americans made up the first contingent of the New York march carrying signs comparing U.S. Vietnam commander General William C. Westmoreland to Custer, and others that said: "Great White Father Speaks with Forked Tongue!" and "Americans—Do Not Do to the Vietnamese What You Did to Us." Chief Lame Deer and Henry Crow Dog of the Rosebud Sioux joined the other notables at the head of the march.

*        *        *

Much of Muste's time in the last days of his life was devoted to working on the formal call for the Spring Mobilization, a process that involved long hours of meetings and rather delicate negotiations to come to agreement within what was by this time a much broader coalition. In its final version the call was politically a stronger condemnation of the very idea of U.S. involvement in Vietnam than those issued by the previous coalitions.

It contained no mention of negotiations and declared: "We

35. *Militant,* April 24, 1967.
36. Ibid.

march to dramatize the world-wide hope that the United States remove its troops from Vietnam so that the Vietnamese can determine their own future in their own way."[37] The committee printed up a variety of slogans for participants to carry, including both the negotiate and withdrawal demands.

The Student Mobilization Committee issued its own call, which explicitly demanded immediate withdrawal, an end to campus complicity with the war, and an end to the draft.

The Spring Mobilization Committee call also reflected the attempt to reconcile the desire for an ongoing multi-issue movement with the central focus of mass action against the war.

We call all Americans to unite and mobilize in a movement to end the senseless slaughter of American GIs and the mass murder of Vietnamese. We call for the enlistment of the men, money and resources now being used to maintain the military machine in a fight against the real enemies of man—hunger, hopelessness, ignorance, hate, fear, discrimination and inequality.

As the war cruelly destroys in Vietnam, so it denies hope to millions in the United States. The need for decent homes, quality education, jobs and fair employment are brushed aside. Our cities smother in smoke and grime, strangle in traffic. Our slums continue to rot. Streams and rivers are polluted, and the very air we breathe is fouled. Our vast wealth could in a short time eliminate these ills. It goes instead to murder and destroy. War contracts and the draft corrupt our campuses and laboratories. And, as the war continues, the ultimate danger of nuclear holocaust hangs over all. . . .

This national mobilization will affirm the will of the American people for peace in Vietnam and a new life for America and for all mankind. We speak to people around the world to mobilize to stop the war in Vietnam We declare not merely a protest but a new beginning.

The sponsors' list was the broadest yet, including a host of peace, radical, and civil rights figures, some prominent ministers, a few labor officials, and even some movie stars like Robert Vaughan and Harry Belafonte. James Farmer, at last, lent his name.

It was obvious, at least in New York, that the major media had a policy of avoiding prominent mention of antiwar demonstrations until the day of the event so as not to help attract

37. "Call to a National Mass Mobilization to End the War in Vietnam Now! April 15, 1967. New York-San Francisco." (Copy in author's files.)

participants. Mortimer Frankel, a professional public relations man who volunteered his services, did the best he could, but by and large April 15 had to be publicized the hard way—by hand-to-hand leaflets, word of mouth, mailings, and a few paid advertisements which required a great deal of organizational work and considerable time beforehand just to raise the money.

Financially the whole operation was bootstrap. We borrowed money to put out the first fund appeal mailings, spent the proceeds, borrowed more, and so it went. We knew we were in somewhat better shape when contributions in response to a coupon on the leaflets being distributed would exceed the cost of printing them. From then on we could distribute freely. The paid staff—which got subsistence ranging from $15 to $75 a week, depending on people's needs—wasn't always paid, and the committee was constantly in debt.

The Parade Committee alone distributed a million leaflets publicizing April 15. Much of this was done by special teams organized by Bernie Goodman, a house painter, about fifty, who was the Parade Committee's master leafleteer. Ron Wolin of Vets and Reservists—which had a special leafletting project directed at GIs—had succeeded in establishing the right to leaflet inside public transportation terminals, like the Port Authority bus building in New York where it had previously been forbidden. This was but one of many ways in which the state of civil liberties was greatly improved through the activities of the antiwar movement.

The nuts and bolts organizational work for the New York affair was done mainly out of the Parade Committee office, which had long since spilled out of the 5 Beekman Street complex into a large loft around the corner at 29 Park Row, off City Hall Park. The SMC operated in the same loft, as did the Spring Mobilization Committee initially, until it got an office at 857 Broadway near Union Square. Lora Eckert, a student from Minneapolis on the Parade Committee staff, and Susan Sutheim for the Spring Mobilization Committee, set up efficient office procedures. The paid staffs were never very large and most of the work was done by volunteers—there were literally hundreds of them—coming in and out at all hours. Marc Paul Edelman, a draft resister, ran the mimeograph machines and never seemed to sleep.

Sutheim put all the volunteers on computer cards—though we had no computer. She notched the holes on the edges for certain skills and availabilities. If we needed a layout artist who could write Spanish and work on a Tuesday evening, for example, she'd push several knitting needles through the holes in the stack of cards, lift them, and out would fall the cards of volunteers with those abilities. Sutheim, incidentally, was a member of SDS who came to work for the Mobilization on her own initiative.

The central offices were only a focus for the operation. A great deal of the building was done by participating neighborhood, campus, occupational, political, and other categories of groups. They organized meetings, fund raisers, buildup demonstrations, mailings, ads in regional newspapers, etc. There came to be a certain air of exhilaration in the movement as a whole during this period and things would move almost on their own with minimal encouragement and direction.

I learned it is important at such a time to be wide open to initiatives and suggestions and not to hesitate to put responsibility on the most recent volunteer if they were willing and exhibited common sense. Actually the operation was expanding faster than anyone could keep up with anyway. Such surges occurred from time to time, but not often, and they did not last more than a few weeks at a time. It was important to make the most of them and that could not be done by trying to keep a tight rein. A few key things—like financial accounting or the training of marshals— had to be watched carefully by the responsible committee, but by and large when the movement had a chance to expand rapidly it was best to rely on the initiative of even the newest activists.

This expansion was not limited to New York or San Francisco, but also occurred to some extent across the country even in places so far away from either demonstration they could send few people to the main marches. New committees were formed, local coalitions brought together, dormant groups activated, and organizations previously not involved brought into antiwar activity. In many areas send-off demonstrations were organized when the buses, trains, or car caravans left for New York or San Francisco and an uncounted number of local demonstrations were held by people who couldn't make the trip.

Almost all the peace and radical political groups were involved, as well as a significant number of local Democratic clubs, moderate religious groups, churches, and so on.

Women Strike for Peace played an important role. Dagmar Wilson became a vice-chairman of the Spring Mobilization Committee (as did Rev. Ralph Abernathy) and WSP organized a whole train to bring demonstrators from Washington, D.C.

Amy Swerdlow, who was Wilson's representative on the working committee, Pauline Rosen, and Cora Weiss sparked the New York WSP participation and the WSP contingent was some 20,000 strong in the march.

National SANE maintained its distance and issued a statement declining to endorse but leaving the door open for local chapters to participate, which a number did including New York SANE. Dr. Spock endorsed as an individual and cochaired the New York rally.

Progressive Labor, whose youth members had entered SDS when they dissolved the May Second Movement the year before, was one of the few groups on the left that did not participate. In the pages of the PL newspaper *Challenge* the mobilization was denounced as a "Trotskyite, revisionist, pacifist, liberal alliance," and PL was not represented among the sponsors. William Epton, however, who was still a member of PL at the time, joined with Paul Boutelle and James Haughton to initiate the Black United Action Front that organized the Harlem contingent for April 15.

Many local SDS chapters were also involved though the National Council did not reverse its previous position until April 5, when it finally voted to endorse. SDS National Secretary Gregg Calvert had become a sponsor in March.

*          *          *

One thing that figured in the SDS endorsement was a draft-card-burning project initiated by Cornell SDS members, which they wanted to make part of the April 15 event in New York. At the same December National Council meeting where it had voted against endorsing the Spring Mobilization, SDS had adopted a draft refusal program and Calvert had coined the slogan "From protest to resistance."

A Cornell "We Won't Go" group that included SDS members who were advocates of nonviolent resistance announced March 2 that they were seeking pledges from draft-age men to burn their cards publicly at the Spring Mobilization. Bob Greenblatt, who taught at Cornell, knew of the plan, as did Dellinger. Most of the rest of us on the Spring Mobilization working committee, however, hadn't heard of it until March 24 when a proposal was made by Mike Margolies that the Cornell group be invited to participate in the rally April 15 and possibly burn their draft cards on the platform. According to the minutes, Abner Grunauer of New York SANE

said that to include the card burning at the rally would be to violate the basis of the coalition because it would involve thousands of persons in an act of civil disobedience to which they had not agreed to commit themselves, and strongly urged that the Committee discourage card burning on the 15th (although by no means on the 14th or 16th or any other given day).

Greenblatt, the minutes continue,

pointed out that he has been working very closely with the organizers of the card burning, and that at this point they have not asked the Committee for any sort of official recognition, approval or inclusion in the Mobilization program.[38]

The issue was put off for later decision and debated at two subsequent meetings. Tim Larkin, one of the original signers of the Cornell pledge, spoke at at least one of these. In the course of this discussion it appeared to some that Dellinger—who attached great importance to the slogan "From protest to resistance"—had made some prior commitment to the Cornell group regarding April 15. In any case these students had made their announcement about "destroying our draft cards at the Spring Mobilization"[39] before it had been discussed in the committee and were obviously disappointed that the committee did not readily accept it.

Previously I had participated in support demonstrations at public draft card burnings, not because I thought the tactic was effective, but because I thought the young men facing jail for an antiwar activity deserved support. But these demonstrations had been announced and built, and endorsers obtained, on the basis that civil disobedience would be a central feature of the action. Not so with the Spring Mobilization.

38. Minutes, Working Committee of the Spring Mobilization, March 24, 1967. (Copy in author's files.)

39. Michael Ferber and Staughton Lynd, *The Resistance* (Boston: Beacon Press, 1971), p. 72. This book contains a more detailed account of the draft resistance aspect of the movement from the point of view of those who considered it crucial.

What disturbed me about this situation was that the Cornell plan—which at best would involve a relative handful—was presented to a much broader coalition as a fait accompli. This threatened the coalition that was building an action of hundreds of thousands in a clear, sharp statement against the war. It was, in my view, a bad omen.

On this aspect of the question a rather bitter exchange occurred between Dellinger and Harry Ring of the Socialist Workers Party, who accused Dellinger of irresponsibility regarding the coalition. Dellinger maintained that a certain amount of "creative tension" was necessary between those who wanted to reach broad sections of the population and those who wanted to sharpen the struggle with civil disobedience.

Recalling the incident later, Ring said he was upset because the attempt to get the draft card burners on the platform "almost seemed like a deliberate move to narrow the coalition precisely at the moment when it was on the verge of a major breakthrough."

We had all worked hard [he said], to bring the additional forces that were needed if we were going to build a movement big enough to actually stop the war. Throughout, we tried to achieve the kind of consensus where the pacifists and individual resisters could do their particular thing, but not impose it on others who would not or could not accept this tactic. But some of the pacifists—and some of the non-pacifist advocates of "resistance" as well—almost seemed to feel that if the movement was making headway in winning new forces it must be doing something wrong. It seemed to be just at those points that some of them were most determined to impose their particular tactic on the coalition.[40]

The compromise which was finally reached was that the Spring Mobilization Committee would not sponsor the draft card burning but that it would take place April 15 in Central Park's Sheep Meadow while the mobilization was assembling there for the march. The card burning was listed in the mobilization program as one of the concurrent activities of participating groups.

On April 15 a few hundred persons gathered near the edge of the assembly and while cameras flashed and plainclothes police waited to pick up the ashes for "evidence," between 150 and 200 cards were burned. Meanwhile, on the other side of the vast crowd, Grunauer was busy with Al Evanoff heading a team of marshals getting the first contingents lined up for the march.

40. Letter from Harry Ring to the author, November 14, 1975.

April 15, 1967, was a chill day in New York with a bit of rain in the morning and threatening more. The march was scheduled to step out of Central Park at noon, go east on Fifty-ninth Street, south on Madison Avenue, then east on Forty-sixth and Forty-seventh streets to the United Nations on First Avenue. The police had cleared the area between Forty-third and Forty-seventh on First Avenue and the sound equipment was set up to cover that as well as Forty-sixth and Forty-seventh back to Second Avenue. For some reason the police were adamant that none of the crowd should go south of Forty-third.

After checking out the technical assignments at the rally area, along the route, the assembly, and the charter bus unloading area—where the drivers had to be given instructions on where to park and the passengers on how to find their buses later—I went to the front of the march to help get it started. The start was delayed by a problem we hadn't anticipated, but which appeared at most of the subsequent large marches as well.

There were so many photographers blocking the way—insisting on "just one more shot"—that the march couldn't move. Professional cameramen, I learned, will not listen to reason while on assignment. You might as well try to reason with the camera. We finally had to shove them aside as gently as possible to get the march started. Fortunately we had a little serious muscle on hand—mostly friendly unionists, as a precaution against possible physical attack on the prominent persons in the front of the march—to accomplish this task. (This incident caused some critical discussion later by some of the Quakers in the coalition. They objected to the fact we had used our hands to move the photographers. They suggested instead that we should have locked arms and simply pushed. The front-line marshals, apparently, were to operate under rules similar to the offensive line in a football game—it was OK to block but not to tackle. In the interests of unity we subsequently adopted that technique, which actually did work better, though I had some difficulty grasping the philosophical distinction.)

The first part of the march made it to the UN along the assigned route without further difficulty, though a few missiles were thrown at the marchers from a tall building under construction along the way. The marshals assigned to that area later told me the missiles stopped after a short time. The perpetrators either ran out of things to throw, or had second thoughts when they grasped the size of the demonstration. For over four hours the street was filled with marchers passing that spot.

The march was more a swarm than a parade. The contingents jammed up on one another and filled the streets from one side to the other. The march began only a little late, but the crowd was so huge and so many arrivals were pouring in—some of them along the long, winding road from Sheep Meadow to the Fifty-ninth Street exit—that it appeared to many in the meadow that the march hadn't even started yet when the first part had already reached the UN.

The all-Black contingent organized by the Black United Action Front marched first through Harlem and then down Eighth Avenue. When it reached the assembly area the field was so full the Black contingent couldn't get in so it swept around the park and down Seventh Avenue, opening up another street. It made the turn from Seventh Avenue toward the UN in good order, but at the intersection where it met the other stream of marchers a jam occurred. Some of the crowd spilled southward and the cops made a mounted charge that briefly disrupted the march. Laura Moorehead, a seventeen-year-old student who was on this part of the Black contingent, later recalled:

We were walking toward the UN, some people were throwing eggs down at us from the apartments. [This was an exclusive, high-rent district.] Some people ahead of us were apparently trying to go somewhere the cops didn't want. The cops came through on horses and we started running, ducking under horses. We found ourselves next to a Women Voters group. They were all these nice ladies dressed up in their Sunday best trying to reason with the cops. We kept getting pushed, almost in a circle it seemed. Finally we made another turn and I looked up and there we were right in front of the speakers' stand. As far as I could see down any of the streets there were demonstrators. It was raining and people were standing there. It was Antiwar City that day. I stood right there and saw Martin Luther King speak. That was a big thrill for me because I had waited so long for him to come out against the war and I became so excited when he actually did. That was one of the main reasons I came—because I knew King was going to speak and publicly identify himself with the demonstration, and I hoped that would help win my parents over.[41]

While all this was going on I was arguing with Chief Inspector Sanford Garelik, who was in charge of the police, trying to get him to move his barricades further north to accommodate the

41. Taped interview with Laura Moorehead, November 12, 1975.

unexpectedly large crowd. It was clear he was under orders not to budge. Finally he lost his temper saying something like, "Look, get off my back. You people have made your point, there's a lot of people against the war." Unfortunately the administration continued to deny that fact, which after April 15 could not honestly be ignored.

At 5:00 p.m. a heavy downpour ended the rally, just as Linda Dannenberg was starting to speak for the SMC. In a few seconds she got soaked to the skin and had to quit. As thousands left they met additional thousands still marching, carrying their placards overhead against the rain. The last two contingents to make the whole march—the students and the medical workers—arrived at the UN, sloshing through the puddles, at 6:00 p.m., five hours after the first section.

* * *

It also rained intermittently in San Francisco that day, but nevertheless 75,000 demonstrators turned out, a record for the city. A contingent of 7,000 trade unionists made the march, many from locals of the International Longshoremen's and Warehousemen's Union (ILWU), which supported the demonstration. As in the East, however, the students were the largest section, and the crowd was mainly young.

In general the West Coast mobilization had somewhat greater success than the East in involving trade unions. It even got the support of the Santa Clara Central Labor Council, a body of delegates from all the AFL-CIO unions in that county. A number of union officials also spoke at Kezar Stadium. One of these was Paul Schrade, West Coast regional director of the United Auto Workers, and later a backer of Senator Robert F. Kennedy for the presidency. Schrade was applauded when he proposed a national debate and referendum on the war, but booed when he called for the U.S. to take up "easily defended" positions in South Vietnam if negotiations did not succeed. This was a variation of the "enclave theory" then being supported by a number of critics of escalation who couldn't bring themselves to flatly oppose the U.S. military presence in Vietnam.

Robert Scheer, who spoke later, commented:

One of the things that disturbs me about more "reasonable" speakers at meetings of this sort is that they always talk about the *complexity* of peace. If someone advocates just getting out of Vietnam, he's told that isn't a complex enough solution. I think it's time we said very clearly that we have to get out of Vietnam, and let's not beat around the bush.[42]

There was no draft card burning at the San Francisco event, but one of the speakers was David Harris, formerly the student-body president at Stanford, who announced the formation of a new group of draft refusers called "The Resistance."

Kipp Dawson, who was executive director of the West Coast Spring Mobilization (Ed Keating was chairman), told the rally:

There's one section of American youth who aren't with us in the stadium today. They aren't in the New York rally. Those are the American youth who have been drafted to fight this dirty war in Vietnam. But because they are not with us today, we cannot assume—and indeed we must not assume—that they are against us. . . . We are here to demonstrate our belief that the soldiers have the right to protest the war in Vietnam. We're extending our hands to them, and taking a lesson from the students who have been . . . making attempts to build links with the soldiers. We are joining with the soldiers in their demand—that they be brought home now.[43]

Another speaker was Rabbi Abraham L. Feinberg of Toronto, who had accompanied Muste and the other ministers on their trip to Hanoi. He said:

Some Americans seem to think that the daily count of Viet Cong corpses, like pheasants in a bag, will somehow lead to victory. A. J. Muste, Bishop [Ambrose] Reeves, Pastor [Martin] Niemoller, and I assure you that even if and when the mightiest nation in the history of the world, namely the United States, decimates, devastates, obliterates, subjugates, pulverizes, North Vietnam, the Vietnamese people will never surrender. . . .[44]

\*       \*       \*

Earlier that day Raul Gonzales, who had just turned thirteen, was walking from his home in San Francisco's Mission district to the Haight-Ashbury area "to watch the hippies" when he heard

42. *Militant*, April 24, 1967.
43. Ibid.
44. Ibid.

the noise of the demonstration. He followed the sound to Kezar Stadium and went inside. Later he recalled:

I didn't know what was going on. So I asked someone. They said it was a demonstration to get the troops out of Vietnam. Personally I was against the war, but I didn't really know why. I thought maybe I was the only one against it. The rally impressed me. So many people behind one thing. And the music and the bands. Country Joe and the Fish were there, and Moby Grape. Country Joe sang, "And it's one, two, three, what are we fighting for?" That's the first time I heard it. Later it was a hit and you could get it on AM even. . . .

I had no arguments against the war. From talking to people at the demonstration, and listening to the speeches, I got arguments. It strengthened my feelings. I took the arguments I learned there and the literature that was being passed out and used that with my friends. Those who were wavering tended to side with me now that I had the facts and figures and the stuff I'd gotten at the demonstration.[45]

It would be two years before Gonzales would engage in another organized antiwar activity—through the Mission High School SMC—but as of April 15, 1967, he knew he wasn't alone in his opposition to the war, and he continually talked to his friends about it. Multiplied many thousands of times, such undramatic and unreported processes played an important part in spreading the antiwar sentiment, and were part of the repercussions of April 15.

*      *      *

Martin Luther King said the New York march was bigger than the 1963 civil rights march on Washington, and that event had enjoyed the approval of the administration at the time and been widely publicized beforehand in the major media. The Spring Mobilization Committee's newsletter reported: "At least 400,000 marched to the UN building in New York, according to Mr. Serge Bourtourline, Jr., a leading professional crowd appraiser, who studied aerial photos of the event." The *New York Times* estimated 125,000 in front of the UN, but there wasn't room for half the turnout there, and some people never did make it out of Sheep Meadow before it was over. The April 16 issue of the

45. Taped interview with Raul Gonzales, November 21, 1975.

*Boston Globe* carried a headline: "400,000 March in New York Against War."

The turnout was the more remarkable in view of the fact that not a single United States congressman or senator had lent his name as a sponsor or accepted the committee's invitation to speak or to march among the notables at the head of the parade. In any case April 15, 1967, in New York produced the largest single march of any kind ever held in the United States up to that time.

# 11

# The Pentagon March

James Bevel was the last speaker at the April 15 New York rally to finish his speech before the downpour. Apparently on the spur of the moment he declared: "We are going to give LBJ one month to stop murdering those folks in Vietnam." Then he announced there would be a confrontation in Washington and massive civil disobedience.[1] This announcement had never been discussed within the committee.

All the speakers were free to express whatever ideas they chose and in this sense Bevel's advocacy of civil disobedience was not out of order. But for the Spring Mobilization Committee's director to commit the group to a controversial action without consulta tion with the committee *was* out of order What is more, it would have been impossible under the circumstances to mount another large action within a month.

The Spring Mobilization Committee, after all, was not an army, or even a trade union with a clearly defined membership and a tradition of disciplined response to a call for action. The commit tee itself was at most a few hundred individuals, with more or less moral authority within the various constituency organizations. It had taken several months of careful preparation to gather together even that much. It had taken another period of concerted campaigning, publicity, local actions, and the building of local coalitions to arrive at the point where broad, essentially unorganized masses would be attracted to the action.

1. "The Spring Mobilization in New York," report by Lou Waronker, New England CNVA mailing, undated. Copy in Spring Mobilization Committee folder, State Historical Society of Wisconsin.

The Spring Mobilization Committee itself was entirely lacking in direct economic or political power, and most of its members had ideologies that hardly had mass followings. The fact that such a group had called an action that attracted huge numbers of people was itself an indication of the increasing breadth of the antiwar sentiment. It was also an indication of the depth of the default by the traditional reformist leadership, including the bulk of the trade union officialdom.

The call for April 15 had struck a chord that swelled to crescendo because it found echo in the mood of immense masses of people with whom the Spring Mobilization Committee otherwise had no authority or connection. If the chord had been off-key the result would have been entirely different—with a few hundred or a few thousand radicals and pacifists especially committed to the particular event. Indeed, on more than one occasion in the future, precisely that was to be the result when the proposed action or the way it was built missed the mark as far as ordinary people were concerned.

The fact that the responsive chord was struck was not due to the genius or authority of any leader, or of a tendency—though some were more in tune with the popular sentiment than others in their advance projections. The success was due to the process of building the mobilization in which several thousand activists who were working with ordinary people had input, and in which differences were argued out and adjustments made.

All this took place in a particular political context—the escalation in the war, and the fact that elections were not near at hand. A change in that context—and the very fact of April 15 itself was one such change—would require another building process. Under the existing conditions there was no substitute for renewing the painful process of conferences and working-committee meetings. Any attempt to substitute a small, relatively closed group of decision makers for this could not develop the required momentum. And least of all could the masses of April 15 simply be called into the streets—for civil disobedience no less—by the arbitrary proclamation of a leader.

A small informal meeting was hastily arranged shortly after Bevel's surprise announcement to discuss what to make of it. Those in attendance included Bevel, Dellinger, Bernard Lafayette, Paul Brooks (who had been one of Bevel's administrative assistants in the building of April 15), Paul Boutelle, Linda Dannenberg, Beverly Sterner, Peter Buch, myself, and one or two others. Dellinger was anxious for a civil disobedience confrontation. I was not, because I thought it would necessarily be small and could not involve the whole coalition. The meeting arrived at a modification of Bevel's announcement, which contained two elements that were generally agreed to and which would make the plan viable—that was, to initiate another building process.

First, the Mobilization Committee would not call for a mass demonstration in a month, but for a delegation to confront President Johnson at the White House on May 17, the anniversary of the Supreme Court desegregation decision. The delegation would include speakers from the April 15 demonstration as well as representatives of various groups that had participated. It would demand the war be stopped in the name of those who marched April 15. Those who wished might commit symbolic nonviolent civil disobedience.

Second, on the following weekend, May 20-21, an antiwar conference would be sponsored by the Mobilization Committee in Washington to develop plans for future action.

This plan was announced at a press conference in New York April 18. Bevel declared: "We're going there with the clear message that the American people are against genocide and if he [President Johnson] doesn't stop it, we'll take steps to stop it."[2]

The *New York Times*, which on April 15 had editorially denounced the demonstration for including immediate withdrawal in its demands, printed a small story on the press conference on an inside page, immediately followed by articles on statements by Mike Mansfield, the Senate Democratic leader, and Leslie M. Fry, commander of the Veterans of Foreign Wars. Mansfield, according to the *Times*, "deplored today the burning of draft cards and flags during antiwar demonstrations in New York City and San Francisco last Saturday." Fry, the *Times* said, urged the prosecution "of all those involved in the burning of the flag during Vietnam war protests in New York and elsewhere over the weekend."[3]

2. *New York Times,* April 19, 1967.
3. Ibid. To my knowledge only one flag was burned April 15. That was in the area of the New York demonstration by individuals unknown to the Mobilization Committee. Msgr. Rice, among others, was convinced it was the work of provocateurs under orders to discredit the demonstration.

This pretty much summed up the public stance of the administration's supporters toward the April 15 event. They latched onto any available excuse to avoid admitting, and to divert attention from, the profound fact that the largest demonstration of any kind in the history of the republic had just taken place, in the midst of a war and against the government's involvement in that war.

For his part, President Johnson pretended to continue to ignore the antiwar movement and proceeded to implement the latest phase of the escalation that had already been planned, and was indeed already initiated with the December bombings of Hanoi. At this time the number of American troops in Vietnam was approaching the authorized 470,000 level. According to the Pentagon Papers, General William C. Westmoreland was requesting 200,000 more, though this was not publicly acknowledged at the time.

Within the antiwar movement there were some who were quick to seize on the fact of the escalation to repeat the argument that demonstrations were useless, that the movement as such was powerless to affect events significantly and should therefore be transformed into a multi-issue radical movement. The Pentagon Papers later revealed, however, that the discussions within the administration over Westmoreland's request were heavily concerned about antiwar sentiment and the effect additional troop calls would have on the American people. On May 19, 1967, Secretary of Defense Robert McNamara sent a memorandum to the president which, according to the Pentagon Papers, "gave a discouraging picture of the military situation and a pessimistic view of the American public's impatience with the war."[4]

This then-secret memorandum was delivered to Johnson while the delegation from the April 15 mobilization was still standing at the gates of the White House and the president was studiously ignoring it. The major media devoted more space to an egg thrown by a heckler, which hit Dr. Spock on the head, than to the delegation's purpose.

Nevertheless, anyone with a serious eye toward the body politic—and this included forces to the right of those that had initiated the Spring Mobilization—could not help but take into account the rising antiwar sentiment that April 15 made mani-

4. *The Pentagon Papers,* as published by the *New York Times* (New York: Bantam, 1971), p. 514. The quote is from the *Times*'s analysis.

fest. Shortly after April 15 two new projects were announced amid considerable publicity. These were "Negotiations Now" and "Vietnam Summer." The fact that Dr. Spock and Martin Luther King, Jr., issued supporting statements at the initial press conference of each of these campaigns gave rise to some impression that they were interconnected and related to the Spring Mobilization. Actually they were each launched by separate groups and neither was connected with the Mobilization Committee except that they were announced in the wake of April 15 and there was some overlapping sponsorship. And, unlike the Mobilization, neither was the result of conferences that were generally open to the movement.

"Negotiations Now" was initiated by the most conservative wing of the old peace forces, the wing that had usually opposed mass actions against government policy and been hostile to both the nonexclusion and immediate withdrawal thrusts of the newer antiwar movement. It had enough financial backing to place large ads in daily newspapers. Its program was contained in a petition for which it sought signatures nationally. The petition called on the U.S. to take the first step and halt the bombing of North Vietnam, and asked Hanoi and the NLF to respond affirmatively and join the U.S. in a standstill cease-fire.

The statement accompanying this petition in advertisements rejected immediate withdrawal, which it said would mean "abandoning responsibility for establishing conditions for a stable peace." The initial signers of the petition included Norman Cousins, who had presided over the purge of SANE in 1960; economist John Kenneth Galbraith; Joseph L. Rauh, Jr., the leading spokesperson of Americans for Democratic Action (ADA); Victor Reuther of the United Auto Workers international affairs office; and Arthur Schlesinger, Jr.

The efforts of this group were aimed directly at bolstering the "doves" in Congress and the critics of Johnson's war policy within the administration. It could be expected to have little influence with the youth activated around April 15.

Vietnam Summer, on the other hand, was aimed directly at such youth, especially the students. Vietnam Summer's policy committee, which was simply announced with no explanation of how it was chosen, was almost entirely composed of persons who then resided in the greater Boston area. It included Gar Alperovitz, a fellow at Harvard's Kennedy Institute; Harvard Professor Martin Peretz; Harvard Chaplain Richard Mumma; Mike

Waltzer, an editor of *Dissent* magazine; Chester Martin, vice-president of Massachusetts Political Action (Mass Pax); Paul Potter, the former SDS president; John Mayer, an old-guard SDS activist; and Ami Roudine, head of the New England draft program of the American Friends Service Committee.

In a printed leaflet the group declared:

> We propose a Vietnam Summer. We urge that students consider repeating the Mississippi Summer precedent—this time not by going South, but by staying in their own university areas to organize the community. Door-to-door in the South worked—but it took time. Now we need to look at problems right at home. If we work this summer, by the fall we will have a solid base. We can hit hard in September to turn out a mass movement which is prepared to blast a major opening in 1968.[5]

In a section labeled "Phase III: Political Action," the leaflet said:

> Once we have covered the community map, block by block, and have a substantial number of volunteer groups, the really crucial organizing can go forward—both to establish solid bases in the community and to focus sharply on 1968: local candidates (with a long running start); Presidential and other primaries; deeply based multi-issue community organization.[6]

In essence Vietnam Summer was a project of a wing of the Conference on New Politics and old-guard SDS radical-liberals. The latter had begun to grasp that they had made some kind of error in abandoning antiwar leadership back in 1965. But once again they tended to view the antiwar issue not as a central political responsibility but as an organizing device for the building of their special conception of a multi-issue political movement.

The Conference on New Politics itself was a grouping of reform Democrats and radical-liberals who had supported Johnson in the 1964 elections but who simply could not see themselves doing so again in 1968. They were looking around for an alternative. Since it was assumed Johnson would again be the Democratic Party candidate, they were considering a third ticket on the presidential level while they would support "doves" on the

5. "Teach Out." (Copy in author's files.)
6. Ibid.

Democratic ticket for lesser offices. There was talk of a King-Spock presidential ticket, though neither King nor Spock had declared a willingness to run. Vietnam Summer claimed to have a budget of several hundred thousand dollars and announced it was seeking antiwar students to work full time on its projects.

In a report to the Socialist Workers Party membership, Jack Barnes took a critical stance toward Vietnam Summer, saying it "represents an attempt to essentially buy off the antiwar activists, and lay the groundwork for 1968 'independent political action inside and outside the Democratic Party.'"[7] The first part of this characterization was perhaps a bit unkind in view of the fact that Vietnam Summer was offering only $25 to $30 a week for a limited number of full-timers. But the characterization of the political thrust was accurate enough. It was clear that Vietnam Summer would be one factor in another period of tension in the same old struggle between those who sought to channel the antiwar movement into liberal electoral politics, and those who sought to keep it independent of the electoral machines and in the streets.

\*            \*            \*

Prior to April 15 the Student Mobilization Committee had already scheduled a national student antiwar conference for May 13-14 in Chicago. Since its founding in December the SMC had succeeded in organizing significant antiwar activity on hundreds of campuses, made a breakthrough into the high schools, and brought out the largest contingents on the April 15 demonstrations. The old divisions between the NCC Madison office and the *Bring the Troops Home Now Newsletter* had been overcome in the building of the Spring Mobilization. The NCC became a local Wisconsin group and the *Newsletter* simply dissolved itself, turning its mailing lists over to the Student Mobilization Committee. Joan Levinson of the NCC staff came to New York to work on the Spring Mobilization. Gus Horowitz, former editor of the *Newsletter*, joined the original staff of the SMC along with Linda Dannenberg and Paul Friedman, a youth associated with the Communist Party. The national office of SDS never did send a staff person to join the SMC, but Bill Snyder of City College of

7. "Antiwar Report," by Jack Barnes, May 3, 1967. (Copy in author's files.)

New York SDS did join the national SMC staff. Maxine Orris, a high school student, headed up the high school work.

The original idea behind the proposal for an SMC conference in May was to map out a summer program of antiwar activity for students. In light of the plan for a national antiwar gathering in Washington May 20-21, however, the student conference one week earlier assumed additional importance. What was decided by the SMC in Chicago could affect what happened a week later at the Washington conference. The opportunity this schedule presented for the mass action perspective was not lost on the YSA.

By this time perhaps the most prominent YSAer in the antiwar movement was Kipp Dawson, who had been the Spring Mobilization executive director for the West Coast. She moved to New York City immediately after April 15 to work in the Student Mobilization Committee national office. She was twenty-one years old at the time. She came from a working class family that had been close to the Communist Party and she had been a political activist since childhood. Kipp was close to her family, and when they disapproved of her joining the Trotskyist YSA she had to argue out the reasons for her political decision. This contributed to a natural inner toughness and a certain earthy political sophistication which were beyond her years, though these qualities were not apparent in casual conversation and were belied by her diminutive size and appearance of being much younger than she was.

In early May, Dawson circulated a position paper among the national staff of the SMC. It declared: "If April 15th taught anything, it should be the lesson that local organizing and large protests are the two sides of a successful antiwar movement: They are interlinked and dependent upon each other."[8] After outlining some suggestions for the summer, the paper presented the following proposal:

We also need to project a place and date—hopefully Washington, October 21st—for a massive action that would culminate the summer and early fall activity. Washington would be ideal because it offers many ways of tying in a variety of activities around the massive action (e.g. a veterans' action at the Pentagon, lawyers' protest at the Department of Justice, etc.), as well as being a good place for showing a united

8. "Proposal for a Summer and Fall Education and Action Antiwar Campaign," by Kipp Dawson, May 13, 1967. (Copy in author's files.)

opposition to the government's policy in Vietnam.

Dawson arrived at the suggested date on purely technical grounds. It fell on a Saturday, which would maximize participation in a demonstration. It was not too close to cold weather, but far enough into the fall school semester to allow a few weeks of organizing on campuses after the students reassembled from summer vacation. Dawson distributed her paper at the opening of the Chicago SMC conference, May 13. It contained the following concluding paragraph:

Because we would need the active participation of adult organizations in carrying out this proposal, we should go to the Spring Mobilization conference in Washington next weekend with the results of our conference and our ideas for a summer project. We should 1) urge them to call for the same kinds of activities within their perspectives for this summer and fall's action and 2) urge them to join us in a call for an October 21st demonstration in Washington, D.C.

In the minds of some, the SMC was merely an adjunct to the Spring Mobilization Committee. From that point of view, the tail was preparing to wag the dog.

\*          \*          \*

By and large the Student Mobilization Committee conference, held on the University of Chicago campus, went smoothly. There were several debates but the differences tended to cut across old factional lines, were argued on the merits, and there was no power fight for control of the organization.

The conference was more broadly representative than the founding meeting six months earlier. It was attended by some 600 persons, with 490 registered from groups on 90 college-level campuses, 24 high schools, and a variety of political, civil rights, religious, draft resistance, and pacifist organizations.

One debate took place over a motion that the SMC oppose the 2-S draft deferment as discriminatory against nonstudent youth. The idea was to make it clear that antiwar students did not seek special exemption from the draft, but opposed the draft across the board. This position was adopted.

A second debate involved a proposed change in the SMC's statement of aims to include "promoting" draft resistance instead of simply supporting "the right of individuals to refuse to cooperate with the military system."

The change was favored by spokespersons for radical pacifist and draft resistance groups, the Du Bois Clubs, and Youth Against War and Fascism. The YSAers did not favor individual draft resistance because they felt it was not politically effective, would be an obstacle to winning support for the antiwar movement among GIs, and was also a hindrance to developing mass participation. As far as they could see, it was mainly important to the individuals involved, and these should be supported. But they maintained that the SMC should not adopt a position of promoting individual draft refusal as a strategy for ending the war.

In this debate a difference once again appeared between the Du Bois Clubs and the youth section of the Communist Party. Mike Zagarell of the CP youth argued that the proposed change would inhibit the broadening of the coalition. In this sense the CP also had its eye on broader masses, but with a fundamentally different strategy from that of the YSA.

The CP had distributed a position paper to the conference emphasizing its view of the importance of antidraft work, but along the lines of "the building of a political movement aimed at abolishing the draft."[9] By implication this was counterposed to a campaign of civil disobedience against the draft. In general the CP's position paper was aimed toward the coming 1968 elections. But their strategy toward these elections faced certain complications.

With Johnson so closely associated with the war and with the assumption that he would be the Democratic Party candidate in 1968, the CP's usual approach of working within the Democratic Party was headed for a crisis. It was similar to the problem faced by the antiwar liberals in the Conference on New Politics. Another complication was the trend within SDS. The new-guard SDSers, now in complete control of the national office, were tending to reject electoral politics entirely. In the context their new slogan "From protest to resistance" contained an implication of this essentially anarchist trend. The CP's position paper was obviously counterposed to this SDS thrust. But the Du Bois

9. "A New Movement." Statement of the National Youth Commission, Communist Party, U.S.A., to the National Student Mobilization Conference, May 13-14, 1967. (Copy in author's files.)

Clubs were still accommodating to the trends in SDS. Said the CP's position paper:

> Struggles around the draft, the high cost of living, and against poverty are struggles of protest. The step from varied protest to a political movement is a significant one. We believe it is time to lay the foundation for a movement that will challenge the political power base of the war and racism in the '68 elections. . . . The choice must be given to the people of the United States in an independent presidential candidate for peace and freedom. To launch such a ticket will need the building of grass roots movements around the country that will also be the base for local candidacies. In the fall on our campuses, as well as in the summer in the communities, we must build from below the organization of sentiment for a *choice* in 1968. Consideration should be given to the creation of a National Student Committee for an independent peace and freedom ticket for 1968.

In essence this was a proposal to convert the antiwar movement into a multi-issue reform political movement, or even a new political party. The thrust was similar to that of the Conference on New Politics and Vietnam Summer. If the CP had attempted to have the SMC adopt this perspective at the May 13-14 conference, there would have been a fight with the YSA and others. But they simply presented it as an idea and did not propose it for a vote. And to leave the door open for their conception of broadening the coalition in the electoral direction they opposed putting the promotion of draft resistance into the SMC statement of aims.

Linda Dannenberg, who was then a pacifist and personally favored promoting draft resistance, also spoke against including it in the statement of aims on the grounds that it would be divisive of the existing SMC coalition and national staff. The proposed amendment was defeated by a vote of 173 to 123.

The conference adopted a summer program that included cooperation with draft resistance groups, helping to get antiwar referenda on the ballot in more cities, cooperation with unions where possible, support to antiwar GIs, and research and planning action against campus complicity with the war.

A fall action proposal was adopted that included the essence of Dawson's suggestion for a march on Washington. This was recommended to the Spring Mobilization Committee conference. The date, however, was not specified, that being left to the Washington gathering.

Shortly after April 15, General William C. Westmoreland, commander of the U.S. forces in Vietnam, made a trip to the United States. The announced purpose was to have talks with the president, secretary of defense, and the joint chiefs of staff. We now know that he presented his case for the additional 200,000 troops at these meetings. It was widely assumed at the time that another reason for the timing of his trip was to counter the antiwar movement.

On April 24 he appeared at a luncheon at the Waldorf-Astoria in New York City during a convention of the American Newspaper Publishers Association. Resplendent in his general's uniform and steel-grey hair, he made a speech in which he declared the U.S. forces were defeating "the enemy" in Vietnam. He continued:

> And yet, despite staggering combat losses, he clings to the belief that he will defeat us. And through a clever combination of psychological and political warfare, both here and abroad, he has gained support which gives him hope that he can win politically that which he cannot accomplish militarily. . . .[10]

Westmoreland said U.S. troops in Vietnam

> are dismayed, and so am I, by recent unpatriotic acts here at home. Regrettably, I see signs of success in that world arena which he cannot match on the battlefield. He does not understand that American democracy is founded on debate, and he sees every protest as evidence of crumbling morale and diminishing resolve. Thus, discouraged by repeated military defeats but encouraged by what he believes to be popular opposition to our effort in Vietnam, he is determined to continue his aggression from the North. This, inevitably, will cost lives. . . .

This speech was a repetition of the oft-used administration argument that the antiwar movement was lengthening the war by sowing false illusions among the Vietnamese "enemy." In response to a question on the "Meet the Press" TV show April 16, Secretary of State Dean Rusk had phrased it this way:

> Well, these [demonstrations] have been called "huge." I suppose they are large, but remember, we have a population of almost 200 million

10. *New York Times,* April 25, 1967.

people and those who speak for the 200 million Americans are the President and the Congress on these issues. We have in our constitutional system an opportunity for lawful and peaceful expression. I am concerned, Mr. [Lawrence] Spivak, that the authorities in Hanoi may misunderstand this sort of thing and that the net effect of these demonstrations will be to prolong the war and not to shorten it.[11]

This argument rested on the premise that it would be a good thing for the U.S. to win the Vietnam War. But the masses who marched April 15 didn't think it would be a good thing. They thought it would be a bad thing—for the United States in particular. By and large they had turned out, not for "bread and butter" reasons but for moral reasons. They did not consider their active opposition to a morally bankrupt government policy to be unpatriotic. On the contrary they thought the decent thing for the U.S. to do was to get out of Vietnam and let the Vietnamese settle their own affairs.

As people who were willing to stand up and be counted in the face of considerable government pressure, they no doubt still represented a minority. But the majority itself was full of doubts and not by any means in support of Johnson's policy. To be sure, a quick victory would have put the issue out of mind—as it had in the case of the Dominican Republic—but this was impossible to achieve in the military and world-political context. Even such extreme methods as an invasion of North Vietnam or the use of nuclear weapons would not have guaranteed it, and would have raised momentous dangers. In the context, Johnson's policy was interminable war. Prowar demonstrations which had the support of daily newspapers, elected politicians, and powerful veterans groups, could muster only a small fraction of what the antiwar movement did. The argument could convincingly be made that the April 15 marchers were representative of a far larger percentage of the population *on this issue* than the president was.

Constitutionally the country is not supposed to be slipped into a war by the secret manipulations of the executive branch. Yet that is exactly what had happened. The war was not even seriously raised in Congress until steadily increasing military force had been committed over several years. Even then the issue was not seriously discussed until widespread opposition had been mani-

11. Cited by Thomas Powers, *The War at Home* (New York: Grossman, 1973), p. 184.

fest among the people, who had been deliberately kept in the dark. Even after that, the congressional critics could not bring themselves to vote against a single war appropriation. The country was clearly in a type of constitutional crisis.

The fact that the courts had consistently refused to touch the constitutional issue—in spite of repeated cases giving them the opportunity to do so—settled nothing. This judicial default and cowardice only compounded the crisis and emphasized its depth. In effect the only part of the constitution still operative on this issue was the Bill of Rights, which with the tradition surrounding its liberties provided some protection for the rights of free speech, assembly, and petition for redress of grievances. And it took considerably more "morale" and "resolve" to use those rights to stand up against the war-makers and all their vast power than it did to go along with them.

A case of resistance in point was Private First Class Howard Petrick, the son of a cafeteria worker and a machinist from Erie, Pennsylvania, who was then stationed at Fort Hood, Texas, and who appeared in uniform at the Chicago SMC conference. He was the first active-duty GI to address a national antiwar gathering. By that time there were a number of GI cases being publicized by the antiwar movement, including that of Captain Howard Levy, a medical doctor who was being court-martialed for refusing orders to train Green Berets for Vietnam.

Levy's defense was based in part on his belief that the Green Berets, who were combat specialists, not medics, would use the instruction for purposes that would violate his Hippocratic Oath.

Petrick had also been threatened with court-martial. But his case was unique in one respect. The other publicized GI cases of the time involved individual acts of conscience and some sort of confrontation with legality such as refusal of orders—civil disobedience by soldiers, so to speak. Petrick, on the contrary, had been careful to carry out all army orders to the best of his ability, and had been rated "excellent" by his immediate superiors. (His regular duties were as a cook.) But he also took every available opportunity to spread the antiwar message among his fellow GIs.

He had been active in the antiwar movement before being drafted. He had also been a member of the Young Socialist Alliance and the Socialist Workers Party. He continued receiving antiwar and socialist literature after being inducted, kept it on his barracks shelf and in his locker, and gave it to other soldiers when the topics came up in the course of normal conversation, which the war often did. After he had been in the army nine months, Petrick's literature was confiscated, he was questioned by Army Intelligence, and told he faced possible court-martial for expressing his views. He immediately contacted the YSA, a defense committee was organized, and on April 7, 1967, Petrick issued a public statement that was widely distributed April 15. It said in part:

I appeal for support from all Americans who agree that GIs are citizens who are entitled to the right of free speech guaranteed by the Bill of Rights. Although I have never disobeyed an order, and have fulfilled all my duties as a soldier, my constitutional rights are now being threatened. All my literature on the Vietnam war, socialism, and other topics (all publicly available in libraries or bookstores) has been confiscated by United States Army Intelligence, my friends and I have been questioned, and I have been assigned an army attorney who informs me of a possible court-martial on charges of disloyal statements or subversion.

Soldiers are also citizens, and should have the same constitutional rights as civilians to hold and express any opinions, including opposition to the Vietnam war. Your support to me at this time . . . can help insure these constitutional rights to all GIs.[12]

Petrick did receive widespread support from the antiwar movement and civil libertarians. In mid-May he got a short leave and went to Chicago where he spoke to the SMC conference. "I figured," he said, "that if General Westmoreland can wear his uniform and speak for the war, I can wear mine and speak against it."[13]

Columnist Murray Kempton commented:

And in Washington, the Defense Department wonders about court-martialing him. It is understandably slow to decide. To try Howard Petrick will be to confess that the war has turned us into a country where a man can be a criminal not for what he does, but for what he thinks and says when asked.

The Pentagon, however, decided to avoid the test case and the publicity which would have inevitably attended it. Eventually it

12. *Militant,* April 17, 1967.
13. *New York Post,* May 19, 1967.
14. Ibid.

simply threw Petrick out of the army without an honorable discharge. (He won that years later on appeal.) In one sense Petrick was unique, which is why he was among the first to do what he did. He had more than his share of "morale" and "resolve" and plain cool nerve, though he didn't have a fanatical bone in his body. And he knew he had an organization in the civilian world that would never let him down and that every move the army made against him would be subject to the glaring light of publicity. But in another sense he was not at all unique. He was of a piece with his generation, which would not prove to be as easily manipulated by the war-makers as previous ones had been.

Central to discussions at the time among Westmoreland, the joint chiefs, and the civilian heads of the administration was the question of a general mobilization of the reserves and National Guard. Westmoreland suggested this as the source of filling his 200,000 additional troop request. But these units, while already organized and trained to a degree, were generally made up of men who were more an established part of the economic and political life of the country than the young draftees. To pull these part-time soldiers out of their civilian lives and send them off to an unpopular war would have immediate and large political repercussions. It was, according to the Pentagon Papers, a political threshold that Johnson felt he could not cross. He turned down Westmoreland's request and instead authorized only an additional 30,000 men for Vietnam, bringing the total to the half-million mark by the end of 1967. Since each soldier generally served only a one-year tour in Vietnam, the draft and the enlistments resulting from its pressure had to be maintained at a fairly high level to provide the replacements.

Little by little—but in far greater numbers than any radical group could possibly muster—the army became sprinkled with youth who had already been affected by the civilian antiwar movement and by the tradition of free speech which it had revived. And increasingly, these youth would find a receptive audience among their peers in the barracks discussions. There was no conspiracy involved. The war-makers and the drafters would have only themselves to blame.

\*              \*              \*

The Spring Mobilization Committee conference, held in the

Hawthorne School in southwest Washington on the weekend of May 20-21, was attended by some 700 antiwar activists, three times as many as the conference that had called April 15. It was more broadly representative of the general antiwar movement than any previous national conference. Only the most conservative section of the old peace movement was not represented, having excluded itself. Even Sanford Gottlieb of the national SANE staff attended as well as Dr. Spock, while Gar Alperovitz made a presentation on the Vietnam Summer project.

The spectrum of forces at the conference, however, could not be expected to agree on very much. The call to the gathering summed up the expectations quite accurately: "The purposes of this conference are to evaluate the April 15 Mobilization, improve co-ordination and communication between various sectors of the movement, and exchange ideas on future programs and actions on the community and national level."[15]

The SWP and the YSA approached the conference with one central goal in mind—to come out of it with a definite call for a mass action in the fall. In our view this was vital, because without it the coalition would not hold together. Other forces, while not necessarily opposed to a mass action in the fall, were centrally concerned with other strategies and tactics. The two most important of these were to prepare for the elections in 1968; and to organize civil disobedience, or, as it came to be sloganized, to move "From protest to resistance" or "From dissent to resistance."

On the surface it might appear that these two strategies were mutually exclusive. But some people in the movement were advocates of both, and an even greater number would swing from one to the other depending on the proximity of the elections, the availability of liberal "peace candidates" who seemed to have a chance of winning or at least of making a major impact, and the level of their own outrage and frustration.

These three strategies—mass action in the streets, reform electoral politics, and civil disobedience or "confrontation"— underlay much of the discussion at the May 20-21 conference, and each tended to be pressed in particular workshops.

Sharp discussion took place within the workshop on political

15. "Draft Call for a National Workshop Conference—Washington, D.C., May 20-21." (Copy in author's files.)

action, where the forces interested in electoral politics were themselves divided over which candidates and parties to support. A proposal was made that the Spring Mobilization Committee urge and endorse a King-Spock ticket for 1968. Some of those most closely tied to the Democratic Party were not willing to go along with this. For entirely different reasons neither was the Socialist Workers Party. On principle the SWP would not support a slate which in effect would be a third capitalist party. In the end a motion put by Judy White of the SWP passed. It declared: "Because of the diversity of opinions within the Spring Mobilization Committee on forms and types of electoral action, the Spring Mobilization Committee takes no stand on any particular candidates, parties or perspective. . . ."[16] The only positive action on which the workshop would agree was to support antiwar referenda.

The question of political action was never discussed in the full sessions of the conference. Instead it was deferred to a special conference later. This meeting, which was small and informal, occurred just prior to the convention of the National Conference on New Politics (NCNP) which took place in Chicago over the Labor Day weekend. In effect, the question of whether the antiwar movement could be transformed into a new multi-issue political movement or party was left to be tested at the NCNP convention itself.

The forces at the May 20-21 conference who were centrally concerned with civil disobedience concentrated in the workshops on draft resistance and on "the strategy and tactics of nonviolence." On recommendation of the draft workshop the conference adopted a position in opposition to the draft, in defense of all draft resisters, and instructing the Mobilization Committee to "make its facilities available for liaison and coordination with those working to resist the draft."[17] The Mobilization Committee, however, was not viewed as a main organizer of this type of activity. That was left to groups composed entirely of advocates of this tactic.

The workshop on strategy and tactics of nonviolence did

16. *Militant,* May 29, 1967.
17. "Preliminary Report on the National Conference of the Spring Mobilization Committee to End the War in Vietnam, May 20-21, Washington, D.C." Spring Mobilization Committee mailing, undated. (Copy in author's files.)

propose a special civil disobedience project which, while being carried out by those committed to the tactic, would be a Mobilization Committee project. The plan was to select a "target city" to be the scene of a "nonviolent radical confrontation . . . to create a social drama that could become the object of national focus."[18] The conference approved this proposal and Washington, D.C., was recommended as the target city. No date was specified for this activity beyond "late summer or early fall." At the time this project was not seen as taking place at the same time as the march on Washington proposed by the SMC. Dave Dellinger was then on a trip to Vietnam and did not attend the May conference. Later he would press for what amounted to a fusing of the two projects.

The workshop on mass action adopted the march on Washington idea overwhelmingly, recommending the date of October 21 and the theme: "Support Our Boys in Vietnam—Bring Them Home!" (The original proposal was for "Bring Them Home Now!" But there were still some forces who objected to the inclusion of "now" in a central slogan. The SMC, however, used the "now" in its publicity and it produced the bulk of the posters, buttons, etc., advertising the event. By the time of the demonstration, the Mobilization Committee itself was including "now" with no objections.)

There was some argument in the workshop over specifying the date. In the wake of the success of April 15, it was not popular at this conference to directly oppose another mass action. Those who either did not really favor it, or who feared it might detract from other projects they were more concerned with, objected to making the project definite by setting a date. This opposition was overcome in the workshop after some discussion and an effective appeal on behalf of the demonstration by Otto Nathan. But the apparently technical detail of specifying the date became the major dispute at the May 20-21 conference, with the SWP insisting on setting the date, and the CP leading the attempt to prevent this.

The reason those of us in the SWP were so adamant on setting the date then and there was that the entire action would otherwise have been left uncertain. We knew from experience that there would be all sorts of hesitations in getting the action off the

18. Ibid.

ground in any case, and much maneuvering within the leading circles of the committee in favor of one or another alternative perspective. If the date wasn't set, the tendency would be to keep putting off preparations until there wasn't adequate time for organizing. Without a specific major action on which to focus, the coalition would tend to dissipate in several directions. A mass demonstration was the only action all the forces in the coalition could support, or at least be pressured into going along with. This was a simple fact of life in so heterogeneous a movement where no tendency had hegemony. But it was not easy for some people to accept, or even to recognize this as a reality.

Another factor in our considerations was that the relationship of forces in favor of mass demonstrations was always much stronger at a large, open conference where rank-and-file activists were present in numbers, than it was in the leadership committees, where not everyone involved was responsible to, or even sensitive to, a real constituency. Also, an action and a date with the authority of the conference behind it would be much harder to maneuver out of. So we concentrated our efforts on nailing down the date.

The mass action workshop took place on Saturday and the proposal was scheduled to go to the plenary on Sunday. Saturday night a long meeting of the conference steering committee was held at the home of Barbara Bick, a Washington Women Strike for Peace activist. Over the years her home would be the scene of many an all-night session in connection with one antiwar activity or another. In the course of this meeting, objections were raised to the workshop proposal for an October 21 march. The argument was that the demonstration should first be discussed with unionists, the Washington peace groups, and the Washington Black community. Those of us favoring setting the date were willing to set a different one than October 21, but not willing to leave it up in the air for fear the further consultations would be interminable and the action would not come off.

The steering committee failed to agree and it appeared that a major fight was shaping up for the Sunday session. The next morning Harry Ring came up with a compromise amendment to the workshop proposal. It read:

the date of October 21 shall be set with the understanding that if practical necessity dictates it can be revised. The date should be finalized within 30 days on the basis of consultation with the Washington peace movement, unionists and leaders of the Black community.[19]

Ring discussed this with Sid Peck, who was to chair the session. Peck thought it was a good compromise that would be acceptable to all concerned and agreed to give Ring the microphone to present the amendment as the first speaker on the mass action proposal.

As the session opened Peck showed the amendment to some of the steering committee members who had opposed setting the date and was besieged with such strong objections that he changed his mind.

The whole conference waited while a swirling discussion took place near the podium between Peck and several of those opposed to setting the date. Finally Ring, who was waiting to be called on, took the microphone on his own and presented the amendment without Peck's support. The issue was at least before the full convention in as clear a form as possible under the circumstances. A full-scale debate ensued. In the course of one major speech against setting the date, the orator asked rhetorically: "What's so sacred about a date?" From the audience came a voice: "April 15!" The convention cheered and the speaker's peroration fell flat.

The voice from the audience was that of Don Gurewitz, a student at Case Western Reserve University who had been chairman of the Case Western Reserve SDS chapter and who had recently joined the YSA, largely on the strength of its antiwar activity.

The major speech against the workshop proposal as amended was made by Archie Brown, a San Francisco longshoreman who had been a Communist Party candidate for public office. He was something of a national figure in left-wing circles, having won a case reversing the federal ban on Communists in union office. His oratory, in the old trade union style, was not without effect. He made much of his credentials as a trade unionist and World War II veteran. At one point he took a Vets for Peace hat from his pocket, put it on his head, and proceeded to explain why the workshop proposal would not appeal to veterans.

The next speaker was Leroy Wollins, a leading Vets for Peace activist in Chicago. "I don't like to argue with Archie Brown; I've known him for years," he began. He brought down the house

19. *Militant*, May 29, 1967.

when he added: "As a matter of fact I just sold him that hat a few minutes ago." Wollins, who was known as an independent figure with no particular factional axe to grind, spoke forcefully for the demonstration and by the time he finished the issue was no longer in doubt. The proposal was adopted with only a scattering of votes opposed.

Within weeks the administrative committee finalized the date. It also dropped the "Spring" from the organization's name, changing it to the National Mobilization Committee. There would be a march on Washington on October 21, 1967. Its exact character, however, was yet to be determined.

\*        \*        \*

On June 23, 1967, President Johnson spoke to a $500-a-plate Democratic Party fund-raising dinner at the Century Plaza Hotel in Los Angeles. The local Peace Action Council (PAC) and the Student Mobilization Committee had called an antiwar demonstration for the occasion. The event began in the afternoon with a "Peace-In" at Cheviot Hills Park featuring rock bands, folk singers, and literature tables. This was followed by a rally that heard SNCC Chairman H. Rap Brown, Dr. Spock, and heavyweight boxing champion Muhammad Ali, who had recently been convicted on a charge of draft refusal. After the assembly there was to be a march to the hotel where Johnson was speaking.

Toward the end of the rally, police distributed to a small part of the crowd copies of an injunction that had just been handed down by a local court. It contained a long list of prohibitions, including a key point that was not part of the permit obtained by the organizers. The march would not be allowed to stop in front of the hotel but would have to proceed past it without stopping. The organizers decided to obey the injunction, but many of the marchers were unaware of the change in plans.

As a further complication, the organizers had planned to lead the march with sound trucks that could give last-minute instructions to the marchers. But the police forbade the use of trucks. One group—composed largely of Progressive Labor Party members in SDS—had brought their own sound truck and attempted to pull it into the street and begin the march about twenty minutes before the scheduled starting time of 7:30 p.m. A few police moved in to stop it and one of them said the truck ran over his foot. The police then smashed the truck's windows, pulled out the driver and passengers, and beat them with clubs.

The main march started on schedule and most of the crowd, which had not seen the encounter, was in a peaceful, even festive mood as it proceeded to the hotel. The turnout was 20,000, by far the largest antiwar gathering yet to occur in Los Angeles. Most of the people were attending their first demonstration. They were largely students and middle-income adults, some with children in strollers. It was certainly not a threatening group.

As the march reached the hotel, some fifty demonstrators, including a number who had been angered by the destruction of the PL-SDS sound truck, sat down in the street, blocking the way. They did this over the protest of march organizers.

The demonstration monitors attempted to lead the march around the sit-downers, so it could proceed on past the hotel. But the police prevented this by blocking off the entire road. They then declared the entire demonstration an "unlawful assembly," and broke it up violently, using motorcycles followed by a charge of hundreds of cops swinging clubs who emerged from the parking lot under the hotel. All told, 1,200 city police were used in the operation, which was obviously carefully prepared.

More than fifty demonstrators were arrested, hundreds were injured, sixty were sent to the hospital, and some were chased all the way to the border between Los Angeles and Beverly Hills. Most of the crowd reacted in shocked disbelief and there was a stampede in close quarters, since the police also blocked off the road further back, toward the rear of the march. The police clubbed several radio and TV personnel and one had his arm broken. The TV coverage was not sympathetic to the police action.

Los Angeles Chief of Police Tom Reddin boasted that it was a perfect police exercise, and he was backed by Mayor Sam Yorty. The city council voted ten to five against hearing spokespersons for the antiwar movement who demanded that the "City of Los Angeles respect the Constitution of the United States, including the Bill of Rights, specifically that section which allows peaceful assembly."[20]

This was the first major antiwar demonstration in the country to be broken up by police. The PAC and the SMC held a meeting immediately after the attack. Mike McCabe, an SMC activist at the time, recalls:

20. *Militant*, July 10, 1967.

After making arrangements for bail and for following up on the people in hospitals, it was decided to have a press conference the next morning. Some people wanted to denounce PL for acting provocatively. It was decided, however, that as inappropriate as the tactics by PL had been, it was clearly the police who had used violence and broken up the demonstration, which was not a threat to either people or property. Publicly pointing the finger of blame at PL would disorient and split the movement when it was necessary to unite against the police attack.

The next morning PL showed up at the press conference anticipating a public attack on them by the PAC and SMC. That didn't happen. PL tried to explain its own tactics, but the other spokespersons concentrated fire on the police attack.[21]

Within the movement, however, a problem was recognized. There was no way of guaranteeing that the police would not have attacked the demonstration anyway, but the sit-down had certainly made the attack more likely and presented an excuse to the authorities, who were obviously prepared to take advantage of it. A small group of people had precipitated a physical confrontation that involved a much larger group that had not agreed to it, and was not prepared for it. It was a problem that would occur more frequently and that the movement would have to learn how to handle.

After Century Plaza it became imperative that the antiwar movement in Los Angeles show it was not to be intimidated. The PAC and SMC called another demonstration for Hiroshima Day, August 6. This time they made careful preparations, including a public campaign in defense of civil liberties and more adequate training and recruitment of monitors, medics, and legal observers.

More than 10,000 people turned out for the August 6 march, which moved in good order down Wilshire Blvd. to a rally at Lafayette Park. The march was twice physically attacked by ultraright groups, first by a small band of American Nazis, and then by some 200 anti-Castro Cubans who charged into the head of the parade armed with wooden stakes. The attackers were surrounded by parade monitors and moved off. This time the police did not interfere with the demonstration. But for years the memory of Century Plaza made it difficult to organize mass demonstrations in Los Angeles.

The summer of 1967 saw widespread antiwar activity on a local

21. Taped interview with Mike McCabe, November 10, 1975.

level, much of it in new places. There was some national coordination through Vietnam Summer and the Student Mobilization Committee, and attempts were made to put antiwar referenda on the ballot in a number of cities. However, as fall approached, only the SMC was seriously publicizing the October 21 march on Washington.

SDS, at its national convention June 25–July 2, gave only grudging support to October 21, if it could be called support at all. It passed a resolution on "Antiwar Activities" which began: "The National Convention of SDS regrets the decision of the National Mobilization Committee to call for a March on Washington in October." It urged SDS chapters to use the demonstration "only as a tool for organizing" and declared: "We feel that these large demonstrations—which are just public expressions of belief—can have no significant effect on American policy in Vietnam. Further they delude many participants into thinking that the 'democratic' process in America functions in a meaningful way."[22]

The National Mobilization Committee itself was in the doldrums. Bevel became ill and in effect dropped out of Mobilization Committee activity. Much time in the group's administrative committee meetings was taken up in soul-searching discussions over how to relate to the spontaneous uprisings that had hit the Newark, Detroit, and other Black ghettos that summer. There was little the committee as such could offer beyond sympathy.

On August 12 the administrative committee held a meeting in Philadelphia at which Eric Weinberger, the treasurer, reported: "Cash on hand $485.01 and a deficit of $12,050.06. The situation is still critical, i.e., people on the staff are hungry."[23]

The group still had no definite plans for October 21 and no project director for the action. By this time it had been agreed to combine some sort of nonviolent confrontation with the mass demonstration, and it was assumed that the march would be on the capitol. There was a standing rule against demonstrators getting any closer than 500 feet to the capitol and the committee considered committing civil disobedience by going further. Abe Weisburd, of Trade Unionists for Peace, moved that the demon-

22. Resolutions, *New Left Notes*, July 10, 1967.

23. Minutes of National Mobilization Committee administrative committee, August 12, 1967. (Copy in author's files.)

stration attempt to enter the capitol itself. According to the minutes, Arnold Johnson "suggested we make it clear we meant the gallery and not the floor of Congress which could be considered insurrection."[24]

The meeting droned on with no enthusiasm and little real agreement. Finally, another meeting was set for August 26 in Washington.

The whole action was hung up waiting for a project director who could at least inspire the committee to get off dead center. In a kind of desperation, I telephoned around the country seeking suggestions. One of these calls was to Peter Camejo in Berkeley, who had been working on something called the Peace Torch Marathon. This involved a torch that had been lit in Hiroshima on August 6, then flown to San Francisco. The idea, originated by a group of moderates in Palo Alto, was to carry the torch by runner across the country to Washington for October 21, with local groups participating in different legs of the marathon. Jerry Rubin had also been working on this, but by the time I called Camejo both he and Rubin had been thrown off the project because they were too radical for the others involved. Camejo told me Rubin was just then at loose ends and might be interested in the Washington project.

I raised this at a small meeting at Norma Becker's apartment, and Dellinger picked right up on it. He called Rubin and asked him to come to New York; Rubin agreed.

In his book on the Pentagon march, Norman Mailer says:

> Some most radical possibilities were already in Dellinger's mind, but to call on Rubin was in effect to call upon the most militant, unpredictable, creative—therefore dangerous—hippie-oriented leader available on the New Left. It is to Dellinger's credit that he most probably did not do this to save the March, since there was no doubt that, doldrums or no, a peaceful demonstration of large proportions could always have been gotten together; the invitation to Rubin was rather an expression of Dellinger's faith in the possibility—a most difficult possibility which only his own untested gifts as conciliator could have enabled him to envisage—of a combined conventional mass protest and civil disobedience which might help to unify the scattered elements of the peace movement.[25]

24. Ibid.
25. Norman Mailer, *Armies of the Night* (New York: New American Library, 1968), p. 225.

True enough as far as Dellinger was concerned. But a large peaceful demonstration was by no means as automatic or easy to achieve as Mailer assumes. I suggested Rubin in the first place for precisely the reason Mailer dismisses. I was soon to have mixed feelings about this initiative.

Rubin came to New York with Stew Albert and Karen Wald, buddies from the Berkeley street scene who immediately joined the Mobilization staff. I hadn't seen Rubin since March 1966 when he still wore a modest haircut and the white shirt and slacks common among students. This time I hardly recognized him. He sported wild, curly hair that stood out half a foot in all directions and he seemed less relaxed than before. He gave a contradictory impression: almost deadly serious and full of outrageous humor at the same time.

Rubin came convinced that the demonstration should go to the Pentagon, an idea he said had already been discussed among street-scene radicals in Berkeley and San Francisco. When I told him I preferred the capitol he gave me a lecture on the mystical practices of certain Native American tribes who were said to use a hallucinogenic drug in their ceremonies and for whom five-sided figures were the symbol of evil. The Pentagon, he declared, was obviously the most famous, biggest, most ominous five-sided figure in the world. It we "exorcise" that, said Rubin, that will really inspire people.

Rubin viewed me as an impossibly straight, "old left" type, and at first I thought he was putting me on when he came across with mystical stuff like that. But after working with him a while I wasn't sure he didn't believe it himself.

\*          \*          \*

The idea of an antiwar demonstration at the Pentagon was not really new. At least five smaller ones had already been organized by pacifists: one by the Quakers in 1960 and four by the Committee for Nonviolent Action. Norman Morrison, a thirty-two-year-old Quaker from Baltimore, had burned himself to death with gasoline on the steps of the Pentagon on November 2, 1965. The most recent Pentagon protest was the CNVA Boston-to-Pentagon Walk which passed through New York on April 15 and was part of the activities connected with the 1967 spring mobilization.

It was Rubin who insisted that it be the focus for the October 21
mass action. Greenblatt and most of the pacifists tended to agree
right away. I still preferred the capitol but accompanied Greenblatt and Rubin to the Pentagon to check out the physical
circumstances. As it turned out, Rubin didn't even know the
Pentagon wasn't in the city of Washington but across the
Potomac river in Virginia. If the authorities blocked the bridges,
the demonstration would never get there.

Rubin was undismayed and entertained us with a description
of crossing the river in rowboats dressed up like George Washington's revolutionary soldiers crossing the Delaware. For different
reasons I viewed the river as no particular problem. It was
unlikely the authorities would not let the demonstration cross. A
confrontation in the city of Washington would present more
problems to them than one on the Virginia side, where there were
open fields for miles except for the Arlington national cemetery
and the Pentagon itself, which they could easily defend. We
agreed that a march on the Pentagon was technically feasible
and the August 26 administrative committee meeting decided to
go ahead, with Rubin as project director. A press conference was
set for August 28 in New York.

*          *          *

One of the first things Rubin did when he got to New York from
Berkeley was to check out the Greenwich Village street scene. He
soon ran across Abbie Hoffman and involved him in the Pentagon project. Hoffman had been a SNCC activist who, like the
other whites in SNCC, had been unceremoniously separated from
the organization when it developed its Black power thrust along
nationalist lines. Hoffman took this quite personally and made
some bitter comments on the subject in the *Village Voice*. He soon
merged with the Village street scene, however, developing a
cultural-radical approach similar to Rubin's. By the time the two
got together Hoffman was already a central figure in this
Greenwich Village milieu. Like Rubin he had a flair for publicity
and was a master of the put-on. He was also a natural clown with
the agility of a gymnast and the face of a mime. He had an
unerring ability to get under the skin of those who took seriously
whatever he chose to make the butt of a joke. I admit he got under
mine from time to time.

Rubin invited Hoffman to speak at the August 28 news

conference. There was some discussion beforehand on what the official statement to the press should say. I sat there in dismay listening to the dreams being spun about how the movement was finally about to take steps to actually stop the war machine and the proposals that we should announce we were going to "shut down" the Pentagon. At one point I shouted: "We don't have the tanks and machine guns to shut down the Pentagon. Let's be serious and not make any statements we can't possibly live up to."

Dellinger replied to the effect that of course we don't have the physical power to shut down the Pentagon but that was our moral intent and it was necessary to state this in order to make clear the movement was going forward to a newer, more serious level of commitment.

Essentially this was the argument behind the whole idea of "From protest to resistance," or "From dissent to resistance." It was common among radical pacifists and new-guard SDSers at the time. It was usually stated as a given, self-evident fact. Somehow the very act of throwing down the gauntlet was expected to spark the masses to action, or result in the development of real power for the antiwar movement.

The approach was wrong in my view because it made a fetish out of a tactic. It attributed some mystical power to the fact of approaching a situation of combat, whether nonviolently or otherwise. I had been through enough of that in labor strikes to know there is nothing magical about facing up to a line of cops. Such confrontations are inevitable at times in the class struggle and ought to be taken seriously, but they are no substitute for program and organization.

My view did not prevail in these discussions and the official press statement contained the following language:

> The National Mobilization Committee today announces that it is beginning to organize a confrontation in Washington on October 21-22 which will shut down the Pentagon. We will fill the hallways and block the entrances. Thousands of people will disrupt the center of the American war machine. In the name of humanity we will call the warmakers to task.[26]

26. "Press Statement of National Mobilization Committee to End the War in Vietnam," for release at Overseas Press Club, New York City, August 28, 1967. (Copy in author's files.)

The press conference certainly made the news. The statement was read by Rev. Thomas Lee Hayes of the Episcopal Peace Fellowship. Among the movement figures present were Amy Swerdlow of Women Strike for Peace; Msgr. Rice; Dick Gregory; Gary Rader, an ex-member of the Green Beret reserve who was then an organizer of the Chicago Area Draft Resisters (CADRE); William Pepper, executive director of the National Conference for New Politics; Carl Davidson of SDS; Lincoln Lynch of CORE; Fred Rosen of Resistance; Lee Webb, the old-guard SDSer who was now codirector of Vietnam Summer; H. Rap Brown of SNCC; Dellinger, Rubin, and myself. But it was Rubin and Hoffman who stole the show with their descriptions of a hippie exorcism and "levitation" of the Pentagon and other hallucinogenic projections.

"We're going to raise the Pentagon three hundred feet in the air,"[27] said Hoffman. And Rubin declared: "We're now in the business of wholesale disruption and widespread resistance and dislocation of the American society."[28] Even Dellinger got a bit carried away in describing the small-scale civil disobedience actions of the Target City project scheduled to begin September 11 and go to October 21. "There will be no government building left unattacked," he declared.[29] It was great theater for the evening TV audiences, though it was bound to exacerbate tensions in the coalition. At least the action was finally off the ground, announced with fairly broad support and considerable publicity. With luck the rank-and-file antiwar activists—on whom the building of the action really depended—would have enough sense of humor not to be sidetracked.

*         *         *

Immediately after the press conference Dellinger left for another trip overseas and some of the rest of us went to Chicago where the National Conference for New Politics convention was about to begin on August 29. The prospect of turning the antiwar movement into a new multi-issue political formation for the 1968 elections went up in smoke at this gathering, which was an

27. Mailer, p. 234.
28. Loc. cit.
29. Loc. cit.

unmitigated disaster for its organizers.

At its start the five-day convention at the Palmer House hotel was the largest gathering of left-wing groups since the birth of the new antiwar movement. Except for the SWP and the YSA— which sent only observers—and a few groups and individuals like Dellinger who were not interested in electoral politics, it was the most broadly representative conference yet, with 3,602 registered participants from 372 groups. The delegates carried bloc votes which theoretically represented 56,000 persons.

At first the idea of a King-Spock ticket got a boost when Dr. Spock indicated he was willing and Martin Luther King appeared for a speech at the opening rally. But King's speech did not deal with the NCNP and he immediately left town without a single public comment on the convention itself.

At the same time a split occurred among the Blacks in attendance as some 350 of them left the gathering and organized a simultaneous Black People's Convention elsewhere in town. This group consisted mainly of the more Black-nationalist-oriented delegates. A position paper circulated by them explained:

Political coalition is a process that implies the total readiness of both sides involved. . . . Black people are not ready for this coalition on many levels, and neither are the so-called white radicals caught up in their psychological, rhetorical and ideological "hang-ups" that have been flourishing since the '30s. We are now immediately aware of the need to begin initiating positive action rather than reacting to various white maneuvers, whether they are establishment oriented or otherwise.[30]

A number of the Blacks remaining at the convention organized a Black Caucus, which, partly in an attempt to outflank the rival meeting across town, adopted a militant thirteen-point program. This was done with the understanding that if the NCNP convention didn't adopt it, the Black Caucus would also leave. More than one point among the thirteen was not welcomed by the liberals, but the thorniest was point five, which referred to the recent Mideast June War as follows: "Condemn the imperialistic Zionist war; this condemnation does not imply anti-Semitism."[31] Martin Peretz, one of the main fund-raisers for Vietnam Summer and the NCNP, threatened his own walkout over this.

30. *Militant,* September 11, 1967.
31. Ibid.

The Black Caucus resolution was adopted, but not as a result of a serious discussion of the issues. Though that would not have led to full agreement, it would at least have been educational. As it was, white paternalism was much in evidence and significant forces supported the motion cynically, just to keep the Black Caucus in the convention. The vote came after a speech in support of the motion by Ed Greer of New Haven in which he said: "People will little note the wording of the resolutions we pass here."[32] Unfortunately for those who by such methods hoped to patch up the unpatchable, the next day newspapers prominently featured the convention's adoption of the anti-Zionist stand, and more of the liberals hit the ceiling.

Meanwhile the convention divided into three blocs over electoral strategy for 1968: those favoring a "third ticket" for president and vice-president, those for launching a new party, and those for no national commitment, who favored concentrating on "community organizing" including local electoral campaigns. The Communist Party was the most determined of the "third ticket" forces, the Independent Socialist Clubs led the fight for a new party, and youth from SDS and Vietnam Summer sparked the "community organizing" position. This last was also supported by those who saw a "third ticket" as diversionary from their emphasis on reforming the Democratic Party.

The fight was bitter and when the three positions were put to a vote none had a majority. The new party position was eliminated and a runoff vote taken between the other two. The convention, using a system of weighted proxy votes, divided down the middle: 13,517 votes for a "third ticket" and 13,519 for "community organizing." A compromise, worked out by the California delegation, was passed. It put the convention on record in favor of a "third ticket" in those states "where local groups and organizations want to run a campaign and feel there is a basis therefor."[33] Since there would be no unified national effort it was a defeat for the "third ticket" forces.

But some of them had another trick up their sleeves, involving the Black Caucus, which by now had shrunk in size and, according to the corridor grapevine, come under the domination of Blacks favoring the "third ticket" position. One of the points of

32. Ibid.
33. Ibid.

the previously passed Black Caucus resolution called for 50 percent Black representation on all convention committees. A majority of the credentials committee brought in a proposal to implement this by considering the convention itself a committee of the whole and giving to the Black Caucus 28,000 votes, half the total originally extant. The Communist Party and the Du Bois Clubs vigorously supported this proposal. One view of the reason is offered by Thomas Powers in his book *The War at Home*:

> If no third-party [or third ticket] effort were mounted, the only antiwar candidate would be run by the Socialist Workers Party, the organ of Trotskyism. The Communists were not about to allow all those antiwar votes, not to mention the publicity, money, and volunteers to go to Trotskyists. If the Black Caucus had 50 percent of the conference votes, some kind of third-party [or third ticket] effort backed by the Communists would obviously be approved. Hence their maneuver.[34]

Be that as it may, the majority of the delegates were not thinking in those terms. The White Radical Caucus, led by youth from Vietnam Summer and SDS, was strongly behind the "community organizing" position, but it too supported giving the Black Caucus half the votes. Once again the debate was shot through with liberal paternalism and cynicism. Renata Adler reported a conversation between Simon Casady, one of the chief organizers of the convention, and *Ramparts* editor Warren Hinckle. Said Casady: "I guess what they're asking is to let them hold our wallet, and we might as well let them." Replied Hinckle: "Especially since there's nothing in it."[35]

The motion to give the Black Caucus half the votes passed. Immediately afterward a delegate from the Du Bois Clubs moved to reconsider the "third ticket" issue "now that our black brothers have rejoined the convention on the basis of equality."[36] Pandemonium ensued and a recess was called for caucusing, but the whole thing left such a bad taste that few took the conference seriously after that.

With it all there had apparently been a miscalculation. After the recess the Mississippi Freedom Democratic Party delegation

34. Thomas Powers, *The War at Home*, p. 264.
35. Renata Adler, "Letter from the Palmer House," *New Yorker*, September 23, 1967.
36. *Militant*, September 11, 1967.

—the major serious force left in the Black Caucus—announced it was opposed to a "third ticket." The spokesperson for the Black Caucus then declared there was no need for reconsideration, and the California compromise was reconfirmed.

The rest was anticlimax. The conference faded out in a mood of demoralization and disgust. Marvin Garson expressed it thus:

> Does anyone still remember the daily leaflets and rallies of the Free Speech Movement, which gave the rank and file a pound of solid fact and reasoning for every ounce of rhetoric? The FSM operated under the principle that any bit of dishonesty or opportunism, however innocuous it might seem at the moment, would grow like a cancer until it killed the movement. . . . The NCNP did not suddenly falsify what had been an honest movement; the style of the movement had been disintegrating for years. Still, it came as a shock to me to listen to the press conference that the new board held as the convention was breaking up. They had boxed themselves in so thoroughly that there was hardly a single question they could answer honestly. . . .[37]

The "New Politics" turned out to be like the old politics of the Democratic and Republican parties where dodging questions is the name of the game. But to be disillusioned one must have illusions in the first place. The NCNP convention failed because the failure was built into the attempt. The movement was simply too heterogeneous in its class composition as well as in the political perspectives of its tendencies, to agree on a single multi-issue program. Any attempt to overcome this problem by mere maneuvers—instead of by the more long-term educational clash of ideas and the tests of experience—was bound to bog down.

In a few states "third ticket" presidential campaigns were mounted. (The Peace and Freedom Party in California was the most important.) But the backers couldn't even agree on a common program or the same candidates for all of these. The NCNP itself soon disappeared.

This fiasco confirmed the fact that mass demonstrations against the war in Vietnam remained the only national tactic that could unify the antiwar movement.

The SWPers and YSAers who attended the NCNP convention did so without voice or vote and played no role in the proceedings

37. *Berkeley Barb,* September 15, 1967.

or caucuses. On the face of it there was no possibility of this convention launching a united socialist or independent working class electoral campaign. We thus did not associate with its stated purpose and attended only as observers.

Paul Boutelle and I had just been nominated as the vice-presidential and presidential candidates respectively of the Socialist Workers Party for the 1968 elections. Our campaign committee rented a room in the convention hotel where we set up coffee and doughnuts and gave the delegates an opportunity to meet the socialist candidates. Boutelle also dropped in on the Black People's Convention.

At one point C. Clark Kissinger cracked to me: "Everybody's arguing about Black power, student power, community power. But you're picking up the pieces with doughnut power." He had a point. We were probably the only tendency at the convention that actually made friends in the course of it, and for a change got none of the blame for the faction fighting.

*          *          *

The National Mobilization Committee as such played no role in the NCNP convention except to publicize the coming march on Washington among the delegates. The staff had rushed out a new issue of the *Mobilizer*, containing the news of the Pentagon demonstration, so the first thousand copies could be distributed to the delegates at the NCNP gathering. The response was less than reassuring.

The issue had been edited by Rubin's buddies, Karen Wald and Stew Albert, and emphasized the confrontation or civil disobedience aspects of the Washington action to the virtual exclusion of anything else. It contained no mention of immediate withdrawal—or negotiations either for that matter—no appeal to the GIs and no political demands at all beyond a brief mention of a committee resolution that called "For the transfer of the billions now being wasted in Vietnam, to a massive decentralized program of aid to America's poor and disinherited."[38] The issue as a whole was an example of the tendency to subordinate the program of the movement to a tactic.

The *Mobilizer* contained an article by Keith Lampe, who had

38. *Mobilizer*, vol. 2, no. 1, September 1, 1967. (Copy in author's files.)

been the Parade Committee's volunteer press agent. Professionally he worked in advertising and public relations and had recently moved into the countercultural scene with a gusto only a Madison Avenue executive type, kicking over the traces, could muster. Lampe's article, entitled "On Making a Perfect Mess," was not without humor, but in the context not everyone in the Mobilization Committee thought it was funny. It said:

A good feeling in the streets of America. Feels like there's going to be a white rebellion too. The work of the black men of Newark and Detroit has freed us honkies (beep! beep!) of a few more scholarly hang-ups and we're getting down into it now.

Now, at last, we're getting past the talk and the analysis and the petitions and the protests—past the cunning white logic of the universities—and we're heading back down into ourselves. . . . In any case, we emancipated primitives of the coming culture are free to do what we *feel* now because we understand that logic and proportion and consistency and often even perspective are part of the old control system and we're done with the old control systems.

There followed a list of things that might happen in Washington in October, including:

A thousand children will stage Loot-Ins at department stores to strike at the property fetish that underlies genocidal wars. . . .
Hey, who defoliated the White House lawn? . . .
Hey, who kidnapped the guard at the Tomb of the Unknown Soldier?
During a block party in front of the White House a lad of nine will climb the fence and piss, piss, piss. . . .

Lampe's article ended with the following note, disturbing even to some of the civil-disobedience-oriented pacifists:

Because as a honkie I have a bully heritage, I dig nonviolence as my best expression. But I know nonviolence is a faith—not a demonstrable truth—and, being ecumenically inclined, I have no desire to impose it on anybody else.[39]

Shortly after the issue came out an emergency meeting was initiated by some of the people in Women Strike for Peace, New York SANE, and the trade unions. Key roles were played in this

39. Ibid.

meeting by Al Evanoff and Bella Abzug, who could be tough as nails. They took on Rubin in no uncertain terms. Evanoff pointed to the place in the issue where his name was listed as one of the several cochairpersons of the National Mobilization Committee, and then to the part about the loot-ins in department stores.

"Do you know what union I am an official of?" he said to Rubin through clenched teeth, "The Retail, Wholesale and *Department Store* Workers. What am I supposed to say when the management of a department store uses this against our union in an organizing drive, or negotiations, or a strike?"

The committee voted to scrap the issue, over Rubin's objection. Sid Peck took charge of putting out the next one, which contained a more balanced projection of the Washington action.

Within the staff there was constant tension—though never personal—between Rubin and me on how the action should be publicized and built. Once he came in with a mock-up for a poster that consisted entirely of a psychedelic design, like something on a piece of paisley cloth. That's all there was to it. No slogan, no indication of what the demonstration was about, no instructions on how to get transportation, not even the date, time, and place of the event. When I objected he said: "Words are bullshit. We don't need words, we need action."

Just to get under *his* skin I blocked out a poster that consisted of nothing *but* words, big block letters on white, with a slogan, the date, time, and place in big type, and a space for local groups to put instructions on how to get bus or train tickets.

Rubin hit the roof and we had a shouting match. He finally agreed to put the date and place on his poster, but he had it done in type so small you couldn't read it from more than a yard away. It was necessary to simply go around him to get out some posters with the necessary information on them in type large enough to be effective. In the end it was the SMC that put out most of the posters anyway, and they were quite clear.

During preparations for the action I worked in the New York office where the Parade Committee was organizing the transportation from New York to Washington. This involved chartering some 500 buses, a number of railroad cars, and organizing car pools. We had to pay in advance for buses and railroad cars and so had to sell tickets ahead of time. There were times when the line into the office stretched around the block.

We were plagued by a rash of cancellations of chartered buses.

Some of the companies bluntly told us this was because of pressure from the administration. The worst single problem was the cancellation of a 1,400-passenger train we had chartered from the Pennsylvania Railroad. After that we told the railroad and the New York City authorities that we'd have our demonstration at the Port Authority Bus Terminal and Pennsylvania Station if we couldn't get transportation to Washington. We got the train back, as well as most of the buses, though some people were stranded and never did make it to Washington.

Meanwhile the committee set up an office in the capital, to work on preparations. The staff there included Maris Cakers, who was in charge of the Target City project and civil disobedience on October 21, and Brad Lyttle, who worked on "logistics" for the major demonstration. This meant all the technical preparations, such as sound equipment, bus parking, monitoring assignments, etc. These two were radical pacifists with a practical bent, long experience in civil disobedience actions, and a sense of responsibility about what they were doing.

*       *       *

Lyttle's attitude had been impressed on me early in our association. Back in October 1965, just before the first Parade Committee march in New York, he had called me into the CNVA office and said he was worried that the demonstration would be violent. He was concerned because it was going to be large, a lot of people would be there who had no nonviolent training, or no such philosophical commitment. He said he was thinking of writing a statement warning of possible violence and even dissociating himself from the event, or asking other pacifists to consider such a stand. He wanted to talk it over with me first. Lyttle was a veteran of many confrontations and arrests and it was clear that personal fears had nothing to do with this conversation. It was concern for principle.

Lyttle had already had a lot of experience organizing nonviolent direct action projects, including demonstrations against atomic missile installations in Nebraska in 1959, the Polaris action projects against atomic submarines, the 1961 San Francisco-to-Moscow Walk for Peace, and the Quebec-Washington-Guantanamo Walk in 1963. But all of these had involved relatively small numbers of committed nonviolent activists. In October 1965 he still had no experience with really large crowds.

I told him I couldn't make any promises about the police and ultra-right-wing groups who might attack the march, but that I and everyone else organizing the October 1965 event agreed on a nonviolent tactic for the occasion and we were doing everything we could to make it go that way. I emphasized that his fears of a large crowd getting out of hand were not well founded. Other things being equal, the larger the crowd, the higher the average level of common sense. He wasn't entirely convinced, but agreed to hold off on the statement so as not to hurt the action. The demonstration went well, and after that Lyttle had no fear of large crowds and made it a point to develop techniques of working with them.

\*          \*          \*

Cakers and Lyttle were anxious to combine the mass action with civil disobedience. But they had a healthy respect for the practicalities and were not inclined to set something in motion and then leave it to chance. They paid attention to setting a nonviolent tone, and to the details—in themselves often tedious—without which the boldest conception will come to naught, or worse. As long as they and others like them were on top of the preparations in Washington, there was reasonable assurance that the civil disobedience would be organized on a nonviolent basis and would not invite confrontation in such a way as to involve people who did not want to be involved.

This assurance was absolutely crucial to the viability of the whole plan as it had developed. Without it, a number of the major groups could not be kept in the coalition and the mass character of the action would be dissipated.

Dellinger was still out of the country and not present at the meeting that scrapped the issue of the *Mobilizer* and called Rubin to order, or tried to. In his book *More Power Than We Know* he telescopes some of the developments prior to the march in the following comments:

Two weeks before the Pentagon action it had looked as if Women Strike for Peace, Dr. Spock, and the Socialist Workers Party on the "Right" and SDS on the "Left" would all withdraw. Dr. Spock and WSP—at this stage of their involvement—had reservations about the practicality of civil disobedience and understandably became apprehensive at the disjointed rhetoric of some of the Left. They needed reassurance that the civil disobedience would be sufficiently separated in time and space from the march and rally to safeguard the "women and children" from police attack.[40]

The SWP never threatened to withdraw from the action. We fought to prevent the legal, peaceful part of the demonstration from being eliminated. Whether the WSP actually threatened to withdraw in the face of the Rubinesque rhetoric I don't know. They did insist on Dr. Spock's endorsement for the action, and I answered a phone call to the New York office from Dr. Spock regarding this. He said he could endorse only if there were a clear separation regarding the civil disobedience because some mothers with children might come on the strength of his endorsement. I assured him there would be such a separation. He seemed satisfied and did endorse.

Dellinger continues with this rather bitter comment:

> The SWP, believing as it does that when the revolution comes it will take place through the armed struggle of the working class, led by the SWP, disapproved of the original plans but went along because they didn't want to be isolated and discredited in the movement. Now they saw a chance to play on the fears of Women Strike and other moderate groups in order to preserve the coalition as a risk-free hunting ground for recruits to their "revolutionary socialist" organization.[41]

The SWP's view of a future American revolution—which Dellinger does not state correctly—was not really germane to the plans for the Pentagon march. Apparently he means to point out that the SWP did not share his anarcho-pacifist perspective, or perhaps that we did not think the revolution was upon us. That much is true. More to the point, we did not agree that a few hundreds or even a few thousands involved in confrontation and arrests—nonviolent or otherwise—could somehow spark a spontaneous wave of decentralized resistance that would then and there dissolve the power of the war-makers. That was a pipe dream in our view.

40. David Dellinger, *More Power Than We Know* (Garden City, New York: Anchor/Doubleday, 1975), pp. 112-13.
41. Ibid., p. 113.

To a certain extent such notions had been encouraged by the experience of the Southern civil rights movement of the early 1960s. In that situation sometimes civil disobedience initiated by relative handfuls did precipitate a widespread national reaction against the segregationists. But there was at least one crucial difference in the context at hand. In the Southern civil rights struggle the civil disobedience had been against local law and local authority that was itself in violation of federal law as ruled by the Supreme Court.

In the Southern struggle against de jure segregation, the most successful civil disobedience was specifically designed to precipitate a confrontation between local and federal authorities. In some cases where the local authorities remained adamant—as in Selma, Alabama—the civil rights movement even demanded— and got—federal troops. The antiwar movement had no such leverage. For the antiwar movement it was much more difficult to make the message of civil disobedience by small numbers clear and the embarrassment it might produce for the federal government was not at all automatic.

If others wanted to experiment with such activity, the SWP would not stand in their way. We had agreed to that at the May conference and more specifically regarding October 21, even before Rubin came on the staff. But we insisted that the other part of the agreement also be honored, that there be a mass, peaceful, legal demonstration as well. Otherwise there would be no mass turnout. And it was the mass action the SWP was chiefly concerned with. We were convinced that the only way the antiwar movement could contribute materially to ending the war was by involving immense and enlarging masses. We voted with others to this end.

As for preserving the coalition as a recruiting ground, we could have set up coffee and doughnuts and irritated nobody if that's all we were interested in. We fought hard to preserve the coalition so the mass character of the action would not be lost.

Dellinger continues:

> The reasons for SDS's aloofness were more complex, but they included growing contempt for all politically deviant and "bourgeois liberal" groups. This contempt, which eventually led to the isolation of SDS from all Americans, including most radical students, was intensified in the weeks just prior to the Pentagon action by the natural timidity and vacillations of middle-class groups that were preparing to make a historic

move forward either into resistance or into close association with it, and
by the hypocritical maneuvers of the SWP, as they tried to prevent these
groups from taking the plunge.[42]

(The term "middle class" is inaccurate here. Some of the groups
referred to were trade unions and none could possibly have been
more middle class in leadership, membership, or political syndrome than SDS itself. What is really meant is "moderate"
groups.)

Dellinger's bitterness toward the SWP in these passages was
not that obvious at the time of these events, as I recall. We had
differences but our relations were still cordial. There may be some
reading back into the situation attitudes that developed later
when the differences reached the point of split. The differences
were present only in embryonic form during preparations for the
Pentagon march. To understand them it is necessary to touch on
the nature of the political problem Dellinger was wrestling with
at the time.

Throughout this period and for some time afterward, Dellinger
paid considerable attention to attempts to involve SDS and the
countercultural milieu in the antiwar movement. Dellinger placed
considerable hope in SDS because its emphasis on "community
organizing," decentralized "resistance," spontanéism, and, at
first, "participatory democracy," were close to Dellinger's own
anarchist approach. Similar trends were present in much of the
countercultural milieu.

A complicating factor was that SDS and the so-called street
people were not necessarily committed to nonviolence. SDS was
beginning to toy with other approaches to direct action, rhetorically for the most part. This was a source of concern to Dellinger.
There is little doubt he pondered the experience of Martin Luther
King, Jr., who had lost influence over the most radical youth in
his own movement and saw them renounce pacifism. All the more
reason for Dellinger to bend every effort to show SDS in life that
nonviolent resistance could be an effective revolutionary force,
and to keep open the lines of approach. The Pentagon march was
the best chance yet to do this.

The SWPers with whom Dellinger had worked closely and to
good effect in the left wing of the coalition were now in a bloc

42. Ibid., p. 113.

with the moderate groups and appeared to stand in the way of the rapprochement with SDS. We supported increasing the influence of the moderates in the general publicity and tone of the event because we agreed with them that this was the best approach to turn out the largest numbers. But it was precisely this tone that drove Rubin up the wall and increased SDS's "contempt" for the coalition. SDS was simply not concerned about the mass action. It had already opted for the idea of a dedicated vanguard substituting itself for the majority and sparking the masses to "resistance" by dramatic example.

SDS was bent on "doing its own thing," which Rubin kept inviting people to do, in line with his dream of initiating wholesale disruption. Dellinger tended to dismiss the wilder statements of SDSers, Rubin, and others in those milieux as idle rhetoric. There was truth to this, but the rhetoric itself was hurting the mass character of the march. It was also the height of folly, in my view, because it gave the police a ready-made excuse to physically attack the demonstration. To counter this the SWP demanded assurances as to the peaceful, legal character of the mass march and rally. We pressed for this to be made publicly clear.

There were also some of the pacifists—like Brad Lyttle and Peter Kiger—who were uneasy about the "do-your-own-thing" rhetoric. They wanted assurances as to the nonviolent discipline. The SWP joined in these demands. But the area of rapprochement with those bent on "doing their own thing" was narrow.

Dellinger in this period was in the unenviable position of negotiating with Rubin and SDS on the one hand and some of the moderate groups on the other. He was, after all, a pacifist committed to nonviolence across the board. The SWPers were not. To him our stand may have seemed like a hypocritical maneuver against Rubin and SDS. But it wasn't. We simply held to the position that the nonviolent tactic was necessary in order to maintain the mass character of the action under the given circumstances. A free-for-all fight—rhetorical or otherwise—was not part of the agreement.

This had nothing to do with "vacillation and timidity." It had to do with keeping the movement's statement clear and attracting the masses. One thing the new-guard SDSers had difficulty understanding was that ordinary people stay away from physical fights they can't possibly win, not because they lack courage or conviction, but because they think it's crazy or too costly.

Dellinger placed great emphasis on personal consultations, negotiations, and understandings with certain leading figures. The SWPers did not. We expressed our views in the large committee meetings and pressed for public statements of tone and policy. In his book Dellinger reveals the impression that the SWP packed these meetings during preparations for the Pentagon march. He says:

> Since the SWP regularly packed meetings with delegates from exciting, new "grass roots" Committees to End the War (the East Twenty-third Street Committee, the West Twenty-eighth Street Committee, the South Philadelphia Committee, the Morningside Housewives Committee), none of whom identified themselves as members of the SWP but all of whom were directed by an SWP floor leader, it was not always easy for a coalition of over 150 national and local organizations to make a decision that ran counter to a decision already made in the SWP caucus.[43]

There is obvious poetic license in Dellinger's illustration, since the Committees to End the War that he mentions are fictional and nobody ever claimed to represent them. Fortunately an actual record survives as to the attendance at most of the meetings of the National Mobilization administrative committee, which was the policy-making body of the coalition during this period. Those in attendance were listed in the minutes.

Neither Democrats, Republicans, Communists, Socialist Workers, nor what have you made a point of mentioning their party affiliation in their speeches. It would have been redundant anyway because in general the people who attended these meetings, and their political views, were well known to most of the others present.

In looking over the minutes from the time Rubin was voted project director, I find the following: At the August 26 meeting, 5 SWPers or YSAers attended out of a total of 31; September 16, 9 out of 87; September 24, 7 out of 48; September 30, 8 out of 57; October 7, 7 out of 69.[44] I have been unable to find minutes for two or three of the meetings, but the pattern would have been similar.

Dellinger may have the impression the meetings were filled with SWPers, but they weren't. When it came to maintaining the

43. Ibid., pp. 113-14.
44. Copies of these minutes in author's files.

mass character of the action, the majority usually agreed with us—or us with them—that's all. We stood out more than some of the others because we were very clear on what we wanted and fought hard for it. Not all the others—including moderates—were bashful about it either. "Timidity and vacillation" were not characteristic of such persons as Cora Weiss, Al Evanoff, and Abner Grunauer—not to mention Bella Abzug.

\*      \*      \*

A good part of this took place in the context of negotiations between the Mobilization Committee and the government over a permit for the legal part of the demonstration. Harry Van Cleve, the top lawyer for the General Services Administration (which maintains federal real estate), was appointed to negotiate for all government agencies involved. These included the city of Washington police, the National Park Police with jurisdiction over such areas as the Lincoln Memorial, and the military itself at the Pentagon. Van Cleve was urbane, businesslike, and after a while polite, but somehow I got the impression he felt he was dealing with people from another planet.

Once, when we told him we were considering a rally at the Lincoln Memorial, he gave us a lecture on how Americans loved to visit that spot, and such a rally would interfere with that. We replied that we intended to increase the visitation on October 21 by some 100,000 Americans who had as much right to be there as anyone.

Dellinger, Rubin, and Greenblatt attended almost all the negotiating sessions, with others including Dagmar Wilson, Brad Lyttle, and Sue Orrin participating from time to time. The original plan presented in the negotiations was for two assembly points in Washington, near the Washington Monument and Lincoln Memorial, marches across two bridges eventually converging in the Pentagon's south parking lot. After a rally there, Rubin wanted to ring the Pentagon with exorcising hippies, pickets, etc. At some point those wanting to commit civil disobedience would approach the building and try to get in.

The very idea of negotiating over a plan like that had an element of the absurd about it, on both sides. But it was important that at least some understanding with the authorities be arrived at for technical reasons if nothing else. For a mass demonstration in the neighborhood of 100,000, arrangements had to be made for bus parking, temporary sanitary facilities, the stopping of traffic on the march routes, etc. Sound and other equipment worth many thousands of dollars had to be rented and put in place, and the contractors were not about to do business if their equipment would be destroyed or impounded. Neither Rubin nor SDS chose to involve themselves in such mundane details, but as in all things the concrete technicalities impose themselves on the abstract plans. The government knew this, of course, and used it for all it was worth.

At a negotiating session October 6 Van Cleve made the following offer: Permits would be granted for an assembly in West Potomac Park (near the Lincoln Memorial), a single march across the Arlington Memorial Bridge, and a rally at the north parking area of the Pentagon. (This was a huge lot across a highway and down an embankment from the grassy mall in front of the Pentagon's administrative entrance, or north face.) But Van Cleve said the government insisted that unless the National Mobilization Committee renounced all illegal activity—meaning civil disobedience—no permits would be granted and no cooperation could be expected for any phase of the demonstration. A confidential memo from the Mobilization negotiators to the administrative committee reported the following ominous note: "His [Van Cleve's] warning: Don't put too high a measure on the Government's unwillingness to fight citizens in its capital."[45]

The administrative committee met October 7 to consider the situation. By unanimous vote it refused to renounce the civil disobedience and decided to proceed with the action. It also launched a civil liberties campaign against the government's refusal to grant permits for the legal part of the demonstration.

The incident had the effect of rallying the movement on both ends of the spectrum. Even the SDS national office finally became enthusiastic about the demonstration.

At the next meeting the government dropped the threat to refuse permits. It added the following to its previous offer: After the rally at the north parking area, demonstrators would be

---

45. Report by Sue Orrin on October 6, 1967, meeting with Van Cleve. Signed by Dellinger, Greenblatt, Lyttle, Orrin, Rubin, and Dagmar Wilson. It had been agreed by both sides that notes from the negotiating sessions would not be published at the time, so this memo was for the administrative committee only. (Copy in author's files.)

permitted to cross the highway to the mall and climb the steps at that face of the Pentagon. Beyond the top of the steps was a small parking area immediately in front of the entrance. Anyone going further than the top of the steps, or trying to go around the building to other faces, would be subject to arrest. All the elements necessary for the three-pronged action—march, rally, and civil disobedience—were present. From then on the negotiations were over details.

For its own reasons the Mobilization Committee decided on a rally at the Lincoln Memorial combined with the assembly. In part this was due to pressure from Dr. Spock and Women Strike for Peace, who wanted a rally separated from the confrontation by the river. A contingent of Black militants also insisted on this on the grounds that they were "prepared to defend themselves in their own community but not at the Pentagon or the bridges where they might be stranded by the white participants."[46] This contingent planned to attend the rally and then go to a Black neighborhood of Washington rather than march to the Pentagon. John Wilson of SNCC, who was a Mobilization cochairperson, was working with this contingent. Though he said he personally did not agree with its decision, he thought the rally at the Lincoln Memorial was necessary considering the problems of the coalition.

The second rally at the Pentagon end of the march was bound to be a redundant affair. It was left in the plan to encourage more people to march across the river and to provide some sort of device for reassembling the marchers prior to the move on the Pentagon.

The Mobilization Committee repeatedly asked for the mall itself, instead of the north parking area for this rally. Rubin was adamant on this, and he had a point. The mall provided a dramatic view of the Pentagon, while it could hardly be seen from the north parking area. The government wouldn't budge on this, however, and most of the rest of us didn't think it was worth breaking off negotiations. In these later negotiations, over this and other details, Rubin kept balking. The affair had been considerably reduced from his dream of wholesale disruption. One got the distinct impression he wasn't too interested in a permit and would have preferred that the whole thing were

46. Minutes of National Mobilization Committee administrative committee, October 7, 1967.

declared illegal. In his eyes that would have been far more dramatic.

Meanwhile the Mobilization Committee negotiators did their best to box in the government on the question of violence. Dagmar Wilson, the soft-spoken Washington housewife who was WSP's most prominent spokeswoman, would spend extended time on this, drawing it out to the last detail: Surely the troops will have no loaded rifles. You don't contemplate using bayonets do you? The whole world will be watching. We want your assurances that those arrested will be treated without brutality. And so on. Looking back, there's a certain humor to this colloquy, but it was dead serious then, and Wilson knew what she was doing.

I was present at the last session of negotiations the day before the march. The permit still hadn't been agreed to and Rubin was still balking. Finally the Mobilization negotiators decided to caucus. It was all very delicate because time was very short, we were in Van Cleve's office, and it wasn't convenient to leave and find a private room on the spur of the moment. Van Cleve offered to leave with his assistant. In their absence an extended argument among the Mobilization negotiators ensued, with Van Cleve knocking on the door every ten minutes or so to see if we were ready. In the end the majority, including Dellinger, voted Rubin down. Then we let Van Cleve back in his office to sign the permit.

\*        \*        \*

The demonstration itself had something for everyone in the coalition. Nobody was entirely satisfied and nobody was entirely disappointed, except perhaps for the few mystics who really thought we were going to levitate the Pentagon, or succeed in shutting it down. The terms of the final permit included a rally at the Lincoln Memorial, a march across Arlington Memorial Bridge and along a small side road to the north parking area for another rally. At 4:00 p.m. those who wished would be legally permitted to cross the highway to the mall and could occupy the steps and the first few feet of the area at the top. Anyone going closer to the building would be subject to arrest and anyone trying to move around the building to another face of the Pentagon would also face arrest.

The rally at the Lincoln Memorial drew over 100,000, by far the largest antiwar crowd up to that time in the capital. It went smoothly except for a brief disruption when some American Nazis rushed the podium while British labor leader Clive Jenkins was speaking. Order was quickly restored.

In his speech Dr. Spock declared: "We do not consider the Vietnamese north or south the enemy. . . . They have only defended their country against the unjust onslaught of the United States. . . . The enemy, we believe in all sincerity, is Lyndon Johnson."[47]

During his speech John Wilson called for a minute of silence— and got it—in memory of Che Guevara, who had been killed in Bolivia earlier that month. Just before the march began at 2:30 p.m., Dellinger spoke. It was a good speech, a before-the-battle speech, and he ended by appealing to the demonstrators to face the troops at the Pentagon without hostility and to carry the antiwar message to them.

Beverly Sterner had organized a group of Washington women to take a collection. We had never had any real success doing this in a large crowd but this time it was different. The collectors stood spaced out across the road as the marchers entered the bridge. They announced the collection over bullhorns and collected the money in buckets as the marchers filed past. They took in $30,000 and for the first time the Mobilization Committee was almost out of debt.

The march had some difficulty getting started and the first part of it moved with painful slowness across the bridge. This heightened the tension because nobody knew exactly what to expect on the other side. The usual press of photographers was compounded by several hundred curiosity seekers and "exorcising" hippies who insisted on getting in front. The line of prominent people, which stretched, arms linked, across the roadway and was the front of the march proper, was actually preceded by this amorphous group of several hundred. In their midst appeared some ultrarightists who attempted to stop the march on at least two occasions as it crossed the bridge. This caused some delay, but no violence as the disrupters were ushered to the side of the road.

At one point a lone man stood in the center of the roadway with a large wooden cross bearing a slogan about killing communists for Christ. He absolutely refused to budge, and, when we started to move him, some spaced-out hippies in front surrounded him

47. *Militant*, October 30, 1967.

shouting, "Don't touch him, let him alone, let him do his thing."
The whole march was halted by one lone nut. I talked it over with
Eric Weinberger who agreed that this was reducing nonviolence
to absurdity. "If you can get him out of there without hurting
him, do it," said Weinberger. So I picked him up, cross and all,
and carried him to the side while Weinberger, with a bullhorn, got
the march going again.

Just behind the front line proper was a huge banner held aloft
on ten poles. It said: "Support Our GIs, Bring Them Home Now!"
A picture of the march crossing the bridge with the banner
clearly legible was carried on the cover of the October 27 issue of
*Time* magazine. It must have been seen by countless GIs, even in
Vietnam.

Peter Buch had been in charge of organizing people to carry
that banner, which they set up behind the speakers' stand at the
rally. Then Buch left to drive some Mobilization lawyers to the
Pentagon. He recalls,

After dropping them off, I parked the car near the Pentagon and started
walking back to meet the march which had in the meantime started off. I
looked for the banner and soon saw it coming steadily toward the
Pentagon. But an almost completely different group of ten were carrying
it. The banner had literally organized itself, as it were! It made it all the
way to the Pentagon walls, where for a time it was still being held by the
students who climbed up, until it fell apart. I later encountered one of the
young women who had carried the banner on the march. She was lying
on the grass, being treated for tear gas which had [temporarily] blinded
her. She lived in Washington, she was not in any radical group, and this
had been her first demonstration. She was not a student, but a young
working woman, supporting her younger sister who was a student. We
were reaching the masses and they were finding their way to us. It was a
great day.[48]

On the Virginia side the march turned south on a road that
wasn't wide enough to hold it. The few police there fell back and
the march spilled off the road and became a swarm toward the
north parking area. The second rally proved to be a clumsy affair.
Many of the demonstrators didn't bother to stop for it, and soon
broke down the temporary fence and rope barricades separating
the parking area from the highway and moved directly over to

48. Letter to the author from Peter Buch, January 1, 1976.

the mall before the appointed time. This left the Mobilization figures who were supposed to lead the civil disobedience still at the rally, while part of the crowd had already moved across the mall and up the steps.

Among the first to make this run was a loose coalition of SDS and a number of small radical groups dubbed the Revolutionary Contingent. This group had been meeting in New York beforehand but had split on the eve of the march. Nevertheless they found themselves more or less in the same place after bypassing the second rally and made a charge up the embankment toward the mall. They were repulsed once, tried again and made it as the troops were ordered back.

Just behind the first demonstrators up the steps were a number who taunted the troops facing those in front, and even threw things over the heads of the first rows of demonstrators at the troops. This brought the wrath of the soldiers down on those in front. There were some in the crowd, however, who appealed for a different approach and began talking to the troops, face to face, or, here and there, over bullhorns. After the steps had been partly filled, a unit of some thirty troops carrying rifles was sent down to block off the steps from below. They quickly found themselves surrounded, perhaps two thousand demonstrators at their backs on the steps and a huge crowd immediately in front of them on the mall. They stood there in a line, their guns pointed at the demonstrators on the mall. Those in the crowd started talking to them while one youth walked along the line putting flowers in the gun barrels. Photos of this became classics. The unit was soon withdrawn.

After the second rally ended at 4:00 p.m. the crowd on the mall and the steps had reached about 35,000. Those who came from the rally and wanted to commit civil disobedience couldn't even get near the "illegal" area at the top of the steps and had to move around the building to find forbidden territory. Lines of troops stood in the way, and behind them federal marshals armed with clubs and pistols. It was the federal marshals who made the arrests.

Actually it wasn't all that easy to get arrested on this demonstration. One had to get through the troops first. They weren't usually standing so close together that people couldn't run between them, but the marshals on the other side sometimes wouldn't arrest demonstrators and would instead chase them back with clubs. Dellinger, Lyttle, and Dr. Spock were on one such sweep past the troops. Dellinger and Lyttle got arrested, but the marshals wouldn't touch Spock. He finally had to give up the effort, unarrested.

From the viewpoint of the crowd in the mall, to the left of the steps and perpendicular to them was a ramp ordinarily used by cars going to the administrative entrance. This ramp was forbidden territory, blocked at the bottom by a barricade and a line of troops. Between 4:30 and 5:00 p.m. a group of several hundred young men and women rushed this barricade. The troops fell back and the demonstrators made it into the small parking area at the top of the ramp where they sat down in "illegal" territory. They were quickly sealed off from the rest of the demonstrators by troops who reoccupied the bottom of the ramp. The ranks of this salient were reinforced by other demonstrators who scaled the wall from the mall level to the top of the ramp, a distance of about fifteen feet, using ropes from dismantled barricades. A bank of perhaps two dozen from the salient made a rush for a door to the Pentagon and a few of them actually made it inside for a brief moment. The charge was quickly clubbed back by forces inside the building. This was as close as any of the demonstrators ever got to blocking the halls of the Pentagon.

At the height of the action at the Pentagon itself several thousand demonstrators were on the steps or in the parking area immediately above them, and another 30,000 or so in the mall. Additional thousands were still making the march from the Lincoln Memorial. As darkness fell, most of the crowd left, walking back over the bridge to Washington. The few thousand who remained talked to the troops, burned draft cards with impunity, wrote slogans on the Pentagon wall with spray cans, and built campfires on the mall. It did indeed have the look of a siege about it, with government officials lining the roof of the Pentagon observing the scene.

At midnight the troops were ordered to begin taking back territory. Arrests, occasional clubbings, and the use of tear gas or mace continued for the rest of the night. By six in the morning 750 or so were still there. The crowd grew a bit during Sunday but by Sunday night when the permit for use of the mall expired a few hundred were still left. These were arrested or chased away in one sweep.

I spent Sunday night standing on a main highway near the Pentagon passing out bus fare to demonstrators who had missed their chartered buses and were stranded without funds. Terrill Brumback, a D.C. taxi driver and one of thousands of unsung movement activists, helped arrange a shuttle of cabs to get them to the bus station. The volunteer lawyers were busy getting people out of jail. The Pentagon march was over.

\* \* \*

According to the Mobilization Committee count, 675 demonstrators were arrested and booked, another 200 or so were arrested but not booked, some just being hauled to the city of Washington and released on the street.[49] Though a number of demonstrators were clubbed by federal marshals or hit with the butts of rifles by some of the soldiers, there were few serious injuries and no one was killed.

The army brought in several thousand troops—in addition to federal marshals and police—to defend the Pentagon. Most of the troops were ordinary soldiers acting as military police for the weekend. Of those who confronted the crowd a few were angry, even brutal. But many were visibly embarrassed by the situation, and some became friendly in the course of contact with the demonstration. Word of this spread among the demonstrators, and afterward throughout the movement as a whole.[50]

Just what direct effect the Pentagon march had on GIs in general is a matter of conjecture. But there is no doubt that the effect on the movement itself in this regard was considerable. Before the Pentagon action, the idea of reaching GIs was pressed by a minority. After October 21, 1967, the movement as a whole began to embrace the idea with some enthusiasm.

Rubin was right about an action at the Pentagon attracting the

49. Report on arrests at the Pentagon October 21-22 and status of those arrested as of November 12, 1967. By the Washington office of the National Mobilization Committee to End the War in Vietnam. (Copy in author's files.) Most of those arrested were released within hours. As of November 12, six were still in jail serving 30-35 days.

50. Stories circulated within the movement that two or three soldiers had joined the demonstrators on the scene. Such a gesture by a soldier would have risked far greater punishment than the civilian demonstrators faced. No names or court cases are known to verify these stories. My own opinion on this is that there was a tendency among some in the movement to underestimate the sense of proportion—not to mention the sense of self-preservation—of ordinary people.

media. The demonstration got far more coverage than any up to that time. Many of the stories were unfriendly but the pictures had more impact than the words. And as the news sifted down to legend, the disadvantage was all on the government's side. Norman Mailer, who was one of the notables who managed to get arrested, even produced something of a work of art out of it— *Armies of the Night*—which won the Pulitzer Prize.

In effect the war-makers had suffered an unprecedented indignity at the hands of Americans. And the government had been forced—by the spreading atmosphere of opposition to the war and the tone set by the Mobilization Committee—to meet it with unloaded rifles.

# 12

## Stop the Draft Week:
## Oakland and New York

Unity between the moderate and radical forces in the antiwar movement often proved more difficult to achieve in the San Francisco Bay Area—and therefore much of the West Coast—than in New York and the East. There were a number of reasons for this difference, including the relative insularity of the Berkeley milieu—long the main radical base in the West. On the other hand, the West did not have the advantage of the direct influence of Muste and the patterns which had been established while he was alive. These carried over to some extent after his death, in New York and the East.

While the march on the Pentagon was being organized in the East there was no comparable unified mass action planned for the San Francisco Bay Area. This was because the West Coast Spring Mobilization Committee—the coalition that organized the April 15, 1967, action in San Francisco—had split and fallen apart in early summer. The National Mobilization Committee never became established on the West Coast.

The Student Mobilization Committee did organize West Coast support for the Pentagon march, but the distances were so great that the number of participants from the West Coast was limited. There was much antiwar activity by various local groups during the summer and fall of 1967 in the Bay Area, but there was no central focus and no unified broad coalition. In the fall of 1967 there did develop in the Bay Area two activities that had national impact. One of these was Stop the Draft Week and the other was an antiwar referendum placed on the ballot in the city of San Francisco for the November 7 elections. Each was organized by different groups with little connection between them.

The referendum campaign was led by a new coalition called Citizens for a Vote on Vietnam. It included some reform Democrats, many of the moderate antiwar groups, the SWP, and some other radicals in the city of San Francisco. Stop the Draft Week involved the Berkeley students and radicals, some San Francisco SDSers (including members of the Progressive Labor caucus within SDS), The Resistance, and a number of pacifists.

The idea for Stop the Draft Week had several origins. As early as April 15, David Harris had announced that The Resistance would organize a national draft card turn-in for October 16, 1967. Later this was incorporated into the activities leading up to the October 21 march on Washington. In July a group of antidraft organizers, including members of SDS, met in the offices of *The Movement,* a Bay Area newspaper affiliated with SDS and SNCC. According to Terence Cannon, one of the group, they wanted "to move opposition to the war and the draft from the level of moral protest to a show of power."[1] They decided to try to halt the activities of the Oakland Armed Forces Examining Station (popularly known as the Oakland induction center), where draftees and enlistees from the Bay Area reported for physical examinations and shipment to training bases. They set up the Stop the Draft Week Committee (STDW) to organize the action for October 16 to 20. According to Cannon, "the STDW organizers rejected traditional pacifist non-violence and emphasized the right to self-defense. The hard-core pacifists broke off and decided to hold a separate demonstration on Monday the 16th at the Induction Center."[2] This was organized by the Civil Action Day Committee, a coalition of pacifists, clergy, and academic figures. Those remaining in the Stop the Draft Week Committee decided to attempt to physically close the induction center beginning on Tuesday and for the rest of the week.

Stop the Draft Week was widely publicized on the Berkeley campus after classes opened in the fall. In an attempt to contain the activity, the university administration granted permission to the official student government for an all-night teach-in on the war and the draft to begin Monday evening, October 16, in a large auditorium on campus. Speakers from different points of view were scheduled and it was clear that some of them would use

1. *The Movement,* November 1967.
2. Ibid.

the occasion to urge participation in the demonstrations at the Oakland induction center.

To forestall this, the Alameda County supervisors went to court for an injunction forbidding the use of any university property by any group for "on campus advocacy of off campus violations of the Universal Military Training and Service Act."[3] This meant that all advocacy of draft resistance or organizing for civil disobedience at the Oakland induction center would be banned on campus for the duration of Stop the Draft Week. It came close to posing the same issue that had initiated the Free Speech Movement in 1964—the right of students to organize on campus to support off-campus civil rights activity, including civil disobedience.

Obviously fearful of precipitating another FSM-type explosion, University Chancellor Roger W. Heyns opposed the granting of the injunction and expressed reluctance to calling police on campus to enforce it.

On Monday, October 16, the first demonstration at the Oakland induction center took place, organized by the Civil Action Day Committee. It consisted of a series of nonviolent sit-downs by groups of about twenty at the entrance, supported by a picket line of several hundred. Some 120 people including Joan Baez and other prominent pacifists were arrested. At noon the demonstrators went to San Francisco where a large crowd gathered in front of the Federal Building to support representatives of The Resistance who attempted to turn in some 300 draft cards. U.S. Attorney Cecil Poole refused to accept them, so they were dumped, according to some reports, over Poole's head. Poole was quoted as calling the demonstrators "rabble."[4]

(The draft card turn-in at Washington, which took place the day before the Pentagon march, was more ceremonious but no less strange. There, over a thousand cards were carried in a briefcase into the Justice Department by Yale chaplain William Sloane Coffin, accompanied by Dr. Spock, Mitchell Goodman, Marcus Raskin, and Arthur Waskow. The distinguished delegation tried to present the cards to Assistant Deputy Attorney General John R. McDonough. McDonough offered coffee, which was accepted, and the delegation made statements of their

3. *Daily Californian,* October 17, 1967.
4. *The Movement,* November 1967.

complicity to encourage draft resistance. But McDonough refused to accept the draft cards. Coffin put the briefcase on a table and Waskow declared: "Here you have just read this statement alleging that we are guilty of crimes for which we offer you proof! And you, the number three man in the Justice Department, refuse to accept the evidence! Where, man, is your oath of office?"[5])

Meanwhile the Stop the Draft Week steering committee had called a rally for Monday night at De Fremery Park in Oakland to mobilize support for Tuesday's action. The turnout was only a few hundred and these marched to the Berkeley campus where the student government teach-in, was scheduled. By that time, the injunction had been handed down, and Chancellor Heyns closed the auditorium and banned on-campus meetings. Some 6,000 students who had come for the teach-in stayed for an impromptu rally in Sproul Plaza, as much to challenge the injunction as to talk about Stop the Draft Week. Such rallies continued through the week. In a sense, then, the injunction itself, and the civil liberties issue which it raised, assured a central focus and large audiences on the Berkeley campus for the Stop the Draft Week organizers.

On Tuesday morning some 3,000 demonstrators converged on the Oakland induction center. Some of them were equipped with shields (from garbage-can lids) and crash helmets or hardhats as protection against police clubs. The police let them occupy the street in front of the induction center and then moved out of a nearby parking building with a solid wedge of cops, using clubs and mace. Some of the demonstrators sat down and the police went to work on them. Some tried to fight back, but the police cleared the area with ease. The demonstration ended in a rout, with the cops injuring several dozens including some medics and newsmen. Among the demonstrators it became known as "bloody Tuesday."

At a Berkeley campus rally later that day it was decided after much discussion to return to the induction center with a large demonstration on Friday, October 20, and in the meantime to have an informational picket line there. On Wednesday some people sat in at the entrance to the induction center and there were ninety-one arrests but no clubbings, and the police did not

5. Thomas Powers, *The War at Home* (New York: Grossman, 1973), p. 194.

interfere with the picket line. The Thursday picket of some 600 was without incident.

On Thursday, Morgan Spector, a nineteen-year-old UC student speaking for the Stop the Draft Week steering committee, announced the plans for Friday: "We're going back with a demonstration like Tuesday's—only smarter—and will attempt to stop the buses." He was referring to the buses used to carry inductees to and from the center. "We don't know if we can prevent the buses from getting through," he added, "but we intend to try. And we intend to give the cops one hell of a run for their money."[6] To almost everyone's surprise, that's exactly what happened on Friday morning.

Early Friday some 10,000 demonstrators showed up in the streets around the induction center, most of them from Berkeley but with contingents from Stanford and other colleges in the area as well as from some high schools. This time they did not concentrate in the street in front of the induction center where 2,000 police, county sheriff's deputies, and state highway patrolmen waited to repeat Tuesday's cleanup operation. Instead the demonstrators approached from all sides, blocking traffic in the streets up to several blocks away. As the police swept down the streets to clear them out they retreated where the attack was heaviest, blocking the street further back, swarming around the edges in small groups, dodging to other streets and intersections, only to return when the police moved to another blockade.

From shortly after 5:00 a.m. (the center opened at 6:00) until 10:30 a.m. the demonstrators kept the police busy and at times controlled the twenty-block area of downtown Oakland surrounding the induction center. They set up barricades using whatever was at hand, including parked cars which they pushed into the streets before letting the air out of the tires. (Somebody spotted U.S. Attorney Poole's car and it was deliberately used this way.)

A few of the buses carrying inductees were stopped for a time. Some of the men gave the demonstrators the V for victory sign with two fingers when the blockade succeeded in stopping the bus they were riding. The demonstrators returned it, and the story is told that this was the origin of the salute of the antiwar movement. In any case after October 20 the V sign quickly spread among antiwar youth in the Bay Area and soon across the

6. *San Francisco Chronicle*, October 20, 1967.

country, becoming the universal and ubiquitous greeting of Americans opposed to the war.

By noon the police had called in reinforcements and the demonstrators had retreated back to the campuses and neighborhoods to spread the word of the fleeting success of their "mobile tactics." They left the area covered with antiwar slogans painted with spray cans. Remarkably, only a handful were arrested on Friday, and fewer than two dozen, about half of them police, were treated for injuries.

Governor Ronald Reagan said he hoped a way could be found to punish the demonstrators under wartime rules in spite of the lack of a formal declaration of war. "There is nothing," said Reagan, a rabid advocate of the slaughter in Vietnam, "that justifies bloodshed, violence, damage to property and harm to individuals."[7] And the "generation gap" widened another notch.

The University of California administration suspended or put on disciplinary probation eleven students who had been prominent in the Stop the Draft Week rallies in violation of the injunction on the Berkeley campus. VOICE, the radical student political party, countered by running these students as its slate for the student senate in early December. In a massive repudiation of the administrative action, the VOICE slate swept the elections, with Peter Camejo and Reese Erlich, the two suspended students, coming in first and second respectively.[8]

\*        \*        \*

During the summer of 1967 attempts had been made to put

7. *San Francisco Examiner*, October 29, 1967.
8. There were ten openings on the student senate. Observers agreed that the students who had been disciplined would have won them all on the basis of simple majority vote, but the rules required seats for any minority party polling 10 percent, so VOICE got only six seats. Camejo, incidentally, was not a member of the Stop the Draft Week Committee. He spoke at the rallies, appealing for violation of the injunction as an affront to free speech. The other disciplined students were: Frank Bardacke, Charles Capper, Marion Cohen, Morgan Spector, Dave Kemnitzer, Hal Jacobs, Jeff Lustig, Patti Iiyama, and Paul Glusman. Later, seven youths, not all Berkeley students, were indicted on charges of "conspiracy" in connection with the Oakland demonstrations. They were Reese Erlich, Steve Hamilton, Bob Mandel, Mike Smith, Jeff Segal, Terry Cannon, and Frank Bardacke.

antiwar referenda on the ballot in many cities, including New York, Cleveland, and Detroit. With two exceptions—San Francisco and Cambridge, Massachusetts—the referenda had been ruled off the ballot as inappropriate for city elections. In San Francisco as well the city administration had first turned down the petitions, but this was reversed by the California Supreme Court. So the San Francisco referendum—on the ballot as Proposition P—was the first time the voting population of a major American city had a chance to vote directly on the Vietnam War issue.

The project had been initiated by members of the Pacific Democrats, a dissident Democratic Party group. A Citizen's Committee for a Vote on Vietnam was set up on a nonexclusive basis, with Ed Farley as chairman and Mary Louise Lovett as executive secretary. Both were Democrats, but Lovett told the *San Francisco Examiner* that "Communists and Republicans, if any, are equally welcome."

From the start the committee took the position that the vote would be meaningful only if the proposition being voted on were clear-cut. On that basis it rejected arguments for an equivocal statement calling for negotiations of some sort, and opted for a straight withdrawal statement. This read:

"It is the policy of the city and county of San Francisco that there shall be an immediate cease-fire and withdrawal of U.S. troops from Vietnam, so that the Vietnamese people can settle their own problems."[9]

The city administration and both major daily newspapers opposed Proposition P, but the committee succeeded in making it a central issue in the campaign. Over 2,000 activists joined in distributing more than 400,000 leaflets at every conceivable public place in the city, including those where GIs gathered. A special project was organized by Catholic students, unionists, teachers, and even a few nuns and priests to distribute 40,000 leaflets in favor of the proposition at Catholic churches. When the *San Francisco Chronicle* published an editorial against the proposition, a hundred workers on that paper took out an ad to rebut it. Two rival talk-show announcers rented a hall and drew 3,000 people to a debate on the proposition.

Shortly after the Pentagon march, I went to San Francisco to

9. *Militant,* November 6, 1967.

help out on the Proposition P campaign. It was a remarkable sight to drive through the streets of the city in those days and see posters in favor of Proposition P in windows of houses and apartments on almost every block. Such a phenomenon would have been unthinkable in the midst of previous wars. Asher Harer commented:

> It is a political axiom that to wage an effective war, the rulers of the country must have a united population behind them, or at least have the voices of dissent isolated and/or muzzled. The extent to which San Franciscans felt free to display these antiwar posters in their windows indicates the extent to which the war "consensus" has been shattered.[10]

The result of the vote was officially reported as 76,632 "yes" and 132,402 "no." Some of us who thought the proposition had a chance to win were slightly disappointed. The election was marred by irregularities and the Citizen's Committee considered demanding a recount, but demurred because of the legal expense involved.[11] But even if the count was honest, 36 percent of the vote in a major American city for immediate withdrawal was still a very impressive showing. It was even more impressive in light of the fact that youths between eighteen and twenty-one could not then vote. The Student Mobilization Committee and the Citizen's Committee set up fifteen polling places where such youth could cast a ballot. Of the 6,149 who did, 4,840, or 79 percent, voted for Proposition P.

10. *Militant,* December 11, 1967.
11. For example, according to the November 18 *San Francisco Chronicle,* there was an "amazing switch" in vote totals between the first official announcement of complete totals and subsequent ones. In addition, prior to the election several mailbags filled with sample ballots being mailed to voters in a heavily Black area—where support to Proposition P was strong—were discovered in a ravine. The sample ballots contained instructions on how to vote and the address of the polling place.
In the United States, cheating in elections is as fine an art as dodging issues. Honest counts in elections where there is something important at stake are assured only by the most complete, meticulous, knowledgeable, and suspicious surveillance of every detail of the process. The Citizen's Committee, unfortunately, did not have a developed electoral machine and could not even provide experienced poll-watchers for many of the polling places. In general it got hostility and no cooperation from the Democratic and Republican machines.
The attitude of the national administration to the Proposition P effort

In Cambridge on the East Coast the referendum was initiated by Vietnam Summer. Its text declared the war "not in the interests of either the American or Vietnamese people" and urged a "prompt return home of American soldiers from Vietnam." The yes vote was 39 percent of the total, 11,316 to 17,688.

The San Francisco and Cambridge referenda—the only chance any Americans got to vote directly on the war in the governmental elections of November 1967—showed a very substantial and growing minority flatly opposed to U.S. intervention in Vietnam. And the majority were by no means in support of Johnson's war policies. A Harris poll released November 14 showed that a whopping 77 percent disapproved. The same poll showed 21 percent favoring escalation and 44 percent for withdrawing from Vietnam "as quickly as possible." Even Johnson stopped claiming he had a consensus, though he continued the war unabated.

\*        \*        \*

There is no doubt that the Friday, October 20, demonstration at the Oakland induction center had an exhilarating effect on the youth who participated. Patti Iiyama, then a UC student and a member of the Stop the Draft Week Committee, still remembered it years later as "the greatest day of my life. For a change it was the cops, not the demonstrators, who were on the run." But there were more than a few illusions. Jeff Segal, a leading SDSer and

---

was indicated in a United Press International dispatch printed in the October 28 *San Francisco Examiner* under the headline: "City Prop. P Upsets LBJ Aides." The story said: "Friends of the Administration failed in their attempt to keep the question off the ballot." But, the story continued, "their concern over this one item on a local ballot indicates the scope of the government's operation to counter criticism of its Vietnam policy." And further: "In the Johnson Administration's counter-attack . . . no target is overlooked."

My own comment at the time was made in a press conference November 3, four days before the election: "San Francisco at this very moment is undoubtedly crawling with CIA agents and other representatives of Washington interested in defeating Proposition P. And they will stop at nothing" (*Militant,* November 27, 1967). When dealing with elections in the United States of America—and other places as well—trust and the assumption of good faith in their managers is badly misplaced.

one of the Stop the Draft Week steering committee members, wrote:

> The action at the Oakland Induction Center during Stop the Draft Week, while not being definitive seems to us to represent a watershed in the course of the antidraft and white student movement analogous to Watts for the black movement. We experimented with tactics that involved direct conflicts with the duly constituted forces of the law—the cops. It was not guerrilla warfare or armed insurrection, for it would be foolish to think that we are prepared either psychologically or materially to launch a large-scale activity of that nature, but the action carried within itself the seeds for all the elements that we will need, when, indeed, our time does come.[12]

Not quite all. The little matter of drawing the masses into action was one thing, among others, that there was a tendency to overlook among those "revolutionaries" who made a fetish out of a moderately successful street fight. And, for some time after the week of October 16-21, SDS and a good part of the student wing of the antiwar movement were preoccupied with discussions of and experiments with "mobile tactics."

There were two such experiments in New York City. The first took place in connection with a demonstration called by the Vietnam Peace Parade Committee for November 14 outside the New York Hilton hotel where Secretary of State Dean Rusk spoke before a Foreign Policy Association banquet.

The Parade Committee planned a mass demonstration outside the hotel. According to the account by Kirkpatrick Sale,

> the SDS Regional Office worked to build it into a major confrontation, and local chapters were alerted that plans were afoot to storm the police barricades, create general disruption, make the night unpleasant for the dignitaries and, some hoped, stop Rusk from speaking altogether.[13]

The broad coalition that still made up the Parade Committee would never have agreed to such plans.

I was not involved in organizing the Rusk demonstration (having left the staff of the Parade Committee after the Pentagon march to devote more time to the socialist election campaign), but, as far as I know, there was no extended discussion of the

12. *The Movement,* November 1967.
13. Kirkpatrick Sale, *SDS* (New York: Vintage, 1974), p. 377.

SDS plans in the Parade Committee meetings. There was, however, a certain accommodation to the mood. It was simply left that SDS would do its own thing, and the Parade Committee leaflet on the demonstration included a small box which said: "There will be various direct actions, sponsored by SDS, at the hotel. For further information call SDS."[14]

The SDS leaflet itself was entirely unspecific, but full of broad hints. It began: "Dine with the Warmakers!" and ended: "Embroil the New York Hilton (6th Ave. and 53rd St.). Revolution Begins: Nov. 14, 5-5:30 p.m."[15]

Since the Parade Committee had long since proven that when it called a massive demonstration it was going to *be* massive, and well ordered, the police had accommodated to the necessities and were generally not obstructive on the technical level. This time it was different.

The Parade Committee had planned to picket directly across the street from the hotel on Sixth Avenue (Avenue of the Americas) and when that area was filled, to overflow to the south. The police had agreed to this, but after a few hundred began picketing directly across from the hotel the cops closed this area off. Further south a huge crowd built up, separated from the Parade Committee marshals. By 5:30 p.m. (Rusk was scheduled to speak at 9:00) there were thousands assembling on the streets near the hotel. With a force of 1,500 men the police pushed the pickets out of the streets and onto the sidewalks behind wooden barricades. They split the demonstration into a number of segments tightly packed on sidewalks in a three-block area near the hotel. The cops limited the crowd by blocking off a number of side streets and refusing to allow anyone to get through. Nevertheless some 10,000 were in the area, lustily jeering the limousines arriving for the banquet, making the peace sign, and chanting slogans.

Around 6:00 p.m. three groups began to try out "mobile tactics." Two, of about fifty each, started outside the immediate area of the main demonstration, one from the north and one from the south, running in the streets, blocking traffic, stopping and banging on

14. Parade Committee leaflet on November 14, 1967, demonstration. (Copy in author's files.)

15. SDS leaflet on November 14, 1967, demonstration. (Copy in author's files.)

cars that looked posh enough to be headed for the banquet. The other, somewhat larger, group gathered at the southeast corner of Fifty-third and Sixth Avenue, as part of the main crowd, and rushed the police barricade, spilling into the streets. The cops charged on horses and forced them back. Some garbage was thrown from the corner at the cops and they attacked from three sides, arresting some and injuring some more. The fourth side—to the south—was packed with demonstrators and those trying to escape were jammed against the main crowd.

The demonstration began to disintegrate and by 7:00 p.m. was dissolving southward down Sixth Avenue. Hundreds of youths ran into the streets, crossing back and forth, stopping limousines, and retreating further south as the cops moved in. The demonstration went as far as Times Square, finally dispersing about 11:00 p.m. Meanwhile, Rusk had been spirited into the Hilton for his speech. Over seventy demonstrators were arrested that night. Three Columbia University SDSers, Ron Carver, Ted Gold, and Mark Rudd, were charged with "inciting to riot."

The Rusk demonstration produced mixed reactions within the movement. Some SDSers, though not all, were elated, and their view was popular among many radicals. Many members of the Parade Committee were less than enthusiastic about the fringe activities, and some of the moderate groups quietly began to take their distance. My own view was that the SDS actions were a lot of damn foolishness which gave the cops an excuse to limit and attack the whole demonstration. The political point could have been made as effectively—and with far less cost—with a straight mass demonstration which would probably have been even larger if it had not been for the shenanigans.

\*         \*         \*

Ten days before the Rusk demonstration there had been a meeting of the National Continuations Committee of the Student Mobilization Committee at New York University. Among other things this meeting decided to call another Stop the Draft Week for December 4 through 8. The proposal was made by Linda Morse (formerly Dannenberg) who used the following language: "I propose that SMC call a national 'Stop the Draft Week' Dec. 4-8, in conjunction with the Resistance, to organize the closing of induction centers or draft boards where possible across the country, a la Oakland style."[16] The proposal passed unanimously. In connection with this action there occurred the second try at "mobile tactics" in New York City.

The plans included a draft card turn-in by The Resistance for Monday, December 4. On Tuesday there would be a traditional nonviolent sit-in at the Whitehall induction center, located near the southern tip of Manhattan between the ferry slips and the Wall Street financial district. Dave McReynolds and the War Resisters League were responsible for coordinating this phase. On Wednesday, Thursday, and Friday an ad hoc Stop the Draft Week Committee, including the Student Mobilization Committee, The Resistance, the Workshop in Nonviolence, and a number of New York SDSers, would attempt to close the induction center.

During the initial organizing discussions the YSAers in the SMC balked at the phrase "to close the induction center." This was unrealistic, they maintained, and they proposed a more defensive formulation for a mass demonstration, to "talk to the inductees." They were in the minority, however, and the final wording on the leaflet was: "BE WITH THOUSANDS TO CLOSE THE INDUCTION CENTER—Talk to the inductees."[17]

The committee sent a telegram to Mayor John Lindsay informing him of the demonstration and saying: "We will be going down to Whitehall Street unarmed and with no intention of violence." It urged the police to "do the same."[18]

On Tuesday, some 5,000 demonstrators showed up before 7:00 a.m. when the inductees were scheduled to report. Thousands of police prevented all but a token number from picketing in front of the center. The demonstrators were herded behind mazes of wooden barricades spread out over a large area. Dr. Spock, who led the first of the sit-downers, once again had difficulty getting arrested. The cops at first wouldn't let him step through the barricade to the front of the building, and the tall, distinguished pediatrician, in a vested suit, had to try to crawl under and push through the cops' legs. They finally relented and let Spock and others walk through to the center entrance to begin the sit-down.

16. "Action Proposals—'Stop the Draft Week.'" Submitted by Linda Morse to the November 4, 1967, SMC Continuations Committee meeting. (Copy in author's files.)

17. Stop the Draft Week Committee leaflet for December 4-8, 1967, demonstrations. (Copy in author's files.)

18. *Militant,* November 27, 1967.

There were so many sit-downers they couldn't all get to the entrance and some sat down in the street. These were attacked by mounted police and one was hospitalized with a brain concussion. Otherwise the sit-down went according to plan and 264 were arrested.

On Wednesday morning, long before sunup, the crowd was also about 5,000, gathering this time in Battery Park a couple of blocks from the induction center. There were literally as many police as demonstrators and they had complete military control of the entire area. The demonstrators marched toward the center in several groups but the cops allowed only token numbers in front of the center where they were tightly boxed in by barricades. One group led by Linda Morse and Gus Horowitz was shunted by police from one side street to another until it was finally dispersed by the cops, utterly frustrated. It was dubbed the "Lost Battalion." One survivor of the adventure recalls:

> There were about 300 of us, and at first everybody was mad as hell at the bullying by the cops. We were peacefully walking toward the Whitehall building when a phalanx of cops marched on us with clubs, pushing us into a side street. We couldn't stop or we'd be arrested and the cops wouldn't say where they were herding us. I was one of the marshals and we decided we had nothing to lose by trying the Berkeley "mobile tactics." So the whole group set out at a dead run down the street away from the induction center, trying to outflank the cops and double back to rejoin the main group. But every time we would turn a corner, with hundreds of cops running after us, we'd sight a new line of police forming up ahead. This went on for several hours as we were driven further and further away, still hoping to run faster than the army on our heels. Finally we realized that the cops not only outnumbered us but were working with radios and a helicopter and knew where we were going before we did. In the end they closed in on us from all sides and we all scattered as fast as we could into stores and alleys just to escape arrest. So much for the Lost Battalion and for "mobile tactics."[19]

Some of the other marchers headed into the financial district, swarming through the streets, their antiwar shouts echoing off the concrete canyons. They were closely followed by cops on all sides. Finally about a thousand broke to the north, marching rapidly through the streets from the financial district to city hall. Chased from there, they half marched, half ran, all the way to the

19. Letter to the author from Les Evans, April 26, 1976.

Waldorf-Astoria hotel, miles uptown, where Dean Rusk was slated to speak at a gathering of the National Association of Manufacturers. Police were massed there as well and eventually dispersed the pickets.

A few hundred stalwarts marched to the United Nations where the cops once again attacked and broke them up. The first day ended in complete frustration for those who had expected to close the induction center, or even have a good try at it. The most encouraging part of the day was the friendly response from people on the sidelines and in windows of buildings as the demonstrators ran past shouting slogans and giving the V sign.

The next two days were similar except that the turnout was much smaller and the cops were proportionately freer with clubs and blackjacks, and more sweeping in their arrests.

On Thursday about 800 demonstrators started out from Battery Park for the induction center. I happened to be in a group of about 100 that the police allowed to picket near the entrance. The pickets were entirely peaceful but at one point the cops put a ring around them and started loading the whole bunch into police vans. Fortunately I was wearing a good overcoat and a tie so I picked up a copy of the *Wall Street Journal* from a trash can and slipped out by asking a cop how I could get through this mess to the Stock Exchange.

The main body of demonstrators once again went north through the streets to Times Square and then east toward the United Nations. Near the UN the cops surrounded the group, by now only about 300 strong, and arrested the whole bunch as Peter Seidman of the Columbia University CEWV was making a speech denouncing the police suppression of the demonstration. The TV cameras happened to catch this and it was shown on TV that evening. The police released without charges all those arrested on this occasion, claiming they'd made a mistake, but 150 others had been arrested and booked during the Thursday activities.

On Friday the crowd was a little larger, about 1,000. They didn't even try to make the induction center but went straight north again. They got as far as Sixteenth Street, in front of an army intelligence center across the street from Washington Irving High School. There the crowd stood for a while waving at the students across the street, who gave the V sign back, and then the cops made the most vicious attack of the week. Plainclothes police inside the crowd took out blackjacks and together with the uniformed cops with clubs beat and arrested anyone they could reach. In a few minutes the sidewalk was spattered with blood. The bulk of the crowd retreated to Union Square where it assembled around a statue and waited for leaders of the demonstration to come up with a plan.

There were perhaps 500 demonstrators left. The police were bringing up vans and surrounding the area. It was obvious that plainclothes police were heavily infiltrating the crowd. A few leaders spoke over portable sound equipment but nobody seemed to have a suggestion. So I asked for the microphone and told the people we were outnumbered by the cops and ought to get out of there quickly by dispersing, go home, and organize a really big demonstration another time.

Art Goldberg, a journalist who was then on the staff doing press relations for the Stop the Draft Week Committee, was angry and said I had no right to do that.[20] To be sure I was not on the committee organizing this demonstration, but I figured three days of puffing through the streets had earned me the right to an opinion. The majority voted with their feet and the bulk of the crowd melted away. A part of it ran north once again and got as far as Rockefeller Plaza where the arrest of seventy-five ended the week's events.

In four days the second Stop the Draft Week had resulted in some 580 arrests (aside from those the cops said were mistakes), uncounted injuries, and no interruption of the business of the induction center. It was not all negative, of course, since the activities did attract a lot of attention and a certain amount of sympathy for the draft protest. But an evaluation of tactics was obviously in order.

20. This Art Goldberg is not to be confused with the longtime Berkeley activist of the same name who was prominent in the radical campus political party SLATE in the early 1960s and in the Free Speech Movement.

# 13

## The Labor Leadership
## Assembly for Peace

Following the Pentagon march, Dellinger wrote an evaluation in which he said:

One of our continuing aims must be to disrupt and block the war machine. There may be a need for other well conceived "disruptions" as well, which will make it increasingly difficult for our society to conduct "business as usual" while the war continues. (We might discuss the implications of trying to disrupt the nominating conventions of the Republican and Democratic parties in order to expose their hypocritical and undemocratic nature.)[1]

The implications *were* discussed and there were objections raised as a matter of civil liberties. Any attempt to disrupt a convention of a political party would put the movement on very dangerous ground, especially since any precedents in that direction were far more apt to be destructive of the gatherings of dissenting political parties or the antiwar movement itself than of the Democrats or Republicans. The parties in power did not lack the means to adequately defend their rights to orderly meetings or to disrupt the meetings of their opponents if that's the way the game was going to be played. (Indeed it *was* played that way covertly by the government through such operations as the FBI's Cointelpro [Counterintelligence Program] which were revealed later.) So the idea of disrupting any conventions was

---

1. *Mobilization Report,* pamphlet published by the National Mobilization Committee to End the War in Vietnam, undated. (Copy in author's files.)

dropped. The idea of a demonstration outside the Democratic Party convention—in the same city at the same time—was, however, considered to be a good one. In fact it looked like a natural.

The president was not only the chief executive, centrally responsible for the administration's foreign policy, but also the commander in chief of the armed forces, a constitutional power that Johnson took literally. It was no secret that he spent hours poring over the maps of Vietnam and even took a personal hand in ordering bombing operations. This sort of thing, and his vigorous denunciation of his critics on the war, had identified Johnson as *the* walking symbol of the war policy. By late 1967 Johnson could hardly appear in public—even on short notice— without being greeted by antiwar demonstrations. If he appeared on a few hours' notice there would be dozens or hundreds; on a few days' notice in a large city, there would be thousands. As a result, Tom Wicker observed in the November 16, 1967, *New York Times,* "going back to at least midsummer, the President of the United States has been in contact with the great American public only in the most limited, guarded and last minute fashion."

People were beginning to wonder how Johnson was going to campaign for the general election in 1968 if, as was almost universally assumed, he was chosen as the Democratic Party's candidate. Conceivably he could continue to avoid public appearances that were announced far in advance even through the primaries, since it appeared he had the nomination locked up anyway. But the convention scheduled for August in Chicago had to be another matter. Johnson's appearance at the convention to accept the nomination—a must, by tradition—would almost certainly be the occasion for an antiwar demonstration of unprecedented magnitude. The place and time frame of his appearance would be known far in advance. The antiwar forces would have not just a few hours, but months to get out the word.

Within the ruling circles of the country, no doubt, there was some trepidation about the natural focus Johnson would continue to provide for a mass surfacing of the growing opposition to the war.

\*         \*         \*

In 1967 virtually all the so-called practical politicians within the two-party system were convinced that Johnson had the nomination sewed up. A rare exception was Allard Lowenstein, a New York reform Democrat. Lowenstein was a friend of Norman Thomas, a member of SANE, and a past president of the National Student Association. Since June, working with people from SANE, Women Strike for Peace, the Inter-University Committee for a Debate on Foreign Policy, and other groups, he had been trying to mount a "dump Johnson" movement based on antiwar sentiment within the Democratic Party.

Through his NSA connections he had involved a number of students, including David Hawk of the Union Theological Seminary and Sam Brown of the Harvard Divinity School. Joseph L. Rauh, head of Americans for Democratic Action and Washington counsel for the United Auto Workers, took a pessimistic view of these efforts, but in September Lowenstein and Curtis Gans, an ADA staff worker, launched the National Conference of Concerned Democrats. Its aim was to unite groups of antiwar Democrats across the country and pledge volunteers for any dove candidate willing to challenge Johnson in the primaries. Local affiliates proceeded to collect signatures and donations from thousands of disaffected Democrats to run ads against Johnson and the war, listing the signers.

On October 20—the last day, incidentally, of the Oakland Stop the Draft Week and the day before the Pentagon march—Lowenstein finally found a candidate. He received a verbal commitment in a Los Angeles hotel from Senator Eugene McCarthy of Minnesota. McCarthy stepped up his speaking schedule, appearing at meetings around the country to criticize Johnson's policy on the war. I was present at one of these appearances two weeks before McCarthy publicly declared his candidacy.

The occasion was a conference of trade union officials in Chicago November 11-12 called the Labor Leadership Assembly for Peace, which was an outgrowth of the Trade Union Division of SANE. It was far broader than the similar conference the year before. This time there were 523 union officials from fifty international unions, including 50 officers on a national level.

McCarthy had not been one of the guests originally scheduled and his appearance gave substance to the rumors then afloat that he was preparing to announce his candidacy. So there was considerable interest as McCarthy got up to speak. The content of the talk was in tune with that particular audience right enough, but the delivery was disappointing, especially compared to the

rest of the program. This included a wit like the economist John
Kenneth Galbraith and the platform mastery of Martin Luther
King, Jr., not to mention Norman Thomas and some of the union
officials themselves, for whom a fighting stance at the podium
was a tool of the trade.

"A nice guy, but a born loser if I ever saw one," commented one
unionist in the hallway after the senator's presentation. I
couldn't resist interjecting: "That's what he's there for, to suck
the kids out of the streets and then lose." After that I had plenty
of empty space around me for the rest of the conference. Even in
those circles, the atmosphere among labor officials was still such
that it was not considered entirely safe to be seen talking to a
bloody Bolshevik.

In McCarthy's talk—it was hardly a speech—he proposed a
bombing halt and negotiations with both the National Liberation
Front and Hanoi.

We are in the wrong [he said quietly]. We must take those steps called
for in order to make things right. . . . There is now no question that the
war is totally immoral and this matter must be brought to the people for
judgment. This is more than just a question of Vietnam. It is a great
reexamination by the American people of what our objectives as a nation
are. It will be very difficult for the people to accept some limitations on
our power. But that is really the question.[2]

In appealing for labor to get more involved for peace, McCarthy
emphasized a point which occasionally broke through elsewhere
at this conference. "This is not the kind of political controversy,"
he said, "which should be left to a children's crusade to save the
country."

The revolt of the youth, and the awareness that the labor
movement had no present influence or control over it, was
something of a specter haunting this assembly. Actually they
could easily have taken the leadership of the antiwar movement
then and there if they'd had the will, by simply calling some
mass antiwar actions and throwing their weight behind them.
They certainly had far more resources at their command than
those who were then leading the movement. The moderate
antiwar groups would have followed them, as would the majority

2. *Labor Voice for Peace,* January 1968. (Copy in Tamiment collection,
Bobst Library, New York University.)

of students. The radicals would have had no choice but to find themselves isolated or remain in the broader movement as a left wing, in all likelihood no longer as central leaders. In spite of the problems this would raise, many of us would have welcomed such a development because of the greater breadth and potential power it would have meant for the movement as a whole.

But the labor leaders in the assembly couldn't bring themselves to take such a plunge. Many of them weren't even thinking in such terms. And those who might have been, had, like Hamlet, all sorts of ramifications to consider and reservations to give them pause.

For one thing they still represented a distinct minority in the AFL-CIO officialdom, though the polls at the time showed the rank and file of labor to be as disaffected on the war as the general population. A successful fight with Meany *within* the AFL-CIO would require redressing the balance of power by involving the rank and file. By nature the officials moved very slowly and with great caution when that sort of thing was involved. No telling where it might lead.

Equally important were their ties with the politicians of the two-party system and their tradition of seeking solutions through the Democratic Party.

Some respect for the student activists was expressed at the assembly, mostly in the corridors but occasionally on the floor. At one point a delegate said unionists attending this conference were putting their heads "on the block." Abe Feinglass, a vice-president of the Amalgamated Meat Cutters and Butcher Workmen, responded:

Our youngsters' heads are on the block. They face the draft and the fight against the war. Yes, our heads are on the block. So be it. Some things are that important. I tell you now, and I don't care who hears it. I sat through that scene at the San Francisco [1965 AFL-CIO] convention [where Meany ordered the sergeants at arms to "clear the kookies out!"], and I admired those kids in the balcony.[3]

But those in control of the conference, especially United Auto Workers Secretary-Treasurer Emil Mazey, made it clear they were very wary of the independent antiwar movement in the streets.

---

3. *Militant,* November 20, 1967. Feinglass was one of the most consistent labor supporters of the antiwar movement.

Their efforts, for the time being, would remain largely confined within the two-party election process, though formally the assembly would not endorse candidates.

For those who were there, the most dramatic development at the Chicago assembly was a talk by Victor Reuther, director of the UAW International Affairs Department, which handled relations with unions in other countries. It was dramatic because it was a description of covert CIA and U.S. State Department activities within the union movement, coming from an authoritative American union leader who was in a position to know the inside story.

Reuther delivered a scathing attack on the AFL-CIO International Affairs Department headed by Jay Lovestone. He described how together with the CIA it participated in the 1964 coup d'etat that overthrew the elected liberal government of João Goulart in Brazil and, in the process, helped weaken the auto workers' unions there. This hurt U.S. auto workers, said Victor, because General Motors, Ford, and Chrysler were all multinational corporations, and auto parts were even being shipped from plants in one country to those in another. The trends in the industry required the UAW to set up arrangements with foreign unions to mitigate the undercutting of wages and union conditions. World auto councils were being formed for this purpose, he said, but the AFL-CIO's blind obedience to the State Department and its associations with the CIA made it difficult for the UAW— which was an AFL-CIO affiliate—to be trusted by legitimate unionists overseas.

The AFL-CIO's "obsession with anticommunism" had led it into "open collaboration" with the most right-wing, antiunion agencies "both at home and abroad." "The listing of organizations with which the AFL-CIO under Meany has affiliated itself," declared Reuther, "comprises the listing of almost all major rightist groups in the U.S. and in South American affairs." He also accused the AFL-CIO International Affairs Department of helping to arrange "fascist corporate-state unions" in several countries.[4]

---

4. The quotes used here from Victor Reuther's speech are from an article I wrote for the November 20, 1967, *Militant,* and were based on notes I took while Reuther spoke. The same story presented in that speech is contained in Victor Reuther's recent book *The Brothers Reuther* (Boston: Houghton Mifflin, 1976). In that memoir Victor says he had

It was no secret at the time that a growing rift had developed between UAW President Walter Reuther and AFL-CIO President George Meany. Both Meany and Walter Reuther were supporting Johnson for the presidency, but Reuther had recently called for a bombing halt and differentiated himself from Meany's all-out support to Johnson's war policy. Victor Reuther's speech laid out the trade union background to the rift. The abuse of the AFL-CIO by the State Department and the CIA, and Meany's unquestioning support to this collaboration, had become a bread-and-butter liability to the powerful UAW. This was a development of great potential importance to the antiwar cause.

Only a small fraction of its potential was developed at the time, however. The top UAW leaders never laid it out before the rank and file of the AFL-CIO the way Victor Reuther laid it out before the Chicago assembly. (Victor Reuther's speech was considered too much of a bombshell to publish in full and only brief excerpts were printed.) They never carried out a full fight *within* the AFL-CIO. Instead the UAW boycotted the upcoming AFL-CIO convention, stopped paying dues to the AFL-CIO, and quietly dropped out of the federation in 1968. The massive impact the issues might have had on public opinion, and on the labor movement as

---

known for years that the AFL-CIO was being used for "disgraceful" purposes by the U.S. State Department and the CIA. He had remained silent because Walter Reuther feared a revelation on the part of the UAW would mean a split in the AFL-CIO and in such a fight Victor "would never be able to produce enough documentation to stand up against the barrage of fabricated documents the agency could produce so easily" (p. 423).

Victor began to disclose some of the story in May of 1966 in an interview for the *Los Angeles Times*. He doesn't mention the point, but this came immediately after the April 1966 issue of *Ramparts* magazine created a national sensation with an exposé of CIA manipulation at Michigan State University. After the *Los Angeles Times* article appeared, Victor Reuther was censured by the AFL-CIO Executive Council for making "irresponsible" charges. He says Walter was disturbed that he had "spoken so openly," but informed the UAW Executive Board he had told the truth. In May 1967, in an attempt to discredit its critics, the CIA revealed that in the early 1950s it had given Walter Reuther $50,000 in $50 bills and Victor had distributed it to anticommunist unions overseas. The Reuthers acknowledged this. Walter said it had been done "reluctantly" and never repeated. Victor says that at the time they were "naive" about the methods of the CIA.

a whole, was muted. They rocked the boat as little as possible. The AFL-CIO convention took place in December 1967 in Bal Harbour, Florida, a suburb of Miami. On December 11 a delegate from the Colorado Labor Council, A. Toffoli, took the floor and read a statement critical of the war adopted by the Labor Leadership Assembly for Peace. Meany declared the Chicago assembly had been "planned in Hanoi," and that he had read the statement before, "every line of it in the *Sunday Worker* [a Communist paper] two weeks before the meeting was held in Chicago."[5] (Actually the *Worker* carried the statement—which had been released to the press—after the Chicago meeting, not before it.)

In his account of this incident in *The Brothers Reuther,* Victor Reuther's memory plays an interesting trick on him. He writes:

> In 1966 [actually 1967], at the first conference, held in Chicago, of the Labor Assembly for Peace, which we helped to found, hundreds of union delegates were addressed by Martin Luther King, Jr., Norman Thomas, and others; and Emil Mazey and I also spoke. At the end of the conference a resolution was adopted, calling for an end to the war. Some of the participants in that conference were elected, by their unions, to be delegates to the upcoming AFL-CIO convention in Miami. When a group of observers at that convention indicated its negative feeling about the Vietnam War, Meany thundered from his rostrum, "Throw the kooks out!" Mazey insisted on speaking, and Meany charged that the resolution we had adopted in Chicago "had been written in Hanoi." This hysterical remark was reminiscent of the most sinister tactics of Joe McCarthy.[6]

The last line is accurate enough, but in the rest, Reuther condenses events which took place in different places and on different days over a two-year period, thus transforming the hesitating Hamlet into the bold and decisive Henry V.

Actually Meany's "clear the kookies out " remark occurred two years earlier at the AFL-CIO convention in San Francisco.[7] At

5. *Proceedings, Seventh Constitutional Convention, AFL-CIO,* Bal Harbour, December 11, 1967, vol. 1, p. 282. Immediately before Meany spoke, Thomas W. Gleason of the East Coast International Longshoremen's Association boasted that "we kept our muscles in shape," by which he meant he had sent some of his goons to help the cops beat up demonstrators during Stop the Draft Week in New York.

6. *The Brothers Reuther,* p. 377.

7. *Proceedings, Sixth Constitutional Convention, AFL-CIO,* December 10, 1965, p. 133. This incident is described more fully in Chapter 10.

that time no one insisted on speaking. Several days later at the same convention Mazey took the floor and did dissociate himself from Meany's earlier action and also from Meany's hawk position. In the context it was an act of courage. Mazey was so careful about it, however, that it is impossible to tell from his remarks whether he voted for or against the resolution being discussed—to endorse Johnson's policy on the war. "We must put ourselves," said Mazey, "on the side of our government in its efforts to negotiate so that we can bring a peaceful solution to this problem. . . . "⁸ In the same discussion, Walter Reuther spoke in favor of the resolution endorsing Johnson's policy.

That was the last AFL-CIO convention Mazey or Reuther spoke at, because the UAW boycotted the next one two years later where Meany made his "planned in Hanoi" statement. Mazey gave his answer to that from Detroit, calling it "libelous." There were those of us at the time who wished the stand had been taken the way Victor Reuther now remembers it. Certainly the tendencies in the largely student-based antiwar movement toward alienation from the labor movement, and toward a lack of stability, would not have been so strong.

\* \* \*

Meanwhile, at a press conference in Washington, D.C., November 30, Senator Eugene McCarthy had made the formal announcement that he would challenge Johnson in at least three state primaries. He was entirely candid about the reasons. After outlining his view that a bombing halt, scaled-down fighting, and negotiations with the NLF were necessary, he declared:

In addition, there is growing evidence of a deepening moral crisis in America—discontent and frustration and a disposition to take extralegal if not illegal actions to manifest protest.

I am hopeful that this challenge, which I am making, which I hope will be supported by other members of the Senate and other politicians, may alleviate at least in some degree this sense of political helplessness and restore to many people a belief in the processes of American politics and of American government.

That the college campuses, especially—on those campuses—and also among adult thoughtful Americans, that it may counter the growing sense of alienation from the politics which I think is currently reflected in

8. Ibid., December 15, 1967, p. 564.

a tendency to withdraw from political action, to talk of nonparticipation, to become cynical and to make threats of support for third parties or fourth parties or other irregular political movements.[9]

The *New York Times* commented:

The decision of Senator Eugene McCarthy of Minnesota to challenge Johnson in the Democratic Presidential primaries now enables those who dissent from the Administration's policy in Vietnam to find political expression for their conviction. Energies that might otherwise be dissipated in marches and demonstrations which often antagonize more people than they persuade can now be used constructively in politics.[10]

How nice.

9. *New York Times,* December 1, 1967.
10. Ibid.

# 14

## The First National Student Strike and the Split in the SMC

The Pentagon march and the Stop the Draft weeks were only the tip of the iceberg as far as the mood among student activists in this period was concerned. In the fall of 1967 there were hundreds of antiwar actions on campuses across the country, some of them involving large-scale strikes and confrontations. Many were dramatic actions against military, CIA, and war-industry recruiters—particularly the napalm-manufacturing Dow Chemical Corporation. These occurred at the University of Wisconsin at Madison, the University of Indiana at Bloomington, New York University, the University of Pennsylvania, Cornell, and UCLA, to mention a few.

Many of these actions involved local SDS chapters, though without SDS national office initiative.

By mid-November, 1967, the SDS N.O. was doing some rethinking about the importance of the antiwar issue and was considering calling a series of actions for April 1968. As for the SMC, the idea of a national student strike had been part of its projection from the beginning but was always postponed at its conferences. By early winter, 1967, however, conditions had ripened to the point where it was assumed a national student strike would be seriously considered at the next SMC conference scheduled for the end of January, 1968, in Chicago.

In November, SDS Inter-Organizational Secretary Carl Davidson wrote to Linda Morse, the executive secretary of the SMC, as follows: "If I am correct in sensing both the mood and the need for less sectarian politics within SDS, then I think we both need to work some things out together." An additional reason for this initiative, according to Davidson, was that "both SDS and SMC are considering similar programs centering around the idea of student strikes."[1]

In early December the SDS newspaper, *New Left Notes*, carried an article by Davidson and Gregg Calvert that said:

> The time has come for SDS to assume a leadership position within the anti-war movement. . . . SDS must develop a positive, although critical, view toward relating to other groups or coalitions within the anti-war movement. To continue our previous position of separating ourselves from other anti-war forces, without advocating an independent program of our own, would be an indulgence in sectarianism which neither we nor the movement could afford. . . .
>
> SDS should have enough confidence in its power and politics to enter into relationships with other groups for the purpose of winning people over to our perspectives, strategies, and tactics. When persuasion fails within certain groups, we should make further efforts within those coalitions to co-opt, neutralize or contain their politics under the hegemony of our own perspective.[2]

Presumptuous phrasing notwithstanding, the SDS overtures were welcomed within both the Student and National Mobilization committees, and SDS was urged to send representatives to the National Mobe administrative committee meeting in New York on December 27. SDS began its own National Council meeting that day in Bloomington, Indiana, so none of the current officers were present in New York. But Rennie Davis, one of the old guard SDSers in Chicago, who was understood to have close relations with the new guard, was present, as well as Steve Halliwell, a recent past president of SDS who had accompanied Dave Dellinger on a trip to Hanoi. Tom Hayden was also there. This was unusual, since he had not been involved in the national antiwar coalitions up to that time, though he would occasionally speak at rallies.

It seemed obvious to me then that this meeting should set a conference to discuss and call a major action for the spring. To my surprise this suggestion was not well received.

Some of the people present preferred to have SDS take the lead on the spring actions. Dellinger took a dim view of a large, open

1. Letter from Carl Davidson to Linda Morse, November 14, 1967. (Copy in author's files.)
2. *New Left Notes*, December 4, 1967.

conference of the antiwar movement. "Everytime there's a conference," the minutes quote him as saying, "there's also a power scramble which with time could cause a fiasco."[3]

(I always had difficulty understanding Dellinger's concept of democracy, which usually did not include resolving disputed issues by debate and vote of the rank and file. Avoiding large conferences did not eliminate either power scrambles or fiascos. It just confined the scrambles to leading circles in isolation from the ranks and their collective feel of what was going on in the broader mass and in the workaday world. That increased the likelihood of fiascos, in my view. Avoiding conferences, however, did give more relative weight to prominent individuals than to organized tendencies, which in part, perhaps, accounts for the differences between Dellinger and me on this point.)

The discussion centered around the possible Democratic Party convention demonstrations, still eight months away. The only consensus we could reach regarding spring was to leave it to "the students [to] set the date and then be backed by adult support."[4] "The students" meant SDS and SMC, or in some people's minds, one or the other.

At this meeting it was clear that the National Mobe was in something of an identity crisis. Questions like "Who are we?" kept on popping up. My answer was that we're the group that called the major mass demonstrations against the war in Vietnam and that we ought to keep doing that sort of thing and not kid ourselves that we—as this particular group—can do much else. This view seemed to satisfy almost no one. Some people thought we should relate directly to the McCarthy campaign and the fight within the Democratic Party. Mike Stein of the Communist Party said:

There is a dual obligation to both the Peace and Freedom movements to form a coalition of the National Mobe, SCLC, MFP [Mississippi Freedom Democratic Party], and the dissenting Democrats to show how to fight within the [Democratic Party] convention.[5]

3. Minutes, National Mobilization Committee administrative committee, December 27, 1967, New York. (Copy in author's files.) The minutes contain brief digests of each speaker's remarks, not direct quotations.
4. Ibid.
5. Ibid.

Dellinger said there was widespread disillusionment with the electoral process, and that National Mobe should encourage the formation of a movement to express that sentiment around many issues in Chicago in August.

In the end the meeting made no decision on Chicago either, beyond leaving it to a subcommittee of the National Mobe officers and some people from Chicago to call a conference of undetermined size and composition to further consider the plans for possible Democratic Party convention demonstrations.

\*        \*        \*

The SDS National Council meeting December 27-30 in Bloomington actually passed a proposal for ten days of antiwar activity beginning April 20, along with a motion to send a representative to the National Mobilization Committee. The original proposal had been made in the December 4 article by Davidson and Calvert under the title "Ten Days to Shake the Empire." It emphasized "resistance" and "confrontation" activities and declared: "The crisis we are confronting is the disruption and dislocation of the political economy of imperialism in the face of wars of national liberation, of which Vietnam is only one front."[6]

This was opposed by the PL-SDSers who proposed developing student power issues on campus in the spring, followed by a summer "work-in" where students would go into factories and try to develop a "worker-student alliance." The PLers appeared at this conference in strength, which surprised the other tendencies in SDS, including the leadership. PL had about 15 of the roughly 80 voting delegates, and in a workshop the leadership proposal was narrowly defeated by the PL-backed resolution.

In part this was due to the fact that the leadership proposal was looked on—and indeed was designed—as encouraging disruptive activities which would involve confrontations with the forces of the law. There was a desire at this conference to at least slow down any process of establishing disruptive actions as a norm. There was some awareness among many of those present that, though SDS was receiving far more publicity than any other youth group and was a household word, in reality it was

6. *New Left Notes,* December 4, 1967.

becoming isolated, not only from the general population, but from the mass of students as well.

A hasty compromise was drawn up by New York SDSers Naomi Jaffe, Bob Gottlieb, and John Fuerst, which kept the "Ten Days of Resistance" to the war, but emphasized that tactics would be decided by local chapters. The leadership group—which included Cathy Wilkerson, Greg Calvert, and Mike Spiegel (Davidson was on a trip to Cuba)—supported the compromise in the plenary and it passed easily over the PL motion. PL, incidentally, also opposed sending a "representative" to National Mobe, arguing for an "observer," but was voted down.

The SDS call was quite vague, specifying only that ten days of resistance to the war were to take place during the period April 20-30. (The fact that this counted out to eleven days, not ten, was later mentioned at the SMC conference, and someone jested: "SDS uses New Math.")

Underlying the discussion at the SDS meeting was the fact that SDS locals were following the SMC's lead on antiwar activity because the SDS national office was not providing any national direction or focus on the issue. But the very vagueness of the SDS call left it squarely up to the SMC to be specific.

In a mid-January report to the YSA membership, Lew Jones expressed the view that the upcoming SMC conference would have the responsibility for setting the dates and general character of the spring actions.

All other national antiwar formations have either delayed or mismanaged the planning of the next actions. As a result the period between the previous action and the calling of the next has been extended longer than before. This delay stems basically from the deepening conflict between contrary perspectives. On the one hand, the ultra-lefts and hard-core "resistance" supporters wish to jettison mass actions for periodic civil disobedient acts. On the other, those individuals and groups who are now supporting McCarthy or are looking for a "peace and freedom" presidential ticket, do not want a major antiwar action that would compete.[7]

In my opinion this somewhat overstated the matter as it stood at that particular moment. These trends existed, but there were many people, especially in the rank and file of the various groups,

---

7. "Antiwar Report," by Lew Jones, January 17, 1968. YSA mailing. (Copy in author's files.)

who were attracted to McCarthy and also to mass action once such actions were called and were clearly building to significant proportions. This was certainly true of the broad layer of youth who responded to the initiatives of the SMC. Most of them would probably have voted for McCarthy if they had a chance to vote at all, but were not at that time in the mood to abandon the streets.

During this period the National Mobilization Committee staff was conducting a poll of local antiwar groups to see if it should "suggest" demonstrations on Saturday, April 20 or 27, as part of the SDS ten days. How long this poll would take was anybody's guess. Rennie Davis and Tom Hayden, who had been co-opted as part of the National Mobe leadership, were heading an office in Chicago and working, not on spring actions, but on the Democratic Party convention demonstration, still six months away. The New York Parade Committee, many of whose affiliates were attracted to the McCarthy campaign, had avoided the question of spring actions, waiting for the National Mobe decision. The Resistance had taken its own initiative and called for another day of draft noncooperation on April 3. Bemoaned Jones:

Such a lack of common perspective and coordination comes at a time when the antiwar movement faces unprecedented opportunites for influencing public opinion and winning new recruits. As the Johnson Administration plans a further, major escalation, opposition to the war and general discontent have risen sharply. A series of actions designed to appeal to major sections of society could have visible results in the coming period.[8]

For its part, the SMC working committee, which at this time included youth from the YSA, the CP, radical pacifists, and independents, had agreed to take the initiative.

These SMCers, regardless of tendency, were quite sincere in wanting to involve SDS both nationally and locally in the spring actions, and they looked upon the SDS National Council decision as an open opportunity. By this time the SMC was working with groups on more than 700 campuses located in every state but Alaska. While they had a variety of views on such matters as the McCarthy campaign and resistance tactics, the SMCers in the national office could feel a groundswell of antiwar sentiment among students generally, and were in pretty solid agreement that, whatever else people might do, this was no time to abandon

8. Ibid.

mass action. They agreed to propose to the SMC conference a national student strike and a day of mass demonstrations in cities across the country, toward the end of the ten days suggested by SDS. This would give focus to the whole thing.

A ticklish problem remained, however. There was still no "adult" call and there might well be resentment if the SMC took it upon itself to call the spring actions in the name of the whole movement, thus formally preempting National Mobe's function. Apparently in informal discussions with the National Mobe office it was agreed that the National Mobe officers would put out a statement endorsing the SDS call, listing any actions the SMC conference might call during the same period, and suggesting that Saturday, April 27, would be a good time for all concerned to unite in demonstrations in various cities for maximum visibility.

With that promise in their pockets, the SMCers prepared for their conference. They invited Carl Davidson to address the plenary and C. Clark Kissinger, who had been SDS national secretary when the first antiwar march on Washington in 1965 was organized, to chair the sessions.

On behalf of the working committee, Linda Morse presented a proposal which included a call for "ten days of campus-based antiwar action to coincide with the SDS-proposed ten days. . . . An international student strike on April 26," and "support of the National Mobilization's call for Mass Actions . . . on Saturday, April 27."[9] Actually the National Mobe call came only after this was adopted at the SMC conference.

*        *        *

The January 27-29, 1968, conference of the Student Mobilization Committee to End the War in Vietnam was the largest up to that time, and the major antiwar conference of the period. More than 900 students and youth from 110 colleges and 40 high schools in some twenty-five states registered. There were even a handful of junior high schools represented. The average age was twenty, with fewer than a dozen registrants over thirty.

Writers Walter and Miriam Schneir were present and observed:

Inasmuch as the President of the United States has publicly accused Movement activists of "storm trooper tactics," it seems worth recording

9. Proposal by Linda Morse for the SMC national working committee to the January 27-29, 1968, SMC conference. (Copy in author's files.)

that the S.M.C. conference was conducted along democratic lines, combining a rather loose preliminary procedure with Quaker meeting-house traditions. On the opening day of the conference, members of various organizations distributed sharply differing position papers on the proposed student strike and other matters, vying for the support of delegates who waited patiently in long lines to register. A room adjacent to the registration area was made available to any group that wished to set up a table for the free distribution or sale of literature. The conference's workshops and steering committee were open to anyone who cared to attend. All ideas were afforded an opportunity to be brought to the floor; any individual or group could mimeograph statements and distribute them. Decisions were reached by majority vote but, where practicable, proposals were modified so that any sizable minority view might be encompassed. At times, sectarian opinions held by comparatively few delegates received considerable attention. For example, the SMC considered at some length a proposal circulated by thirty-seven individuals to "expose, repudiate and reject" the S.M.C. . . .[10]

This motion was prompted by Progressive Labor. It was put on the floor in opposition to the student strike proposal, and in the process of answering it, some effective education was done regarding the nature and purpose of the student antiwar coalition. The PL motion received only a handful of votes and the strike proposal passed overwhelmingly. The previous day, Carl Davidson had appeared as a guest speaker and in the course of his remarks had said that though the SDS National Council had not taken a position on the proposed strike, local SDS chapters were free to decide for themselves whether or not to participate and he was confident many would.

The major dispute and the longest debate at the conference centered around proposals by the CP delegates to change the SMC from mainly an antiwar group into a "peace and freedom" group—that is, a combination antiwar and civil rights organization. As part of this perspective the CP and the Du Bois Clubs put forth an organizational proposal to give the Black caucus—attended by sixty of the more militant Blacks at the conference—parity on all bodies, including 50 percent of the conference vote.

The SMC had always taken a position against racism. Its main contribution to this struggle was its fight against the racist war. It did not, however, pretend that the SMC as such was a part of the leadership of the Black freedom struggle in the United States,

10. *Liberation,* March 1968.

and it did not adopt as its own position any of the competing strategies for fighting racism then being argued out within the Black movement. There had been indications before the conference that a change in this policy would be proposed. For example, a position paper circulated by the Du Bois Clubs, in support of the student strike idea, declared:

The issue of racism cannot be tacked onto the peace slogan as an afterthought. We must understand the organic connection in today's realities. This must be reflected in the composition of all the planning meetings and committees for this strike beginning with the Chicago [SMC conference] meeting at the end of January.[11]

In his January 17 report Lew Jones of the YSA declared:

The CP wants the SMC to emulate the practices of the National Conference for New Politics convention by giving half the vote to a black caucus (where they will be heavily represented) and thereby "prove" that the SMC is "really" against racism. Both the CP and the DBC [Du Bois Clubs] are mobilizing for the conference for this purpose and to put forward the demand that the SMC adopt the slogan "end racism" and conduct the student strike under the banner of "freedom and peace."

The CP has seized on the most emotional and guilt-ridden issue in American politics as a means of jamming their class collaborationist politics down the throat of the antiwar movement.

Jones charged that the CP wanted to change the character of the SMC so that it would become involved in support of Democratic Party candidates or, on the presidential level and after the Democratic Party convention, in support of a "peace and freedom" ticket.

This proposal [continued Jones] must be debated politically. . . . On the organization side, it is important to point out that it is a crass and foolish error for a predominantly white organization to try to mechanically achieve "black-white unity." As Malcolm said, there can only be such unity when first there is black unity. Moreover such unity must flow from a concrete political agreement, which does not exist at present. If there is no political agreement, then parity voting or other organizational measures will not solve the problem.

The CP proposal for parity appeals to those interested in individual

11. *For a Student Strike.* Du Bois Clubs pamphlet, undated, circa early January, 1968. (Copy in author's files.)

soul-cleansing. . . . Do they practice what they preach? Does the CP have 50 percent black representation on its own bodies?[12]

At the conference itself the proposal for parity to the Black caucus was made and passed in a workshop on "racism and the war" which was predominantly white. But the Black caucus rejected the idea. As it turned out the Black caucus was convened by John Wilson of SNCC, and the delegates who attended it were largely militants inclined toward a Black nationalist rather than a liberal approach. Gwen Patton, who was on the national SMC staff, declared in a position paper she presented at the caucus:

black militants find it necessary to coerce the Peace Movement to call for certain demands which in fact can have only black implementation. This is one of the greatest contradictions that exists in the total Movement. . . . The only way we can solve these contradictions is by the establishment of a black base that will deal with imperialism. . . .
Without such a base, black people will forever be absorbed by the Peace Movement. . . . With this black base black people will be their own dictates for action and will be the keepers of their own works.[13]

The Black caucus founded the National Black Antiwar Antidraft Union (NBAWADU), which issued its own call to the April 26 student strike as well as other actions specifically aimed at the oppressed national minorities. The call included certain statements which not all the other SMCers were ready to agree to, such as solidarity with the Arab revolution. NBAWADU was established as an independent organization with fraternal relations to the SMC but not subordinate to its policies. John Wilson and Gwen Patton were chosen national officers of the group.

The debate over whether the SMC should continue as an organization centrally concerned with getting the U.S. out of Vietnam began in the Sunday plenary, January 28, in a somewhat confused form. Spokespersons for the CP introduced a motion that the title of the student strike should be "Against the Vietnam War, Racial Oppression and the Draft." YSAers accused the CPers of trying to slip in their multi-issue perspective, and put a countermotion that the strike should be "Against the Racist War in Vietnam." The CPers then accused the YSA of refusing to

12. Jones, "Antiwar Report."
13. *Militant,* February 5, 1968.

take a stand against racism. In the heated debate which followed, C. Clark Kissinger in the chair did a good job of keeping tempers down and bringing the issues out. It turned into a discussion of the various strategies for fighting racism, from electing better Democrats to projections for an independent Black political party, from pacifism to self-defense, from the difference between voluntary separation and imposed segregation to the difference between integration and self-determination. If nothing else it was educational.

Finally the chair gave precedence to a motion declaring: "The purpose of the Student Mobilization Committee is to fight against the racist war in Vietnam." When that had passed by overwhelming vote, the YSAers withdrew their countermotion and the first motion on the title for the strike was adopted. It was also voted that the SMC would circulate the National Black Antiwar Antidraft Union call.

The ten days of April action and the April 27 mass demonstrations were also adopted, as well as endorsement of the idea of massive demonstrations at the Democratic Party convention in August. The last day of the conference was devoted to brief working sessions to get the program rolling. Some of the New York delegates left early to get back for an important rally taking place that night.

\*       \*       \*

The New York meeting, sponsored by a broad range of antiwar groups, including the SMC, was scheduled for Manhattan Center. Its purpose was to greet Dr. Benjamin Spock, Rev. William Sloane Coffin, Jr., Michael Ferber, Mitchell Goodman, and Marcus Raskin. These five were most of the delegation that had presented the draft cards of resisters at the Justice Department the previous October. They arrived at the New York rally after having been arraigned that day in Boston on charges of "conspiring to counsel, aid, and abet" young men in refusing the draft.

Long before the start of the meeting more than 3,000 antiwar activists jammed the hall. A hastily rented annex was quickly filled with another 1,800, and 800 more stood outside in a dark street listening to speeches over a loudspeaker, and expressing solidarity with the defendants. One of the speakers, attorney Arthur Kinoy, who had also spoken at the SDS National Council

378   *Out Now!*

and the SMC conference along similar lines, warned that a comprehensive program of government repression was under way. It had been signaled by the indictment of H. Rap Brown, said Kinoy, and, while aimed first and most heavily at militant Black groups, included the antiwar movement as a primary target. The use of catch-all "conspiracy" indictments, he said, could be expected to increase.

\*     \*     \*

Between the time of the SMC conference and the spring actions which it called, there occurred a series of interconnected events that shook the world, or at least the American position in it. The first of these began in Saigon on January 31, 1968, during the lunar New Year holiday known in Vietnam as Tet, that culture's major celebration of the year.

For months the United States military spokesmen had been telling the American public that there was light at the end of the tunnel. The "Viet Cong," as they called the NLF forces, were being defeated and had lost control and even influence in the major population centers of South Vietnam. A November 1967 public report by General Westmoreland claimed that of the total South Vietnamese population of 17.2 million, only 2.5 million remained in NLF-controlled areas. These had been reduced mainly to border areas near "sanctuaries" in Cambodia, Laos, or North Vietnam, and isolated sections of jungle, mountain, or swamp, according to the U.S. claim.

If only North Vietnam would cease its "aggression," the Johnson administration's argument went, by stopping the supply and infiltration of fresh troops into these areas, the pro-American Saigon government would have little trouble securing them, and the U.S. could retire in peace, having saved the new country of South Vietnam for the "free world."

In truth, in the three years since the major U.S. escalation began, the devastation of the countryside by incessant U.S. air raids and ground "search and destroy" missions had driven some two million peasants into refugee camps and overcrowded poor districts of the cities. All the cities were occupied by the 600,000-man Saigon army and defended by half a million U.S. troops. It is necessary to bear in mind that the NLF forces at this time had no air cover at all and were forced to rely almost exclusively on light infantry weapons. The peasants were sometimes reduced to farming at night around the edges of bomb craters, supplementing their diet with minnows that grew in the flooded craters. The Americans bombed and strafed virtually with impunity in South Vietnam.

Meanwhile, in the richer sections of the cities an artificial economy based on massive American military spending and imports created a meretricious boom for the well-to-do and the hangers-on of the puppet regime. Saigon was flooded with con artists and salesmen of every kind from the United States and Japan.

Let two American newsmen, present when the chain of events began, set the scene. Charles Mohr, the *New York Times* Saigon bureau chief, wrote:

> The great majority of Saigon's residents live in tortuously twisted alleys, many of which end in cul-de-sacs and most of which have no formal names. From the air, it becomes even more apparent than from the ground that these are incredibly jammed areas.
> The roofs overlap like playing cards in a fanned deck. It is sometimes impossible even to detect the twisting alleys, because they are so closely hemmed and constricted by shantys. . . .[14]

And *Los Angeles Times* correspondent John Randolf, in the accepted American jargon of the time, described another aspect of the city that fateful morning:

> Saigon presented a picture that, for the capital of a small, poor, weak country in its ninth year of a war for national survival, could only be described as disgusting.
> At a time when the country is desperately short of doctors, hospitals, clinics, schools, teachers—and almost everything else—the roar of idiotic firecrackers to celebrate Tet, the lunar year, was costing Saigon at least tens of thousands of dollars per day. . . .
> Combined with this was a New Year's buying spree for gifts of the most luxurious nature. There is much poverty in Saigon, but much prosperity too. Vietnamese were either badgering their American friends to pick up choice items in the post exchange, or failing that, were paying triple prices for legally imported, tax exempt luxuries.
> Genuine luxuries, too—Paris perfumes, cognac, choice Scotch, rich materials, TV sets, cameras, watches—and only the very best, too, no second-rate merchandise wanted.[15]

14. *New York Times*, February 10, 1968.
15. *Los Angeles Times*, February 10, 1968.

The American irritation at the firecrackers is also explained by the fact that they obscured the first warning sounds of the NLF guns that morning. Its forces set up barricades in the twisted alleys and attacked the American embassy in downtown Saigon—not from "sanctuaries" on the borders, but from within the capital city itself. Thus began the Tet offensive.

The Americans were taken by surprise. Their Vietnamese "friends," it became obvious, had either neglected to tell them, or were themselves so isolated from the general population that they did not know, that the NLF had organized and equipped an army under their very noses. The NLF captured the embassy. They held the compound for only the first day, but it was soon apparent that the NLF controlled whole sections of the city. The attacks quickly spread to every city and almost every town in South Vietnam. Within a few days the NLF held thirty-six cities and major towns, including Hue, the ancient capital and the third largest city in the South. The Saigon regime's army proved incapable of holding up under the NLF attack. Indeed it was obvious that not a few members of these forces, as well as the general population, had to have cooperated with the NLF, at least to the extent of keeping its preparations secret from the Americans. Only the American bases proper remained secure, and fighting occurred within the confines of some of those.

The American military reaction was quick and brutal. They began pulverizing with bombs, shells, and rockets the urban areas held by the NLF, regardless of civilian casualties. In two weeks another half million Vietnamese civilians—those lucky enough to flee in time from the American holocaust—became refugees. Whole sections of Saigon itself were reduced to rubble.

The methods by which the American forces recaptured many of the urban areas were summed up in an Associated Press dispatch February 7 from the Mekong Delta provincial capital of Bentre, which the U.S. military had just retaken. That is, they had occupied the rubble and were digging out over a thousand bodies of men, women, and children. AP quoted an American major: "It became necessary to destroy the town in order to save it."

That statement reverberated around the world, and more than a few Americans who until that time had gone along with their government turned against the war.

When the Tet offensive was over, the NLF losses were severe, the casualties of U.S. ground combat units heavy, and the civilian casualties enormous. The Americans had recaptured the cities, and militarily the war was stalemated once again. But the American expedition in Vietnam had suffered a major political defeat. And henceforth no one would credit another statement from General William C. Westmoreland about victory being just around the corner.

\* \* \*

The country-western bards among the American ground troops in Vietnam—no one knows exactly when—added another verse to an endless GI ballad sung to the tune of "The Wabash Cannonball."

The forward air controller[16]
Is a warrior without match,
With his monogrammed flight jacket,
And his F-100 patch.
Put napalm on a hamlet,
And burned the whole thing flat.
Killed a hundred noncombatants,
And he's sorry about that.

\* \* \*

The Tet offensive convinced many additional Americans that the war was morally wrong. It convinced others that the war was unwinnable, and not worth the cost. It caused General Westmoreland to request an additional 206,000 troops, and the joint chiefs of staff to request a mobilization of the United States military manpower resources, which meant calling up the National Guard and reserve units. These requests were not made publicly, but there were rumors to that effect which fueled the public debate.

All these developments precipitated a major secret debate among presidential advisers and the joint chiefs of staff, and a reevaluation of the war strategy by the highest ruling circles.

16. The jets that did the tactical bombing moved too fast to pick out their own targets. This was done by a forward air controller in a light plane who made the judgments and indicated the targets by radio and smoke flares.

Clark Clifford. the Du Pont interests' chief lawyer, who had just replaced Robert McNamara as secretary of defense, headed a task force to advise Johnson on Westmoreland's troop request. The task force consisted of twelve men, most of them appointed government officials, none of whom had ever held elective office, and all of whom had close ties to the Eastern big business Establishment. This group laid out the essential outlines of what would become the U.S. strategy for the rest of the war. It later became known as "Vietnamization." Essentially it meant retraining and reequipping the Saigon forces (known as ARVN for Army of the Republic of Vietnam), then cutting back on the American ground role, backing the ARVN with American airpower, and using the bombing of North Vietnam as a negotiating ploy in the hope of reducing or halting Hanoi's support to the insurrection in the South. This strategy rejected the idea of general mobilization and massive additional U.S. troop levels in Vietnam. Domestic opposition to the war was a major consideration in this approach.

While this strategy was being decided in secret and within top ruling circles, the effect of the Tet offensive was being reflected in the primary election campaign and in Congress.

The first primary was scheduled for New Hampshire on Tuesday, March 12. The McCarthy forces had managed to mount an effective campaign apparatus sparked by young volunteers who came to the state in large numbers to set up canvassing operations and storefront offices in every major city and town. (Sam Brown and David Hawk were involved in this.) Nevertheless it was still assumed that Johnson would win handily.

Then, two days before the New Hampshire elections, a report of Westmoreland's request for an additional 206,000 troops, and the fact that this might mean the calling up of reserves, was published by the *New York Times*. The next day Secretary of State Dean Rusk appeared before the Senate Foreign Relations Committee for open hearings on foreign aid. The hearings became a debate on the war between Rusk and the committee's chairman, William Fulbright. Rusk failed to add anything to the rationalizations for U.S. involvement and refused to say whether the Westmoreland request would be granted. It was a dismal show for the Johnson administration.

The next day the New Hampshire primaries were held. McCarthy's vote was beyond all expectations. (When the absentee ballots were counted later, McCarthy had a plurality over

Johnson.) It was widely regarded as a rejection of Johnson's war policy. Its immediate effect was to convince Senator Robert F. Kennedy, who had also been making dove speeches, that Johnson could be beaten. Kennedy announced his own candidacy on March 16. Under those conditions Johnson was by no means assured the nomination. To try to win it he would have to campaign, and he faced the uncomfortable prospect that his every appearance would be the occasion for an antiwar demonstration.

On March 22, General Westmoreland was recalled as U.S. commander in Vietnam and kicked upstairs to the post of army chief of staff in the Pentagon.

On March 31, Johnson appeared on national TV to announce, "I shall not seek, and I will not accept, the nomination of my party." He also announced a suspension of the bombing of Vietnam north of the twentieth parallel—that is, over most of North Vietnam—and offered to negotiate with Hanoi. On April 3, 1968, Hanoi accepted.

This series of events, initiated by the Tet offensive, dramatically changed the immediate political situation in the country and the context in which the antiwar movement operated. On the one hand the breadth of antiwar sentiment increased considerably. On the other hand there were illusions that the war would soon be over.

This latter effect did not manifest itself all at once, or to the same degree in all parts of the antiwar movement. For one thing, Johnson's declination speech contained an announcement of an additional 10,500 U.S. troops to Vietnam, and military analysts pointed out that a bombing halt north of the twentieth parallel was not that significant since the overall U.S. bombing was not decreased, just concentrated in the remaining areas of North and South Vietnam. What is more, the talks had hardly begun when they became bogged down in a long dispute over technical matters such as the shape of the bargaining table.[17]

17. The official U.S. position maintained that it was in Vietnam at the request of the Saigon regime, so it couldn't leave Saigon out of the negotiations. In return it was understood that NLF representatives would join the Hanoi delegation. But Saigon and the U.S. balked at seating arrangements that implied direct negotiations with the NLF, so the shape of the table became a disputed issue.

So amidst hope and anticipation that the war would soon be over, there was also considerable understanding of the need to keep up the pressure, at least for a while longer. The SMC, then, continued to find good response to its preparations for the student strike and the April 27 mass demonstrations. Many of the moderates, however, while giving some support to the spring actions, were anxious to concentrate their efforts on the elections, behind either Kennedy or McCarthy. And many of the radicals were expressing concern over what would become of "the move-ment" when the war was over. There was widespread feeling in the "new left" milieu that liberal politicians had co-opted the antiwar cause, that it wasn't radical anymore, and that those who wanted to build a radical base had to shift quickly to other issues and other methods or organizing.

It should be recalled here that the National Mobe administra-tive committee meeting in December had appointed a subcommit-tee to arrange a conference to plan the anticipated demonstra-tions at the Democratic Party convention in August. This conference was scheduled for March 23-24, and by the time it occurred McCarthy had won in New Hampshire, Kennedy had announced his candidacy, and Westmoreland had been recalled.

The conference was by invitation only. It took place at a summer camp at Lake Villa outside Chicago, and was attended by some 200 persons, mostly from the SDS milieu, both old guard and new.

The meeting was not really an antiwar conference at all. It seems that the original subcommittee, which included Dellinger, Greenblatt, Hayden, and Rennie Davis, considered itself a kind of steering committee for a new multi-issue coalition. The conference adopted a program for this "new coalition" which stated in part:

We call for an election-year organizing campaign to be carried into cities, towns, and counties across America. Our purpose is to generate massive popular support against the war, the draft, imperialism, racism, repression, poverty, and unrepresentative government.[18]

Further: " . . . we need to develop independent electoral alternatives based on radical programs and centered on local organizing."

18. Cited in a "Report on the Lake Villa Conference," by Lew Jones, March 28, 1968. (Copy in author's files.)

Interestingly, the conference put off any decision on demonstrations at the Democratic Party convention. The conference voted not to support Kennedy or McCarthy, but most of those present wanted to wait until after the California primary in June—which would determine whether Kennedy or McCarthy were front-runners—before deciding on the nature of demonstrations at the Democratic Party convention.

Nothing ever came of the "new coalition" and the Lake Villa conference turned out to be pretty much a waste of time. But it indicated some of the thinking going on among the active officers of the National Mobilization Committee, and it was a portent of tensions to come. The few YSAers who happened to be invited to this conference were angry at the lack of interest there in the spring actions.

A week later SDS held a National Council meeting on March 29 in Lexington, Kentucky. The "ten days" of antiwar actions the previous NC had adopted, and which this meeting should logically have been devoting itself to building, were hardly mentioned. In effect the SDS NC simply abandoned them. According to Sale,

the new shift of focus was expressed for the NC in a moving and persuasive speech by Carl Oglesby, who told the young delegates that the job of SDS now was to turn from the issue of the war to that of racism. Radicals have done all they can now toward ending the war, he suggested, and adventures like the Chicago convention demonstration or schemes for involving working-class communities around the draft were not really going to help much. Radicals now should turn to the questions of black liberation and white racism, fighting not only for the sake of the oppressed blacks, but also because this struck a blow at one of the pillars of the system.[19]

What was wrong with this was not the recognition of the importance of the Black struggle in the United States, but—among other things—the abandonment of the antiwar cause.

\*         \*         \*

Yet another event, this one unconnected with the Tet offensive,

19. Kirkpatrick Sale, *SDS* (New York: Vintage Books, 1974), pp. 418-19.

would shake the country as the spring antiwar actions were being prepared. On April 4, while in Memphis supporting a strike of Black sanitation workers for union recognition, thirty-nine-year-old Martin Luther King, Jr., was assassinated by a hired killer. It had only been twelve years since his role in the Montgomery bus protest had gained him national prominence. Within hours spontaneous rebellions occurred in the Black ghettos of more than a hundred American cities, and there were peaceful demonstrations in countless others. In the capital, smoke from fires set by enraged Blacks hung over the city, and in Chicago the fires were said to be the worst since the great fire of 1871. Some 65,000 national guardsmen and federal troops were called out to reinforce local police. Thirty-eight people were killed and more than 15,000 arrested. One of those killed was Bobby Hutton, the seventeen-year-old treasurer of the Black Panther Party, shot down by Oakland police while surrendering from a house they had surrounded.

\*            \*            \*

Joe Miles, a nineteen-year-old Black militant in Washington, D.C., was vice-chairman of the local Black Antiwar Antidraft Union. When the news of King's death broke, he was called by students at a high school to organize a protest. He went to the school and joined with a hundred students in a march to Howard University, a virtually all-Black campus. On the way they picked up 200 more high schoolers. At Howard about 1,000 students gathered for a rally. Someone had brought a Black nationalist flag, and everyone cheered as the American flag was lowered from the flagpole and the Black nationalist flag was raised over the campus. We shall meet Miles again in the course of this narrative, after he has been drafted into the army.

\*            \*            \*

In spite of the inaction of the SDS national office, the month of April saw widespread antiwar activity and preparations for the strike on campuses across the country, initiated by the SMC, local SDS chapters, and other groups. On Friday, April 26, a million students participated in the first national student strike since the 1930s and the largest up to that time in the history of the country. At a few universities, most dramatically at Columbia in upper Manhattan near Harlem, the strike coincided with actions initiated earlier around specific demands directed at the university administration. But for the most part it was a one-day political strike in opposition to the war. As a rule the students did not simply stay out of class, but engaged in leafletting, picketing, marches, rallies, sit-ins, discussions, teach-ins, and other educational activities against the war.

Involved were over a thousand schools, including at least fifty major universities, and many high schools from Maine to California and from Washington State to Florida. The spread of the actions was particularly significant. Schools in every part of the continental United States were drawn in, and there were some surprising results in areas previously considered conservative and prowar. At the University of Arizona at Tucson, for example, 11,000 students, half the enrollment, stayed out of class.

The most remarkable feature of the April 26 strike was the participation of high school students, especially in New York City. The city board of education estimated abnormal absenteeism that day at 200,000, according to the *Student Mobilizer*. There was large participation from high schools in every kind of community—Black, white, and Puerto Rican, working class and middle class. The *New York Times* put the number of strikers in city high schools and city-operated colleges at 200,000. The SMC estimated an additional 60,000 students were out at private colleges and universities in the New York area.

Paradoxically, the national media paid little attention to the strike, perhaps because it was overwhelmingly peaceful, orderly, and even businesslike. Local media tended to treat the actions in their areas as local news without pointing up the fact that similar events were taking place across the country at the same time. A few local actions, particularly the Columbia events, got far more national publicity than the national strike itself.[20]

20. The Columbia events began with a building occupation April 23, spread to a partial strike April 25, and included a police assault April 29 that kept the full strike going well into May. The events had not been planned by either the SMC or the SDS National Council despite highly inventive reports to the contrary. They climaxed a long history of struggles by Columbia SDS, the Student Afro-American Society, and other groups against the encroachment of the university on a park used

Nevertheless the national strike had a profound and lasting effect. It tapped new layers of student activists as some of the older ones were getting tired or disoriented. And it helped establish a new atmosphere in the high schools and previously unaffected colleges. This was true even where only a relatively few students on a particular campus participated. These used the occasion for teach-ins, setting up literature tables, and so on, to begin the process which had taken place elsewhere two or three years earlier.

In effect the April 26 national student strike took advantage of the changed atmosphere initiated by the Tet offensive to spread the antiwar word to new layers of people who had previously been immune or indifferent to it.

The strike helped deepen and widen the level of student activism in general. And in this atmosphere the struggles of the students from oppressed national minorities around their own special demands began to assume significant proportions. In the beginning these were almost always combined with some antiwar action. A new movement for the right of high school students as such to engage in political activity—first of all against the war— also made its appearance in the wake of this strike.

Internationally, the April 26 student strike was a part of the student ferment sweeping many parts of the world in 1968. Student strikes and demonstrations around April 26 occurred in Canada, Mexico, Puerto Rico, Japan, Italy, France, Germany, and many other countries, including Czechoslovakia, then enjoying the brief "Prague Spring." In Copenhagen some 30,000 marched April 27 to the American embassy. There was no direct connection with the SMC call, but it is interesting to note that the famous May events in France—in which a student uprising

---

by the nearby Black community, and against war research by the Institute of Defense Analysis. The general atmosphere of the April days, however, was part of the background which allowed a bold action by a relative handful of Black students and SDSers to precipitate a major confrontation. SDS lost the leadership very quickly, but Mark Rudd, the chapter chairman, never forgot the moment. The will to throw down the gauntlet regardless of objective realities would become a political principle, summed up in the later Weatherman slogan "Dare to struggle, Dare to win," and Rudd would try again. Such moments, however, are fairly rare, and do not present themselves as the result of the efforts of any small group, however resolute.

ignited a general strike by the working class and a near revolution—were the culmination of a chain of events which began with a demonstration in solidarity with the Vietnamese revolution. There *was* a direct connection between NBAWADU and SMC calls and the prolonged student strikes which shook the whole Japanese higher educational system in 1968. On April 26, seventy-two Japanese universities were shut down. This was only for one day, but the solidarity showed the Japanese students they had more power than they knew and gave an impulse to the already developing revolt against their own conditions.

\*            \*            \*

The April 27 demonstrations were not concentrated in one or two cities but took place across the country. They were generally the largest yet for that kind of decentralized arrangement. The numbers in most cities were still in the hundreds rather than tens of thousands, but the movement was obviously growing. In New York the turnout amounted to some 200,000 for dual marches down Fifth Avenue and Central Park West to a giant rally that more than filled Central Park's Sheep Meadow. The range of the speakers was broad, with notables such as Manhattan Borough President Percy Sutton and Mayor John Lindsay putting in brief appearances.

I marched and was one of the speakers at the demonstration in San Francisco, which drew some 30,000. Significantly, that march was led off by a contingent of about forty active-duty GIs, in civilian clothes. Some of them were air force reservists who had recently been called for active duty. In spite of all the pending negotiations between the two sides, the bombing was being stepped up and shortages of manpower had appeared in certain categories, so the military was selectively calling up some reservists.

It is interesting to note that the early links between the civilian antiwar movement and *groups* of antiwar GIs, rather than just individuals, began among these levies of reservists.

\*            \*            \*

In Chicago a demonstration of 7,000 April 27 was broken up by police without provocation. C. Clark Kissinger was chairman of the ad hoc committee of the Chicago Peace Council and other groups that organized the demonstration. From the beginning the city administration was hostile to the committee when it tried to negotiate permits. These were denied until the last minute when the crowd was gathering in Grant Park. Even so, the march was permitted in the street for only a brief distance and then was forced onto the sidewalks into smaller sections. After the first of these reached the civic center the cops attacked them, throwing some of the demonstrators into a reflecting pool. About eight demonstrators were arrested and many injured.

A detailed analysis of this affair was later published by an independent commission of distinguished citizens unconnected with the peace movement. It declared that

the police badly mishandled their task. Brutalizing demonstrators without provocation, they failed to live up to that difficult professionalism which we demand. Yet to place primary blame on the police would, in our view, be inappropriate. The April 27 stage had been prepared by the Mayor's [Richard J. Daley] designated officials weeks before. Administrative actions concerning the April 27 Parade were designed by City officials to communicate that "these people have no right to demonstrate or express their views." . . . The police were doing what the Mayor and Superintendent had clearly indicated was expected of them.[21]

It was a portent of things to come.

\*        \*        \*

Martin Luther King, Jr., had agreed before his death to be the featured speaker at the April 27 demonstration in New York. Though only three weeks from her personal bereavement, Coretta

---

21. *Dissent and Disorder,* a report to the Citizens of Chicago on the April 27 Peace Parade, August 1, 1968, pp. 30-31. The commission was funded by the Roger Baldwin Foundation, but was autonomous. Its members were: Warren Bacon, vice-president of Inland Steel; Dr. Edgar H. Chandler, executive director of the Church Federation of Greater Chicago; Earl B. Dickerson, president of the Supreme Life Insurance Co.; Monsignor John J. Egan, pastor of the Presentation Church; Dr. Joseph P. Evans of the University of Chicago medical school; Professor Harry Kalven, Jr., of the U. of C. law school; Rev. E. Spencer Parsons, dean of the Rockefeller Memorial Chapel; and Rabbi Edgar E. Siskin, president of the Chicago Board of Rabbis.

King took her husband's place. She had always been, and would continue to be, a consistent antiwar activist. All the more significant was the view of the immediate future that she expressed that day.

She pointed out that Martin had made his major address against the war in Vietnam only one year to the day before his death, and how he had been maligned for it. She continued:

Now one year later, we see almost unbelievable results coming from all of our united efforts. Had we then suggested the possibility of two peace candidates as front-runners for the presidency of the United States, our sanity would certainly have been questioned.

Yet, I need not trace for you how many of our hopes have been realized, in these twelve short months. Never in the history of this nation have the people been so forceful in reversing the policy of our government in regard to war. We are indeed on the threshold of a new day for the peacemakers. But just as conscientious action has reversed the tide of public opinion and government policy, we must now turn our attention and the soul force of the movement of people of good will to the problems of the poor here at home.[22]

I wasn't any better at short-term prophecy than Coretta King was, though I had no confidence whatever in the government, in the "peace candidates," or in the pending negotiations. In my speech to the San Francisco rally I said:

We are told that we can't get out of there now, that we have to negotiate and that we have to stay there because we've got to somehow shore up the Thieu-Ky regime so they can carry on the war themselves. . . .

Now, we're supposed to expend GIs' lives to shore up that regime. Let me tell you that that's not exactly why they are expending GIs' lives. They are being expended to save face for some cheap politicians who first got us in there because they were sending the American military around the world to defend big business. And that's a very poor reason to lose 21,000 young men dead, and it's a very poor reason to kill all those Vietnamese.

We don't own that country. And we never did. And we never will. And we shouldn't. It doesn't belong to us. And the fighting over there is not in our interest and it has absolutely nothing to do with the defense of this country. . . .

And the way we're going to end this war: We don't have to wait till the election. And we shouldn't quit then either. But we don't have to wait

22. *Liberation,* April 1968.

until then necessarily. If we stay in the streets and if the GIs keep coming on demonstrations. And if we get out and talk to them, and if we talk to the young men that are facing the draft. And if we keep building that pressure, then we can stop the war. Not by trusting some other liberal Democratic or Republican politician. . . .

Don't get fooled. Don't get sucked back into their structure. Stay independent. Stay in the streets. Build black power. Build brown power. Chicano power. Student power. High school student power. Independent political action. Labor power. . . . Keep building that independent power and we'll end this war and make this country a decent place to live in. And if that be revolution, make the most of it.[23]

The war was not to end for years and it would yet cost over twice as many lives as it had up to that point. The expectation that it would end soon, however, was widespread at the time, especially among antiwar leaders, and that was part of the basis for the severe crisis that hit the movement immediately after the spring actions.

\*        \*        \*

The student strike and the April 27 demonstrations, especially in New York, were successful beyond expectations, and for those who favored mass actions the SMC had certainly proved its worth. Yet immediately after the actions, trouble developed within the SMC national office. Kipp Dawson, who was one of the national coordinators and on the national staff, recalls that the first sign of this was immediately after the demonstrations, when she suggested that the SMC hold a press conference the following Monday, to present a summary of the student strike.

At the time [she says], I thought of this as obvious and routine. We had always done something like that after a major action. But this time most of the others said no. Linda [Morse] said we couldn't do it because the press would ask what we planned next and we couldn't answer that. When I said we could at least say that another conference would be held

23. The transcript of this speech was published by the Socialist Workers Campaign Committee under the title "*. . . if that be revolution make the most of it.*" (Copy in author's files.) The *Militant* of May 10, 1968, published excerpts, leaving out the part about not necessarily having to wait until the elections for an end to the war. The editors, it seems, were less optimistic than I on that point.

in the near future to decide on future action, she said no, we couldn't do that because there was no agreement on what we should do. The SWP and YSA, she said, saw the SMC as a group for just organizing mass demonstrations and conferences to call them, and she said it had to be more than that.[24]

On May 8, 1968, less than two weeks after the student strike, a meeting of the SMC working committee adopted the following motion:
"The staff shall be composed entirely of independents in order to relieve some major tensions in the office."[25]
This excluded any member of a radical political organization from the SMC national staff. There were only three persons (out of about a dozen) on the staff at the time who were acknowledged members of radical political groups. Phyllis Kalb, who was a CPer, voted for the motion and immmediately resigned from the staff. Syd Stapleton and Kipp Dawson, who were YSAers, voted against the motion, and were considered fired from the staff, though Dawson and Kalb remained SMC coordinators. Neither Dawson nor Stapleton had any prior notice that this motion was going to be raised at this meeting and they were shocked.

It was clear in the discussion that the reason for the motion was to get rid of Stapleton and Dawson. There was no accusation that they hadn't worked hard and efficiently. It was generally agreed that both had played key roles in building the mass actions and the strike. On the contrary, the accusation was that they were too effective, too hard-driving, and that they were carrying out YSA policy, not SMC policy. The two YSAers replied that there was no contradiction between YSA policy and SMC policy as adopted by the SMC conference, that they had never attempted to transform the SMC into a socialist group, or have it adopt or carry out the YSA's multi-issue program.

That, however, was just the problem. A majority of the others present—including the CPers and radical pacifists—thought it was high time the SMC did adopt a general multi-issue radical program, though they weren't too clear on what it should be. Kipp and Syd had opposed that. Considering the differences within the SMC, they felt that any such platform would be too nebulous to

24. Letter from Kipp Dawson to the author, May 15, 1976.
25. Minutes, SMC working committee, May 8, 1968. (Copy in author's files.)

be meaningful and would mean abandoning opposition to the war in Vietnam as the SMC's central focus.

Shortly after the May 8 meeting, some informal discussions were held with non-SMCers in an attempt to mediate the dispute. Those present included radical pacifists Dave Dellinger and Eric Weinberger, and SWPers Harry Ring and myself. SMC staffers Linda Morse, Irwin Gladstone, Brent Garren, and Jane Baum also participated, as well as Dawson and Stapleton.

During these discussions it became clear that the blatant exclusionary motion was simply indefensible in a movement which had fought so hard for the principle of nonexclusion. Linda Morse declared that it was their intention to withdraw that motion, but insisted on the dismissal of Dawson and Stapleton. She and the other staffers, backed by Dellinger, insisted that it was a matter of personalities. They said they were not opposed to all YSAers being on the staff, but had to exclude Kipp and Syd because they were too "hard line," too "insensitive" to the feelings of the "independents." In this discussion they kept repeating how important personality and sensitivity were, and saying, now there's no problem with *you* (meaning Harry and me) or with Lew (meaning Lew Jones, who had previously been active in the SMC but was currently YSA national chairman). *Our* personalities, it seemed, were all right, but Kipp and Syd's were not.

Harry and I talked it over during a recess, and in our view what was involved here was a serious political difference which ought to be discussed out on the merits without chewing up people personally in the process. In an attempt to maneuver out of the bind they had gotten themselves into on the question of exclusion, Dellinger and Morse had put Kipp and Syd in the position of having their personalities attacked. Dave and Linda tried to be as gentle as possible about it, but Harry and I knew damn well this whole turn of events hurt Kipp and Syd personally. The problem was to get the dispute off that tack and to make it as clear as possible that political differences were at issue.

So Harry and I threw the maneuver back. We told the others that we would suggest to Lew Jones that he seek a leave of absence as chairman of the YSA and, if that were possible, make himself available for the SMC staff.

If the working committee would clearly demonstrate its adherence to nonexclusion by rescinding the exclusionary motion, the resignation, and the firings, Kipp and Syd agreed they would withdraw voluntarily from the staff and be replaced by Lew Jones. It was fairly obvious the others didn't like this but in light of what they had just been saying they initially agreed to it. It was also agreed that Howard Petrick, the YSAer and antiwar GI who had just been kicked out of the army and was then on a speaking tour fighting for an honorable discharge, would also join the staff when he was available.

By the time of the May 16 working committee meeting, however, Morse had caucused with the majority on the working committee and they broke the agreement.

First a motion was put to "rescind last week's staff motion and to reaffirm the principle of non-exclusion and to specify that individual merit rather than political affiliation shall be the basis for hiring and firing of staff."[26] This passed unanimously.

Then another motion was put to "accept Phyllis Kalb's resignation from the staff and to dismiss Kipp Dawson and Syd Stapleton from the staff." This passed seventeen to six. Those voting in favor included most of the staff and the representatives from Hunter College, New York University, CCNY (later City University of New York), New York High School SMC, The Resistance, the War Resisters League, the Workshop in Nonviolence, and the Communist Party.

Those opposed were Dawson and Stapleton, Martha Harris of the staff, and the representatives from Columbia University, the SWP, and the YSA.

This vote, essentially reaffirming the exclusionary policy adopted May 8, was the key action of the May 16 meeting. The rest was anticlimax. A motion to hire Lew Jones was defeated, in spite of his impeccable personality, by fourteen to seven, with two abstentions. The essence of the issue, at least, was considerably clarified.

The May 16 meeting also passed a motion to hire Howard Petrick "because of his general ability and his particular experience in organizing GIs." But he wasn't immediately available anyway. In a letter to Linda Morse, Petrick commented:

> How could you expect me to function as window-dressing for a grouping that has introduced political discrimination and exclusionism into the antiwar movement? . . .

26. Minutes, SMC working committee, May 16, 1968. (Copy in author's files.)

I wasn't in New York and frankly don't know all the details about the charges and counter-charges. But I *did* read the *Mobilizer* that Syd edited and used it to get support in the army. I *did* read the correspondence that Kipp sent out to build the strike, and I *did* see the results of this work and the effect of the strike on GIs! I also know that if witch-hunting and exclusions are brought back into the movement it will kill it—and this is a hell of a time to do that.

The war, as every GI knows, is still going on. During the last two weeks, despite the "negotiations," there have been more deaths in Vietnam than in any two previous weeks of the war. . . .[27]

\*        \*        \*

The national SMC structure at this time consisted of biannual conferences, a continuations committee authorized to meet between conferences, and a working committee which met every week or so in New York. The continuations committee hadn't actually met, but theoretically it was composed of one person from each local or campus antiwar group that supported the SMC and sent a representative, plus representatives of each national group, and a few prominent individuals. The working committee was a more or less accidental body composed of staff, the six national coordinators, and the members of the continuations committee who resided in New York and attended meetings. The working committee usually consisted of from a dozen to thirty youth and was supposed to operate on consensus, referring disputed issues of substance to one of the other bodies.

After the May 16 meeting it was obvious that the majority of the working committee was no longer willing to operate on consensus on major questions. This contained an inexorable logic. The coalition of forces that made up the national SMC had very limited agreement. Even the current majority of the working committee was not a homogeneous grouping. It was a bloc united temporarily by a common irritation with the YSA, and an abstract agreement on going multi-issue. Even this point was extremely nebulous. Perhaps some of the majority had a clear idea in mind of what the specifics of the new multi-issue program should be, but others were simply expressing a mood of frustration rather than a thought-out perspective. Any serious attempt

27. Letter from Howard Petrick to Linda Morse, May 27, 1968. (Copy in author's files.)

to specify in action a particular multi-issue program would bring out the substantial differences in the current majority and would in turn have had to be settled by the domination of one multi-issue tendency over the others. The losers would inevitably drop out or become disinterested.

The YSA was accused of "dominating" the organization, even though it was a small minority within it. And in a sense the so-called YSA line had, until then, tended to dominate. But this had come about, not because of the YSA's alleged hardness or insensitivity, or even its notorious efficiency and caucus discipline. The reason was that the "YSA line" consisted precisely in sticking to the central point of agreement, the point that everyone in the SMC at least paid lip service to—mass action for immediate withdrawal from the war in Vietnam.

If allowed to stand, the new direction would mean the end of the SMC as a group capable of broad mobilizations, whether the YSA stayed around to be outvoted or not. The YSA was now faced with two hard choices: bow out gracefully, or fight back. To fight was not a pleasant prospect. Normal people at peace with themselves—even those with a fighting instinct—do not relish faction fights, any more than physical ones. Kipp Dawson recalls that she had a "sinking feeling in the pit of my stomach" at the prospect.[28] But the war was still going on, and the YSAers were convinced that they were faced with a tendency to liquidate the SMC as an antiwar mobilizing group, so they chose to fight.

Dawson and Stapleton demanded that a full conference be called in a central part of the country so the character and future activity of the SMC could be argued out and decided by the ranks. The majority of the working committee refused to call a full conference, but did call a continuations committee meeting for June 29 in New York City. The struggle, then, turned around that meeting.

The first problem was getting the issues out to the ranks. At the May 16 meeting a motion had been made to send out the minutes with two cover letters, one approved by the five coordinators in the majority, and one by Kipp Dawson, the minority coordinator. This was defeated and a motion passed to send only the majority cover letter.

Shortly thereafter, Dawson, who had compiled the SMC mailing lists in the first place and felt no obligation to exclude herself

28. Letter from Dawson.

from them, made copies, and sent out an open letter from herself and Stapleton giving their interpretation of the dispute.

The letter urged SMC supporters in each area to call meetings to discuss the decisions of the May 16 working committee meeting, to protest to the SMC national office, and to demand a full conference. It declared:

> We feel the differences over staff and its functions reflect deeper policy differences over what path the antiwar movement should take. . . . We are for organizing other international student antiwar actions, even larger and more extensive than the spectacularly successful international student strike of April 26.
>
> Others on the Working Committee do not agree with this perspective. They would either junk the SMC by crippling it with the policy of exclusionism and witch-hunting . . . or dilute its character as an antiwar organization. If they succeed, the fight against the war will be set back at the very time it has become imperative to step up the pressure on Washington.[29]

The letter was printed in the *East Village Other*, one of the so-called underground papers in New York.

Some of those in the working committee majority reacted in anger. "YSA has been screaming," said a letter signed by Art Goldberg and others from the "Independent Caucus" and printed in the next issue of the same paper, "that Miss Dawson and Mr. Stapleton were 'excluded' from the staff because they were Socialists. That is horseshit. They were kicked off the staff because they were SCUMBAGS. . . ."[30]

Whatever else it was, this letter was not written in the traditional style of the antiwar movement. It should be noted that none of the SMC coordinators supporting the Independent Caucus signed it. It would have been out of character for any of them. But it was indicative of a degeneration in the character of argument by some within their group to a nonpolitical, emotional level. For another example, they put out a button that said: "Sour Grapes is Not Exclusion."

The statement sent out by the majority of the coordinators characterized previous SMC activity as follows:

29. *East Village Other,* May 31, 1968, letters column.
30. Ibid., June 7, 1968.

Our focus has been almost completely on the war, and very little on the draft, racial oppression, and university complicity. . . . Major national or international actions are of vital importance and almost no one has suggested that we stop organizing them. However, it is equally important for SMC to help groups increase their campus base and effectiveness on a continuing basis, around all *four* issues. . . .[31]

Note that even the draft is considered a separate issue from the war. This was in line with the theoretical approach then shared by SDS, the Du Bois Clubs, and some of the pacifists, that the draft, in and of itself and even *rather than* the war was a key to radical organizing among youth.

The statement outlined a four-point summer program: working on draft resistance through the SDS Draft Alliance; working with GIs through the "Summer of Support" (a fund-raising project set up by Rennie Davis and others to finance "movement"-style coffeehouses near army bases); working to "Intensify antiwar organizing"; and working to "Organize local projects aimed at combating white racism, and the hysteria that is liable to flow from it this summer."

On antiwar organizing the only things specified were the production of fact sheets each week emphasizing that the war wasn't over, and "an emergency demonstration plan in event of escalation or if the talks are broken off."

This program confirmed the worst fears of the YSAers, not for what it included, which was too vague to have any practical meaning anyway, but for what it left out—mass mobilizations against the Vietnam War.

Meanwhile, the discussions proceeded in antiwar groups across the country, and dozens of letters and resolutions objecting to the actions of the May 16 working committee were coming into New York. From Berkeley came a resolution passed by the official student senate June 3, which did not mention the dispute in the SMC directly, but declared:

WHEREAS, the war in Vietnam being waged by the United States government is an imperialist war;

31. SMC mailing, May 20, 1968. Signed by Linda Morse, executive secretary, and four national coordinators: Clark Lobenstine, Phyllis Kalb, Gwen Patton, and Leslie Cagan. (Copy in author's files.)

WHEREAS, the war in Vietnam has resulted in more than 150,000 GIs killed and wounded;

WHEREAS, the war expenditures are needed for humanitarian projects such as the elimination of poverty, sickness and illiteracy;

WHEREAS, it must be demonstrated in mass street actions that the mass of American people are against the war;

NOTING, that the antiwar movement has been built through democratic national conventions to call antiwar demonstrations and decide policy questions;

AND FURTHER NOTING, the antiwar movement has also been built on the basis of non-exclusion;

BE IT RESOLVED, the Student Senate of the Associated Students of the University of California declares its opposition to the war;

DEMANDS, the immediate withdrawal of U.S. troops from Vietnam;

DECLARES, its support for mass demonstrations such as those on April 15, 1967; October 21, 1967; April 26, 1968; and April 27, 1968;

DECLARES, its support for the antiwar coalition responsible for calling and coordinating these actions on the national level, the Student Mobilization Committee;

DECLARES, its support for the fundamental foundation of the antiwar movement, non-exclusion in membership and democracy in decision making.[32]

The YSA itself never presented the "YSA line" on the antiwar movement more clearly. It is difficult to avoid the conclusion that the YSAers at Berkeley had something to do with this resolution, but no one ever claimed that the YSA dominated the Berkeley student senate, least of all the YSA's detractors. Dawson promptly made copies and mailed them around the country.

The SMC continuations committee meeting on June 29 was held in the ballroom of the old Hotel Diplomat in midtown Manhattan. Some 400 observers and delegates from campus committees across the country attended.

I was one of the observers, as was Jerry Rubin, who came with a small group of other Yippies.[33] Jerry and I were always friendly

32. Resolution of the Senate of the Associated Students of the University of California at Berkeley, June 3, 1968. (Copy in author's files.)

33. Yippies: the Youth International Party, a countercultural group formed by Jerry Rubin, Abbie Hoffman, and others earlier in 1968. It claimed to be running a pig for president of the United States.

to one another but we were rooting for different sides in this arena. I had no idea how it would come out. I knew that Dawson did not expect a resolution of all the issues at this meeting. She was hoping for a reversal of the firings and the calling of a full conference.

From looking around I guessed the two sides were fairly evenly matched in numbers, with the Morse group, which called itself the Independent Caucus, heavily represented by New Yorkers, and the Dawson group, called the Antiwar Action Caucus, perhaps stronger from the outlying areas. But I guessed a large number present were confused and undecided, and these would make the difference. I expected to listen to a full day of serious discussion. But the showdown came quicker than anyone expected.

It started off quietly enough. An impartial chairman, Myron Shapiro of Veterans and Reservists to End the War in Vietnam, was agreed to. It was obvious there was going to be some questioning of credentials of voting delegates, so a motion was made and passed to elect a credentials committee by regional caucus, to be convened when the first substantive vote was called.

There followed a couple of hours of discussion on procedural matters, on the firings, and on the principle of nonexclusion. There had not yet been any discussion on the perspectives of the SMC when a vote was called on some point. The chair recessed the meeting for the election of the credentials committee and a recommendation on voting.

The delegates divided into regions and elected one representative for each area. In the New York regional caucus the vote was so close it had to be taken three times. Finally, Maris Cakers of the Workshop in Nonviolence won against Kipp Dawson. Then the six members of the credentials committee met while the rest of the meeting killed time.

In the committee it quickly became apparent that Cakers was outnumbered. As a matter of fact, all the others were YSAers. Maris was shocked, and accused the YSA of packing the committee and the conference. Actually, according to a YSA caucus report when the conference was over, about ninety of the delegates were members of the YSA, a substantial bloc but by no means a majority. The fact is, the Independent Caucus was very weak outside of the New York region, and the YSAers tended to be prominent activists in committees around the country. In the regional caucuses they were strong candidates anyway, and the

YSAers voted en bloc. It just came out that way. But it didn't look good. One of the YSAers on the committee felt so bad he sided with Cakers on the spot. That made it four to two.

The majority of the credentials committee questioned the legitimacy of a host of votes from New York, especially claims by single delegates that they should be able to cast multiple votes they said had been given them by proxy. Unable to resolve this, the majority then decided to propose to the body simply to accept all delegates who were present. Cakers requested a minority report.

No vote was ever taken on the credentials committee reports, and to this day I don't know how it would have come out. In his report Cakers described the composition of the credentials committee as indicating that the YSA had packed the conference. There followed some sharp discussion. Suddenly Linda Morse took the microphone and called for a walkout of the "independents." A sort of march around the room began, gathering forces, with Rubin and the Yippies lighting firecrackers and throwing them here and there. Some of the marchers started chanting: "Up Against the Wall, YSA!" Spontaneously, from the other side, the chant began: "Bring the Troops Home Now!"

For what seemed like a very long moment, "Up Against the Wall" competed with "Bring the Troops Home Now." Then and there, the walkout lost any chance for a majority. It was hardly a reasoned discussion, but the politics were clear enough for most of the undecided.

*          *          *

At the utmost, perhaps a third of the delegates walked out. Those remaining proceeded with the agenda. Outside the hall Linda Morse passed a sheet around among those who walked out, and she later said that eighty-five had signed. That night the walkout group held a meeting in a church near Washington Square. I dropped by to observe. There were about sixty-five people present. The meeting had already excluded a few YSAers who had also gone there. A motion was made to exclude me from the hall as well, but that was a bit much for the majority of those present and the motion was defeated. After that they stopped excluding people. I said nothing, just observed. They were clearly unsure of themselves, but seemed somehow greatly relieved to be done with the SMC. Nothing was decided that night and they met again the next morning. They made some vague plans for a new multi-issue organization to be established later after a summer of groundwork, and constituted themselves the Radical Organizing Committee (ROC) with an office in Philadelphia.

A delegation from the SMC continuations committee headed by Howard Petrick and Robin Maisel appeared at this meeting to offer cooperation on whatever level possible in antiwar activity. They suggested that whatever multi-issue program ROC adopted for its own activities, it could still affiliate with the SMC and join in mass antiwar activities as well. This delegation was received politely, but coolly. No action was taken on its suggestions.

\*            \*            \*

The story went around that Linda Morse later described the walkout to Irving Beinin of the *Guardian,* a consistent advocate of the multi-issue perspective for the antiwar coalitions. He shook his head sadly and said: "You have just succeeded in snatching defeat from the jaws of victory."

ROC itself never got off the ground. It set up an office in Philadelphia which closed after a short time. Linda Morse went back on the staff of the New York Parade Committee, and ROC simply disappeared by the end of August.

\*            \*            \*

Meanwhile, the SMC continuations committee meeting rescinded the firings of Dawson and Stapleton, reaffirmed the principle of political nonexclusion, and the central task of the SMC as mobilizing mass actions against the war. It declared the next main SMC task to be building actions already called around Hiroshima Day in August, and called a national SMC conference for the first weekend in September.

\*            \*            \*

That night, after the continuations committee meeting was over, there was a YSA caucus meeting, which I also observed, to go over what had happened. The spirits were good and there was a determined mood. But it was hardly a victory celebration. The YSA was now the only major radical youth group supporting the SMC. The accusations of YSA domination could be expected to increase, and the pull of unity would be gone, at least for a while. The pressures of the elections and illusions in the negotiations would make the next period very difficult. Speaker after speaker carefully explained that even though the other radical groups were no longer in, the door should be left wide open, the YSA should not make the mistake of using its weight in the SMC to turn it into a socialist group. In spite of the mood of the so-called new left milieu, the sentiment against the war was still rising among ordinary people, and that's what the SMC should be geared to. Sooner or later, the illusions in the government's tricks would be shattered, and mass response could be expected to calls for action. In the meantime the YSA would have to switch some people from other assignments to do everything it could to help keep the SMC alive.

It would be guided by the policy resolution adopted by the continuations committee meeting that declared:

We emphatically reaffirm the basic political position of the antiwar movement—for immediate and unconditional withdrawal of U.S. troops from Vietnam. The Vietnamese have the right to determine their own future. American imperialism has no rights in Vietnam. It has absolutely nothing to negotiate there.

The Paris negotiations are being used by Washington as a screen for further escalation of the war. The negotiations are meant to disorient the antiwar movement in an election year. We will not fall for this ruse. We will retain our independence and continue our mass actions demanding withdrawal of troops.

The Vietnamese, of course, have every right to use the negotiations as they see fit. But our duty, as Americans committed to self-determination for Vietnam, is to press all the more tenaciously to bring the GIs home.

We reject any action that would lend credence to the U.S. role in the Paris negotiations. Our job is to expose Washington's war aims, not to try to convince the warmakers that if they were just a little more reasonable their aims could be negotiated. . . .[34]

34. *Militant,* July 12, 1968.

# 15

## The Chicago Democratic Party Convention Demonstrations

The California primary on June 6, 1968, resulted in a victory for Robert F. Kennedy, which would have given him an excellent chance at winning the Democratic Party nomination for president. But he was assassinated the night of the primary. It soon became apparent that Vice President Hubert Humphrey was the choice of the major elements of the Democratic Party machine. McCarthy was still a candidate but considered to have little chance. The major ambiguity that had faced the Lake Villa conference, then, was pretty well cleared up by mid-June. Nevertheless, there was no widespread agreement among the antiwar forces about demonstrating at the Democratic Party convention.

Dellinger, Bob Greenblatt, Rennie Davis, and Tom Hayden, who were actually running the National Mobilization Committee at the time, were still very anxious for a series of multi-issue demonstrations at the convention.

The SWP and the YSA were now opposed to demonstrating at the Democratic Party convention. What had changed their attitude was the declination of Johnson. In their view the whole idea had been to take advantage of the appearance of Johnson, who was a major symbol of the war. But after Johnson's withdrawal there would be no such clear focus and any demonstrations by the antiwar movement at the convention would be seen as support to the doves within the Democratic Party, in particular as pro-McCarthy demonstrations. On principle the SWP and the YSA wanted nothing to do with supporting any Democrat or Republican for public office, and they opposed the antiwar movement being co-opted to reform of the Democratic Party.

It would be better, said the YSA, for the antiwar movement to concentrate on organizing demonstrations around Hiroshima Day and in the fall. This position was presented at the SMC continuations committee meeting on June 29 and it passed. (It is anybody's guess whether it would have carried if there had been a full SMC conference and no walkout.)

The moderate forces, like Women Strike for Peace and the local SANE chapters, were generally heavily involved in the McCarthy campaign. They were not necessarily against demonstrations at the Democratic Party convention, but they viewed them precisely as pro-McCarthy efforts and attempts to influence the platform of the Democratic Party. To be effective in that sense, however, the demonstrations would have to be orderly.

This approach was in some respects in sharp contrast to that of Jerry Rubin, Abbie Hoffman, the rest of the Yippies, and other ultraleft and anarchist-type forces attracted to the Chicago actions. For months Rubin had been going around speaking publicly in deliberately outrageous terms about what might happen in Chicago. For example, in a public debate with me, before Johnson declined, Rubin presented a scenario as follows.

The time: August, 1968. The place: Chicago. Chicago is in panic. The American Youth Festival has brought 500,000 young people to Chicago to camp out, smoke pot, dance to wild music, burn draft cards and roar like wild bands through the streets, forcing the President to bring troops back from Vietnam to keep order in the city while he is nominated under the protection of tear gas and bayonets.[1]

My reply was, if the leaders of the demonstrations talked like that, there would be no chance of getting a half-million demonstrators to Chicago, or anything more than a few thousand.

Rubin also frequently articulated the theory of provoked repression—which was not unique to him. In the same debate he told the audience:

Repression turns demonstration protests into wars. Actors into heroes. Masses of individuals into a community. Repression eliminates the bystander, the neutral observer, the theorist. It forces everyone to pick a side. A movement cannot grow without repression. The Left needs an attack from the Right and the Center. Life is theater, and we are the guerrillas attacking the shrines of authority, from the priests and the

1. *Militant*, January 8, 1968.

holy dollar to the two-party system. Zapping people's minds and putting them through changes in actions in which everyone is emotionally involved. The street is the stage. You are the star of the show. And everything you were once taught is up for grabs.

Though the motivations of Dellinger and Rubin were not identical, their approaches had a lot in common, and neither one changed his mind in the least regarding Chicago after Johnson's declination. For them the tactics dominated over the politics, or rather the tactics had *become* the politics. The same was more or less true of Rennie Davis. Davis, however, had practical organizational talent and much of the detail rested on his shoulders.

Tom Hayden stood between the moderate, pro-McCarthy forces and those bent on confrontation, or, to be more accurate, he viewed the one approach as complementary to the other.

(It was later revealed that, as the demonstrations came near, he sought an arrangement with McCarthy's campaign. The nomination of the presidential candidate was scheduled for Wednesday, August 28. According to Sam Brown, who was on McCarthy's staff, "Hayden suggested . . . that if McCarthy appeared to have a good chance by Monday or Tuesday—and if that chance might be hampered by public activity [the demonstrations]—then we could meet to decide whether to go ahead with the public activity.")[2]

Hayden personified the betrayed liberal turned enraged ultra-left, a not uncommon phenomenon in those days. Such people, for all their inflamed rhetoric, never became revolutionary in the sense of seeking to build a new power that could effectively challenge the old, but looked throughout to the Establishment liberals, and the Democratic Party in particular, as the real source of power for change. Their object seemed to be to shock, or threaten, or frighten the ruling circles—particularly in the Democratic Party—into changing their ways. They were therefore inclined to advocate superficially shocking acts. Occasionally I would lose my temper in movement discussions and refer to this approach as the "spoiled brat syndrome of politics," like children creating a mess so their parents would pay attention to them. Those in this frenzied frame of mind had broad common political ground with the moderate groups in the antiwar movement but were often at odds with them on the level of tactics. (The

2. *Washington Post*, January 22, 1970.

relationship between the SWP and the moderate groups was generally the other way around.)

In all probability it would have been impossible to reconcile the differences that existed at a large conference, even among those who favored demonstrations at the Democratic Party convention. As it turned out there never was a conference which decided upon, and called, those demonstrations. Dellinger, Greenblatt, and Hayden simply held a steering committee meeting and authorized themselves to hold press conferences calling the demonstrations in the name of the National Mobilization Committee.

The only record I have found of this meeting is a coordinator's report by Bob Greenblatt which describes the actions taken, but not those in attendance beyond Greenblatt, Dellinger, and Hayden. According to this document, both the meeting and the public announcements—by Rennie Davis in Chicago and Dellinger and Hayden in New York—took place on the same day, June 29. (Perhaps coincidentally, perhaps not, this was the same day as the walkout from the SMC.)

The same steering committee meeting also set July 20 "as the time for a full meeting of the Administrative Committee in order to make further decisions about the political and strategic nature of the Chicago demonstrations."[3] But the administrative committee was presented with a *fait accompli* as far as the initial public announcement of the demonstrations was concerned.

The July 20 meeting, held in Cleveland and attended by about seventy-five people, was fairly broad as administrative committee meetings went. Representatives of the major elements of the coalition were there. Lew Jones debated Tom Hayden, but the YSA objections to the demonstrations were brushed aside. The SWP and the YSA were badly isolated at this meeting, and all they could do was make the record. For one thing, they found themselves in the uncomfortable position of opposing an action. But more important, the majority simply didn't agree with their objections. The moderates favored the demonstrations precisely because they would be seen as pro-McCarthy. Many of the others were either not really against being seen as pro-McCarthy, or considered that an unimportant consideration, which could be

---

3. "National Mobilization Committee Coordinator's Report," by Robert Greenblatt, undated. (Copy in author's files.)

overcome by simply declaring that the demonstrations were in support of issues, not candidates.

While Dellinger insisted on such a declaration, he tended to straddle the McCarthy question, considering the chance for a confrontation to be the important thing. For example, in a public statement printed in the *Chicago Tribune* he wrote:

> In relation to the McCarthy candidacy, it is doubtful that McCarthy would have adopted his mildly antiwar position, would have entered the New Hampshire primaries or would have received sufficient support to have kept his candidacy somewhat viable, except for the turmoil and pressures created by the teach-ins, street demonstrations and active resistance. To abandon these tactics now would cut down the Movement's leverage and weaken McCarthy's bargaining power. . . . The Movement's power comes from those who refuse to be drafted, refuse to pay war taxes, desert or refuse orders in the Army, fill the streets, occupy buildings at Columbia, etc. Any candidate who is worthy of our support had better have plenty of such "troops" visible if he is to be taken seriously before or after election. Given the history of previous peace candidates, we shall need *more* troops. The future will determine whether we need them to support a McCarthy, to keep him honest or to combat him.[4]

The July 20 meeting approved the plans as outlined by Hayden and Davis for the Chicago demonstration. But these were fairly vague and did not resolve the tensions between the moderate groups and the ultralefts. What is more, there was little countervailing influence in the Mobilization staff, since neither the SWP nor the moderate groups had been represented there for several months. The Rubinesque rhetoric had far freer play than before the Pentagon march.

As the demonstrations approached, the moderate groups, as well as some of the pacifists, took their distance from the actions. What is more, the McCarthy campaign canceled most of its own plans for activities outside the convention, and McCarthy himself appealed for his followers not to come to Chicago for demonstrations.

One reason for this may have been that the McCarthy campaign had gotten wind of how Chicago's Mayor Richard Daley—a key figure in the Democratic Party and a strong Humphrey backer—intended to deal with the demonstrators.

4. *Chicago Tribune*, August 9, 1968.

Consequently, the turnout for the demonstrations was far smaller than anyone had predicted, perhaps 15,000 all told, and only some 10,000 on hand for the largest single gathering. This was in the face of the fact that beforehand the Mobe announced it was making housing arrangements for 50,000 and printing up 100,000 copies of a demonstrators' guide, while the Mobe applications for permits had estimated 150,000.

On Sunday, August 25, the day before the convention opened, a rally of 5,000 youthful supporters welcomed McCarthy to town. This rally was not sponsored by the Mobe and the only mention of opposition to the war at this affair was in several thousand leaflets distributed by the SMC, advertising one of its meetings. The same day there was the first of a series of workshops and movement centers around town called by National Mobe, in which different groups discussed whatever they wanted and made plans for various street actions. Several of the largest of these workshops took place at Lincoln Park near the Old Town section of the near north side.

The Yippies had previously announced a camp-in in Lincoln Park as part of their "Festival of Life," but the authorities had refused a permit. At 11:00 p.m. police announced over bullhorns the closing of the park. Some 1,500 persons had gathered there by shortly after midnight when the cops moved in. The police used tear gas and clubs, and threw people in the park pond. A number of newsmen were targets of police attack. Gas wafted over into Old Town, an area of cafes and shops frequented by student-aged youth, while the police moved through the area roughing up people who looked like hippies or demonstrators. Taunted by shouts of "pig" and greeted with occasional missiles, they responded by indiscriminate clubbings. This scene was repeated Monday night, and that pretty much set the tone for the rest of the week. According to a later report drawn up by a team of investigators under the direction of Daniel Walker, then president of the Chicago Crime Commission, "To read dispassionately the hundreds of statements describing at first hand the events of Sunday and Monday nights is to become convinced of the presence of what can only be called a police riot."[5]

During the daylight hours of Monday and Tuesday there were several marches, ranging from a few hundred to 1,500 persons or

5. *Rights in Conflict*, a study directed by Daniel Walker. Quoted from *Life*, December 6, 1968.

so. Some were peaceful and some involved scuffles and a few arrests. But they were followed by general police thumping of youths, including bystanders, in the Old Town area after dark, as well as sweeps of the park after closing hour. On Monday and Tuesday night the demonstrators built makeshift barricades in the park and tried to hold their ground at least for a time.

None of the demonstrations got anywhere near the Amphitheatre where the convention was being held, which was about four miles southwest of the Loop at Halsted and Forty-third streets. A thirty-block area around the Amphitheatre was sealed off by chain-link fence and police checkpoints. National guardsmen were encamped in several parks nearby. The city administration had refused all permits to march to the Amphitheatre. Prefabricated plywood walls were set up along some approaching routes, apparently so the delegates coming from the Loop hotels to the convention couldn't see parts of Chicago's slums.

On Wednesday, August 28, the day of the nomination, some 10,000 demonstrators gathered at a National Mobe rally in the bandshell area of Grant Park, a mile or so south of the center of the Loop. The rally was orderly until a young man lowered the American flag from a flagpole. Some cops moved to arrest him and were heckled by members of the crowd seated in that area. Seizing on this incident, a phalanx of about forty cops waded into that part of the crowd, clubbing freely. People scrambled out of the way, desperately climbing over overturned benches. Some were hurt. Another part of the crowd began to face off at the police.

Rennie Davis, who unlike Rubin was inclined to be in the thick of things even after they got sticky, moved with a line of marshals between the crowd and the cops, facing the crowd and trying to get people back in their seats. Some of the cops charged again and Davis was clubbed from behind and knocked unconscious.

At this point it is necessary to set the geographical scene. Grant Park lies between Lake Michigan on the east and Michigan Avenue on the west. Across Michigan Avenue from the park are hotels where many delegates were staying and where convention caucusing was going on. The strip of park directly on Michigan Avenue is separated from the rest—including the bandshell area—by a deep railroad channel which must be crossed by bridges.

Dellinger wanted to lead a nonviolent march from the rally

across the nearest bridges, then south on Michigan Avenue toward the Amphitheatre. This route would not have taken the marchers directly in front of the convention hotels, since they would have emerged onto Michigan Avenue somewhat south of the hotel area.

He proposed that the crowd divide into two parts: those who were willing to face arrest would march to the Amphitheatre, and those who did not could either go north through the park or disperse. As the march to the Amphitheatre moved west it found the bridges blocked by police and National Guard units, including military vehicles with racks of barbed wire attached to their fronts. Dellinger then started a sit-down.

Tom Hayden, however, had delivered an impassioned speech to the rally after Davis was knocked out, which was not entirely in line with Dellinger's plan. According to the *Chicago Daily News,* Hayden said:

> This city and the military machinery it has aimed at us won't permit us to protest in an organized fashion.
>
> Therefore we must move out of this park in groups throughout this city and turn this excited, overheated military machine against itself.
>
> Let us make sure that if blood flows, it flows all over the city; if they use gas against us, let's make sure they use gas against their own citizens.
>
> If the police run wild, let them run wild all over Chicago—not just over us sitting in the park. If they are going to disrupt us and our march, let them disrupt the whole city.[6]

Part of the crowd following Dellinger did not sit down. Some of them simply dispersed, especially after tear gas was used. But part of them swung around and joined the group moving north, making about 3,000.

They found each bridge blocked until they reached Monroe Drive, about a mile north, where they swarmed across. By coincidence at just that time a parade of about a hundred Blacks and a mule wagon, led by the Rev. Ralph Abernathy of the Southern Christian Leadership Conference, was coming south on Michigan Avenue. This group had a parade permit and a police escort. The crowd from Grant Park joined in a move south along with the mule wagon toward the hotels on Michigan Avenue.

Then the police made what would appear later as a first-class blunder. Instead of letting the march continue south on Michigan

6. *Chicago Daily News,* August 29, 1968.

Avenue, at least as far as some more isolated spot, they halted it in front of the Conrad Hilton, one of the main convention hotels, where a lot of McCarthy delegates were staying. Meanwhile another couple of thousand people, not all of them demonstrators, had gathered in the general area of the Hilton. Speakers in the crowd shouted to move on with the march. While TV cameras rolled, the cops waded in with clubs swinging.

Some of the action was later described in the Walker report:

A part of the crowd was trapped in front of the Conrad Hilton and pressed hard against a big plate-glass window of the Haymarket Lounge. A reporter who was sitting inside said, "Frightened men and women banged . . . against the window, that it might get knocked in. As I backed away a few feet I could see a smudge of blood on the glass outside."

With a sickening crack, the window shattered, and screaming men and women tumbled through, some cut badly by jagged glass. The police came after them.

"I was pushed through by the force of large numbers of people," one victim said. "I got a deep cut on my right leg, diagnosed later as a severed artery. . . . I fell to the floor of the bar. There were 10 to 20 people who had come through. . . . I could not stand on the leg. It was bleeding profusely.

"A squad of policemen burst into the bar, clubbing all those who looked to them like demonstrators."

The report described the beating by police outside the Hilton of a youth who looked about fifteen years old, and then continued:

A well-dressed woman saw this incident and spoke angrily to a nearby police captain. As she spoke, another policeman came up from behind her and sprayed something in her face with an aerosol can. He then clubbed her to the ground. He and two other policemen then dragged her along the ground to the same paddy wagon and threw her in.[7]

Meanwhile Dellinger and the group he was with had finally made it to the street in front of the Hilton. He remembers the scene as follows:

As I approached, several vans came up a side street and unloaded police reinforcements. The new arrivals jumped out of the vans and charged into the crowd, swinging their clubs and chanting, "Kill, kill, kill."

7. *Life*, December 6, 1968.

We had no sound system capable of reaching the crowd, no plan of action, no training of marshals (most of whom were scattered, arrested, or bleeding from previous assaults) adequate for the occasion. All day long I had felt betrayed by the absence of most of the movement's pacifist leadership, some of whom had stayed away from Chicago altogether, some of whom had engaged in a small, separatist "pacifist action" the day before, aloof from the major dynamics of the week's struggle. Meanwhile a number of the more vocal, visible leaders had been arguing for several hours that "This is the end of nonviolence in America. It simply won't work anymore." I felt completely defeated by the situation, incapable of doing anything useful.

I shall never forget the spontaneous actions of the demonstrators. Of course, some rocks flew and some fists went into action in attempts to ward off the attackers—desperate acts of angry self-defense. But mainly the protestors parried the blows while retreating slowly and in remarkably good order, then surged forward again as each police attack momentarily spent itself. . . . It took a long time to push us back, to clear the streets for a couple of blocks. And when the streets were finally cleared and lined with police, the demonstrators were still there, massed on the grass across from the hotels, chanting antiwar slogans, singing movement songs, shouting to the delegates.[8]

Meanwhile, back at the convention, Humphrey had been nominated, McCarthy defeated, and a number of the delegates had returned to their hotels, only to become swept up in the melee around the Hilton.

Mayor Daley would later complain that his administration and the Chicago police did not get sympathetic press and TV coverage from their actions of Wednesday night.

On Thursday, August 29, a crowd of some 5,000 gathered in the strip of park opposite the Hilton for another rally sponsored by National Mobe. According to the original schedule this was to have been a "massive People's Assembly to project the directions and tasks"[9] which were supposed to have developed out of the workshops and activities of the week. But McCarthy turned out to be the principal speaker.

Formally, the National Mobe rally was adjourned before McCarthy was introduced, but neither the major media nor the bulk of the crowd drew the fine distinction. The crowd gave

8. Dave Dellinger, *More Power Than We Know* (New York: Anchor Press, 1975), p. 186.
9. *Mobilizer*, August 15, 1968.

McCarthy a standing ovation, and he emerged as the martyr of the hour.

After McCarthy spoke, another attempt was made to march to the Amphitheatre. This time some 2,000 people led by Dick Gregory and Eric Weinberger, as well as a number of accredited delegates to the convention, made it as far as Michigan Avenue and Eighteenth Street where they were stopped by police and National Guard units. Only delegates would be allowed beyond this point, they were told.

About twenty-five of the delegates, including columnist Murray Kempton, removed their badges, moved forward with Gregory and some fifty others, and submitted to arrest. Then police and guardsmen tear-gassed the rest of the crowd and chased it north, back toward the Hilton and Grant Park, where sporadic demonstrating and attacks by the police and National Guard continued until early morning.

About 5:00 a.m. Friday, police raided a suite on an upper floor of the Hilton rented by John Kenneth Galbraith and others and used as a McCarthy headquarters. (The cops claimed that ever since Wednesday night people in the hotel had been throwing ashtrays, beer cans, and other things out the windows at them, and that they had pinpointed this suite as a source of such missiles.) The last of the demonstrators were leaving the street by 8:30 in the morning. The Chicago Democratic Party demonstrations were over.

Some 660 people had been arrested in connection with the actions, probably over 1,000 injured, and one killed. He was Dean Johnson, a seventeen-year-old Native American from South Dakota who was in Old Town when the police made a sweep. He allegedly drew a gun on them and was shot down.

\*     \*     \*

There was enormous publicity around these demonstrations, both in the United States and worldwide. Millions of people watched the police attack at the Hilton Wednesday night on TV. Some twenty-two newsmen, including reporters from such prestigious media as Associated Press, United Press International, the *Washington Post,* and *Business Week,* accused the police of assaulting them, and in the early reports at least, the Daly administration did not get a good press. Daly himself played an important role in the convention, and the controlling machine within the Democratic Party came off with a black eye.

An article in the *Chicago Daily News* declared:

> The antiwar "movement" came to Chicago, hoping to establish in the public's mind, that the nation's ruling party is plagued by a militaristic over-reaction—at home and abroad.
>
> And while their heads are bloodied, they may have succeeded—with an unexpected boost from Mayor Richard J. Daley and the Chicago police.
>
> The "medium became the message" as their threats of massive demonstrations against militarism elicited the largest display of military force in the history of political conventions. Even the TV commentators and liberal delegates have dubbed this convention city a "police state."[10]

In that sense the leadership of the action counted it a victory, and were at first euphoric. Not for nothing did Rubin have a reputation for exploiting the publicity media. But the antiwar movement itself was in something of a shambles, badly divided, and that part of it which had organized this action soon entered a prolonged crisis.

Years later Dellinger would write:

> Despite the small turnout for the convention protests, the government partially saved us when it decided to withhold permits and to turn loose the Chicago police. . . .
>
> There was a limit, however, to how far a repressive government and rampaging police could save a movement that was as divided and confused as we were. They could save us from immediate public embarrassment, even cause a temporary outpouring of sympathy in our behalf, but they could not heal our internal wounds. In practice they exacerbated them. They helped create a movement mystique of revolutionary derring-do and heroic street encounters as goals in themselves. This polarized the movement around the question of street violence and gradually led to a tragic separation between the organized movement and large sections of the antiwar public. Although the immediate result of the Chicago police riots was to increase antiwar sentiment, the long-run effect was to make it more difficult for that sentiment to express itself in an organized, effective fashion.[11]

When Dellinger speaks here of "a tragic separation between the organized movement and large sections of the antiwar public," he

10. *Chicago Daily News,* August 29, 1968.
11. Dellinger, *More Power Than We Know,* p. 125.

is—consciously or not—referring to only a part of the "organized movement," the part that at the time of Chicago he considered most important. This included the de facto current leadership of National Mobe, a group of graduate SDSers, and the current SDS leadership and milieu. All these were deeply involved in the Chicago actions.

When Rennie Davis and Tom Hayden set up the Chicago operation they enlisted the efforts of a number of graduate SDSers, including Kathy Boudin, John Froines, Carol Glassman, Vernon Grizzard, Paul Potter, Jeff Shero, and Lee Webb. Much of the work involved in the Chicago actions was done by this force. Carl Oglesby also played a certain role through the SDS national office, for which he still worked.

The new SDS leadership, elected at the East Lansing convention in June, included Mike Klonsky as national secretary and Bernardine Dohrn as inter-organizational secretary. Both had recently announced themselves as "revolutionaries."

The SDS national office at first opposed the Chicago actions, in part because it rejected antiwar demonstrations and in part because it rejected McCarthy and electoral politics in general. But as the demonstrations approached, the SDS leadership became attracted, precisely because the publicity of confrontation was building. They decided to mobilize several hundred SDSers to come to Chicago as organizers to try to recruit among the large number of McCarthy youth expected to attend. They set up several workshops, the largest in the Old Town area, and found themselves in the thick of the confrontations when they occurred. They were enraptured by the whole experience, particularly by the fact that a certain number of ordinary Black and white Chicago youth, looking for adventure or angered at the police riot in their haunts, became involved in the street fighting.

The SDS leaders exaggerated this and drew the most romanticized conclusions from it. At the Grant Park rallies both Mike Klonsky and Jeff Jones, a leader of the New York regional office, declared that a new revolutionary force had been tapped and the way to organize it was to get into more such street action. The September 9 issue of *New Left Notes* carried a wall poster which made the same point, along with an outline of street fighting techniques, and even suggested that it might be possible to expose the national election the way they felt they had succeeded in exposing the Democratic Party convention.

At the time, Dellinger himself considered the Chicago demonstrations to be a victory, though he noted and warned against a tendency among some of the leading participants to draw conclusions that were deeply disturbing to him.

We came off well in Chicago [he wrote shortly after the events]. It was a clear-cut victory because the police acted abominably and our people showed courage, aggressiveness and a proper sense of values. But if street fighting breaks out when the police are restrained and if we act contemptuously of other people's rights, the sentiments of those who should be our allies could turn against us. More important, we will begin to lose sight of our objectives and develop a Movement style that attracts lovers of violence rather than lovers of justice and brotherhood. . . .

There is of course a delicate line to be drawn here. The war makers would like nothing better than to carry on "business as usual," challenged only by token dissent and static demonstrations. . . . But to be effective, disruption and disorder must be discriminating and purposeful.[12]

Once again we come to the problem that Dellinger had wrestled with in the Pentagon march and which still occupied much of his attention. He rejected the mass action approach of the SMC as "token" and "static." Perhaps he did not agree that under the given circumstances demonstrations had to be orderly to be massive. But in any case he considered the mass aspect to be less important than the disruption, and tended to sacrifice the one for the other. He viewed the SDS milieu, which was attracted to disruption, as very important.

But to that milieu the "delicate line" essential to Dellinger's disruptive nonviolence was becoming more and more difficult to draw. What was involved here on the movement side was not real violence. There was very little of that during or even after Chicago. What was involved was provocative rhetoric and romantic fantasies about reliving in the modern United States the guerrilla warfare experiences of some colonial revolutions. Thus removed from reality, a "movement style" of escalating rhetoric developed which fed on itself, contributing to a more and more sectarian syndrome.

Dellinger tried to counter this after his fashion, but in my view he had a fantasy of his own. In his October 1968 article analyzing the Chicago events he said:

"Our aim is to destroy power, dissipate it, decentralize it,

12. *Liberation,* October 1968.

democratize it if you will. This process must begin here and now in the organizations and institutions which we set up as training centers and pilot projects for the new society."[13] As if the time had come for pure anarchy. Unfortunately this approach was far more effective in dissolving the authority of the National Mobilization Committee than that of the government. Dellinger's concept of democracy did not include the formalities, and his concept of struggle did not include organizational discipline. What materialized in life was the transformation of the National Mobilization Committee from a broad coalition into a name used by a self-appointed group of prominent figures with an organizational norm of do-your-own-thing.

Dellinger attempted to influence the SDS milieu by accommodating to its mood, and by having National Mobe call actions designed to attract SDS toward nonviolent resistance. It didn't work. The denouement would unwind in the course of the next year and would not be without its element of tragedy. But all this concerned only a part of the organized movement.

*     *     *

Other parts of the antiwar movement drew different conclusions from the Chicago actions. Lew Jones commented in a report to a joint SWP-YSA meeting:

> It's important to see this demonstration [Chicago] in the context of the history of the struggle within the antiwar movement for a line. . . . There are essentially two alternative lines before the antiwar movement. Our line says that around two or three simple themes, such as end the war, bring the GIs home now, the movement should go out and mobilize people into mass actions in the streets. The other line, which Dellinger has more and more deepened and tried to organize around, is the idea that what is necessary is to get small brigades of youth, confront armed authority, by doing that expose the real nature of the system, and by doing that masses of people are influenced. It's the so-called spark theory. That's what was really involved in this demonstration. . . .
>
> Now, what do we say to people about this demonstration? First, we condemn the Daley machine up and down for being brutal, suppressing every notion of civil liberties with the most brutal police methods. Secondly, we solidarize with those youth there on their civil liberties.

13. Ibid.

But. . . . more of these kinds of demonstrations are not going to radicalize people. On the contrary, it will have a demoralizing effect and it will turn out to be a self-fulfilling prophecy about repression in this country.[14]

The Student Mobilization Committee held a conference in Chicago on August 31–September 1, immediately after the Democratic Party convention demonstrations. Only about 300 youth were present. A significant number of these were former McCarthy supporters, some of them nursing wounds from police attacks of the previous week. None of the major radical groups outside the YSA were present. This showed the effect of the walkout from the SMC as well as the general state of disarray of the organized antiwar movement after the Chicago demonstrations.

The conference called for fall antiwar actions the week of October 21-27 with mass demonstrations on October 26. This timing was set, partly because groups in other countries had already scheduled activities against the war in Vietnam in that period. The most significant of these were to be in Japan, where a number of Japanese peace groups and the major trade union federation, SOHYO, had called for an antiwar strike on October 21, and England, where the British Vietnam Solidarity Campaign was preparing for a mass demonstration on October 27.

Linda Morse appeared at the workshop where this proposal was discussed. On behalf of the National Mobilization Committee office she requested that specific dates not be set for the fall actions. National Mobe would be meeting in a few weeks, she said, and it would be better to wait to set dates at the meeting. The conference adopted the call anyway, with the proviso that the SMC would give serious attention to any proposals that came out of the National Mobe meeting.

The SMC conference reflected optimism in spite of the organizational difficulties. It was obvious that antiwar sentiment in the country as a whole had never been greater. For the first time, a panel of active-duty GIs and recent veterans was part of the program and the whole conference discussed for several hours the problem of effective approaches to GIs by the antiwar movement.

14. Report on the Democratic Party convention demonstration to a joint meeting of the SWP and YSA in New York, September 4, 1968, by Lew Jones. (Copy in author's files.)

The panel included Pvt. Steve Dash, Sp/4 Sherman Sitrin, Howard Petrick, and Vietnam veterans Ron Alexander and Bob Wilkinson. The fall action proposal emphasized the growing antiwar sentiment and activity among GIs and declared:

> The GIs are an important ally for the movement, have a constitutional right to oppose the war in words and deeds, have more reason than anyone else to oppose the war, and can be reached and won over to an antiwar position. . . . The fight for immediate withdrawal of U.S. troops from Vietnam, against the draft, against campus complicity with the war and in solidarity with American soldiers can be built on an unprecedented scale.[15]

The conference also moved the national office of the SMC from New York to Chicago. The move was precipitated by the fact that the SMC had been told to leave the office space it shared with the New York Parade Committee. Part of the majority that voted this demand did so because they supported the walkout; others because they just didn't want to be involved in the tensions around the split. The New York SMC continued to be represented on the Parade Committee, but the incident was another indication of the coldness the SMC now faced from much of the organized radical milieu. A few prominent figures, however, demonstratively supported the SMC. Dr. Otto Nathan, Ruth Gage-Colby, who was the United Nations correspondent of the Women's International League for Peace and Freedom, and Harlem attorney Florynce Kennedy signed a special SMC fund appeal.

The program adopted by the SMC conference was not designed to accommodate to the concerns of the radical milieu as such and least of all to the latest fashion in SDS. It was designed to appeal to, and mobilize, the increasing antiwar sentiment in the general youth population. The organizational limitations and isolation now imposed on the SMC, however, would make it impossible to accomplish more than a bare beginning in that direction in the course of the fall actions.

A Chicago-area working committee was set up and the conference approved four staff members: Syd Stapleton, Tom Kozden,

---

15. "SMC Working Committee Action Proposal," August 30, 1968. (Copy in author's files.)

Howard Petrick, and Michael Maggi. All but Kozden were also members of the YSA, not because the YSA wanted it that way, but because nobody else would take on the job. One of the first projects the new Chicago SMC office threw itself into was helping to mount a mass demonstration in Chicago within a month to protest the police suppression of dissent, and to reestablish the right to demonstrate against the war.

\*       \*       \*

The Chicago Peace Council had supported the convention demonstrations but was only nominally involved in their leadership. Immediately afterward, however, the National Mobe office was more or less inoperative from a combination of exhaustion and euphoria, SDS was fantasizing about organizing street gangs into guerrillas, and a lot of the cleanup fell to the Peace Council. Sylvia Kushner, an old-time CPer who was the central person on the Peace Council staff, made sure lawyers were found, bail was put up, transportation arranged for people stranded without funds, and so on. Kushner and others on the Peace Council understood that armies that leave their wounded lying around the battlefield undermine their own morale. Moreover, the Peace Council was going to have to continue operating in Chicago.

There was widespread feeling in antiwar and civil liberties circles in Chicago that the movement had to reassert the right to demonstrate as soon as possible. A series of informal meetings were held involving Kushner; Max Primack, also of the Peace Council; Michael Maggi and other SMC staffers; Sid Lens; and representatives of an ad hoc group called Citizens for a Free Chicago. This last was largely composed of civil libertarians and dissident Democrats interested in political reform in Chicago. These meetings planned a demonstration for September 28 which was built on the themes of withdrawal from Vietnam and opposition to police repression of dissent. The demands included amnesty for all those arrested in connection with the convention demonstrations.

Primack announced that the sponsors were applying for a permit to proceed down Michigan Avenue to a rally in Grant Park across from the Hilton, that the affair would be orderly, and that they would march, permit or no. The permit was granted.

Speakers included representatives of the Peace Council, the SMC, Vets for Peace, civil liberties and civil rights groups, the Black Panther Party, and political reformers. Neither the Chicago National Mobe office nor SDS bothered to build this demonstration. The National Mobilization Committee was represented among the speakers by Sid Lens, who was still one of its cochairmen and also active on the Peace Council.

Twenty-five thousand people participated in this demonstration, the largest antiwar gathering yet in Chicago. The crowd was overwhelmingly young, but included people in business suits, parents with children, nuns, priests, and even a few soldiers, sailors, and marines. The cops were on their good behavior that day, and the whole affair was without violence or arrests. It did not, of course, receive the avalanche of publicity of the events a month previous.

# 16

## The First Counterinaugural

One demand of the September 28, 1968, demonstration in Chicago was amnesty for a group of forty-three Black GIs at Fort Hood, Texas, who were facing court-martial for demonstrating against being sent to Chicago for riot duty during the Democratic Party convention. More than half of these GIs were veterans of Vietnam.

The background to the incident included the fact that units from Fort Hood had been sent to Chicago during the uprisings immediately following the assassination of Martin Luther King, Jr., in April. Shortly before the Democratic Party convention, troops at Fort Hood were again alerted for possible use in Chicago. Obviously the authorities feared that the demonstrations might precipitate another rebellion in the Black ghetto.

On the night of August 23-24, more than a hundred Black soldiers from the First Armored Cavalry Division gathered outdoors in a protest against being ordered to Chicago. The commanding general spoke to them at midnight, but many of them stayed where they were. In the morning MPs showed up and arrested forty-three. For whatever reason, the Fort Hood units were not sent to Chicago.

The case of the Fort Hood Forty-three received widespread publicity and support, especially in the Black community and the antiwar movement. The NAACP also provided legal aid. Eventually, twenty-six were convicted and given relatively light sentences, the longest being ten-months hard labor. This was in contrast to the six- and ten-year sentences given the year before to William Harvey and George Daniels, Black marines at Camp

Pendleton, California. During the Detroit uprising in the summer of 1967, Harvey and Daniels had called a meeting to discuss whether Black men should fight in Vietnam. When they and twelve other marines requested a hearing before their commander, the two were charged with insubordination, isolated, court-martialed, convicted, and sentenced. The case received little notice. But by August of 1968 the antiwar sentiment was widespread enough, and the contacts between GIs and various parts of the antiwar movement were sufficient, to make it very difficult for the military authorities to keep such incidents quiet.

When the Fort Hood Forty-three were arrested, there already existed an antiwar-oriented coffeehouse, the Oleo Strut, in Killeen, the town just off base, and a GI newspaper, *Fatigue Press,* published by GIs with the aid of civilians at the coffeehouse. The Black GIs who took part in the protest were not involved in this activity, but within hours of their arrest, the GIs who were had made contact with various antiwar organizations, helping to arrange lawyers, publicity, and so on.

The first of these GI coffeehouses near bases was set up late in 1967 by Fred Gardner and Donna Mickleson in Columbia, South Carolina, near Fort Jackson. Gardner, a former editor of the Harvard *Crimson,* had conceived the idea while on a tour of active duty as a reservist. The object was to provide something besides saloons or the semiofficial USOs, where GIs could hang out when off duty, meet students and other antiwar activists, and have available a certain amount of movement literature.

The Columbia coffeehouse was called the UFO. Gardner and others set up the Oleo Strut in 1968, and within the next year the coffeehouses spread, with various groups establishing them near bases across the country. These establishments were usually quite low-key, with little antiwar organizing taking place on the premises. In part this was because the coffeehouses were often subject to severe harassment by local officials, obviously acting in collusion with military authorities. There was also a certain tendency after a while for some of these coffeehouses to develop a kind of in-group atmosphere, to become hangouts for radicalized GIs who set themselves apart and had little confidence that their peers in the army were capable of organizing against the war. But the coffeehouses did provide some means for GIs at isolated bases to make contact with the antiwar movement, particularly in emergencies. The UFO and the Oleo Strut were among the more successful of these efforts.

An even more important development was the growth of antiwar GI newspapers. The first of these were published by civilians and aimed at GIs. The most influential in the early period was *Vietnam GI,* published in Chicago by Vietnam veteran Jeff Sharlet, who managed to accumulate a mailing list of thousands of GIs in Vietnam itself. Another was *Veterans Stars and Stripes for Peace,* also published in Chicago by the Veterans for Peace. Another was the *Bond,* originally put out in Berkeley and distributed by Berkeley radicals at bases in the area. After Bill Callison, the publisher, was arrested for draft resistance he gave the name and mailing list to Pvt. Andrew Stapp at Fort Sill, Oklahoma.

Stapp, with the aid of the Youth Against War and Fascism, was the founder of the American Servicemen's Union (ASU). He was given an undesirable discharge from the army in early 1968 for organizing, and he put out the *Bond* from New York as the organ of the ASU. The ASU was largely a one-man publicity operation, but the *Bond* was widely distributed. It developed a significant circulation and was published more consistently, and for a longer period, than any other antiwar GI paper.

By August 1968, papers published by GIs themselves on particular bases had begun to appear. *Fatigue Press* and *FTA* at Fort Knox, Kentucky, were among the first to make a go of it.

The spread of these papers was the more remarkable since the GIs who put them out were invariably subject to more or less severe harassment by the military brass or civilian authorities in collusion with them. It wasn't illegal for GIs to publish a newspaper, but it made enemies of people in a position to retaliate. Arbitrary transfers to break up the editorial boards of these papers were common and were among the milder countermeasures taken. Pvt. Bruce Peterson, the first editor of *Fatigue Press,* for example, was arrested in August 1968 and the lint in his pockets was sent to a laboratory which allegedly detected traces of marijuana. Marijuana was so widespread at Fort Hood at this time that the base was commonly referred to as "Fort Head." Yet Peterson was convicted of possession of an illegal drug and sentenced to eight years at hard labor. He served two years before being released on appeal.

GI organizing was no idle pastime. It didn't mix well with the "revolution for the hell of it" atmosphere of much of the countercultural milieu.

I was not present in Chicago for the Democratic Party convention demonstrations because I was on a trip overseas as the socialist candidate for U.S. president. The main reason for this trip was to talk to American GIs in South Vietnam. But I also stopped in Japan, and since Vietnam is halfway around the world from the United States, I returned by way of Europe and spoke to GIs in Germany.

In Japan I attended conferences of several Japanese antiwar groups, and was a little taken aback to find that a common approach among Japanese peace activists toward American GIs was to encourage them to desert. Helping GIs who had already deserted or who felt a moral imperative to do so was one thing, but encouraging antiwar GIs to desert was quite another. The practical effect would be a tendency to behead the movement inside the military services. An antiwar GI inside could spread the word to dozens and possibly hundreds of other GIs, but as a deserter he could do little or nothing beyond the initial publicity that some deserters managed to get. What is more, the penalties for desertion were very harsh.

A GI who deserted overseas in all probability would not be able to return to his country in the foreseeable future. His family would lose his allotment, and if they were dependent upon him they would be destitute. For these reasons and others, most ordinary GIs tended to look on people who advocated desertion as people to be avoided. Desertion massive enough to actually interfere with the war was simply not in the cards.

I argued along this line time and again with people in the movement in the United States. With some people this was a point of difference on which there just seemed to be no meeting of the minds. Looking back, it seems clear that the deadlock was not so much a matter of logic as of two different philosophical approaches. They looked upon it as some kind of victory every time a GI deserted because he opposed the war. I looked on it as an opportunity lost. Even in Vietnam an antiwar GI could do far more for the antiwar cause—and even to prevent killing if he handled himself right—than he could in exile or as a fugitive. As far as I was concerned the antiwar movement was in the business of making the antiwar sentiment and activism as pervasive as possible. It was not in the business of accumulating sacrifices or transforming individual souls.

One of the groups in Japan centrally concerned with organizing against the Vietnam War was Beiheiren (Japan Peace in Vietnam Committee). Jeff Sharlet and I were among several Americans who attended the August 1968 Beiheiren conference. Sharlet's general political approach was closer to that of the graduate SDS milieu than to mine, but on the question of desertion our views at the time were similar. He took the floor to caution the group about encouraging desertion, explaining that what the American movement needed was as many antiwar GIs as possible inside the military. (Tragically, Sharlet discovered shortly afterward that he had cancer. He died in 1969.)

In conversation with Japanese activists, and later with European ones, I tried to explain that from a practical point of view it would be better if they would encourage American GIs to read antiwar literature, to become experts on why the U.S. intervention was wrong, and impart that knowledge to their fellow GIs. The GIs themselves would have to decide how far they could go in organizing petitions, letters home, demonstrations, and so on. Whatever they could do in that regard would have great effect back home.

*    *    *

My trip to South Vietnam, where I was accompanied by SWP leader Barry Sheppard, was smooth enough. We had no illusions that in a few days we could reach enough GIs to make any appreciable difference, but I wanted to see for myself and demonstrate to the antiwar activists back home that with a sensible approach the movement could get a good reception from GIs even in the war zone. As a candidate I figured the American authorities might not keep me out because that would give me more publicity than just letting the visit take place. So it turned out.

Years later a court order forced the FBI to reveal documents that showed they had attempted to interfere with this trip. In the words of an FBI letter at the time, a "blind memorandum" was sent "to the intelligence branches of the Armed Forces by Liaison which would hamper the efforts of the leader of the Socialist Workers Party in trying to contact members of the Armed Forces abroad."[1] The memorandum contained a provocative smear of

1. Nelson Blackstock, *Cointelpro: The FBI's Secret War on Political Freedom* (New York: Vintage Books, 1975), p. 65.

the SWP and the following obvious incitement to violence: "It should be an interesting experience for Mr. Halstead, when he encounters the men who have served both their own country and others in the interests of freedom."

In spite of the FBI's efforts I encountered no hostility on the part of the GIs I talked to in Vietnam. Some still favored the war, more were opposed, and the majority seemed just confused on the question. But the GIs were polite and willing to discuss.

This was important because the official reasons for the American intervention simply couldn't stand up against the facts, and under discussion could not be made to coincide with the interests of the GIs themselves, either personally or as working class Americans. The spreading of an awareness that the folks at home did not expect them to sacrifice for this war, and did not want them getting killed in it, was also important.

There is a strong psychological tendency for soldiers facing combat to rationalize that there is some good reason for their participation. Nobody wants to die for nothing. This is reinforced by a self-generating morale factor in combat squads and platoons. On that level, each man depends on the others and they fight to save their buddies if for no other reason. This becomes the highest morality, and it is not to be violated. Those who would reach combat soldiers must understand this. But when all the other rationales for fighting are no longer tenable this combat solidarity can turn into its opposite, and the violator of the highest morality is he who gets the unit into combat.

This mood started in small ways. Later I interviewed Spec/4 Robert Mall, who was with the 173rd Airborne Brigade in Vietnam in 1968. I asked him where he was during the Tet offensive. He replied:

At Bien Hoa on long-range patrol. In February, our intelligence sources said there was going to be an offensive in the area and we were sent out about five miles to watch a trail, which intelligence said was heavily used. Fortunately this wasn't true. We found no traffic on the trail at all. In fact, the grass was about three feet high on it. So we just pulled off the side of the trail and waited for anything to come by. Nothing did. We were there watching that grass when we heard the mortars hitting Bien Hoa. That was the start of the Tet offensive.

*Q.* Did you rush back into Bien Hoa?

*A.* No, we stayed out for a few days. I had no desire whatsoever to go back into Bien Hoa and get mortared when I could sit there and watch the grass on the trail.

Q. Is this a common attitude?

A. Definitely. The attitude of the American soldier in Vietnam is if you can stay the hell out of the way of the VC that's exactly what you want to do.[2]

No one predicted it then, but this process would eventually turn the American ground forces in Vietnam into a net liability to the war effort. But it was only beginning in 1968.

While in Vietnam I did not present myself to the public relations officers of the command. Nor did I meet with any Vietnamese, because that would have attracted the attention of the Saigon regime, and might have meant immediate deportation. I just talked to ordinary American GIs on the streets of Saigon, in the USO, in the bars, and at the huge American base at Long Binh. I distributed copies of one of my election campaign brochures entitled "A Letter to GIs on the '68 Elections." It stated in part:

No one has a better right to oppose the war than a combat GI. And while I understand that GIs are in a tight spot, I also know that there is no law that says GIs have to be brainwashed, or that they do not have the right to think for themselves, or to read different points of view on the war, or to discuss the war. I also believe they ought to have the right to demonstrate against the war. . . .

The Johnson administration and the warmakers in general expend a great deal of effort trying to stir up hostility between GIs and the antiwar movement at home. But the fact is that millions of ordinary Americans have demonstrated against the war, and probably very close to a majority are opposed to it.

These Americans don't want to see our men being hurt and killed in an unjustified war. It's these Americans who are opposed to the war who are really on the side of the GIs. They want to support the GIs by bringing them home.[3]

The only close call Barry and I had when we were in Vietnam was in a bar near the Saigon docks. A bunch of soldiers were drinking while a convoy of trucks they were guarding was being loaded. They had automatic rifles which they propped against the bar and in the corners of the booths. (This unnerving practice

2. *Militant,* June 13, 1969.

3. "A Letter to GI's on the '68 Elections," by Fred Halstead, Socialist Workers Campaign Committee, 1968.

was common in Saigon at the time.) A big sailor came in and sat down next to Barry. I was talking to a Black GI when we overheard the sailor say something to Barry using the word "niggers." The Black GI knocked the sailor off his stool with one punch and the place erupted in a fight. Fortunately the guns did not come into play, and some of the other GIs finally pushed the fight outside. Barry and I took off.

Looking back on the incident in light of the exposures about the FBI's SWP disruption program, the sailor might have been sent into the bar to get us into trouble. But on the other hand it could have been just a piece of America abroad.

\*       \*       \*

On September 14, 1968, a meeting of the National Mobe administrative committee was held at which Rennie Davis and Tom Hayden, supported by Dellinger, presented a program of action for the fall. It was quite different from that already adopted by the Student Mobilization Committee conference. The SMC had called for an international week of protest from October 21 to 26, with emphasis on supporting the right of GIs to speak out against the war. The SMC approach was to proceed with massive, orderly demonstrations and not repeat the experience of the Chicago Democratic Party demonstrations.

The Hayden-Davis proposal declared "the need to create two, three, many Chicagos." The "strategic purpose" of the proposal was described as "to display a growing militant defiance of the authority of the government." It included a call for a strike on election day: "On November 5, we must show the world that our 'democratic process' is a contemptible mockery and that a political strike against the Presidential election has wide American support."[4]

In an obvious attempt to counterpose something to the SMC's GI emphasis, the Davis-Hayden proposal also contained a "national GI week" including visits to military bases November 1-5. Its purpose, said the proposal, was "to dramatize American support for the right of soldiers to return to civilian life." This

4. "Politics After Chicago," proposal to September 14, 1968, National Mobilization Committee steering committee by Rennie Davis and Tom Hayden. (Copy in author's files.)

＊

was a euphemism for encouraging desertion by individual GIs. Suggestions that the dates of the "GI week" be made to coincide with the SMC fall activity were brushed aside. There was no general consensus at the September 14 meeting on this program, but it was later announced as decided by the officers.

This fall program had been arrived at in good part as the result of consultations with SDS and people around its milieu. It was an attempt to accommodate to plans SDS was already forming on the idea of repeating the Chicago experience on a national scale around the elections.

A proposal to that effect was later passed at the SDS national council meeting October 11-13. It called for a two-day student strike November 4-5 with the slogan: "No class today, no ruling class tomorrow." The first day was to be devoted to rallying forces on campus for excursions into the streets on election day. A special issue of *New Left Notes* was distributed containing a wall poster that declared: "The elections don't mean shit. Vote where the power is. Our power is in the street."[5]

＊          ＊          ＊

The activities called by the SMC for October 21-26, 1968, were hardly massive. A national election period was always a difficult time to organize major antiwar actions. The disarray following Chicago, and the lack of a unified call within the antiwar movement, contributed to the difficulty. In most areas the turnout was in the hundreds, with crowds of a thousand or two in several cities. In a number of places the marches were led by GIs. In some areas the activities consisted of GI-civilian conferences or teach-ins rather than marches, and the overall approach was to defend the right of GIs to speak out against the war. While not very large, the activities did succeed in making the point—to the public, the GIs, and the movement—that antiwar sentiment among GIs was widespread. There was therefore some sense of accomplishment in SMC circles. What is more, on an international scale the actions were very large in some places. In London, 100,000 marched, and in Japan, 800,000 participated in demonstrations and strikes against the war in Vietnam and the use of Okinawa as a U.S. war base. This helped keep up the spirits of SMC activists.

5. *New Left Notes,* October 25, 1968.

The most effective fall 1968 antiwar action in the United States was an October 12 "GIs and Vets March for Peace" in San Francisco, where 500 active-duty GIs and some 15,000 civilians demonstrated. The main civilian support for this effort came from the SMC, the Vets for Peace, and some of the organizers of the April 27 demonstration. The activity originated with a group of GIs from Hamilton Air Force Base and Fort Ord who had attended the April demonstration. Together with Ken Shilman, an ex-paratrooper who worked with the SMC, and Ron Alexander, a Vietnam vet, they organized a successful teach-in at Berkeley in the summer and laid plans for the fall demonstration.

These preparations gave birth to another GI paper, *Task Force,* edited by active-duty GIs and veterans. The first issues were widely distributed at bases in the area to advertise the march. Some of the GIs involved worked on the military airlift and were able to get bundles into Vietnam. (*Task Force* continued irregular publication through 1969. In general, the publication of GI papers dependent on active-duty GIs was tenuous because of transfers and harassment of the editors. In the course of the war several hundred such papers appeared, but many were short-lived. During the height of the GI movement—from mid-1969 to mid-1972—the number of papers averaged around ninety.)[6]

At one point during preparations for the October 12 demonstration the commander of the Military Airlift Command sent a message to the Pentagon asking permission to discharge one of the march organizers, air force 2nd Lieut. Hugh F. Smith. The message also declared: "Strongly believe this demonstration should be quashed if possible because of possible severe impact on military discipline throughout the services." But, the message noted, "There is no AFR [Air Force Regulation] specifically proscribing this type of activity."[7]

This message was copied by GIs somewhere along the transmission and sent to *Ally,* a GI newspaper published in Berkeley.

6. See David Cortright, *Soldiers in Revolt* (Garden City, New York: Anchor/Doubleday, 1975), pp. 282-84, for a graph showing the average number of GI papers by service branch and year.

7. Reprint of the original text, unclassified message received August 28, 1968, at Headquarters USAF Communications Center, headed "Personal for General McConnell from General Estes. Subj. 2nd Lieutenant Hugh F. Smith, FV3179560." (Copy in author's files.)

It was recopied and distributed by antiwar students at the military bases in the Bay Area.

In the end the military authorities called inspections and special duty for October 12 at the nearby bases to prevent GIs from attending the demonstration. This did keep a lot of them away, but it also made more GIs aware of the activity.

The demonstration was entirely peaceful, and great care was taken to keep it that way so GIs could attend without being arrested. Two of the leaders of the march, Airman 1/c Mike Locks and navy Lieut. (j.g.) Sue Schnall, did suffer disciplinary action for their participation. They had decided to wear their uniforms in spite of the regulation on that point. Schnall, a nurse, also faced court-martial for dropping leaflets from a rented airplane on several naval installations and the aircraft carrier *USS Ranger,* then berthed at Alameda.

(Schnall was convicted at a general court-martial, but the sentence was relatively light—in effect, six-months duty without pay, followed by dismissal from the service. A much more serious victimization indirectly associated with the march was the case of the so-called Presidio Mutiny. Two days after the October 12 demonstration, twenty-seven inmates of the stockade at the Presidio, an army base at the tip of the San Francisco peninsula, held a brief nonviolent sit-down strike. They were protesting conditions in the stockade and the shotgun killing by a guard of a mentally ill inmate a few days earlier. This protest was in part inspired by the show of solidarity at the October 12 demonstration. The army authorities seized on the incident in an attempt to terrorize GI dissent, and charged the men with mutiny, meting out sentences of more than fifteen years in the first convictions in the case. The army would later have to retreat, however, as the case became a cause célèbre.)

The significance of the October 12 march went beyond the fact that 500 GIs had managed to participate in a demonstration for immediate withdrawal from Vietnam. That was remarkable enough and would not prove easy to repeat in the face of punitive transfers, restrictions, and harassment of GI organizers. But a whole new atmosphere was established in the Bay Area, which was a major embarkation point for Vietnam. Henceforth friendly contact between the antiwar youth in the area and GIs who passed through was taken for granted.

A similar atmosphere developed in the Seattle area, another major point of embarkation for Vietnam. Wendy Reissner, who was with a team of leafleters advertising an October 26 GI-civilian antiwar conference, described one scene at Fort Lewis:

MPs refused to allow the teams to distribute leaflets, but Friday night before the conference, we tried a new tactic. We decided simply to talk to the GIs without leafleting. Carloads of antiwar activists arrived on base and headed for the USO dance.

Our carload chose the snack bar as a base of operations. We filed in, ordered coffee, and spread out to cover as many tables of GIs as possible. Most of us started with, "I'm here to talk about the war in Vietnam." The GIs were friendly and quite eager to talk. After 20 minutes, almost every table was the scene of discussion and debate, and the time and place of the conference was being scribbled down on scraps of paper.

Four MPs marched up to the table where I was talking with three GIs and demanded my military ID card. On finding that I was not in the armed forces, they asked me to leave. All discussion stopped, and eyes were riveted as I walked across the room to leave.

After about 30 seconds, the soldiers I was talking to and others followed me out. As the others in our group were kicked out of the snack bar, more GIs came outside with them. They were indignant. Many offered to invite us in as their personal guests. As the crowd gathered, the MPs tried to disperse it. But each antiwar person went in a different direction with several soldiers and kept on talking about the antiwar movement for about an hour, while the MPs were frantically trying to keep up with all of us.[8]

Reissner and others were finally barred permanently from Fort Lewis, but there were always more students, and always other places to meet GIs. Two hundred GIs, incidentally, attended the October 26 conference in Seattle.

\* \* \*

The National Mobe–SDS "election offensive" was a failure. There were no successful strikes anywhere because the students didn't respond. Most local SDS chapters didn't even try to organize strikes at their own campuses. There were a few small picket lines and rallies. Here and there, where other groups, including the SMC, were involved, there were modest peaceful antiwar demonstrations. The confrontations SDS had counted on did not occur.

8. *Militant*, November 8, 1968.

The failure of their plans was particularly demoralizing within SDS, where the national leadership and its followers lost ground to the Progressive Labor faction. The PL-SDSers had opposed the strike call.

The high point of the National Mobilization's "GI week" was supposed to have been a mass "be-in" just outside Fort Dix, New Jersey. Ordinarily this phrase described a gathering of counter-cultural youth in a park for a day's outing. For the Fort Dix affair they distributed a leaflet with a picture of a woman in Vietnamese dress and the title: "HANOI ROSE yearns for you." The text continued: "Join her in the freedom booth. . . . All GIs who join us get free ham sandwiches, music, love, dope, surprises, civvies, money, bus tickets, flowers, theater, hippie wigs. . . ."[9]

A Freedom Booth [said the *Mobilizer*] at first glance looks like an election booth but inside instead of the levers, knobs, toilet paper and other irrelevant machinery, the Freedom Booth contains civilian clothes, bus tickets and subway tokens, civilian ID cards and other great choices for the American serviceman.[10]

It might have seemed funny in Greenwich Village, but it was harebrained foolishness under the circumstances at Fort Dix. The affair was a flop as GIs avoided it like the plague.

Harry Ring commented in the *Militant:*

Now, it has been recognized by the most obtuse that there is significant antiwar sentiment among GIs and that there are an impressive number of servicemen and women ready to assert their constitutional right to voice their views on the war.

Finally compelled to recognize this reality, a turn toward the GIs was finally made by those like the present operators of the National Mobe (which, incidentally, for all practical purposes has virtually stopped functioning as a coalition). But they made the turn to the GIs in such a damagingly irresponsible way that one is tempted to think it might almost be better if they hadn't.[11]

The military authorities could limit direct GI participation in

---

9. This leaflet was reproduced in the *Militant,* November 22, 1968.
10. National Mobilization Committee *Mobilizer,* October 25, 1968. (Copy in author's files.)
11. *Militant,* November 22, 1968.

demonstrations, harass the coffeehouses and GI editors, but they couldn't eliminate contact between GIs and the general population of their age group, which by this time was heavily against the war. The SMC emphasis on supporting the right of GIs to oppose the war helped assure that the antiwar movement was not isolated from this communication.

The interplay went both ways. This was particularly important in the fall and winter of 1968-69 when, in spite of the growing antiwar sentiment, the organized antiwar movement was largely in disarray and a lot of the previous activists were confused, demoralized, or turning inward into sectarian concerns and abandoning antiwar activity as such. Though the number of GIs who could attend antiwar meetings was small, they had a healthy influence on the movement.

They were far less inclined than civilians to have illusions in the negotiations or the occasional U.S. bombing halts, or to believe that the war was practically over. Their material interest in the growth of the antiwar movement was more direct. What is more, GIs were being rotated in huge numbers from a year's duty in Vietnam and many brought with them stories of the war— including descriptions of corruption and atrocity and a remarkable respect for the "VC"—which spread throughout the bases in the United States and turned even more GIs against the American intervention. The fact that significant numbers of GIs were participating in the antiwar movement was a new factor which added great authority to the antiwar arguments.

The SMC did everything it could to take advantage of this new factor to rejuvenate and regroup the antiwar movement. In line with this it initiated a GI-Civilian Antiwar Action Conference in Chicago on December 28. Among other things it was hoped this conference could give impulse to a call for unified mass actions in the spring of 1969.

The Chicago Peace Council agreed to cohost the GI-Civilian Antiwar Action Conference, and the SMC was able to get fairly broad sponsorship for it. But the building of the conference was difficult because of the divisions within the movement. To some extent these were also reflected among GIs who had connections with one or another radical tendency. A number of forces, including the Dellinger-Davis-Hayden grouping in National Mobe, the Du Bois Clubs, SDS, Youth Against War and Fascism, and others, took a dim view of the conference and kept their distance from it. Some PLers campaigned against the conference beforehand.

The editorial board of one GI newspaper, the *Last Harass* at Fort Gordon, Georgia, wrote an open letter to Howard Petrick of the SMC staff accusing him of using the paper's name as a sponsor of the conference without the permission of the full editorial board. Petrick answered that he had been assured by the one editor he had spoken to that it was okay to list the paper as a sponsor, but Petrick apologized and removed it from the list.[12]

In their letter to Petrick, the *Last Harass* editors argued against the conference on the grounds that it would expose dissenting GIs to the military authorities.

We hope you will become aware of the security precautions that are necessary in order to prevent organizations from being effectively wiped out by a few swift moves by army intelligence when certain individuals' connection with certain things have been confirmed.[13]

In his reply Petrick summarized the specific context in which activist youth in the U.S. military services found themselves, concluding:

I think that it's fair to say that a good-sized majority of active duty GIs are against the war in Vietnam. Our task, then, is to find some way to organize this sentiment, to find ways in which GIs can organize and protest that won't get them into legal trouble and will have a real effect towards ending the war. . . .

Anyone who has been in the military service knows that one of the things the brass tries to do is make it seem that citizens lose their constitutional rights once in uniform, and that free speech and assembly do not apply to GIs. Although they try to make GIs believe this, and although many do believe this, the facts are just the opposite—at least according to the constitution. GIs do have the legal right to free speech; GIs do have the right to speak out against the war; GIs do have the right to demonstrate. True enough, the brass will attempt reprisals against the first GIs who speak out but experience shows that with proper legal defense, GIs can win, and can assure their rights.

In order for GIs to organize against the war, we have to publicize the

12. Letter from Howard Petrick to the *Last Harass,* December 14, 1968. (Copy in author's files.)

13. Letter from the *Last Harass* to Howard Petrick, November 29, 1968. (Copy in author's files.)

fact that GIs have the right to do so. The only way to publicize that fact is to act; to be very careful to exercise legal rights and thus minimize the chance of victimization; and to be prepared for an adequate defense in case the brass tries illegal reprisals. In that way antiwar GIs who speak out can show the others what can be done. This publicity is also necessary for organization.

In this sense, it seems to me that the main aspect of the "necessary security" that should be undertaken is the security of carrying out legal actions [as opposed to illegal ones], so that any attempted victimizations can be fought. I don't deny the need for security, but too much secrecy can hurt organizing efforts. If a GI is to be actively engaged in antiwar activity (more than in his private thoughts) then I don't think that that activity can really be kept secret from military "intelligence" unless it is also kept secret from the very same GIs you want to reach. And you can't organize GIs to act out against the war unless you explain what you want to do. GIs who are willing to speak out now can reach others who are silent only if they do actually speak out. . . .

The conference, I hope, will place a very strong emphasis on the responsibility the civilian antiwar movement has to help in the defense of GIs' civil liberties. In addition, I should hope that the conference will repudiate any attempt by anyone to foster a "freak show" spirit onto the proposed GI-civilian action, or any attempt to call illegal actions which could maximize the chances that GIs who take part will get into trouble with the brass.[14]

In general, the drift toward escalated rhetoric and sectarian practices in SDS circles was reflected in the GI movement in a tendency to emphasize an underground approach. Superficially, this tactic might have appeared more militant, but in practice it was an escape from the real opportunities that presented themselves.

The GI-Civilian Antiwar Action Conference itself was poorly attended, in part due to a severe snowstorm that hit the Midwest and made travel to Chicago difficult that weekend, but mainly because of the crisis in the movement.

Some 300 people attended the first night's session, which heard a number of GIs, including Rudy Bell, one of the Fort Hood Forty-three; his mother, Nettie Bell, who was active in the defense; Reber Boult, the Atlanta ACLU attorney who was working on the case of Captain Howard Levy; Chicago Alderman Sammie Raynor of Vets for Peace; Sid Peck; and others.

14. Letter from Howard Petrick to the *Last Harass*, December 14, 1968.

Both Peck and Sid Lens attended the conference though they were obviously not entirely comfortable with it. They did not want to close the door to the possibility of unified mass action in the spring.

Some 270 persons registered for the working sessions on the second day. An absolute majority of these were members or close sympathizers of the YSA. This was not by design, but because the YSA and the SWP were the only radical organizations that gave full support to the conference and made sure their people got there, snowstorm or no.

The conference did propose mass GI-civilian demonstrations for the spring, suggesting that they be held in six or seven cities: New York, Chicago, Seattle, Atlanta, Austin, San Francisco, and possibly Los Angeles. The suggested date was to be Easter Sunday, April 6, 1969. This holiday was chosen to make it more difficult for military authorities to restrict GIs to base on the day of the demonstrations.

C. Clark Kissinger, who chaired one of the sessions, wrote an article for the *Guardian* in which he characterized the conference as a failure. Said Kissinger:

> The boycott of the conference by national GI papers like the *Bond* and *Vietnam GI,* as well as by local groups, resulted in a conference pretty much limited to the YSA and its supporters. In this setting the unanimity and boredom was not surprising.
>
> The GI-Civilian Antiwar Action Conference ended late Saturday afternoon, so the national conference of the Student Mobilization Committee, which was to have begun Sunday morning, was called to order after a dinner break. The entire SMC conference lasted one hour and 10 minutes. Only a shadow of its former self, the SMC (mostly YSAers) heard brief reports, endorsed the actions of the GI-Civilian Antiwar Action Conference, and adjourned.[15]

Yet the SMC leaders were convinced that the demonstrations called by the GI-Civilian Antiwar Action Conference would be successful, and in the process the SMC would be rebuilt. The reason was as simple as it was profound. The war was not about to end, and the American people were turning more and more against it.

The outgoing Johnson administration, and the incoming ad-

15. *Guardian,* January 11, 1969.

ministration of Richard M. Nixon, who had been elected in November, were united in a determination to continue trying to win the war. This is not what they said, but it was the way they acted, as the GIs well knew from the preparations they saw under way. Nixon had promised he had a plan to end the war, the details of which he kept secret. But neither the Democrats nor the Republicans made any sign of doing the only thing that would end it—getting out of Vietnam. By spring the illusions that the war was about to end would be dissipating.

*     *     *

Meanwhile the National Mobilization Committee had called for a series of antiwar activities in Washington around the inauguration of President-elect Nixon on January 20, 1969. These came to be known as the Counterinaugural. The experience of the "election offensive" had a somewhat sobering effect and this time the projections were more realistic, and an attempt was made to involve broader forces. The central leaders of the National Mobilization Committee now were Davis, Dellinger, and Paul Potter. Hayden had moved to the West Coast, and was only nominally involved.

Essentially, Davis's and Dellinger's approach remained the same—to court the SDS and countercultural "confrontationists" while attempting to keep at least some moderate forces involved. But in this case most of the concessions tended to be to the moderate side. Some of the others resented this and made no secret about it.

The final plan was for three days of activities: a series of workshops on a wide variety of subjects on Saturday, January 18; a march along Pennsylvania Avenue on January 19; a "Counterinaugural Ball" that night featuring rock bands and a light show in a huge circus tent; and a "movement presence" along the route of the inaugural parade itself on Monday, January 20.

The tension during the preparations revolved mainly around whether there should be a physical confrontation, particularly on Monday at the inaugural parade. The New York Parade Committee, as well as the few moderate groups and individuals who had become hesitantly involved, opposed this. A milieu of small radical groups, some SDSers, and the self-proclaimed "Crazies" (an offshoot of the Yippies) continued to press for a confrontation.

In New York, the Coalition for an Anti-Imperialist Movement (Co-Aim) devoted itself to organizing this milieu for the Counterinaugural. Co-Aim itself was largely a bloc between Youth Against War and Fascism and Walter Teague's Committee to Aid the National Liberation Front.

The SDS national office did not support the National Mobe's call for the inaugural demonstrations. According to Dellinger the SDS national office wasn't opposed to the action, but would not join the call because of the internal dispute with PL.[16] Things had reached the sorry point where public support to a coalition antiwar demonstration had become a point of embarrassment in the faction struggle within SDS.

The SMC supported the Counterinaugural although it was not involved in the planning or on the Washington staff. I returned to the staff of the Parade Committee for the Counterinaugural preparations but worked from the New York end, not on the Washington staff of the Mobe. This was not accidental. If I had been on the Washington staff it would have been uncomfortable for everyone concerned. It was no secret that I was not in a mood to equivocate with the advocates of getting small bands of youth into street fights with the armed forces of the state. That was neither more militant nor more anti-imperialist than peaceful demonstrations as far as I was concerned. It was just damned foolishness.

Once again, Dellinger—and in this case much of the staff— found themselves in the position of trying to smooth things out between the moderates on the one hand and Co-Aim and those of like mind on the other. To reassure the moderates, the National Mobe literature emphasized that the affair would be peaceful and that the confrontation would be political, not physical. This was the policy agreed upon among the major forces participating. There was, however, a certain fuzzy area. In the words of a staff statement: "Groups that were seeking more militant kinds of action were also aware that there would be other opportunities during the weekend for militant tactics to be employed."[17]

Just what these "other opportunities" were was not quite clear, and in any case Co-Aim and the Crazies did not want to do their

16. "Summary of Administrative Committee Meeting, Washington, December 14, 1968." See report by Dellinger. (Copy in author's files.)

17. *Liberation,* February 1969.

thing by themselves—they could never muster very many people on their own—they wanted to involve the larger crowd.

As it turned out, the National Mobe's activities for the Counterinaugural came off more or less as planned. The Saturday workshops were well attended with perhaps 2,000 persons taking part. On Sunday there was a short rally in the circus tent (it was too cold for an outdoor rally) followed by a march of 13,000, more or less the number projected.

The last speaker at the rally was Derrick Alexander, a GI who had been seriously wounded in Vietnam only two months before. He had literally gotten out of his bed at Walter Reed hospital to take part in the antiwar activity. Throughout the program, a group of hecklers kept interrupting speakers, demanding "action." It was clear they hoped to win the crowd at the rally to their perspective of physical confrontation. The atmosphere of hostility among these types toward the Mobilization Committee had reached the point where some of them even allowed themselves to be led into trying to shout down Alexander in an effort to get the crowd running through the streets after their fashion. It didn't work. Alexander finished his talk and led off the march together with other GIs, though he was clearly suffering physically.

That night some 10,000 people stood in and around the tent attending the Counterinaugural Ball. That event went smoothly, except for a superabundance of mud. But while most of the National Mobe staff was at the tent, a group of about thirty people from the Co-Aim group raided the office and took it over physically. Apparently the raiders hoped this coup would allow them to determine the tactics for the following day at the inaugural parade. Some of them put out a press release along those lines.

In practical terms the raid was nonsensical because the press release couldn't possibly have been published before the next morning's events, and street demonstrations cannot be directed out of an office anyway.

Dave Dellinger was called back to the office from the tent and negotiated with the raiders, assuring them that National Mobe had always intended to provide "legal, medical and communications help for all groups on Monday."[18] A physical free-for-all in the office was narrowly avoided.

18. Ibid.

On Monday the inaugural parade was heavily guarded by troops as well as police. Squads of well-trained soldiers in battle dress, with rifles and bayonets, were moved quickly into position opposite any area along the route where demonstrators appeared to gather in force. The crowd was heavily infiltrated with plainclothes cops. But they generally didn't interfere with the demonstrators as long as they stayed on the sidelines.

Several thousand demonstrators stood along the route, chanting antiwar slogans and giving the peace salute. Some had gotten tickets in the grandstands and held up antiwar signs as the parade went by. One group spelled out "Vietnam for the Vietnamese," one letter per person.

Meanwhile the Co-Aim forces concentrated at a certain place along the route. Rumor had it they would attempt to rush the president's motorcade when it passed, but there was nothing more than a little pushing and shoving and a few wads of paper and small stones thrown into the street. Anyone gesturing as if to throw something was apt to be pounced upon by the plainclothes cops. Incredibly, in this situation, a group of Crazies wandered through the crowd passing out marijuana cigarettes. One of them tried to hand one to me and it took considerable restraint to keep from laying him out right there.

After the presidential motorcade passed, several hundred youths broke away from the rest of the demonstrators and moved north, away from the parade route, running through the streets of downtown Washington, turning over trash cans and breaking windows here and there. The cops chased them through the streets for a couple of hours until they were dispersed after several dozen arrests. So ended the Counterinaugural.

\*        \*        \*

In one sense the Counterinaugural had been a modest success. Except for the trashing at the end—which wasn't really all that serious—it had gone according to the agreed plan, and the turnout, while small, was just about what had been expected. What is more, at the workshops on Saturday there had been widespread support for the idea of the projected Easter GI-civilian demonstrations, though the workshops had not been structured to make decisions.

I hoped the National Mobilization Committee would take over the national coordination of the Easter actions after the Counter-inaugural. The December GI-Civilian conference had left this to a

"Liaison Coordinating Committee" with me as convenor. But so far, aside from me, only an SMC representative and Sid Lens had agreed to serve on this body. (This was another of those times when Sid Lens's anxiety for unity at all costs played a positive role.) Involving the National Mobe as such, in spite of its current narrowness, would be very important because it would signal a greater unity around the spring actions and make it much easier to get the New York Parade Committee to sponsor the New York regional affair, and for other local coalitions to be constituted or refurbished.

But the National Mobilization Committee was roundly criticized after January 20 by both the moderates and the ultralefts. The bad feeling involved around the Counterinaugural—highlighted by the raid on the office—apparently had a traumatic effect on the National Mobe staff. Of great importance here, considering the general approach of Dellinger and Davis, was the fact that after the Counterinaugural, National Mobe was sharply derided in SDS circles.

By that time the level of polemic within SDS was rapidly deteriorating and plain slander had become part of the style. For example, an article on the Counterinaugural in *New Left Notes* complained that the Saturday march had not resulted in a confrontation, and declared:

> The reason that the pigs could perform so smoothly and in such reserved fashion on the Mobilization march, using only four or five motorcycle cops per block to keep us on our side of the street, was because the Mobilization marshals effectively functioned as cops. In fact, several of them drew knives on demonstrators who were trying to rip down the flag in front of the HEW [Health, Education and Welfare] building.[19]

But what rattled Dellinger and Davis wasn't so much the fact that the specific charges were largely false and unfair—we had all developed rather thick skins by then—but that the Counterinaugural had the effect of repelling rather than attracting the SDS milieu to National Mobe.

The same *New Left Notes* article declared:

> In the past the Mobilization has played an important role as an antiwar coalition, and has organized actions which have built SDS and the

19. *New Left Notes*, January 22, 1969.

movement in general. It is clear that it is no longer able to deal with the radical movement's development in terms of political analysis and militance.

It is difficult to avoid the conclusion that Dellinger and Davis agreed with this part of the criticism. In effect they deferred to it. During the preparations for the Counterinaugural, Davis and Paul Potter had responded to a similar criticism as follows:

> The Mobilization came into being and has continued to exist through all its travails not because anyone *ever* "looked to the Mobe for political leadership" or the correct line, but because there was a simple, powerful sense of urgency about the war that was strong enough to bring into a working coalition groups that distrusted, even hated one another.[20]

But after the Counterinaugural, Dellinger and Davis acted as if the National Mobilization Committee had become a liability.

*      *      *

On February 7, 1969, an enlarged steering committee of the National Mobilization Committee met in Norma Becker's apartment in New York. Those present included Becker, Dellinger, Davis, Hayden, Potter, Irving Beinin, Eric Weinberger, Barbara Bick of Washington Women Strike for Peace, Sid Lens, Sid Peck, Carol Lipman, who was the acting executive secretary of the SMC, and myself.

This meeting rejected my proposal that the National Mobe take over coordination of the Easter GI-civilian demonstrations. Both Dellinger and Davis advanced the argument that in the coming period, considering the mood of "the youth," it would not be possible to organize mass demonstrations without their getting out of hand. Lipman and I argued that their view of "the youth" was too narrow. Co-Aim, the Crazies, others in a similar mood, and even SDS were a tiny part of the American youth willing to actively oppose the war. If we set the proper tone and were unequivocal as to the discipline, we could organize mass peaceful demonstrations.

Dellinger and Davis had no proposal for the spring and seemed

20. *Guardian,* January 11, 1969.

preoccupied with news leaks that a number of movement figures would soon be indicted by a federal grand jury in connection with the Chicago Democratic Party convention demonstrations. The important thing, in their view, was to make the most of that case. (Later they would write: "We believe exciting, new energy can be released by a positive political offensive against the indictments of the movement's action in Chicago. . . ."[21] My own view was that defense of the indictees would be important, but that the case could not be a substitute for—and was not likely to be a precipitator of—mass action, which it seemed to me was objectively possible.)

Potter and Hayden expressed no interest in another set of antiwar demonstrations, nor in the continuation of a national formation to call and organize them. Both seemed in an introspective mood and would soon drop out of national antiwar activity as such for an extended period.

Peck, Lens, and Bick were dissatisfied with the recent course of the National Mobe. They saw the need for rebuilding a national antiwar coalition, but didn't think the National Mobe would serve their purpose. Bick said it no longer had any authority among Women Strike for Peace groups. The discussion turned around dissolving the National Mobilization Committee. It was decided not to do this for the simple reason that such an announcement might be used by prowar forces and publicized as a sign of weakness of the antiwar movement. But in effect the activity of the group was suspended.[22]

The only national antiwar coalition effort remaining was the Liaison Coordinating Committee for the Easter GI-civilian actions. I had previously sent out a letter to prominent activists and

21. Letter to "Dear Friend" from Dave Dellinger and Rennie Davis, February 24, 1969. (Copy in author's files.)

22. Unfortunately, no minutes of this meeting were produced, as I recall, precisely because the major decision it made was not to be announced. My account is based on memory refreshed by two documents which reported the results of the meeting at the time, referring to the central decision only by implication. The accounts in the two documents emphasize different points but are not contradictory. The documents are a National Mobilization Committee mailing of February 24, 1969, entitled "Inauguration, Chicago Indictments, Antiwar Directions: A Mobilization Report," and an internal SWP mailing of February 15, 1969, entitled "To Antiwar Directors and Organizers." (Copies in author's files.)

local coalitions calling a meeting of this body for February 9 in
Chicago and had hoped to present it with the news that the
National Mobe would join the effort. This was now not possible.
The Chicago meeting was poorly attended. Present were representatives of the Chicago Peace Council, Vets for Peace, the
Women's International League for Peace and Freedom, the SWP,
and regional coalitions in Cleveland, Detroit, and Minneapolis.
Of the seven regional centers where the Easter actions were
supposed to take place, only Chicago was represented by a local
coalition. The New York Parade Committee had not yet discussed
the Easter actions, and I was not empowered to represent it at
this meeting. So I represented the SWP.

The meeting received a supporting telegram from the national
board of the Women's International League for Peace and
Freedom. The text is interesting in that by implication it touched
on the tactical differences the moderate groups had with the
recent approach of National Mobe. It said:

WILL ENCOURAGE LOCAL BRANCHES COOPERATION IN CIT-
IES CHOSEN FOR NON-VIOLENT, LEGAL DEMONSTRATION
EASTER SUNDAY. CONCUR WITH EMPHASIS ON ENDING THE
WAR IN VIETNAM, LEGAL RIGHTS FOR GI'S, ABOLITION OF
DRAFT, AND GENERAL REDIRECTION OF RESOURCES FROM
WAR TO PEOPLES WELFARE.[23]

Sid Lens and Sylvia Kushner assured the meeting that the
Chicago Peace Council would sponsor the demonstration in
Chicago, though on Saturday, April 5, rather than Easter
Sunday. That left six cities to go. Lens reported that Stewart
Meacham of the American Friends Service Committee had
organized a National Action Group (NAG) of pacifists, mostly
Quakers, which would be holding some actions in early April.
Lens was sure NAG would not consider these in competition with
the Easter efforts, and that Meacham would be supportive of the
GI-civilian actions. So would Sid Peck, but for the moment he did
not want to be directly involved.

The meeting set up a committee of five, instructed to broaden
the sponsorship and participation in organizing the Easter

---

23. Cited in letter "To Antiwar Directors and Organizers" from Gus
Horowitz, for the SWP's national antiwar steering committee, February
15, 1969. (Copy in author's files.)

demonstrations. They were: Sid Lens and Sylvia Kushner, Leroy Wollins of Vets for Peace, Howard Petrick of the SMC, and myself. All told, the results of the meeting were not much to go on, and the five of us knew it. But the war was continuing, the opposition to it was growing and needed a focus to surface. The most significant point about the Chicago meeting was that it was held at all, and that it decided to proceed.

\*          \*          \*

On March 29, 1969, a federal grand jury in Chicago indicted eight people on charges of conspiracy and "traveling in interstate commerce to incite a riot." The defendants faced up to ten years in prison and $20,000 fines. Those indicted were: Dave Dellinger, Rennie Davis, and Tom Hayden of the National Mobilization Committee; Bobby Seale of the Oakland Black Panther Party; Jerry Rubin and Abbie Hoffman of the "Yippies"; graduate SDSer John R. Froines; and Lee Weiner, a research assistant at Northwestern University.

In effect what was left of the National Mobilization Committee dissolved into the "Conspiracy," a group set up by Dellinger and other indictees to publicize the case and the variety of political views and approaches held by the defendants.

# 17

# The Easter 1969 GI-Civilian Demonstrations and the Birth of the New Mobilization Committee

The lack of an authoritative national coalition made it difficult to get the preparations for the Easter 1969 actions under way in most of the seven cities for which they had been projected. The initiative nationally was largely left to the Student Mobilization Committee. Insofar as the resistance among adult leaders to following this initiative was overcome, that was largely attributable to a sense of urgency about the war itself. In spite of Nixon's promises, there were over half a million U.S. troops in Vietnam and the bombing was still escalating. More than a few local figures in the antiwar movement swallowed their doubts and went along because "We just have to do something."

This factor was certainly uppermost at a well-attended meeting of the New York Parade Committee February 13 where I reported on the Easter actions and proposed that the Parade Committee organize the New York demonstration. The bitterness of the SMC split had deeply affected the Parade Committee, and the staff was generally hostile to what was considered an SMC-originated proposal. Dave Dellinger and Norma Becker, the Parade Committee coordinators, were not expected to be friendly to the idea but did not speak against it. Becker simply encouraged full discussion. She was a working schoolteacher who somehow always made me feel like a slightly errant schoolboy whenever she chaired a meeting, a feeling which was heightened on this occasion. The sentiment, however, was clearly in favor of the action, and toward the end of the meeting both she and Dellinger gave their approval. For some reason the opponents centered on the fact that the proposed date was Easter Sunday, April 6. They were taken aback when we agreed to change it to April 5 and the proposal was adopted overwhelmingly.

A GI planning board for April 5 was set up in New York by active-duty GIs. It worked jointly with the Parade Committee and the SMC. Key figures in this formation were Sp/4 Allen Myers of Fort Dix, New Jersey, and Pvt. David Cortright, a member of the army band at Fort Wadsworth at the entrance to New York harbor.

It may appear odd that this unit, whose duties included playing patriotic music at military and state occasions in the country's largest city, would develop into a nest of antiwar sentiment and activity. Cortright later explained:

> Most of the members of the 26th Army Band stationed within the Fort Hamilton complex at Fort Wadsworth were professional musicians who had enlisted for duty as bandsmen to avoid a draftee infantry assignment in Vietnam; many were decidedly anti-military and outspoken in their views against the war.[1]

The embarrassment this caused the army brass eventually resulted in a number of punitive transfers, no doubt to the detriment of the quality of the music-making.

With both the Chicago Peace Council and the New York Parade Committee as well as the SMC firmly committed, the Easter actions now had enough authority behind them to allow the drawing together of local coalitions to organize the demonstrations in other cities, including San Francisco, Los Angeles, and Austin, Texas. The project got a boost when on February 16 Seattle jumped the gun and some 200 GIs there led a march of 4,500 civilian supporters demanding withdrawal from Vietnam. The march was organized by the GI-Civilian Alliance for Peace (GI-CAP), which had grown out of an SMC-initiated conference in October 1968.

The spring actions were larger than expected. Some 100,000 marched in New York April 5 in spite of rain. The Chicago turnout was 30,000, the largest yet for that city. In San Francisco April 6 some 40,000 marched to a rally at the gates of the Presidio, demanding an end to the war and freedom for the Presidio Twenty-seven. The Atlanta turnout was 4,000. Los Angeles had 6,500, and Austin had a march of 1,200 including a

---

1. David Cortright, *Soldiers in Revolt: the American Military Today* (Garden City, New York: Doubleday, 1976), pp. 68-69.

hundred GIs. The Austin and Atlanta marches were also the largest to date in those cities. Active-duty GIs were speakers at all these demonstrations.

In addition, the Quaker-inspired National Action Group (NAG), which had originally projected April actions in half a dozen places, found itself organizing them in more than thirty cities. These were smaller than the GI-civilian demonstrations and generally involved some sort of nonviolent civil disobedience, but they received considerable publicity and had a wide impact, particularly among church groups. (Many Quakers, incidentally, were particularly concerned over Nixon's war policy because the president professed the Quaker faith.)

In general the spring 1969 antiwar actions were far more successful than originally anticipated. Organizationally the effect went beyond the cities in which the major demonstrations were held. Local coalitions were refurbished or built in many other areas where supportive activities took place and new GI groups were organized on a number of bases. The Student Mobilization Committee emerged greatly strengthened compared to its condition in December, particularly among high school students. It was increasingly, though sometimes grudgingly, recognized as the main organizer of antiwar youth on a national scale.

*            *            *

An incident occurred at the April 5 New York demonstration that further increased tensions between Dellinger and me and had a certain effect on subsequent developments. In the Parade Committee it had been agreed beforehand that Dellinger would speak on behalf of the defendants in the Chicago "Conspiracy Eight" indictments; if other defendants were present they would be introduced, but neither Jerry Rubin nor Abbie Hoffman would speak. Both Hoffman and Rubin made no secret of the fact they considered peaceful demonstrations a waste of time, and the majority of the committee—especially the trade unionists and GIs then involved—didn't trust the two Yippie leaders to refrain from appealing for an ultraleft confrontation then and there.

On the march, there was a small group of Crazies carrying poles on the end of which were speared the heads of pigs they'd gotten from butcher shops. They taunted the cops with these along the route and generally comported themselves in a provocative fashion. The march itself was so massive that this small group was lost in the crowd, but at the rally a steady rain thinned the audience and the Crazies managed to elbow their way to the front, just behind the contingent of active-duty GIs seated in front of the speakers' stand.

During Dellinger's speech he invited Rubin and Hoffman onto the stage and then handed the microphone over to them. They proceeded to make deliberately outrageous appeals to the Crazies and the crowd to attack a few police lined up nearby. The GIs were between the Crazies and the cops.

Fortunately the crowd didn't respond and the GIs held the Crazies back. But if a melee had resulted some of the GIs would undoubtedly have been caught in it and arrested. That would have given the military authorities just the excuse they were looking for to victimize another group of antiwar GIs. As chief marshal for this demonstration I was livid at what I considered Dellinger's irresponsibility. He was roundly criticized by Al Evanoff, myself, and others at the next Parade Committee meeting. It is not that Dellinger agreed with what Rubin and Hoffman did. He criticized that himself. But he apparently just couldn't bring himself to say "no" to these self-appointed representatives of the wildest countercultural youth.

*       *       *

One of the speakers at the April 5 GI-civilian demonstration in Chicago was Pvt. Joe Miles, then on a weekend pass from Fort Bragg, North Carolina. Miles was the National Black Antiwar Antidraft Union (NBAWADU) organizer who had led the high school students' demonstration in Washington, D.C., at the time of Martin Luther King's assassination a year earlier.

Miles had been drafted into the army in the fall of 1968 and was sent to Fort Jackson, South Carolina, in early January, 1969, for advanced training. There, in the company he was assigned to, he found a ready receptivity to his Black nationalist and antiwar views, and began organizing among his fellow GIs. One of these was Pvt. Andrew Pulley, a big, tough seventeen-year-old who had been arrested in a Black uprising in Cleveland's Hough ghetto and given the choice by the judge of going to jail or enlisting in the army. Pulley later recalled:

It started when Joe Miles suggested to some of us in the barracks at B-

14-4 [B Company, 14th Battalion, 4th Brigade] that we listen to some Malcolm X tapes. It started as all black and Puerto Rican just listening to the tapes and talking about it afterward. The first night about fifteen GIs came. The second night it built up to thirty-five.[2]

Miles later commented:

It was like Malcolm had been made for this kind of audience and we were ready for him. It was like walking around during one of the rebellions, just saying, "Oh my, I'm so glad I'm black.". . . So guys were running around there in brotherhood. The brotherhood there, you could cut it, cut it in the air. We'd hug each other, greet each other, spend ten minutes shaking each other's hands. Guys would grab the PA [public address] system and announce, "All you brothers on the third floor, black and proud, let me hear you." And guys would come yelling down the steps, "black and proud."[3]

It wasn't long before some of the officers and noncommissioned officers became disturbed and began to harass these Black GIs. Pulley and Miles lodged a complaint with the Inspector General (IG) about a lieutenant calling Miles "boy" and some of the lifers (career soldiers, usually noncoms or officers) trying to provoke Pulley into physical fights so they could court-martial him. The IG, in effect, told them to go to hell. Soon fights were breaking out. According to Miles:

Brothers were going around and every dude they considered a racist was wasted. . . . That's when the army made the charges against several black guys who had been in the meetings, charges for assault and so on. Actually the guys they charged hadn't done anything. But there was a general situation around there of fights happening. Then guys started discussing it. "We're all going to end up in jail if this keeps up," and "What are we going to do about our relations with the whites?" We had to have a serious discussion about all this at the next meeting. It was by far the best meeting we had had. Sixty guys showed up.[4]

They made a calculated decision to organize white GIs as well and to appeal to them to join in a struggle against the war. Miles

2. Fred Halstead, *GIs Speak Out Against the War* (New York: Path-finder Press, 1970), pp. 31-32.
3. Ibid., pp. 81, 84.
4. Ibid., p. 97.

was a member of the YSA before he was drafted, and one of the whites he invited to the next meeting—attended by eighty GIs—was Pvt. Joe Cole, a tall, soft-spoken Georgian who had been in the YSA in Atlanta. Cole later recalled:

I was Permanent Party [attached to the base staff, not a trainee] and there's a post regulation that prohibits Permanent Party from associating with trainees, and I had on a Permanent Party patch and insignia on my hat, [so] when some sergeants from my company came by the meeting, some of the guys took my hat off and crowded around me so the sergeants wouldn't see me. The automatic response of those guys at that meeting was just fantastic for me to see. Everything was just perfect. It was an experience I'll always remember. And all the other meetings were just like that.[5]

Out of these meetings grew an organization, GIs United Against the War in Vietnam, which later spread to other bases. At Fort Jackson the authorities attempted to stop the meetings by restricting the men to barracks, and so on. GIs United circulated petitions—first in defense of other antiwar GIs who were facing court-martial, and then requesting an open meeting on post "at which all those concerned can freely discuss the legal and moral questions related to the war in Vietnam and to the civil rights of American citizens both within and outside the armed forces."[6]

Meanwhile, Miles was transferred on three hours' notice to Fort Bragg, North Carolina. The organizing continued, however, sparked by Pulley and Pvt. Jose Rudder, a Puerto Rican from Washington, D.C., and a Vietnam combat veteran.

(This was actually Miles's second tour of duty at Fort Bragg. The fact that he and Jose Rudder were in Fort Jackson at all was itself the result of an attempt by the command at Fort Bragg, where they had done their basic training, to suppress dissent. Both Miles and Rudder had been assigned after their training to Fort Bragg's base staff as permanent party, where they became friends with another soldier, Pvt. Keith Jones, a Black socialist from Washington, D.C. In November 1968 Jones was visiting student friends at the University of North Carolina at Chapel Hill and sat down behind an antiwar literature table set up on the campus. He was in uniform and attracted the attention of a local

---

5. Ibid., pp. 33-34.
6. Ibid., p. 102. The petition is reproduced in full.

TV station which did an interview with him. The brass at Fort Bragg became alarmed and transferred out to other bases not only Jones but a number of other GIs known to have some radical political past. Thus, Rudder, who had protested the war while in Vietnam, and Miles, who was in the YSA, found themselves suddenly assigned to Fort Jackson.)

GIs United was constantly harassed, but it also constantly sent its material to the press and TV, called press conferences, and began to receive significant publicity. On March 3, Cole and another YSAer at Fort Jackson who was not in a training company, Steve Dash, walked up to the post headquarters to present the petition for an open meeting. The presentation had been announced to the press and the army had placed the training companies on restriction, so Cole and Dash had to do it. In front of the press the commanding authorities refused to accept the petition and Cole and Dash were given direct orders to return to barracks. The news reports attracted considerable attention. Shortly thereafter the Huntley-Brinkley TV news show sent a crew to Fort Jackson to interview GIs United and this was on national TV.

On March 20 an impromptu meeting outside the B-14-4 barracks took place. Over a hundred GIs attended and Rudder, Pulley, and others spoke. Within a few days eight members of GIs United were put in the stockade, or under barracks arrest, all under charges stemming from the meeting. Thus began the case of the Fort Jackson Eight. The defendants were privates Pulley, Rudder, Cole, Edilberto Chaparro, Dominick Duddie, Delmar Thomas, Tommy Woodfin, and Pfc. Curtis E. Mays.

The case became a cause célèbre and proved a major embarrassment to the war-makers. The men had committed no crimes, violated no orders, and were being held because they spoke out against the war. A ninth GI, Pvt. John Huffman, who had been arrested along with the others and had retained the same defense counsel, surfaced in the court hearings as an agent planted in GIs United by Army Intelligence. He had sat in on meetings between defendants and counsel and this created something of a legal scandal.

Cole later recalled:

We were always aboveboard legally. We realized that if we didn't operate that way it would be a quick trip to the stockade for no good cause. So we had gotten our heads together and decided that our best bet was not to operate underground but to let as many people know about us as possible.

We knew there were a lot of agents around anyway so we decided we wouldn't fall for the normal GI escape of using drugs and so forth. Huffman was always trying to convince us to use LSD and so forth. We told him it was illegal. . . . He also tried to get us to cold cock a barracks sergeant. That is, hit him in the head with a boot when he was asleep. We told him that was illegal too. At that point we had questions about Huffman because he didn't seem to understand what GIs United was all about. We weren't after any individual sergeant or anything like that. We weren't after any products of the system. We were after the system, after the war that was killing us and killing Vietnamese.[7]

A vigorous publicity and legal-defense campaign was launched by the GI Civil Liberties Defense Committee, whose secretary was Matilde Zimmermann. A representative of the committee, Helen Schiff, and her husband, attorney Mike Smith, went to Columbia and maintained frequent contact with the defendants. Students from the University of South Carolina demonstrated at the federal courthouse in Columbia when the men were brought there for hearings. The case was featured at all the GI-civilian demonstrations in April, and received support from the broadest antiwar and civil liberties circles. The legal defense was handled by a team of lawyers including Leonard B. Boudin, David Rein, Dorian Bowman, Diane Schulder, and Thomas Broadwater.

Under pressure of the publicity and legal work, the army finally dropped the charges against all eight defendants. The last to be released—after sixty days in the stockade—were Rudder, Pulley, and Cole. They were booted out of the army with undesirable discharges in spite of the fact that there were no charges against them. All three became activists in the civilian antiwar movement.

Meanwhile Joe Miles started another GIs United at Fort Bragg, this time not mainly among trainees, but among GIs who were combat veterans of Vietnam. The army retaliated by putting him on a one-man levy to a base above the arctic circle in Alaska. The fight against this was only partially successful, and he was eventually sent to Anchorage, where he finished out his hitch in the army, flying into the lower forty-eight for antiwar conferences whenever he could get a leave.

7. Ibid., p. 46.

Shortly after the spring demonstrations, the radical weekly *Guardian* declared in an editorial:

> It is clearly time for the general antiwar movement to recognize in theory what it is in practice—a mass radical movement with Vietnam as its central but not exclusive thrust. . . . Any effort to revive the old left-liberal coalition as it formerly operated—resulting in a watering-down of radical politics, compromise and caution born of conservatism—or to push the movement back to a Vietnam-only perspective, could bring things to a standstill again. . . .
>
> Being against the war is not enough. The newly radicalized antiwar movement must struggle against the source of imperialistic war and it must conduct that struggle here and now against the capitalist system, its institutions, politicians and policemen which make such wars inevitable. The movement, simply, must struggle for power to the people.[8]

This approach wasn't new, of course, and it was widespread among the so-called new left radicals, as well as a lot of the old ones, including radical-liberals. One of the main problems with the suggested reorientation was that they couldn't agree among themselves what the program of the new multi-issue radical movement ought to be, and always fell out among themselves whenever they tried to work that out within a particular coalition. This was one of the factors that had paralyzed the National Mobilization Committee.

Writing in the *Militant,* SWPer Gus Horowitz answered the *Guardian* editorial as follows:

> No thank you. We don't want to scrap the antiwar movement for demonstrations that are *limited* to the select few. We prefer the present method which calls on everybody who is ready to act against the war to come out in the streets and demonstrate. . . .
>
> What the *Guardian* incorrectly and disparagingly calls the "lowest common denominator" is, in actuality, the only basis on which independent *mass actions* can be built against the imperialist war in Vietnam. . . . Furthermore, when it is possible, in the midst of an imperialist war, to mobilize masses of people—including members of the armed forces!—in militant demonstrations demanding the immediate withdrawal of the imperialist forces and self-determination for the "enemy," that is far from a "lowest common denominator." It is concrete, meaningful struggle against an imperialist war—not hollow verbiage.[9]

8. *Guardian,* April 12, 1969.
9. *Militant,* April 25, 1969.

In a report to the SWP branches across the country Horowitz declared:

It is clear that it is possible to organize another major mass mobilization against the war. To do so will require the rebuilding of the national antiwar coalition, since the National Mobilization Committee is no longer viable, has lost considerable authority, and did nothing for the April 5-6 demonstrations. In the next few weeks we hope to lay the groundwork for another major antiwar conference. It is important that such a conference be representative of the groups in the antiwar movement. Accordingly, we are proceeding immediately to initiate the necessary preliminary discussion with other forces to obtain agreement for the idea of such a conference and to build it with adequate time and preparation to insure a representative attendance. It would be helpful if preliminary discussions about the idea of such a conference could be held among the central antiwar figures in each area, so that we can have a clear picture of what to expect.[10]

Horowitz recalls:

We [the SWP] thought there was enough of a changed mood in the masses that a big demonstration could come off. Two, we thought there was enough receptivity for this idea in the antiwar movement as a whole that, if a call to a conference were issued, it would be successful. The problem was to get some authoritative coalition body within the antiwar movement to call it. The best bet seemed to be the Cleveland Area Peace Action Council (CAPAC).[11]

CAPAC, like many other antiwar formations, had virtually ceased to function in the fall of 1968, after the Chicago Democratic Party demonstrations. But it had been refurbished during preparations for April 5-6. The Cleveland SMC had done remarkably well recently, especially among high school students, and worked closely with CAPAC. In addition Cleveland had been the site of the conferences which gave birth to the great national demonstrations of April 15, 1967, and it was hoped this would increase the interest in the conference. This would be enhanced if Sid Peck, who had played a central role in those previous conferences, would back the idea.

Peck had helped found CAPAC and had been its chairperson

10. "Antiwar Report" by Gus Horowitz, April 16, 1969. (Copy in author's files.)

11. Taped interview by author with Gus Horowitz, August 25, 1975.

until shortly after the August 1968 Chicago demonstrations. He had not been active in it recently, though he still lived in Cleveland. He had been preoccupied with other matters, including his own defense in a case stemming from the confrontation outside the Hilton hotel during the 1968 Chicago events. He had, however, demonstratively announced his support for the April 1969 actions and had chaired the April 5 rally in Chicago.

The current chairperson of CAPAC was Jerry Gordon, a forty-year-old practicing attorney with a background of some years as an active trade unionist before he finished law school. He favored a conference.

Horowitz made several trips to Cleveland to discuss the proposed conference with Gordon, Peck, and others. Everyone said they were in favor of reconstituting a national antiwar coalition and for major fall demonstrations. On May 10, CAPAC unanimously passed a motion to host the conference and proceed with the preparations, first by sending a letter to the major regional coalitions requesting their approval for the idea and tentatively setting the date for the July 4 weekend. Peck, however, was not present at the meeting and balked at signing the letter, though he had helped edit it beforehand. Gordon strongly favored calling the conference but was reluctant to proceed without Peck's approval. The letter was not sent.

Peck in turn was anxious to get the agreement of Dellinger and others with whom he had worked in the National Mobilization Committee, and they were obviously expressing reservations. The whole thing was tied up in one hesitation after another.

During this period Dellinger called me and asked to talk things over. We met in a cafe in New York along with Rennie Davis and my companion, Virginia Garza. Dellinger pleaded with me not to press the national conference. He and Davis said something important could soon be expected from SDS in connection with the opening of the trial of the "Conspiracy Eight" in Chicago. The trial was set to begin in September, and this, they said, would be the proper focus for a major fall action.

I told them I didn't trust SDS—which had not even been able to bring itself to discuss, let alone support, the April 5-6 actions—to take the lead for the antiwar movement. If we didn't press for a national conference, we could end up without a fall action, or with one that would repel the broad forces that could now be involved.

It seemed clear to me that we had a weighty difference on the character of the fall action. Dellinger and Davis wanted a confrontation, Chicago 1968 style, and Garza and I wanted a major mass action that could involve the broadest forces. Dellinger insisted that on the basis of nonviolence the two perspectives could be reconciled. I didn't believe so, and certainly not if the initiative were left exclusively to forces like SDS, the Yippies, and the "Conspiracy."

The fall mass actions would require a certain level of discipline, particularly if nonviolent civil disobedience were involved. "Do your own thing" would simply not work. If there weren't enough damn fools around to mess it up, the government's political police agencies would provide some. In my view we had to present our different perspectives before a conference that was open to the whole antiwar movement and let the conference decide one way or the other, or else work out a compromise in terms which would be widely understood before the organizing began.

We finished our talk without agreement, and for Dellinger and me, who had worked together for a long time, with a touch of sadness at the growing parting of the ways.

\*     \*     \*

Shortly thereafter, in early June, Gus Horowitz left for another trip to Cleveland. This time I went with him to help break through the hesitations there. Farrell Dobbs, then national secretary of the SWP, told us as we left: "Don't come back until the call to that conference is in the mail."

In Cleveland, Gus and I had some preliminary discussions with Gordon, Professor Richard Recknagel, and others, and it was clear that CAPAC was more than anxious to proceed if only Peck would agree. The whole thing finally came to a head in a meeting at Peck's house that lasted far into the night.

To avoid disturbing the rest of the household we met in the kitchen. Those present included Peck, Gordon, Horowitz, and for part of the time, Don Gurewitz of the Cleveland SMC and Louise Peck, who was active in Women Speak Out for Peace and Justice. In addition Dellinger was consulted several times in the course of the meeting by long-distance phone.

The Pecks agreed to a conference, and Dellinger apparently understood it was going to happen without him if he didn't go along. But both Sid Peck and Dellinger insisted it be a small conference, by specific invitation, rather than a large, open one. Horowitz, Gurewitz, and I insisted on an open conference, with every antiwar group invited to send delegates since there was no structure for democratically selecting a small group of invitees. Also we wanted the differences that we were convinced existed over tactics argued out before the largest possible audience. Neither Peck nor Gordon thought that the differences were as great as we feared.

Gordon recalls:

I favored an open conference, but I urged that we agree with an invitational one primarily for two reasons. One was that it became clear to me that a unified conference could not be held unless it was on the basis of an invitation. The movement was in a weak state, and we needed each other; we needed the unity. Secondly I anticipated that out of a conference, even an invitational one, a mass action would result. I simply could not believe that Dellinger and Peck and the others of that milieu— because the movement had been left in such a shambles as a result of Chicago—would come to this national meeting, and in effect propose the same thing, another Chicago.[12]

The impasse was broken when someone came up with the idea that observers be welcomed, while only the invited delegates would have vote. Peck and Gordon agreed. So did I. Gurewitz and Horowitz drew me aside. They didn't like the compromise. "We've got to break the impasse," I told them. "If the call gets out with observers welcome, all sorts of activists will be there and the arguments will take place in front of them. By then decisions will be up to the conference, not to a handful of people in a kitchen and one on the phone." So we agreed to an invitational confer-ence with observers welcome.

Then Sid Peck, Gordon, and I, with Dellinger on the phone, drew up the list of those who would be delegates at the next national conference of the American antiwar movement. I made it clear I considered the procedure lacking in democratic virtue and was only going along with it to break the deadlock.

We finished early in the morning with a list of sixty-six names, plus allocations of delegates to a number of groups and regional coalitions. Gordon did manage to convince Peck to allow a certain flexibility in the formula in case we had overlooked something. Additional names could be sent to CAPAC and presumably decided upon by the credentials committee of the conference. The next day we drew up a call to the conference. Peck and Dellinger phoned around the country and got twenty individuals, including many from the old Mobe steering committee in its better days, to act as the steering committee and initial endorsers of the conference. This was very important because it insured continuity and eliminated any effective charges of divisiveness against the CAPAC initiative.

After all that was agreed to, Gus and I stayed around the CAPAC office until the call to the conference was in the mail to the list of invited groups and individuals. In fact we watched while it was being dropped into the mailbox. Then we returned to New York.

After the national office of the Student Mobilization Committee received the invitation, it sent out its own call for a national student antiwar conference, also in Cleveland and on July 6, the day after the close of the other conference. This would allow the SMC to take immediate action on the results of the preceding conference and begin building the actions without delay. But there was also an element of pressure involved. The SMC call had the following paragraph:

> The Cleveland Area Peace Action Council (CAPAC) has called a national conference July 4-5 to broaden and unify the antiwar forces in this country and to plan coordinated national mass actions this fall. The SMC urges all student organizations and individuals to participate in this conference as observers or representatives (write CAPAC if your group wants delegate status).[13]

The SMC call was given wide distribution, assuring that the movement generally would be aware of the July 4-5 conference. Dellinger and others on the conference steering committee took a dim view of this action of the SMC, but the word was out and there was nothing they could do to reverse it.

\*        \*        \*

While preparations for the national antiwar conference were getting under way, SDS held its ninth annual convention in

13. SMC leaflet, undated. (Copy in author's files.)

Chicago June 18-22. The central feature of this gathering, attended by some 1,500 youths, was an irreparable split between the supporters of the Progressive Labor Party (PL) on the one hand and the SDS national office on the other. PL led the Worker-Student Alliance (WSA) caucus and the national office supporters were organized as the Revolutionary Youth Movement (RYM) caucus.

Antiwar activity as such was not central to the split arguments, though the issue of the Vietnamese revolution itself was. PL had developed a line characterizing both North Vietnam and the South Vietnamese National Liberation Front as "revisionist" because they accepted aid from the Soviet Union. RYM, on the other hand, insisted that anyone who did not support the NLF and North Vietnam and accept their programs across the board was not really opposing U.S. imperialism.

Specific activity at home against the war was not discussed. Actions designed to involve broad masses of Americans who were willing to demand immediate U.S. withdrawal, but not necessarily to take positions on Vietnamese politics, were discounted by both sides in the dispute. The upcoming national antiwar conference was not mentioned, except in leaflets distributed in the corridors by the SMC and other groups.

(The YSA distributed a leaflet headlined "Comrades, where were you?" It pointed out that SDS had abstained from the April demonstrations and appealed for participation in the July conference and the fall actions. It quoted a message sent by the NLF to the organizers of the April 6 demonstrations which said: "What more to say than that we are entirely pleased with your suggestions to concentrate on the themes: TOTAL AND UNCONDITIONAL WITHDRAWAL OF AMERICAN TROOPS! VIETNAM FOR THE VIETNAMESE!")[14]

The argumentation between the PL-WSA and RYM supporters could hardly be characterized by any such dignified term as "debate." The discussion consisted largely of each side trying to shout down the other with chants. By this time the SDS national office, lacking a consistent program of its own with which to answer PL's ideology, had begun to mirror the Stalinist-type polemics as well as the organizational methods of its opponent. RYM had even adopted Maoist trappings.

14. The entire leaflet is reproduced in the *Militant,* July 4, 1969.

Only a small part of the RYM supporters were entirely serious about this ideological transformation. Others accepted it cynically in a desperate attempt to get some sort of edge on their factional opponent in the heat of the fight. Still others, including one group that stood on chairs shouting nonsense and waving the little red book of Mao quotations, acted with tongue in cheek. But any genuine polemics were on such a low level that not everyone caught the satire of this bit of guerrilla theater, and the audience was further confused.

RYM was expected to have a strong edge over PL on two points. PL took a dim view of both Black nationalism and the women's liberation movement, then taking hold among SDS women. RYM claimed to support both, and in this respect was far more in tune with the bulk of the delegates than was PL. A key move in the RYM attack was the appearance of a delegation from the Black Panther Party, which was allied with RYM and bitterly hostile to PL. But Panther spokesmen Rufus Walls and Jewel Cook not only denounced PL, they also derided women's liberation, using such expressions as "pussy power" and "the position for you sisters [in the revolution] . . . is *prone.*"[15] Neither Walls nor Cook were able to finish their talks over the shouts of "Fight male chauvinism," and pandemonium broke loose in the hall.

"The Panthers," comments Kirkpatrick Sale, "had humiliated not PL but their own supporters, and in doing so had neatly managed by a single stroke to turn to dross both of RYM's chief theoretical weapons: its alliance with the vanguard Panthers and its support for women's liberation."[16]

Finally, with the convention in disarray, the RYM caucus stalked out of the main hall and met for a day and a half by itself. On Saturday night, June 21, the caucus voted to expel the PL-WSA supporters from SDS and to exclude from SDS all those who did not accept a set of points adopted by the caucus. RYM then returned to the main hall where its spokesperson, Bernardine Dohrn, announced this to the full convention. Without taking a vote, RYM retired to another hall to proceed with the "real SDS" convention.

RYM SDS then did discuss and adopt a proposal for a fall national action against the war. It was to be in Chicago at the time of the opening of the trial of those under federal indictment

15. Kirkpatrick Sale, *SDS* (New York: Vintage Books, 1973), p. 567.
16. Loc. cit.

in connection with the Democratic Party convention demonstrations in August 1968.

But the leaders of RYM found themselves dividing into two increasingly antagonistic factions—Weatherman and RYM II.[17] Weatherman was based on the style of the local SDS "action factions" such as that at Columbia University in the spring of 1968. Its main thrust was the notion that it could inspire masses of youth to revolutionary action by its own dramatic example. The courting of physical confrontation with the police was central to its approach.

RYM II had certain theoretical differences with Weatherman and began to draw back from the tactical implications of the Weatherman approach as soon as the split with PL was consummated. The most prominent spokespersons for RYM II were Mike Klonsky and Bob Avakian, the latter of the Bay Area Radical Union and author of the "out-Mao-the-Maoists" strategy in the fight with PL. The leaders of the Weatherman faction included Bernardine Dohrn, Mark Rudd, Bill Ayers, and Jeff Jones.

In the elections which completed the RYM SDS convention, Weatherman took all three national officers and a decisive majority of the National Council.

Meanwhile, the PL-WSA caucus proceeded with its part of the convention by declaring itself the "real SDS." It elected national officers and moved its version of the SDS national office to Boston, where its support was strongest.

More than one observer commented that the split convention of the major organization of the "new left" exhibited the worst features of the old, with none of the virtues.

Stew Albert, one of the veteran Berkeley street people and a sidekick of Jerry Rubin, wrote in the *Berkeley Barb*: "The scenes on the convention floor were out of a reactionary newspaper cartoon satirizing the New Left." Albert quoted Jerry Rubin saying: "If the ruling class wanted to destroy SDS they would televise their convention for free at prime time." Then came the

---

17. The names of these factions came from titles of documents distributed at the convention: "You Don't Need a Weatherman To Know Which Way the Wind Blows" and "Revolutionary Youth Movement II." The former is a line from Bob Dylan's song "Subterranean Homesick Blues."

ultimate Rubinesque putdown: "Everyone watching would be bored."[18]

In the wake of the convention SDS was shattered, the bulk of its activists following none of the factions, just drifting away. SDS as a major youth group was no more, though it would take some time for this self-destruction to become generally apparent. In the meantime Weatherman was left in charge of the SDS national office in Chicago and of preparations for the national action in the fall.

\* \* \*

The 1969 Cleveland national antiwar conference was held July 4-5 at Case Western Reserve University. The night before, the twenty-member steering committee met to make final preparations for an agenda.[19] Dellinger and Rennie Davis brought several observers to this meeting, including Mark Rudd and Kathy Boudin, Weatherpeople representing the SDS national office in Chicago. They said little beyond the fact that SDS was planning a national action in Chicago on the opening date of the "Conspiracy Eight" trial, and some regional actions in November.

Dellinger proposed in effect that the steering committee recom-

18. *Berkeley Barb,* June 27, 1969.
19. The members of the steering committee were: Norma Becker of the New York Parade Committee; Barbara Bick of Washington Women Strike for Peace; Professor Douglas Dowd of Cornell; Rennie Davis of the "Conspiracy"; Dave Dellinger of *Liberation* magazine; Al Evanoff of District 65, Retail, Wholesale and Department Store Workers; Rev. Richard Fernandez of Clergy and Laymen (later Laity) Concerned; Jerry Gordon of CAPAC; Fred Halstead of the SWP; Arnold Johnson of the CP; Professor Donald Kalish of UCLA; Sidney Lens of the Chicago Peace Council; Carol Lipman of the SMC; John McAuliff of the Committee of Returned Volunteers (Peace Corps veterans); Stewart Meacham of the American Friends Service Committee; Professor Sidney Peck of Case Western Reserve; Maxwell Primack of the Chicago Peace Council; Carl Rogers of the Committee for the Presidio Twenty-seven; Irving Sarnoff of the Los Angeles Peace Action Council; and Cora Weiss of New York Women Strike for Peace. Only Davis, Lipman, McAuliff, and Rogers were under thirty, and only Lipman was from a student group.

mend to the conference that it consider these the major actions of the fall and help build them. Jerry Gordon presented a fall proposal from the Cleveland Area Peace Action Council for a mass demonstration in Washington, D.C., without civil disobedience so that the broadest participation could be organized.

After some tense discussion Sid Lens proposed a compromise: that the steering committee should recommend both actions. This was one time I didn't appreciate Lens's penchant for patchwork unity. I insisted on counterposing a vote for the Washington action against Lens's compromise, on the ground that we should clearly reject any attempt to build into the fall actions an ultraleft confrontation. In the discussion that followed, Dellinger, Lens, and others insisted that the Chicago action could be built so as to include both mass action and nonviolent civil disobedience, and need not be a relatively small street-fighting affair. Under the given conditions, that was impossible, in my opinion, and I pressed for the vote. Only Gordon, Carol Lipman of the SMC, and I opposed the Lens motion. The three of us then insisted on a minority report to the conference.

The next morning on the way to the auditorium where the conference was gathering, I passed a group of Weatherpeople sitting on the grass Indian fashion. Mark Rudd got up from the circle and approached me. "Well Fred," he said, "looks like we're going to have a fight." "Looks that way," I replied, "but let's keep it clean and make the differences as clear as possible." "Right," said Rudd, and we shook hands and parted. One thing I appreciated about the Weatherpeople, at least those I had anything to do with, was that they were not given to obscuring their positions.

This would prove important in the discussion at the conference. The majority of the steering committee had voted to recommend the SDS actions not because they agreed with the Weatherman approach, but because they didn't really know or were unwilling to accept as accomplished fact the direction Weatherman was determinedly pursuing. The illusions that SDS represented "the youth" still persisted among many of them.

Then too there was a certain tendency among these older radicals and radical-liberals to be attracted to ultraleft confrontation. They were more than half convinced it might do some good. Dellinger's dream of a nonviolent Narodniki provided a certain ideological ground on which they could hope to have it both ways. In addition most of the members of the steering committee were reluctant to find themselves in direct opposition to Dellinger, even more so in company with the representative of the Socialist Workers Party.

Gordon was an exception. For one thing he had not been a part of the old Mobe steering committee and was a new element in the situation. But mainly he was just very clear on what he wanted: the broadest possible mass action for immediate withdrawal, unencumbered by any opening for ultraleft adventures.

Gordon was a bit formal, with a stubborn streak. He would sometimes say that as a practicing lawyer he could not participate in violations of the law, not even nonviolent civil disobedience, though he recognized those who did as part of the movement and would defend them. He was not easily swayed by fashion nor inclined to revolutionary romanticism. If he did any dreaming it was in the direction of getting the labor movement involved. The others had mixed feelings about Chicago in August 1968. Gordon was just appalled.

A sort of keynote address was given to the conference by Leo Fenster, who had been invited by CAPAC in its capacity as host group. Fenster was the elected head of the Ohio regional district council of the United Auto Workers union, and he appealed to the conference to adopt the tactics of "a majority movement." He said the majority of both the leadership and membership of the UAW now favored withdrawal from Vietnam "posthaste."[20] In his view this was true of the majority of the country's union members generally, in spite of the hawk position of George Meany and the AFL-CIO Executive Council. This in turn, said Fenster, reflected a change in the population as a whole. The antiwar movement, he said, should organize this sentiment, not isolate itself from it.

On the fall action, Dellinger reported for the steering committee majority, and Gordon for the minority. But Mark Rudd gave a supplementary report on the SDS action in Chicago. The clashes at the August 1968 Chicago Democratic Party convention demonstrations had been more damaging to imperialism than all the mass peaceful demonstrations put together, Rudd said. What was needed, he declared, was an "anti-imperialist movement" in the United States acting as the American arm of the National Liberation Front of South Vietnam and led by such groups as the Black Panthers, the Young Lords (a Puerto Rican group which

20. Cleveland *Plain Dealer,* July 5, 1969.

originated as a street gang in Chicago but whose best-known section was a split-off of the same name in New York), and SDS. The Chicago national action would build such an alliance, he said, because it would prove that SDS was a white radical group that would fight, literally. The broad-based coalitions that until now had led the antiwar movement must be willing to follow this leadership. (Later both the Panthers and the Lords would reject the Weatherman action as suicidal.)

It was not enough, declared Rudd, to demand immediate U.S. withdrawal from Vietnam. Instead, the movement must "Bring the war home."[21] He made it clear that SDS was going to run the Chicago action and determine its character.

Rudd's presentation was received with dismay by the great bulk of the audience, including the members of the steering committee. Lens turned to me with a pained look and jested bitterly: "Did you pay him to say that?"

Meantime much heat was being generated over the question of delegates' credentials. There were about a hundred originally invited voting delegates at the conference. But over 800 other activists also registered, some two hundred of them requesting delegate status, and the rest as observers. The steering committee had set up a credentials committee, and over the objections of Gordon, Lipman, and myself, took the position that the steering committee itself should be the final source of appeal on credentials. The first morning a motion that the conference itself be the highest body of appeal was defeated 55 to 44. It later proved to be almost the undoing of the steering committee.

The members of the credentials committee from the steering committee majority were apparently afraid that the SWP and YSA would pack the conference with voting delegates. They started by challenging almost every delegate they didn't know. The result was that all sorts of people were challenged, and they were fighting mad. The credentials committee majority even challenged some people who had been elected by their local

---

21. There is no literal text of Rudd's speech. It is paraphrased here from my rough notes. But he took part of it from an SDS position paper distributed at the conference and entitled: "Bring the War Home." (Copy in author's files.) The same essential line as Rudd's speech appeared in an article by Kathy Boudin, Bernardine Dohrn, and Terry Robbins in the August 23, 1969, *New Left Notes* (Chicago) entitled "Bringing the War Back Home: Less Talk, More National Action."

unions to attend the conference—a bold step for a local union in those days—and these just wouldn't take no for an answer. By the middle of the second day, even I was feeling sorry for the members of the steering committee who were being besieged by irate petitioners. In the end a sizable number of additional delegates were accredited, but by then it didn't really matter as far as the relationship of forces on the issues was concerned. The discussion had been full and there was no question the great majority supported Gordon's approach and rejected Rudd's in spite of other differences.

In truth the SWP and YSA had made no attempt to pack this conference in the sense of having SWPers and YSAers who were not legitimate representatives of antiwar groups demand delegate status. We were a minority of the voting delegates throughout. We made no secret of the fact that we encouraged antiwar groups to send participants, either as delegates or observers, but we had no desire to go through the exercise of capturing ourselves. We wanted a representative conference that would be a real test of where the activists stood on the issues, and that would have the authority to call masses into action on an unprecedented scale.

By the middle of the second day it would probably have been possible for Gordon to push through the CAPAC resolution without compromise. He considered this but was dissuaded by arguments of Harry Ring and others that it would be much better to get an agreement for a joint majority-minority resolution that would commit the whole steering committee behind the program adopted by the conference.

Lens had been negotiating back and forth and finally came up with a compromise that both the majority and minority on the steering committee agreed to support. It included both the Chicago and Washington actions, as well as others. What made it acceptable to Gordon was the following wording regarding Chicago: "Planning on this action was initiated by other groups. It will therefore be necessary to negotiate on tactics and means of collaboration with these other groups to assure the development of plans and tactics capable of mobilizing the largest number of people."[22] Participation in the Chicago action, then, would be

22. "Steering Committee Proposal for Joint Majority-Minority Resolution." Cleveland national antiwar conference, July 5, 1969. (Copy in author's files.)

conditional on whether SDS could listen to reason.

Just how this worked out in real life would depend heavily on who was in charge of the various actions. Dellinger proposed that he head up the Washington action and Rennie Davis take Chicago. This was unacceptable to most of the others, including me. After a long period of painful negotiating we came up with the following: Project directors for Washington would be Fay Knopp of the Philadelphia Friends staff, and Abe Bloom, the chairman of Washington SANE and a leader of the Washington Mobilization Committee.

That put the central responsibility on Bloom, who was resident in Washington. This was a crucial choice because Bloom was firmly committed to the mass action perspective. Whatever happened elsewhere, proper preparations for the Washington action could proceed. Project directors for Chicago would be Rennie Davis and Sylvia Kushner of the Chicago Peace Council staff. Kushner's participation was a built-in safety valve. She would not be inclined to let SDS lead the Chicago Peace Council into suicide, and she was tough enough to put her foot down when necessary. In addition two cochairpersons of the new national coalition would be assigned to the Chicago project and two to Washington. For Chicago it would be Douglas Dowd and Sid Lens; for Washington, Sid Peck and Stewart Meacham. Dellinger would be liaison coordinator between the two projects.

All this was negotiated in the corridors between members of the steering committee and a few other people, while the rest of the conference stalled for time and wondered what was going on. Gordon found the process offensive, and the rank and file of the conference—already angry with the steering committee majority—was resentful of the behind-the-scenes negotiating.

The joint resolution on activities was attractive enough on its own merits to pass without difficulty, especially since the issues involved had already been well discussed by the conference. But the structural proposal was another matter. This included the project directors, cochairpersons, and the steering committee for the new coalition, which we proposed be the same as the old one with some additions. The ranks of the conference were angry enough by then to vote for throwing out much of the old steering committee. But this would have amounted to a virtual split. It wasn't necessary. It would have destroyed the pull of unity, and the members of the old steering committee had much to contribute to building the actions.

The steering committee majority was afraid the structural proposal would not pass if one of them presented it, so they insisted one of the minority do it. I presented it to the conference, appealing for acceptance in the interest of a unified coalition. There were a few groans and a lot of tight lips, but it passed overwhelmingly.

Gordon, as chairman of the host group, spoke at the conclusion of the conference, thanking the people who had done the technical work, praising Lens for his unity efforts, and finally telling the audience that he shared their exasperation at the "invitational" character of the conference and the "high-handed" way it was run. The place exploded in applause. Gordon said he would do everything he could to see that future conferences were run democratically, and the meeting ended with the crowd giving Gordon an ovation.

That night the steering committee met to take care of some details, including adopting a name for the new national coalition—the New Mobilization Committee to End the War in Vietnam. But the conference had been something of a traumatic experience for the steering committee majority, and the meeting began with virtually every person in the room except Lipman, me, and the new members excoriating Jerry Gordon for playing to the crowd. Gordon later commented: "Cheered by the ranks, denounced by the bureaucratic leadership. What an experience that day was!"[23]

\*      \*      \*

One of the activities the conference decided to participate in was called the Vietnam Moratorium. It had been presented to the plenary by David Hawk, a former staff member of the National Student Association and one of the leaders of the youth for McCarthy in the 1968 presidential primaries. The idea was for a "moratorium on 'business as usual'" on October 15, a Wednesday and a regular workday, "in order that students, faculty members and concerned citizens can devote time and energy to the important work of taking the issue of peace in Vietnam to the larger community." A month later another moratorium was to be held, this time for two days, and so on, expanding by one day

23. Letter from Jerry Gordon to the author, July 23, 1975.

each month "until there is American withdrawal or a negotiated settlement."[24]

This project had already been publicly announced a few days before the Cleveland conference, but few delegates had heard of it until Hawk presented it in Cleveland and asked for support. The idea was received with skepticism, as I recall. It seemed at one and the same time either too mild—some dispersed and unfocused educational activities by students here and there across the country—or unrealistically ambitious—something like a cumulative general strike.

The Vietnam Moratorium was added to the Cleveland conference's call for actions, not so much out of enthusiasm for the idea itself as out of a desire on the part of Lens and others to develop friendly relations with the forces that had initiated it. The original Vietnam Moratorium announcement had been made in Washington June 30 by Hawk; Sam Brown, a fellow at Harvard's Institute of Politics; and David Mixner, then serving on the Democratic Party reform commission headed by Senator George McGovern. All three had been principal organizers of the youth for McCarthy in 1968. In addition almost 500 college student-body presidents and school newspaper editors had signed the student call to the Moratorium.

The Vietnam Moratorium proposal also had some influence on the Cleveland conference's choice of a date for the mass demonstration in Washington—Saturday, November 15. That would be around the time of the second month's moratorium. It was hoped this would maximize the possibility of the Moratorium forces tying in with the Washington action. Participation in the Vietnam Moratorium was adopted by the Cleveland conference without much discussion and almost as an afterthought. But it would prove to be one of the most important decisions the conference made. For it placed the New Mobilization Committee and the Student Mobilization Committee—which adopted the same set of actions at its own conference July 6—in a position to take advantage of a major opening to their right.

24. "Student call for a Vietnam Moratorium," undated. (Copy in author's files.)

# 18

# The Vietnam Moratorium

Less than a week after the July 4-6, 1969, Cleveland conferences a peculiar confrontation occurred between the Nixon administration and the antiwar movement in Seattle. In June Nixon had announced that as part of the plan to "Vietnamize" the war, 25,000 American troops would soon be withdrawn. (At the time there were some 535,000 uniformed U.S. military personnel in Vietnam.) Seattle was chosen as the city to host a parade of the first of the withdrawn GIs to reach the United States by ship.

On July 10 some 800 soldiers from Vietnam were marched through the streets of Seattle to the public library, where they were to stand at parade rest and listen to speeches by General William C. Westmoreland and Secretary of the Army Stanley Resor. As they neared the library they were greeted by chants of "Welcome home, Bring them all home!" from a crowd of antiwar demonstrators carrying signs that said: "It's a Trick, Dick. Bring Them *All* Home!" and "Welcome Home GIs. Join the Antiwar Movement."

The authorities had gone to some lengths to assure a "patriotic" rally. A girls' school had been let out and the students equipped with American flags to wave. There were about as many "patriots" as antiwar demonstrators, and the scene was emotionally charged. Wendy Reissner and Gwynn Vorhaus, who were there, reported:

Many of the "patriots" really wanted to believe that the war was over, and were very upset by the demonstration which brought home the reality of the situation. An incident typified this mood. A young girl with an American flag stepped up to block a sign saying, "We Want Them *All*

Home." She said, "How can you do this!" The demonstrator explained that the war was not over, and she was demonstrating because the token pullout was being used to fool people; that it would take 20 years to bring them home if 25,000 were withdrawn annually, and that three normal days worth of replacements could make up for 25,000 withdrawn. The girl with the flag began to cry and stepped aside.[1]

What had been planned as a public relations coup for the administration's Vietnam policy fell flat. Even the *New York Times* was constrained to report that when the antiwar demonstrators shouted about bringing all the GIs home, "to some people in the crowd, the chant appeared to express their private feelings."[2]

*          *          *

On July 13 a flotilla of six rowboats, three rubber rafts, and a canoe, filled with youths calling themselves the Free the Army (FTA) forces, set out from a public beach on one shore of American Lake outside Tacoma, Washington. They rowed to the other side for a landing at the enlisted men's beach on the Fort Lewis military reservation. They had previously issued a statement to the press declaring their intention to "liberate the 40,000 men held prisoner at Ft. Lewis." The statement added, "if it becomes necessary to destroy Fort Lewis in order to save it, *we shall not shrink from that task.*"[3]

The landing force, most of them women, alighted on the beach and started passing out leaflets inviting the soldiers to a meeting of the GI-Civilian Alliance for Peace. FTA "General" Stephanie Coontz, twenty-four, stood in her rowboat a safe distance off-shore, her shirt bedecked with medals, shouting orders and telling newsmen she could see light at the end of the tunnel. As military police moved down the beach toward the invaders, one demonstrator came up to them and unfurled a banner which read, "You are surrounded. Lay down your guns."[4] When the MPs

1. *Militant,* July 25, 1969.

2. *New York Times,* July 11, 1969.

3. *GI Press Service,* July 24, 1969. A set of this publication of the Student Mobilization Committee is on file at the State Historical Society of Wisconsin.

4. *Counterpoint,* August 7, 1969. (Copy in author's files.)

refused, an FTA frogman who had swum ashore floating a round table with him asked to be taken in with the others, so that negotiations could be held around his table.

The invaders were hauled to the provost marshal's office and given letters warning them not to come on base again. From her rowboat "General" Coontz, already the possessor of several such letters, declared the invasion a success. According to the *Seattle Post-Intelligencer*, "A reporter asked how the operation could be considered a success when all the invaders were captured. 'Well,' she shot back, 'we certainly were as successful today as the United States has been in Vietnam.' "[5]

\*        \*        \*

The New Mobilization Committee and the SMC built rapidly after the Cleveland conferences. So did the Vietnam Moratorium, and by July 30 Dave Hawk was able to report to a New Mobe steering committee meeting that the Moratorium had active workers on 225 campuses and contacts on 75 others. That was just the beginning. The Vietnam Moratorium had set up its national office in Washington, D.C., in a suite on the eighth floor of 1029 Vermont Avenue, N.W. After the Cleveland conference, the New Mobe's Washington Action Committee moved into the ninth floor of the same building. This soon became the national office of the New Mobe. The SMC followed suit, moving its national headquarters to the same building in the capital.

Relations between the three organizations were not without some tension, but willy-nilly they were all cooperating on the October 15 Moratorium and, as far as the general public was concerned, there was little distinction between them. This was a source of concern to the wing of the Democratic Party that was backing the Moratorium. But in spite of initial wariness, the youth on the Moratorium staff and those building it across the country by and large willingly accepted the cooperation they got from the other two groups.

The steering committee of the New Mobe was greatly expanded in late July as interest in the fall antiwar offensive widened. At Stewart Meacham's initiative, Ron Young of the Fellowship of Reconciliation was added as a co-project director of the Washington action, and Young moved to Washington to take charge of the New Mobe staff.

5. *Seattle Post-Intelligencer*, July 14, 1969.

Negotiations with SDS over the Chicago action—now set for October 11—broke down as Weatherman SDS insisted on complete control. Just what they had in mind was made clear by a widely distributed leaflet drawn up by Detroit SDS. It declared: "We're going back to Chicago, tougher and more together than ever. . . . And the time is right for fighting in the streets! . . . SDS is recruiting an army right now, man, a *people's* army, under black leadership, that's gonna fight against the pigs and *win!!!*"[6] (The reference to "Black leadership" was pure fantasy since no Black organization would support the action, and SDS had no Blacks in its leadership.)

At the New Mobe steering committee August 17-18 a motion was passed "That we not actively build the SDS action on October 11 but that we publicize it by including it in listings of fall actions and informing our constituencies about it."[7] Jerry Gordon opposed even the listing, but the majority voted for it on the ground that we should leave the door open for a possible change in developments. As it turned out, the New Mobe had nothing further to do with the SDS Chicago action.

Meanwhile, a wave of demonstrations and other antiwar activities took place during the summer as local coalitions were expanded and new ones developed. High officials of the Nixon administration began to be greeted with the same sort of antiwar demonstrations that had plagued President Johnson.

On August 17, 1969, the first of the actions directly endorsed by the Cleveland conference was held as 8,000 demonstrators from around California, including a few dozen antiwar marines from nearby Camp Pendleton, converged on the so-called Summer White House at Nixon's home in San Clemente. The area was not noted for radical sentiment, yet in spite of much talk beforehand, a right-wing counterdemonstration drew only half a dozen pickets. The antiwar affair was organized by the Los Angeles Peace Action Council and the SMC and was carefully marshaled and entirely peaceful.

Another kind of demonstration that was widespread in those days was known as "reading of the war dead." These antiwar memorials were often staged by church organizations and con-

6. *Militant*, September 19, 1969, emphasis in original. The full text of the SDS leaflet is carried.
7. New Mobilization steering committee minutes, August 17-18, 1969. (Copy in author's files.)

sisted of groups of people standing in a public place taking turns reading the list of American GIs killed in Vietnam. At the end of August 1969, there were some 38,000 such deaths and the names were read into the *Congressional Record* as the Pentagon released them.

In spite of the negotiations and announced withdrawals, the GI death rate was an average of 244.8 per week in the first six months of Nixon's term, some 30 percent higher than during the last six months under President Johnson.[8] And the Vietnamese casualties rose far higher under the massive U.S. bombing.

The object of the "reading of the war dead" demonstrations was to bring home the fact that the war was not "winding down" and that the statistics represented individual human beings.

*    *    *

"'SIR, MY MEN REFUSE TO GO!'—Weary Viet GIs Defy Order" That was the headline in the New York *Daily News* of August 26, 1969. There followed an Associated Press dispatch by Peter Arnett and Horst Faas which was featured in papers across the country about the temporary refusal to continue fighting by Company A of the Third Battalion, 21st Infantry, in Vietnam. There were no reported victimizations of the GIs, and the company commander was relieved of his command. Oddly enough, one argument used to downgrade the significance of this incident was that it was not really unusual and that the company commander was green and didn't know how to cover it up without making waves.

James Reston commented in the August 27 *New York Times* that Nixon

has been worried about the revolt of the voters against the war, and even about a revolt of the generals if he humiliates them by pulling out too fast. But now he also has to consider the possibility of a revolt of the men if he risks their lives in a war he has decided to bring to a close.

Reston here assumed that Nixon really was trying to get out "gracefully" when in truth he was still trying to win the war. But

8. *Armed Forces Journal*, August 2, 1969.

the *New York Times* vice-president did put his finger on a major contradiction in the Nixon public relations effort. The more the government tried to defuse the antiwar movement by talking about the war being almost over, the less tolerable facing death in Vietnam was for the GIs.

\*          \*          \*

As the universities and high schools opened in the fall it became apparent that the sweep of support for both the October 15 Moratorium and the November 15 activities was unprecedented and actually far beyond what the national offices of the antiwar groups could keep track of. Some of the initial campus organizing meetings for the Moratorium drew over 1,000 participants. The first campus SMC meetings of the fall semester drew three and four times as many as before, and many new campuses were involved.

An example of the mood is what happened at the University of Michigan at Ann Arbor where a teach-in was held Friday night, September 19. The next day some of the participants leafletted football fans as they entered the stadium for the Michigan-Vanderbilt game. As the game ended, more than 15,000 people joined in an antiwar march from the stadium to a rally at the center of campus to launch the local fall offensive against the war. Dave Dellinger and ex-Private Andrew Pulley were among the speakers.

The teach-in itself had filled the auditorium to well over its 4,500 capacity, and the president of the University of Michigan, Robben Fleming, was one of the speakers. He called U.S. involvement in Vietnam a "colossal mistake" and advocated a staged withdrawal of troops—all but 100,000 by the end of 1970. Rennie Davis spoke next and counterposed the New Mobe's position of immediate withdrawal. A group of SDSers attempted to physically disrupt the meeting, denouncing those who would allow Dr. Fleming to speak. They were repulsed.

This incident was indicative of the stance taken by Weatherman-SDS, RYM II-SDS, and PL-SDS toward the opportunities for broadening the antiwar movement that presented themselves at this time. All three denounced the Moratorium, for example, as nothing more than an attempt by Establishment liberals to co-opt the student movement.

There is no doubt that a section of the Democratic Party and some Republican doves hoped to use the Moratorium to co-opt the antiwar movement in preparation for the 1970 congressional elections. But in so doing they were—however hesitantly—throwing their authority behind an antiwar action. This provided openings of an entirely new dimension. The Moratorium was not an election for public office but a date for antiwar activities across the country. Their character would be determined by the participants in each locality.

The New Mobe and the SMC, instead of turning their backs on this development, threw themselves into building these actions. They did not oppose the appearance of prominent Establishment figures as sponsors and speakers. They took advantage of the opportunity to speak to larger audiences with their own more radical positions, welcoming the element of debate involved, and drawing more people into preparations for the November activities.

And the truth is that while the major splinters of SDS were sinking ever deeper into sectarian and obscurantist methods—setting up Stalin as an example to follow, excluding and slandering rivals within the movement, trying to settle ideological arguments by physical force—the liberal youth organizing the Moratorium by and large went along with the principle of nonexclusion. In building the October 15 activities and selecting speakers, the more moderate elements did not go along with attempts by some of the older Democratic Party politicians to exclude the radical antiwar forces. In part this was due to the presence of the SMC, which was constantly hammering away at immediate withdrawal and nonexclusion and getting a good response from students generally.

Remarkably enough there was very little competitive hostility on a local level between the Vietnam Moratorium Committee and the SMC. One reason was that the Moratorium was not really an organization in its own right. Nor was it a coalition of constituent groups. It was a self-appointed initiating group of liberal youth with connections to a section of the Democratic Party and some dove Republicans. It also had a wide following among student government figures. But it had no democratic structure and was not responsible to a rank and file. Indeed it had no rank and file; its national decisions were made behind closed doors among a small group of people in contact with the politicians. These were informally discussed and sometimes influenced by the national staff, a somewhat larger number. On a local level its structures were ad hoc, informal groupings around figures who were in contact with the national office and with local politicians.

The SMC, on the other hand, had a formal, representative structure on both the local and national levels, responsible to conferences of the rank and file. And it actively sought to build and extend this foundation.

In the greater Boston area, for example, a regional SMC conference was held October 2 in connection with the October 15 preparations. Six hundred activists attended. At that time, there were twelve SMC college chapters on Boston-area campuses, nine more in formation, and several high school chapters. The Greater Boston SMC membership was estimated then at 2,000, and a budget of $10,000 was approved for the immediate period ahead, all of it raised locally. It was reported that an October 15 SMC button had sold out the original Boston run of 2,000 in three days.

Once organized, an SMC chapter held weekly meetings where decisions were made by majority vote. The chapter had an open steering committee composed of working committee chairpersons and those members willing to devote a large amount of time. A citywide steering committee was made up of representatives from the chapters. Occasionally, when major decisions were involved, it would convene a regional meeting like that in Boston, October 2.

The SMC national office also published the *Student Mobilizer* and the *GI Press Service*, which was set up to make it convenient for local GI papers to lift whole articles, cartoons, and so on. It was edited by ex-Sp/4 Allen Myers, founder of the *Ultimate Weapon* at Fort Dix, New Jersey, who had finished his hitch in the army in June.

The result of all this work was that in the course of building the October 15 events the Moratorium as an organization remained little more than a national office, while the SMC as an organization expanded manyfold.

\*         \*         \*

Throughout this period, the Nixon administration maintained a public posture of dismissing the antiwar movement as irrelevant. On September 26 the president held a press conference in which he announced that the "Vietnamization program" was "moving forward."[9] At the time, Senator Charles Goodell (Republican-New York) had introduced a bill calling for a 1970 deadline on the withdrawal of U.S. troops from Vietnam, and there were stories of caucusing among congressmen to discuss support to the Moratorium. Nixon denounced these congressional moves as "defeatist" and declared that "under no circumstances" would he be affected by antiwar demonstrations.

There is now ample documentation that the White House was on the contrary very much disturbed by the demonstrations. For example: Jeb Stuart Magruder, one of those later convicted in the Watergate scandal, was at the time just going on the White House staff. To acquaint him with the president's thinking, he was given some memos on public relations that Nixon had dictated on September 22, 1969. In his book *An American Life*, Magruder says:

> The President's memos had been inspired by the fact that two great antiwar demonstrations were approaching, the national moratorium on October 15 and the rally at the Washington Monument on November 15. We all felt threatened, put on the defensive, by the imminence of these two well-organized, well-publicized demonstrations, and the President was taking the initiative in suggesting how we might counter our critics.[10]

The sections of these memos that Magruder quotes are mainly concerned with managing the news, planting stories implying that congressional critics were dupes of Hanoi, and so on. But one such memo—to "Mr. Haldeman"—contains the following: "I wonder if you might game plan the possibility of having some pro-administration rallies, etc. on Vietnam on October 15, the date set by the other side. Inevitably, whenever we plan something, they are there to meet us; perhaps we can turn the trick on them."[11]

The proadministration rallies intended for October 15 never materialized. The government did, however, use other much dirtier and downright illegal tricks to attempt to derail the antiwar demonstrations.

9. *New York Times*, September 27, 1969.
10. Jeb Stuart Magruder, *An American Life* (New York: Atheneum, 1974), p. 78.
11. Ibid., p. 80.

For example, in August 1969, copies of a letter purporting to be from an organization called the Black United Front in Washington, D.C., were received by the New Mobe steering committee and Abe Bloom. The letter demanded an initial payment of $25,000 on a levy of one dollar for each demonstrator the New Mobe would attract to Washington, "because of the expressed strong opposition to any white-led convention in our Black City. . . ." And "As a show of good faith from the New Mobilization of its commitment to assist black people to end colonial rule."[12]

The reference to colonial rule dealt with the fact that the local government of the District of Columbia was appointed by the federal authority, and its citizens had no effective vote in national elections since they did not reside in a state. Proposals for a change in this status, such as "home rule" or "statehood," were important issues among the city's predominantly Black population. The Mobe was aware of this, of course, and more than willing to publicize such demands and invite local speakers in support of them on its platform. But the Black United Front's demand for money for itself, in the name of the whole Black community, was something quite different.

Over two years later a disaffected FBI agent, Robert Wall, wrote an exposé in the *New York Review of Books* in which he revealed that this letter had been written by the FBI. Wall further explained:

At the same time we instructed some informants we had placed in the black organization to suggest the idea of a security bond informally to leaders of the organization. The letter we composed was approved by the bureau's counterintelligence desk, and was signed with the forged signature of a leader of the black group. Later, through informants in the NMC [New Mobe] we learned that the letter had caused a great deal of confusion.[13]

It certainly did. Some of us on the Washington staff were opposed from the beginning to having anything to do with this demand. Not because we had any proof that it was a government provocation, but because it was politically wrong on the face of it. We stressed that those who presented themselves as spokesper-

12. Letter from Black United Front to the New Mobilization Committee, undated. Copy on file at Library of Social History, New York.
13. *New York Review of Books*, January 27, 1972.

sons for the BUF didn't have the authority to speak for the whole Black community of Washington, much less collect money for it. Also that the New Mobe didn't have that kind of money anyway. But the main point was that the Blacks of Washington were generally against the war for the same reasons other people were; if anything more so. The notion that any large number of them would oppose the right of people to come to the capital for a peaceful antiwar demonstration didn't hold water.

But some people on the New Mobe steering committee, despite our opposition, thought it best to negotiate with the BUF on this matter. In his book *More Power Than We Know*, Dave Dellinger, who was in Chicago when he first saw the letter, recalls the circumstances this way:

> I was informed by Washington black intermediaries, whom I had asked to check out the situation, that the letter writers seemed dead serious and threatened, in the absence of such a payment, to wreck arriving cars and buses and attack disembarking passengers. This threat was repeated in lurid terms a week or so later when I went to Washington. . . .[14]

Dellinger writes that he and a few other New Mobe officers, including Stewart Meacham and Ron Young,

> met with about a dozen angry blacks. After some initial sparring, they ostentatiously locked the door and told us that if we knew what was good for us we would give them a check for the first ten thousand dollars then and there. Fortunately, we didn't yield [had they done so, the check would have bounced. F.H.], and probably because most of the blacks present were honest revolutionaries who responded to honest dialogue, a couple of hours later we emerged unscathed, without paying or promising to pay any money but with a better understanding of the problems of the black community, including those exacerbated by insensitive white protesters.[15]

The negotiations extended over several weeks. At the September 13 meeting of the New Mobe Washington Action Committee, Meacham proposed that the New Mobe "ask every marcher to withhold one dollar from taxes and turn it over to the BUF." The quote is from the minutes, which continue:

14. Dave Dellinger, *More Power Than We Know* (Garden City, New York: Anchor/Doubleday, 1975), p. 71.
15. Ibid., p. 72.

Most who spoke did not support Meacham's proposal. Several speakers emphasized the importance of clearly identifying those with whom we are negotiating and who they represent. [Bob] Haskell reported on discussions with several prominent black militant leaders who cautioned against giving in to demands for money. Someone suggested that we should send copies of all future communications to *all* BUF steering committee members, especially when those communications deal with upcoming meetings between New Mobe and BUF spokesmen.[16]

The problem dragged on until the decisive intervention of Julius Hobson, a venerable figure in the Washington Black community, a leading advocate of statehood, and an antiwar activist himself. Hobson had been contacted earlier and had said the BUF demand was ridiculous. He finally told the New Mobe that if they didn't quit giving credence to it, they could take *his* name off the New Mobe sponsors' list. After that the demand was rejected.

In early October Abe Bloom got a letter from John P. Carter of the Black United Front which said:

After thinking about the Black United Front's proposal. . . . I've decided that the money is coming from the wrong source. To ask the mobilization for it, is like taking money from allies. We should be asking enemies for it instead. . . . We all know we must put a stop to the war and death machine. Part of that machine's death has been the death of Black Americans. . . .[17]

Carter pledged support to the October 15 Moratorium and the November antiwar activities. The incident was over.

There were too many such government political provocations to recount in detail here, so crude as to be obvious even at the time. But this was one of the more crafty ones. It was designed to play on a situation where there was a lot of anger among Black militants and a certain paternalistic "white guilt syndrome" among some elements within the antiwar coalition. In this case the trick didn't do nearly as much damage as it might have, thanks especially to Julius Hobson.

The SDS national action in Chicago was finally set as a series

16. Washington Action Committee of the New Mobilization, minutes, September 13, 1969. (Copy in author's files.)
17. Letter from John P. Carter to Abe Bloom, October 1, 1969. (Copy in author's files.)

of demonstrations October 8-11 which came to be called the
"Days of Rage." Few people showed up, however, and some of
those who did had second thoughts and bowed out at the last
minute. It began Friday night, October 8, when some 500 youths
gathered in Lincoln Park. Tom Hayden spoke there, but did not
go along on the action that followed. At a signal from the
Weatherman leaders, perhaps 300 ran south through the Gold
Coast, an exclusive apartment district, breaking windows and
smashing cars. It took about an hour for the police to disperse,
arrest, or beat them down. Six were hit by police gunfire, dozens
more clubbed or injured by patrol cars which drove pell-mell into
their ranks, and over sixty were arrested.

Over the next few days a few smaller activities took place. RYM
II, which by this time had publicly split with the Weatherman,
carried out a few orderly marches with a couple of hundred
participants. On Saturday no more than 200 Weatherpeople
gathered at Haymarket Square for what was to have been the
major mass march. Surrounded by a much larger force of police,
they walked toward the Loop, then broke through to smash
windows, bang on cars, and fight the cops. It took the police
about fifteen minutes to mop up. The "Days of Rage" resulted in
more than 200 arrests, as many injuries, and serious charges
against almost all the Weatherman leaders. Their bail was over
$2 million dollars.

A different sort of demonstration occurred on October 12 at
Fort Dix, New Jersey. Several thousand youths gathered for a
rally at the GI coffee house in Wrightstown, demanding freedom
for antiwar GIs held in the Fort Dix stockade. They marched onto
the base through an open field. Led by a front rank of a hundred
women, they made it a mile inside before being stopped by special
military police. They were driven back under a barrage of tear
gas. The retreat was orderly and there were no serious injuries.
This demonstration had been organized in good part by people
from the former SDS milieu who had given up on the idea of
participating in the Chicago action.

In general, the SDS chapters across the country turned away
from both Weatherman and RYM II SDS, and, except for a few,
from PL-SDS as well. They either dissolved, became independent
local groups, or affiliated with the SMC or other national
organizations. SDS (Chicago) was destroyed. Weatherman would
soon go underground, its leaders fugitives.

On October 15, 1969, the antiwar movement for the first time reached the level of a full-fledged mass movement. Before that there had been huge demonstrations, but only a large vanguard of the whole population of the country was directly involved. On October 15, millions of ordinary Americans were out in the streets demonstrating, canvassing door to door, picketing, leafletting, and so on.

As the October 24 *Life* magazine reported: "It was a display without historical parallel, the largest expression of public dissent ever seen in this country."

Hundreds of major universities were turned over to antiwar activities. In almost every city the size of the major rallies was unprecedented: 100,000 in Boston; over 50,000 in Washington, D.C., drawn from the local area only; 25,000 in Ann Arbor, Michigan; 25,000 in Madison, Wisconsin; 20,000 in Minneapolis; 20,000 in Philadelphia; 20,000 in Detroit; 11,000 in Austin, Texas; 5,000 in Salt Lake City; to name but a few.

There were Moratorium events in virtually every state, in Puerto Rico, and the Virgin Islands. Even in Anchorage, Alaska, where it was already winter, there was an indoor rally of 600 with the prominent antiwar GI Pvt. Joe Miles the featured speaker.

The scope and variety of the events defy full description. In New York City, for example, hundreds of thousands took part in rallies all over the city, many occurring at the same time—10,000 at Columbia, over 5,000 Manhattan high school students in Central Park, 4,000 at a rally of people who worked in the city's publishing houses, 7,000 in the financial district, and so on. The city's board of education estimated 90 percent absenteeism in high schools and 75 percent in junior high and elementary schools that day. Four of the city's TV stations suspended all regular programming to cover the activities nationally. More than one plane flew over the city writing peace slogans in the sky.

In the late afternoon more than 100,000 New Yorkers gathered in and around Bryant Park creating a monumental traffic jam. The rally there was chaired by Shirley MacLaine and Tony Randall; other entertainment stars including Janis Joplin appeared. There were speeches by Mayor John Lindsay and three U.S. senators as well as representatives of the antiwar movement. This crowd was largely moderate in temper but gave massive applause to New York SMC coordinator Joanna Misnik when she said, "October 15 is just the beginning. . . . We're going to stay in the street until every last GI is brought home."[18]

By the time the major events for October 15 had been set, there were so many that the Moratorium, the New Mobe, and the SMC, as well as all the New Mobe's constituent groups that chose to do so, were able to schedule all the speakers they could muster for large rallies and there still weren't enough to go around.

I appeared at several demonstrations in Philadelphia October 15 and was the featured speaker at a rally that night at Villanova, a major Catholic university in eastern Pennsylvania. It was hard to go anywhere in Philadelphia that day without coming across some sort of antiwar event. The mood was not tense or angry, but more like a holiday, with a lot of friendly banter between demonstrators and passersby. In many localities the October 15 Moratorium had a semiofficial character about it, with school administrations going along, here and there city councils endorsing, and local elected politicians making appearances at demonstrations.

At the Villanova rally that night I pointed out that Nixon's stated policy was to use force to extract concessions from the Vietnamese in negotiations. I said that it would be immoral for the U.S. to either win the war or to succeed in extracting any concessions. I was surprised at the applause these points evoked from that not very radical audience. There was a Democratic Party politician on the platform who squirmed and gritted his teeth, but the rally ate it up. Even the nuns were clapping.

The response of that audience convinced me that the antiwar movement had indeed made some profound changes in America. Henceforth it was a question of how much damage the government would do to itself, and unfortunately to the victims of the war, before it caught on to that fact.

At the huge rally on Boston Common, Senator George McGovern got a standing ovation when he appeared. The enthusiasm was repeated only once in an otherwise dull speech, when he said: "The most urgent responsible act of American citizenship in 1969 is to bring all possible pressure to bear on the Administration to order our troops out of Vietnam *now*."[19]

There had been an unsuccessful attempt to exclude Peter Camejo from the Boston Common speakers' list because some of

18. *Militant*, October 24, 1969.
19. Ken Hurwitz, *Marching Nowhere* (New York: W.W. Norton, 1971), p. 140.

the Democratic Party politicians objected. Ken Hurwitz, one of the insiders in the Boston Vietnam Moratorium group, later described the scene as Camejo got up to address the rally:

> The last speaker of the day [was] Peter Camejo, the Venezuelan revolutionary who had had us all ready to write a press release of disassociation. [Camejo was born in the U.S. of Venezuelan parents and spent some of his youth in Venezuela.] Still a step or two away from the microphone, he started on his speech. He didn't want a single person to leave the Common before he had a chance to work his spell. The words came in a high pitched, stacatto cadence, and his whole body vibrated to the rhythm.
>
> Vietnam, he said, isn't a mistake but an absolute inevitability of the system.
>
> "And to those politicians who are joining the bandwagon," he continued, "this antiwar movement is not for sale. This movement is not for sale now, not in 1970 and not in 1972." I expected the next shot of the crowd [The rally was televised.—F.H.] to show five thousand people sitting in front of the platform and ninety-five thousand people heading for the Park Street subway station. But that wasn't so. People were listening and responding. Certainly the majority wasn't agreeing entirely with the revolutionary stance, but they were listening. . . . It didn't matter whether we were socialist revolutionaries or not. He made us hate the war perhaps more than we ever thought possible. It was a scourge, a plague— there could be no "timetable" for ending it, it had to be ended now. Camejo spoke with such easy power, it was demagogic and frightening. This was a day of peace, but he made me see just how close the peace in the antiwar movement always is to something far more charged and militant. Our own latent emotionalism and contempt surprises us all. Camejo ended his speech at the peak, and the crowd applauded until their hands were weary.[20]

Except for the fact that Camejo was an especially gifted speaker, this incident—and Hurwitz's reaction—was not atypical. The Establishment politicians who had jumped on the Moratorium bandwagon, and even some of the liberal youth who had initiated it, were not entirely comfortable with what they helped set in motion October 15. This would soon become evident as the Moratorium Committee—which had not yet officially endorsed the New Mobe's November march on Washington—came face to face with that decision.

20. Ibid., pp. 143-44.

# 19

## The March Against Death
## and November 15, 1969

The period between the October 15 Moratorium and November 15 was one of tension within the antiwar movement. In part, this reflected the fact that the movement had reached the point where it was putting great pressure on the government. The government in turn was putting its pressure on the movement.

For some time the Vietnam War had been the central focus of U.S. foreign policy and, in a sense, of world politics. The American ruling class itself had become sharply divided on what to do about Vietnam. That was the reason for the backing the Moratorium got from a significant section of the Establishment. The inside details were not then public, but it was generally assumed that the administration was in the throes of making major decisions about the war, and, in spite of Nixon's public stance, the antiwar movement was one of the factors that had to be taken into account in these secret deliberations.

Some facts have subsequently come to light about the nature of these decisions. Roger Morris, then an assistant to Henry Kissinger, Nixon's chief foreign-policy adviser and troubleshooter, has revealed that in the fall of 1969 "there was an NSC [National Security Council] study of the mining of Haiphong and the carpet bombing of Hanoi—a 'savage' blow, as he [Kissinger] told his staff, to bring a 'fourth-rate' industrial power to its 'breaking point.'. . ."

But "the option" was set aside, according to Morris, "complete with draft presidential speech."[1]

Daniel Ellsberg, the Rand Corporation expert who worked with

---

1. *Washington Monthly*, July-August, 1974.

the Pentagon Papers and later made them public, was still on speaking terms in 1969 with Vietnam advisers within the administration. Later, in commenting on Kissinger's attitude toward the 1969 "savage blow" plan, Ellsberg declared: "And he [Kissinger] said then as he'd said on other occasions, when his staff told him this wouldn't work, as I'd told him essentially . . . in December of '68, his answer was: 'Are you telling me that this is the first country in history with no breaking point?' "[2]

It is Ellsberg's view that the antiwar offensive of October 15 and November 15 contributed materially to the shelving of the 1969 "savage blow" plan.

I think [said Ellsberg in a 1974 Harvard speech] it seems to have derailed a plan to mine Haiphong in the fall of '69, and postponed it for what turned out to be two and a half years. That probably saved hundreds of thousands of lives in North Vietnam and probably— speculation here, but I think a good bet—probably kept us from invading North Vietnam and using nuclear weapons ultimately. That's more speculative. The life aspect in North Vietnam I think is not really speculative.[3]

Evidence to substantiate this view is contained in Jeb Stuart Magruder's memoir, where he quotes from a long memo from White House aide Dwight Chapin to H. R. Haldeman, Nixon's chief White House staffer. The date of the memo is October 16, 1969, and it deals with plans for countering the antiwar movement through November 15. A major presidential speech on Vietnam had been scheduled for November 3. The memo said in part:

For example, if the President should determine the war has to be escalated and it is announced November 3, unless the stage is properly set, the action will only fuel the November 15 movement. (If the President de-escalates the war on November 3, then the action can be built upon in order to head off November 15.)[4]

The rest of the memo is a game plan for dealing with the threat of November 15. Since its key suggestions were actually imple-

2. *Harvard Crimson,* November 12, 1974.
3. Ibid.
4. Jeb Stuart Magruder, *An American Life* (New York: Atheneum, 1974), pp. 87-88.

mented, though not always with success, it is worth quoting from it at length:

. . . The objective is to isolate the leaders of the "Moratorium" event and the leaders of the "Mobilization" committee. They are one and the same and their true purpose should be exposed. At the same time, those people who are loyal to the country and who have been disillusioned by the war should be pulled back into the fold of national consciousness. . . .

*PROPOSITION:*

Only the President can work out the peace. He must be given the nation's support, trust, and understanding. Unity during the next few months is of primary importance.

*ACTION TIMETABLE*

*October 17 to 20.* Tone—very low key.

1. Congressmen and Senators who endorsed the October 15 activity are approached by moderates within their parties—told not to rush off on the November 15 thing—it is different.

2. The media is contacted—maybe by rumor—the same as above. Friendly columnists should be given the line—for Sunday stories and next week's articles.

3. The Cabinet, agency heads and other appropriate officials should be given some facts about the November 15 mobilization groups—they should start talking it down in private situations.

4. The Business Council in Hot Springs should adopt a resolution of Presidential support and put out a resolution to ask the business community to rally to the President at this time.

*October 20-26*

1. Congressional activity should be pressed hard—resolutions of support until November 3. Try to quiet all except the real fringe—talk responsibility. Congressional support is the main mode of public support for the Moratorium group.

2. A full-fledged drive should be put against the media. . . . Letters, visits to editorial boards, ads, TV announcements, phone calls. (In New York, the networks should be visited by groups of our supporters tho highest level—and cold turkey should be talked.)

3. A representative of the Justice Department and a spokesman for the FBI should hold a press conference on Monday, October 20. They would brief the press with documented information on the leaders of the two movements. . . .

A Monday, October 20, press meeting should point up a dedicated President—not detoured by the Moratorium . . . a man who has been working for peace and has stepped up the activity. It should not be an appeal—it is fact, he is strong, confident, undeterred. . . .

*October 27 to November 3*

*Setting*—speculation will be building.

All of the activity of the preceding week would be sustained at a higher pitch. The President would spend most of the week meeting advisors and talking about keeping the country together.

*November 3 and after*

The time to go for a display of support to the President is immediately after the November 3 speech. . . . If properly handled, many of those who might be considering becoming involved in the November 15 activity can be won over. It will also tend to make the November 15 group more vocal—less rational and appear properly as the fringe groups they are.

This would also be the right time for the appearance of pro-Administration sentiment. It should be shown by all—each in their own way—but what they do must be visible. . . . It might be an idea to ask the networks to tell it to Hanoi—what if the networks were set as the sounding board for the vast segment of American people who support the President and his peace efforts. Thousands of wires, letters, and petitions to the networks. . . .

On Saturday—November 15—most Americans will do what they normally do on a Saturday—go shopping, work on the lawn or go to the ball games. Football games—half times—are the things to shoot for—and the President should also attend a game that weekend. It would work.[5]

Nixon's November 3 speech did not announce a major escalation, and was couched in terms to imply de-escalation, but essentially it offered more of the same, indicating that U.S. forces would stay in Vietnam as long as necessary to keep the Saigon puppet regime firmly in power. I. F. Stone commented:

"Those who say there was nothing new in the Nixon speech are badly mistaken. Never before has he disclosed how committed he is emotionally and ideologically to this war."[6]

\*          \*          \*

One event that helped cut across the administration attacks was that a large number of church groups across the country were involved in a special project that was part of the November mobilization. The proposal for this had been adopted at the founding conference of the New Mobe in July at the suggestion of Stewart Meacham, then community peace education secretary of the American Friends Service Committee. The idea developed out of the reading-of-the-war-dead demonstrations, with the amend-

5. Ibid., pp. 87-90.
6. *I. F. Stone's Weekly,* November 17, 1969.

ment proposed by Meacham, that each name be represented by a demonstrator. As eventually developed, the plan was for each of some 43,000 people to start outside the Arlington National Cemetery on the Virginia side of the Potomac, carrying a placard with the name of a dead GI or of a Vietnamese village, and walk single file across the Memorial Bridge to Washington, past the White House, and on to the capitol where the placard would be placed in a coffin to be carried in the November 15 mass march. The project was to begin Thursday evening, November 13, and end as the Saturday march was assembling. The object, of course, was to show in graphic terms the cost of the war in human lives.

In early October, Meacham, Susan Miller of the Episcopal Peace Fellowship, and I attended a meeting in Philadelphia where Meacham presented the idea to a group of Quakers and other religious peace activists. They decided to organize church groups across the country to take part in the project. Miller was put in charge of it on the New Mobe staff, assisted by Trudy Young. The project was given the name "March Against Death" and became a major part of the plans for the Washington action.

\* \* \*

The remarkable thing was not that the Nixon administration red-baited the antiwar movement at this time, but that this smear had so little effect within the general population. The opening salvo occurred on the eve of the October 15 Moratorium. The excuse was a letter of greeting from Pham Van Dong, the premier of the Democratic Republic of Vietnam (Hanoi). It was released in Paris, October 14, with copies cabled to the Moratorium, the New Mobe, and the Student Mobilization Committee. The message declared:

The Vietnamese people demand that the United States Administration withdraw totally and without conditions American troops and those of foreign countries in the American camp out of Vietnam and let the people of Vietnam decide themselves their own affairs.

It also wished "the progressive American people" success "in your autumn offensive."[7]

The letter came unsolicited and was not the first such greeting

7. Letter from Pham Van Dong to the New Mobe, October 14, 1969. *New York Times,* October 15, 1969.

sent to American antiwar groups. On this occasion, however, Nixon decided to use it to red-bait and drive a wedge between the congressional supporters of the Moratorium and the rest of the movement. Vice President Spiro Agnew appeared at a White House press conference, denounced the Pham Van Dong letter, and challenged the backers of the Moratorium to "repudiate the support of a totalitarian government which has on its hands the blood of 40,000 Americans." He declared the Moratorium leaders and the members of Congress who supported them "were now chargeable with knowledge of this letter" and must differentiate their position from that contained within it.[8] This was reminiscent of the blackmail demand made by witch-hunting Senator Dodd back in 1960 on the leaders of SANE that they "clearly differentiate" their position on atmospheric nuclear testing from that of the Soviet Union, which was calling for a bilateral halt to the tests.

The Agnew attack had little effect on October 15 itself, an indication that red-baiting simply didn't carry the same punch as before.

The Moratorium did its best to ignore the attack. Their public response was a two-sentence statement: "October 15 is an appeal to the conscience of the American people. It is regrettable the Administration would seize this straw in an attempt to discredit the patriotism of the millions of Americans who sincerely desire peace."[9] Some of us in the New Mobe thought a much stronger stand was called for. We felt that the basic assumption in Agnew's argument ought to be challenged. Accordingly, at the October 16 New Mobe steering committee meeting, I introduced a motion to send a public reply to Pham Van Dong, acknowledging receipt of his message and saying we agreed the U.S. ought to get out of Vietnam. The motion passed without dissent. The proposed reply also said:

Vice President Agnew, speaking on behalf of President Nixon, said that such a message from you to Americans was a "shocking intrusion into the affairs of the American people." We wish President Nixon's intrusion into the affairs of the Vietnamese people was limited to letters.[10]

8. *New York Times,* October 15, 1969.
9. Ibid.
10. Draft answer to Pham Van Dong from the New Mobilization Committee, October 16, 1969. (Copy in author's files.)

After the meeting, however, Stewart Meacham told Ron Young, who was in charge of the office, not to release anything to the press on this matter. I hit the roof, but Young and Meacham wouldn't budge and stalled for over a week. Meantime the SMC released its own reply to Pham Van Dong—similar to the New Mobe's—but the moment had been missed for a big news break in reaction to the Agnew attack.

Meacham's motive for this behavior had to do with the negotiations he was involved in with the Moratorium leaders over their support to November 15. The congressional doves were wavering and the Moratorium had apparently demanded of Meacham that the New Mobe not play up the Pham Van Dong message. Meacham wanted to remove any obstacle to joint action that he could. So did I, but our tactical instincts in this matter were different. From the point of view of developing the mass movement—which was not necessarily the same thing as currying favor with congressmen—it would have been better to take the red-baiting head on.

What is more, for a couple of officers of the Mobe to override the decisions of the coalition on so important a matter of substance was an ominous development, especially when pressures from the right could be expected to increase. To inhibit such unilateral actions in the future I took the unusual step of circulating a letter on the incident to all members of the New Mobe steering committee. A subsequent meeting of this body once again voted to send out the Pham Van Dong reply.

In the meantime, the Moratorium finally endorsed November 15, at a joint press conference with the New Mobe on October 21. It soon became clear that there were other elements in the deal that had been made over the Moratorium endorsement. The Moratorium leaders were anxious to be more heavily involved in the decision-making process regarding November 15. In itself this was perfectly understandable and entirely in order. But on October 25 a meeting of the New Mobe executive committee—which was made up of the officers and project directors but not the other members of the steering committee—was held. The four coordinators of the Moratorium committee were invited, but when the SMC also asked to attend, it was excluded by a vote of 9 to 5.

The SMC protested this exclusion in a letter to movement activists. It declared in part:

Some of the more establishment-oriented forces have been pressuring the New Mobe to remove from the speakers list the more militant spokesmen of the antiwar movement, including the Student Mobilization Committee. To invite a Senator is one thing, but to remove the Student Mobilization Committee or anyone else because the Senator may object, is quite another.

Our generation has given more than numbers to the peace movement. Even more important has been our contribution in helping to establish the political principles which have built the movement and kept it strong. These principles include the following points on which the SMC is based. (1) For immediate and unconditional withdrawal of U.S. forces from Vietnam; (2) for non-exclusion, for rejection of red-baiting of any form; (3) for mass legal peaceful demonstrations which are independent of any political parties or candidates; and (4) for democratic decision making in the movement.

Some of the new forces that are speaking out against the war do not agree with all these points. This makes it all the more imperative that in welcoming their support to the antiwar cause, and strengthening the unity of the movement, we do not alter or abandon these principles which can really force an end to the war.[11]

As it turned out, the struggle over speakers in Washington for November 15 ended without the exclusion of the radicals, and the final list included Carol Lipman of the SMC and several others, as well as two U.S. senators, the Democrat George McGovern and Charles Goodell, a New York Republican.

The pressures brought by the White House on members of the House of Representatives proved effective, however, and only one endorsed November 15, compared to sixty-five for the October 15 Moratorium. That one was Allard Lowenstein, who had been reported as using his influence to attempt to exclude the radicals, and as being very annoyed by the New Mobe's refusal to do so. Murray Kempton caught the frightened mood in Congress when he commented that "Allard Lowenstein of New York . . . being closer to the movement than any other Congressman, was more conspicuous for the agony and calculation that preceded his choice and got less credit than he may deserve for finally making it."[12]

The problem of exclusion had developed to a much greater

11. Letter to "Dear Friend" from Carol Lipman for the National Interim Working Committee of the SMC, October 31, 1969. (Copy in author's files.)

12. *New York Review of Books,* December 18, 1969.

extreme in San Fransisco than in Washington. There the Moratorium was weak. It was another grouping—which included forces around the Communist Party, acting as self-appointed proxies for the liberal Democratic politicians—that made the attempt to bar the radicals.

The delegates from San Francisco who had attended the founding conference of the New Mobe in July began preparations for the West Coast action by calling a meeting to which all ninety-nine antiwar groups in the Bay Area were invited. About 150 activists showed up and established a coalition open to building the action. A group led by Terence Hallinan and Karen Talbot, however, refused to participate. Hallinan was the son of prominent San Francisco attorney Vincent Hallinan, and was likewise a lawyer. He was widely known in his own right as the defense attorney for some of the GIs in the Presidio Twenty-seven case. He was also a founder and leading member of the Du Bois Clubs. Talbot was associated with the *People's World*, a West Coast weekly that expressed the views of the Communist Party.

In August, Sid Peck went to California, chaired a meeting of the coalition, and then set up a small working committee headed by Hallinan and Donald Kalish, the UCLA professor who was a member of the national New Mobe steering committee. Peck also used his influence to have Kalish and Hallinan appointed as temporary New Mobe cochairmen for the West Coast. There was some logic to this step since both Kalish and Hallinan were fairly widely known, and apparently Peck did it to make sure Hallinan and his group would participate. Out of deference to Peck, the coalition agreed to this arrangement. The working committee was known as New Mobe West and the coalition was called the Bay Area Peace Action Coalition and sometimes the New Mobe Membership Committee, the Bay Area affiliate of New Mobe West. Both groups were set up in the same San Francisco headquarters, which also housed the San Francisco SMC.

The Membership Committee proceeded to build the action through large, open meetings of activists who volunteered for subcommittees such as publicity, finances, Third World task force, labor task force, the SMC women's task force, and so on. The working committee concentrated on plans for the program for November 15 itself.

Hallinan and Kalish were adamant that there be only one political speaker and the rest of the program be devoted to cultural events, poetry readings, music, and the like. Hallinan dubbed it "Woodstock West," after the famous rock music festival that had taken place in upstate New York in August. According to Hallinan, the single political speaker would outline a program of "what next" for the antiwar movement. Since this perspective had not even been discussed, let alone decided, the Membership Committee viewed this as an attempt to stifle all points of view but one.

In a memo to the national New Mobe steering committee, New Mobe West co-project director Marjorie Colvin complained:

> The obvious question—what would the "what next" speaker say, and what was the money [from the collection, if any were left after expenses] to be used for. This was left vague; it would be worked out by some small committee. In my opinion, the Hallinan group has in mind some sort of preliminary work for the 1970 gubernatorial election campaign here.[13]

It was no secret that Hallinan's group favored channeling the antiwar movement into partisan electoral activity within the Democratic Party. Colvin, a member of the SWP and a consistent advocate of keeping the antiwar coalitions out of partisan electoral campaigns, commented: "It is their right to try and build such a movement on their own, but not to use the antiwar movement for their own factional purposes."[14]

The idea of limiting the list of speakers to a small number had a certain attraction to those who had listened through the long parades on the platform that seemed to be the norm at big antiwar rallies. But when it came down to deciding who the speakers would be it had always been impossible to come to agreement on one or two alone in a genuine coalition. The antiwar movement was just too heterogeneous. The New Mobe officers in the East—who, unlike Hallinan, had a lot of experience organizing big demonstrations—had reconciled themselves to this reality and opted for a list long enough to be more or less representative, interspersed with cultural features. But Hallinan and Kalish tried to take the bull by the horns by exerting purely mechanical control as the cochairmen. Hallinan declared that the Membership Committee had no decision-making authority.

He was voted down on the number of speakers even within the

13. Memo to all New Mobilization Committee steering committee members from Marjorie Colvin, October 24, 1969. (Copy in author's files.)
14. Ibid.

working committee, which on October 11 decided on a list of five plus a chairperson, with two or three to be added later. Hallinan, a former Golden Gloves boxer, shouted: "Anyone who wants to fight with me over this, meet me outside."[15] Nobody took him up on this challenge, but after the meeting Hallinan lost his cool and threw a couple of punches at Roland Sheppard, a representative from Painters Local Union 4, who had voted against him.

On October 16 a meeting of the Membership Committee reaffirmed the list as adopted by the working committee. It was also announced that the San Francisco cast of *Hair*, the popular rock musical of the time, had volunteered to perform. So had singer Buffy St. Marie and other top artists. But those who thought this was a reasonable compromise had underestimated the obsession of the Hallinan group.

Late the next night Hallinan's supporters removed all the New Mobe West and New Mobe Membership Committee desks, tables, chairs, leaflets, and posters from the office. In the morning the staff discovered the phones had also been disconnected and the mail stopped—by order of Terence Hallinan as New Mobe cochairman. Hallinan and Kalish set up a new "Regional Working Committee"—by invitation only. At its first meeting a squad led by longshoreman Archie Brown of the Communist Party kept out the members of the old working committee who had not been invited, including the SMC representative, and many others.

The Membership Committee refurnished its offices, had its phones turned on, and proceeded to build the action as before. But two weeks before November 15 both groups were applying for permits for the demonstration and the city was holding them up pending resolution of the dispute.

\*       \*       \*

Meanwhile the New Mobe in Washington had no permits either, not because of a split among the organizers, but because the Nixon administration was holding them up on the allegation that the demonstration would lead to violence. This was also a major theme of the stories planted in the press by the White House game planners.

15. Ibid.

In the midst of this atmosphere, Jerry Rubin, Abbie Hoffman, and a few others around the "Conspiracy" came bouncing into the New Mobe Washington office one day with the news that they had just called a demonstration of their own to protest the trial of the "Conspiracy Eight." The trial was then in progress in a federal courtroom in Chicago and the Justice Department, of course, was responsible for the prosecution. The demonstration, then, would be held in front of the Justice Department building in Washington at 5:00 p.m. November 15, at the end of the major mass march and rally. Rubin and associates wanted our endorsement. Before telling us about it, however, they had unilaterally announced their intention at a press conference outside the Justice Department, with Rubin posing for pictures wearing boxing gloves.

I was not amused. Neither was the SMC, and the Moratorium was outraged. My own feeling was that Rubin and company had just handed Nixon exactly what he was looking for, on a silver platter.

Brad Lyttle, who along with me was in charge of logistics and marshals for the November 13-15 Washington activities, later described his apprehensions at the time:

My own position was based on a scenario that seemed inescapable. The Justice Department demonstration had been set up with the symbolism and tone of angry combativeness. At the Monument rally [where the major crowd of the day would be assembled] there would be references to the cruel treatment of Bobby Seale [the defendant who had been bound and gagged in the Chicago federal courtroom] that would anger many. At least one major speaker would urge people to go to the Justice Department. At 5:00 p.m., at dusk, and after a cold, tiring day, tens of thousands of angry people would flow toward Pennsylvania Avenue and the Department. The authorities had made clear that they feared an attack on the White House and government buildings in that area. They would meet the crowd with a line of heavily armed police backed up with troops. Justice Department rally speakers would taunt the police as "pigs" and perhaps invite an attack on them. Probably there would be government provocateurs in the crowd who would see violence and a riot to be in the government's interest; a means to discredit the New Mobe and the demonstrators. They might curse and throw things at the police. At some point, the police, many of whom would be rightists and out of sympathy with the demonstrators—possibly also in league with the provocateurs— would attack the demonstrators. They would use at least gas and perhaps clubs as well. In the darkness and the dense crowds there would be a good deal of brutality. The disorganized demonstrators might panic and run, or there could be a riot.[16]

Within the New Mobe there were some who favored the Justice Department demonstration, particularly Dellinger. By that time RYM II and some other groupings from the dissolving SDS had been attracted by the November 15 buildup and were sending representatives to the New Mobe steering committee. They were strong backers of the Justice Department demonstration, though not all of them wanted a physical confrontation.

The issue was fought out at the steering committee meeting November 2, and a motion that we not endorse or sponsor passed handily, in part because the Moratorium was present in force. We considered the possibility that New Mobe should sponsor and try to assure the peaceful character of the Justice Department demonstration by, in effect, taking it over. This was rejected as too risky. Brad and I agreed on this. Later, after the New Mobe marshals proved so effective in organizing the other events November 13-15, Brad would express the opinion that full sponsorship might have been better. But I still think we made the right choice.

The success of the marshals depended on the whole tone that was set in building the action. But the very conception of the Justice Department demonstration was dead wrong from the start, and in blatant contradiction to the decision of the July conference that rejected a repeat of Chicago, 1968. In effect it was an attempt by a small group to reverse that decision. The wrong tone had already been set for the Justice Department demonstration and continued to be built up in the small meetings of ultraleft groups that were mobilizing for it. The best we could do was discourage it and isolate the trouble as much as possible. New Mobe endorsement or cosponsorship would have cut across that, giving some authority to small groups bent on sucking the large crowd into a reckless confrontation.

On the other hand we couldn't put ourselves in the position of denouncing anybody's right to hold a peaceful demonstration. What we did was refuse to endorse or sponsor the action, and instruct the chairpersons at the New Mobe rally to make that point clear in case any speaker urged people to go to the Justice

16. Bradford Lyttle, *Washington Action, November 13-15. A report and comments from the viewpoint of a practical organizer,* February 10, 1970, p. 48. (Copy in author's files.)

Department. We also insisted on expressions of peaceful intent
from the sponsors of the Justice Department affair. They could
hardly refuse without splitting among themselves. On that basis
we agreed to allow those who were concerned with the technical
details—which in the nature of things excluded Rubin and
Hoffman—to recruit their marshals from the New Mobe pool. As
it turned out, these marshals did help keep the trouble down and
relatively isolated—and got a good dose of police tear gas for
their pains—but they couldn't work miracles.

*                    *                    *

On November 9, the GI Press Service of the Student Mobilization Committee ran a full page ad in the Sunday edition of the
*New York Times.* It was signed by 1,365 active duty GIs, many of
them stationed in Vietnam. The ad, which carried the name,
rank, and station of each signer, appealed for Americans to
attend the demonstrations in Washington and San Francisco
November 15. It also stated: "We are opposed to American
involvement in the war in Vietnam. We resent the needless
wasting of lives to save face for the politicians in Washington.
We speak, believing our views are shared by many of our fellow
servicemen. Join us!"

Nothing like this had ever happened before in American
history, and, according to Washington correspondent William
McGaffin, "the Pentagon obviously does not like it one bit."

"Pentagon officials," wrote McGaffin, "were frankly surprised
that this many GIs would permit their names to be used in a
protest ad."[17] This only showed the Pentagon's blindness to the
real mood among rank-and-file GIs. Although the Pentagon tried,
it failed to find signers who would declare their names had been
used falsely. (The GI Press Service had each authorization in
writing before it published the ad.) Lawyers from the Judge
Advocate sections of the army, navy, air force, and marine corps
were assigned to find something illegal in what the GIs had done.
The best they could come up with was that signing might be
construed as "conduct of a nature to bring discredit upon the
armed forces," which was a quote from the catchall Article 134 of
the Uniform Code of Military Justice.

The GI Civil Liberties Defense Committee threatened to sue

17. *New York Post,* November 11, 1969.

against persecution of the GI signers. The Pentagon dropped the matter rather than precipitate another cause célèbre.

This incident was only one item in the veritable crescendo of antiwar activities, publicity, and interest that was generated between October 15 and November 15, in spite of the counterefforts of the Nixon administration. One of the most dramatic of these was the breaking into the major American news media of the story of the My Lai massacre.

My Lai was a hamlet in the village of Son My (sometimes written "Songmy" and occasionally referred to by Americans as "Pinkville") in South Vietnam. On the morning of March 16, 1968—that is, a year and a half before the story surfaced—My Lai was occupied by a unit of U.S. infantry from the Americal Division. The villagers offered no resistance and none of them bore arms. They were ordered out of their houses, which were dynamited if made of stone and burned if made of wood. All this was standard operating procedure on American "search and destroy" missions in Vietnam. What followed was more unusual. The villagers—799 men, women, and children—were assembled in groups and some of the Americans fired directly at them with automatic rifles until not one seemed left alive. That was the My Lai massacre.

As it turned out, 132 of the Vietnamese survived, lying under the bodies of their relatives and neighbors, until their murderers left. Some of them reported the story to local Vietnamese officials who were, however, under U.S.-Saigon control. But the atrocity was no secret. In addition to those who ordered it, and committed it, there were other Americans who had evidence of the crime. Nevertheless it was covered up as far as the American press was concerned.

One reason for this was that the indiscriminate killing of noncombatants was not uncommon in Vietnam, especially by American air strikes. My Lai was just an especially brutal example of the kind of counterrevolutionary war against a whole population that the U.S. military machine was engaged in.

An American GI, Ronald Lee Ridenhour, heard about the My Lai massacre and for his remaining eight months in Vietnam devoted his free time to gathering and sifting accounts of the affair. He returned to the U.S. with a substantial dossier and wrote a summary of his findings. In early 1969 he sent this to the White House, the secretary of defense, and a number of "dove" senators. He received one visit from an army investigator.

In June 1969, tired of waiting for official action, he gave his report to a literary agent who offered it to major newspapers, magazines, and at least one of the three major TV networks. None were interested. Ridenhour gave up.

In September 1969, the army, as unobtrusively as possible, announced through the command at Fort Benning, Georgia, that an army officer had been charged with murder in the death of an unspecified number of civilians in Vietnam in 1968. The Associated Press carried this on its wire September 6, but few papers picked it up and none assigned an investigative reporter to follow up. It was not until shortly after the October 15 Moratorium that a reporter began to pursue the affair. He was Seymour M. Hersh, a free-lancer, operating on a $1,000 grant from the Foundation for Investigative Journalism, funded by Philip M. Stern, a resident of Washington and a supporter of the Moratorium and the New Mobe. Incidentally, Stern was one of many Washingtonians who offered housing to antiwar staffers from out of town, and Brad Lyttle was staying at Stern's home at the time.

Hersh resurrected Ridenhour's memorandum and found three GIs who had witnessed the My Lai massacre. He arranged for one of them, Paul Meadlo, to appear on television.

*Militant* reporter Robert Langston later commented:

> The capitalist media had been wholly indifferent to Ridenhour's report, and to the September AP dispatch. Two months earlier, they could and would have given the same treatment to Hersh's story. . . . But in the second week of November that was virtually impossible. The antiwar movement's activity had made the Songmy story the hottest piece of merchandise in the journalistic market.[18]

The day the first installment of Seymour Hersh's My Lai series broke into the major dailies was November 13, 1969. The macabre story would be in the news for years and haunt the war-makers as no other publicity in the history of the war had done.

\*          \*          \*

The cold split of the antiwar forces in San Francisco was never fully resolved, though a modus vivendi was worked out to allow the permits to be released and the demonstration go off smoothly.

18. *Militant,* December 12, 1969.

David Warren

Above, Fred Halstead speaking at rally of 30,000 in San Francisco, April 27, 1968. Below, left to right, Norma Becker, Sidney Peck, and Rennie Davis.

Brian Shannon          Brian Shannon          Howard Petrick

Dick Gregory

Harry Ring     Brian Shannon    
Carol Lipman     Jerry Gordon     Dave McReynolds

Brian Shannon

The Democratic Party convention demonstrations, Chicago, August 1968. Above, Mayor Daley's cops, clubs swinging, wade into an antiwar rally in Grant Park, August 28. Below, "dove" presidential candidate Eugene McCarthy speaking at a New Mobilization Committee meeting August 29 in a park opposite the Hilton hotel.

Brian Shannon

Above, left to right, Airman First Class
Michael Locks, Lt. (j.g.) Sue Schnall, and
Gen. Hugh Hester, Ret., followed by 500
active-duty GIs in October 12, 1968, San
Francisco march. Below, part of crowd of
50,000 in San Francisco, April 5, 1969.

New York Press Service

Above, press conference for the Fort Jackson Eight, New York, June 1969. From left, Matilde Zimmermann of the GI Civil Liberties Defense Committee; Privates Jose Rudder and Joe Cole, two of the eight GIs charged for having participated in an antiwar rally on base in March 1969; and Pvt. Joe Miles, founder of GIs United Against the War. Below, Austin, Texas, SMC rally, August 3, 1969.

Frank Lord

Brian Shannon

Washington, November 15, 1969. Above, part of the crowd of some 750,000 in Washington. With the simultaneous demonstration of 250,000 in San Francisco this was the largest political demonstration of any kind in American history and would be exceeded in the course of the antiwar movement only once, on April 24, 1971. Below, left to right, Dr. Spock in the March Against Death; out-of-towners the morning of the demonstration; D.C. police going after stragglers at the end of the day.

Dick Roberts          Betsey Stone          Brian Shannon

Brian Shannon

Harry Ring

Top, Black Moratorium, Riverside, California, January 23, 1970. Middle, left, SWP national secretary Jack Barnes; right, radical pacifist leader Brad Lyttle. Bottom, 3,500 people at February 14-15, 1970, SMC conference, Case Western Reserve University, Cleveland, Ohio.

CWRU Observer

Kent and Jackson, May 1970. Above, national guardsmen fire tear gas at Kent State University students in Kent, Ohio, May 4, during nationwide protests against U.S. invasion of Cambodia. Later that day they would shoot and kill four students, wounding many others. Below, student peers from bullet-riddled window of women's dormitory at Jackson State University, Jackson, Mississippi, where two students were killed in a barrage of police gunfire during an antiwar demonstration May 15.

Cleveland, May 5, 1971

ACTIVE
DUTY
OFFICERS

Above, Los Angeles police in attack on Chicano Moratorium, August 29, 1970. At left, antiwar army officers in civilian clothes demonstrate in Washington, D.C., October 31, 1970.

John Gray

National Chicano Moratorium, Los Angeles, August 29, 1970. Part of the demonstration of 25,000 Chicanos against the Vietnam War, broken up by L.A. police, who left three protesters dead.

John Gray

Above, founding conference of National Peace Action Coalition (NPAC), Cleveland, June 19-21, 1970. Below, United Auto Workers contingent in May 5, 1971, New York NPAC demonstration on first anniversary of Kent State killings.

Howard Petrick

Veterans. Above, Vietnam vets on march from Morristown, New Jersey, to Valley Forge, Pennsylvania, September 4-7, 1970. Below, a wounded Vietnam veteran on the capitol steps in Washington addresses a veterans' demonstration a few days before the massive April 24, 1971, antiwar mobilization.

Stuart Kiehl

Stuart Kiehl

April 24, 1971. The largest of all the antiwar demonstrations, the simultaneous rallies on East and West Coasts drew more than 750,000 in Washington and over 300,000 in San Francisco. Photos on this page and facing page are from the Washington rally.

Harry Ring

E MAJORITY IS NOT SILENT
HE GOVERNMENT IS DEAF!

Mark Satinott

Mark Satinoff

Marching in the rain. New York, April 22, 1972.

Terrill Brumback

Washington,
Spring 1970

The Hallinan group kept control of the program but had to resign itself to eight speakers, including two nominated by the Membership Committee. These were Corky Gonzales of the Chicano Crusade for Justice in Denver, and Dan Seigel, student body president at the University of California at Berkeley. Hallinan had originally opposed both as too radical. In addition it was agreed that the expenses both groups had incurred in building the action would be paid out of the collection and anything left over would go to national New Mobe. The SMC provided most of the marshals, concentrating on the march, while the Hallinan group's marshals concentrated on the platform.

In Washington, unlike San Francisco, a comprehensive permit covering a maze of jurisdictions had to be negotiated directly with the federal administration. On this occasion the government liaison negotiator was Assistant Deputy Attorney General John Dean, later to become famous as the counsel to the president who refused to take all the blame as scapegoat for the Watergate coverup.

Dean was assisted by Ken Tapman, a lawyer for the Department of the Interior. They were both quite young and not at all like the tall, grey-templed aristocrat Van Cleve, with whom we had negotiated the Pentagon march. At the first meeting, in October, they asked for assurances against violence. We weren't planning any and said we hoped the government wasn't either. As I recall, Tapman made some crack about putting us in jail if we broke the law. From what we learned later this was out of character for Tapman, or perhaps he was just making a lame try at a bad joke. The idea that it would be Dean, not us, who would later be going to jail was the last thing in anyone's head at the time.

The negotiations themselves were polite enough, in spite of the tensions generated by the government's stalling, which was a decision made at higher levels anyway.

Before the negotiations were completed, I remember encountering Tapman hanging around the New Mobe office without a tie and sporting antiwar buttons. It seemed a strange way to spy on us, since the government no doubt had us well covered by less conspicuous types. In fact, Tapman had become sympathetic with the movement. In one sense this was purely incidental. In another it was more meaningful. The antiwar sentiment was so pervasive that we kept finding friends in the strangest places, including within the Pentagon.

It got so we even knew what military moves the government was making in preparation for the demonstrations because GIs in the units they were ordering around told us about them.

We first asked for a march from the area of the capitol, along Pennsylvania Avenue, around the White House, to a rally south of the White House. It was Brad Lyttle's opinion that on the basis of their conceptions of military security alone, the authorities would not agree to part of this. As he put it: "I believed that the U.S. government would rather see a riot in Washington than allow 'the White House to be surrounded by a mass march."[19]

The route around the White House was left in abeyance while the major sticking point became Pennsylvania Avenue. It was the traditional prestige street for parades and the administration didn't want us on it. We had broad public support, however, and even the *Washington Post* expressed some outrage at the government's refusal.

Lyttle, who favored holding out for Pennsylvania Avenue to the end, later recalled:

To me, the most surprising feature of these negotiations about Pennsylvania Avenue was the attitude of Phil Hirschkop [the New Mobe's attorney]. Phil was asked again and again if we shouldn't take the matter to court. He always replied emphatically No, that to do so would be a major error. It would take the government negotiators off the political hook and we would almost certainly lose in court. Furthermore, Phil recommended that we hold out for Pennsylvania Avenue to almost the last moment. He was nearly as hard-nosed as I. Never in more than ten years of demonstrating had I known a lawyer to have such an attitude. Every attorney I had worked with before would have recommended, indeed insisted, that we go at once to court, and all would have urged that we give in to the government at an early stage.[20]

Finally, on Wednesday afternoon, November 12, the government agreed to Pennsylvania Avenue, provided we would turn south on Fifteenth Street and march directly to the Washington Monument area, avoiding the loop around the White House. We accepted.

Hirschkop reported that the mayor of the city, Walter Washington, had intervened personally with President Nixon to get him to

19. Lyttle, *Washington Action*, p. 11.
20. Ibid., p. 13.

agree to this arrangement. The November 15 march could now proceed without a built-in confrontation.

*        *        *

There was no special difficulty about the permits for the March Against Death, since only a single-file line on the sidewalk would be passing the White House. The big problem was technical. We had to maintain a flow of more than 1,000 people per hour for forty-two hours, and we couldn't let all 45,000 stand at Arlington Cemetery awaiting their turn. We set up a series of tents on the Arlington side of Memorial Bridge, where buses from around the country arrived on a staggered schedule. There the passengers had a chance to stretch, use toilets, get refreshments and instructions before stepping off one by one on their two-and-a-half hour walk across the bridge, past the White House, and on to the capitol. At night they carried candles, as well as a placard with the name of a deceased GI, or a Vietnamese village, and as each passed the front gate of the White House the name was called out. Incidentally, very few relatives asked us not to use the names of their dead in this antiwar demonstration, and a sizable number of relatives participated, carrying the names of their own deceased loved ones.

In the city, a series of reception centers were set up for people whose buses arrived too early, or who came on other transportation. These were taken to Arlington on shuttle buses. One kind of bus or another arrived at the Arlington tents every three minutes around the clock. At the capitol end, those who completed the march could board shuttle buses to mass housing accommodations in churches or gymnasiums. Or they could go to movement centers where various groups held programs, meetings, and so on.

There were all sorts of sticky details involved in the logistics of this huge operation. For example, the problem of how the sleeping bags and hand luggage of tens of thousands of people, which were left at the Arlington end before the walk, would connect with their owners later. This was in the province of the Mass Accommodations committee. As Brad put it: "We in Logistics looked at Mass Accommodations with awe. Our problems were child's play compared with theirs."[21]

21. Ibid., p. 31.

The New Mobe had little money to pay for rent, and the space used for housing, movement centers, marshal training, and so on was donated. The city opened up its heart, another indication of the depth of the antiwar sentiment. The New Mobe's Local Arrangements committee, sparked by Alice Arshak, handled this as well as numerous other details. Arshak had a voracious appetite for work and responsibility, and sometimes absorbed matters Logistics was supposed to handle, not without a certain irritation. It was probably just as well, since Brad and I were almost overwhelmed. In fact, during the last week of preparations the Moratorium became convinced the task was over the heads of the New Mobe staff. There was a grain of truth to this, though it was also born of prejudice that people who had such a cavalier attitude toward the sensitivities of congressmen to red-baiting couldn't be very practical organizers.

Writer Murray Kempton talked to Moratorium backer Adam Walinsky during this period and quoted him as saying of the New Mobe:

> They don't know what they are doing. They announced that they would start the March against Death some place near Arlington Cemetery. They picked an island where there's no access, where you can't even put in telephones. They didn't even go out and look; some Trotskyite picked it from the map. I don't know what would have happened if thirty-five of our kids hadn't come in, without complaining, and just gone to work on the logistics.

Kempton continued: "The Mobe had not, he [Walinsky]clinched his point, even thought about toilets."[22]

Actually, it was Deputy Assistant Attorney General John Dean who had picked that spot, on the advice of traffic experts, and Brad had carefully inspected it personally along with Ken Tapman and Chief Inspector Bye of the Park Police, before we made the decision. And we had thought about the toilets until the problem gave us nightmares. We just didn't have the money to rent them and were counting on the D.C. Health Department to provide them out of desperation, which it finally did. But we needed all the help we could get and the Moratorium volunteers did a splendid job.

Finances posed a constant headache for the New Mobe. A day

22. *New York Review of Books,* December 18, 1969.

or two before the demonstration Sid Peck had to take up a collection in the office to keep the phones from being shut off before the day was out. At that time the New Mobe had barely enough money in the bank to keep the account open, and was tens of thousands of dollars in debt. I didn't envy Dick Fernandez, who spent this time bent over the phone, arranging more loans. Brad despaired of getting any money to operate the marshal center and hopefully set up a collection box there. It worked, and we ended up paying for the whole marshal operation, with a few hundred dollars left over to apply to the general debt.

Some 700 marshals were used on the March Against Death, including replacements and backup. Each worked two five-hour shifts and was dispatched out of a marshals' center at the Ebenezer Methodist Church southeast of the capitol. There was one night attack by a small group of American Nazis, but that was quickly isolated.

Except for some confusion in the first hour or so, the March Against Death went smoothly. The mood was solemn and determined, and for many of the participants it was obviously a deeply felt spiritual experience.

The scene at the White House at night had an eerie and ominous quality because the floodlights, which ordinarily light up the building, were turned around to blare at the approaches. A mercury vapor lamp about ten feet long was added and the glare almost blinded anyone looking toward the building. Brad later recalled:

Those nights, the White House reminded me of the descriptions I had read of Special Forces camps deep in VC territory. It was easy to imagine machine gunners stationed in the building's windows ready to mow down the first wave of high school students who breached the fence. I could scarcely think of a grosser expression of the Nixon Administration's fear of the people than these security precautions at the White House.[23]

\*        \*        \*

It rained intermittently, but hard, Friday night, November 14, and I was driving along the route of the March Against Death making sure marshals who got soaked had relief, when a news

23. Lyttle, *Washington Action*, p. 11.

report came over the regular car radio. According to this, a riot had broken out at Du Pont Circle, a couple of miles to the north.

RYM II and some other small groups loosely united in a "Revolutionary Contingent" had planned a march from the circle to the Saigon embassy, and it was a reasonable assumption that Weatherman would also be involved. There had even been a report—for which I personally had no firsthand knowledge or verification—that Weatherman had demanded without success $25,000 from the Moratorium as its price for staying out of Washington over the weekend.[24] Weatherman later boasted of its activities on this occasion as follows:

We were the people our parents warned us about. We moved through the streets in groups, marching, dancing, running, chanting, singing, downing jugs of wine. Running together with the people we knew well and trusted a lot. We carried VC flags and used the flagpoles as weapons. Trashing windows and pig cars. Setting fires at street corners.[25]

I drove to Du Pont Circle, but saw no riot. The cops had just broken up the small march and swept back through the circle, using tear gas and chasing away youths hanging around. It was all over by the time I got there. About twenty were arrested, and there couldn't have been more than a few hundred in the action. But the radio was still reporting the incident in the most exaggerated terms. A listener could have the impression that the whole town was about to go out of control. I checked out the March Against Death again. It was going smooth as silk. And the rest of the city was quiet, in spite of the ominous tone set by the radio reports. I headed back to the marshals' center to make some final preparations for the big march the next morning.

\*            \*            \*

The March Against Death marshals made up the core of the teams for the mass march November 15. In addition, we had planned to organize some three thousand more marshals for that event. The process started weeks ahead of time, with training

24. An account of this demand is contained in the article by Murray Kempton in the December 18, 1969, *New York Review of Books.*

25. *Fire,* November 21, 1969. Reprinted in *Weatherman,* edited by Harold Jacobs (Palo Alto, California: Ramparts Press, 1970), pp. 275-76.

sessions in cities as far away as Chicago. Various Quaker organizations, including A Quaker Action Group, the American Friends Service Committee, and the Friends Peace Committee played a key role in this preparation. They developed, and provided instructors in, effective techniques of preventing violence without using it. This was in line with the tactical agreement of the coalition on this demonstration.

The key to the success of the operation was to have this policy—of a peaceful demonstration—clearly understood, not only by the marshals, but by the mass of the demonstrators, the rest of the public, and the government as well. For that reason the point was stated over and over again in the New Mobe literature that advertised the demonstration, and in the technical instruction for groups sending people to Washington. Nor was this policy imposed from the top. It was discussed and argued out, again and again in organizing meetings. Even within marshal training sessions, questioning of this policy was invited so the reasons for it could be reiterated and volunteers sincerely convinced. In the vast majority of cases they were. If not, they were discouraged from being marshals.

There were several reasons for adopting this policy. Among the most important was that it was the best way under the circumstances to put the government on the defensive. We weren't naive about what might happen. We knew, however, that if the authorities used violence against us, we couldn't effectively reply in kind. The most effective defense against that possibility was to put the government in a position where the political repercussions would be prohibitive, and the demonstrators in a position to react without panic.

As for concerted violent attacks by hostile ultraright groups, we knew these would be tiny compared to the size of the demonstration. The tactic was to isolate the trouble, outnumber the attackers with sturdy marshals, and by means such as locking arms and surrounding them, move them out.

We knew our main problem would be with relatively small groups of ultraleftists who did not agree with the policy of the demonstration, and the government's political police provocateurs, who often masqueraded as ultralefts. Here again, the number would be very small compared to the demonstration as a whole. The technique was to isolate the trouble with marshals, some of whom just talked it down, face to face, reducing it to the hard core, and others of whom restrained the hard core with a mass of sturdy bodies. These marshals were trained not to strike anyone. The object was to stop fights, not get involved in them.

We made it a rule never to adopt a hostile attitude and never to accuse anyone causing trouble of being an agent provocateur. That would only make them fighting mad, and justly so if they weren't, which was usually the case. It would also contribute to an atmosphere of paranoia. We just treated them as people who didn't agree with the policy and who might be convinced to restrain themselves. They usually were, at least for the occasion. If not, they were isolated.

Above all, the success of the marshals depended on the fact that they were demonstrators themselves, in tune with the mood of the vast majority of the crowd.

The marshal center was opened Wednesday afternoon, November 12, and ran continuous training sessions—organized by Candy Putter, Bob Levering, and others from A Quaker Action Group in Philadelphia—through Friday night. Brad conceived the idea of recruiting additional marshals from people who had completed the March Against Death, and this worked well. Almost too well, in fact, for by Friday night the center was so crowded training broke down for a time. Putter estimated that 4,000 people went through the center. Many of these were also housed there and in another church, so we always had plenty of volunteers on hand.

There were also a number of specialized groups involved, including the Hog Farm community from New Mexico, who were experts at gently cooling problems in the countercultural milieu at rock concerts, and a large squad of trade unionists to protect the speakers and prominent guests. This latter group was not Quaker trained, but they weren't armed either.

The Hog Farmers also staffed the kitchen at the marshal center and kept everyone filled with hot soup.

Set up separately from the marshals' operation were several hundred legal marshals—lawyers and law students—organized by Hirschkop and Sheila O'Donnel; and hundreds of medics—nurses, doctors, and medical students—organized by the Washington Chapter of the Medical Committee for Human Rights.

The Ebenezer Methodist Church took a beating from all the activity and some of the plumbing broke down from overuse. It was indicative of the attitude of the pastor, Reverend Harris, and the church board—who were Black, incidentally—that when I later offered to raise money to pay for repairs, they refused. "We all have to do whatever we can to end this war," was Rev. Harris's comment.

\*         \*         \*

At six in the morning, November 15, Bill Handley, probably the best big-crowd sound man in the business, was getting his huge amplifiers adjusted at the rally site. John Gage. and a crew of volunteers was working on the stage, the press tent, and a set of bleachers for the speakers, entertainers, and their guests. Brad Lyttle was checking out the assembly area on the Mall west of the capitol where the march would begin. He remembers it thus:

The sky was overcast, the temperature about freezing. A chill, hard, unrelenting wind drove over the Mall from the northwest. Except for a couple mummified in sleeping bags at the foot of a tree, no demonstrators were in sight. "This day," I said to myself, "will be a bomb." By about 8:30, people began to arrive in small groups. The wind abated. The sun broke out from behind purple clouds. By 9:30, people were flowing in from all sides, and I thought about 20,000 were there. By noon Pennsylvania Avenue was filled and the Monument area was two thirds full. Waves of marchers, many carrying banners that billowed and waved, were surging up from buses parked near the Potomac. "A quarter of a million," I thought. From then on, people poured in from every point of the compass. The entire grassy Mall and Monument area seemed overrun. All these people came in about six hours.[26]

The Moratorium had arranged for Senator Eugene McCarthy to make a brief speech at the assembly area. That done, the march stepped off in good order, in spite of the usual initial confusion, and the first part made it to the speakers' stand at the southwest corner of the Washington Monument grounds without incident. As the day proceeded, however, more than once a contingent of ultralefts tried to lead it toward the White House instead of south at Fifteenth Street. This maneuver had been anticipated, and there were more than 300 marshals packed several deep at that point.

Ordinarily, we would handle some group that insisted on taking the wrong route by letting them go their way and make sure the rest of the march wasn't misled into following them. In this case, however, the marshals were instructed to be a wall, not

26. Lyttle, *Washington Action*, pp. 45-46.

a sieve. When I gave the marshals their instructions I told them it was their humanitarian duty. We knew very well the authorities had also anticipated this problem and had special forces lying in wait, no doubt to trap those going toward the White House. They'd have gotten the hell beaten out of them, or worse. So these marshals held their ground, though it was a little like being on a gigantic football team making a last-ditch goal-line stand.

Aside from that, the march itself was quite orderly, and the police kept a low profile (except later at the Justice Department) while the troops were kept inside the buildings, not to be seen. The White House area itself was surrounded by a wall of steel, made of huge buses parked bumper to bumper, but these were never stormed.

The turnout was too large for everyone to make the march along Pennsylvania Avenue, and thousands got tired of waiting and just poured across the Mall toward the monument area. For a while, then, there were two streams moving toward the rally area. At the height, around 1:00 p.m., from the crest of the hill at the base of the monument itself, one could see the slopes of the hill filled and the rally area packed until it looked as though there was no room for more, yet there were still tens of thousands crowded into the assembly area near the capitol while Pennsylvania Avenue was filled with marchers.

The mood was different than it had been on October 15; more serious, less like a holiday, but not a generally angry tone either. These people resented the administration's attitude—exemplified by Vice President Agnew, who had been making speeches calling antiwar critics "effete snobs" and "rotten apples"—but they had not come in a violent mood. Indeed, if they had, as the *Washington Post* later noted (in a November 18 editorial), their numbers were such that the police could not have stopped them.

They had come to petition for a redress of grievances, and most of them still expected, or at least hoped, the government would respond and get out of Vietnam. The dominant mood was summed up by a popular song, "Give Peace a Chance," which arose spontaneously from the march as it first moved along Pennsylvania Avenue and was later started at the rally by Pete Seeger. The whole crowd sang while Mitch Miller—whose TV show had made him the most popular sing-along artist in the country—appeared on stage to join in leading the colossal chorus.

Chaired by the venerable Dr. Spock and Rev. William Sloane Coffin, Jr., the rally, in spite of a windy speech or two, was impressive and at times a deeply emotional experience for those who were there. The artistic side was arranged by Peter Yarrow, who put on an array of star attractions that would have had any TV network jumping at the chance to carry it in full—under normal circumstances. But the White House campaign had its effect not only in the House of Representatives. The heads of the American networks were afraid to show the rally program and they carried only brief excerpts on regular news programs.

There were rumors that ultralefts were planning to disrupt the rally. Senator McGovern was concerned enough about this to send a member of his staff to monitor New Mobe's preparations before accepting the invitation to appear. In fact, some groups did plan to rush the stage, choosing the moment when McGovern got up to speak as the signal for the attack. In their view it was a bad thing to have senators (Charles Goodell also spoke) at an antiwar rally. I myself didn't agree with the senators' support to the capitalist system, but their right to speak against the war when invited, and the coalition's right to invite whomever it decided on without a physical disruption, was worth protecting. And that was part of my job. (It is interesting to note that not a few of the self-proclaimed "revolutionaries" who were bent on disrupting November 15, and who denounced me for organizing marshals to stop them, were two years later supporting McGovern for the presidency on the Democratic ticket and denouncing me for insisting on voting socialist.)

The attacking forces, which numbered a few hundred at the most, were not hard to spot as they came weaving their way through the huge crowd—which was then seated on the grass—carrying colorful flags on long poles and dressed in helmets and padding. The marshals at the perimeter of the stage area expected this move and were reinforced where the attackers concentrated. I wasn't worried, but John Hartwell, whom the Moratorium had assigned to accompany me with a walkie-talkie, insisted I check out the situation just before McGovern spoke. I had been explaining to Hartwell all day that a marshaling operation in a crowd of this size couldn't be directed by anyone; the necessary elements had to be built in beforehand and the marshal captains had to think for themselves. But Hartwell insisted, so we went to the affected area.

In general, the marshals were holding well, but at one spot were weakening. The problem was a real, though peculiar, one. The ultralefts at that point were not physically rushing the line but trying to talk their way through to make a breach. They had given up arguing against civil liberties and had developed a special political twist. They were accusing the marshals of protecting special privilege, namely, that there was a portable toilet nearby inside the speakers' area, and none that close for the crowd assembled outside the line. They were screaming that they couldn't hold their water, and the marshals—who, after all, weren't disciplined soldiers but demonstrator-volunteers who wouldn't stay fast unless they felt justice on their side—were beginning to buckle.

Of course, once the attackers had breached the perimeter on any excuse, they would try to disrupt the speakers' area. The attackers would then still have to face the trade unionists, but it was better to forestall that encounter.

The leader of this thrust was wearing a helmet with a face guard over his nose that made him look a bit like a medieval knight and partially hid his face. I finally recognized him as Walter Teague of the "Committee to Aid the NLF." I knew him well. I made my way to the front of the line, put my arm around Teague in a friendly way, and in a loud voice said: "What's the matter, Walter, want to go to the bathroom? I'll take you." So I ushered Teague to the toilet while the marshals stiffened, closed behind us, and held fast.

When I brought Teague back, the danger of a breach was over. The marshals had set up a system to usher one person at a time to the toilet, and not another until the first was ushered out. Hartwell was duly impressed. Actually this was about the only important thing I did all day, after helping get the march started. It was the ranks, not the generals, who determined the course and character of the events.

\*                \*                \*

Flanked by Jerry Rubin and Abbie Hoffman, Dave Dellinger spoke in the latter part of the program to represent the "Conspiracy Eight" defendants. This time it was well understood beforehand that he was not to turn the mike over to Rubin or Hoffman. But Dellinger did announce the Justice Department demonstration and urge people to go there. Although the great majority ignored this appeal, the thin line of colorful flags was seen once again, weaving its way back through the crowd toward the Justice Department.

By that time it was cold, and the edges of the main crowd were melting away. There were still almost a hundred thousand people left when the East Coast cast of *Hair* took the stage to sing and dance the musical's top song, "Age of Aquarius." The whole audience, on its feet now, joined in, dancing. I felt like a killjoy having to cool this on the temporary bleachers next to the stage because the rhythm was building to the danger of collapse. But it was a climactic moment, the other side of the March Against Death. An affirmation of life while the dour, frightened man in the White House sat behind his steel wall, according to his press releases watching a football game on TV.

The New Mobe demonstration ended on that high note. As the crowd was leaving, the tear gas blew over from the Justice Department location, sending people running, but there was no panic.

*         *         *

Several thousand people, some of whom had gone to demonstrate at the Justice Department and some of whom were just walking away from the monument area in that direction, found themselves near the building when the trouble began. Some say a part of the crowd rushed the building and threw rocks. In any case the cops broke up the demonstration with tear gas and clubs, then swept slowly southwest, across the Mall and into the monument area, scattering and gassing the remnants of the main crowd. Some cops went as far as the New Mobe stage area, where they gassed the crew dismantling the equipment. There was hell to pay getting additional volunteers to finish the job.

The next day, at the building housing the antiwar offices, I happened to find myself alone on an elevator with Abbie Hoffman. "You know, Fred," he said, "the trouble with you is you're too straight. You ought to try some LSD." Fortunately somebody else got on the elevator before I lost my temper.

Later, in his booklet *Washington Action*, Brad Lyttle devoted a section to the Justice Department demonstration. Characteristically, he was more charitable than I, but some of his conclusions are worth repeating. Wrote Brad:

> An argument made in categorical support of the Justice Department demonstration is that some outlet for people's frustration and anger must be provided by a movement. If the movement can't provide a completely peaceful outlet, then it should go along with what exists, even if that is

far from ideal. This isn't a completely sound strategy.

The argument also has paternalistic overtones. It tends to regard demonstrators as children. . . . Adults are supposed to have the intro-spection, self-control, sense of humor and imagination that give them freedom from such mechanistic dependencies. . . .

It has also been argued that demonstrators are morally justified in being angry and abusive. This argument is true, but misses the point. The point is not what is justified, it is what are the best strategies and tactics for dealing with political realities? A mature movement doesn't waste time whitewashing itself. It seeks the most effective ways to reach its goals.[27]

\*         \*         \*

November 15 in San Francisco was also the biggest yet, and entirely peaceful. The New Mobe's official estimate was a quarter of a million in San Francisco and three quarters of a million in Washington. The newspapers generally gave lower figures, but these were still unprecedentedly large. My own view is that the New Mobe figures were closer to the fact. Some 4,000 chartered buses came to Washington, which would account for close to 200,000 alone, not to mention those who came by car, train, and airplane, and those from the Washington area itself.

While November 15 focused on the two cities, there were numerous antiwar activities elsewhere in the same period. The Student Mobilization Committee called a national student strike for November 14, and it was widespread as well, though not as solid as October 15 since it did not have the semiofficial charac-ter of the Moratorium. In a matter of months, the idea of another national student strike—with or without the support of school administrations—would explode, catching many people by sur-prise. But such things are never completely spontaneous and always have a preparatory background. The November 14 SMC strike was part of what was to come.

In any case, Washington on November 15 saw the largest political demonstration in the history of the United States up to that time. Outwardly, President Nixon pretended to ignore it, and administration spokesmen hinted prosecution of the leaders of New Mobe, citing the sideshows at Du Pont Circle and the Justice Department as part of the excuse.

27. Ibid., pp. 49-50.

The November 18 *Washington Post* ran its lead editorial with a one-word title: "No." It began:

> The effort by this administration to characterize the weekend demonstration as (a) small, (b) violent, and (c) treacherous will not succeed because it is demonstrably untrue. If citizens had had the opportunity to witness the weekend on television, they would know it to be untrue; as it is, they will have to ask those who were there—either cops or kids, no matter.

The *Post* further observed:

> It seems clear from their statements, and from the accounts of participants at the command post in the Municipal Center over the weekend, that the Nixon administration was less interested in trying to keep the march peaceful than in trying to make it seem less large and more violent than it really was, and in trying to scare the daylights out of that putative Silent Majority at the same time.

The editorial concluded with this comment about President Nixon:

> It was a fine afternoon for watching football, he is quoted as saying on Saturday, and for sheer piquancy, we have not heard the likes of that since Marie Antoinette.

# 20

# The Invasion of Cambodia and May 1970

In light of the success of the November 13-15, 1969, demonstrations, it seemed obvious to me that we should prepare for more of the same and at least call another national antiwar conference, which would plan and set a date for mass actions in the spring of 1970. But this view was by no means shared by all the leaders of the antiwar movement.

The mood at the time was characterized by frustration. The inside facts about the impact of the demonstrations on the administration were not then public knowledge and Nixon's charade about ignoring the antiwar movement had its effect. So did the announced U.S. troop cutbacks in connection with the "Vietnamization" ploy. In truth, the pace of withdrawals was much slower than the highly publicized announcements. By the end of 1969 there were still 472,000 U.S. troops in South Vietnam, and the tonnage of U.S. bombs being dropped, as well as the number of people being killed—including U.S. GIs—was higher than in 1967. But hopes were raised that the war would soon be over. Though the antiwar sentiment was deeper than ever, a lull in visible antiwar activity occurred after the November demonstrations.

In addition, there was an increase in government repression against radicals, including not just prosecutions but secret police provocations and assorted dirty tricks. In northern Illinois, to cite only one of many examples, a protofascist group called the Legion of Justice made a series of violent raids on various radical and antiwar groups, including the SWP and the YSA. It was later revealed that this was done in collusion with Chicago police and the army intelligence apparatus in the region.[1] This connection was not known at the time, though it was ominously clear to the victims that this group operated with some sort of official assistance or immunity.

The Chicago "conspiracy" trial was then in progress, as well as a series of prosecutions against Black militants, especially the Black Panther Party, which by the end of 1969 had suffered some two dozen members killed in police raids. It was during this period that Chicago Black Panther leader Fred Hampton was shot to death in bed during an unannounced predawn attack December 4 by officers of the Cook County Attorney's office.

Draft resistance was increasing, but this was not very clear at the time, since the most publicized draft resistance organizations, including The Resistance and CADRE, were in a state of disarray, or became transformed into prisoner aid groups with their leading younger activists in jail.

GI opposition to the war was also increasing and had already become an important factor in the military situation in Vietnam. But this development too was not all that obvious at the time to people not on the scene. By its very nature, antiwar organizing by

1. Details of the Legion of Justice attacks were described at the time in "A Further Alarm Signal from Chicago—An Open Letter from Fred Halstead," December 15, 1969. (Copy in author's files.) Also in a report by the Commission on Civil Liberties and Law Enforcement of the Independent Voters of Illinois (IVI) summarized in the *Chicago Sun Times*, April 9, 1970.

For subsequent revelations of official collusion see: a series of articles by reporters Larry Green and Rob Warden in the *Chicago Daily News* in March 1975, in particular March 24; the *Militant* of September 26 and December 5, 1975; and a report by a Cook County grand jury released November 10, 1975.

The grand jury declared: "There is no question that some members of the Security Section [of the Chicago Police Department] maintained a close working relationship with the Legion of Justice" and that the police "either condoned or directed" the attacks. The grand jury indicted no police or government officials, however, on the grounds that crucial physical evidence had been destroyed, that the statute of limitations had expired on some of the crimes, and that the guilt of high ranking officials would be "obscured by a criminal trial of a few patrolmen." The *Chicago Sun Times* of November 12, 1975, commented editorially: "The grand jury said it did not indict because that would draw attention away from the systematic seriousness of the problem. That was well meaning. It was also nonsense."

active-duty GIs was transitory even as it proliferated. The sentiment was there but its organized expressions tended to be short-lived because of the usual troop movements and expired tours of duty, as well as punitive transfers and more severe forms of repression.

These factors contributed to the widespread frustration which in some radical and radical-liberal circles led to a certain desperation.

The problem of the apparent inability of the movement to materially inhibit the war once again came to the fore and a wide variety of schemes were suggested in an attempt to overcome this. Sid Peck and Stewart Meacham circulated a proposal that the antiwar movement itself prepare to call a general strike in the spring, but withdrew it as unrealistic.

Much time was spent discussing various ideas for confrontation, civil disobedience, encouraging desertion, and so on. Many of those who advocated this supposed "higher level of commitment" also, in apparent contradiction, raised the idea that the war itself was not a major issue for "radical organizing," or at least that there was no longer room for a coalition focused centrally on the war.

In a repeat of the old arguments within SDS, this view was rationalized in two opposite ways, sometimes by the same person: There is nothing we can do to stop the war anyway, so we should concentrate on building a radical movement on other issues; or, the war is practically over and the attention of the antiwar forces should be turned elsewhere.

The latter variant was most starkly expressed by Weatherman, which in an article criticizing the November 15 demonstrations declared:

THE VIETNAM WAR ISN'T THE ISSUE ANY MORE. Mainly because the war is over. The Vietnamese people have won a military victory over the most powerful empire in the history of the world. They have regained control of the entire countryside and most of the cities, while the American troops have retreated to a few of their most defensible bases (40 percent of the U.S. troops are now stationed in Saigon). The only thing left is for Nixon to find the American ruling class a diplomatic way of admitting defeat.[2]

2. *Fire,* November 21, 1969. Reproduced in *Weatherman,* edited by Harold Jacobs (Palo Alto, California: Ramparts Press, 1970), p. 276.

While the Weatherman tactical approach had no support within either the New Mobe or the Moratorium, similar, though less ridiculously exaggerated, views of the state of the war were reflected there. The Moratorium Committee was not interested in "radical organizing." Its forces were pointed toward the Democratic Party and the congressional elections in the fall of 1970. It abandoned its original idea of adding a day of moratorium each month. "What could we do for eight days in May?" commented Marge Sklencar, one of the Moratorium's coordinators.[3] Instead, it decided to call decentralized activities for April 15, the income tax deadline, as a way to emphasize that the war was costing people a lot of money.

The Moratorium Committee's climactic point had been October 15, 1969. After the administration's counterattack, many Moratorium activists were disoriented because the mass media did not give them the publicity they had before, and most of the Democratic and Republican dove politicians who had previously been friendly ran for cover. Except for New York and Boston, where the local Democratic Party machines hoped to recruit some activists for the fall elections, the Moratorium did very little to build the spring antiwar actions.

\*       \*       \*

On December 13-14, 1969, a meeting of the New Mobe steering committee took place at Case Western Reserve University in Cleveland, in the same hall where the first of the Mobes had been founded back in 1966. This meeting was dominated by a caucus led by radical-liberals such as Art Waskow of the Institute for Policy Studies in Washington and a number of people from the former SDS milieu who were new to the coalition. (RYM II had decided in late November to enter both New Mobe and the Student Mobilization Committee.)

Their caucus was not formally announced but referred to itself in the corridors as the "radical caucus" or the "new left caucus." It was supported by Dave Dellinger and Rennie Davis and other

---

3. *New York Times,* December 10, 1969. Sklencar, who ran the Moratorium's Washington office with efficiency and a kind of refreshing bluntness, seemed to have a penchant for guessing wrong, in light of what actually developed in May 1970.

advocates of confrontation of the Chicago 1968 variety, by people around the *Guardian,* and by a number of pacifists who advocated the more traditional forms of nonviolent civil disobedience. This bloc was not very clear—and certainly not unified—on what it wanted the New Mobe to do, but it was united in opposition to having the Mobe focus centrally on another set of mass demonstrations against the war. This, it was felt, would dominate the Mobe's activities. Other concerns—such as organizing civil disobedience or building a radical constituency around a multi-issue program or "community work," and so on—would tend to be shunted aside.

A motion supported by the "radical caucus" proposed a variety of scattered activities with no central focus and no mention of demanding immediate withdrawal of U.S. forces from Vietnam.

We had been through this argument so many times in the past—and more than once in this same room—that I took the floor, shouting: "Haven't you learned anything?" I made the point that while all of us in this small meeting considered most of the proposals worthy causes, the motion left out exactly what this particular coalition had proven it could do effectively—provide a central focus for mass mobilization against the war. I was exasperated, and the ranting speech was not well received.

"Radical caucus" spokespersons put amendments to include a day of decentralized demonstrations on April 15, and to consider all the activities as "functionally carrying out our demand for immediate and unconditional withdrawal of all American troops from Vietnam and withdrawal of support for the Thieu-Ky regime."[4] But these items were put in as afterthoughts, in an attempt to blunt the opposition, and it was made clear that mass antiwar demonstrations were not to be the focus of New Mobe activity.

An amendment by Harry Ring that "these activities build toward and culminate in a series of coordinated anti-war demonstrations on a selected day in the spring" was supported by Sid Peck but nevertheless defeated. The vote was 29 to 25.[5] Another amendment that the New Mobe call a conference for the end of January, inviting representatives from each antiwar group in the

4. New Mobilization steering committee minutes, December 13-14, 1969. (Copy in author's files.)
5. Ibid. The vote count is not in the minutes but comes from the December 26, 1969, *Militant.*

country, was defeated by a greater margin. Some of the "radical caucus" spokespersons candidly explained that such a conference might overturn the decisions of the steering committee. The "radical caucus" perspective was adopted. Subsequently, Jerry Gordon, chairman of the Cleveland Area Peace Action Council, resigned from the steering committee on the grounds that the new perspective included civil disobedience as New Mobe policy, and he didn't wish to be committed to that.

Some fairly effective literature was put out by the New Mobe office in support of a variety of actions, mainly organized by other groups, but the New Mobe itself became increasingly narrow. Its steering committee was effectively replaced by a smaller coordinating committee dominated by the "radical caucus." Except in Philadelphia, the New Mobe—like the Moratorium—did little to build the spring antiwar actions.

\*        \*        \*

Once again, as in the spring of 1969, it was the Student Mobilization Committee that carried the weight of the organizing for the April activities. On its own the SMC held a youth antiwar conference in Cleveland February 14-15. The turnout was 3,308 registered participants plus a few hundred more, less than 10 percent of whom had participated in a previous SMC conference. It was the largest working conference in the history of the antiwar movement, and a major indication that the campuses were going to be far from quiet that semester on the war issue. It was also a powerful objective rebuke to the "radical caucus" policy.

The conference discussed perspectives similar to those that had been counterposed at the New Mobe steering committee meeting in December. A formation not unlike the "radical caucus" also appeared at the SMC gathering. This time it was called the Independent Radical Caucus. It opposed the "Mass Action Focus for Spring" proposal introduced by SMC Executive Secretary Carol Lipman. In his book on SDS, Kirkpatrick Sale describes it this way:

> The critical point in SMC's development came at a conference it called in Cleveland in February 1970, when some 3500 people showed up, many of them independent radicals hoping to broaden SMC's politics, inject an anti-imperialist analysis into its antiwar policies, and turn it into a multi-

issue organization that could succeed SDS. But the YSA and SWP vigorously resisted any changes in what had been a very successful front group for them and by maintaining rigid control over the proceedings were able to beat back the challenge and keep the SMC to the narrow antiwar path.[6]

The strategy pressed by the YSA prevailed at the conference not because of any "rigid control" but because it won a majority after full discussion in a wide-open debate. The SMC was never a front for the YSA, though during ebb periods it was mainly the YSA that kept it alive. Throughout, the YSA worked to build the SMC as a broad, nonexclusionary antiwar formation, striving to bring in all antiwar tendencies and leaving the basic decisions up to votes at open conferences after full debate. This conference was simply the most successful example of this democratic procedure.

I was present at the conference—as were Sid Peck and Jerry Gordon, both of whom gave speeches of greeting—and I estimated some two-thirds of the participants were uncommitted at the outset and were neither former SDSers nor members of any other organized radical tendency. Most of the radical youth groups were represented, however, and the debate over perspectives generally found the YSA caucus on one side and most of the other organized tendencies—including RYM (by this time no longer called RYM II), the Independent Socialists, Youth Against War and Fascism, and the recently organized Young Workers Liberation League (which succeeded the Du Bois Clubs), on the other.

No caucus exercised mechanical control. Carol Lipman and Don Gurewitz—two of the chairpersons—were members of the YSA, but the conference parliamentarian was C. Clark Kissinger, a spokesperson for RYM, and one of the chairpersons was U.C. Berkeley Student Body President Dan Seigel, a supporter of the Independent Radical Caucus.

There was much baiting of the YSA in attempts to rally opposition to the Lipman perspective on grounds it was "a YSA proposal."

Robin Maisel took the floor to explain the contribution the policy of nonexclusion had made to overcoming the cold war, witch-hunt atmosphere, and that nonexclusion meant judging ideas and individuals on their merits, not on their political

6. Sale, *SDS,* p. 622.

associations. Even C. Clark Kissinger, speaking for the RYM-backed motion, commented:

> We don't want anyone voting for our proposal out of opposition to the Young Socialist Alliance. We are firmly opposed to anticommunism and it's been manifested greatly at this conference.[7]

Some participants tried to disrupt the proceedings in the fashion that had been common at SDS gatherings during that organization's death throes. An account by Jim Gwin in the *Great Speckled Bird,* one of the important alternate newspapers of the time, caught the scene accurately:

> "Free John Sinclair" and "bullshit" rang out many times during the conference, summing up the sentiment of a number of hip anarchists who despite their numbers were never able to generate a program other than organizing against the *organization* of the SMC.[8]

Withal, it was a full and democratic debate. "Despite the emotional fervor with which most of the students embraced their ideas," the February 16 *Cleveland Press* reported, "an almost overwhelming democracy prevailed. Nearly everyone who wished got a chance to speak."

The opponents of the Lipman proposal were at a distinct disadvantage as the debate proceeded. They tended to agree on the idea of some kind of multi-issue approach but once again couldn't agree among themselves on what such issues should be. Shortly before the vote, the Independent Radical Caucus, RYM, YAWF, and a group calling itself the Grass Roots Community Coalition announced they were combining their various proposals in an attempt to defeat Lipman's. They had difficulty agreeing on what to include in their joint proposal, however, and were unable to present it coherently to the gathering. The Lipman proposal passed overwhelmingly.

The Lipman proposal did not ignore other issues and tactics, and left local chapters free to engage in civil disobedience if they

---

7. *Militant,* February 27, 1970.

8. Atlanta *Great Speckled Bird,* March 2, 1970. John Sinclair was the leader of a small, somewhat bizarre countercultural group in Ann Arbor called the White Panthers. He had been railroaded to prison for a long term on a marijuana charge.

chose to do so. The crucial dispute was not over whether other
issues than the war would be acted upon or whether other tactics
in addition to mass demonstrations would be utilized, but
whether the task of organizing the broadest possible mass
actions against the war would remain the SMC's central orientation. The conference took positions on many other issues—
against racism; for women's equality; against the oppression of
homosexuals; in defense of the Black Panther Party, the "Conspiracy Eight," and other victims of government repression; and so
on.

The SMC had already been involved with other issues. During
the fall and winter of 1969-70, for example, both the national
office and certain local chapters spent considerable energy in
support of the 147,000 striking employees of the General Electric
Corporation. In the narrow sense, the strike was for new union
contracts with wage provisions to counteract inflation. But GE
was the second-largest military contractor in the U.S. and the
eleven unions involved went on strike despite pleas that this
would interfere with war production. The SMC viewed this class
action as an opportunity for the antiwar movement to relate more
concretely to labor. The unions had called for a boycott of GE
products so the SMC organized along this line on campuses, as
well as engaging in other activity against university complicity
with GE. Officials of both the International Union of Electrical
Workers and the United Electrical Workers publicly welcomed the
SMC support.

One of the notable features of the SMC conference was the
heavy turnout of high school students and their participation in
leading capacities. The conference adopted a "High School Bill of
Rights," which had been developed out of experiences in Cleveland and elsewhere. Though the SMC thrust was to extend the
rights of high school students to organize against the war, the
High School Bill of Rights dealt with student rights in general,
from dress codes to student control of school newspapers. It was
effectively used in many places in the struggle to extend high
school student rights.

For example, in New York the SMC joined with the General
Organization City Council (the city-wide high school student
government body), the Afro-American Student Association,
ASPIRA (a Puerto Rican student group), and others to form the
High School Student Rights Coalition. This coalition adopted a

similar bill of rights which became an important demand in the April 15 student strike in New York.

\*        \*        \*

The SMC went forth from its conference keyed up to build the spring actions on the scale of the previous fall events. The lack of unified national antiwar leadership, however, was reflected on a local level, where most of the coalitions suffered divisions, hesitations, and abstentions. Even in Boston, where the Moratorium Committee did make an effort, it was half-hearted.

Boston staffer Ken Hurwitz caught the mood in the local Moratorium office as April 15 approached:

> I sat on the phone, making calls, trying to help piece things together, but all the time knowing it was a useless, irreparable mess. Literally no one was signing up to do community canvassing, no major antiwar politicians would be speaking, SDS [the PL wing, which opposed any liberal speakers at the rally] was laying plans to take the stage by force, and the November Action Coalition [composed of groups that had demonstrated at the Justice Department November 15] was allegedly organizing for the burning of Harvard Square. And on top of this it was clear that the great numbers involved in October all over the country simply weren't going to duplicate their efforts on this fifteenth of April. This time around, the Moratorium was going to be smaller, lacking cohesion, and perhaps even violent. . . .
>
> Not that I particularly cared, but April 15 was a sun-filled day in Boston. We all knew that the weather's only significance was that it would determine the exact degree to which this day would fall short of October 15. No matter what, the evidence would show that over the last six months our movement [the Moratorium] had not expanded or even maintained its position, but had contracted—fatally. In Washington, [Sam] Brown and his friends were already preparing for a press conference to announce the disbanding of the Vietnam Moratorium Committee. Excepting a sudden change in events, the day would determine only how graciously the Moratorium would take its leave.[9]

Nevertheless, the April 15 demonstrations proved to be massive and widespread, actually more so than any previous decentralized demonstrations except for the preceding October 15. In Boston the major demonstration on the Common was variously

9. Ken Hurwitz, *Marching Nowhere* (New York: W. W. Norton, 1971), pp. 187-88.

estimated at 65,000 to 100,000. New York had a rally of 35,000 run by the Moratorium to which marches organized by the Parade Committee and the SMC fed. Chicago had 25,000; San Francisco, 20,000; Houston, 6,000; Seattle, 8,000; Orlando, Florida, 2,500; Detroit, 12,000; San Diego, 5,000; and so on.

There were some disruptions, however, which further soured the Moratorium. PL-SDS did not succeed in taking over the stage by force in Boston, but it did in New York and the Moratorium rally there had to be cut short. Ultralefts led a march from the Boston rally to Cambridge which ended with a few hundred "plate glass revolutionaries" breaking a lot of windows in Harvard Square.

The April 15 student strike was more on the scale of November 14 than October 15. It shut down few schools, though half the New York City high school students went out. Actions took place on hundreds of campuses and in every region of the country, and while few schools were struck solid, the idea of a student strike became much more current.

In many places the actions focused against the Reserve Officers Training Corps (ROTC) through which civilian colleges provided well over half the army's levy of new officers. The campaign against this institution—in which many radical and pacifist groups as well as the SMC had been participating—was already giving the military trouble. At a number of campuses, building takeovers were involved, with mixed results.

At the University of Colorado in Boulder, for example, the local SMC led 500 students in occupying the administrative offices April 15, demanding that ROTC get off campus. The sit-in swelled to 2,000 in a few hours while university officials rounded up several hundred police from nearby areas.

Joanie Quinn, then an SMC activist at Boulder, later recalled: "They [the police] formed up outside the building and sent a representative inside. 'You have two choices, you can line up quietly and take your summons' or, they added, brandishing their clubs with expectation, 'we will come serve the summons on you.'" Jim Lauderdale, one of the leaders of the SMC, grabbed for the mike and explained that the demonstrators had another choice, "We can walk right out of here, and be free to struggle tomorrow."[10] With the authorities looking on perplexed, the

10. Letter from Joanie Quinn to the author, June 1, 1976.

demonstrators filed out of the building, between two massive phalanxes of cops, and marched through the dorms to arouse other students and spread the demand for an end to ROTC on campus. The groundwork was laid for winning the demand during the next upsurge, which would come sooner than anyone expected.

At Miami University in Oxford, Ohio, matters took a different turn. There, following an SMC rally April 15, students broke into the ROTC building for a sit-in, which, since a band also entered, became more like a dance. Cathy Hinds, then the local SMC chairperson, recalls:

> Everyone was having a good time, with a few speeches thrown in, until the administration got tough. . . . they called in all the surrounding police forces in Butler County and the State Police; 176 students were arrested that night, and tear gas was over the entire campus. . . . they tear-gassed the Fiji Fraternity House and let loose a police dog in there which bit one of their members. The result: the frats were our biggest supporters in the strike that began the next day.[11]

The strike was about 80 percent solid and included demands of the Afro-American Students Association for increased Black enrollment (of 12,000 students, only 200 were Black) as well as protests against ROTC and other university complicity with the war. Some serious errors were made out of inexperience, peculiar to that particular campus but not so unusual in their unintended self-defeating character.

For one thing, the strike leadership put a twenty-four hour picket line at the commissary and asked the union truck drivers to honor it. They did and the cafeterias, where most of the students ate, received no fresh food. For another, the strike leadership—which had been careful to head off such tactics as fire bombings—allowed one strange suggestion to go unopposed. On April 21, at the daily strike rally of some 5,000 students, somebody got the mike and called for everyone to flush their toilets at the same time to empty the water tower and back up the drains. The leadership forgot about this project but a sound truck later appeared announcing the time for the "flush-in," and it caught on.         .

11. Letter from Cathy Hinds to the author, April 3, 1976.

Recalls Hinds:

It was so successful that the entire town was without water for as long
as 24 hours. . . . We got national news coverage of this event. Unfortunately, this great "success" also broke the back of the strike. . . . That
night I called my roommate from another rally we had, and she was
hysterically demanding her water back. I tried to explain that I couldn't
do anything to get her water back, and offered that I hadn't even flushed
a toilet. That didn't help, but she did warn me that the women in my
dorm were awfully angry, and that I better not come in alone. . . .
Instead of opening up the university for strike activities and support, we
attempted to close it down, a mistake made unconsciously by many
activists across the country.[12]

Campus protests of this size and strength, though scattered on
April 15, were portents of things to come a short while later.

In the meantime, of the three major national antiwar organizations, only the SMC viewed the results of April 15 as indicating
both the possibility and the need for organizing more mass
demonstrations against the war in the near future.

\*         \*         \*

The Geneva Accords of 1954 resulted in the division of the
former French colony of Indochina into four parts: the two zones
of Vietnam, Laos, and Cambodia. Theoretically, both Laos and
Cambodia were neutral, but by the late 1960s a civil war was
raging in Laos between the left-wing Pathet Lao, supported by
North Vietnam, and the right-wing Royal Laotian Army, supported by the United States.

Some of the mountain paths over which supplies were carried
from North Vietnam to the NLF in the South—the so-called Ho
Chi Minh Trail—passed through Laotian territory and these
areas were steadily bombed by American planes. In addition, the
U.S. had been covertly involved in the Laotian civil war from the
beginning.

In early 1970 Washington sharply escalated its military involvement in Laos, mounting some of the heaviest bombing in
human history over central Laos far from the border trails, using
B-52s as well as fighter bombers from U.S. bases in Thailand.

12. Ibid.

The purpose was to stave off a military victory by the Pathet Lao, which had gained control of two-thirds of the country.

Until 1970 the situation had been different in Cambodia, where the head of state, Prince Norodom Sihanouk, walked a shaky tightrope maintaining a "neutralist" policy. The South Vietnamese NLF used certain Cambodian border areas—where there was a large ethnic Vietnamese population—for supply and regroupment. Sihanouk tolerated this presence for fear that if he tried to force the NLF out, they in turn would be forced to back Cambodian revolutionaries in taking over at least the border areas, and Cambodia would become another zone of war and revolution.

In mid-March, 1970, Sihanouk was ousted by a coup. Rightist General Lon Nol took over and was quickly backed by the U.S. The Cambodian army began cooperating with the U.S. and Saigon forces in border area raids on the NLF. Lon Nol's forces were soon in deep trouble, however, from previously isolated Cambodian guerrillas called the Khmer Rouge, now backed by North Vietnam, the NLF, and even Sihanouk, who was preparing to set up a government in exile in Peking.

On April 3, the *Wall Street Journal* carried the following ominous report from Washington:

arguing for U.S. involvement in Cambodia, a senior American general with much Vietnam experience, insists the communists couldn't keep up their warfare around Saigon and the Mekong Delta, without these sanctuaries.

Through the month the tension around the Cambodian situation continued to mount.

On April 19, Sam Brown announced the disbanding of the national Vietnam Moratorium Committee. The group's activists, it was suggested, could devote themselves to electoral campaigns of liberal candidates. Marge Sklencar declared that mass demonstrations were "a political fad that has worn off."[13]

The next day the SMC national office issued a statement declaring:

The Student Mobilization Committee finds it regrettable that such steps were taken in face of the clear expansion of the war into Laos, Cambodia and the rest of Southeast Asia by the United States government. . . . We

13. *New York Times*, April 20, 1970.

are urging all antiwar organizations and leaders in the antiwar movement to jointly call a national conference where the entire antiwar movement can discuss and project further nationally coordinated actions against the war.[14]

On April 29, the coordinating committee of the New Mobe met at Cora Weiss's house in New York City. Several members of the steering committee, including Carol Lipman and me, were also present by invitation. The idea of a national conference was raised and once again rejected.

But early in the meeting, news came that caused all of us to set aside our differences for the moment. Major U.S. military forces from South Vietnam were invading Cambodia. We did not know from those early reports how extensive the escalation was or what the reaction of the American people would be, but it was clear we had to do something.

The meeting unanimously agreed to issue a call in the name of the New Mobilization Committee for a mass demonstration at the White House for Saturday, May 9, a little more than a week away. A number of us agreed to put aside other commitments and go to Washington to begin preparations. Brad Lyttle and I were once again put in charge of logistics, including marshals.

\*         \*         \*

The next day, the SMC issued a statement addressed to "Antiwar coalitions, SMC chapters and other opponents of the war." It declared in part:

Clearly, the movement is obligated to organize a massive public outcry of protest against this new move, one loud enough to force the administration to reverse itself. . . . If we begin work immediately we can turn the Cambodian escalation into a major political defeat for the administration and a massive new upsurge for the antiwar movement.[15]

That evening, Thursday, April 30, President Nixon appeared on television to acknowledge that he had ordered the invasion of Cambodia. Its purpose, he said, was to destroy what he described as the central military headquarters of the communist forces in South Vietnam, which he claimed was hidden in Cambodian

14. *Militant,* May 1, 1970.
15. Student Mobilization Committee statement, April 30, 1970. (Copy in author's files.)

territory. The move was couched in terms of shortening the war, but the American people had been told the same on the occasion of every previous escalation. It became clear to millions who had hoped the administration was backing out of the war that in truth it was widening it in quest of quicker military victory. The angry mass reaction began before Nixon finished his speech.

The biggest of these first spontaneous outbursts occurred at Princeton, New Jersey, where some 2,500 students and faculty (out of a university community of 6,000) met immediately and voted to strike the college. By morning the strike was virtually solid.

Throughout that day, May 1, wherever young people gathered, there was angry discussion of Nixon's speech. Mass meetings and rallies took place on hundreds of campuses and the strike idea spread. At Yale in New Haven, Connecticut, a partial strike was already in progress in protest against the New Haven Black Panther trial, and a defense rally had previously been scheduled for the weekend of May 1. It had been publicized beforehand and supported by the New York Parade Committee and other groups. As a result, there were people in attendance from many places in the eastern part of the country.

The Cambodian invasion prompted the New Haven gathering to call for a nationwide student strike around three demands: immediate withdrawal from Southeast Asia, freedom for political prisoners, and an end to campus complicity with the war.

In addition, a strike information center was hastily set up at Brandeis University in Waltham, Massachusetts, over the weekend, and the SMC as well as the National Student Association also spread the strike call. But in truth, no national group initiated, controlled, or directed the strike. It simply exploded with unprecedented force across the country, organized on each campus by whatever local activists there were. By Monday, the SMC national office had contacted groups at over a hundred universities and virtually all these campuses were on strike or making plans to take a strike vote.

*          *          *

The national spotlight was turned on one of the most unlikely places to become famous in a national student upsurge. That was Kent State University in northern Ohio. The nonstudent population of the immediate area tended to be conservative, even right-wing. The bulk of the 20,000 students at Kent, while generally opposed to the war, were not noted for their radical activism. In addition, events during the spring 1969 semester had dealt a severe blow to student political rights at Kent State.

In April 1969, the local SDS chapter carried out a series of small actions isolated from the mass of the student body by ultraleft rhetoric. Using a combination of police, right-wing civilian ruffians, red-baiting, and spurious felony charges against the students, the school administration broke up the SDS demonstrations, revoked the SDS charter, and derailed an attempt by several thousand non-SDS students to defend the civil liberties of the victims. This attempt ended in disarray partly because the SDS leadership demanded that concerned students and faculty participate in the defense on the basis of a "revolutionary" program or not at all. An atmosphere of fear and intimidation established by the school administration was still in evidence a year later.

Nevertheless, at noon on the day following Nixon's speech, some 300 Kent State students rallied in protest. In the afternoon the Black United Students held another rally. A pent-up anger soon became apparent. That night, Friday, a rally of about a thousand people took place in downtown Kent in which a large number of windows were broken. The following night, Saturday, May 2, the National Guard was called out. Later the same evening some two thousand students marched on the ROTC building and some of them set it afire. While it burned, the guardsmen were given orders to shoot anyone cutting fire hoses. There was no shooting then, but a tone had been set.

On Monday, May 4, at noontime, students gathered around a bell mounted in the Commons, an open field in the center of the campus. A speaker mounted the base of the bell and called for a strike. A state trooper with a bullhorn pronounced the gathering illegal and told the crowd to leave. A few of the more than a thousand students in the area threw rocks. Guardsmen arrived and gassed the crowd, which retreated, but did not fully disperse. Gas canisters were lobbed; some students lobbed them back; the students retreated again, toward a parking lot. Some students were throwing small rocks at a group of guardsmen on a hill. A line of the soldiers got to their knees and aimed their rifles. Two students, Mike York and Fred Kirsch, who were present, later recalled:

At first no one was sure what was happening. There was a steady, loud rattle, like machine guns. Someone yelled, "Those are only blanks." Then we heard bullets whistling past our heads. Dirt flew up in our faces, where bullets were hitting the ground, landing only a few feet from us. There was a tree about fifteen yards behind us. There were repeated sounds of thuds and splintering noise as bullets hit the tree. More bullets hit the cars in the lot, smashing the windshields, hitting the fenders and the sides of the cars. . . .

A girl was screaming. "They're not using blanks. They're not using blanks." Another student fell over, dead. A student collapsed to the ground, hit. Suddenly, after about 30 seconds, the shooting stopped. We got up and looked around. One girl was lying on the ground, holding her stomach. Her face was white. There were others, lying on the ground. Some moved. Some didn't.

The whole area was one of panic. We heard a girl crying hysterically. "Get an ambulance, get an ambulance," others were shouting. A guy picked up one girl and held her in his arms. The front of her was covered with blood. "She's dead," he was shouting. "She's dead. I know she's dead."[16]

*   *   *

Four students were killed and many wounded, one crippled for life, in that fraction of a minute. The guardsmen claimed they had been fired upon, but this was later proven false. Some of the students who were shot had not even been in the demonstration but were simply passing through the parking lot. The dead were Allison Krause, 19; Jeffrey Glenn Miller, 20; Sandra Lee Scheuer, 20; and William K. Schroeder, 19. Schroeder had been attending Kent on an ROTC scholarship, though like many such students, he was critical of the war.

That evening, tens of millions watched television interviews with some of the dead students' anguished parents. The bereaved parents were not hostile toward the student demonstrators and bitterly denounced the government.

The news of the Kent State massacre gave further impetus to the already spreading student revolt. Within a few days some 350 universities across the country were on strike.

At Brown University in Providence, Rhode Island, the student

16. *May 1970: Birth of the Antiwar University* (New York: Pathfinder Press, 1971), p. 13.

government reserved a hall with a capacity of 1,000 for a meeting to take a strike vote on Monday night, May 4. Some 4,000 showed up, 80 percent of the campus community, and the meeting was moved outside to the Quad, where sound equipment was hastily rigged. Brown SMC activist Toby Emmerich recalled:

> There was a lot of discussion and debate over whether to strike. This was not going to be a one-day affair. People were worried about what we were going to do about the end of the semester, finals, classes, credits, grades, and so on. When it finally got to the point where people thought we were ready to vote, we suddenly realized we had no way to do it, no ballots or boxes, and it was too dark to see hands in the crowd. At last we decided people should leave through two different arches, one for strike, one against. Thousands waited to walk through the strike arch while only a few walked through the other one. The next morning we met again, taking over the hockey rink, the only place big enough for mass meetings.[17]

The first hockey rink meeting took over some sacred prerogatives of the university administration. The strikers decided to keep the university open but there was to be no complicity with the war. Professors who so desired could continue teaching and students could attend classes, but there were to be no credits lost and no reprisals against students or faculty devoting part or full time to antiwar activity. The faculty was asked to give grades for the entire semester according to work done as of the beginning of the strike. The faculty meeting later that day agreed, and the administrators had to go along. Similar arrangements were being made elsewhere across the country.

*    *    *

At the Berkeley campus of the University of California, the Academic Senate—the official body of the faculty with over 1,200 members, and normally a moderate group—met Monday, May 1, and voted to call for a Wednesday convocation to "discuss appropriate responses of the campus community to the grave consequences of the recent widening of the war."[18]

The next day a noon rally of over 5,000 was held on Sproul

17. Taped interview by the author with Toby Emmerich, November 18, 1974.
18. *May 1970*, p. 20.

Plaza. The student body president, Dan Seigel, who spoke on the need for the whole campus to become a massive antiwar center, received a standing ovation. The six-member faculty steering committee was enlarged to include Seigel, Jean Savage of the SMC, and Matthew Ross of the People's Coalition, a group that in recent weeks had led several anti-ROTC confrontations.

Fifteen thousand attended the Wednesday convocation May 6 in the Greek Theatre. The high point came when faculty member Sheldon Wolin summarized the student-faculty demands in a seven-point motion, which was adopted by a wildly enthusiastic crowd. It said:

1. This campus is on strike to reconstitute the university as a center for organizing against the war in Southeast Asia. We are curtailing normal activities for the remainder of the quarter. We pledge our time, energy, and commitment to stopping this war. We will open the campus to mobilize our resources—our knowledge and skills, our manpower and facilities. We will organize not only against the war, but against the structures in society that facilitate that war. And we will organize to end our university's complicity with that war.

2. We will immediately press to end our university's relationship with ROTC, the Livermore and Los Alamos [nuclear weapons] laboratories, and the Thailand Counterinsurgency Project. [The SMC had published a sensational exposé of this project in the April 2, 1970, *Student Mobilizer*.]

3. We will organize and cooperate with antiwar activity in the community and across the nation, and use the summer to prepare for a national strike, in which colleges and high schools in particular would refuse to resume their normal activities in the fall if the war has not stopped by that time.

4. We will resist with all our resources the repression of antiwar and other dissenting activity on the campus and off.

5. We will protect ourselves by taking steps to minimize our risks and to aid each other when we engage in necessary risks. We will make every effort to protect the jobs and wages of university staff and to enable the faculty to discharge the minimum responsibilities required to protect the present and future academic status of students.

6. While our antiwar actions will be disruptive of normal activities, it is not our intention to encourage destructive action.

7. We strongly urge the faculty and students of other institutions to organize for the end of accomplishing the above objectives.[19]

Thus a different sort of strike strategy—of great potential

19. Ibid., pp. 22-23.

importance for revolutionary student movements generally—
emerged in the midst of the May 1970 upsurge: not to shut down
the universities but to take over their facilities and use them to
spread the antiwar activism to other sectors of the population.
Once it began to appear, this concept was most vigorously
pressed and publicized by the SMC, which proclaimed it "the
antiwar university."[20]

In an obvious move to head off this development, California
Governor Ronald Reagan—an all-out hawk on the war—
announced after the Berkeley convocation that the entire state-
owned university system, including the Berkeley campus, would
be closed until Monday, May 11. That night the Berkeley Strike
Coordinating Committee session turned into a mass meeting of
3,000, which voted to continue antiwar activities at the campus.

\*         \*         \*

In Chicago, a city-wide strike council meeting of 1,500 students,
representing some forty colleges and twenty high schools, met
Tuesday night, May 5, and voted to strike. Campuses throughout
the city held mass meetings of three, four, and five thousand
people on May 6. The strike was solid at the University of Illinois
Circle Campus near the center of Chicago, where the SMC
implemented the antiwar university strategy. Decisions were
made and forces mobilized at daily mass meetings on campus.
The students demanded—and got—telephone lines, printing
facilities, and ample space to organize strike activities. The Art
and Architecture Institute on campus voted unlimited use of
facilities and was open twenty-four hours a day producing a
variety of artistic antiwar posters that were placed all over
Chicago.

Students were dispatched throughout the area with different

20. This general approach appeared earlier in France in the near-
revolution of May-June 1968 and in the Japanese student strikes of the
same year, particularly at Tokyo University. There attempts were made
to institute student-faculty control of the universities in order to transform them into educational catalysts of social change and place their
facilities and talents at the service of the oppressed, rather than of
privilege. The idea of the "red university" originated with the student
occupation of Belgrade University in Yugoslavia in June 1968 and the
phrase "antiwar university" was derived from this precedent.

special leaflets to distribute to GIs at nearby bases, workers at factory gates, high school students, and the general public. The students also held a mass memorial service for the Kent State dead; rallies in the Black, Chicano, and Puerto Rican communities; and, in cooperation with the Chicago Peace Council, a citywide mass demonstration in the Chicago Loop May 9.

\* \* \*

On Thursday, May 7, the SMC held a press conference in Washington for a number of strike leaders from Berkeley, Wayne State, Case Western Reserve, and Tufts universities. They issued a statement which said in part:

> On a growing number of campuses, the strike has advanced from "shut it down" to "open it up" as the antiwar university. Campus facilities have begun passing into the hands of the campus community—students, faculty members and campus workers. They are using these facilities as centers from which to organize and mobilize in effective action this daily mounting antiwar sentiment of the population as a whole. This is a revitalization of the colleges and the beginning of their reconstruction in accordance with the proclaimed humanistic goals of higher education.
>
> The established ruling authorities of some campuses now on strike have declared "their" campuses "closed." They hope thereby to split the campus community into a "responsible" part that will meekly do their bidding and go home, and the "bums" [President Nixon had used this term to refer to student demonstrators] whom they hope to turn into targets of government violence. This attempt to divide the campus community must be defeated. . . .
>
> We call on the campus communities that have not yet taken control of their campus facilities to do so and join with their sisters and brothers across the country in utilizing the facilities to mobilize noncampus communities against the war.
>
> We call on the united campus communities to reach out into all communities—into the neighborhoods, the labor unions, the Afro-American and other Third World organizations, the churches and synagogues, the women's groups, the political associations, the military installations—and organize the new, united antiwar movement that will have the power to actually compel an end to the killing abroad as well as at home.[21]

In New York City, where the major universities were all on

---

21. *Militant,* May 19, 1970.

strike, the high schools and even junior highs were also in turmoil in early May. Laura Garza, then twelve years old and a student at IS 70, a junior high school in the Chelsea district of Manhattan, described part of the scene:

> When I arrived in front of the school there was another student a few years older, maybe from a nearby high school, with a bullhorn talking about the bombing in Vietnam, Laos and Cambodia and urging everyone to stay outside and follow along to see some demonstration. About two-thirds of the student body hung around listening until he started the march, and we all followed along. The local police seemed exasperated by the whole situation and could think of nothing to do but follow us through the streets in their cars, shouting that we would get in trouble and upset our parents if we didn't go back to school. Mostly we ignored them, and as we got further along and more exhilarated you could hear shouts of "Get lost, pigs." I didn't know the streets outside my neighborhood and didn't know where we were going. I recognized one place though, Washington Irving [an all-girls high] where my sister went. We stood chanting outside until they closed it down, and the students came out to join us. By that time our group, which started out on the sidewalks, had fused into a march that filled the street for blocks. Eventually, we ended up near city hall where there was a rally, and a woman spoke. I think it was Jane Fonda.[22]

On Friday, May 8, one of these marches going through the city hall district was attacked by a gang of about 500 men from construction sites nearby. The attackers injured some seventy persons, and the police made no arrests. The officers of the building-trades unions did not denounce the attack. On the contrary they encouraged additional "patriotic" forays into the street by construction workers, arranging that the men would lose no pay for the time off the job for this purpose.

In the background of these incidents was the fact that the construction sites involved had been the scene of organizing by ultraright, racist groups opposed to demands by Blacks and Puerto Ricans for jobs in certain virtually all-white skilled construction trades.

Shortly after the May 8 attack, Peter Brennan, president of the New York Building Trades Council, called a mass demonstration for later in the month, essentially in support of President Nixon and also to embarrass Mayor John Lindsay. The mayor was not

22. Letter from Laura Garza to the author, April 20, 1976.

only a dove on the war, but under pressure to apply the law requiring integrated city hiring on city construction jobs.

While Brennan's support of Nixon during the crisis over the Cambodian invasion was in accord with the AFL-CIO Executive Council's hawk position, it obviously likewise involved some rather crude political dealing. Brennan was later rewarded with an appointment to Nixon's cabinet as secretary of labor.

The Building Trades demonstration took place May 20 and was large, drawing some 50,000. Many of the construction workers were required by their unions to attend and received pay for time off the job. Right-wing organizations such as the John Birch Society and New York's Conservative Party also mobilized. The event was not billed as prowar, but as a display of "love for the only flag we have." Its thrust was clearly blind support to government foreign policy, but the war itself was so unpopular that even Brennan was constrained to remark in his speech: "We are all against the war and we want to see it ended."[23]

In a countermove, a dozen other New York unions organized a demonstration against the war and the repression of dissent. These included District 65; the Drug and Hospital Workers; District 37 of the American Federation of State, County and Municipal Employees (AFSCME); District 3 of the International Union of Electrical Workers; the Amalgamated Clothing Workers; and the Jewelry Workers (all AFL-CIO affiliates).

This demonstration, for which workers were not paid, drew about half as many as the Building Trades affair, but in one sense it was more significant. It was the first antiwar demonstration organized formally and officially by unions since the war began.

In fact, the Cambodian invasion and the student reaction to it at last broke the solid front of the official labor movement's support to the war. Until that time, with minor exceptions, American unions had at best maintained official silence and at worst echoed the prowar position of AFL-CIO President George Meany. Even the Labor Leadership Assembly for Peace—which had operated only briefly anyway—spoke officially only for the individual officers involved, not in the name of their unions.

That began to change in May 1970. For example: At its national convention in Denver, May 7, the American Federation of State, County and Municipal Employees, one of the larger

23. *Militant,* June 5, 1970.

unions in the country and then the fastest-growing, adopted a resolution calling for the "immediate and total withdrawal of all United States armed forces from Southeast Asia consistent with the safety of our armed forces and without regard to the willingness or ability of the Thieu government to carry on the war."[24]

In San Francisco, 452 elected labor leaders signed their names to a full-page ad in the May 18 *San Francisco Examiner* demanding immediate withdrawal from Southeast Asia.

Jacob S. Potofsky, president of the 417,000-member Amalgamated Clothing Workers of America, condemned the war in Indochina and the Nixon administration in his keynote address to the union's national convention in Atlantic City May 25. Potofsky was a member of the AFL-CIO Executive Council.

Patrick Gorman, secretary-treasurer of the half-million-member Amalgamated Meat Cutters and Butcher Workmen of North America, accused AFL-CIO President Meany of being "out of step" with the thinking of workers on the war. In an editorial in the union's newspaper Gorman declared: "No rational segment in the makeup of America puts the stamp of approval on our war involvements."[25]

United Auto Workers President Walter Reuther broke his union's official silence on May 7—two days before he was killed in an air crash—with a telegram to President Nixon endorsed by the union's top officers. It declared:

On behalf of the UAW I wish to convey to you our deep concern and distress. . . . Your decision to invade the territory of Cambodia can only increase the enormity of the tragedy in which our nation is already deeply and unfortunately involved in that region. . . . Many Senators are understandably aroused. . . . However this dangerous adventure turns out militarily, America has already suffered a moral defeat beyond measure among the people of the world. . . . At no time in the history of our free society have so many troops been sent to so many campuses to suppress the voice of protest by so many young Americans. . . .[26]

24. *Labor Voice for Peace,* May 28, 1970. This was the newsletter of the Madison, Wisconsin, Labor Against the War group. (Copy in author's files.)

25. *The Butcherworkman,* June-July 1970. The editorial was written in May.

26. "UAW President Walter Reuther's Last Public Statement." Reprinted by the UAW International Affairs Department. (Copy in author's files.)

Meanwhile in Washington, D.C., the New Mobe was making preparations for the May 9 action. A coordinating committee met, usually at Barbara Bick's apartment, almost continuously from Sunday, May 3, until the Saturday, May 9, demonstration itself. People had to drop out from time to time for other tasks or an hour's sleep, and this may have contributed to the confusion that was to develop. The meetings were in almost constant crisis because different perspectives for the demonstration couldn't be resolved.

In these discussions, Rennie Davis and I were probably the most sharply opposed. Davis was convinced the country was on the verge of explosion. He had earlier come closer to predicting the upsurge over the Cambodian invasion than any of the rest of us. Immediately after Kent State, he predicted such clashes would be so widespread that martial law would be declared in the capital by the time of our demonstration. (As it turned out, serious clashes between students and police or troops occurred at twenty-six universities during the upsurge and the National Guard was sent to twenty-one.) He had his heart set on May 9 in Washington being a repeat of Chicago, 1968, in a more pregnant situation, and thought such a confrontation might impel the movement beyond "symbolism" and electrify the country.

My view was that nothing we artificially set up in Washington May 9 was going to have that effect. May 9 was just another mass demonstration, primarily educational. The bigger and the less costly in victims, the better. The ultraleft confrontations— violent or otherwise—were also essentially "symbolic," just much smaller and more costly.

Where the movement had finally moved beyond "symbolism" was where the student strikes developed the scope and the organization to take over universities, to deny them to the war-makers, to force longer-term concessions from the university administrations, and to transform the universities into antiwar organizing centers aimed at the rest of the population. That directly affected the war effort. It was also a step toward independent power. If that pattern should spread to other strata of the population, we would be involved in a new ball game.

But even if that should come about, it would be a complicated and drawn-out process in which masses broke from following the political leadership of the Democratic and Republican parties. It could not be some sort of immediate, generalized, spontaneous uprising.

I viewed both the ultraleft adventures and the usual pacifist nonviolent civil disobedience as proceeding from similar fallacies. They both tried to substitute the actions of a comparative handful for the actions of immense masses. However, there was an important difference between the two. Nonviolent civil disobedience did not make it easy for the war-makers to put the onus for violence on the antiwar movement. What is more, its manifestation required discipline, not anarchy. For these reasons I was willing to go along with nonviolent civil disobedience as part of a mass demonstration. If the civil disobedience could be massive, so much the better.

But I was adamant against "do-your-own-thing" confrontational activity, which was wide open to provocation, tended to take the government off the hook as far as the responsibility for violence was concerned, and could involuntarily catch up other demonstrators.

Dellinger, of course, was insistent on nonviolence. But in his quest to prove its effectiveness to Davis and similar youth, and in sympathy with their anarchist tendencies, he tended to bend in their direction. In the proposals of Davis and Dellinger, the line between nonviolent civil disobedience and "do-your-own-thing" confrontation once again became exceedingly thin and readily crossed.

The original call for the demonstration implied at least the possibility of civil disobedience. There was a regulation requiring fifteen days' notice for the use of the federal park land, including Lafayette Park, just across Pennsylvania Avenue from the White House. Since President Nixon hadn't given us fifteen days notice of the Cambodian invasion, we called the demonstration at the White House anyway.

The first leaflet mentioned the fifteen-day rule and declared:

Public outrage at the invasion of Cambodia is so great we will go to the White House in spite of these regulations. . . . The police may block us. If they also decide to arrest us, we will maintain a militant nonviolent discipline, and options will be provided for those not prepared for arrest.[27]

This formula was unanimously agreed to.

27. New Mobilization Committee leaflet announcing May 9, 1970, demonstration in Washington. (Copy in author's files.)

Brad Lyttle and I were the cochief marshals. It was agreed that in addition to regular marshals we would organize a group of several hundred prepared for arrest who would lead the civil disobedience part of the demonstration. The idea was for people to step across the police line and face arrest.

At first we expected a crowd of ten thousand. This would fit into Lafayette Park, or if that were denied, into H Street on the north, with plenty of room to evacuate the crowd in the event of a police charge or gas attack.

Later it was clear we would have a much bigger crowd. We decided to ask for the Ellipse, a field just south of the White House, where there was room for 100,000 or more. This was done over Dellinger's objections, made on the grounds that if we got the Ellipse there would be no built-in confrontation and less opportunity to draw a large part of the crowd into civil disobedience.

The government adamantly refused both the Ellipse and Lafayette Park, saying it would keep us out of both areas, but not out of H Street, just north of the park, or the Washington Monument area, south of the Ellipse. The monument area was too far from the White House, so we proceeded with arrangements on the H Street plan, though Brad and I were not pleased with it.

A crowd of 100,000 would jam not only the H Street area adjacent to the park but the streets leading into it for several blocks back. According to Lyttle,

most of the crowd would be hidden by buildings from any speakers' platform on H Street. Communications between the speakers' stand and remote parts of the crowd, or from the north to the south edge of the crowd, would have been unreliable or impossible.[28]

We also knew, from officials in the mayor's office and other sources, what the government planned to do. They would trap the crowd between a double horseshoe of police and troops. The inner shoe would be around the White House area including Lafayette Park. The outer one would be hidden inside buildings at first and

28. *May Ninth* (New York: Lafayette Service Company, 1970), p. 10. This pamphlet included commentaries on the demonstration by David Gelber, Fred Halstead, Arthur Waskow, Bradford Lyttle, and David Dellinger.

appear after the crowd gathered. It would be placed west, north, and east of the crowd. If trouble began, the government intended to apply pressure, by gas or otherwise from the north, hold fast on the east and west, and the crowd would have to escape south on Fifteenth and Seventeenth streets all the way to what was called a "home free" area on the Washington Monument grounds. The rationale for this was that trouble was expected and the government didn't want an angry crowd dispersing into the city.

All this entered into the crisis in the coordinating committee. The experience of the Mexican students at Tlatelolco in 1968— where a demonstration was trapped and hundreds killed—was mentioned. At one point the New Mobe's attorney, Phil Hirschkop, brought Norman Mailer, who happened to be in town, to the meeting. Mailer said there was something he felt he had to tell us. We should not underestimate the perfidy of President Nixon, he said, who was perfectly capable of ordering a military attack on the demonstration, and might even view it as a political opportunity to cripple the movement and polarize the country to the right. Mailer suggested we call the whole thing off. We couldn't have done that if we had wanted to, but this is an example of the crosscurrents in which the discussions were taking place.

On Friday afternoon, less than twenty-four hours before the demonstration, a group of the Quaker marshal-trainers, including Carl Zietlow of the Nonviolent Training and Action Center in Chicago and Bob Levering of the AFSC in Philadelphia, spoke to me. They were part of the team working on plans for the civil disobedience and the evacuation problem. They calculated it would take well over an hour to evacuate a crowd of 100,000 down Fifteenth and Seventeenth streets. There was a distinct possibility that a gas attack could cause a stampede, which would be disastrous. They said they could not in good conscience proceed with the H Street plan if the overall crowd exceeded 20,000, which it obviously would.

This later became bandied about as the "revolt" of the marshals. But it was the most experienced practitioners of nonviolent civil disobedience who "revolted."

I told them to talk to the coordinating committee. They were doing that when Phil Hirschkop—who had been negotiating vigorously up to the wire—called to say the government had finally agreed to the Ellipse. By that time we had trained some 3,000 marshals, mostly at campuses in the area. With great relief and no time to lose, we started making assignments on the Ellipse plan.

Meanwhile, in the coordinating committee meeting, Davis and Dellinger in particular acted as if something had gone wrong. Davis started coming up with a series of plans to build a confrontation back into the demonstration, including one to surround the White House. That night I told them I preferred to leave well enough alone, that it was too late to change most marshal assignments, but that the civil disobedience marshals would gather at a designated spot in the morning so they could tell them whatever civil disobedience plan was agreed to.

The committee met all night and into the next day without a definite decision. I took no part in these discussions. It was the advocates of civil disobedience themselves who could not agree. Preoccupied with their meeting, the New Mobe officers didn't even show up at the Ellipse rally until two hours after the huge crowd had gathered and an hour after the scheduled starting time. Brad Lyttle and I, of course, were there early, working on the defense, sound system, etc., and had to stall the rally. Brad later recalled:

> Acting out of our sense of responsibility to the Coordinating Committee, Fred limited himself to announcements and non-controversial political exhortations like "Spread the strike!" I didn't use the mike.[29]

At one point I noticed Professor Noam Chomsky of MIT, whose writings on the war had earned him the respect of virtually all sections of the movement. I suggested that Brad ask him to speak while we waited for the New Mobe officers, who were in charge of the speakers list, to arrive. According to Brad:

> I found Noam sitting in the shade behind the speakers' platform and invited him. He looked at me through his shiny spectacles, the honesty of a scholar beaming forth, and replied, "Oh no, I wouldn't want to upset the delicate balance of the coalition."[30]

There were over 100,000 present when the New Mobe officers finally arrived. They asked Dr. Spock to chair and the speaking

29. Ibid., p. 14.
30. Loc. cit.

began while the officers and a few others continued a swirling discussion, right on the platform, about the civil disobedience. Their managing of the program itself left much to be desired from the point of view of the "delicate balance of the coalition." For example, a leader of the Black Panther Party had been invited to speak but couldn't make it. Two other people claimed the Panthers had designated both of them to take his place and the officers put them on. One of these was John Froines from the "Conspiracy" and neither a Panther nor Black. His contribution at the mike was to attempt to start a chant of "Fuck Nixon," which only caused the TV cameras—covering the event live—to turn off.

Aside from several such exercises in "revolutionary" rhetoric, the rally went smoothly enough. At one point an unidentified infiltrator managed to leap to the podium to attack Dellinger. Walt Shaffer, one of the marshals, stopped him with a flying tackle. There were literally hundreds of cases of prostration from unseasonable heat, but we had plenty of medics on hand. As for the civil disobedience, according to Lyttle:

At 3:30, the moment of truth had come. It was then or never. The Committee wasn't in agreement. In 20 minutes the decision was made and unmade to have a civil disobedience march. Finally, Stewart Meacham called the civil disobedience marshals to the west side of the Ellipse to prepare for a march up 17th Street to the White House. A few minutes later, Co-Chairman Dave Dellinger directed the march . . . to go up 15th Street and sent the demonstration off the east side of the Ellipse. No clear instructions were given concerning where or how the march should sit down. The march had been deprived of the civil disobedience marshals, and, a final mistake, none of the Committee members was leading the march.[31]

The marshals stationed at Fifteenth Street were not expecting civil disobedience in that area. They knew nothing of the last-minute decision for a march north on Fifteenth Street. They didn't stop it, but discouraged it, warning people there might be trouble north of the White House. Only a thousand or two made the march. The cops played it cool and didn't stop them, so there was no clear point for a sit-down, and most of the march just kept walking until people got tired. A few hundred did sit down in the street, and a smaller group tried to push a mock coffin over one of

31. Ibid., p. 13.

the buses surrounding the White House area. There was some tear gas, and some "trashing," but not much. Some 400 were arrested, the great majority in the nonviolent sit-downs.

As the main demonstration was dispersing with people drifting back into the city, there were some provocations but the demonstrators generally handled them well. In one case a small ultraright group using clubs and blackjacks attacked the building housing the New Mobe and SMC offices. Those on duty at the entrance managed to get the doors secured with the attackers outside. One carload of the attackers was being surrounded by demonstrators when I got there. The attackers were trying to start a riot, showing Nazi symbols, brandishing blackjacks, and shouting racist epithets at the demonstrators. There were police cars nearby but they wouldn't arrest the attackers. No doubt they'd have arrested us if we had started fighting. I finally found a legal observer from a group organized by former Attorney General Ramsey Clark, who had become a critic of the war. The observer introduced himself to the cops and started writing on a big legal pad. Only then did the cops take away the carload of armed attackers.

*     *     *

The May 9 demonstration was over. I thought it had gone well under the circumstances. It had been of unprecedented size on such short notice. It had been disciplined and overwhelmingly peaceful. Nobody got killed, and nobody seriously injured. Without the marshals we had trained that would not have been possible. Brad Lyttle later observed:

> This massive marshals' training program had an unexpected and profound influence on the entire Washington campus community. Early in the week, Rennie Davis reported that students on the campuses were so angry over Cambodia and Kent State that he predicted martial law in Washington by Thursday. I attended one of the campus rallies at George Washington University and could see how he came to this opinion. After the marshals' training sessions were started, hundreds of these outraged activists were drawn into them. They believed that a peaceful demonstration May 9 would be best. By Saturday, these students had become an organized force of determined, peacekeeping marshals. They cooled off not only the great rally on the Ellipse but the streets of Washington afterwards and all the campuses.[32]

32. *Ibid.*, p. 12.

But at a meeting that night, Davis, Dellinger, Art Waskow, and others were bitterly disappointed that there hadn't been another Chicago, 1968. They blamed the marshals for allegedly preventing massive civil disobedience. In particular, they blamed me. My reaction was a bit subjective. I called them generals without armies who could talk themselves into anything but who didn't know east from west. Essentially, I told them to go to hell, and then walked out.

\*        \*        \*

In a written discussion shortly thereafter, Dellinger offered the following view:

> If marches and rallies take place every few weeks and are self-perpetuating activities which fail to prepare people for more militant forms of resistance, they must surely operate under the law of diminishing returns. The resulting frustration helps promote the illusion that what is needed is to break away from the next march and trash windows or battle cops. . . .
>
> The New Mobe had no difficulty in rejecting the Monument site but had made the mistake (as I believe and as I had argued to no avail on long-distance telephone) of asking for the Ellipse. The decision to ask for the Ellipse had been made for honorable reasons: it was close to the White House, and there was a danger that the alternative areas constituted a military trap. But if there was a "failure of nerve" and a "betrayal" that weekend, it occurred when this decision was made.[33]

I wrote:

> There should be no entrapment games played with the masses who attend antiwar demonstrations. . . . If [Rennie] Davis or anyone else wants to invite people into such a situation, clearly stating what is involved and doing it in his own name, that is his business. I might advise against it, but it would not be my place to try to stop it. But I will not be a party to inviting people to what is presented as a peaceful demonstration while behind the backs of most of those coming an attempt is being made to structure a confrontation in which many people would be involuntary participants. . . . and probably wouldn't have come if such a plan had been the stated policy of the demonstration. This is not because the mass of the demonstrators are any less committed or brave than those who are bitter when things go peacefully and smoothly. It is

33. *Village Voice,* June 4, 1970.

because many people just don't believe such deliberately provoked confrontation between unarmed demonstrators and heavily armed police is politically productive. . . .

The purpose of these mass demonstrations is not to provide catharsis for frustrated "radicals" who have not yet learned that to stop this war, or to make any fundamental change, much less a revolution, you must involve immense masses. Nor is the purpose of such demonstrations to provide victims for additional examples of ruling-class violence. Their purpose is to provide a visible form in which dissent on the war can manifest itself; and to provide a form whereby new sections of the population can become involved.[34]

Brad Lyttle, who strongly favored civil disobedience and who criticized himself for not having led it on May 9, wrote:

For reasons already given, I think May 9 was a step forward for the movement. . . . If they [the New Mobe officers] didn't come up with a dramatic, massive civil disobedience effort, at least they avoided a disastrous explosion that would have torn the movement to bits, given [Attorney General] Mitchell a hundred clubs to beat us with, and panicked the public into the arms of Agnew and the Pentagon.[35]

Art Waskow wrote:

Who can be blamed for the actions of the marshals [at Fifteenth Street]? My first thought was of Fred Halstead, who was one chief marshal and whose politics were anti-C.D. It should be clear that I vigorously disagree with SWP politics, have battled them in the Mobe, and have been bitterly attacked by the SWP. I would have been overjoyed to find evidence that Halstead had ignored the Coordinating Committee's decisions, and instead trained the marshals "his way." *But I can find no such evidence.*[36] [Emphasis in original.]

But Waskow drew the following conclusion:

The wing of the anti-war movement that wants to concentrate on the war as the only issue cannot easily cohabit with that wing which wants to join the war to anti-corporate, anti-inflation, anti-welfare, anti-repression, or similar issues. That wing which wants legal rally demos only cannot easily co-exist with that wing which believes militant nonviolence absolutely required at this stage. Both wings (or more) exist.

34. *Militant,* June 5, 1970.
35. *May Ninth,* p. 17.
36. *WIN* magazine, June 15, 1970.

Keeping them in an unnatural embrace only stultifies them all. So the Mobe requires at least major reconstruction, and quite possibly a divorce.

This was a self-fulfilling prophecy. The New Mobe had already ceased acting as a broad coalition when the "radical caucus" took it over. The Cambodian invasion revived it momentarily, but May 9 would be its last demonstration. By June it would split.

*        *        *

May 9 in Washington was only one in the biggest wave of mass demonstrations ever to sweep over the country. The spread was even wider and, with few exceptions, the crowds much larger than the previous October 15. For example, there were 50,000 in Minneapolis, 60,000 in Chicago, 12,000 in San Diego, 20,000 in Denver, 20,000 in Austin, Texas, all May 9; 10,000 in Sacramento, 50,000 in Boston, 10,000 in Providence, all May 8; 25,000 in Seattle May 6 and 12,000 in DeKalb, Illinois, the same day. The list could go on and on. All this came on top of the student strike.

The upsurge tore an open rift in the ruling class. Powerful sections made it clear to the administration that it was too dangerous to try to handle opposition to the war with the kind of public approach Nixon and Agnew had been using. This schism was manifested even within the Nixon cabinet. On May 6, for example, a letter was released to the press in which Secretary of the Interior Walter J. Hickel warned President Nixon that "youth in its protest must be heard."[37] The doves in the House and Senate suddenly found their voices again and were joined by a number of sobered-up hawks.

Such divisions in all likelihood were a factor in the decision to grant the Ellipse to the Washington demonstrators. Max Frankel, Washington correspondent of the *New York Times,* reported May 7 that

until yesterday morning, it was still this administration's clear intention to ride out the protest with appeals to patriotism, the President's duty as commander-in-chief, and the long range benefits of his decision to move troops into Cambodia.

37. *New York Times,* May 7, 1970.

But by May 7 the White House mood, wrote Frankel, was "fear and the anxious activity inspired by fear."[38]

Unlike November 15, Nixon did not pretend to ignore the Washington demonstration this time, but made a show of going out of the White House to the Lincoln Memorial early Saturday morning to say a few words to some of the encamped young demonstrators. Nixon also pledged, to a nervous delegation of university administrators, to halt the use of the kind of language he and Agnew had previously directed at student demonstrators. More important, at his press conference Friday night, May 8, Nixon promised to have all U.S. troops out of Cambodia by the end of June.

\*        \*        \*

On May 9, in Augusta, Georgia, a sixteen-year-old Black youth was beaten to death in the county jail under mysterious circumstances. There were demands for an investigation and a series of demonstrations which became increasingly angry as county officials turned deaf ears to this and other long-standing grievances in the Black community. On the evening of May 11 a gathering of about a thousand youths, from elementary to college age, was fired upon by police. The crowd erupted. Windows of white-owned stores were broken and some were set afire.

Governor Lester Maddox branded the disorders "a Communist plot" and ordered state troopers and national guardsmen airlifted to Augusta. Through the night of May 11-12 police and troopers roamed the Black community firing at will, killing six and wounding dozens. As at Kent State, some of the police claimed they were firing at snipers, but none of those killed were carrying weapons and a coroner's report said all six were shot in the back. No police or guardsmen were wounded.

\*        \*        \*

Next, on May 13 in Jackson, Mississippi, some 300 students held a demonstration at Jackson State College, a Black school, protesting the war and the drafting of Black students. Five were arrested in a minor incident. The mayor called in the National

38. *New York Times,* May 8, 1970.

Guard and ordered blockades around a thirty-block area of the
Black community. (The mayor's reckless alarm was not unique at
the time. The day before, the University of Alabama at Tusca-
loosa was put under martial law in response to an entirely
peaceful rally of 1,500.)

There was no demonstration at Jackson State the night of May
14, but a small crowd of students gathered near some dormitories
on campus. A large contingent of city police and state highway
patrolmen arrived somewhat after 11:00 p.m. There were shouts
of "pigs go home" and a bottle or two and a dustpan were thrown
from dorm windows, landing harmlessly. A cop with a bullhorn
warned the students that they were looking for trouble and not to
stick their heads outside the windows. Another bottle was
thrown, crashing on the pavement, and suddenly the police
opened fire. Bullets raked the ground level as well as the windows
of Alexander Hall, a women's dorm. Two students were shot dead
and fourteen wounded, including a number of women in the
dorm. The dead were Phillip L. Gibbs, a junior at Jackson State,
and James Earl Green, a senior at Jim Hill High School nearby.

*        *        *

A number of Black colleges, not previously involved, joined the
strike at this time, including Howard University in Washington
where regular classes were suspended for the remainder of the
semester and turned over to discussions on the problems of Black
people. Antiwar groups, especially the SMC, incorporated Augusta and Jackson into their calls for protest. New York City
high school students demanded—and got—an official one-day
closing of the city schools in memorial to the Jackson State dead.
But demonstrations in response to the Jackson State killings took
place at only some fifty college campuses, many of them predominantly Black schools.

More than a few observers bitterly noted that the protest
response to Jackson State where the dead were Black was a ripple
compared to the wave of indignation over Kent State where the
dead were white. But there were other factors involved, in
addition to the weight of America's racism, in the relatively
subdued response.

For one thing, the killing of demonstrators does not automatically evoke larger demonstrations. More often than not, quite

the contrary. For another, Kent State occurred when the student strike over the Cambodian invasion was just beginning and strongly on the upbeat. By the time of Jackson State the strike fervor was already on the ebb.

This ebb was due to many factors. The strike had *not* spread to other sectors of the population, in particular to the labor movement. There was only so far it could go so long as it was confined to a student base. Moreover, the strike had already won important concessions at many universities and had forced a change of stance by the Nixon administration. Thus the emergency did not appear so acute by May 14.

In addition, where schools were closed as a result of the upsurge, the students for the most part quickly dispersed and were no longer concentrated in readily mobilizable form. Some schools had been struck only until certain concessions were granted, then the students went back and by mid-May were devoted to final examinations. Even where the antiwar university strategy developed, there was a tendency for some of the students to drift away to begin summer jobs or vacation trips early, a tendency which fed on itself in the absence of a dramatic spread of the strike wave after a week or so.

Still another element was a change in the approach of important sections of the ruling class toward the crisis. As the Cambodian invasion began, Establishment critics of the move were anxious to put pressure on a White House they were not sure was acting rationally. An editorial in the May 1 *New York Times*, for example, called the invasion a "military hallucination." The major news media virtually campaigned in protest of the Kent State killings, in good part no doubt because the more farsighted sections of the Establishment wanted to bring the administration to its senses. This adjustment appeared to have been accomplished by May 8. From then on, the central and immediate concern of the entire ruling class—and therefore of the major news media—was to dampen the student protest. The national TV news carried no interviews with parents of those killed at Jackson State, for example, and the major media as a rule played down the Augusta and Jackson events.

At Princeton, where the first strike against the invasion occurred, a move was begun early to keep the protest out of the streets. A meeting of the university assembly May 4 voted to condemn the invasion by a vote of 4,000 to 200. But a proposal by the strike committee to use the campus facilities to organize the general population against the war—essentially the antiwar university strategy—was defeated by a four to three margin. In order to defeat the strike-committee proposal the university administration made a number of concessions which included declaring itself on the students' side against the invasion, and an agreement that the students could cease class attendance, exams, and so on without penalty.

The Princeton administration supported a counterplan that the students should direct themselves to "concrete political action," by which was meant support to the electoral campaigns of Democratic and Republican "peace" candidates. Known as the Princeton Plan, this diversion called for the university to recess for two weeks before the elections in November to allow students to campaign for candidates. Similar recesses were promised by administrations at a number of other schools. A Movement for a New Congress was initiated which worked to channel the student protest into this sort of innocuous electoral activity.

This kind of approach was encouraged by the media, politicians, and by the Congress where measures were even introduced to lower the voting age in federal elections from twenty-one to eighteen. (This resulted later in the Twenty-sixth Amendment to the U.S. Constitution.)

All of these factors contributed to the decline of the student strike and the wave of demonstrations, though these continued to some extent here and there through the end of May.

On May 16 there were a number of significant actions by GIs which forced the military to close some thirty bases to the traditional Armed Forces Day open house. Jane Fonda, who was active in support of these demonstrations, shortly afterward aptly declared:

"Nixon's worried about being the first president to lose a war. He might be the first president to lose his army."[39]

In Atlanta, 10,000 attended a rally May 23 against the war and against repression at Kent, Augusta, and Jackson State. It was sponsored by the Southern Christian Leadership Conference and supported by the Atlanta antiwar movement as well as a number of unions.

Earlier the Student Mobilization Committee had called demonstrations for Memorial Day, May 30. But by that time the strike was virtually over and many schools had closed for the summer.

39. *Militant,* June 12, 1970.

These demonstrations were of modest size, the largest being 10,000 in New York City.

* * *

The May upsurge shut down or took over for a period of time some 536 college campuses, with something over 350 of them on strike and the rest closed down by school officials. Protest demonstrations of significant impact occurred at over half of the 1,350 college-level institutions in the country. Sixty percent of the college enrollment of 7.5 million, that is, over 4 million students, were involved.[40] In addition, uncounted high school, junior high school, and even elementary school students participated. By all accounts it was the biggest student strike in world history.

The magnitude of these events showed clearly that the opposition to the war had passed far beyond a radical vanguard and now embraced virtually an entire younger generation.

The strike itself did not draw in other sectors of the population, though the antiwar consciousness was certainly enhanced. Henceforth the mood of the country would not be quite the same. Antiwar referenda in the scattered places where the movement could get them on the ballot would carry by majorities rather than just receiving large minorities. Significant trade union endorsement of antiwar activities would become the rule rather than the exception. The great bulk of the young soldiers going to Vietnam as replacements would be opposed to the war even before they got there. And the ruling class lived in fear of another upsurge which might go further than that in May 1970.

Columnist James Reston, writing from Washington for the May 17 *New York Times,* gave this informed testimony:

This capital is more divided and pessimistic today than at any time since the beginning of the Vietnam war. . . . For, since the Cambodian invasion, everything has changed in Washington. The strategic problem in Indochina may be the same, but the political problem at home has been transformed. The Cabinet and the Congress are different. The universities are now organizing against him [Nixon] instead of merely demonstrating against him. His war policy is not helping the economy but hurting. . . . His advisers recognize the changed mood in the capital.

40. Statistical details appear in "May 1970: The Campus Aftermath of Cambodia and Kent State," a study by the Carnegie Commission on Higher Education, 1971.

They thought, when they came to power, that they were dealing with a foreign war, and they now see that they are dealing with a rebellion against that war, and maybe even with a revolution at home.

McGeorge Bundy was then president of the Ford Foundation. As an adviser to President Johnson he had been one of the authors of the major Vietnam War escalation in 1965. His estimate of May 1970 was widely shared in high circles and its essence would be repeated again and again by top ruling class advisers. On May 15 he said:

Not only must there be no new incursion of Americans across the Cambodian border, but nothing that feels like that to the American public must happen again. . . . any major action of this general sort, if undertaken in the same fashion as the Cambodian decision—now that the domestic effects of that decision are visible—would tear the country and the administration to pieces. At the very least the Congress would stop money for the war, and the chances of general domestic upheaval would be real.[41]

As for the invasion itself, in spite of Nixon's rationalizations, it was a military dud—and a political fiasco in Southeast Asia as well as the United States. The central military headquarters of the South Vietnamese revolutionaries, which Nixon had alleged to be in Cambodia, was not "cleaned out" for the simple reason that it wasn't there. The Lon Nol regime was saved for a time by American military backing, which continued in the form of supply and heavy bombing for years after the invasion was withdrawn. The net result of this "incursion" was to spread a terribly destructive war—and a revolution—to Cambodia.

41. *New York Times,* May 17, 1970.

# 21

# The Split of the Antiwar Coalition

What turned out to be the last meeting of the steering committee of the New Mobilization Committee to End the War in
Vietnam took place in Atlanta, May 22-23, 1970. By then the
Cleveland Area Peace Action Council (CAPAC) had already set a
date—June 19-21—to host an open national antiwar conference.
CAPAC Chairman Jerry Gordon promised he would hold off
announcing the conference call to the press until after the
Atlanta meeting in the vague hope that New Mobe would sponsor
the Cleveland conference. But Dellinger remained adamantly
opposed, and this time—unlike 1969—he was supported by Sid
Peck and the other New Mobe officers.

At the Atlanta meeting it became clear they could not deter
CAPAC from going ahead, so they hurriedly initiated a different
conference—by invitation—to take place in Milwaukee June 27-
28. The Milwaukee meeting was not called as a New Mobe
conference, but its sponsors included the officers of New Mobe as
well as Sylvia Kushner of the Chicago Peace Council, Norma
Becker of the New York Parade Committee, and Irving Sarnoff of
the Los Angeles Peace Action Council. The Cleveland meeting
was called by CAPAC, the Student Mobilization Committee, and
a number of people who were members of the New Mobe steering
committee, including James Lafferty of the Detroit Committee to
End the War in Vietnam, and Helen Gurewitz and Abe Bloom,
who were leaders of the local Washington, D.C., area coalition.

The gathering in Cleveland was billed as the National Emergency Conference Against the Cambodia-Laos-Vietnam War, and
the one in Milwaukee as the Strategy Action Conference. These
two meetings, a week apart, amounted to an open split in the

coalition that had organized the major national antiwar demonstrations under various names—November 5-9 Mobilization, Spring Mobilization, National Mobilization, and New Mobilization—since the original Cleveland conference of 1966. (The New Mobe itself was not formally dissolved at the time of the split; it just faded away.)

There were a number of differences between the Cleveland and Milwaukee groups, but the major cause of the breach was the disputed issue of confrontationism versus mass action as the main strategic line for the antiwar movement.

The call to the Cleveland conference was released to the media May 24 at a press conference in Detroit attended by Gus Scholle, president of the Michigan AFL-CIO. Scholle said he "learned in 1933 that you don't throw rocks at armed militia" and declared that labor leaders had a "moral responsibility" to help organize student protesters.[1] This pointed up one of the main motivations of Gordon and Lafferty in initiating the conference. They wanted to involve more unionists in antiwar activity and Gordon was convinced this aim could not be accomplished unless the orderly and legal character of the demonstrations was firmly established.

The Milwaukee conference was not called to plan further antiwar demonstrations, but, according to an open memorandum by New Mobe Cochairman Sid Peck, "for the specific purpose of working through the strategy and tactics for a multi-issue struggle against the war, repression, racism and poverty."[2]

By contrast, the purpose of the Cleveland conference, as stated in its call, was "to plan anti-war demonstrations and other antiwar activities of the most massive kind centering on the crucial issue of withdrawal from the war and conducted in a peaceful and orderly fashion." The Cleveland call added:

This conference is not intended to solve or even necessarily to discuss all the problems of our crisis-ridden society. It is not a conference to hammer out the strategy or tactics of social revolution or to found a new political party or movement. . . . IT IS A CONFERENCE TO ORGANIZE MASSIVE OPPOSITION TO THE WAR.[3]

1. Detroit *Free Press,* May 26, 1970.
2. "Memorandum to All Concerned from Sidney Peck, Re: Cleveland Antiwar Conference," undated, circa June 1970. (Copy in author's files.)
3. "A Call to an Emergency National Conference Against the

There was much rancor associated with the split.

The main thrust of Sid Peck's memorandum, for example, was to denounce the Cleveland conference. Among other things he declared it was "essentially initiated by the Socialist Workers Party." The same thing could have been said of the conference that founded the New Mobe itself. The difference this time was that Jerry Gordon needed no persuading to go ahead, whereas Peck couldn't be persuaded at all. Gordon denounced Peck's memorandum as red-baiting.

The Socialist Workers Party had no reason to apologize for the fact that it frequently played a strong role in initiating antiwar conferences. But in my view Gordon was correct in his characterization of Peck's attack because it seemed to suggest that the SWP was out to set up a narrow "front" which it would control behind the scenes. In reality, in collaboration with many people like Gordon, the SWP worked to build the broadest coalition possible under the circumstances, as it had previously done in collaboration with Peck and others.

In a letter replying to criticisms of the Cleveland initiative, Gordon declared:

The New Mobe leadership apparently feels that it would have no chance of passing a civil disobedience perspective at an open conference. For that reason, they avoided the idea of a conference like the plague. That is, they did so until our conference got off the ground.[1]

Gordon made the following appeal:

Of course, you could take a different tack. You could come to Cleveland on June 19-21 and bring with you as many of your followers as possible. You could fight for your point of view at the conference and whatever that point of view is you will receive a respectful hearing. You could help build a broader anti-war movement, one in which proponents of civil disobedience are warmly welcomed even though the movement *as a whole* does not advocate or practice civil disobedience. And you could advocate and practice civil disobedience in the name of those who agree with it but not in the name of the movement as a whole until and unless the CD advocates prevailed at an open conference. You could even use the

Cambodia-Laos-Vietnam War," June 19-21, Cuyahoga Community College, Cleveland, Ohio. (Copy in author's files.)

4. Letter from Jerry Gordon to Allan Brick, June 5, 1970. (Copy in author's files.)

opportunity to invite those in Cleveland who support CD to go to the Milwaukee meeting.

The New Mobe officers were generally averse to such suggestions, and except for Sid Lens—who always had a feeler out for unity—they either attacked or ignored the Cleveland conference. The two conferences did, however, have some overlapping sponsorship and attendance.

Some 1,500 people registered at the Cleveland affair, most of them students. Among those attending were several hundred unionists, including a number of officials. Of the major radical tendencies, only the SWP and the YSA seriously supported the Cleveland conference. PL-SDSers were there in force—solely for the avowed purpose of disrupting. They demanded the exclusion of liberal politicians and trade union officials and vainly did their utmost to shout down such speakers when they took the floor.

On the final day, the new assemblage constituted itself as the National Peace Action Coalition (NPAC), with a specific perspective based on a few simple principles. Its central demand was "the immediate and unconditional withdrawal of all U.S. forces from Indochina and the dismantling of all U.S. bases in Southeast Asia."[5] This was frequently summed up in the slogan "Out Now!"

In addition, NPAC was founded on the basis of "non-exclusion by which is meant all who oppose the war are welcome in the movement irrespective of their views on other questions and regardless of other affiliations."

On tactics, the conference declared:

The antiwar movement employs a variety of tactics to win adherents to its program of immediate withdrawal. But whatever tactic is used, the movement must function in a peaceful, organized and disciplined fashion. Confrontational adventures hurt the movement by alienating otherwise sympathetic sections of the population, particularly labor and Black and Brown peoples. . . . The antiwar movement must counter the violence-baiting directed against it. But mere announcements stating our peaceful intentions are not sufficient. All demonstrations need careful preparation . . . to insure that these events occur as planned. Then it can be

5. "Peace Action Coalition," undated packet of proposals adopted at National Peace Action Coalition founding conference, June 19-21, 1970. (Copy in author's files.)

made clear that the responsibility for any violence or disorder rests with the warmakers.[6]

The conference held that

> Mass demonstrations remain the antiwar movement's most effective method for communicating its message to, and involving, the largest numbers of people. . . . Demonstrations by themselves do not end the war. Nor do other methods of protest suggested by those who disparage demonstrations. The war will end when its catastrophic consequences become unbearable to those waging it and those burdened by it; and when workers, GIs, and Third World people act decisively to end the killings. The job of the antiwar movement is to educate, organize and mobilize tens of millions of people to hasten the day when those with the power to change governmental policy use that power to end the war.[7]

On elections the conference did not support any parties or candidates but urged antiwar referenda as a means to "further accelerate the process of demolishing Nixon's claim that he has the support of the 'silent majority.'"
It also stated:

> Because the movement includes in its ranks people of a variety of political persuasions, it cannot endorse candidates. . . . But individuals and constituent groups within the movement are free to endorse and work for political candidates of their choice and to try and convince others in the movement. Such a formula permits unity of the movement in mass actions and simultaneously allows those within it to follow their own political bent.[8]

The conference also declared that: "The decision-making process can never be the private reserve of a limited few. Periodic conferences, open to the entire movement, are indispensable to democracy within the movement."

The conference elected a steering committee for NPAC and five national coordinators: Jerry Gordon of the Cleveland Area Peace Action Council; James Lafferty of the Detroit Committee to End the War Now; Ruth Gage-Colby of the Women's International League for Peace and Freedom; Don Gurewitz of the Student Mobilization Committee; and John T. Williams, who was vice-

6. Ibid.
7. Ibid.
8. Ibid.

president of Teamsters Local 208 in Los Angeles and a prominent figure in the Black community there.

An action proposal was adopted which included activities on August 6-9, the twenty-fifth anniversary of the atomic bombing of Hiroshima and Nagasaki, and a call for mass demonstrations in a number of urban centers on October 31, 1970. "These demonstrations," said the proposal, "should relate the war to the issues of racism, inflation, unemployment, political repression, GI rights and women's liberation."[9]

\*          \*          \*

The Milwaukee conference a week later was marked by considerable confusion about its objectives, evident in the workshops that took up the first day. Some 800 people registered initially, though only about 350 stayed for the plenary on the second day. I attended as an observer and made no attempt to speak at either the workshops or the plenary. A sign of the tensions that existed was that my mere presence at a workshop led by Sid Peck was so disturbing to him that he asked me to leave the room, which I did.

Discussion at the plenary turned mainly around two proposals for civil disobedience "direct action." One of these, supported by Rennie Davis and Art Waskow, called for "collectives" to march on Washington to "stop" the city by blocking bridges, occupying buildings, and the like.[10] The other proposal, according to Douglas Dowd, who presented it, called for actions aimed at creating "as much upheaval and disruption as possible" in the event of a major escalation of the war.[11]

There was no consensus on these proposals. In addition to the New Mobe officers, the major forces at the Milwaukee conference were confrontationists such as Rennie Davis, Art Waskow, and Michael Lerner of the Seattle "Conspiracy"; traditional pacifists

9. Ibid.

10. "A Proposal for the Formation of Liberation Collectives and Brigades and for the Disruption/Liberation of Washington," presented at Milwaukee Strategy Action Conference, June 27-28, 1970. (Copy in author's files.)

11. *New York Times,* June 29, 1970. Also, in this author's files on deposit at the State Historical Society of Wisconsin there is a copy of the Milwaukee Conference "Emergency Perspective Workshop Proposal" by Douglas Dowd.

such as Brad Lyttle who favored civil disobedience "direct action" but were especially concerned that the nonviolent nature of the activity be firmly established; a group from the National Welfare Rights Organization whose spokespersons declared that they hadn't understood the nature of the conference and made it clear they would not participate in the "direct action" plans; some leaders of the Southern Christian Leadership Conference; and a number of people around the Communist Party and the Young Workers Liberation League. These last took a dim view of the civil disobedience perspective but went along with the Strategy Action Conference in hopes that some sort of multi-issue political formation would emerge that might channel antiwar activists toward election campaigns, mainly of liberal Democrats.

The conference voted support to several activities already being organized by other groups, including a June 30 demonstration of the National Welfare Rights Organization and an antigenocide petition to be presented to the United Nations in the fall. It proved impossible for the conference to agree on any definite plans of its own beyond projecting a series of regional conferences to further discuss "direct action" proposals.

There were eight such gatherings, all small, and then another Strategy Action Conference on September 11-13, again in Milwaukee. This meeting, of sixty people, representing six of the regional meetings and a number of the national groups, set up a new organization called the National Coalition Against War, Racism and Repression (NCAWRR, sometimes satirically referred to as "knockwurst" or the new coalition against everything). This group had difficulty agreeing on what to do with itself. Its major activity was the building of a demonstration at the United Nations on November 15 when the antigenocide petition was presented. This drew 1,500 people, and Brad Lyttle led the nonviolent civil disobedience part of the activity, in which twenty-six persons were arrested.

But the founding conference of NCAWRR was significant for something else. It adopted a proposal presented by Sid Peck and backed by Rennie Davis and Michael Lerner that called for massive civil disobedience actions in Washington, D.C., in May 1971. NCAWRR as such would not survive until that date. But, through NCAWRR's founding in September 1970, Rennie Davis finally obtained formal backing—such as it was—for his pet idea of a massive disruptive action in the nation's capital. He would spend the next half-year parlaying this small beginning through a remarkable series of maneuvers designed to make the idea bear fruit.

*      *      *

There was one major exception to the relative ebb in demonstrative antiwar activity during the summer of 1970. This involved the Chicano community, and the actions were organized under the name of the Chicano Moratorium.

The background to this development was described at the time by National Chicano Moratorium Chairman Rosalio Muñoz, a former UCLA student-body president and a draft resister. Muñoz, who had been active with a group of other Chicanos in draft counseling work, explained:

We saw right away, once we got involved in this full-time, that the draft wasn't really the issue, that if Nixon's [projected plan for a] volunteer army comes, it's going to be purely Chicanos, Blacks and other minority people because of the immense social and economic pressures on Chicanos and on poor people. Especially the economic incentive, because there's really no job opportunities for Chicano youth at that age. . . . These economic pressures are reinforced by the welfare and court systems. If a guy who's seventeen or eighteen gets a good job or—and this actually happened at UCLA—if he gets a scholarship to go to college, they'll take the welfare money away from his mother, but if he goes to the [military] service, his mother will keep the welfare and get a little check from the service too. Or if a guy gets picked up for sitting on the street and drinking with his buddies . . . the cop or the judge or the probation officer says, "We'll put you on probation for three or four years, but if you sign up for the Army you're off free and it's off your record."

And in the Chicano high schools, we've got the worst facilities for college prep—but the best ROTC facilities.

Also, we found in getting Chicanos to do draft counseling there was a traditional attitude of Chicanos toward war that comes out of our own experience in this country. During the 1930s it was the policy of the U.S. to deport Chicanos [to Mexico] to make jobs available for white people. . . . Then came World War II, and the Chicano was very welcome out on the front lines, and we became the best soldiers. We came back with more Congressional Medals of Honor, more Distinguished Service Medals, and, of course, high death rates. . . .

With that, we had something that, in a sense, we could be proud of, something that we did within society, and we had a political rhetoric. Chicanos came back from World War II, and they started throwing bricks through windows that said, "No Dogs and No Mexicans." They put on their uniforms and medals and they'd say, "We served; you can't call me a wetback, you can't tell me where to go."

So we developed this cultural and psychological thing. You prove yourself, you become a human being, by going through the service, by being a *macho,* and you get a political rhetoric that way.

And so, there's all this funneling of the Chicano youth right into the service. We figured that given all these social and economic pressures, draft counseling isn't the most relevant thing. You have to get the whole community, the whole culture of the Chicano, involved in the thing! And because of the Chicano's *machismo* that pushes him into the service— "You've got to be a man; prove yourself"—we had to go *directly* the other way against it, if we were going to relate to what was happening.[12]

Muñoz and other Chicano antiwar activists attended the November 15, 1969, demonstration in San Francisco where Corky Gonzales of the Denver Crusade for Justice spoke and were impressed with the possibility of using mass demonstrations to unite and educate the Chicano community against the war. Shortly thereafter, at a conference on the draft hosted by the Crusade for Justice in Denver, they formed the Chicano Moratorium Committee. On February 28, 1970, this group held a demonstration in East Los Angeles, which in spite of pouring rain drew 6,000 marchers. A film of this spirited event was shown in Denver at a National Chicano Youth Conference in March, which projected a National Chicano Moratorium demonstration for August 29 in Los Angeles.

To build toward this, there were Chicano Moratorium demonstrations in Coachella, Fresno, San Bernardino, San Francisco, Santa Barbara, San Diego, San Fernando, and Stockton, all in California, and others in Texas, New Mexico, Colorado, and elsewhere. These ranged from several hundred to several thousand marchers. In some places, where significant numbers of other Latinos were involved, they were known as La Raza Moratoriums.

Muñoz spoke at the Cleveland NPAC founding convention as well as at the Milwaukee Strategy Action Conference. Both endorsed the August 29 action. But the National Chicano Moratorium was organized independently by a broad Chicano coalition. The fact that Chicanos were dying in Vietnam at a rate far greater than their proportion in the general population—even greater than Blacks—made the Moratorium's appeal very power-

12. *Militant,* September 4, 1970.

ful in the Chicano community. And the Moratorium itself created an unprecedented unity in action among the various factions among Chicanos who through its demonstrations raised not simply the war question but many other burning issues facing this oppressed nationality.

The National Chicano Moratorium was supported by such organizations as the Raza Unida parties in Texas, California, and Colorado and also by more Establishment-oriented groups not previously involved in the antiwar movement, such as the Congress of Mexican-American Unity, the Mexican-American Political Association, and the GI Forum, the major organization of Mexican-American veterans. Most, however, came from the Chicano student movement through such groups as the Movimiento Estudiantil Chicano de Aztlán (MEChA).

The August 29 demonstration took place in the East Los Angeles barrio, an unincorporated area under the police jurisdiction of the Los Angeles County sheriff's department. The demonstrators assembled at Belvedere Park, went south to Whittier Boulevard, then west to a rally in a field then known as Laguna Park, near Indiana Street.

It was the largest antiwar demonstration up to that time in the Los Angeles area, with some 25,000 marchers and thousands more lining the streets applauding and joining in chants. The marchers were overwhelmingly young, but all sections of the Chicano community were represented, including elderly persons and mothers with small children. There were mass chants of "Chicano Power," "Raza Si, Guerra No!" and "Viva La Raza"; and thousands of banners with slogans such as "Chicanos: 18% Dead in Vietnam, 23% in Las Pintas [prisons], Is This Justice?", "Brown is Beautiful," "Our Fight is in Aztlán, not in Vietnam," "Bring All the Carnales [brothers] Home!"[13]

The march itself was peaceful, though sheriff's deputies were out in force and some hostile words were passed. At the rally site the crowd was in a festive mood. Food was provided and a picnic atmosphere was generated as people listened to the entertainment and awaited scheduled speeches by Muñoz, Corky Gonzales of the Crusade for Justice, César Chávez of the United Farm Workers, and others. The rally was cut short, however, before Muñoz, the first speaker, finished.

---

13. Aztlán in Aztec myth is a land of origins to the north. The word is used by Chicano nationalists to refer to the Southwestern United States.

Nearby on Whittier Boulevard a minor incident occurred at a liquor store where a number of spectators and demonstrators who had finished the march had gone to buy beer and soft drinks. The manager of this particular store wouldn't let them in and they stood outside pounding on the door. When a squad of deputies arrived they were greeted by a shower of beer cans. The sheriff called in massive reinforcements waiting nearby who, instead of dispersing the small crowd at the store, drove it back to the rally site two blocks away. Part of the crowd there was attracted toward the disturbance and there was some fighting. The Chicano Moratorium monitors locked arms and placed themselves between the sheriff's men and the rally. Then about 500 deputies poured out of special buses on Whittier Boulevard, lined up, and charged the mass rally.

Later a Moratorium Committee news release declared:

This charge was conducted in such a way as to enclose the multitude between an impassable line of buses and a police line of club-swinging deputies. The crowd naturally panicked, and many sought refuge inside the buses and in nearby houses. The police charged into the buses and private homes and proceeded to evict and systematically beat and club the people. Tear gas cannisters were shot indiscriminately into the crowd striking many and seriously injuring several.

Fifteen minutes later, the crowd had been dispersed with injury to at least 70 people. As the crowd fled from the area, the police gave chase, firing tear gas grenades and guns.[14]

Carolina Salcedo, an eighteen-year-old picture-frame-factory worker, had just arrived from Pico Rivera with a carload of relatives to attend the rally. They had left their car a few blocks north and were walking toward Laguna Park when they came across a one-sided pitched battle between youths on the north of Whittier Boulevard and well-armed deputies on the south side of the street. Salcedo recalled:

Old ladies, children were in shock, did not know what was going on, running for their lives. It was ugly. We never made it to the park. The police had barricades up on Whittier Boulevard; some cars were crashing through them. You could see people coming down Whittier Boulevard breaking windows in stores, dumping over trash cans. This was immediately after they had chased the people out of the park. People were just

14. *Militant,* September 11, 1970.

enraged. You could see people out in the streets asking "What is going on?" and the cops were slapping people. People weren't being treated like people at all. All that area for days afterwards, you could drive through and see people being dragged out of their houses. Mothers would come out saying, "Where are you taking my child?"—or my husband, or whatever. And the answer would be, "Get back in your house." And if they didn't, they'd take that person off to jail also.[15]

One of those who attended the demonstration was *Los Angeles Times* columnist Ruben Salazar, who was also news director for the Spanish-language television station KMEX. Salazar had been a reporter on the *Times* for ten years when James Bassett, the editorial-page editor, decided it was time to "close an information gap" by carrying a column about Chicano life in Los Angeles. "Instead of writing bland descriptions of Mexican-American family life, Salazar regularly turns in hard-hitting weekly columns attacking 'Anglo racism' and voicing serious Mexican-American grievances."[16] *Newsweek* quoted Salazar as saying, "Bassett keeps telling me to explain the Chicano to the (white) community, but more important things keep coming up. When you've been a reporter this long, you go for more significant, hard-hitting stuff than telling why people eat enchiladas."

Salazar was very popular in the Chicano community. After the August 29 rally was broken up, he was in the Silver Dollar Cafe relaxing with friends over a drink when a sheriff's deputy on the sidewalk fired a tear-gas grenade launcher point-blank into the cafe. The grenade struck Salazar and killed him.

Two other Chicanos died later of wounds sustained in the course of the police attack—Angel Gilberto Diaz, of multiple wounds from shots fired by sheriff's deputies, and Lynn Ward, fifteen years old, as a result of injuries received when a police tear-gas grenade exploded near him.

Later, the community renamed the site of the short-lived rally of the National Chicano Moratorium the Ruben Salazar Memorial Park.

\*       \*       \*

The National Chicano Moratorium was the largest and most

15. Taped interview by the author with Carolina Salcedo, May 13, 1976.
16. *Newsweek,* June 22, 1970.

significant action of any oppressed nationality in the U.S. against the war in Vietnam. Moreover, it was the largest demonstration of Chicanos as such during the period of the rise of Chicano nationalism. Along with the other Chicano antiwar actions preceding it, it had a profound impact on the Chicano people, on the Establishment's attitude toward them, and on the course of the antiwar movement itself.

These actions graphically linked the imperialist war in Vietnam to the oppression Chicanos and other oppressed nationalities suffer in the United States. They helped to undercut the impression manufactured by the major media that the antiwar movement was just a white, middle-class, student phenomenon that Chicanos, Blacks, other oppressed groups, and working people as a whole were not interested in.

The American government was terrified of this development—and of its potential repercussions in the Black and labor movements—and it concentrated its dirty tricks, illegal provocations, and disruptions in an attempt to head it off.

\* \* \*

Though the National Peace Action Coalition was more successful than the Strategy Action Conference-NCAWRR grouping, the antiwar demonstrations in response to its call for October 31, 1970, were smaller than those of the previous fall, not to mention the May upsurge. They took place in something over thirty cities and involved about 100,000 demonstrators all told.

The split in the movement was only one factor in this reflux. For one thing, 1970 was an election year. Since the inception of the movement against the Vietnam War, election periods had always proved to be the most difficult for organizing mass demonstrations. This was true in the fall of 1966 and 1968 as well as 1970. As each biennial November election approached, substantial numbers of the various forces participating in local and national antiwar coalitions turned away from demonstrations to devote their energies to electioneering for one or another major party "peace" candidate.

This process was compounded in the summer and fall of 1970 by the White House campaign to convince the American people that the administration was intent on getting the country out of the war. The capitulation of the Democratic and Republican "doves" to this subterfuge gave an additional boost to the administration's propaganda.

During the student upsurge in May, senatorial doves launched a campaign touted as an attempt to reassert congressional power over foreign policy. This centered around an appropriations-bill amendment sponsored by senators George McGovern (Democrat—South Dakota) and Mark Hatfield (Republican—Oregon) that set a 1971 deadline for U.S. withdrawal from Vietnam. After the May upsurge receded, the campaign lost its steam and on September 1 the McGovern-Hatfield amendment was defeated in the Senate by 55 to 39. That same day the Senate—doves included—voted 85 to 5 for the full military funding Nixon requested for fiscal 1971.

This default by the legislative doves was typical. They consistently declined to invoke the power of the purse strings and voted in favor of war appropriations, using the excuse that American fighting men could not be left without the means to defend themselves as long as they were in Vietnam. This was precisely the same pretext Nixon—and Kennedy and Johnson before him—used to justify every escalation of the war. The argument was entirely specious since even American military spokesmen acknowledged that the U.S. forces already had everything they needed to defend themselves if attacked during any withdrawal, and in any case the NLF and North Vietnamese wouldn't attack U.S. forces if they were actually quitting the war.

The real reasons behind the excuses of both Nixon and the doves was that the president was not prepared to give up the attempt to save the puppet regime in South Vietnam and the doves were not prepared to admit that the U.S. had no right to be in Vietnam at all. The administration strategy was to stall for time, hoping the piecemeal withdrawals of some American troops would mollify the American public while the terrible punishment of American firepower, defoliation, bombing, and forced displacement to the cities of the rural population would compel the Vietnamese to agree to at least a Korea-type stalemate arrangement. This would leave the Thieu-Ky regime in power backed by sufficient American military presence to assure its continued existence.

During this period the rationalizing of the doves was slippery. Senator Ted Kennedy (Democrat—Massachusetts), for instance, declared opposition to the use of plant-killing chemicals solely for the destruction of crops, but supported their use in areas which allegedly involved the security of American personnel. That formula, of course, left the war-makers latitude to drop herbicides anywhere they chose.

The capitulation of the doves was virtually total immediately after October 7, 1970, when Nixon again tendered a highly publicized "peace" proposal. Its major feature was for a standstill cease-fire leaving the U.S. and Saigon forces in military control of all the major cities of South Vietnam. There was nothing essentially new about the proposal. It envisaged a piece of Vietnam remaining under U.S. military control for the foreseeable future. Yet almost all the doves in Congress rushed to endorse it. A resolution was unanimously passed by the Senate hailing the Nixon message.

NPAC denounced Nixon's speech, characterized it as demagogy, and warned that Nixon was planning to escalate the war again. In this period it fell mainly to NPAC and the SMC to keep alive the demand for immediate withdrawal—which could not be equivocated—and provide national focus for some visible antiwar activity in the streets.

Some of the moderate forces in the movement were hostile to this effort. For instance, at a September 14 meeting of the Greater Boston Peace Action Coalition, representatives from Mass PAX, the Newton Coalition for New Politics, the Voice of Women, and Citizens for Participation Politics announced their intention to publicly repudiate October 31 and encourage their memberships not to participate, on the grounds that the demonstrations would embarrass the "peace" candidates and divert energies and funds from their campaigns. The coalition defeated the proposal to abandon October 31, but the action was hampered.

In another example, at the NPAC steering committee meeting in Philadelphia October 11, a proposal was made to postpone the October 31 demonstrations "at least in Detroit" until November 11, that is, after the elections. The motion was put by Mort Furay, president of Detroit Local 880 of the Hotel and Restaurant Workers, who made it clear that the proposal came from Emil Mazey, secretary-treasurer of the powerful United Auto Workers. In an earlier letter Mazey had expressed concern that any disruption or violence October 31 would hurt the chances of candidates critical of the war in the November 3 elections.

Mazey knew very well there was little danger of disruption or violence at these NPAC-sponsored events. If that were his real concern he need only have taken up NPAC's request that the

UAW supply marshals. Actually Mazey wanted to channel all efforts toward the election of Democratic Party "friends of labor." That had been his approach with the Labor Leadership Assembly for Peace, which at its founding conference in 1967 had made him its convenor. He put that grouping on ice shortly thereafter in deference to support of Lyndon Johnson, and later Hubert Humphrey, in the 1968 presidential election. Mazey believed that anything but working for the election of Democrats, and possibly an occasional liberal Republican, was at best irrelevant and at worst a dangerous flirtation with radical elements. (Mazey was one of those former left-wing militants who had long since buried the idealism of his youth and was supersensitive to the presence of radicals.)

Mazey himself was not an endorser of NPAC but expected the NPAC steering committee to defer to his wishes. In a sense resistance to his pressure was a moment of truth for NPAC, whose founders were more than anxious to find common ground with the UAW. The idea was even raised that if Mort Furay could offer some assurance that Mazey and the UAW would mobilize for a November 11 demonstration, NPAC would defer to Mazey's request and postpone the action. Furay said he could make no such promise. After extended discussion the steering committee voted overwhelmingly to proceed without postponement, with the understanding that the Detroit coalition could change the date of its demonstration if it felt that by so doing it could secure greater trade union participation.

The top UAW officials remained aloof, however, and the Detroit coalition went ahead with the original date. Lafferty told the press:

> The doves on Capitol Hill have sold out time and time again, most dramatically now after Nixon's speech. I put my trust in the people of this country to pressure the administration to end the war, not the politicians.[17]

For the time being, cooperation between the UAW and the Detroit antiwar coalition was more or less limited to support to a referendum for immediate withdrawal that the coalition had placed on the city ballot for the November election.

17. Detroit *Free Press,* October 20, 1970.

Though the October 31, 1970, demonstrations were of modest proportions they were the largest yet in the fall of an election year. This was a test of NPAC's effectiveness and it emerged substantially strengthened.

The biggest action was in Austin, Texas, of all places, where over 10,000 joined a march headed by a contingent of 400 GIs. Elsewhere the marchers numbered from a few hundred to several thousand. Five thousand massed October 31 at the Ohio state capitol in Columbus to protest the war and the indictment earlier in the month of twenty-four Kent State students and one faculty member in connection with the May events.

Incredibly, the special state grand jury in Portage County had exonerated the National Guard on the grounds of "self-defense" and blamed the May 4 massacre on the victimized students. It attributed the violence to "laxity" on the part of the university administration as exemplified in the fact that "Students for a Democratic Society (SDS), Young Socialist Alliance, Red Guard, Student Religious Liberals (SRL), and other groups who advocate violence and disruption" had been allowed to have chapters on campus.[18] Those indicted included Craig Morgan, the student-body president, and others obviously selected for their radical political activism, though they hadn't thrown a pebble at the guardsmen. Nor had the four students who were shot dead.

The grand jury action flew in the face of previous investigations, in particular that of the Scranton Commission. Shortly after the May events and under pressure from troubled sections of the Establishment, Nixon appointed a prestigious President's Commission on Campus Unrest. This group, headed by former Pennsylvania Governor William Scranton, had concluded that while some of the students had broken laws and others acted "irresponsibly," "the indiscriminate firing of rifles into a crowd of students [at Kent State] was unnecessary and inexcusable."[19]

The Kent State indictments were the most outrageous in a series of attacks on student rights perpetrated or encouraged by the Nixon administration during this period. A few weeks before, Attorney General Mitchell and Vice President Agnew had censured the Scranton Commission report which had attempted to

18. *Militant,* October 30, 1970.
19. *Report of the President's Commission on Campus Unrest* (The Scranton Commission Report) (Washington: U.S. Government Printing Office, 1970), p. 289.

analyze the student unrest with some objectivity. Nixon requested a special FBI appropriation to send 1,000 agents onto the campuses in the fall. The Internal Revenue Service issued a new set of "guidelines" that schools had to abide by to retain their tax-exempt status and that could serve as a basis for restricting student rights, including censorship of college newspapers.

On September 20, 1970, FBI Director J. Edgar Hoover released a statement in the form of an "Open Letter to College Students" expressing "concern about the extremism which led to violence, lawlessness, and disrespect for the rights of others on many college campuses during the past year." Hoover's letter sought to counterpose the "small minority of students and faculty members who have lost faith in America" to the "vast majority" of legitimate critics who had been lured into joint action with the "extremists." These, he emphasized, "may be associated with the Student Mobilization Committee to End the War in Vietnam (SMC), a Trotskyist-dominated antiwar group."[20]

The SMC replied,

The violence and repression perpetrated by Hoover and the forces he represents is the real "extremism" in America—and if Hoover is really concerned with "disrespect" for authority, he should realize that the "problem" will not go away until he and Nixon and Agnew put an end to their attacks on the rights of the American people and until *all* the troops are brought home from Indochina.[21]

The YSA, which was mentioned in Hoover's letter along with SDS and the YWLL, issued in reply its own "Open Letter to U.S. Students" which was widely circulated. It declared that "Hoover's letter is one component of a generalized assault being launched by the Nixon administration on the basic democratic rights and civil liberties of students." It concluded by calling upon the entire student movement "to join us in repudiating Hoover and Nixon and in building united fronts to defend the gains of the student strike last May."[22]

When the Kent indictments were announced, the *Kent Stater,*

20. *Congressional Record* (House), September 21, 1970.

21. Statement by SMC national office, September 28, 1970. (Copy in author's files.)

22. "An Open Letter to U.S. Students from the YSA," September 1970. (Copy in author's files.)

the student newspaper, called the grand jury report "demented" and the Student Senate demonstratively passed a unanimous endorsement of the October 31 demonstrations. October 19, the day the arrests began, NPAC coordinator Jerry Gordon spoke to a thousand Kent State students who wildly applauded when he said: "There will be no moratorium on dissent."[23] Subsequently defense meetings of up to four thousand were held on that campus. The Association of Student Governments, the National Student Association, the SMC, and student government officials around the country pledged support to the defense.

Of the Kent State Twenty-five, three were convicted of minor misdemeanors, one was acquitted, and charges against the rest were eventually dropped, but not before another massive spring offensive against the war.

23. *Militant,* October 30, 1970.

# 22

# April 24, 1971, and the May Days

At the October 31, 1970, demonstrations NPAC spokespersons announced another national antiwar conference for December 4-6 in Chicago. While preparations for this gathering were in motion, its importance was increased by two developments: First, in the biennial elections of November 3, 1970, antiwar referenda passed by majorities in the scattered places they were on the ballot. Second, after the elections Nixon began another major escalation of the war.

The preelection moratorium by Democrats and Republicans on criticism of Nixon's "Vietnamization" policy, together with the endorsement by the doves of his October 3 "peace" plan, left the voters with no way to register any clear-cut sentiment on the war when voting for major candidates. The referenda did, however, show that Nixon's "silent majority" in favor of the war was fictitious. In Detroit, a referendum calling for immediate withdrawal passed by 63 to 37 percent. The United Auto Workers Community Action Program had recommended a "yes" vote.

In San Francisco, a similar referendum, also backed by important unions, won by a majority of 107,785 in favor to 102,731 opposed. This in spite of a virtual press blackout on the issue during the campaign, broken only when the two biggest papers editorialized against a withdrawal vote. In Marin County, to the north of San Francisco, a withdrawal referendum passed by 39,940 to 33,827.

The vote on a three-way statewide referendum in Massachusetts equally underlined the unpopularity of the war. The results ran 558,975 for "withdraw our armed forces in accordance with a planned schedule"; 347,462 for "withdraw all our armed forces immediately"; and 150,984 for "win a military victory." The Massachusetts vote in favor of military victory amounted to less than 15 percent of the total. The immediate withdrawal position carried a majority in the working class districts of the Boston area.

These results did not support the image promoted by the administration and the press—especially since the "hard-hat" demonstrations in Manhattan—that the working class was behind the war. They confirmed the conclusions of a survey of voting patterns in earlier referenda in seven cities reached by Dr. Harlan Hahn, associate professor of political science at the University of California at Riverside. According to his studies, when given the opportunity, working class voters, by and large, expressed strong disapproval of the war. This, he said, "suggests that antiwar feelings have not 'trickled down' from upper-middle-class sources as much as they have 'percolated up' from working-class citizens."[1]

Shortly after the 1970 elections, Morton Halperin, deputy assistant secretary of defense under Johnson, and until May 1969 a member of the National Security Council staff under Henry Kissinger, wrote a prophetic article which appeared on the opinion page of the *New York Times,* analyzing the implications of Nixon's so-called "peace plan":

President Nixon's Vietnamization policy, far from getting us out of Vietnam, will at best lead to an indefinite presence in Vietnam of thousands of American troops. It could well drive the President to massive escalation. . . . The Joint Chiefs of Staff will tell the President, as they told his predecessor, that they can win the war if given permission to bomb all targets in North Vietnam, mine Haiphong, and invade Laos. The President could well order them to implement this plan.[2]

On November 20, Nixon resumed massive bombing of North Vietnam, striking major population centers. This type of bombing had supposedly been ended in 1968, just before the Paris negotiations began.

On December 1, the *New York Times* reported that the Pentagon had a new policy "of striking North Vietnamese missile sites along the Laotian border when they threatened American planes operating over Laos."

1. *San Francisco Labor,* November 13, 1970.
2. *New York Times,* November 7, 1970.

By the time of the NPAC national convention December 4, then, the antiwar forces were aware that a further escalation was being mounted, possibly involving an invasion of Laos. The convention, held in the Packinghouse Labor Center in Chicago, was attended by 1,500 delegates. All antiwar groups had been invited. The National Coalition Against War, Racism and Repression (NCAWRR) in particular had been urged repeatedly to participate. A number of its leaders did show up, but, except for Sid Lens, did not register for the convention or participate in its debates. Most even declined to enter the convention hall. Instead, they stood outside in the lobby negotiating with Jerry Gordon and other NPAC figures.

The NCAWRR representatives were Sid Peck; Sid Lens; Jack Spiegel, an official of the Shoe Workers union in Chicago; Ron Young of the Fellowship of Reconciliation; Irving Beinin, Carl Davidson, and Abe Weisburd, all three from the weekly *Guardian;* and Gil Green of the Communist Party. They urged that the NPAC convention defer any decision on the date for the major spring demonstrations until a smaller, invitation-only meeting that NCAWRR planned for January. They said they intended to recommend there a series of actions in April and May which would include commemorations for Martin Luther King on April 3 and 4 and a "culminating action May 1st or May 8th of demonstrations throughout the country but with some emphasis on Washington and special activities by government employees."[3]

The NPAC coordinators had prepared a proposal for submission to the convention centering around mass marches on Washington and San Francisco April 17. They agreed to amend this to include the King commemorations and to change the Washington–San Francisco date to April 24 since April 17 was too close to the April 3-4 actions and followed a vacation week on many campuses. The NPAC negotiators pointed out that Rennie Davis had already received wide publicity for his plan to disrupt Washington on May 1, and expressed the view that a broad mass action was impossible in conjunction with that sort of protest.

---

3. There were no minutes of these negotiations, but there is a written record of the proposals made by the NCAWRR representatives in the form of a "Motion on a Unified Spring Action" written by Sidney Lens and later presented by him on the floor of the NPAC convention. The quote is from the document. (Copy in author's files.)

A tentative agreement was reached that the united action should be nonconfrontational while NCAWRR would be free to organize other activities, including civil disobedience, on a different day. NCAWRR then proposed May 8 for the major mass demonstration. The NPAC coordinators argued that the April 24 date was preferable for two reasons. May 8 was too close to final examinations and the end of the school term for maximum student participation, and the atmosphere for building a large demonstration would be more favorable if it was scheduled for before, rather than after, the projected disruption at the nation's capital. Nevertheless, the NPAC coordinators finally agreed to May 8, in the interests of having a united action.

To our great astonishment [the NPAC coordinators later reported], the other group said no, the convention should not set any date! . . . we were asked to leave the date up in the air for an unstated period pending negotiations with people some of whom were not at the convention and whose views were not known to the people attending the convention.[4]

Jerry Gordon observed that

all this caused a lot of resentment among the more than a thousand people there because these negotiations were going on behind the scenes. Many people insisted that this never be repeated, that the whole character of NPAC was resolutions openly discussed, openly debated, and not these back-room, behind-doors negotiations. The convention was almost in a state of suspension as these negotiations were going on.[5]

The NCAWRR group insisted that they were not authorized to agree on any date but had to consult with others—which obviously included Rennie Davis—not present. They held to their proposal that the definite calling of the spring action be postponed until their January meeting. According to the NPAC coordinators:

The proposal did not mesh with our idea of democracy within the antiwar movement. How do you invite 1500 people to a national gather-

4. Letter from the NPAC coordinators to Kay Camp, president of the U.S. section of the Women's International League for Peace and Freedom, December 9, 1970. (Copy in author's files.) Camp was an endorser of the NPAC convention but was unable to attend.
5. Taped interview by author with Jerry Gordon, November 14, 1976.

ing of the antiwar movement to decide a future course for the movement and then urge them to delegate to others (some known and some unknown) the power to decide important questions which the 1500 people thought they were to decide? What happens if the negotiations on the major political questions . . . are not productive and what if agreement is not reached? Who decides what, if not the people convened at an open, all-inclusive and democratic convention? . . . Anyone could have come to the convention, could have brought anyone he or she wanted, and could have proposed any resolution. The question posed for us was: Should people who did not come to the convention be given a veto power over people who did come? We felt they should not.[6]

Behind these formalities of democratic procedure—which had their own importance—lay two vital issues: the dynamic of the mass mobilization and the character of the action. The exact date was a secondary consideration. The point was that the action had to be called; without at least a tentative date it would not clearly be in the works. The maximum momentum could only be assured if that call had behind it the authority of the extensive body of activists present at the convention who were ready, willing, and able to build it. To allow the Chicago gathering to disperse without setting in motion the energies of those present on a specific project would dissipate the steam to drive the mobilization forward.

NPAC's coordinators were proposing a massive, peaceful, legal demonstration designed to involve the largest numbers and the broadest sponsorship possible. By contrast, the character of the main action being worked upon by those in the NCAWRR milieu was Rennie Davis's projected disruption of Washington, D.C. The two actions were incompatible. Either there would be adequate separation or the major unified action simply would not occur. What NCAWRR's stand amounted to was that NPAC not settle that question with the authority of the convention but leave it to a smaller meeting of invited "leaders" in which the confrontationists would have much greater political weight.

With the patience of the convention body wearing thin, the NPAC coordinators decided to present their proposal for April 24 for its consideration. The others were urged to offer their motion and debate the matter out on the floor. Only Lens chose to do so. Though his motion still used the phrase "a culminating action

6. Letter to Camp.

May 1st or May 8th," its essence was contained in the following paragraph:

A meeting to finalize these plans will be held next month and will include leading figures of the student, Church, community and trade union elements. . . . In view of this prospect the Conference [the NPAC convention] hereby endorses the Spring Campaign and will take steps to join with it in a single effort. In no event will the Conference set any dates or promote any plans which will conflict with that effort.[7]

This motion had the obvious defect of not specifying the tactics of the "effort," not to mention the dates.

The debate was a bit one-sided since only Lens spoke on behalf of his motion. It was almost unanimously defeated. The NPAC coordinators' proposal was adopted. It centered around the following:

The week of April 19-24 to be designated NATIONAL PEACE ACTION WEEK to culminate in massive, peaceful and orderly national demonstrations in Washington, D.C., and San Francisco on Saturday, April 24.[8]

The text boldly declared that "the antiwar movement now speaks for a majority of the American people."

It underscored the dilemma facing the administration and the guidelines for the peace forces:

Even if Nixon is permitted to stretch out the period for his declared policy of troop withdrawals, a crisis of major proportions looms ahead. If, to preserve the South Vietnam military dictatorship, he puts a stop to withdrawals, he will expose his true intentions and evoke an astronomical growth of "out now" sentiment. If on the other hand he continues periodic withdrawals, the peoples of South Vietnam, Cambodia, and Laos will quickly put an end to the domestic tyrannies maintained by the Nixon administration. Whatever the future holds, the demand of the United States antiwar movement must remain at all times crystal clear: immediate, unconditional and total withdrawal of all U.S. military forces from Southeast Asia.[9]

7. "Motion on a Unified Spring Action," Sidney Lens, December 1970. (Copy in author's files.)

8. "Action Proposal Adopted by the Convention," undated. (Copy in author's files.)

9. Ibid.

The January 8-10 meeting initiated by NCAWRR, which also took place in Chicago, had 300 in attendance. It was inconclusive. Sharp differences appeared over an action program for the spring. Rennie Davis and Dave Dellinger were above all concerned with pressing "direct action" in Washington. Another grouping, which embraced Sid Peck and Ron Young, favored some form of national mass action but with civil disobedience as the main feature. Gil Green of the Communist Party took the floor late in the first day's plenary session to declare that he was greatly dissatisfied with the direction the conference was taking. Unless it projected a broad mass demonstration as part of its program, he warned, its efforts would end in failure. He did not, however, advocate joining in on April 24.

Carl Davidson of the *Guardian* observed that the conference was attempting to function "with its head in the sand" in not seriously discussing NPAC's call for April 24:

> April 24 will occur whether you relate to it or not. How will you explain to the Vietnamese why you weren't there? Will you tell them you weren't there because it was only a mass march for immediate withdrawal?[10]

(The *Guardian* itself subsequently endorsed April 24, and appealed for unity around it.)

The conference adopted a vague proposal including a week of activities May 1 to 8 which would be "nonviolent and militant, going beyond rallies and demonstrations, but also including them, into active struggle."[11] The exact relationship between this and Rennie Davis's plan for Washington was left unclear.

The NPAC coordinators had not ruled out all possibility of reaching agreement on a broader and more unified demonstration and had stated that if this involved a date other than April 24, an emergency convention of NPAC could be held to reconsider. A week after the NCAWRR meeting, leaders of the two groups conferred and again failed to agree.

Pressure from local groups and rank-and-file activists for a unified national action was very strong. For instance, the Lower East Side Mobilization for Peace Action (LEMPA) in Manhattan addressed an imploring letter January 26 to both NPAC and NCAWRR:

10. *Militant,* January 22, 1971.
11. Ibid.

Can any of you seriously argue that these [differences] are overriding in the face of the urgency of united action? What madness has brought this upon our movement? . . . We therefore plead—we urge—we demand—we shout to you: Halt this headlong drift towards division, towards splintering, towards tragedy. Join together—it is not too late—to deal President Nixon and his war policy a mighty blow, and accelerate the drive towards peace in Vietnam.[12]

\*        \*        \*

At the end of January 1971, under cover of a heavy censorship imposed on newsmen in the war zone, the U.S. command increased its bombing and massed American and Saigon troops and equipment on the Laotian border for an invasion. The extraordinary secrecy shrouding this escalation revealed in the sharpest way the administration's fear of public opposition to the war. As a *New York Times* correspondent sarcastically commented on the press embargo:

The command says that the objective is to prevent disclosure of valuable military information to the enemy. However, the enemy does not have to see American news reports to learn about large military operations; enemy commanders cannot fail to be aware if the bombs are falling around them.[13]

As of February 3, reports had filtered through that at least 25,000 South Vietnamese (Saigon) ground troops, backed up by 9,000 U.S. combat troops, were poised on the Laotian border while the heaviest round-the-clock bombing of the war was in progress.

Since the news had dribbled out bit by bit, word of the invasion itself, which began on February 8, came more as an anticlimax than a sudden shock. Nevertheless, a wave of demonstrations took place nationwide on February 10.

The Student Mobilization Committee reported that over 50,000 people took part in these actions, braving severe winter weather

12. Letter to NCAWRR and NPAC from Evelyn Wiener, LEMPA chairperson, and LEMPA Planning Committee members Ruth Bloch, Paul Dietrich, Tom Farley, Paul Goldberg, Morris Goldin, Ester Gollobin, Harry Lippenholtz, Margaret Morrison, Ted Reich, Helen Rueben, Sylvia Silber, and Angel Velez, January 26, 1971. (Copy in author's files.)

13. *New York Times,* February 2, 1971.

in much of the country. The demonstrations ranged from 100 picketing the federal building in the aftermath of a blizzard in Cleveland to 10,000 on the Boston Common with feeder marches from MIT, Harvard, Boston University, and Northeastern. Several universities went on strike, such as the University of Wisconsin at Madison, where daily mass meetings of 1,500 to 2,000 took place. In Boston, SMC spokesperson Mike Arnall told reporters: "I would characterize the reaction now as a slow burn which will, without question, grow."[14]

\*          \*          \*

Rennie Davis was the only one of the original SDS leaders, of either the old or the new guard, who consistently saw the Vietnam War issue as the key to his organizing. He also developed a clear tactical conception and persistently pursued it.

He considered the May 9, 1970, demonstration in Washington a failure because it did not result in another confrontation like Chicago 1968 on a larger scale. Immediately after the 1970 May events he began to press for another try along this line without limiting its promotion through the New Mobe or NCAWRR.

That August he attended the National Student Association (NSA) convention at Macalester College in St. Paul, Minnesota, which adopted a proposal to send an American student delegation to meet with student organizations in both North and South Vietnam. The object was to "negotiate" a symbolic peace treaty as an attempt to show that a real one could be accomplished. This became known as the "People's Peace Treaty."

Davis, who had previously visited Hanoi, assisted NSA president David Ifshin in arranging the trip to Vietnam. He also attempted to get the NSA to take on his project for disrupting Washington the following May, but its officials cautiously demurred. The undaunted Davis utilized the organization of the Vietnam trip to initiate a "Student and Youth Conference on a People's Peace" that *was* endorsed by and organized through the NSA. Its coordinator was Frank Greer and its explicit purpose was to ratify the "treaty."

The student visit to Vietnam was completed in December 1970. The ratification conference took place on the weekend of February 6, 1971, in Ann Arbor, Michigan. This was in the midst of the

14. *Christian Science Monitor,* February 12, 1971.

growing tension over the Laos invasion. The attendance therefore was quite large—some 1,600 at the outset—and the participants were angry and eager to take a slap at the administration. (One thing they did was to set the date for the emergency demonstrations February 10.)

The "peace treaty" plans of the NSA leaders were almost lost in the shuffle as Rennie Davis and other organizers of "May Day" sought the endorsement of the conference for their Washington project. The May Day proposal was put forward by a caucus led by Mike Lerner and other members of the "Seattle Eight," who were defendants in a case similar to the Chicago "conspiracy" trial. The exact scenario for May Day was vague in the written motion, but its character was defined in the remarks of Davis, who said the object was to give the government until May 1 to ratify the People's Peace Treaty and if it didn't, to tie up Washington.

There was sharp disagreement, but on the second day, after about half the people had left, the conference adopted the project. The NSA itself did not endorse or take responsibility for it.

While the NSA was the official sponsor of the Ann Arbor meeting, the actual moving force there was a grouping Davis had pulled together the previous December during the Vietnam trip. It was called the May Day Collective—sometimes later called the May Day Tribe. This formation won the leadership of the People's Peace Treaty conference and Rennie Davis finally had the vehicle he sought, dedicated to carrying out his tactic in Washington and backed by the authority of a sizable national conference.

\*　　　　\*　　　　\*

Just prior to the Ann Arbor conference, the NCAWRR leaders met, dissolved their group, and set up a new organization named the People's Coalition for Peace and Justice (PCPJ). Its coordinators were Dave Dellinger, Sid Peck, Rennie Davis, Brad Lyttle, Ron Young, and Bill Douthard, a Black community organizer from New York. Carol Henderson Evans was added at a PCPJ steering committee meeting February 27. She was the only one of the seven not previously associated with NCAWRR. As administrative assistant to NSA President Ifshin, Evans had done the technical organizing on the Vietnam trip and had shifted to the staff of the May Day Collective before the Ann Arbor conference.

Evans went to work full-time for PCPJ, which established its national headquarters on the ninth floor of the building at 1029 Vermont Avenue in Washington, where the New Mobe and later the NCAWRR offices had been located. NPAC and the SMC already shared the whole eighth floor of the same building, having taken it over after the Vietnam Moratorium Committee dissolved. The Washington Area Peace Action Coalition, an NPAC affiliate, was on the fouth floor, while the May Day Collective took an office on the tenth floor. In addition, the Vietnam Veterans Against the War, which had called its own action for Washington, shared space in the SMC complex and later in the PCPJ offices. For all their divergences, these forces came together physically under one roof, though they still had not come to agreement on the forthcoming actions.

The relation between May Day and PCPJ was indicated by a press conference February 8 in which Dave Dellinger on behalf of PCPJ announced a week of intensive actions beginning Saturday, May 1, in Washington. He stated: "We must move from expression of opinion to action. We have to move to the stage of force without violence." At this news conference, staged directly across the street from the White House, Rennie Davis reiterated, "Unless Nixon commits himself to withdrawal by May 1—that is, if he won't stop the war—we intend to stop the government."[15]

\*          \*          \*

The Student Mobilization Committee had rented facilities at Catholic University in Washington for a national student antiwar conference February 19-21 which promised to be a big one. Suddenly its staff was plagued by arbitrary technical demands from the university administration, which threatened cancellation of the arrangement. For example, a stipulation that the SMC take out a million-dollar insurance policy against possible damages caused by "riots." No American insurance company would write this policy. According to John Studer, then an SMC staff coordinator:

It was crystal clear they [the university administration] had changed their minds and wanted us out. But they didn't want it to appear as a

15. *Militant,* February 19, 1971.

political move. They didn't think we would do it, but we got the policy—
from Lloyd's of London.[16]

These well-informed insurers obviously knew that the chances
of violent destruction at an SMC-organized affair were minimal.
Years later, FBI documents released by court order disclosed
that behind the obstruction lay some of the "dirty tricks" the FBI
had used to try to paralyze the peace movement. They show that
even the Catholic church was a target of political police operations designed to impose the ideology of the FBI officials upon
private organizations.

The San Antonio, New York, and Washington, D.C., FBI offices
connived to try to prevent the February 1971 SMC conference.
San Antonio wrote that it had a contact in the local archdiocese
who was an "enthusiastic supporter of U.S. policy in Vietnam"
and that there was "strong resentment" among local Catholics
against funding Catholic University in Washington. It suggested
taking advantage of this to pressure the school to refuse accommodations to the SMC.[17]

Referring to the radicalization being manifested in Catholic
circles, the San Antonio FBI office wrote:

It is strongly felt that at the emergence of the so-called permissive
attitude [in the Catholic church] that if effective counterintelligence
actions had been taken, the Bureau's investigation in New Left and other
such matters would not have been as great as it is today.

In other words, had the political police intervened earlier to
manipulate church policy, the effort would have been more "cost
effective."

Washington agents proposed that the FBI, using "commer-
cially purchased paper to protect Bureau as the source," write
anonymous letters about the SMC and Catholic University to
such groups as the Knights of Columbus, Daughters of Isabella,

16. Ibid., April 15, 1977.
17. FBI internal memorandum, February 1, 1971, based on a January
26, 1971, report from the San Antonio office. These and related documents
were obtained from the FBI by the Political Rights Defense Fund as part
of its suit on behalf of the Socialist Workers Party. They were released to
the press by PRDF on April 6, 1977, and copies were kindly made
available to the author.

Catholic Daughters of America, Catholic War Veterans, the Catholic Youth Organization, as well as to the *Catholic Standard* newspaper.[18]

One story the FBI prepared for circulation in this attempt to whip up a campaign against Catholic University pointed to the recent arrests of antiwar Catholics like Father Philip Berrigan and Sister Elizabeth McAlister. They had been indicted with several others January 12, 1971, on incredible charges of conspiring to kidnap presidential adviser Henry Kissinger and blow up the heating system of federal buildings in the nation's capital.

In an internal memo, FBI Director J. Edgar Hoover, whose overheated imagination had cooked up the charges against Berrigan, et al. (later known as the Harrisburg Eight), commented:

considering financial support CU receives from Roman Catholics throughout U.S., majority of whom are undoubtedly anti-communist and loyal Americans, it appears unique counterintelligence situation presented with potential to have SMC conference cancelled.[19]

Hoover also said:

It is opinion of Bureau decisive, agressive, timely and well-organized counterintelligence operations invaluable in disrupting or altering, to our advantage, activities which are clearly against U.S. public interest.

Difficulties notwithstanding, the SMC conference took place at Catholic University, attended by some 2,500 young antiwar activists. To the satisfaction of Lloyd's of London, the sessions were entirely orderly; the participants made sure that not even a set of initials was scratched on the walls or furniture. In addition to mapping plans for campus antiwar activity over the next period, the conference undertook to build student support for April 24.

Discussion during the weekend was heated and extensive, and the bulk of the participants, as before, were not committed in advance to any single course of action. The open debate in front

18. Teletype message to New York FBI director, February 11, 1971, from Washington field office. (Copy in author's files.)
19. Airtel message, February 10, 1971, from FBI director to San Antonio, Washington, and New York field offices. (Copy in author's files.)

of the ranks that the NCAWRR leaders had avoided at the NPAC convention did occur here. Following preliminary presentations, twenty-two different proposals were sifted down by straw vote to half a dozen for the major debates.

Two of these were adopted. One called for a day of coordinated antidraft actions across the country March 15. (The draft law was coming up for renewal the following June.) The other adopted proposal, submitted by Don Gurewitz and Debby Bustin, who had recently come on the national staff from the Houston University SMC, emphasized:

The spring offensive to stop the war should focus on the April 24 demonstrations for immediate withdrawal of U.S. troops in Washington and San Francisco.[20]

Much of the debate revolved around this proposal, which was counterposed to three others: the May Day action in Washington, endorsement of the People's Peace Treaty, and a motion that the SMC call for more immediate actions by the entire antiwar movement sometime in March to counter the threat of a possible additional escalation beyond the Laos invasion, which was going badly for the U.S. side. This last was presented by Tony Monteiro of the Young Workers Liberation League and initially received wide support. However, in the workshops and on the floor, most of those originally attracted to the idea were persuaded by the arguments that the best preparation against another escalation of the war was an escalated process of building for April 24, which had already become a central focus for broad antiwar forces.

The People's Peace Treaty, May Day, and March emergency-action proposals were all backed by spokespersons for PCPJ; one of its coordinators, William Douthard, introduced the May Day motion.

The People's Peace Treaty placed certain conditions on the Vietnamese—defining the nature of the government that would replace the puppet regime, for example—and was equivocal on the question of immediate withdrawal of all U.S. forces. Most of the SMC leadership therefore opposed endorsing it on the ground that Americans had no right to impose anything on the Vietnamese. Mike Zagarell, youth director of the Communist Party,

20. *Intercontinental Press*, March 1, 1971.

pointed out that the Provisional Revolutionary Government, political arm of the NLF, had indicated it would accept such terms. This was answered with the argument that while the Vietnamese—who were under the gun—might make compromises to relieve the pressure on them, the American peace movement should not put its stamp of approval on any conditions extorted by force from the Vietnamese. The People's Peace Treaty obtained only a scattering of votes.

At the end, the Gurewitz-Bustin proposal was overwhelmingly adopted. It stated:

It will take a giant, independent mobilization of the American people to force the withdrawal of troops from Southeast Asia and to prevent the U.S. government from continuing its policy of destroying Southeast Asia in order to "save it." . . . Without such independent mass action, Nixon can continue indefinitely to talk about "peace," while continuing the aggression.[21]

Scores of correspondents from campus newspapers were present. One of these, Elton Golden of the New York University *Ticker,* wrote in the February 24 issue: "What impressed me most about the national meeting of the SMC in Washington last weekend was the political maturity of the left."

Hy L. Dubowsky commented in the February 25 York College *Pandora's Box:*

The American public was very calm and silent during the invasion of Laos. It would seem as though our mouths have finally been sealed by the tactics of the Nixon administration. We walk along and shrug our shoulders, there is nothing else we can possibly do to end the war. This sentiment was thoroughly discussed at the conference, and it was unanimously concluded that come April 24, Nixon and company will not get much sleep, amidst the shouting voices of a concerned people.

\*        \*        \*

Support to the April 24 demonstrations built rapidly following the SMC conference. By late February, according to Jerry Gordon, some 400 organizations and prominent individuals had endorsed, including an unprecedented number of unionists and a

21. Ibid.

list of members of Congress that was growing daily. The feminist leader Kate Millet, members of Congress Ron Dellums and Shirley Chisholm, and other well-known figures signed fund appeals for April 24.

The pressure on PCPJ to join in on April 24—whatever else it did—was becoming irrresistible. PCPJ's difficulty flowed in part from the fact that the forces composing it did not see eye to eye. In public pronouncements as well as in negotiations with NPAC they sometimes gave different dates for the projected attempt to block the streets of Washington and sometimes quite different scenarios for the first week of May. There was considerable tension between the pacifists in PCPJ and Rennie Davis over the character of the anticipated civil disobedience—referred to in the movement simply as "CD."

Moreover, the forces around the Communist Party were not much interested in the CD anyway. They were more interested in the political line of the People's Peace Treaty and were concerned lest PCPJ be left standing on the sidelines while NPAC on the one hand and the May Day Tribe on the other kept driving ahead with their actions.

At one point PCPJ agreed that the attempt to disrupt Washington would not start on May 1, which was a Saturday, but on Monday, May 3. They proposed a unified non-CD demonstration on Sunday, May 2. That way it would be easier to get more people to stay over for the Monday action. But NPAC considered this not enough separation, and by that time April 24 was already so broadly endorsed it would have been very difficult to switch the date.

The logjam was finally broken at a PCPJ meeting toward the end of February, according to Bob Levering. A caucus of pacifists which included himself, Stewart Meacham, Dave Dellinger, and Chris Meyer brought forth a proposal based on an idea suggested by Dave McReynolds: They could use the period between April 24 and May Day for a series of well-organized CD actions to train demonstrators in nonviolent techniques and set the desired nonviolent tone for the May events. They pressed this through, and PCPJ adopted the following plan:

It would support April 24. It would call for people to stay over in Washington for a week-long "people's lobby" on behalf of the People's Peace Treaty and other demands. During that week the pacifists would carry out several CD actions in Washington, training all the participants instead of a selection of marshals.

On Monday, May 3, the May Day Tribe would begin its attempt to block the streets of Washington, and PCPJ—including the pacifists and the demonstrators they had trained—would participate.

NPAC and PCPJ issued a joint press statement February 28 declaring they would cosponsor the April 24 demonstrations in Washington and San Francisco. "In addition," the statement said, "the People's Coalition will sponsor sustained actions in Washington during the last week of April and the first week of May."

Both coalitions agreed that the central demands of the April 24 Washington demonstration would be "Immediate withdrawal of all U.S. troops and materiel from Southeast Asia," and "End the draft now." The document noted that:

> In addition, the People's Coalition will, on its own, project other central demands: "Immediate withdrawal of all U.S. military air, land and sea forces from Vietnam and that the U.S. set the date for the completion of that withdrawal," "$6,500 Guaranteed Annual Income for a family of four—set the date," and, "Free All Political Prisoners—set the date."[22]

Ever since the McGovern-Hatfield amendment was introduced in 1970, some sections of the movement had begun advancing the slogan "set the date" in place of "immediate withdrawal." The old dispute over the implications of "negotiations" versus "immediate withdrawal" reappeared in this new form, with the advocates of "set the date" claiming it was more realistic and those of "immediate withdrawal" maintaining that it was a matter of principle and most effective to be unequivocal about the U.S. military not having any right to be in Vietnam for any period of time. PCPJ's rather clumsy formulation was an attempt to reconcile both positions.

The May Day Tribe and NPAC entered into a tacit agreement to simply stay out of each other's way—no May Day civil disobedience on April 24 and no attempt by NPAC to interfere with it on the May Days. This arrangement was honored.

The Quakers, including Levering, Carl Zietlow, and Brian Jaffe, who were training demonstrators for the civil disobedience

22. "Joint Statement of the National Peace Action Coalition, People's Coalition for Peace and Justice," February 28, 1971. (Copy in author's files.)

in late April and early May, were anxious to recruit and train as many participants as possible beforehand. NPAC was recruiting a lot of people to serve as marshals for the twenty-fourth and wanted the Quakers' assistance in training them. So an arrangement was worked out whereby the two types of demonstrations would be explained to these recruits, and those who volunteered to do so would be demonstrators in the subsequent CD actions as well, after some special nonviolent CD training. Aside from that, NPAC played no role in the May Days.

As occurred in the period before November 15, 1969, the weeks before April 24, 1971, saw an eruption of local demonstrations and other manifestations of antiwar sentiment from coast to coast.

On March 19, for instance, the Wisconsin state senate voted twenty-four to four for a bill challenging the right of the federal government to draft Wisconsin citizens to fight in an undeclared war. In the course of organizing the King commemorations, the NAACP and the Urban League were involved for the first time officially in antiwar actions. NPAC published a full-page ad in the April 11 and 14 editions of the *New York Times* signed by forty-nine members of the First Air Cavalry Division which declared:

"We urge you to march for peace April 24. We'd do it ourselves but we're in Vietnam," (An asterisk after the division's title noted in traditional movement style: "Organization listed for identification purposes only.")[23]

By mid-April, four central labor councils representing hundreds of thousands of unionists in Northern California had endorsed

23. A few days after this ad appeared, a UPI story sent from Saigon attempted to create the impression the ad was a hoax. In reply NPAC released a letter sent by Sp/4 Charlie Whithers, one of the ad signers, to the NPAC press secretary, Cathy Perkus. The letter was dated April 19, 1971, the same day *Pacific Stars and Stripes,* the armed forces newspaper, ran the UPI story under the headline: "Antiwar Ad Unread by 49 GIs." Whithers wrote: "We have seen an article saying that we who signed didn't know what we were doing. Some of us are deeply concerned having higher-ranking personnel making statements like that. If you could, make it known that we did know what we were doing. All of us have been very pleased to hear that our signatures have helped. . . . If this reaches you after the march, I hope and pray that it was a success. Thank you and all the people who came in support for trying to end this war and bring us home." (Full text reprinted in the *Militant,* May 14, 1971.)

the San Francisco demonstration. Such a motion was passed by the San Francisco Central Labor Council after a heated debate and over the opposition of some of the top officials. Council Secretary George Johns urged that the approval of AFL-CIO President George Meany be sought before taking any action. Shouts of "To hell with Meany" went up throughout the room. "You want to evade the most crucial issue facing the nation," declared Ann Draper of the Amalgamated Clothing Workers. "Quit being copouts," Mike Schneider of the Electrical Workers argued. "A lot of us didn't speak out earlier and a lot of kids are dead because of it!"[24]

In a city election in Madison, Wisconsin, on April 6, a referendum for immediate withdrawal was passed with a 66 percent majority, 31,526 to 15,977. The proposal had been backed by the AFL-CIO Committee on Political Education (COPE). Unions in New York chartered an entire train to take members to Washington for April 24.

A Harris poll conducted in mid-April showed 60 percent favoring withdrawal "even if the government of South Vietnam collapsed." For the first time in such surveys, a majority (58 percent) believed that it was "morally wrong" for the U.S. to be fighting in Vietnam. This stand was taken in face of the fact that the same poll showed 57 percent believed that a communist "takeover" would result if the U.S. pulled out.[25]

Congressional opposition to Nixon's course in Indochina was again revived. A number of bills to this effect were introduced. One, called the "Vietnam Disengagement Act of 1971," cosponsored by nineteen senators and more than fifty representatives, called for withdrawal of American armed forces by December 31, 1971.

Senator Vance Hartke of Indiana even introduced a bill for immediate withdrawal, endorsed April 24, and spoke at NPAC press conferences building it.

The March 28 *New York Times* carried what was said to be the longest book review in its history, by Neil Sheehan, its former correspondent in Vietnam. It dealt with thirty-three books, mostly by antiwar authors and committees. His theme was: "Should we have war crime trials?"

Sheehan was evidently shocked by the evidence compiled in

24. *Militant,* April 23, 1971.
25. *New York Post,* May 3, 1971

these volumes and ashamed of his own previous tacit acceptance of Washington's intervention. He singled out for special attention the publication of the proceedings of the 1967 Bertrand Russell War Crimes Tribunal, titled *Against the Crime of Silence.* "The proceedings," he pointed out, "were widely dismissed in 1967 as a combination of kookery and leftist propaganda. They should not have been. Although the proceedings were one-sided, the perspective was there." This was partial rectification of the ridicule originally heaped on the tribunal by the editors of the *New York Times* itself.

Sheehan now saw U.S. strategy in Vietnam in a different light than when he had been a correspondent there.

I remember asking one of the most senior American generals in the late summer of 1966 if he was not worried by all the civilian casualties that the bombing and shelling were causing. "Yes, it is a problem," he said, "but it does deprive the enemy of the population, doesn't it?" . . .
So this was the game. The firepower that only American technology can muster, the General Motors of death we invented in World War II, was to defeat the Vietnamese Communists by outright military attrition, the body count, and by obliterating their strategic base, the rural population.

Such reevaluation was going on in many circles. Indeed, the opposition became so deep that large numbers of Americans, far beyond those already radicalized, found themselves rooting for the other side to win the war. The strangeness of the feeling was perhaps best expressed in the poem "What Kind of War?" by Larry Rottmann, a Vietnam vet.

*Ask what kind of war it is*
*where you can be pinned down*
*all day in a muddy rice paddy*
*while your buddies are being shot*
*and a close-support Phantom jet*
*who has been napalming the enemy*
*wraps itself around a tree and explodes*
*and you cheer inside?*[26]

26. *Changing Hearts and Minds: War Poems by Vietnam Veterans,* edited by Larry Rottmann, Jan Berry, and Basil T. Paquet (New York: First Casualty Press, 1972), p. 97.

Endorsements of the April 24 marches poured into the NPAC office. National SANE for the first time formally endorsed an action organized by a coalition which it did not dominate. Many members of the House of Representatives and eight senators as well as numerous state legislators, mayors, and whole city councils registered their support.

The city of Washington opened its arms to the organizers of April 24. Dozens of churches lent their facilities for various preparations. Antiwar committees proliferated among government employees, who formed special contingents for the march. The antiwar offices at 1029 Vermont Avenue were crowded with volunteers, some of them belonging to the military services stationed around the city.

\*        \*        \*

Matilde Zimmermann of the GI Civil Liberties Defense Committee and I were in charge of the logistics and marshals for April 24 in Washington. At one point we looked for a volunteer who could come in regularly and handle a lot of arrangements. The office manager directed us to a person who had been on hand consistently and who took hold of matters well. I called him into the logistics office and started to lay out our plans when he interrupted me to explain that he was a lieutenant-colonel in the air force currently on duty at the Pentagon. He hated the war but he was a career officer who had only a short time to go to qualify for his pension. For this reason he didn't want to resign from the air force but felt obligated to do something against the war.

In this mood he had come down to the NPAC office and started stuffing envelopes. He wanted to make sure I knew who he was before I confided anything to him. I told him that ours was not a secret operation, that the authorities undoubtedly had us covered like a blanket anyway, and that his own situation was the only thing to worry about. Just in case any attempt was made to victimize him, we got it on the record that everything was aboveboard. He was included on the committee that negotiated such technical problems as bus parking with the city authorities and federal agencies involved. And in signing the attendance sheet at these official negotiations he used his real name. He did excellent work and from then on was a regular antiwar activist, both before and after his release from the military.

His case was not unusual. A marine corps captain had helped

us in the marshaling operation for the November 15, 1969, action and later was a founder of the Concerned Officers Movement, composed of active-duty military officers opposed to the war. The government apparatus became permeated with antiwar sympathizers. Even the CIA was infected. In their 1974 book, *The CIA and the Cult of Intelligence,* Victor Marchetti and John D. Marks related:

After the U.S. invasion of Cambodia in 1970, a few hundred CIA employees (mostly younger officers from the Intelligence and Science and Technology directorates, *not* the Clandestine Services) signed a petition objecting to American policies in Indochina. Director Richard Helms was so concerned about the prospect of widespread unrest in the agency's ranks and the chance that word of it might leak out to the public that he summoned all the protesters to the main auditorium and lectured them on the need to separate their personal views from their professional duties.[27]

The CIA protest was hushed up at the time, although there were reports of demonstrations by personnel at the State Department. Ten months later, during the preparations for April 24, we came on a case of the FBI firing its personnel for engaging in antiwar activities. Three young women, who had been helping out in the NPAC office after work, came in one day close to tears and confided to me that their employer had told them to stop their antiwar activity or resign. When I enquired where they worked, they said they were clerks at the FBI building. I carefully explained that they could not be legally fired for that reason, but that if they chose to fight it, they would probably face considerable harassment such as being publicly accused of associating with "reds" like me.

For family reasons one decided not to contest the matter, but the other two did. They received a letter from J. Edgar Hoover himself firing them. Attorney Phil Hirshkop took their case and the *Washington Star* broke the story with a front-page banner headline in the midst of the preparations for April 24. The clerks eventually won the case and, though by that time they didn't care to return to the FBI, they did get back pay.

Early in April, the Nixon adminstration, aided by right-wing

---

27. Victor Marchetti and John D. Marks, *The CIA and the Cult of Intelligence* (New York: Alfred A. Knopf, 1974), p. 272.

elements in Congress and compliant columnists, launched witch-hunting attacks of a Joseph McCarthy type in an attempt to discredit the antiwar movement. Representative Richard Ichord, chairman of the House Internal Security Committee (formerly HUAC), charged on April 6 that the April 24 demonstrations, NPAC, and PCPJ were "dominated mainly by two Communist factions, the Communist Party and the Trotskyite Socialist Workers Party." He also stated that April 24 would be violent because of the leading role of socialists in organizing it.

Noting that a number of senators and congresspeople had publicly endorsed the April 24 demonstration, Ichord said, "I wonder if my colleagues are prepared to accept the chaos which these antiwar groups are proposing to unleash?"[28]

On April 19, the columnists Evans and Novak singled out one of these endorsers, Senator Edmund S. Muskie of Maine, who was then considered to be the leading contender for the Democratic Party nomination for president in the 1972 election, as a special target, accusing him of acting blindly. They wrote: ". . . he had no idea whether Trotskyite Communists were or were not running NPAC nor did he show much interest in that question."[29]

They went on to say:

> What makes all this significant is that the Trotskyists are not the few bedraggled malcontents of a generation ago but the most dynamic, most effective organization on the American far left. . . . The Young Socialist Alliance has replaced the faction-torn SDS (Students for a Democratic Society) as the most important radical organization on college campuses and is now a prime mover in national antiwar demonstrations. . . . The result is what would have been unimaginable a few short years ago: Hundreds of thousands of Americans marching in their capital under Trotskyist command.

Frank Boehm, national chairman of the YSA, replied:

> The implication of the article "Muskie and the Trotskyists" is that by some fantastic maneuver the majority of the American people have been duped and manipulated by the YSA and SWP. The truth is that on the question of the Indochinese war, the American people agree with us, not Nixon, not Muskie, not Evans and Novak. Furthermore, the fact is that the American people have been manipulated, duped, and lied to by four

28. *Washington Post,* April 15, 1971.
29. *Boston Globe,* April 19, 1971.

consecutive administrations about the war. This Saturday we, along with hundreds of thousands of Americans, will march in Washington and San Francisco demanding an immediate end to the lying and manipulation and an immediate end to the slaughter in Indochina.[30]

At the next big NPAC press conference, with all the media present, Jerry Gordon pointed out that the organization's steering committee of about 150 members consisted not only of socialists, but also a broad range of Democrats, Republicans, and politically unaffiliated persons. Then, taking the red-baiting head-on, he made a point of introducing me as an SWP member on the staff and inviting any questions on this matter from the reporters. To our pleasant suprise, the press corps didn't show any more interest than Muskie had but focused their queries on the real news: how April 24 was building. To me this was a telltale sign of the changed atmosphere in the country. Nixon's red-baiting techniques that had been so poisonously effective for more than two decades had finally lost their potency. As Watergate later revealed, however, Nixon's aides had other "dirty tricks" in store for Muskie's primary campaign.

\*          \*          \*

In the last five days before April 24, a series of actions by Vietnam veterans set the stage for the massive antiwar march. The Vietnam Veterans Against the War (VVAW) pitched an encampment on the Mall a few hundred yards from the capitol and from there sent out squads to lobby Congress, to enact guerrilla theater, and to talk with people in the streets. They called this project "Operation Dewey Canyon III," mimicking the military code name for the Laos invasion, Operation Dewey Canyon II. Some twelve hundred veterans, bearing proof of their Vietnam service, were involved. Wearing combat fatigues, brandishing dummy weapons, and occasionally accompanied by actors and actresses dressed up as Vietnamese peasants, they reenacted "search and destroy" missions in the streets of Washington and on the capitol grounds. They also had a silent march past the White House led by legless veterans.

30. "Statement of Frank Boehm, National Chairman of the Young Socialist Alliance, for Press Conference, April 21, 1971." (Copy in author's files.)

About sixty of the Vietnam vets even tried to turn themselves in at the Pentagon as war criminals. This gesture was related to the recent court-martial of Lieutenant William Calley, who was convicted of murdering twenty-eight of the victims of the My Lai massacre. Calley was the only man convicted in this case while the higher-ups responsible for the My Lai operation and countless other war crimes were protected.

Some of the vets testified before the Senate Foreign Relations Committee, bitterly denouncing the war and the atrocities being committed by American forces. That televised hearing was memorable for the impassioned testimony of VVAW member John Kerry, a former navy lieutenant, who said the men did not want Vietnam to be just "a filthy obscene memory" but "mean instead the place where America finally turned and where soldiers like us helped it in the turning." Kerry also answered the proponents of setting some distant date for withdrawal by pointing out that Vietnamese and U.S. GIs were being killed every day: "how do you ask a man to be the last man to die in Vietnam? How do you ask a man to be the last man to die for a mistake?"[31]

The Justice Department obtained a court injunction against the VVAW encampment, but the men refused to evacuate even after the Supreme Court upheld the order. "Vets Overrule Supreme Court," blared the headline in the April 21 *Washington Star.* The whole city waited in suspense to see whether something like General Douglas MacArthur's forcible removal of the World War I Bonus Marchers in 1932 would be repeated.

That night I walked through the encampment.

Discussions were going on among informal groups sitting in circles. At one spot, where a flatbed truck was parked, a continuous camp meeting was in progress, with speakers mounting the truck to say words of encouragement to the vets or to express defiance of the authorities. Visitors had come from around the city, including many active-duty GIs stationed nearby.

I heard one square-shouldered young man with close-cropped hair identify himself and a few companions as members of the honor guard at the Tomb of the Unknown Soldier who were bringing a message of solidarity to the vets. "If they try to call the troops out against you, there'll be hell to pay!" he said.

The next day the Justice Department attorneys went back to

31. *Congressional Record,* Senate, April 23, 1971, p. 11739.

the district court to say they had changed their minds and got a reversal of the unenforced ban.

On April 23 I was checking on the erection of apparatus at the speakers' area on the west steps of the capitol where the rally would be staged the next day. With me was Dr. Ichi Moritaki, professor emeritus of Hiroshima University and chairman of the Japan Congress Against A- and H-bombs, who was scheduled to be one of the speakers on April 24. We watched while about 600 Vietnam veterans filed by the steps. One by one they called out the names of buddies who had been killed and they flung at the base of the capitol medals and decorations they had been awarded for fighting in Vietnam. Some broke down and wept. Some hurled the decorations shouting curses at the government, their faces distorted with rage.

Our Japanese visitor, a white-haired, gentle old man, a survivor of Hiroshima, said to me quietly when the ceremony was over: "Perhaps humanity shall yet save itself from the nuclear holocaust."

That night the Concerned Officers Movement sponsored a memorial service at Washington's National Cathedral for all who had fallen in the Indochina war. In spite of a Pentagon ban, on the grounds that the services were "political," over 400 GIs attended in uniform as well as hundreds more in civilian dress. In addition, many of the veterans, a group of Gold Star mothers whose sons had been killed in Vietnam, and other civilian supporters were present. The crowd overflowed the cathedral, one of the nation's largest churches, and heard Sp/5 Charles Balent say: "We are the ones who have listened to our brothers rolling bleeding on the ground and cursing those who sent them there to die."[32]

This climaxed the buildup for the next day's demonstration. All these activities received broad publicity in the media and were doubtless responsible for inducing many thousands to decide in the final days to come out and join the April 24 action.

*            *            *

We had the Ellipse, close by the White House, for assembling the marchers, a parade route down Pennsylvania Avenue, and

32. *Militant,* May 7, 1971.

the rally on the capitol steps. The latter had never before been granted to the antiwar forces. This time, unlike previous occasions, government officials did not hold up permits until the last minute, which gave us adequate time for the technical preparations.

But neither we nor the government negotiators had anticipated the unprecedented size of the turnout. It was the biggest demonstration in American history! Without any intention, the sheer bulk of the masses of people pouring in blocked the city's traffic.

Buses bringing demonstrators that morning were backed up for twenty miles—all the way to Greenbelt, Maryland. Uncountable numbers of cars and buses filled with demonstrators didn't get to Washington until after the march and rally were over.

The confusion arising from the crush of people was so great at the starting point that we had to array about 200 marshals into a double line to manage the takeoff. This formation elbowed its way until it stretched from one side of the street to the other. Then, facing each other, the marshals, holding hands with those on either side of themselves, backed out to make a huge empty square into which we guided the notables. They and part of the first contingent, composed of active-duty GIs and wounded veterans, headed the procession.

As we stepped off, the GIs and vets let out whoops and whistles that reverberated from the buildings and gave the sendoff an eerie, almost frightening quality. These were angry men. Different from November 1969, there was no hymnlike singing of "Give Peace a Chance." American flags, so plentiful on earlier demonstrations, were hardly to be seen.

The original plan had been to leave one lane open on Pennsylvania Avenue for emergency vehicles, but that provision went by the board as marchers filled the broad avenue from building to building, sidewalks and all. Withal, it was entirely peaceful. There were no troops and very few police in evidence. The authorities were not so foolish as to irritate an assemblage of that mood and magnitude.

After the first contingents reached the capitol, I ascended its steps and turned to gaze upon the spectacle of Pennsylvania Avenue jammed with marchers as far as the eye could see. It stayed that way for hour upon hour, long after the grounds of the capitol were packed with people. The continuous overflow took over every available patch of space in the general area.

The capitol authorities had constructed a high chicken-wire

fence cutting off intruders from a triangular space adjoining the building itself. This area contained shrubbery they wanted to protect and the side wall of the upper level of the steps prevented any view of the podium, from that vantage point anyway. The surging crowd soon broke down this fence. Dozens of human flies, realizing they couldn't see the program, started scaling the wall, a feat that landed them squarely on the level serving as the speakers' platform. All afternoon the trade unionists guarding the speakers were kept busy in the contradictory endeavor of helping the climbers over the difficult rim of the wall, lest they fall, and ushering them out by a different route. This frustrated any provocateurs among them. Remarkably, the shrubbery remained intact.

The most serious trouble of the day was concentrated at the fence around the area set aside for speakers, the news media, the TV and sound technicians, and so on. Throughout the four-hour proceedings, repeated attempts were made by provocateurs to incite elements in the crowd to break through the fence. They did not succeed, though at one tense moment they concentrated their forces and shoved one of their number onto the top of the fence where he clung to the inside struggling to pull that section of it down with him. Lenny Selig, a vice-president of the New York Hospital Workers union, and another marshal heaved him back to his cohorts. Selig and Bill Nuchow of the Teamsters had been instrumental in recruiting sturdy and level-headed union members who volunteered to protect the platform at antiwar rallies and such personages as Coretta King against possible bodily harm or assassination. The FBI, incidently, visited some of these good men and tried to pressure them not to be involved.

Back at the Ellipse, the Cincinnati contingent was coping with another problem involving the White House, which was certainly one place that was fully guarded. Mary Zins and Ellen Faulkner were contingent marshal captains. Faulkner recalled:

Cincinnati was a pretty big contingent: thirteen buses. It was well-organized and well-behaved. It was even, you could say, earnest, with lots of middle-aged people. It was mid-American. It was waiting in the Ellipse behind the White House for its turn to march down to the rally. Our scouts returned with the message that some ultralefts were going to rush the White House. . . .

Mary and I saw how they would be coming. We saw the gathering up of their strength and their intended direction. They had about thirty people. We had thirteen busloads. We moved our people in the way and sat down and had a huge immobilizing lunch. . . . There was some embarrassment in the contingent about behaving so unheroically and with such apparent conservatism—here we are defending the White House from the red flags—and there was some self-depreciating joking going on about the situation. But the rush was stopped.[33]

A part of the Cincinnati contingent merged with the ultralefts and diverted their direction into the main line of march. "So they had to go where the masses told them to go after all," said Faulkner.

\*       \*       \*

Tensions between PCPJ and NPAC did not vanish with the cosponsorship compact but surfaced in the negotiations between them over such matters as the speakers' list. It was therefore decided that the rally be chaired by a neutral committee mutually agreed upon. This was made up of several trade union officials, including Abe Feinglass of the Meatcutters and David Livingston of the Distributive Workers, who had collaborated with both coalitions. Jerry Gordon for NPAC and Dave Dellinger for PCPJ spoke at the rally but did not chair it.

The program started around noon, an hour earlier than scheduled, because of the immense crowd already at the site. The order of speakers kept changing, and new ones were added as the rally progressed. It was not unusual for the chairpersons at such rallies to be hard-pressed by groups and influential individuals who insisted, at the last minute, on having a voice. Thus, as John Kerry, the best-known figure of VVAW, was delivering his talk, a different VVAW faction strenuously demanded a spokesman who more closely represented their views. The chairman resolved the tussle by yielding the next place to them. Such rearrangements went on all afternoon. Brad Lyttle, who was scheduled and usually had something important to say, never did get the mike.

Debby Bustin of the SMC recalled:

I had arranged for the National Student Association and the Association of Student Governments, the two big student government groups, to have their presidents speak. The three of us were waiting to speak and kept being preempted. No one under the age of thirty-five or forty had

33. Letter to author from Ellen Faulkner, undated, circa 1975.

spoken by three o'clock after the first three hours of the rally. . . . So I literally harangued each of the four chairpeople individually before we finally got on.[34]

At one point Sid Peck wanted to enter the roped-off enclosure set aside for the next people on the program and the chairpeople, in order to similarly pressure them on behalf of some speakers he was concerned with. He called me over to have the marshals pass him through. Because of the hard feelings between NPAC and PCPJ, I refused until he had appealed to the chairpeople, and only when they told me to let him through did I do so.

Peck never forgave me for this affront, and on reflection I came to regret it myself. Peck was, after all, a coordinator of one of the sponsoring groups and had played a key role in the antiwar coalitions for a long time. It doesn't necessarily pay to be hard-nosed, and spite is always a poor adviser.

The breadth of the antiwar forces was manifest not only by the size of the crowds but in the diversity of the organized contingents. Almost every element of the American population had its representation. Present were older veterans of earlier wars, along with Vietnam vets and GIs. There was an all-Black contingent and a Third World section embracing Blacks, Latinos, Asian Americans, Iranians, and Palestinians, each bearing their own banners. There was also a group of left-Zionists. In the procession in addition were a delegation of Native Americans; religious groupings; students from scores of colleges; political parties and organizations; hundreds of local and regional antiwar committees and coalitions; pacifists; gays; lesbians; Women Strike for Peace; Another Mother for Peace; Women's International League for Peace and Freedom; the National Welfare Rights Organization; Business Executives Move for Peace; professional bodies of doctors, teachers, lawyers, and law and medical students; multitudes of government workers; a contingent of reservists and national guardsmen; high school students; handicapped people; and others.

All these groups carried banners against the war. With encouragement from the sponsors many also seized the event to proclaim their own special concerns, grievances, and demands. The gay rights movement, for example, was just beginning to

34. Taped interview by author with Debby Tarnopol (Bustin), April 15, 1977.

assert itself in a dramatic public way. It still wasn't easy in most places for gays to demonstrate by themselves. But on antiwar demonstrations during this period, and especially on the April 24 marches in Washington and San Francisco, they could come out in full force without fear of harassment and show themselves to be a significant part of the population.

I noticed a few of their signs: Columbus, Ohio, Gay Liberation; Northwestern University Gay Liberation; Gay Feminists Against the War; Gay Liberation Front of the Tri-Cities (Albany, Schenectady, and Troy, New York); and the SMC Gay Task Force, among others.

Tens of thousands of trade unionists marched, their affiliations identified by placards and banners, in many cases defying top union officials. They also bore slogans condemning Nixon's recently imposed wage freeze. One of the most popular was: "Freeze the War, Not Wages."

Almost from the start the antiwar movement had been agitated by the controversy over "single issue" versus "multi-issue." Here in gigantic living reality was a practical resolution of that false dilemma. NPAC and the SMC had maintained against their critics that the largest, broadest, and most effective action could be achieved by focusing on the question of the Vietnam War itself. This was certainly realized. At the same time, the united movement provided a vehicle for every element of the deepening radicalization in American society to mobilize itself as such, feel its strength, and bring forward its own claims for justice. This they could do, not only by themselves in isolation, but together with virtually all other forces intent upon social and political progress. Here was multi-issue diversity in a single common cause and unifying thrust. That's one of the essential features of an authentic united front of the masses.

This point was driven home in San Francisco, where the Chicano, women's, and gay contingents were the largest Northern California demonstrations ever of these groupings under their own banners.

Several of the contingents, including the SMC Gay Task Force, the United Women's Contingent, and the Third World Task Force, were initiated by NPAC or the SMC. While these formations had the same positions on the war as the umbrella organizations, they were autonomous. They acted on matters and raised slogans that went beyond the commitment of the parent bodies.

The SMC, for instance, expressed no view on the Middle East apart from opposing U.S. military intervention there. A more defined position was out of the question if the SMC were to remain nonexlusive and to continue to embrace Palestinians and left-Zionists as well as people who did not take sides in the Arab-Israeli conflict. The constituents of the Third World Task Force, however, had no difficulty agreeing among themselves on solidarity with the Palestinians, and the task force presented that position.

Among those addressing the assemblage that afternoon were Congresswoman Bella Abzug, Senator Vance Hartke, Coretta King, Rev. Ralph Abernathy, Teamsters union international Vice-President Harold Gibbons, Andrew Pulley, Juan-Mari Bras representing the Movement for Puerto Rican Independence, along with Black nationalist, Chicano, high school, male and female gay liberation, and women's liberation speakers. Most of them argued for immediate withdrawal, but some, such as Coretta King, Abzug, and Abernathy, took the set-the-date position. Hartke called unequivocally for "Out now!"

John Kerry was loudly applauded when he referred to the attempt to oust the vets from their encampment and denounced a "government more worried by the legality of where we sleep than by the legality of where we drop bombs."[35]

Forecasting that the antiwar movement would tie the hands of America's rulers in any further military adventures in the colonial world, Charles Stephenson, a national organizer of the Third World Task Force of the SMC, quoted Malcolm X on Vietnam and then stated:

What next? The Middle East, Africa, where will the next target of this insane war machine be? I must take time to formally express solidarity with my Arab and Palestinian sisters and brothers who recognize that their country could very well be the next Vietnam. All people of color regardless of what corner of the world they may be from understand this racist regime makes its prey on those colored nations that are moving to decide their own destiny.[36]

When she finally got to the mike, SMC National Coordinator Debby Bustin declared:

35. *Intercontinental Press,* May 3, 1971.
36. *Militant,* May 14, 1971.

Another nightmare for Nixon is the draft. There's only one reason why Nixon won't abolish the draft. He *needs* that draft to keep on fighting this war. Drafted youth in Vietnam, and many of the [volunteer] enlisted men, have literally stopped fighting this dirty war. We must make something very clear to Nixon. You keep drafting us, and you're going to draft tens of thousands of young people who hate your filthy war.[37]

Bustin drew the biggest ovation of the day as she hammered away:

You keep drafting us, and you aren't going to get a bunch of soldiers, you're going to lose an army. You keep using the American Army against revolutionary struggles of people seeking self-determination, and the GIs will take the Army away from you.

\*                    \*                    \*

It became an open secret that the White House, alarmed by the demonstration, insisted that government agency estimates of its size be as small as possible. Since the heads of the Washington city administration were at that time not elected but were federal appointees, they were obliged to comply. Police Chief Jerry Wilson stuck to his estimate of 200,000 before incredulous reporters. But some of the press also quoted Bill Jepson, a civilian police information officer who apparently hadn't gotten the White House signal:

"I would say from my knowledge there were more here than ever before. We had liaison men out and they said it just dwarfed anything they'd seen."[38]

The official NPAC estimate was "over half a million"—and that was modest. I think anyone involved with the technical side of the demonstration was aware that this was the biggest of all, surpassing November 15, 1969.

The impact of the event was not lost on the Establishment.

The effect [commented *New York Times* Washington bureau chief Max Frankel] of any single outpouring like today's cannot be measured, but the cumulative effect of the popular protest here over the years is

37. Ibid.
38. *Philadelphia Inquirer,* April 26, 1971.

abundantly clear. The marching minority now feels itself becoming a national majority.[39]

\*　　　　\*　　　　\*

By all accounts the San Francisco demonstration was indisputably the largest in the history of the West Coast. News media estimates ranged from 150,000 to 350,000. According to the organizers, over 300,000 came out in the crisp weather. For a time the demonstrators stretched across the entire seven-mile route from the Embarcadero to the Polo Grounds in Golden Gate Park.

As in Washington, the breadth of the antiwar spectrum was shown in the variety of the organized units, which included GIs and vets; many unions; Business Executives Move for Peace with 500 marchers; the American Psychological Association, which was then holding its annual convention in San Francisco and which voted to adjourn to join the march; a Raza contingent that assembled in the Mission District; a gay contingent; women's groups; a genuine marching jazz band; church groups, and so on.

"Make Wine, Not War" proclaimed the banner of the Napa Valley Committee for Peace. A huge "Jesuits for Peace" banner was carried in front of a group of young seminarians from the Jesuit School of Theology. A row of yellow buses, with Berkeley Parent-Teachers Association banners on their sides, pulled up and emptied students, parents, and teachers out into the procession. Ten chartered buses marked "United Auto Workers" let out their passengers along the route.

By the time the three-hour program at the main rally was under way, the huge oval-shaped Polo Grounds was filled to overflowing. Most of the crowd was not aware of it but a continual commotion took place directly in front of the speakers' stand where the "Anti-Imperialist Contingent" kept striving to take over the stage.

At one point, a scheduled speaker assisted the disrupters by inviting several of them onto the platform and turning over the microphone to them. He used a lot of ultraleft rhetoric which had been conspicuously absent when he had run in the Democratic primaries for the state assembly in the previous election. It took over half an hour before the planned speakers' list could be resumed.

39. *New York Times,* April 25, 1971.

As a result the rally ran out of time so that four scheduled speakers—gay liberation leader Morris Kight, pacifist Davi Harris, James Lafferty of NPAC, and Congressman Pau. McCloskey—could not be heard. Most of the immense crowd was unaware that anything out of the ordinary had happened until they picked up the San Francisco *Examiner* the next morning, which featured the disruptive incident as though it was the principal feature of the day.

Those who did get to speak included Paul Schrade, Western regional director of the United Auto Workers; Warren Widener, the new mayor of Berkeley; Phillip Veracruz of the United Farm Workers; John T. Williams of the Teamsters; Don Gurewitz of the SMC; Eileen Hernandez of the National Organization for Women; and Linda Jenness, SWP candidate for president of the United States in the 1972 elections.

One of the most popular speakers was Dick Gregory, who delivered a bitingly humorous attack on Nixon and Agnew. He announced he was embarking on a solid-food fast until the war was over. (He kept this pledge.) This famous Black comedian was a consistent and nonsectarian antiwar activist, often accepting speaking engagements without fee if his calendar allowed.

Another speaker in San Francisco was Delia Alvarez, sister of the first American prisoner of war captured back in 1964 and the longest-held POW. She charged Nixon with using the prisoner issue as an excuse to continue the war. "My brother is a victim of our government's inhumane policies, not those of the Vietnamese," she said.[40]

\*         \*         \*

Unlike November 15, 1969, when the White House had successfully pressured the networks to give minimum coverage, on April 24 both the East and West Coast actions were carried live on national TV, which alternated reports from one city to the other. Some of the speeches were carried in full and were interspersed with shots of the crowds and interviews with participants. It made an impact like a colossal mass meeting across the country. The effect was reinforced by local actions on the same day in communities at a considerable distance from Washington and

40. *Militant,* May 7, 1971.

San Francisco. For instance, 6,000, including a 1,000-strong Chicano contingent, marched on the state capitol in Phoenix, Arizona.

\*      \*      \*

The post-April 24 demonstrations in Washington began as planned with civil disobedience actions at the Justice Department; at Health, Education and Welfare; and at Selective Service headquarters. These were carried out in the traditional style with people sitting down or standing at the entrances and accepting arrest when ordered to move. The numbers involved ranged between 200 and 500.

The night of Saturday, May 1, a rock concert sponsored by the May Day Tribe was held near the Lincoln Memorial. It was attended by 50,000 people, almost all of them youth, including many GIs from nearby bases. This event was not planned to involve civil disobedience and when it was over the great majority left and did not return for the rest of the May Day activities.

Nearby in West Potomac Park was a May Day encampment where several thousand demonstrators gathered expecting to spend their nights. Very early Sunday morning the police declared it an illegal assembly.

The encampment was loosely organized by regional collectives and affinity groups, with very little coordination between them. Probably the largest was the Indiana Collective with over 500. Jot Kendall, a student from Indiana University in Bloomington, recalled the scene:

The police started encircling the camp and then there was a long wait. Finally they moved in on horseback and broke it up, using clubs and tear gas, but not many arrests. Their action was definitely to disperse. It was a blunder on their part, I think. We were isolated to an island; they had us surrounded and could have kept us there. But as they broke us up we had to find accommodations around the city, in private homes, churches, dorms, whatever. So when we did start the attempt to block traffic, we came from all directions.[41]

41. Taped interview by author with Joseph (Jot) Kendall, October 25, 1976.

No civil disobedience was planned for the rest of Sunday, but the cops refused to permit a scheduled "soul rally" on the Washington Monument grounds. A May Day women's march was dispersed and some arrests made.

On Monday morning, May 3, the attempt to "stop the government" began. The actions were to be of two kinds: PCPJ-organized civil disobedience marches on the Pentagon and the Justice Department; and the May Day Tribe, using "mobile tactics," blocking traffic at intersections and bridges during the morning rush hour.

The places to be blocked were announced beforehand in a throwaway—complete with map—distributed by the Tribe. The government, of course, was ready and waiting with Washington's 5,000-strong police force, supplemented by 2,000 national guardsmen and 8,000 soldiers and marines, as well as federal marshals. There were perhaps 12,000 demonstrators, all told. The actions were not well organized, partly because meetings previously planned for Sunday at the encampment could not be held.

Dave McReynolds, who was part of the PCPJ group that was to march across the Fourteenth Street Bridge to the Pentagon, described the scene:

The cops were in a very nasty mood. Very early, as we were just arriving, they were zipping back and forth, gunning their motorscooters. God, I never saw them in such a nasty mood.

Incredibly, we had not worked out with the May Day not to close the Fourteenth Street Bridge, so May Day was busy trying to close it while the pacifists and the "older generation" were trying to move across it. An extraordinary tactical blunder! We were moving into our allies. Of course no one got across the bridge. Dr. Spock was ahead of us and then there was a line consisting of William Douthard, Ralph DiGia, Dotson Rader, Barbara Deming, myself, and some others.

We reached a line of cops. I remember William said to a cop, "Arrest us," and they just pushed us off to the side. So we reformed and started again. This time in the confusion I was not in the front, fortunately for me. A cop hit someone in the front line over the head with a club. The tear gas started going off all around us. There was a Black kid shouting that the cops had broken his arm. There was no way to hold the march together. Some of the May Day kids by this time had started trashing, throwing sticks at the cops. The gas was too thick. We ran.[42]

42. Taped interview by author with Dave McReynolds, December 1, 1975.

A few miles north, Jot Kendall and a dozen Indianans had spent the night at a private home and were walking southwest in the direction of the capitol. Kendall recalled:

When we got near DuPont Circle we could see very few demonstrators going into the street. They were either getting arrested, or, if they resisted, beaten or tear-gassed. So our group didn't stay there; we went down side streets toward the capitol. Along the way we could see other people at different intersections getting rounded up and arrested. Truckloads of troops were zipping back and forth. Carloads of federal marshals in Civil Defense cars were jumping out with clubs and beating people. I didn't see them arrest anyone, just beat them. A Washington cop told me they were Maryland county sheriff's deputies, appointed as federal marshals for the occasion.

At one point a carload of about six of them—huge men—jumped out and went for four young kids who were just walking down the street, holding hands. I ran right up to one of the men and said: "What do you want us to do officer? Walk?" He didn't expect that. It must have blown his mind. I had this long beard and all. I turned to the kids and said, "OK, you go that way," and then to the federal marshals: "OK, you drive off." They got back in their car and drove off. But that was an isolated instance. Usually they just used their clubs. . . .

When we got within sight of the capitol there was a pretty good traffic jam. Some sympathetic motorists had stopped their cars in the street. But some demonstrators were using wooden staves—closet rods—to swing at cops. That approach was very foreign to me. Our collective had had a special nonviolent training weekend at a farm near New Castle, Indiana, where the pacifist trainers came down from Chicago. I ran up to the people with the staves to try to talk them out of it because I didn't think it was productive. One demonstrator with his back to me was winding up to hit a cop. As he swung back, the pole caught me on the bridge of my glasses and knocked me out. My friends got me out of there and we dropped out of the demonstration. Even so we were chased by cops and ducked into a shop. The rest of the morning we watched the action through store windows. It was wild. They were picking up people at random.[43]

Over 7,000 people were arrested that morning. In effect the cops used preventive detention, suspending their normal procedures and making no pretense of concern for civil liberties. Yet they declined to make orderly arrests of groups committing traditional nonviolent CD. Instead they waded in with clubs, tear gas, and sometimes speeding vehicles, scattering such demonstrators. For

43. Kendall interview.

a while this served to increase the numbers using "mobile tactics"—rushing into traffic and retreating before the inevitable police charge, only to try again until clubbed, gassed, or hauled off. Despite sporadic blockages, the major commuter arteries were kept open.

Many innocent bystanders were arrested, including an army lieutenant, an off-duty cop, a law professor, a *Washington Star* reporter, numerous businessmen, and even a couple on their way to get married. With the jails so full, detainees were herded into a Washington stadium and the Coliseum and were left without food or sanitary facilities for many hours.

White-coated medics were on the streets to administer first-aid. The cops even arrested a number of them, raided and confiscated their medical trucks, and destroyed their supplies.

McReynolds, having escaped from the approach to the Fourteenth Street bridge, was walking around watching the action.

There was tear gas all over the city, there were helicopters flying around [he recalled]. The May Day action was totally ineffective but the police managed to gas a large part of the population of Washington. There was tear gas going up to the tenth floor. The police arrested all kinds of people. I had beads and a beard but I looked old, I guess, and somehow I didn't get picked up.[44]

At a press conference that afternoon Rennie Davis declared:

Our biggest problem was not appreciating the extent to which the government would go to put people on the skids.[45]

He was arrested by FBI agents immediately after the press conference on conspiracy charges.

Tuesday morning there were about 700 arrests and no traffic stoppages. Later, about 3,000 demonstrators gathered in Franklin Square for a noon rally that preceded a march to the Justice Department led by Sid Peck, William Douthard, and other PCPJ personages. The march was spirited and orderly and even drew in some passersby along the way, many of them Black. The crowd grew to 4,000 outside the Justice Department building.

"Attorney General Mitchell was standing on the balcony,

---

44. McReynolds interview.
45. *Militant,* May 14, 1971.

holding his pipe, looking at us," observed McReynolds.[46] After the rally had proceeded for about an hour, John Froines, the Chicago "Conspiracy" defendant, was spirited away by FBI agents to be indicted on the same charges as Davis. Then the police ordered the gathering to disperse. Twenty-seven hundred stayed, and were arrested, among them Jot Kendall, who recalled:

It was a humorous situation down on the street until the cops moved in. People were looking up at Mitchell, standing there like an emperor or something. While people were being arrested you could see about 20 or 30 percent of the cops did *not* want to be there; you could see it on their faces, one, about twenty feet from me, was actually crying; and all these were Black. Then there were others who were doing their duty with a vengeance, using clubs occasionally. We were being a little resistive, but nothing violent.[47]

This demonstration was the largest single CD action in the history of the movement. But Dave McReynolds again missed getting arrested. He expected the police to move later than they did and had left the gathering temporarily to stock up on cigarettes and candy bars in preparation for a stay in jail. By the time he got back it was over.

Jot Kendall was taken to a police substation:

They packed seventeen of us in one small holding-cell for forty-eight hours. It was dirty, no water in the toilet. We had to organize rotation to lie down. It was so tight one person at all times had to stand on the toilet, or sit on it if they could bear it. The Red Cross sent us sandwiches the first day, but the jailers didn't give them to us until the next day and they were loaded with mayonnaise. A lot of us got very sick from it. I still think the cops did that deliberately.[48]

The evening after the Justice Department demonstration there was a meeting of some 800 demonstrators. Rennie Davis, who had been released on bond, spoke for a nationwide strike, "not for one day but on and on."[49] Hosea Williams of the Atlanta SCLC suggested going to the capitol the next day and staying there until Congress ratified the People's Peace Treaty. Impa-

46. McReynolds interview.
47. Kendall interview.
48. Ibid.
49. *Militant,* May 14, 1971.

tience and dissension mounted over the vague plans presented by Davis and others.

It was pointed out there was no structure to coordinate the actions of the various "affinity groups" with the body as a whole. The chair retorted that everyone should feel free to do their own thing. The leading lights were accused of hogging the microphone. There were complaints that no women had spoken at the meeting. Many people walked out with an open display of frustration. The remainder of the meeting broke up into small groups contending over what to do.

Around noon on Wednesday about a thousand demonstrators congregated in front of the capitol and were addressed by Congresspersons Ron Dellums, Parren Mitchell, John Conyers, and Bella Abzug—three Blacks and one woman. "The capitol police very carefully announced that you're all going to be arrested if you don't move," recalled McReynolds. "That was a very orderly arrest right on the steps of the capitol." Virtually the entire crowd except for the members of Congress were arrested and incarcerated in a sports arena where they were held by the National Guard and some Washington police. McReynolds, at last, was among those arrested. He continued:

Our accommodations were better than for those arrested on previous days. Actually it was a very exciting thirty-six hours. Most of the detainees were the May Day kids who by the middle of the second day had accepted the old leadership and marched in formation, giving up the mobile tactics. There were a thousand people locked up in the arena and except for a handful like myself they were all young. When the police would try to make announcements, there would be a general uproar and the police couldn't organize things. They refused to bring any food other than bologna sandwiches and water.

Later on the first day, carloads began appearing from the Black community bringing chicken sandwiches, fruit, and so forth. Some came from the Black Panthers, but most of the food was from churches. It was the first time the Blacks had ever seen masses of whites get arrested and it changed a lot of attitudes.

The kids turned the whole thing into a festival. They made music out of nothing. They tossed one another up in the air with blankets. They organized singing.

The troops kept watching this. The kids began to exchange salutes with those guys at the changing of the guard. The guardsmen started bringing us cigarettes and soft drinks. When the guardsmen were pulled out on the third day, we gave them all a standing ovation.

Then there came some very tense moments. We were left alone with the cops, who were sullen and had a different attitude. They realized that now they had us to themselves. The kids were restless, ready to start something. Some of the cops were frightened.

Hosea Williams was sleeping and we woke him up. "I don't think the kids realize these cops are going to crack skulls," I told him. We held a little teach-in, theoretically for ourselves but actually because we wanted to reach the cops. Hosea started it with a good radical socialist talk, Southern Baptist style of oratory, and he held the kids' attention for about an hour. The cops, most of them Black, were also listening. Then a couple of us white pacifists spoke. Then we broke and the tension was gone. The cops were changing the position of their chairs to sit down and talk with the demonstrators.[50]

\*     \*     \*

The maximum estimate of the number of demonstrators involved in the post-April 24 PCPJ-May Day Washington actions was 15,000. There were some 12,000 arrests, some individuals being arrested more than once. It is possible there were more arrests than demonstrators.

(Few of the arrests held up in court. There were fewer than a hundred convictions. A suit by the American Civil Liberties Union resulted in a ruling granting $12 million in damages to some of those arrested.)

The civil disobedience happenings in the national capital received the most press attention but they were not the largest antiwar actions during early May. May 5 had been set by NPAC, PCPJ, SMC, the National Student Association, and the Association of Student Governments as a day for actions throughout the country to commemorate the Kent State and Jackson State killings the year before. Tens of thousands demonstrated in marches and rallies; memorial meetings were held in many universities; some campuses went on strike. The memorial at Kent State itself took place on May 4, and 7,000 participated. A rally of over a thousand at Wayne State in Detroit on May 5 climaxed a day of activity in which half a dozen high schools were closed down by antiwar strikes.

The main rally in Boston May 5 drew 35,000 and one in New York 10,000. Some of the larger protests occurred in smaller cities such as Flint, Michigan, with 7,000; East Lansing, Michigan,

50. McReynolds interview.

with 4,000; Tempe, Arizona, with 4,000; and at Vanderbilt University in Nashville, Tennessee, with 3,000.

In a statement for the SMC in Washington May 5, Debby Bustin declared: "The student antiwar movement is telling the warmakers: 'No more Kents! No more Jacksons! Free the Washington, D.C., 12,000! Bring All the Troops Home Now!'"[51]

The antiwar actions focused on the military during the official Armed Forces weekend May 15-16. GI demonstrations took place outside more than a dozen military installations around the country. Salt Lake City saw the largest antiwar demonstration yet staged there on May 15 when 6,000 marched, led by a contingent of active-duty GIs. There were rallies at Fort Dix, New Jersey; Wright-Patterson Air Force Base near Dayton, Ohio; Great Lakes Naval Training Station near Chicago; Fort Bragg, North Carolina; and elsewhere.

Over a thousand active-duty GIs marched May 15 through the streets of Killeen, near Fort Hood, Texas. The leadership of the Fort Hood Spring Offensive Committee that sponsored the demonstration had been arrested a few days before on charges of loitering while standing outside an antiwar coffeehouse in the town. That harassment swelled the ranks of the marchers.

The Armed Forces Day demonstrations rounded off the spring offensive.

\*　　　　\*　　　　\*

"We have just come through what has probably been the longest, broadest, deepest, and most intense period of antiwar activity in the history of this country," wrote SMC staffer Jay Ressler in the June-July issue of the *Student Mobilizer*.

The central focus of this activity was the April 24th March on Washington and San Francisco. April 24th generated tremendous amounts of antiwar energy which was brought into motion throughout the spring. This energy made possible all other antiwar actions that took place. The intense activity that we have witnessed is confirmation of what we in the SMC have been saying for a long time: that most people in this country oppose the war, and that as time goes by and the dilemma of the warmakers deepens in Southeast Asia, the opportunities open to the antiwar movement become greater and greater for mobilizing this antiwar majority and finally forcing withdrawal.[52]

This view of the spring events was decidedly more optimistic than that of most other commentators critical of the war. May Day received the worst press of any demonstration from the beginning to the end of the movement. The administration, the congressional witch-hunters, and conservative opinion-makers uniformly exaggerated the violence attributed to the demonstrators and tried to use it as a stick to beat the whole movement with. The liberal media, except for a few antiwar columnists, were no less harsh on May Day itself.

In a long article defending May Day in the June 17, 1971, *New York Review of Books,* Noam Chomsky referred to an editorial in the liberal *New Republic* which declared it "paradoxical" that the May Day demonstrators should be "indignant" over the violations of their legal rights, and another in the *Christian Science Monitor* that commented on the "ironies" of the situation as "demonstrators who sought to suspend the process of law and impose anarchy on Washington are now demanding the protection of the law." Wrote Chomsky:

This remarkable view seems to be widely held. Is it also "ironic" or "paradoxical" for the murderer of dozens of Vietnamese civilians to expect the full protection of the law? [A reference to the My Lai massacre trials.] If President Nixon were to be charged with war crimes, should he first be beaten bloody by arresting officers? In fact, if an embezzler, a burglar, or a murderer caught in the act were subjected to the abuse and violence directed as a matter of course against a person violating traffic ordinances to protest the war, the press and public would be appalled by this savagery. But there is slight attention when those committing this crime are brave and decent young people, with no thought of personal gain, who are simply demonstrating their commitment to end a miserable, criminal war. Those who are attracted by ironies and paradoxes would do better to look here.

The major media were predictably full of hypocritical complaints about the damage done to the cause of peace by May Day. Typical was an article, cited by Chomsky, by *Time* magazine's Washington correspondent Hugh Sidey: "The pressure of public opinion drawing the President toward the end of the war has

52. *Student Mobilizer,* June-July 1971.

been deflected by witlessness." Because of the "scenes in Washington," he continued, it may be that "the war may go on just a bit longer than it might have otherwise."

To this Chomsky replied:

> Sidey's assumption that the President is ending the war is about as persuasive as his claim that public opinion, formed by the mass media, is the main factor forcing the President in this direction, or his further claim that the Pentagon march of 1967, for example, helped to ease pressure on the White House to end the war more quickly. . . .

For their part, NPAC and the SMC refused to join the chorus depicting May Day as the villain rather than the victim. Their public pronouncements at the time concentrated on denouncing the police violence and the illegal arrests.

Rennie Davis, characterizing the May 3 action as a military defeat, declared a temporary retreat. At the May 3 press conference he maintained:

> This is literally a beginning. We are coming back again. They are going to have to jail every young person in America before we can be stopped.[53]

But this was pure bravado.

Jot Kendall recalled:

> The general effect of May Day on the people I went with from Indiana was demoralization. I would say 95 percent were out of antiwar activity from then on. You just never saw them again. I had some guilty feelings about this because I had helped organize them to participate and had attended the national meetings of the May Day Collective.[54]

Carol Evans was subpoenaed before a federal grand jury, granted immunity, and questioned about Rennie Davis, Sid Peck, and Dave Dellinger. She refused to testify and was jailed without opportunity for bail. An appeals court later released her on her own recognizance and the Supreme Court threw the case out by a vote of five to four on the grounds of illegal wiretaps. The remnants of the May Day Collective had one more meeting—in mid-August in Atlanta—which degenerated into infighting and fell apart.

53. *Militant*, May 21, 1971.
54. Kendall interview.

There were those in and around the movement who believed that May Day was more than a tactical defeat and thought it was a serious setback for the movement as a whole and had undone the positive effects of April 24 and the rest of the spring offensive. That was the tenor of an editorial in the May 4 *Hatchet*, the student newspaper at George Washington University (which had been invaded by the police in their roundup May 3). It asserted that April 24 had been a great victory but that May Day had destroyed it all because "one good day of street violence and thousands more Americans from all levels of society eagerly look towards the next presidential election and the candidacy of a two-bit hatemonger like [Alabama Governor] George Wallace." The editorial damned both a violent Establishment and "violent rebels."

SMC spokesperson Jay Ressler rebutted:

It is a mistake for us to place the blame for violence on the doorstep of any part of the movement—the purveyors of violence are the warmakers. The May Day actions did not cancel out the impact of April 24th and the veterans' demonstrations. It's not that easy. Antiwar sentiment in this country is too deep for that.

May Day showed that civil disobedience will remain as an approach of many people within the movement. The SMC does not organize or endorse civil disobedience actions, but we do support the right of people who feel that their conscience demands they engage in civil disobedience to show their moral commitment. We believe that mass action is the instrument, the tactic, which will enable the movement to bring to bear the power necessary to force the government to end the war. . . .

It is wrong to view mass actions as being for people new to the movement and civil disobedience as the next step for anyone sincere about ending the war. On the contrary, many of the most committed people in the movement chose not to engage in civil disobedience because they believe in the efficacy of mass action. . . .

In a real sense civil disobedience is an attempt to show a moral commitment to ending the war and thereby persuade the warmakers to end the war. But the warmakers do not understand moral persuasion; they understand only power—the power of the masses of the American people. April 24th did what May Day couldn't do.[55]

55. *Student Mobilizer*, June-July 1971.

# 23

# The Crumbling of U.S. Military Morale

Following the spring 1971 actions, I wrote an article for the *International Socialist Review* explaining why the SWP did not endorse the May Day activities in spite of the fact that, for civil disobedience actions, they were "quite large and cannot be dismissed as isolated actions of a handful of ultralefts."[1] Apart from the unrealistic May Day rhetoric and some of the tactics, the SWP abstained because it disagreed with the stated central political demand of the May Day actions—support to the People's Peace Treaty. The "treaty" defined the post–cease-fire government of South Vietnam as a coalition, which in the context meant that it would include elements of the U.S. client regime in Saigon. We considered this a violation of the right of the Vietnamese people to determine their own government without U.S. intervention.

(Incidentally, it also implied a governmental coalition between bourgeois forces and socialists, or a "popular front," committed to maintenance of the capitalist social system, something the SWP has consistently refused on principle to endorse anywhere.

The Communist Party had precisely the opposite view. Such fine points of Marxist theory were not widely taken into account by the antiwar movement as a whole, in spite of the SWP's efforts to present them. They did have considerable indirect effect, however, since they hardened the SWP and YSA antiwar cadres against any dilution of the immediate withdrawal slogan.)

My article elaborated on these points:

1. Fred Halstead, "Some Comments on the Mayday Actions," *International Socialist Review*, July-August 1971.

To be sure the treaty contains essentially the same position as that offered by the Provisional Revolutionary Government of South Vietnam in the Paris negotiations. But slogans pegged to particular conjunctural phases of the Paris talks are not necessarily more effective as demands for the American peace movement than "out now." Indeed, they are less so, as far as appealing to the broad mass of the American people is concerned. The Paris talks, after all, also involve demands made by Nixon on the Vietnamese—some of which are conceded to in the "Peace Treaty." One of the great lessons the American people are now learning is that they don't have the right to determine other people's governments. . . .

The People's Peace Treaty has a quality, however, which made it particularly attractive to the organizers of the Mayday actions. Mayday leader Rennie Davis explained this point repeatedly when the actions were called. He pointed out that the stated position of many congressional doves—as reflected in such documents as the McGovern-Hatfield amendment—is very close to the Peace Treaty proposal. The liberal politicians who have endorsed the "treaty" have explained this by saying that it promises concessions by the Vietnamese as well as by Washington and thus doesn't commit Washington to unilateral withdrawal.

It seems clear that the political demands of the Mayday action were designed to appeal to a wing of the ruling class rather than the mass of the American people who just want the war to end as soon as possible.

Strange as it may seem, the tactics chosen for the Mayday actions were aimed at the same audience, at least as advertised by the organizers of the Mayday Tribe. The call to action was a threat: if the government doesn't stop the war, the demonstrators will stop the government by tying up Washington. Behind all the escalated rhetoric and left-sounding verbiage lies a clear attempt to get the attention of the ruling class, *not to mobilize the mass of the American people.*[2]

This aim of convincing the powers-that-be by shock methods was accompanied by a tendency to tailor the antiwar movement's demands to the tactical discussions within the Establishment and to the elections within the two-party system.

In my view the electoral contests between the two major parties in the United States were irrelevant as far as getting the U.S. out of Vietnam was concerned. These contests decide which set of politicians get which share of the pork barrel but do not determine policy decisions, especially in foreign policy.

Another related motivation of the May Day participants, particularly some of the pacifists involved in the CD, was to

2. Ibid., emphasis added.

appeal to the humane feelings and decency of the American policy makers. While I had learned more than a little from working with the pacifists, this was one of the points where we had deep philosophical and political disagreement. Morality is not strictly an individual but very much a class question. For example, privileged classes depend on social inequality. Their members as a rule tolerate this wrong, despite any discomfort to their consciences. Ordinary working people can be different, not because they are superior individuals or incorruptible, but because their human decency, their sentiments of human solidarity, don't contradict their long-term material interests as a class.

History testifies that most of the individuals who comprise a ruling class in decay will rationalize brutality and corruption as the way things have to be done. The closer they are to an impasse, the stronger the tendency will become. The wealthiest families of America, who control the two-party system, are no exception. The standards and practices of the CIA and the Pentagon, for example, exemplify the morality of their masters. There are individual exceptions, of course, both among the ruling rich and among the Democratic and Republican politicans they control. But these people were not chosen—nor could they be—by the class as a whole to make or implement major policy. "The time chooses the man" is an old saying. "Whom the gods would destroy, they first make mad," goes another.

The American ruling class has not reached the point where it deliberately selects madmen to rule, though it came surprisingly close to that in the early 1970s, as Nixon and some of his aides personified.

Deputy to Henry Kissinger, General Alexander M. Haig. could nonchalantly speak in those days of "brutalizing" the Vietnamese in order to gain a point or two in the negotiations for a truce.[3]

The tendency for some sections of the antiwar movement to focus their appeal on the Establishment and to trim their demands to the confines of two-party politics was not without its logic. The U.S. government was the one force which could have stopped the war any time it wanted to. But neither the threat nor the unsuccessful attempt to tie up Washington, nor the sacrifices of those who committed civil disobedience, nor, for that matter,

3. Tad Szulc, "How Kissinger Did It—Behind the Vietnam Cease-fire Agreement," *Foreign Policy,* Summer 1974.

the huge mass demonstrations, succeeded in improving the morality of the American power structure. For all their tactical disputes, its leaders never did change their minds about their right to "brutalize" Vietnam to keep a piece of it under U.S. domination as proof of their ability to police the world. This was in keeping with *their* morality.

America's rulers were never persuaded morally. They were *forced*—first of all by the resistance of the Indochinese peoples but also by the American antiwar movement and the international opposition to the U.S. role—to maneuver within ever more restricted bounds. They backed off reluctantly, bit by bit, "brutalizing" as much as they could get away with, all the way to the end. The function of the American antiwar movement was not to blusteringly threaten them or cajole them, but to add as much weight as possible to the relationship of forces working against them.

In the article cited above, I expressed the view that, in evaluating the relative effectiveness of April 24 and May Day, there were serious questions to be asked:

How many new forces were involved in antiwar activity as a result? How many minds were opened? How many minds were changed? How many young men facing the draft attended this demonstration, or know someone who did, and what effect will this have on the armed forces? How many GIs participated, or saw the demonstration, or heard about it, and what effect will that have on them, and even on battles in Vietnam?

How many workers participated, or watched, or heard about the demonstration and what effect did it have on their attitude toward the administration's attempts to get them to sacrifice for the war? Will they be more or less inclined to accept a wage freeze, for example? More or less inclined to strike in their own interests? More or less inclined to back up GIs who oppose the war?

I concluded that from this point of view the April 24 and the immediately preceding veterans' actions were "tremendously effective," while the effectiveness of May 3-5 in Washington was "questionable."

In any case the disastrous spring 1971 Laos invasion plus the spring 1971 antiwar offensive further restricted Washington's power, and the war in Vietnam took on a different complexion. Nor was the international situation specifically the same. The American policy makers were finally forced to undertake the "agonizing reappraisal" of the cold-war approach, spoken of and rejected with such distaste in 1954 by then-Secretary of State John Foster Dulles.

In tracing the history of Henry Kissinger's secret diplomatic maneuvers culminating in the 1973 accords, *New York Times* foreign correspondent Tad Szulc locates the date of the first major U.S. concession at May 31, 1971, that is, shortly after the spring 1971 antiwar offensive. The moves, Szulc wrote, took place

> against the background of increasingly hostile public opinion at home— the antiwar movement was at its apex by 1971—and in the context of Kissinger's conviction that the key to a Vietnam settlement was a détente with both the Soviet Union and China. Conversely, Kissinger believed that détente could flourish in the long run only with the liquidation of the Vietnam war. Thus, in 1971, the strands of U.S. policies toward Moscow, Peking, and Hanoi began coming together as Kissinger wove an intricate diplomatic fabric in the Communist world.[4]

Kissinger's strategy was predicated on the hope that as part of the price for détente he could get Moscow and Peking to pressure Hanoi and the NLF to accept his terms, or at least avoid intervening as he proceeded to "brutalize" the Vietnamese to achieve that end. That this hope was not baseless was highlighted by his—and Nixon's—subsequent cordial receptions in Peking and Moscow while the U.S. air war was reaching new intensity.

Szulc continues:

> There were also two other cardinal concepts governing the Kissinger policy: one was that the United States had to extricate itself from Vietnam sooner or later . . . and the other was his unshakable belief, expressed privately in 1969, after his first secret meeting with the North Vietnamese, that the breakthrough in negotiations could come only after a final paroxysm of battle. He was, of course, proved right in 1972.

The "unshakable belief" was a self-fulfilling prophecy.

No such "final paroxysm of battle" (there would actually be more than one) would have been necessary if the U.S. did not keep insisting on retaining a piece of Vietnam, under some form of U.S. satellite control, as a part of the peace pact.

What Kissinger hadn't counted on in 1969, however, and what he was forced to accept by 1972, was that the final battles would

4. Ibid.

occur without the participation of major U.S. ground-combat forces.

The Laos invasion of 1971, which had begun in February, was over by April. The operation was aimed at cutting the supply and replacement routes to the NLF areas from North Vietnam and was supposed to prove the success of the "Vietnamization" policy. That is, the ability of the refurbished Army of the Republic of (South) Vietnam (ARVN) to hold its own against the NLF, Pathet Lao, and North Vietnamese army (NVA) units.

The ARVN, however, was badly mauled and retreated in wild disorder. The American command was surprised at the heavy losses of its own helicopters flown by American crews. Here and there American ground units refused orders to advance and in general dragged their feet. The Pentagon was unable to rescue the operation by using massive numbers of additional American ground troops. The American antiwar movement made that course too socially explosive at home, especially since the move would have to come just as the spring antiwar offensive was building. The specter of May 1970 haunted the American Establishment.

Instead, the administration issued rose-tinted reports of the Laos operation and continued to try to defuse the antiwar sentiment by cutting draft calls, sending word to field commanders to reduce GI casualties, and stepping up the withdrawals of American troops. This worked to some extent, but at a military cost. In the spring of 1971 there were over 330,000 U.S. military personnel in Vietnam, two-thirds the March 1969 peak. By the end of the year the level was down to one-third the peak with very few involved in ground combat. As the U.S. ground-combat role melted away, the Pentagon fixed its hopes on air raids to keep the Saigon regime in business. The antiwar movement had forced this shift along with spreading opposition to the war among GIs in Vietnam itself. Even before the large-scale withdrawals of 1971, the American ground-combat effectiveness in Vietnam was already disintegrating from within.

Until 1968, most American GIs in Vietnam still rationalized that the war had some good purpose. But when they returned to the U.S. after the regular one-year tour of duty, they inclined to turn against the war, in part because they could now think about it without the psychological trauma of admitting they were facing death for no good reason, and in part because by 1968 the antiwar sentiment had penetrated deeply among the American youth population.

After the spring of 1968, the rank-and-file replacements to Vietnam tended to be antiwar, or at least very doubtful before they went over, and their experience on the scene tended to reinforce this attitude. While the U.S. troop level did not exceed 550,000 in South Vietnam, because of the one-year tour of duty some 3 million American military personnel served there in the course of the Second Indochina War. From 1968 on, this constant coming and going reinforced the antiwar sentiment among Americans both in Vietnam and at home, and by 1971 it reached a critical point in Vietnam itself.

This crucial interrelationship between the antiwar movement in the U.S. and the antiwar sentiment in the army in Vietnam was expressed in a letter sent to President Nixon in early 1971 by forty young army officers, mostly infantry, en route to Vietnam. Of civilian antiwar activists it said:

Many of these "troublemakers" at home are our younger brothers, or our friends, our girl friends, our wives. We share many of their views.

Now we are asked to lead men who are unconvinced into a war in which few of us believe ourselves. This leaves us with only survival—"kill or be killed"—as a motive for our mission. If the war continues much longer, young Americans may simply refuse to co-operate. You must have us out of Vietnam by then.[5]

The young officers added:

We know [the letter] will be seen by our military staff and also that punitive action has been taken against officers who have written to you: nevertheless, we must take our chance.

The American operation in Vietnam was always top-heavy, with only about 10 percent of the men sent out on combat missions on any particular day. The great bulk of the remainder were rear-echelon troops, manning bases, handling supplies, maintaining aircraft and other machinery, and so on. To be stationed at some big base in Vietnam, like Cam Ranh Bay, was not much different from being on duty at a comparable base at home, except that boredom, frustration, drug addiction, and the

5. *London Observer,* April 18, 1971.

atmosphere of colonialist corruption saturated the place. These bases were obviously designed and built as permanent American installations, right down to landscaping, Post Exchanges that resembled supermarkets at home, and regular housing for officers' dependents. There were no fixed fronts in this war, and there was always an edge of danger, particularly when duty took a GI off the base for whatever reason. But it was not a bad life in the view of some career officers and noncoms.

For the ordinary combat soldier ("grunts," as they were known) it was another story. The draft supplied only a small part of the U.S. military personnel around the world. In combat infantry units in Vietnam, especially after 1968, the ratio of draftees was far higher, sometimes 90 percent, and heavily weighted toward the poor, the Black, and other oppressed nationalities. As the war dragged on, people with any kind of pull tended to avoid that duty. Exceptions were officers fresh out of school and some more experienced career noncoms and officers (lifers) seeking quicker personal advancement through combat. The average grunt was not inclined to empathize with these latter types or to consider them safe to have around.

Ron Ridenhour, the GI who collected the file on the My Lai massacre when he was in Vietnam in 1968, returned on a visit over two years later.

By January, 1971 [he wrote], latrines throughout Vietnam bore the epithets of smoldering, sullen rebellion. *Fuck the Army—Smoke Scag.* One hundred thousand of them took to heroin in less than two years. A curious kind of brilliant, apropos nonsense danced on their tongues. "It don't mean nothin'," they said. "Not even." They turned it the way of all slang, machine-gunning it at everything they dealt with, creating a temporary articulation of a newly emergent American *volksgeist.* When their superiors—officers or NCOs—objected, reacting, as always, as if the symptom were the cause, responding with force, threats of force and repression, the grunts returned it in kind. They murdered their oppressors at will, feeling only, apparently, satisfaction. "If I frag [throw a fragmentation grenade at] a lifer, man," one told me, "that's not murder. I just fragged his animal ass, that's all. Don't mean nothin', man. Not even."⁶

Another factor in the disintegration of combat effectiveness was described this way by *New York Times* correspondent James P. Sterba:

6. *New Times,* August 8, 1974.

In the early days of the war, when American units were pouring into the country and moving off into the jungle to do battle, the morale of front-line troops was generally high. In those days, their leaders—from captains all the way up through to colonels and occasionally even generals—actually led. The command structure was tight. Ranking officers were in the field with the young men they commanded.

But gradually the leadership pulled away from the fighting, leaving young, inexperienced captains and sergeants on the ground.

Higher ranking officers preferred to oversee the battlefield from the comfort and security of helicopters hovering above the range of small-arms fire. Grunts spent the year in their line units. Officers were replaced every six months. Leadership became loose, with orders often given from a hilltop fire base protected with barbed wire and machine guns—too far away for commanders to know what their troops on the ground were going through or even what they were doing.[7]

It was the habit of the American command to count progress in terms of "body count," supposedly the number of NLF and NVA soldiers killed. These statistics were notoriously exaggerated, sometimes including simple falsifications on paper as commanders sought to make themselves look "good." On many operations there was little if any distinction drawn between combatants and the civilian population in "VC territory." These areas were frequently designated "free fire zones." My Lai was small potatoes compared to the kind of slaughter that took place in these areas.

Some Americans even relished this sort of thing. One of the most notorious was John Paul Vann, an ex-army lieutenant-colonel who was a long-time "pacification adviser" in Vietnam.

In the beginning [wrote war correspondent Kevin Buckley], he was bitterly opposed to the use of massive force. He wanted to win the war "politically" by making the Saigon government more appealing to the people than the NLF. But in his last days on earth he worked endless hours setting the targets for B-52 strikes in the hills around Kontum and Pleiku. Always a man who followed through, he insisted on inspecting the craters from his helicopter after a strike. . . . He told visitors that when the wind blew in the right direction from the hills it often brought him good news—the smell of many rotting bodies.[8]

(Vann was killed in 1972 when his helicopter was shot down.)

7. *New York Times,* May 1, 1975.
8. *New Times,* August 8, 1974.

But the moral disintegration that Vann symbolized was only one side of the story. I know of an artillery spotter who made his choice when a commander radioed him to place a barrage on a village where he could see many civilians, including children. After he reported this situation, the order was reiterated. He directed the strike to an empty area and reported a heavy "kill." From then on he misdirected fire as a matter of course, except when the lives of GIs were at stake. Solidarity with his buddies was still the cardinal rule, and if it hadn't been, he wouldn't have lasted very long.

It was a common occurrence for a patrol out of sight of the command to fire their weapons in the air, then report "kills" where there had been no action at all. For all these reasons, the American ground-combat force in Vietnam had become a net liability by 1971, and this reality, above all, forced Nixon to continue the withdrawals in spite of the failure of "Vietnamization."

Col. Robert D. Heinl, Jr., (Ret.), a marine corps historian, was one of the many American military experts who considered the force the U.S. had in Vietnam in 1967 to have been the best American army ever put into the field. Yet, in the June 7, 1971, *Armed Forces Journal,* he made the following astounding statements:

The morale, discipline and battle-worthiness of the U.S. Armed Forces are, with a few salient exceptions, lower and worse than at any time in this century and possibly in the history of the United States.

By every conceivable indicator, our Army that now remains in Vietnam is in a state approaching collapse, with individual units avoiding or having refused combat, murdering their officers and non-commissioned officers, drug-ridden, and dispirited where not near mutinous.

Elsewhere than Vietnam the situation is nearly as serious.

The author cited some evidence to substantiate his conclusions and then continued:

All the foregoing facts—and many more dire indicators of the worst kind of military trouble—point to widespread conditions among American Forces in Vietnam that have only been exceeded in this century by the French Army's Nivelle Mutinies of 1917 and the collapse of the Tsarist armies in 1916 and 1917.

The effects of the antiwar sentiment were thus ominously deep-

going just when Nixon's troop withdrawals were being bally-
hooed as the winding down of the war. While Nixon's gambit
gave him more maneuverability at home, it had a different effect
among the section of the population most directly involved—the
ground-combat GIs in Vietnam. They were disposed to seize upon
the stepped-up "peace" propaganda as further—indeed, as
definitive—justification for avoiding combat. This was one of the
factors accounting for the wholesale deterioration of the effectiveness of the American army in Vietnam in 1970 and 1971.

A popular song titled "Bring the Boys Home" was released in
1971 and became a hit. The Pentagon had it banned in Saigon.
Freda Payne, the singer on the record and by no means an
antiwar activist, reacted:

> When I heard the song was banned in Saigon . . . I was offended at
> first. It was as if they were calling me a traitor, or disloyal, or something.
> And that really made me feel bad. I wanted to go off and picket or
> demonstrate at the Pentagon, or maybe the White House, since they claim
> they are doing what the song is about, bring the boys home. I thought it
> was unfair.[9]

Col. Heinl pointed out that the "search and destroy" missions
had acquired a new name among troops. He wrote: " 'Search and
evade' (meaning tacit avoidance of combat by units in the field) is
now virtually a principle of war." The "enemy" accommodated to
this evasion, said Heinl. He pointed to "the VC recent statement
at the Paris Peace talks that communist units in Indochina have
been ordered not to engage American units which do not molest
them."

One example of the "search and evade" tactic was the fires that
American units frequently lit on patrol. When asked why they
would do such an apparently foolish thing, the GIs explained it
was to let the opposing units know where they were so they
wouldn't pass through where the Americans were. That way
nobody got killed.

Similar accommodation among opposing troops has been a
temporary and episodic phenomenon in many wars. But it was
endemic in Vietnam and became the norm. A process called
"working it out" started in Vietnam and spread even to training
exercises by American troops in the U.S. and Europe, especially

9. *Militant,* November 12, 1971.

in places to which men from Vietnam had been reassigned. The procedure was simple and was even filmed by television crews. A unit or a GI would refuse to take an order or to advance. Everybody, including the officers, would sit down and talk. The order would be modified or a safer route agreed on. Officers and sergeants in Vietnam who refused to take part in these discussions risked being "fragged"—having a hand grenade tossed into their bunk by one of their own men.

According to Heinl, "in the morale-plagued Americal Division fraggings ran one a week" in early 1971. This division was disbanded toward the end of the year. Heinl also reported that "word of the deaths of officers will bring cheers at troop movies or in bivouacs of certain units." He indignantly described some literature circulating among GIs on the West Coast that quipped: "Don't desert. Go to Vietnam and kill your commanding officer."

Author Arthur Hadley, who visited the war zone during this period, quoted an unnamed general in Vietnam:

> Lieutenant Colonels [the usual rank of battalion commander] also must expend themselves dealing with the ten per cent, the hard core, the anti-authority people, both black and white. They must continually explain why, because men will not move from A to B merely on the basis of an order. That's all very well now, but in an emergency it may kill us. And it drains good men.[10]

Hadley reported that a majority of the battalion commanders he talked to in Vietnam had been threatened with murder: "Such threats were occasional in World War II; now they are more common and hold more terror." Hadley visited an NCO [non-commissioned officers] club in Vietnam frequented by "lifers." The NCOs had just finished singing "God Bless America," a World War II favorite—when their stomachs sank as someone outside tossed a grenade against the wall. Fortunately for Hadley it was a dud.

The various reports of that time on this subject all made the same point: that the army everywhere, not just in Vietnam, was in trouble. Enrollment in ROTC, which had provided the army with a majority of its officers, had declined from 165,000 in 1961 to 74,000 in 1971. Reenlistments by ROTC graduates were also

10. *Washington Post,* August 15, 1971,

down sharply. In 1961, one in three reenlisted; in 1971, one in five.

Some military observers took comfort in figures showing a decline in certain kinds of antiwar activities in the armed forces during 1971. According to the Pentagon, the number of underground GI newspapers dropped from around sixty at the end of 1970 to some thirty at the end of 1971. The brass did not accompany these statistics with the explanation that they had been doing everything they could to suppress such newspapers and other organized antiwar actions by groups of GIs.

The hard statistics traditionally used by the army itself as morale indicators, including Absent Without Leave and desertion figures, all showed trouble. The all-army desertion index (absent over thirty days) stood at 74 per 1,000 men according to the September 5, 1971, *New York Times.* This was an all-time high, surpassing the previous peak of 63 per 1,000 toward the end of World War II.

Some military men were also reassured by the fact that the desertion rate in Vietnam was much lower than the all-army rate. This merely indicated the difficulty of getting out of Vietnam or of living there for any length of time off post. Drugs were the routine form of individual escape in Vietnam.

The Vietnam War drastically increased the problem of hard drug use among Americans both in Vietnam and in the U.S. The usual figure cited was that 15 percent of U.S. GIs in Vietnam in 1971 were on heroin. Marijuana wasn't even counted. In September 1971, a nine-part *Washington Post* series, entitled "Army in Anguish," observed: "Ironically, many officers in the drug field believe the army would be a lot better off if the heroin users could be converted back to pot."

It had been a scandal since 1964 that private planes carrying opiates from the so-called "Golden Triangle," a drug-producing area in Southeast Asia, had the protection of both the CIA and the Saigon regime. In 1970 the command pilot of the U.S. embassy in Saigon got sloppy and was caught with $8 million worth of heroin in his plane at the Saigon airport; he was convicted and sent to prison.

Armed forces other than the army were likewise affected by the antiwar sentiment. The marine corps was pulled out of any major ground-combat role in Vietnam before 1971 in an attempt to insulate this branch from the disintegrative effects.

Nor was the navy immune. To cite but two examples: On a

suggestion from David Harris, a group of activists from Non-Violent Action, the People's Union in Palo Alto, and the Concerned Officers Movement organized a poll among military personnel and civilians in the San Diego area around the question of whether or not the aircraft carrier *Constellation* should go, as scheduled, to Southeast Asia in October 1971.

The results were that 54,721 voted, and 45,060 thought the ship should stay home. Of these, 6,951 people in the military voted that the ship should remain as against 2,575 who voted it should sail. Ten percent of the crew of the *Constellation* itself voted, 354 to 292, not to go to Vietnam.

As a followup in the San Francisco Bay Area, a group of sailors and civilian supporters calling themselves "Stop Our Ship" organized a petition drive among the crew members of the carrier *Coral Sea*. Their petition read:

TO THE CONGRESS OF THE UNITED STATES
FROM THE BROTHERS OF THE CORAL SEA
  In our opinion there is a silent majority aboard ship which does not believe in the present conflict in Vietnam. It is also the opinion of many that there is nothing we can do about putting an end to the Vietnam conflict. That because we are in the military we no longer have a right to voice our individual opinions concerning the Vietnam war. This is where we feel that the majority of the Coral Sea has been fooled by military propaganda. As Americans we all have the moral obligation to voice our opinions. We, the people, must guide the government and not allow the government to guide us. In our opinion this action is even more justified for the military man because he is the one who is taking personal involvement in the war.
  The Coral Sea is scheduled for Vietnam in November. This does not have to be a fact. The ship can be prevented from taking an active part in the conflict if we the majority voice our opinion that we do not believe in the Vietnam war. If you feel that the Coral Sea should not go to Vietnam, voice your opinion by signing this petition.[11]

In spite of the seizure of petitions and other repressive measures by the brass, over 1,000 members of the crew of the *Coral Sea* put their signatures to this statement. It is interesting to note that duty on these carriers—except for air crews—did not involve getting shot at by the other side, which had no means of attacking these giant ships. These sailors were not trying to save

11. *WIN* magazine, December 1, 1971.

their own lives but their country's moral standing.

The ships were sent anyway, of course, and were used as platforms from which part of the "brutalizations" were launched. But fighting ships are not just expensive piles of machinery. Whatever the surface appearance, the more complicated the technology the less effectively they deliver their punch without the wholehearted participation of the crews.

*            *            *

The defeat of the Laos invasion, the spring antiwar offensive, and the symptoms of "the worst kind of military trouble" within the U.S. armed forces alarmed an influential section of the Establishment. The administration was warned that time was running out and it should proceed posthaste with the withdrawals and measures to extricate itself from an untenable predicament. These circumstances prompted a bold decision by the *New York Times* to risk publication of the Pentagon Papers in June 1971.

As early as 1967, Robert S. McNamara, secretary of defense, began to have second thoughts about the effectiveness of the war in Indochina. He accordingly instructed a team of top administration officials, men who had been responsible for the planning and implementation of U.S. policy, to prepare a comprehensive history of U.S. involvement there. The result was contained in forty-seven volumes containing some 7,000 pages of historical narrative and documentation and an estimated 2.5 million words entitled "History of U.S. Decision Making Process on Vietnam Policy." The compilation covered the period from the beginning of U.S. involvement to mid-1968 and was intended only for the eyes of top advisers.

No more than fifteen authorized copies of the study were made. Daniel Ellsberg and Anthony Russo, researchers at the Rand Corporation, a government-subsidized "think tank," obtained a copy, secretly xeroxed the entire study, and made it available to the *New York Times* in March 1971. Ellsberg himself, transformed from a partisan to an opponent of the war, was already participating in the spring antiwar offensive of 1971.

The *Times* edited the material for three months, deleting items it considered too sensitive, and then prepared to publish the story. Only the top editorial staff at the *Times* knew what was going on.

Even the typesetters were isolated and sworn to secrecy, apparently for fear that the government might find out and attempt to prevent publication.

The *Times* began publication on June 13. After the first three installments appeared, the government obtained a court injunction against the *Times* preventing further publication. Other major newspapers, including the *Washington Post,* the *Boston Globe,* and the *Los Angeles Times,* proceeded to carry excerpts. Congressional committees demanded copies of the papers and could not be refused. Senator Mike Gravel (Democrat-Alaska) prepared to read the text into the *Congressional Record.* On June 30, the U.S. Supreme Court decided by a six to three vote that publication by the *Times* could continue.

The government's unsuccessful attempt to prevent publication provoked a wide outcry and further isolated the administration in the country.

These, said Neil Sheehan in his introduction to the *New York Times* edition of the Pentagon Papers, "are the written words of the men who set the armies in motion and launched the warplanes." The documents revealed that the government in Washington, from Truman through Johnson, whether under Democratic or Republican administrations, had consistently and secretly deepened U.S. involvement to prevent Vietnam from falling into the hands of the Vietnamese.

They also undercut the official propaganda that the war was a result of an invasion of the South by North Vietnam. As the *St. Louis Post-Dispatch* summarized:

> While the United States was busy denying that the struggle in South Vietnam was a revolutionary civil war, secret documents that later came to light among the Pentagon Papers indicated that aggression was something of a cover story and the real enemy was seen as popular revolution.[12]

The documents further showed, in the words of Sheehan, that:

> The segments of the public world—Congress, the news media, the citizenry, even international opinion as a whole—are regarded from within the world of the government insider as elements to be influenced. The policy memorandums repeatedly discuss ways to move these outside

12. *St. Louis Post-Dispatch,* April 30, 1975.

"audiences" in the desired direction, through such techniques as the controlled release of information and appeals to patriotic stereotypes. . . .
The papers also make clear the deep-felt need of the government insider for secrecy in order to keep the machinery of state functioning smoothly and to maintain a maximum ability to affect the public world.[13]

The Pentagon Papers disclosed how fearful Washington was of the American public's perception of its Saigon puppet regime. Saigon had been plagued by repeated plots and coups against its various administrations in the early 1960s following the overthrow of the hated Diem regime. At a meeting of senior National Security Council members in Washington on December 24, 1964, a day after one such coup, Secretary of State Dean Rusk "raised an issue that was high among Administration concerns—namely that the American public was worried about the chaos in the GVN [Government of Vietnam], and particularly with respect to its viability as an object of increased U.S. commitment."[14]

In Saigon, the same day, General Maxwell C. Taylor, the U.S. ambassador, summoned the Saigon generals, including Nguyen Cao Ky and General Nguyen Van Thieu who had attempted to overthrow the government of Premier Tran Van Huong the previous night, and read them "the riot act."[15]

Excerpts from a transcript of Taylor's meeting with these generals included the following:

Ambassador Taylor: Do all of you understand English? (Vietnamese officers indicated they did . . . )
I told you all clearly at General Westmoreland's dinner we Americans were tired of coups. Apparently I wasted my words. Maybe this is because something is wrong with my French because you evidently didn't understand. I made it clear that all the military plans I know you would like to carry out are dependent on government stability. Now you have made a real mess. We cannot carry you forever if you do things like this.[16]

The fact that the real power in Saigon didn't even give orders in Vietnamese symbolized in itself a central reality of the colonialist war.

13. *The Pentagon Papers: As Published by the New York Times* (New York: Bantam Books, 1971), p. xiii.
14. Ibid., p. 337-38.
15. Ibid., p. 336.
16. Ibid., p. 337.

The Pentagon Papers exposed the way in which the war-makers calculated. As Sheehan pointed out in his analysis: "The restraints, the limits of action perceived, are what the body politic at home will tolerate and the fear of clashing with another major power—the Soviet Union or China."[17]

"What the body politic at home would tolerate." So Washington was not able to ignore the antiwar movement, as it kept pretending.

The publication of the Pentagon Papers created a sensation, exciting discussions on an unprecedented scale, which sharpened distrust and indignation about Washington's course and fueled the deepening antiwar sentiment.

17. Ibid., p. xv.

# 24

# NPAC and PCPJ—
# the Uneasy Partnership

In practice—though not in occasional polemic—April 24 and May Day more or less settled the question of do-your-own-thing confrontation. Such proposals were still ventured by Rennie Davis and others, but after May 3, 1971, they didn't attract much following.

There would still be several major mass demonstrations and many smaller civil disobedience actions but with only one significant exception—Miami during the 1972 Republican Party convention—these would be separated and the civil disobedience carried out along traditional pacifist lines.

As the differences over tactics receded in practice, political differences came to the fore. These took the form of "Set the Date"—or some variation of this approach—versus "Out Now"; attempts to build a popular-front political force versus focusing on the war; and de facto support to the Democratic Party versus nonpartisan antiwar activity.

After the spring 1971 antiwar actions, discussions were initiated between NPAC and PCPJ. Abe Feinglass, Moe Foner, and David Livingston acted as mediators. (Together with Leon Davis, these made up the group of unionists who had served as chairpersons in Washington April 24, 1971.) An agreement was reached on a series of "peaceful, orderly non-confrontation actions" for the summer. These were: local Hiroshima-Nagasaki commemorations August 6-9, a national moratorium on October 13 with activities in every community where they could be organized, and a "series of regional massive antiwar demonstrations in the streets in [a] selected number of metropolitan cities" on November 6.[1] It was understood that each coalition would raise its own demands and carry out additional activities, including other tactics, on its own. The joint statement concluded: "The parties look upon this common program of action as the beginning of a unification of the peace forces." The common program was adopted by a national PCPJ conference in late June and by an NPAC convention a week later.

Still there was no fusion between NPAC and PCPJ and the tension between the two national coalitions continued almost unrelieved. The PCPJ conference, attended by over 1,000, was held June 26-29 at the Milwaukee church of Father James Groppi, then nationally prominent as an opponent of racism. The conference was dominated by discussion over the proposed unified actions. Former members of the May Day Tribe were opposed, arguing that the agreement was a capitulation to NPAC's strategy. Their forces were relatively weak and disheartened and could not block adoption; Rennie Davis did not even attend. The conference also reaffirmed PCPJ's multi-issue political approach and projected additional actions, including an ambitious program of civil disobedience. (Most of this did not materialize and by fall had sifted down to a series of activities in Washington, D.C., as part of launching an "Evict Nixon" campaign in preparation for the 1972 elections.)

The NPAC convention took place July 2-4 at Hunter College in Manhattan with 2,300 registered participants. Support was overwhelming for the unified action proposal. NPAC's nonpartisan stand on electoral candidates and its emphasis on mass action in the streets, focused on immediate withdrawal from the war, was reaffirmed. There was a general feeling of optimism that the November 6 demonstrations could be the biggest ever.

One episode in the July 1971 NPAC convention remains especially vivid in my mind. The gathering was physically attacked by the Progressive Labor Party and the remnant of SDS which it controlled. (By this time, incidentally, PL was in the process of breaking from Maoism. It had extended Mao's analysis of the USSR as "revisionist" and "capitalist restorationist" to China itself, as well as to Cuba and North Vietnam. It denounced the NLF for engaging in negotiations with the U.S. and advo-

1. Joint memorandum by PCPJ and NPAC. Attached to "NPAC Coordinator's Proposal" to NPAC convention, July 2-4, 1971. (Copy in author's files.)

cated the slogan "No Negotiations" for the antiwar movement.)

The use of physical means to settle political differences within the movement had become a PL-SDS hallmark since they had succeeded in taking over the stage at the Moratorium rally in New York April 15, 1970, ostensibly on the grounds that prominent liberals had been invited to speak.

This time their initial rationalization was that Senator Vance Hartke and Victor Reuther, international affairs director of the United Auto Workers, were among those scheduled to address the NPAC preconvention rally. Later they added David Livingston, president of District 65 of the Distributive Workers and one of the NPAC-PCPJ mediators, to their forbidden list.

PL-SDS had held a series of public meetings beforehand in Boston—the group's main base—where they recruited people to go to New York for the express purpose of preventing such invited speakers from being heard at the NPAC convention. One Progressive Labor Party leaflet declared: "Working people in this country will fight until every creep that NPAC builds, and the NPAC leaders themselves, are either behind bars or buried."[2]

An SDS leaflet stated:

Hartke and Reuther shouldn't be allowed to speak at all. These guys will scream "freedom of speech" but there should be no freedom to speak for people who ride the anti-war movement for their own personal gain.[3]

I had not been involved in the convention preparations and expected to have no particular assignment there. At that time I was living in Chicago working on a job at my regular trade as a cutter in a garment factory. The preconvention rally took place Friday night. I flew to New York after a full day's work and arrived at the Hunter College auditorium after the rally had begun. I planned to get accommodations at the housing table, listen to a speech or two, and leave early for a night's sleep. But the PL-SDS disruption was under way when I arrived.

Over a hundred of their followers were standing up in the audience making threats and shouting "Dump liberal politi-

2. Cited in the *Militant,* July 16, 1971.
3. SDS leaflet entitled "Dump Liberal Politicians. Dump Union Bureaucrats. Build Worker-Student Unity." Undated, circa July 2, 1971. (Copy in author's files.)

cians!" and "Dump union bureaucrats!" Explanations from the
chair that PL and SDS were welcome to present their ideas at the
convention for discussion and vote were to no avail. One of the
rally speakers was Bob Mueller, an antiwar Vietnam vet in a
wheelchair. He managed to restore order temporarily by suggesting a vote on whether the scheduled speakers should be heard. A
PL spokesperson was allowed to motivate the group's opposition.
The vote was overwhelmingly in favor of hearing the scheduled
speakers. But the disrupters were not dissuaded.

A representative of the presiding committee sought me out and
told me that if it got so bad that the program could not proceed,
the disrupters would be removed. It would be no easy task to
remove over a hundred people determined to fight, without
destroying the meeting, which is just what PL counted on. The
removal would be directed by the chair, but the presiding
committee wanted me to be prepared to make the first move on a
signal from them. The object was to get the disrupters out without
people getting hurt or a free-for-all developing.

When Hartke spoke, PLers used electrically amplified bullhorns
to drown him out. We removed the bullhorns in a brief scuffle and
Hartke finished his speech over the PL-SDS shouts and curses.
When Reuther was introduced, the disrupters' frenzy reached a
new pitch and the committee gave me the signal. I selected a
disrupter near the back of the group, put a nonpunishing hold on
him, and started ushering him out toward the rear of the hall. A
dozen of his cohorts rushed me, literally tearing off my jacket as
they grabbed and punched. They also knocked off my glasses.
But in going for me, they attracted their forces toward the back,
away from the platform. NPAC and union marshals, assisted by
much of the audience, just kept them going in the same direction.

The scuffling was over in about ten minutes with the hundred
hard-core disrupters on the street and the meeting back in
session.

I spent the next couple of hours helping to organize the defense
for the remainder of the convention, since we had every reason to
expect further attacks. (They occurred but were easily repelled.)
After the rally the NPAC steering committee met and unanimously voted to exclude those who had disrupted from the rest of
the convention. There was no exclusion of PLers or SDSers as
such, only those who had attempted to prevent the program. (PL-
SDSers were given the floor of the convention several times and
used the opportunity to argue against the steering committee

motion when it was put to the plenary on Saturday. It was adopted overwhelmingly.)

By the time the Friday night steering committee meeting was over, the housing committee had left. It was well after midnight and I had no place to stay and no money for a hotel. I accompanied some students to an apartment where they had been assigned. The beds were already full. I was bone-tired from the day's work, the trip from Chicago, the tension of the night's events, and ached from blows received in the fracas. The floor felt hard as I lay down amongst the kids in sleeping bags. Suddenly I realized I was in my mid-forties and wasn't young anymore.

By the time the fall antiwar demonstrations came around, it appeared to many that the war was finally about to end. Though the air war was proceeding apace and increased fighting was going on in Laos and Cambodia, this did not involve many American ground-combat GIs. U.S. casualties were at their lowest rate since the major escalation in 1965. Draft calls had been cut drastically to a total of 10,000 for the last three months of the year combined, compared with 17,000 per month for the first quarter of 1971. This was an 80 percent reduction since April.

A sense of urgency about the war was also defused by the fact that a Nixon trip to China, scheduled for early 1972, had been announced in the summer, and the U.S. had ceased its efforts to block the admission of China to the United Nations. A fear of war with China—which might include the use of nuclear weapons—had always been a weighty underlying factor in the antiwar activism.

Within the movement there was increasing pressure to become involved in two-party politics in preparation for the 1972 presidential elections. NPAC continued its campaign to build the November 6 demonstrations, whereas PCPJ centered its attention on launching its "Evict Nixon" efforts through a series of actions, including civil disobedience, in Washington, D.C., October 25-27. Though some of its local affiliates continued to build November 6, its national literature hardly mentioned these actions and characterized the "Evict Nixon" campaign as "perhaps the most serious political project ever undertaken by the antiwar movement."[4]

4. *Militant,* October 29, 1971.

There was much comment, both in the radical press and the major media, about the alleged moribund state of the antiwar movement, accompanied by estimations that the war was no longer a major issue in American politics. In an analysis of the PCPJ's election-year strategy Rennie Davis wrote: "Whatever it is that describes our movement, this much is clear: There is no motion in this country for Vietnam."[5]

Davis advertised the October 25-27 actions in escalated rhetoric similar to that he had used for May Day, declaring that the offices of the presidency would be "closed" by demonstrators who would surround the White House.

He revealed the opportunist side of this ultraleft posture during a speech October 15 at George Washington University when he was asked how he would vote in 1972. "I'll probably vote Democratic," he replied, "but it turns my stomach."[6]

The October 25-27 PCPJ actions were quite small, the largest being a rally of 800 near the Washington Monument, 300 of whom were arrested while nonviolently approaching the White House to serve an "eviction notice" on the president.

In spite of the difficulties—which included a virtual press blackout—the November 6 demonstrations were big, larger than the previous fall, though not on the scale of the spring of 1971. Over 40,000 turned out in San Francisco, 30,000 in New York, 15,000 in Denver, and 5,000 in Houston in the largest antiwar demonstrations ever in the two last-named cities. In Boston, 10,000 marched; 8,000 in Chicago; 8,000 in Minneapolis, in the face of a subfreezing thirty-mile-an-hour wind; and crowds in the thousands in a dozen other cities.

These demonstrations had by far the broadest trade union endorsement of any previous antiwar actions, in part because Nixon had recently imposed a wage freeze. Most endorsing union leaders, however, did little to turn out their ranks and the crowds were overwhelmingly youthful, including many high school students. The major media downplayed the actions, frequently reporting them inaccurately or not at all. Nevertheless, November 6 showed that the antiwar movement was far from dead.

Interestingly, one of the buildup actions for the November 6

5. Ibid., November 5, 1971.
6. *New York Post*, October 16, 1971. (In Mary McGrory's column.)

San Francisco demonstration was a rally of Asian-Americans in Chinatown. According to Milton Chee, one of the organizers, it was the first antiwar demonstration in Chinatown not broken up by gangs controlled by the so-called Six Companies, the Kuomintang-oriented association that dominated much of Chinatown's business and political life.

\*　　　\*　　　\*

On October 16 the coordinators of NPAC sent an open letter to PCPJ proposing a united convention in early December to "plan and implement massive antiwar demonstrations for the spring and as long afterwards as is necessary to end the war." The letter stated that "we of course recognize that participating groups, such as the Peoples Coalition for Peace and Justice, would retain complete freedom to independently carry out campaigns on all issues with which they are concerned."[7]

The overture was rejected, however, and on November 6 NPAC announced its own convention, open to all antiwar activists, for December 3-5 in Cleveland.

PCPJ held a national steering committee meeting of about eighty people in Chicago November 27-28, which I attended as an observer. The question of the strategy to defeat Nixon in the 1972 elections dominated this meeting. The forces around the Communist Party particularly pushed the idea that the antiwar movement should be channeled into election campaigns to defeat "the most reactionary" candidates. It was obvious that this meant working for the Democratic Party "peace" candidate for president, as well as other liberal Democrats and an occasional liberal Republican in the congressional races.

Dellinger and others present were not interested in electoral activity as such. Yet they did consider it important that Nixon be defeated. Dellinger put a motion, which passed, that PCPJ not endorse a presidential candidate, but that it work locally in the primaries. Since the primaries' sole function was to select or to recommend candidates within the Democratic and Republican parties, the motion was rather odd. However, its implication was

---

7. Open letter from NPAC to PCPJ, October 16, 1971. (Copy in author's files.)

obvious enough. PCPJ would in effect work for the Democrats to win the presidency, withholding formal endorsement, at least for the time being.

A motion also passed to hold demonstrations at both the Democratic and Republican Party conventions in the summer of 1972, with emphasis on the Republican in order to embarrass Nixon as much as possible. Rennie Davis had already projected mass civil disobedience outside the Republican convention, then scheduled for San Diego. He made no secret of the fact that he hoped this would help the Democrats win.

There was very little support at the PCPJ meeting for mass antiwar demonstrations in the spring, though Abe Weisburd of the *Guardian* and Brad Lyttle urged this. It was decided simply to endorse activities by local groups on April 15, tax payment day.

I, of course, was not in agreement with the results of the PCPJ meeting. The SWP position was expressed in these terms in the December 3, 1971, *Militant:* "It is the mass actions of the antiwar movement, organized independently of the two parties responsible for prosecuting the war, that can force delivery on the promises of the politicians *no matter who is in power*" (emphasis in original).

Undoubtedly many supporters of NPAC, including some of its coordinators, would be voting for the Democratic Party presidential ticket, especially since it was reasonably certain that the head of the ticket would be a "dove" like McGovern or Muskie. The SWPers were in a small minority as far as voting socialist was concerned. But while PCPJ's position on the elections was fuzzy, with implied support to the Democrats, NPAC's position as a coalition was clear: nonpartisanship toward the elections and emphasis on independent activity for immediate withdrawal from the war.

This policy was fully discussed and reaffirmed at the December NPAC convention. At the rally that opened the proceedings, several of the speakers, including John Sweeny, an Ohio state legislator, and Arnold Pinckney, president of the Cleveland Board of Education, urged the assembled antiwar activists to get involved in the Democratic Party. This approach was outlined most clearly in a resolution submitted to the convention by SANE Executive Director Sanford Gottlieb. It directly counterposed working "to elect peace-oriented candidates to Congress and the

Presidency" to the organization of mass antiwar demonstrations.[8]

This was opposed to a resolution introduced by Ruth Gage-Colby, James Lafferty, Jerry Gordon, and John T. Williams which said:

It is crucial that demonstrations take place during the 1972 presidential election year and beyond if necessary. While constituent groups within the antiwar movement are, of course, free to follow their own electoral bent with respect to candidates or political parties, the movement as a whole must stay independent. The task remains to unite greater numbers of people—on the basis of nonexclusion—in an ongoing intensive struggle to end the war.[9]

This position was adopted overwhelmingly.

In addition to other activities, the convention projected major mass demonstrations for April 22, 1972, in New York and a West Coast city to be designated after further consultation with West Coast groups. Los Angeles was the choice.

Incidentally, this NPAC convention was the first at which there wasn't some attempt at physical disruption. At an open steering committee meeting the afternoon before the convention, several PL and SDS representatives appeared and demanded assurances that they would be allowed to participate. These were given after I asked their spokesman directly if they intended to try anything physical. "We've decided that's an ineffective tactic toward NPAC," he said.

\*      \*      \*

Beginning the day after Christmas, 1971, navy planes from carriers offshore and other American jet bombers flew some 1,000 sorties in five days against targets in North Vietnam. This was the most concentrated bombing attack against North Vietnam since 1968, though according to the Pentagon it was limited to the area south of the twentieth parallel. This marked the beginning

8. "Resolution on Peace Politics of 1972, Adopted by Executive Committee of SANE, November 17, 1971." Submitted to National Antiwar Convention, December 3-5, 1971. (Copy in author's files.)

9. Resolution submitted by Gage-Colby, Gordon, Lafferty, and Williams, December 4, 1971. (Copy in author's files.)

of a major escalation of the air war. In the first three years of his presidency, Nixon had already dropped more bomb tonnage on Indochina than had been dropped in all theaters of World War II and the Korean War combined. By February 1972 the bombing over South Vietnam, the southern part of North Vietnam, Laos, and Cambodia had reached new heights. Whole populations in some of these areas were living in underground tunnels, emerging briefly between raids.

A glimpse of the destruction was provided by Southeast Asia expert T. D. Allman, who had flown over the Plaine des Jarres in Laos. He wrote:

> Until recently the area provided a living for a population of more than 20,000. Now it is empty and ravaged, a striking example of what less than three years of intensive U.S. bombing can do. . . . In large areas the original bright green has been destroyed and replaced by an abstract pattern of black and bright metallic colors. Much of the remaining foliage is stunted and dull from the use of defoliants. Black is now the main color of the northern and eastern reaches of the plain. Napalm is dropped regularly to burn off vegetation, and fires burn constantly, creating giant rectangles of black. . . . Along the main Communist access routes leading into the plain, the innumerable pockmarks of 500-lb bombs give way to the giant crater patterns created by the B-52s. The saturation bombings are used in an attempt to extinguish all human life in the target area, and to create landslides to block roads. . . .
>
> Now, even if the war ended tomorrow, it might take years for the ecological balance to restore itself, and just as long to rebuild towns and villages, and recover fields. Even then the plain would for decades, if not longer, present the peril of hundreds of thousands of unexploded bombs, mines, and booby traps.[10]

Most of the major American media down-played such facts, but they were widely known among antiwar activists, thanks in good part to the efforts of Project Air War, a research group headed by Fred Branfman in Washington, D.C., which frequently distributed papers on the subject.

On January 2, President Nixon declared that the bombing of North Vietnam would continue until the American prisoners of war were released. The cynicism of this appeal was truly monumental, since the more sorties over the North there were, the more

10. *Manchester Guardian Weekly,* January 1, 1972.

American planes were downed, and, therefore, the more U.S. airmen were captured.

There were a number of emergency actions in response to the escalated bombing, by both NPAC and PCPJ as well as other groups, though PCPJ still refused to join in building April 22, or any other common date for a major mass antiwar mobilization in the spring.

They insisted that this would be a diversion from their attempts to develop "an American left." Another argument advanced by some in PCPJ against April 22 was that NPAC still used the slogan "Out Now" instead of "Support the Seven-Point Peace Plan" which referred to the current proposal by the Provisional Revolutionary Government of South Vietnam at the Paris negotiations. The NPAC leaders considered this a lame excuse since PCPJ was free to raise the seven-point slogan as part of any unified action. NPAC did not substitute the seven-point slogan for "Out Now" for the same reason it hadn't done so with the People's Peace Treaty.

The various "anti-imperialist" contingents and groups which featured NLF flags and slogans like "Victory for the NLF" and "The NLF Is Gonna Win" became adamant insisters on the seven-points slogan. They even accused those who declined to use it of being anti-NLF. Their rhetorical support to the NLF became translated into mimicking its negotiating position in Paris. This, by its very nature as a compromise proposal, was less radical than "immediate withdrawal" and quite complicated. It was also far less effective as a slogan for mobilizing Americans than "Out Now."

That's where the matter stood when both the PCPJ and NPAC were invited to send delegations to an international conference February 11-13 in Versailles, France. Known as the Paris World Assembly for the Peace and Independence of the Indochinese Peoples, this meeting was convened by the Stockholm Conference on Vietnam and the World Peace Council. Twelve hundred delegates attended, including groups from every part of the world except China. Substantial delegations from Laos, Cambodia, and both North and South Vietnam were there.

The conference convened at a moment of sharp worldwide focus on the Indochina crisis. Nixon's trip to Peking was to take place the following week. The "brutalization" of the Vietnamese from the air was under way. Both Moscow and Peking were under criticism from their left for not reacting with more than routine verbal rebukes to the U.S. and for doling out aid to Hanoi and the NLF so parsimoniously. Combined Soviet-Chinese aid sent to Indochina amounted to less than one-twentieth of what the U.S. provided to its clients there.[11] Using the excuse of protesting the Versailles conference itself, the U.S. walked out of the Paris truce negotiations, postponing them indefinitely.

The World Peace Council was heavily influenced by the Moscow-oriented Communist parties, and gatherings under its auspices were cut-and-dried affairs not noted for nonexclusion or full debate on matters the major Communist parties didn't want aired.

Since the American CP supported PCPJ but not NPAC, PCPJ had the inside track at this conference.

Nevertheless NPAC was invited, since the NLF wanted the whole American movement to be represented there. It decided to send a delegation including myself and six NPAC coordinators: Ruth Gage-Colby, Jerry Gordon, John T. Williams, James Lafferty, Stephanie Coontz, and Debby Bustin, who also represented the Student Mobilization Committee.

Ruth Gage-Colby, who was not unknown at such international gatherings and was not easily overawed by anything, got the floor in a large workshop and on behalf of the NPAC delegation proposed a World Peace Week beginning April 15 and culminating in mass demonstrations internationally on April 22 against U.S. involvement in Indochina. To our pleasant surprise this was well received.

PCPJers countered with a proposal for endorsement of various demonstrations on a variety of issues taking place in the U.S. between April 1 and May 15, the whole six weeks to be considered a period of international solidarity with the Indochinese. We knew from experience that you simply wouldn't mobilize great masses of people around such a diffuse program. You had to focus on a single day or week to get the momentum going. Then the other events would also get more attention. The matter was referred to the action commission. At the final plenary session, the commission reported out a resolution which included April 22

11. From 1966 to 1972 Russia sent $2.4 billion in aid to Indochina while China sent $1.7 billion. During the same period the U.S. sent $101 billion. In 1973 the figures were: Russia, $175 million; China, $115 million; U.S., $5.26 billion. Sources: U.S. Department of Defense Intelligence Agency and U.S. Department of Defense. Cited in *New Times*, August 8, 1974.

as part of the six-week array, but included no specific date for international actions.

Jerry Gordon and Jim Lafferty took the floor to make an amendment, for a sharper focus, but the idea of debating different proposals and letting the delegates decide was not exactly the way things were done in the purview of the World Peace Council. In fact, the plenary had no provision for discussion at all, just ratification. You could have heard a pin drop when Gordon and Lafferty rose. The atmosphere was as if some heretic had gotten up in St. Patrick's Cathedral during high mass and proposed an amendment to the Pope's latest encyclical. Gordon and Lafferty were ruled out of order after giving it a good try, and the resolution was duly ratified.

Withal, the adopted resolution represented progress from NPAC's point of view. It included April 22 as a day of "national mass actions in New York and Los Angeles to demand an unconditional end to U.S. involvement in the war in Indochina" and also stated:

> The delegates to this Assembly have decided to organize, simultaneously with the most important initiatives of the U.S. movement, big multiform rallies and actions, aimed at demonstrating the political and material support to the peoples of Indochina fighting for peace and independence.[12]

If all the organizations represented at the conference had really done that, the war could have been over much sooner than it was. But that was not to be. Still, the resolution was useful to some extent in building actions in the U.S. and elsewhere.

Another interesting aspect of this conference was the role of the Cambodian delegates, who were, of course, opponents of the Lon Nol regime that had called in the American bombers against its own population. Moscow maintained a shockingly cynical stand in this matter. It had recognized the American client government after General Lon Nol's coup and still had relations with it. By this time Lon Nol controlled little more than the capital and its supply routes. The rural population was being subjected to some of the worst heavy bombing in history.

These Cambodian delegates made no waves at the plenary, but

12. Resolution of the Action Commission, Paris World Assembly for the Peace and Independence of Indochinese Peoples. (Copy in author's files.)

they singlemindedly buttonholed whomever they could and their almost frantic bitterness could hardly be masked. They did succeed in getting some compromise wording in the resolution which said: "the delegates to this Assembly will strive to exert a pressure on the governments of their countries" to recognize the Sihanouk-Khmer Rouge government and cease any support to the puppet regime.[13]

The final act of the assembly was to join a march through the streets of Paris. This grew to about 15,000 people. I marched with a contingent of 2,500 organized by the French Indochina Solidarity Front (FSI). It had been excluded from the Versailles conference in spite of numerous protests, including NPAC's, at the insistence of the powerful French Communist Party—no doubt because it included French Trotskyists among its constituent groups. But it couldn't be excluded from the march.

One feature of this demonstration struck me. When the marchers sang the *Internationale,* the working people on the sidelines, including accidental passersby, joined in and they knew all the words. In the United States it would have been a rare marcher, let alone the people on the sidelines, who knew the words to *that* historic song.

---

13. Ibid.

# 25

# The Blockade of North Vietnam and Nixon's Visit to Moscow

Even after the Versailles conference PCPJ refused to co-sponsor April 22, though there were divisions within its ranks over the issue. A February 21 fund-raising letter, describing its program for "this election year," did not mention April 22 or several other features of the resolution PCPJ had endorsed in Versailles.[1]

The opposition to a united action was particularly strong in Los Angeles, where the election-oriented leaders of the PCPJ affiliate, the L.A. Peace Action Council, were against it. At a March 2 meeting of April 22 West, a number of PCPJ supporters presented themselves as the "Third World Caucus." This was an old contrivance used by the CP at the National Conference on New Politics in 1967 and on other occasions. In Los Angeles this peculiar improvised formation, sparked by Deacon Alexander, a prominent CPer, included whites who were leaders of the Peace Action Center but excluded Blacks, Chicanos, and Asians who were NPAC supporters.

The caucus demagogically submitted a list of demands obviously designed to blow up the meeting. These included the following:

I. The existing literature, which is mostly irrelevant, must be discarded and a committee of Third World people be organized to rewrite it. . . . V. The April 22 rally must support the rally to be held at the Republican

1. Letter to "Dear friends" from Dave Dellinger, Jane Fonda, Bradford Lyttle, Sidney Peck, Benjamin Spock, and Cora Weiss, February 21, 1972. (Copy in author's files.)

National Convention in San Diego [where it was then scheduled].
VI. Total and unequivocal support must be given to the PRG 7 point
program. . . . VIII. The NPAC must be completely restructured, across
the board with 80% Third World representation.[2]

After these proposals were voted down, the caucus stormed out,
declaring April 22 "racist." In contrast, the *Guardian* from the
East Coast declared:

> We support the actions called for by PCPJ—and NPAC should too. But
> none of them as yet appears capable of growing into truly massive
> protests. April 22, in fact, may prove to be the only vehicle this spring for
> manifestations in the tens and hundreds of thousands.
>
> We assume PCPJ's delegates to the World Assembly will be discussing
> this question in coming days. The only conclusion they can come up with
> that is consistent with the needs of the Indochinese and American
> peoples is to join enthusiastically with NPAC and the entire antiwar
> movement in building April 22.[3]

By mid-March some sections of the movement in the San
Francisco Bay Area who were bitterly hostile to NPAC had
nevertheless become convinced, since the escalation of the air
war, that they had to do something April 22. So they issued a
separate call in the name of an ad-hoc group for a demonstration
in San Francisco on that day, emphasizing the seven-point
demand. This group, which became known as the Anti-
Imperialist Coalition, was endorsed by the San Francisco PCPJ
affiliate. At first NPAC condemned this as a splitting move and
tried to get the San Franciscans to join the Los Angeles demonstration. Failing in that, NPAC helped build the Northern
California action as well, under its own demand of "Out Now."
Both groups also proclaimed "Stop the Bombing." April 22 was
now centered on three cities. However, PCPJ nationally still
withheld formal endorsement.

Hanoi and the NLF gave their answer to the air war on March
30 when they launched a major offensive on the ground in South

2. "Third World Caucus Proposal to the April 22 West NPAC," undated,
copy appended to letter from NPAC April 22 West Coordination Committee to PCPJ and Los Angeles Peace Action Council. (Copy in author's
files.)
3. *Guardian*, February 23, 1972.

Vietnam. In the past, North Vietnam had sent only supplies, replacements, and small units equipped with light weapons to aid the NLF. In this Easter offensive, as the Americans referred to it, fully equipped main-force units of the North Vietnamese army (NVA) fought alongside the NLF forces in the South.

The offensive began with infantry and artillery attacks on bases across the northernmost province of South Vietnam. Within a few days the only major base in the province held by the Saigon forces was in Quangtri City, the provincial capital, and it was under siege. The revolutionaries also advanced on two other fronts: the central highlands, and toward Anloch, the capital of Binhlong province, fifty miles northeast of Saigon. Heavy guerrilla fighting broke out elsewhere, especially in the Mekong Delta.

Nixon's hopes of keeping the war off the front pages while the "brutalization" proceeded were knocked awry. Though American intelligence had predicted some sort of offensive, it missed badly on the location of the initial attacks and on the strength and staying power of the operation. Large numbers of tanks and 130-millimeter guns, which outranged the U.S. artillery, showed up unexpectedly, even far to the South. The NLF and NVA forces advanced openly in conventional rather than just guerrilla formations for the first time in the Second Indochina War. The ARVN was badly beaten in the initial attacks, which were slowed only by massive American air strikes and naval shelling near the coast.

The NLF and NVA in South Vietnam had no naval or air support at all. Heavy fighting continued through the spring, especially at Quangtri and Anloch, where large parts of the ARVN were surrounded. American air power took a heavy toll of the NLF forces in this set-piece conventional warfare, but did not break them.

By this time the American ground troops still in Vietnam were supposed to be restricted to guarding U.S. bases. The Nixon administration launched trial balloons about the possibility of ending the promised continued withdrawals of U.S. troops and even probed using American ground-combat units in the battles. This met with alarmed objection from important sections of the Establishment.

Notably, an April 4 editorial in the influential *Los Angeles Times* declared:

Victory in Indochina is not the will of the American people. This nation has long since perceived the futility of this war. If a way out can be negotiated in Paris, fine. But the frustration of negotiations is no cause to slow the withdrawal. There is only one way out. It includes pilots and bombardiers and airborne electronics technicians as well as infantry. If Saigon cannot survive without them, the sooner that is acknowledged the better.

The most ominous rebuke came from the infantry GIs directly involved, on the same day one of the trial balloons was released. On April 12, Gerald Ford, then the House Republican leader, told reporters of a briefing he had just received from Nixon. Ford claimed: "There has never been a commitment" to further withdrawals. And, he went on, "I don't think you can assume anything at this point."[4]

On that same day (April 11 in Vietnam) a company of the 196th Light Infantry Brigade was flown from Danang to Phubai air base near Hue, believed to be a main target of the Easter offensive. They were ordered into trucks to be taken outside the base for patrol. The number refusing was variously reported as between 50 and 100 out of the 142 in the company, and those who complied did so only after assurances there would be no fighting. UPI quoted one of the soldiers as saying: "Man the war stinks. It's a damn waste of time. Why the hell are we fighting for something we don't believe in?"[5]

*     *     *

Across the Pacific the antiwar movement was again on the rise. On April 1, 10,000 marched in Harrisburg, Pennsylvania, protesting the war and the trial of the Harrisburg defendants. This action was organized by the Harrisburg Defense Committee and PCPJ and was supported by many groups including NPAC, SMC, and even the National Federation of Priests' Councils. Daniel Ellsberg was a featured speaker.

The campuses again began to stir, with significant antiwar actions breaking forth at hundreds of universities and large mass meetings and strikes at several dozen of them.

Nixon escalated the air war further, including the use of B-52s from bases in Thailand and Guam. On April 15 these planes

4. *New York Times*, April 13, 1972.
5. Ibid.

struck Hanoi and Haiphong. This was the first time since Johnson suspended the bombing of North Vietnam in 1968 that these principal population centers came under heavy attack. Five B-52s were shot down in the initial Hanoi-Haiphong raid.

James Reston summed up Nixon's policy in his *New York Times* column of April 11:

> The military crisis in Vietnam has at least clarified the policy of the Nixon Administration. In the name of protecting the withdrawal of American troops and prisoners from the battlefields, the President is now directing a massive air offensive against the enemy in order to prevent the defeat of the South Vietnamese Army and the overthrow of the Saigon Government.
>
> This is at least a policy; but it is not a policy for getting out, it is a policy for staying in; not a policy for defending our troops, but a policy for defending General Thieu's command and his regime.

The Pentagon attempted to black out the news and the major media did not play it up, but antiwar activists, through their contacts with GIs, became acutely aware that Nixon was preparing yet another big escalation. In Boston an Ad Hoc Military Buildup Committee was set up to compile and publicize such information. On April 11 the PCPJ leadership met and at last adopted a statement calling "on everyone to join in vigorous support" of the April 22 actions.[6]

On April 14 Dave McReynolds wrote an article for publication by the Manhattan weekly *Village Voice* in which he pointed to the inadequate coverage of the crisis by the leading newspapers, including the *New York Times*. McReynolds said:

> The depth of the present crisis became clear enough to the Pentagon when the entire defense line just south of the DMZ [demilitarized zone separating North and South Vietnam] was cracked wide open. The depth of the crisis became clear to the peace movement very soon afterward. For, unlike other wars, there is now a resister of some kind on virtually every military base and every ship at sea. Calls began to come in to our various offices: Iwakuni, Japan—on alert; one guided missile cruiser, Norfolk, Virginia—on alert; Third Marine Air Wing, El Toro Marine Corps Air Station—ordered to Vietnam; 82nd Airborne at Fort Bragg—on standby; Long Beach, California, six guided missile destroyers left April

---

6. "Statement by the People's Coalition for Peace and Justice," National Interim Committee, PCPJ, April 11, 1972. (Copy in author's files.)

10—emergency orders without warning, destination unknown. One could go on for pages. . . . Nixon has now assembled the most massive air fleet in the history of war for deployment over North and South Vietnam.

This article was carried in the April 20 issue of the *Voice*, with the following additional comments by McReynolds inserted in a box:

After I wrote this on Friday, the massive air strikes took place in Haiphong and Hanoi, creating the gravest crisis in the war since Nixon took office. [Since Russian freighters called at Haiphong harbor there was danger they might be hit.] Those attacks were of course reported by the media, but the *Times* buried deep on an inside page of the Sunday edition the report that 300 demonstrators were arrested at the White House on Saturday, in an emergency action called by the People's Coalition.

At this writing, April 17, I've just returned from a joint press conference called by the People's Coalition for Peace and Justice and the National Peace Action Coalition, to announce their planned response to the crisis. The *Times, Post,* CBS, NBC, and ABC had no one at the press conference. The only reporters present were from the *Guardian,* Voice of America (!?), the *Militant,* Tass, WOR-FM, and the *Daily World.* The public should know that while the *Times* is silent the movement is not. For the news that no longer fits, call the Vietnam Peace Parade Committee, 255-1075. And be sure to make it out to the mass demonstration this Saturday.

*       *       *

It was unseasonably cold in New York on Saturday, April 22, and it rained hard. Ordinarily that would have been enough to reduce a mass demonstration—especially one that had been blacked out of the major media—to a few bedraggled organizers. Yet a hundred thousand people marched that day to a rally on the Avenue of the Americas between Thirty-eighth and Forty-second streets, spilling over into the side streets and Bryant Park.

This was the largest demonstration in New York in two years, and those on hand report it was the most disciplined and determined crowd of them all. Under their umbrellas and improvised rainwear they hung on through the day's events in spite of the cold wind and rain. The most notable Democratic and Republican doves were conspicuous by their absence, the highest ranking politicians present being a few congresspeople and the borough president of the Bronx.

The speakers were mostly from the movement, plus a number of celebrities, including John Lennon and Yoko Ono. Daniel Ellsberg, then under indictment for exposing the Pentagon Papers, spoke and said the turnout showed "it is a slander and a lie that the American people care only about American deaths." Youth dominated the gathering and the most popular chants expressed their mood: "Peace Now," "Out Now," "Join Us," and "1, 2, 3, 4—We don't want your fucking war!"

The Los Angeles and San Francisco demonstrations turned out some 25,000 each, with the participants in a similar determined mood. Smaller demonstrations took place in other cities around the country; the National Student Association estimated that some 200 college campuses had ceased "business as usual" on Friday, April 21.

I had gone to Los Angeles a few weeks earlier to help organize the events there, partly because of the difficulties being encountered. The movement was plagued during this period by frequent squabbles and provocative activities that did not fit any pattern of political logic. That's usually a sign of some sort of concerted efforts by agents provocateurs, but it can't be effectively countered by accusing anyone merely on suspicion or encouraging paranoid attitudes. A week before the march we knew of at least four different planned attempts to foul up the April 22 demonstration from within, as well as a countermarch on the same street in the opposite direction by the Nazis. The latter did not involve a lot of people, but it was clearly designed to start a fight.

The situation was complicated by another problem in the greater Los Angeles area. Many people were wary of coming out because Chicano Moratorium actions, not only in August 1970 but later demonstrations under its sponsorship, had been broken up by police. Tension was further heightened by the hostility of Los Angeles Mayor Sam Yorty, who, after the April 22 demonstration was announced, publicly slandered NPAC as being responsible for violence in Washington.

A while before, one Frank Martinez, an agent provocateur connected with the Alcohol, Tobacco and Firearms Division of the U.S. Treasury Department, had made a public confession of his disruptive role within the Chicano Moratorium Committee. He had wormed his way into its chairmanship, ousting Rosalio Muñoz by demagogic incitement to ultraleft actions. The committee had become defunct under his chairmanship. In his confession, given before newsmen, Martinez described how he had provoked fights with police on demonstrations. I obtained a copy of a newsclipping on this and kept it in my shirt pocket.

When the NPAC West delegation met with the Los Angeles police about the march route for April 22, the officer in charge insisted on assurances that there would be no violence.

"There won't be any from us," I said, "and our monitors will be well organized." (In the West the word "marshal" was not used in movement circles.) "But," I continued, handing him the clipping, "I trust you'll demand the same assurances from the Feds." As it turned out, the LAPD was on its good behavior the day of the march and the antiwar monitors handled the attempted disruptions easily. Most of the crowd never knew they had occurred.

\*         \*         \*

The April 22 actions were viewed by the movement not as culminating a spring antiwar offensive as before, but as the springboard for a sustained and mounting antiwar upsurge. Precipitated by the escalated bombing, it was to be aimed at putting the maximum pressure on the Nixon administration in what was obviously a crucial turn in Vietnam.

The situation there was described April 25, 1972, by Nguyen Van Tien, deputy chief of the PRG's delegation to the negotiations in Paris. A group of sympathetic Americans interviewed him in Paris and asked: "What are the aims of the current offensive? Why this timing?" Tien replied:

U.S.-ARVN must deploy almost all their forces in the battle areas, on the three fronts in Quangtri province, Binhlong province, and the central highlands. This provided the people of the Mekong Delta and the coastal plains with favorable conditions to chase out the Saigon control units, and the situation there is changing greatly. . . . This is just part of our struggle for a peaceful, independent, democratic, and neutral South Vietnam. Our specific purpose is to advance the struggle for that goal. As to timing—the struggle will be stepped up whenever there are favorable conditions. As usual, you will notice, the offensive takes place in the dry season.[7]

The next question was: "What about the danger of commando

7. *Militant*, May 12, 1972.

raids, mining Haiphong Harbor or the use of tactical nuclear weapons?" Tien replied:

We have to be prepared for all possibilities. But we are sure of one thing: Nixon cannot retrieve his situation even by recourse to the worst. And I think the American people will take active measures to stay Mr. Nixon's hand. Americans also share responsibility in this regard.[8]

As the Pentagon Papers indicated, the limits of U.S. military escalation in Vietnam were set by two basic factors: what the American public would tolerate and fear of precipitating conflict with the Soviet Union or China. Expectations of what these powers would do was, in turn, an important underlying factor in the expression of opposition to the war among the American people. From the beginning most observers and commentators on the war had listed four possible specific moves by the United States that Peking and Moscow would not put up with and that were likely to cause them to take immediate and grave countermeasures against the U.S. in Southeast Asia or elsewhere.

These four "forbidden" measures were: a U.S. invasion of North Vietnam; the use of nuclear weapons; extensive destruction by bombing of the dikes in the Red River Delta of North Vietnam; and the blockade and mining of Haiphong Harbor, which was the major source of outside supplies for North Vietnam and frequented by the ships of many nations, including the Soviet Union.

On May 8, President Nixon announced on TV that he had decided on one of these steps—the sealing off of North Vietnam's harbors—and that U.S. planes were already dropping mines in and around the port of Haiphong, as well as smaller ones. Nixon said he took this move because

the risk that a communist government may be imposed on the 17 million people of South Vietnam has increased, and the Communist offensive has now reached the point that it gravely threatens the lives of 60,000 American troops who are still in Vietnam.[9]

The president made a special appeal to the American public to

8. Ibid.
9. *New York Times*, May 9, 1972.

support him in this new escalation, declaring: "It is you most of all that the world will be watching."

Following April 22, even before this announcement, there had been widespread actions by thousands of participants in cities across the country and large demonstrations in many parts of the world protesting the U.S. bombing. Nixon had hardly finished his May 8 speech when spontaneous demonstrations began to break out in the U.S. The *New York Times* reported: "The coast-to-coast outburst of demonstrations was the most turbulent since May, 1970, when protests over the United States invasion of Cambodia closed universities across the country."[10]

To give a sampling: On the night of May 8, right after Nixon spoke, 3,000 students at Boulder, Colorado, blocked the main highway into town all night long. In Berkeley, police tried to break up a crowd of thousands May 9 with tear gas and rubber bullets. At the University of Wisconsin in Madison, 10,000 participated in a candlelight march May 9 and some 4,000 later marched on the state capitol.

Some 200 antiwar Vietnam veterans barged into the United Nations May 9. During the morning rush hour that same day a group of protesters abandoned their cars on Chicago's Eisenhower Expressway, causing a massive traffic jam. In Albuquerque, New Mexico, two students were wounded with shotgun pellets when state police opened up on a crowd of 300 blocking a freeway. Two days later thirteen more were wounded in another blockade near the same spot. On the evening of May 9, Vice President Spiro Agnew's limousine was pelted with potatoes when he arrived at the Ohio State Fairgrounds in Columbus. That night he took a plane to Honolulu and was picketed by antiwar protesters there.

Three hundred chanting young protesters prompted officials to close the visitors' gallery of the House of Representatives in Washington May 10. National guardsmen were called to the University of Minnesota that day when more than 2,000 demonstrators had taken over a Minneapolis street. At Northwestern University in Evanston, Illinois, hundreds of students fanned out into the surrounding community to publicize a rally the night of May 10, which was attended by 8,000.

On May 11, a thousand persons blocked the entrance to

10. Ibid., May 10, 1972.

Westover Air Force Base in Massachusetts. Five hundred were arrested, including John William Ward, vice-president of Amherst College. Two U.S. senators and twenty-one members of the House filed suit in federal court the same day, asking for an injunction to stop the administration from carrying out the mining of North Vietnam's harbors.

On Saturday, May 13, massive emergency demonstrations occurred across the country, the largest being the 25,000 who marched nine miles through Minneapolis in spite of rain. Ten thousand rallied in Central Park after a march from Times Square in Manhattan where demonstrators had surrounded the military recruitment center chanting: "One point peace plan: U.S. Out of Vee—et—Nam!" Eight thousand marched through the Loop in Chicago, 2,500 in Seattle, 3,000 in Boston, 7,000 in Denver, and so on.

On May 10 an emergency meeting of antiwar leaders had convened in New York to plan a response to the Nixon move. Present were representatives of NPAC, PCPJ, Americans for Democratic Action, SANE, Business Executives Move for Peace, the Student Mobilization Committee, the New York Peace Parade Committee, Greater Boston PAC, Philadelphia PAC, Women Strike for Peace, and others. The meeting, which took place in the District 65 headquarters, was welcomed by the union's president, David Livingston, who appealed for unity. It was chaired by Al Evanoff.

The bitterness and disputes that had characterized the pre-April 22 period were swept aside in the urgency of the moment. Among other things, the gathering quickly agreed on calling a march on Washington for May 21, and a number of us left for the capital city to prepare for what we anticipated could be one of the biggest mobilizations of all. The pacifists also planned a civil disobedience march on the Pentagon for May 22.

In the meantime all eyes were on Moscow. Peking's reaction to the mining of Haiphong was subdued, so it was clear that Kissinger's strategy and Nixon's February trip to Peking had paid off. But the president's visit to Moscow hadn't yet taken place; it was scheduled for May 22. Moreover, the mining of Haiphong put Moscow more directly on the spot than Peking, since Russian ships were involved.

It was widely assumed that, as a sign of its displeasure, Moscow would at least cancel or postpone Nixon's trip in face of the new escalation, with the massive bombing of Hanoi and Haiphong. This expectation—mingled with trepidation at further Russian or Chinese moves—lay behind the sharper initial questioning of Nixon's actions within the American Establishment. As the May 9 *Wall Street Journal* put it: "The move—never before attempted in the long Indochinese fighting—risks a direct confrontation with the Soviet Union."

However, Moscow's first response was no less subdued, and no mention was initially made of the Nixon trip. The whole world waited, almost literally with bated breath. Moscow maintained silence even after Hanoi and Agence France-Presse reported that at least two Soviet freighters had been damaged by U.S. bombs and several crewmen wounded.

The tipoff to Moscow's attitude came on May 11. A "courtesy call" on the White House was scheduled for that day by Soviet Foreign Trade Minister Nikolai S. Patolichev. The White House had not informed the press beforehand of this for fear that the visit would be demonstratively and embarrassingly canceled. But it wasn't. The administration hastily summoned correspondents and photographers to report the "cordial atmosphere" of the visit and photograph Nixon with the Soviet official. On his way out, Patolichev was asked by a newsman whether Nixon's trip to Moscow was still on. "I don't know why you asked this question," the May 12 *New York Times* reported him replying, "Have you any doubts?"

It took a few days for the full import of this diplomacy to be absorbed by the antiwar forces around the world. But the consternation was well voiced immediately by Bertil Svahnström, chairman of the Stockholm Conference on Vietnam. This group had cosponsored the Versailles conference, worked closely with the World Peace Council, and was not noted for disputing Kremlin policy. All the same, in a letter to antiwar groups internationally, dated May 12, Svahnström cried out:

At this moment world opinion should be able to play a decisive role in stopping this criminal attempt . . . by Nixon and his councillors. . . . It must not be possible that one of the makers of the destiny of the world who tries to annihilate a whole people which does not want anything but to live peacefully on its own little part of the globe, is treated as an honourable statesman and is received as a guest by other nations. Rumors that Nixon will come to Stockholm on the occasion of the UN conference on the human environment are not true. The whole Swedish people would raise in revolt against such a visit, and everybody knows that it is physically and politically impossible in the present circumstances. . . .

This morning I heard on the radio from Washington that the circles around Nixon regard the reaction of the other world powers to his latest actions rather as an "encouragement," as the governments restrict themselves to protests without indicating any counter measures, and as Nixon's visit to Moscow is not even cancelled.

Nixon is allowed to move one step after the other, and in the meantime he spreads death and horror in Vietnam.[11]

On May 16 the Kremlin answered such critics in a commentary over Moscow television by Viktor Shragin, who explained why the Nixon trip had not been put off. The Soviet leadership, Shragin declared, is

steadfastly keeping to its principle of peaceful coexistence [the Kremlin's code word for its pursuit of the policy of détente] despite the stormy course of international events and despite the twists and turns in the world situation.[12]

Shragin continued:

There are, of course, forces in the world that would like to stop the positive trend in international relations. These forces are not beyond urging upon our country a course of action dictated by the situation of the moment. But such attempts cannot be successful.

The refusal of Moscow to cancel or postpone Nixon's trip, gleefully trumpeted by Washington's spokespeople, struck like a dagger in the ribs of the antiwar movement. Antiwar activists in the U.S. and abroad felt double-crossed. They did not want warlike acts on the part of the USSR, but to wine and dine Nixon under these conditions was a terrible blow.

The official opinion-makers congratulated the administration on its cleverness and spread illusions that a negotiated settlement would soon be reached with the Kremlin's assistance. As early as May 10 Max Frankel had commented in the *New York Times:*

11. Letter to international antiwar groups by Bertil Svahnström, May 12, 1972. (Copy in author's files.)

12. *New York Times*, May 17, 1972.

If the Moscow meeting still begins on schedule two weeks hence, then the situation in Vietnam will now be a principal item on the agenda. . . . In the name of "saving the peace" between themselves, the major powers could finally attempt to impose a bargained peace on Indochina.

*       *       *

It was a gray, cold, drizzly day on May 21 when the march on Washington took place. Nixon was on his way to Moscow and a great deal of steam was out of the antiwar offensive. The demonstration, which marched east on Constitution Avenue to a rally on the west steps of the capitol, was 15,000 strong, far less than had originally been expected. This was also one of the few demonstrations of the period that was not predominantly made up of college students.

The schools were then in the midst of final examinations. The student strikes, which had erupted immediately after Nixon's May 8 announcement of the mining of Haiphong, fizzled out upon the news that the trip to Moscow was going ahead. Relatively few students decided to leave their examinations for the journey to Washington. A large part of the demonstrators were members of District 65, the Hospital Workers, AFSCME, the UAW, and other unions, along with a turnout of older radicals. It was lucky these people were there for they had a lot of much-needed discipline and we had more trouble on this action than any other nonconfrontational demonstration we'd ever organized in Washington.

To begin with, I made a mistake in planning out the assembly area. The contingents were to line up in a large open field in several columns parallel to each other, and all perpendicular to Constitution Avenue. Each column was supposed to move into the avenue one after another, make a ninety-degree turn, and start marching. This was standard procedure when a march was assembling in side streets.

However, this was an open field with no discernible lines, and rain had made the field muddy and uncomfortable to stand in. The mass tended not to line up in the designated perpendicular columns but along the sidewalk parallel to the avenue. When the sidewalk filled up, the crowd spilled, in no order, into the street before traffic had been stopped. The cops got uptight and charged the crowd with horses. If the bulk of the demonstrators had not shown exceptional self-control, anything could have happened.

But we managed to get the horsemen to back off after their first couple of forays, got a first contingent in some kind of order and started the march. The rest of the crowd just swarmed in behind.

The specific weight of the ultralefts bent on a confrontation with the cops was much greater among the students who did come than it would have been in a larger body. Along the route several hundred of these broke away and headed for the Justice Department on Pennsylvania Avenue, where a number of windows were broken.

The main group was proceeding with the rally at the capitol when the breakaways, chased by D.C. police, ran into the fringe of the larger crowd at the edge of the capitol grounds, and the cops lobbed tear-gas grenades after them. The main crowd managed to hold together.

A little later the breakaways split again, running to the Health, Education and Welfare building at Third Street and Independence Avenue where more windows were broken. Once more they returned to the central rally with cops in pursuit. Dwindling in size with each foray, the group continued this pattern of behavior for most of the afternoon, repeatedly drawing the cops and the tear-gas attacks into the edge of the main crowd. The police on the capitol grounds proper, however, were a special unit, controlled by Congress, and the executive branch of the government had little influence with them. They strictly maintained their jurisdiction and, apparently to avoid rioting on the capitol grounds, refrained from attacking the assemblage. At the same time the rally had to cope with the constant tear-gassing at its fringes.

I could see all this quite clearly from the top of Capitol Hill. The city cops were obviously allowing the trashers to regroup and march back, with banners flying, to the rally, saving their main tear-gas attacks for when the ultralefts reached the edge of the capitol grounds. I felt a little like a monster dispatching squad after squad of antiwar marshals down the hill to keep the edge of the rally crowd separated as best they could from the melee, only to see them return in few minutes, stumbling and crying, to have their eyes washed out by medics.

The rally chairpersons, as well as the speakers, did a remarkable job of keeping the crowd calm and determined in the face of these difficulties. I particularly remember the venerable Julius Hobson—who was then quite ill with cancer—holding himself at the podium with his arms, appealing against the provocations and raising the spirits of the listeners.

The speakers included Jerry Wurf, international president of AFSCME and the only member of the AFL-CIO Executive Council to consistently vote against Meany's hawk position; Victor Gotbaum, executive director of AFSCME District Council 37; Victor Reuther; Dick Gregory; Congresswoman Bella Abzug; Cleveland Robinson, international vice-president of the Distributive Workers; Tran Khanh Tuyet, a Vietnamese student; Paul Kuntzler of the Gay Activists Alliance; Dr. Barbara Roberts, national coordinator of the Women's National Abortion Action Coalition; Bert Corona, California Chicano organizer; Andrew Pulley, who was then the SWP vice-presidential candidate; Sergeant Gordon Youngs of the GI Alliance; and Gus Hall, presidential candidate of the Communist Party.

It was the first time Hall had spoken at a major antiwar rally, and he was one of several speakers who discussed Nixon's Moscow trip.

Having also just returned from Moscow and Warsaw [said Hall]—I can tell you on the highest authority—that the continued all-out support of the Soviet Union and the other socialist countries to the just struggle of the people of Indochina—will not be up for discussion or negotiations when Tricky Dick visits those cities. . . . Anyone who says different is an unmitigated liar.[13]

PCPJ National Coordinator Sid Peck stated in a somewhat different vein:

The blockade of Haiphong and the bombing of Hanoi is part of a desperate risk to escalate the conflict into an international crisis, and then attempt to effect a political settlement in Moscow and Peking favorable to U.S. interests. But Nixon will not be able to settle the war in Moscow or Peking. The Vietnamese will not allow any foreign power to dictate the terms of settlement. The American people should not be fooled by Nixon. He cannot end the war in Moscow, just as he was not able to end it in Peking.[14]

NPAC Coordinator Jerry Gordon said that Nixon

goes there as he went to Peking in hopes of achieving what he couldn't

13. *Daily World*, May 23, 1972.
14. *Intercontinental Press*, May 29, 1972.

win on the battlefield. Nixon wants a continuing U.S. presence in Vietnam, a presence strong enough to thwart the liberation of the Vietnamese people.

But the Vietnamese continue to resist despite everything. They have made it clear that despite the terrible toll, they will determine their own destiny. They and no one else. They have told the world that the fate of Vietnam will be determined in Vietnam and nowhere else. And as we of the peace movement rally here at this crucial moment in world history, we must rededicate ourselves to continuing, intensified support to the inalienable right of self-determination for the Vietnamese people.[15]

The rally ended in good order, which was an accomplishment in itself. Some 200 persons had been arrested in the surrounding melees. As demonstrators from the main rally were walking peacefully back to their buses, carrying their signs, over a hundred of them, including many members of the United Furniture Workers and District Council 37, were arrested on the specious charge of "parading without a permit."

All in all, it was a difficult day, and one that portended an uncertain future for the American antiwar movement.

The day following, May 22, Nixon arrived in Moscow. Thousands of American flags were set up to greet him on his route from the airport. That same day just outside Washington PCPJ sponsored a "People's Blockade" of the Pentagon where 500 antiwar activists were arrested in nonviolent civil disobedience.

During the three previous days, U.S. bombers flew 1,000 sorties over North Vietnam, including the heavily populated area of Hanoi and Haiphong.

15. Ibid.

# 26

# The Second Counterinaugural

Though Moscow's reception for Nixon threw a wet blanket over the mass antiwar demonstrations in the U.S., the war itself was more unpopular than ever. In many ways the efforts of the administration to work up enthusiasm—or just cooperation—for the war effort were thwarted. The rise in draft resistance for this period compared with earlier years is revealing of the underlying mood.

By 1972 it superficially appeared that the draft was no longer a major issue in American life. Draft calls in fiscal 1972 (the year ending June 30, 1972) were down to about 12 percent of the fiscal 1968 peak and student protest on the issue was sharply reduced. There was little of the earlier dramatic publicity about draft resistance—which was now being organized, if at all, by the traditional pacifist groups—but the men still being called were more or less quietly evading the draft at an unprecedented rate.

In fiscal 1965 the proportion of youth charged with violation of the Selective Service Act compared with those actually inducted was an insignificant .003 percent. In fiscal 1968 the proportion had increased tenfold but was still only .035 percent. For fiscal 1972, however, the figure mounted to 18 percent.[1] In that same year twice as many as those charged with violating the draft law avoided induction in other ways after being called. These were truly alarming figures from the government's point of view. The military options available to the administration were further restricted.

1. In absolute figures, 341 men were charged with violating the Selective Service Act in 1965. This number grew steadily during the war,

The unpopularity of the war was so pervasive that for some time, we now know, the president and White House staff felt themselves besieged by enemies on every side. Though it was not public knowledge in the spring of 1972, the White House had already established a special, secret, illegal task force for electronic surveillance, burglary, and "dirty tricks."

This group, largely composed of former CIA employees and veterans of the 1961 Bay of Pigs invasion of Cuba, was known as "the plumbers." Following the publication of the Pentagon Papers, members of this group had been dispatched to California to burglarize the office of Daniel Ellsberg's psychiatrist and steal the file of the former Rand Corporation expert who had helped reveal the documents. Precisely what these broken-down James Bonds were expecting to find was never completely clear. (Could it have been some mental aberration that turned Rand Corporation robots into decent human beings?) Shortly before the mining of Haiphong, Ellsberg appeared at a small antiwar demonstration in front of the capitol to explain his educated reasons for

---

reaching 4,906 for 1972 (*Statistical Abstract of the United States, 1973* [Washington: U.S. Government Printing Office], from table 445, p. 274). In the same period, the total number inducted grew from 102,555 in 1965 to 339,596 in 1968, then began to decline, hitting 27,083 in 1972 (*Selected Manpower Statistics* [Washington: Department of Defense, May 15, 1974], pp. 27.60 and 27.61).

These figures show the progression over time of deepening opposition to the war among prospective draftees, but they give only part of the picture of the scale of this opposition. Later, in 1974, when the government proposed an amnesty for draft resisters, it gave a figure of 113,000 for those eligible, of whom 90,000 were men who had received less-than-honorable discharges for having gone Absent Without Leave (AWOL). These figures were disputed by the American Civil Liberties Union, mainly on the grounds that they left out hundreds of thousands of men who had simply never registered for the draft. These men, while they had never been charged or arrested, were still subject to prosecution if the government caught up with them. In a January 6, 1976, press conference the ACLU gave its own estimate of 750,000 persons who should be covered by the government's amnesty. Former Attorney General Ramsey Clark, who was among the ACLU officials at the news conference, said that he considered even the ACLU's estimate conservative. His own estimate of those still in legal jeopardy was some 2 million. (*Facts on File*, January 10, 1976, p. 4.)

expecting a major escalation in the war. The plumbers were sent to beat him up.

Such was the state of mind of the White House as the 1972 election campaign was getting into swing, and as the Democrats were making a partisan issue of the war.

In the early hours after midnight, June 17, 1972, a security guard in an office building in the Watergate complex in Washington, D.C., was making his rounds when he noticed tape across a door latch, a possible indication of burglary. He called the city police, who responded routinely with a search of the building. Five men were discovered burglarizing the offices of the Democratic Party's National Committee headquarters. They were arrested and booked. It soon became apparent to the police reporters, however, that this was no ordinary burglary. Four of the five had prior links to the CIA and Cuban counterrevolutionary activities, including the Bay of Pigs; and one, James McCord, Jr., was a former CIA employee, then on salary as a "security aide" for the Republican Party's Committee to Reelect the President.

The arrested burglars had in their possession extensive photographic and electronic surveillance equipment and were caught installing a bugging device near Democratic Party Chairman Lawrence O'Brien's office.

O'Brien called it a "blatant act of political espionage" and announced a suit against the Committee to Reelect the President. Nixon's press secretary, Ronald Ziegler, flippantly dismissed the affair as a third-rate burglary that deserved no comment from the White House. The *New York Times* reported June 24 that the group of Cuban counterrevolutionaries involved had met in Miami with "American friends from Washington" and had agreed to undertake "direct action to combat what they viewed as left-wing causes in the United States." For years both Democratic and Republican administrations had countenanced such illegal activities against left-wing, antiwar, civil rights, and other dissident groups and individuals. Now the Democratic Party National Committee itself had become a target. On June 21, the *Washington Post* editors noted their concern over the affair "in a time of waning confidence in the processes of government."

\*        \*        \*

Nixon's summitry in Peking and Moscow did not end the war

on Kissinger's terms or otherwise. But it did give the administration much more maneuverability in the election campaign at home and in the bombing of Indochina. "To speak plainly," wrote I. F. Stone in the June 15, 1972, *New York Review of Books,*

the chief running dogs of US imperialism now seem to be Brezhnev and Chou En-lai. This is how it must look from Hanoi. Ignominious as Hitler's appeasers were in the Thirties, he was never dined as an honored guest in Paris, London, or Washington while he bombed Guernica and destroyed the Spanish Republic.

Stone further stated:

True, without Soviet and Chinese supplies, the North Vietnamese and the NLF would soon be forced back to low-level protracted warfare, as they may be in any case if the bombing and blockade continue long enough. But without the enormous resolution and courage of the Vietnamese, what would Moscow and Peking have to offer Nixon, *what would they have to sell?* Peking bought its admission to the United Nations, bought its way out of containment, with the blood of the Vietnamese people. The same commodity—in such plentiful supply—has brought Nixon to Moscow. All those bright hopes of expanded US trade and credits which Nixon's emissaries have been dangling before the Kremlin since Secretary of Commerce Stans went there last year rest on Nixon's desire to buy some Soviet "restraint" on Hanoi. If it were not for Hanoi, Moscow too would have little to sell. [Emphasis in original.]

A glimpse of what the continuing bombing meant was provided by *New York Times* writer Anthony Lewis, who had just been in North Vietnam, in his July 3, 1972, column:

Most Americans thought it grotesque and horrifying when Gen. Curtis LeMay [of the Strategic Air Command] spoke in 1965 of bombing the North Vietnamese "back in to the Stone Age." But something very like that is happening right now. Two weeks ago it was said that 60 per cent of North Vietnam's industry, such as it was, had been knocked out. . . . [The French daily] *Le Monde*'s highly respected correspondent in Saigon, Jean-Claude Pomenti, wrote recently: "North Vietnam is returning to the Stone Age at a gallop."

\*         \*         \*

The decline in organized antiwar activity under the pressure of Nixon's visit to Moscow and the impending presidential elections emboldened many opponents of the movement, sometimes from unexpected quarters. One example cropped up in Washington, D.C., where an ad hoc group of women, led by folksinger Joan Baez, had scheduled a women's and children's "Ring Around the Capitol" demonstration for June 22.

On June 16, a group of prominent local Black political figures held a press conference to denounce the antiwar movement as a whole as "racist" and to demand cancellation of the June 22 action. A statement was distributed to the press, signed by some sixty Blacks, mostly from the Washington area. The language of the statement had a militant, and even Black nationalist, ring to it:

We, the black residents and the black workers in the Washington, D.C. community, have long since demonstrated our protest against the military government of the U.S.A. in its attempts to bomb Southeast Asia into submission or face genocide and total annihilation. . . . We clearly understand that the oppressor abroad is the oppressor in this country and the oppressor of our city.[2]

But its main point was an "indictment" of the peace movement, claiming that antiwar demonstrations did not point out that the war in Southeast Asia was racist, that "the cost for demonstrations is paid out of the local D.C. budget which comes from the taxes of D.C. workers," and that the antiwar movement did not offer "substantial backing of black political candidates."

The signers of this manifesto were mainly Black Democratic Party politicians, including Walter E. Fauntroy, the District of Columbia's nonvoting delegate to Congress; Louis Stokes, chairman of the Congressional Black Caucus; Marion S. Barry, chairman of the D.C. school board; and John Gibson, assistant director of the Washington Urban League. Other signers included representatives of the Young Republicans, several religious organizations, the Congress of African People, and some individuals in the orbit of the Communist Party, including officers of several Young Workers Liberation League chapters.

Barry, at the press conference, demanded that in place of the June 22 demonstration, a group of selected leaders of the antiwar movement meet with him and other signers of the manifesto in a "summit conference" to decide what the antiwar movement was

2. Press release, undated. (Copy in author's files.)

prepared to do for Washington Blacks in general and for the Black Democrats in particular.

The charges were immediately picked up by all the Washington press and were debated down to the wire until the demonstration finally took place. Julius Hobson, one of Washington's best-known Black political activists, called the accusations "idiotic" in a telephone interview with the *Washington Post*. He called the press conference "a form of blackmail," declaring that "The present peace movement has not excluded blacks."[3] The *Washington Post* added:

> At one point Hobson said yesterday's press conference was actually organized by Fauntroy and that the persons subscribing to the statement constituted a "front group for his political tightening up of this city."[4]

The accusing group was quickly dubbed the "Fauntroy Sixty," but their attack still proved disorienting for some within the antiwar movement. On June 19, Dave Dellinger held a press conference at the All Souls Unitarian Church. As the *Washington Post* reported:

> Dellinger, at a Monday press conference with the blacks, confessed that he, too, thought the peace movement showed signs of being racist and announced he was cooperating in planning the summit meeting.[5]

Julius Hobson's comment on this was to call Dellinger a "fool," adding, "I really blame the peace movement for what this is becoming. They shouldn't give the attack credibility." He said he believed the motive of the "Fauntroy Sixty" was to implement a "promise . . . to keep people quiet here and off the streets in exchange for votes in Congress for home rule for D.C."[6]

Though neither NPAC nor PCPJ had initiated the June 22 demonstration, both were drawn into the fracas because of the wholesale character of the accusations against the antiwar movement. PCPJ's approach was to seek to participate in the proposed June 22 "summit meeting," although the organizers of it announced that no one would be permitted to attend who took

3. *Washington Post*, June 18, 1972.
4. Ibid.
5. Ibid., June 21, 1972.
6. Ibid.

part in the "Ring Around the Capitol" demonstration. NPAC was also prepared to attend the "summit," but not at the price of publicly opposing an antiwar action. As a result, Jerry Gordon was refused entrance into the meeting, as were Sam Manuel and Herman Fagg (later Omari Musa), both Black representatives of NPAC's Third World Task Force.

NPAC distributed an open letter to the meeting, which said in part:

> At a time when the Nixon administration is intensifying its brutal war of extermination against the Vietnamese and other peoples of Indochina, it is more important than ever for Americans who oppose the war to be out in the streets in visible, massive, militant protest. An antiwar demonstration called by women peace activists is scheduled for noon today at the Capitol. This conference you are attending was called to conflict with that demonstration. *In effect, you are participating in a counter demonstration, a demonstration against the peace movement.* . . .
>
> The giveaway as to what is taking place today is shown by one charge contained in the "indictment" issued by the organizers of today's "summit." They say the antiwar movement has failed to give "substantial backing to Black political candidates." They want you ringing doorbells for particular politicians rather than in the streets building an independent, non-partisan mass antiwar movement which demands that the bombing be stopped and that the U.S. get out of Southeast Asia NOW![7]

A long article on the whole affair in the "underground" *D.C. Gazette* afterward concluded that, apart from the question of motives, "the most cogent critique of the ['Fauntroy Sixty'] statement—on the basis of what the statement itself said—came from Herman Fagg, the Socialist Workers Party candidate for delegate."[8] He had written:

> You, sisters and brothers who initiated and signed the statement, claim to be in complete solidarity with oppressed nations, among them Vietnam, Cambodia and Laos. You correctly state that the "oppressor abroad is the oppressor in this country and the oppressor of our city." But rather than confront the enemy that wages the war, you attack those who are fighting to end it. . . . You blame the antiwar movement for the inequali-

7. "An Open Letter to the Participants of this Conference from NPAC," June 22, 1972, emphasis in original. (Copy in author's files.)
8. Sam Smith, "Fight of the Generals," *D.C. Gazette*, July 12, 1972.

ties and ills of capitalist society. You claim that the "cost for demonstrations is paid out of the local D.C. budget which comes from the taxes of D.C. workers. . . ." This is more than bad logic and folly. The U.S. government spends 60% of every tax dollar to kill people around the globe. The U.S. government is the real criminal, not the antiwar movement. And it is an outrage to say anything else. . . .

Black students at Eastern High walked out of school and held rallies and marches in support of the Vietnamese and against the mining of Haiphong Harbor. The students sought the support of the D.C. School Board. The board (presided over by Marion Barry) was asked to call, on May 19th (Malcolm X's birthday) assemblies in the schools throughout the city to discuss the war and its relation to the struggle for Black liberation.

How did the School Board respond to this demonstration of Black solidarity with the Vietnamese and against the U.S. government?

Did they place support for the Eastern students at the top of the agenda? No!

Did they place the resources of the School Board at the disposal of antiwar Black students? No!

Did they call on the Black Community to follow the lead of the students and go into the streets against the genocide denounced in the statement of June 16th? No!

Where were you, brothers and sisters, when the Black students needed your support in their actions against the war?[9]

In the end the demonstration took place as scheduled, with Joan Baez leading some 3,000 women and children in a march around the capitol building, followed by lobbying of representatives and senators. Across town, Rennie Davis, Ron Young, Dave Dellinger, and Sid Peck met with Marion Barry and several other signers of the June 16 statement. Walter Fauntroy did not attend. The attempt to stop people from petitioning the government for a redress of grievances, on any grounds, had been so badly received that he withdrew his name from the document, claiming he had never read it and had signed on Barry's advice. Except for whatever impact it had in reducing the size of the June 22 demonstration, nothing else was achieved by the "summit" meeting. As one Black community organizer, Willie J. Hardy, put it, "I do not recognize the 60 Fauntroy people as my leaders or as the leaders of black people. They don't speak for black people any more than I do."[10]

9. Ibid.
10. *Washington Post*, June 21, 1972.

This episode raised the obvious question: who did speak for Black people? It is true that the "Ring Around the Capitol" demonstration was particularly vulnerable to the kind of maneuver pulled by the Washington Black Democrats. This flowed from the ad hoc character of the action and the political lull, so that it was guaranteed to be a small turnout at best, without a significant Black component. Such baiting would have been impossible at the April 15, 1967, New York march, where Martin Luther King and Stokely Carmichael spoke. It would have fallen flat at the April 24, 1971, Washington mobilization, where the NPAC Third World Task Force was an impressive contingent in its own right, not to mention the large Black turnout in trade union contingents, such as the Meat Cutters, the Distributive Workers, the Hospital Workers, and the State, County and Municipal Employees.

Unfortunately, there was no ongoing counterpart in the Black community to the nationwide coalition represented over the years by the various Mobilization committees. To be sure, many prominent Black figures were involved in this work and many tens of thousands of Blacks came to the demonstrations. What was missing was an authoritative Black organization that could have participated in the coalition but had an independent existence of its own.

The antiwar movement arose at a time when the existing Black organizations, after having won important victories in the antisegregation battles of the early 1960s in the South, had gone into decline. Long-established groups such as the NAACP shared much of the attitude of the trade union leadership, in seeking to avoid conflict with Washington on foreign policy issues in exchange for the hope of domestic reform. More militant organizations in the civil rights movement, such as the Southern Christian Leadership Conference, the Congress of Racial Equality, and the Student Nonviolent Coordinating Committee, lost ground rapidly after 1965 and were generally on the defensive by the late 1960s, unable to take significant initiatives on any question, the war in Vietnam included.

Both the SCLC and SNCC did adopt antiwar positions. SNCC, however, took the position of refusing induction into the army, which made it vulnerable to persecution, especially in the South. It ultimately evolved into ultraleft, "pick-up-the-gun" rhetoric. It then became the target of a concerted police-agency attack. Lacking a clear perspective on tactics and strategy for the Black movement, it was torn apart and ceased to play a role in the antiwar movement as well.

SCLC went into a prolonged crisis after the assassination of Martin Luther King, Jr., in 1968, and though its leaders, such as Rev. Ralph Abernathy, occasionally participated in antiwar actions afterward, it lost much of its national attraction.

The northern, ghetto-based Black nationalist movement suffered a similar fate after the murder of Malcolm X in 1965. It came to be represented by the Black Panther Party, which lacked Malcolm's hard-headed realism and sense of the mood of the Black masses.

Under the circumstances, there was no way that individual Black leaders, small local organizations, or Black committees within the broad antiwar coalitions could overcome the general leadership vacuum that had developed in the Black movement by 1968. Moreover, at that time the nucleus was missing through which conscious Black radicals could have created a new channel for organizing the deepgoing antiwar feelings of American Blacks. No group comparable to the radical pacifists existed as an all-Black organization. Nor did the Socialist Workers Party at the outset of the antiwar movement have enough Black members to get the ball rolling for a Black antiwar movement.

What did exist as an expression of Black opposition to the war within the broader coalition were groups such as the NPAC Third World Task Force. This was set up by antiwar activists who were members of Black, Hispanic, and other oppressed national groups. The idea was to provide a form through which these communities could mobilize themselves against the war and at the same time address their own specific concerns and demands.

Its efforts, however, were only moderately effective. Its greatest success was among Black high school students. Another formation—called the Black Moratorium, organized in Riverside, California, and in Detroit in 1970 on the pattern of the Chicano Moratorium—had similar results. Maceo Dixon, an organizer of the Black Moratorium, later recalled:

The major problem we faced was that many prominent spokespersons within the Black community were opposed to organizing our people in the streets in alliance with the antiwar movement. A tremendous vacuum existed in terms of Black leaders organizing against the Vietnam War. This in spite of the fact that most of these spokespersons were themselves against the war. They had a thought-out political position against organizing Blacks in the antiwar movement, and actively opposed such efforts. This was our major problem.

This attitude came partly from Black elected officials and others looking to the Democratic Party or to government agencies and the like for careers and favors. It was a question of "You don't bite the hand that feeds you." Opposition also came from the sectarian Black nationalist groups. At one point the Black Panther Party would say, the thing to do is to recruit and send Blacks to North Vietnam and fight with the Vietnamese against American troops. This was unrealistic and a rhetorical substitute for organizing the Black population against the war. Some leaders of the League of Revolutionary Black Workers would say the war had nothing to do with Black people. That was just turning their backs on the facts and missing an opportunity to take advantage of a serious weakness in the white power structure, which was in trouble with its war. The various polls always showed Blacks more heavily opposed to the war than whites.[11]

Omari Musa (then Herman Fagg) had helped organize the Third World Task Force in Washington for the April 24, 1971, demonstration. He had also helped to deflate the "Fauntroy Sixty," which did not ingratiate him with the city's Black Democrats (they were not exactly polite when they told him he wasn't welcome at the June 22 "summit"). He later commented on the general difficulty of bringing masses of Blacks into the antiwar movement:

Except for the Harlem feeder march on April 15, 1967, there was never a mass antiwar demonstration of Blacks as such. There were always demonstrations going on in the Black communities against the war, but these were small, a few hundred at most. The organizations that called them were almost always based on Black youth who were moving in an ultraleft direction. Even though they weren't necessarily confrontations, the rhetoric was ultraleft and couldn't appeal to broad numbers. Had Martin Luther King and Malcolm X stayed alive, that might have shortened the war, because their kind of authority tapped just about everybody in the Black community. Both King and Malcolm were against the war and might have been willing to do something about it. If they had done it together, that would have been exceptionally powerful and undoubtedly would have made both the antiwar movement and the struggle against racial injustice more effective.[12]

11. Author's taped interview with Maceo Dixon and Omari Musa, February 20, 1978.
12. Ibid.

Nixon presented himself for reelection during the 1972 campaign as the candidate most likely to end the war quickly and to bring about a general relaxation of tensions among the world powers. This was done with remarkable success judging from the public opinion polls before the election. And he did it while carrying out the heaviest bombing yet of Indochina. The summitry is only part of the explanation for his ability to get away with this swindle. The other major factor was the usual effect of the two-party electoral game in defusing and derailing the organized antiwar activity.

During the 1972 election campaign this factor was greatly magnified. In spite of the fact that the antiwar forces in the U.S. were horrified by the bombing, during the period between Nixon's May trip to Moscow and six weeks after the November elections, protest demonstrations were relatively small within the United States. Much of the organized antiwar movement abandoned independent activity and devoted itself to campaigning for dove candidates, particularly Senator George McGovern.

McGovern won the nomination handily on the first ballot July 13 at the Democratic Party convention and the Democratic leaders calculatingly attempted to identify the party and the convention with the mood of dissent in the country. Even Jerry Rubin showed up on the convention floor—as a reporter for the alternative press—and was interviewed on TV praising the show. The Democrats' object was to steer the activist protesters out of the streets and into the Democratic Party election campaign. They succeeded, by and large.

At its own convention in July, NPAC reaffirmed its nonpartisan position on candidates and called for a series of national actions before and shortly after the election, demanding an end to the bombing and immediate U.S. withdrawal. But it proved impossible to get any unified national call and the demonstrations were small, running only in the hundreds in most places. Momentary unity was achieved for one demonstration in Los Angeles, where 15,000 picketed the Century Plaza Hotel September 27 when Nixon was there for a fund-raising dinner.

PCPJ—which worked to turn out votes for McGovern—concentrated on the Republican Party convention in Miami in August as far as demonstrations were concerned. These activities were organized by the Miami Convention Coalition, which included PCPJ, the VVAW, a New York group called the Attica Brigade, and PL-SDS. Rennie Davis advertised them in the most exaggerated terms, sometimes predicting a million protesters. They did get a lot of publicity, but the turnout numbered three or four thousand at the height. Twelve hundred people were arrested, most on August 23 when over a thousand demonstrators blocked the approaches to the convention center.

The Indochina Peace Campaign was formed in this period by Jane Fonda and Tom Hayden. It sponsored a series of meetings, which attracted audiences in the thousands and usually featured Fonda, who had recently been to North Vietnam where she had witnessed the effects of the bombing and spoken to American GIs on Hanoi radio. After McGovern's nomination, the Indochina Peace Campaign concentrated its activities in several key states where the vote was expected to be crucial, in an attempt to assure a McGovern victory.

While many antiwar activists were devoting their energies to the McGovern campaign, his stated position on how to get out of the war became more and more indistinguishable from Nixon's. McGovern actively discouraged antiwar demonstrations, reneged on his previous statements for immediate withdrawal, and promised he would get the U.S. out of the war in Vietnam within ninety days of his inauguration if elected. Nixon kept claiming he would end it sooner than that.

The Democratic Party presidential campaign was not only plagued by the "dirty tricks" later uncovered in the Watergate scandal but was remarkably inept in itself. For instance, shortly after the nominations it was publicized that McGovern's vice-presidential choice, Senator Thomas Eagleton of Missouri, had in the distant past been hospitalized for a nervous breakdown. After declaring himself behind Eagleton "a thousand percent," McGovern replaced him in mid-campaign.

Having given up independent antiwar activity in pursuit of the illusion of ending the war through the Democratic Party, the organized antiwar forces supporting McGovern found themselves backing a candidate with a credibility gap that appeared— momentarily at least—as big as Nixon's and, what is more, a candidate the polls said had little chance to win. In the end, the Democrats were far outstripped by Nixon in their competing promises for peace.

The weeks preceding the election saw a flurry of diplomatic activity, including meetings between Henry Kissinger and North Vietnamese negotiators as well as between Kissinger and General Thieu in Saigon. The substance of the talks was secret but the whole world knew they were taking place. On October 22 the United States announced it was suspending air strikes over Hanoi and Haiphong and the rest of North Vietnam above the twentieth parallel. World capitals were rife with rumors that an agreement had been reached and a cease-fire in Indochina was imminent. Reporters in Washington virtually besieged the White House waiting for Nixon to announce peace to the American people.

On October 26, Radio Hanoi cut through the rumors and announced that an accord had indeed been reached October 20 which would be signed within a few days. At a press conference October 27 Henry Kissinger essentially confirmed this by declaring: "We believe that peace is at hand." In Saigon, General Thieu balked at the agreement, but according to the Nixon administration only a few "linguistic" details remained to be ironed out before the formal signing when the cease-fire would go into effect.

As McGovern hailed the development, there was virtually no difference left between the stated positions of the two major candidates on the issue that had secured McGovern the nomination and was expected to have been the crucial plank in his campaign. Except that Nixon was in power and appeared to have delivered on his promise.

Nixon won reelection November 7, carrying every state except Massachusetts. The significance of the election was anything but clear-cut. The Democratic Party retained its majority in both houses of Congress and gained two Senate seats in the process. The results showed no decisive changes and no distinctive trends to the right or left within the makeup of Congress.

It had certainly been an odd campaign. A man who was already the most isolated American president in modern times ran for reelection while the greatest scandal ever to hit the presidency had begun to unravel, presented himself as a lover of peace while carrying out the heaviest bombing in history in a war the majority of the people had repudiated, and carried the election in an unprecedented sweep while his own party lost ground. I leave it to supporters of the two-party system to explain that anomaly.

\*　　　　　\*　　　　　\*

The election came and went but the cease-fire accords still were not signed. Kissinger was obviously demanding additional concessions to shore up the Saigon regime. Meanwhile the bombing of Laos, Cambodia, and North- Vietnam south of the twentieth parallel continued apace. So did the ground fighting as each side tried to establish claim to as much territory as possible before the cease-fire. The accords, as revealed in October, called for a cease-fire in place upon the signing, withdrawal of U.S. military forces from South Vietnam within sixty days, and return of prisoners of war during the same period.

The political solution to the civil war in South Vietnam and the nature of the social system to be established there was essentially left up in the air. South Vietnam would be occupied by hostile Vietnamese armies, with the Thieu regime in control in some areas and the NLF in others. Many of the areas were in dispute. The accords also stipulated that the U.S. and North Vietnam would supply no additional military equipment to the respective sides, but that the equipment each possessed at the time of the cease-fire could be replaced piece for piece as used up.

As the secret negotiations over the final version of the accords dragged on, the U.S. flooded South Vietnam with new equipment, especially by air, to the point where the Saigon regime's air force suddenly became one of the four largest in the world in terms of aircraft, though not of trained mechanics and pilots. Reports appeared in the American press that thousands of U.S. instructors and advisers, under the technicality of being civilians working for private firms under contract to the U.S. Defense Department, would remain in Vietnam after the troop withdrawal. It was also made clear that the U.S. would maintain its bases in Thailand and its fleet off Vietnamese shores.

For six weeks after the election the world waited in expectation that the accords would be signed momentarily. During this period a sharp dispute occurred within the American antiwar movement, with NPAC continuing to raise the demand for total, immediate, and unconditional U.S. withdrawal—"Out Now"—and PCPJ demanding that Nixon "Sign the Agreement Now," or "Sign Now."

NPAC declared that if the accords were signed it would welcome the halt to the bombing and the withdrawal of U.S. troops, but that while Hanoi and the PRG had the right to make any agreement they felt necessary, the American antiwar movement should not endorse the concessions wrested by the U.S. from the Vietnamese by force.

PCPJ maintained that since Hanoi and the PRG had agreed to the accords, the important thing was to demand that Nixon sign them. The efforts of neither group evoked much following at this time.

Demonstrations for "Out Now" on November 18 had been planned months ahead by NPAC and were well prepared. They took place in twenty-one cities with the largest a march of 2,000 in New York. The mass of the American people considered U.S. involvement in the war virtually over, felt no urgency about it, and were not responding to antiwar calls no matter what the slogans. At a combined meeting of the steering committees of NPAC and SMC December 2, these groups—for the first time since their founding—decided not to press for mass demonstrations in the coming spring, at least for the time being.

The secret negotiations were broken off December 13 with Hanoi and the PRG still declaring they would sign the accords originally agreed to in October. On December 18 the U.S. resumed bombing north of the twentieth parallel. It soon became clear this was the worst bombing of the war, concentrating on Hanoi and Haiphong with B-52 bombers. The December 20 *Washington Post* reported:

> The B-52s are viewed as a terror weapon by many U.S. officials. The crushing raids have been cited as a psychological depressant. . . . Almost 100 B-52s and about 25 F-111s a day are hitting the North. . . . Neither plane has a reputation for pinpoint bombing.

In approximately ten days, 100,000 tons of bombs were dropped in these raids, the equivalent of five Hiroshima-type bombs. Hanoi and Haiphong had already been two-thirds evacuated, but the toll in human life was still severe. On December 26, for example, Kham Thien Street, one of Hanoi's major thoroughfares, was hit by B-52s. An Agence France-Presse dispatch from Hanoi reported that when clean-up squads got to the area, they found 1,445 bodies.[13]

On December 18, the Nixon administration acknowledged that the bombing of North Vietnam above the twentieth parallel was under way and warned that the raids "will continue until such

13. *New York Times*, January 8, 1973.

time as a settlement is arrived at."[14] Once again the light at the end of the tunnel had dimmed.

At an NPAC press conference the next day Jerry Gordon called for massive antiwar street demonstrations in major cities across the country and said that a date in January would shortly be announced for a coordinated national protest. A specific national focus was not immediately set in hopes of achieving a unified call, particularly with PCPJ. In view of the disagreement over the slogans "Out Now" and "Sign the Agreement Now," NPAC proposed a unified action around "End the Bombing, End the War" with each group free to raise the other slogans in banners and speeches. PCPJ spokespersons expressed difficulty with this.

\*           \*           \*

Some forces within PCPJ—particularly the Communist Party and some Maoist-oriented groups—had been insisting that there could be no cooperation with NPAC because it did not endorse the October accords and make "Sign the Agreement" a central demand. Ever since Nixon's trips to Peking and Moscow were completed, and before the October accords were announced, the same groups had taken a similar attitude with regard to the PRG's seven-point negotiating position. In both cases NPAC was slandered as being anti-PRG. In fact NPAC took no position on internal Vietnamese politics, only holding that the U.S. had no right to intervene and should cease its invasion and its support to the puppet Thieu government.

Neither NPAC nor the SWP ever criticized Hanoi or the PRG for agreeing to the accords. For its part the SWP unconditionally supported victory for Hanoi and the NLF-PRG against American imperialism and its puppet regime. At the same time the SWP had never been uncritical of the politics of Hanoi and the NLF. It frankly stated its disagreement with their statements that the accords were "just."

The victim of an armed robbery has every right to yield his wallet to save his life. For one reason or another—like the threat of being shot—he may even feel it necessary to declare that the robber has some rights in the disposition of the victim's property.

14. Ibid., December 19, 1972.

But it doesn't help for the victim's supporters to endorse that statement.

Since the Vietnamese were held in awe because of their heroic struggle, the pressure within the movement to uncritically accept everything attributed to them was especially strong. The American Stalinists of both the Maoist and Moscow-oriented varieties played upon this sentiment for all it was worth, insisting that the slightest criticism of the leadership of the Vietnamese revolution was tantamount to opposition to the Vietnamese revolution. This was in line with their standard methods of answering criticism from the left of Moscow and Peking: those who said that Moscow (or respectively, Peking) was wrong to wine and dine Nixon were called anti-Soviet (or anti-Chinese).

The SWPers were accustomed to bearing the brunt of that kind of Stalinist slander and standing up to it. There were some in the antiwar movement, however, who were intimidated by such accusations and drew back from common action in the face of the barrage of smears that NPAC was "anti-Vietnamese."

All this was a key factor in PCPJ's initial refusal to work together with NPAC in response to the Christmas bombing. In fact, the American CP—which like Moscow considered the maintenance of détente to be central and the Vietnamese revolution strictly secondary to it—did not initially want a major demonstration. The CP and the Maoists did not control PCPJ, but for the moment they had other forces within it hesitating.

*      *      *

NPAC refused to wait further and issued a call for a mass antiwar demonstration in Washington, D.C., to take place January 20, the day of Nixon's second inauguration. NPAC was then censured by some in PCPJ for acting unilaterally. In a December 26 letter to the PCPJ interim committee, Jerry Gordon explained:

we decided we had no other choice. When the bombing was resumed last week, we wanted to meet with you immediately, the same way we got together right after the May 8 blockade. We felt the situation was urgent and that a united response was imperative. However, when you told us that PCPJ was not prepared to meet with NPAC and that you would not consider the matter again until December 26, we could not wait. *The antiwar movement needed a focus* and those members of Congress calling for mass demonstrations coinciding with Inauguration Day were helping provide it. Our statement (enclosed) was framed to support their call for January 20 demonstrations, not to stake out a claim on the date for ourselves. There has been a fantastic response to the call, as the enclosed list of sponsors, secured in just a few hours, clearly shows. We had a picket line at the White House yesterday of 500-700 people, nearly all of whom evinced a real desire to help build the January 20 demonstration.

We are very anxious to move together with you in building mass antiwar demonstrations on January 20.[15]

After some soul-searching, the PCPJ leadership responded favorably and an agreement was reached for cosponsorship.

The CPers within PCPJ went along. This caught some of their own followers by surprise. For some time the CP leaders had been sensitive to the numerous reports and analytical articles appearing in the major media as well as movement periodicals to the effect that Moscow was not doing all it could to support Hanoi and was pressuring the North Vietnamese and the PRG to make concessions in the negotiations. Such statements in the *Wall Street Journal* and the Paris daily *Le Monde* were even characterized in the *Daily World* as "Trotskyite Nixonism."[16] NPAC and especially the SWP were special targets of the CP's tortured polemics on this point, but the criticism of Moscow was widespread within the movement and even popped up within CP ranks.

After NPAC and PCPJ—CPers included—began jointly building January 20, the CP found it necessary to explain its rather abrupt change. A statement by CP National Peace Commission Chairman Matthew Hallinan declared in part:

The question is not how bad are the Trotskyites but, rather, will certain forms of unity with them under certain conditions help to compel U.S. imperialism to end its oppression in Vietnam? . . . The Inauguration Day actions are a challenge to Nixon's attempt to interpret his election victory as a mandate for continuing the war. . . . Under these circum-

15. Lettter to interim committee, People's Coalition for Peace and Justice, from Jerry Gordon, December 26, 1972, emphasis in original. (Copy in author's files.)

16. An editorial in the January 6, 1973, *Daily World* said: "One strain of the Nixonite CBW [chemical-bacteriological warfare] is Trotskyite anti-Sovietism. It crops up in the oddest places, but is none the less noxious for that. . . . The Wall Street Journal said . . . in its editorial that 'peaceful overtures to Russia . . . have cut into Hanoi's . . . support.' That is Trotskyite Nixonism."

stances, the issue of what slogans are on the lead banner is not the central one. Indeed, the mass of the American people are not even aware of this debate over slogans.[17]

The latter observation at least was accurate.

Nevertheless, the dispute over slogans around the January 20 demonstration was not just a tempest in a teapot. It reflected the uneasiness around the world among those who followed the Stalinist ideology in the face of Peking's and Moscow's wooing of Nixon.

Lest Hallinan's statement be interpreted as conciliatory, it was accompanied by a campaign of systematic misrepresentations of the SWP position, typified by an article on the same page of the *Daily World* that carried Hallinan's piece. By Mike Zagarell, national education director of the YWLL, this was headed, "Trotskyite friends of Nixon's trickery." Wendy Reissner, then SWP antiwar director, commented:

They have been forced to whip their people up into identifying NPAC and the SWP as agents of Nixon, in order to stave off criticisms in their own ranks which are similar to criticisms that the SWP raises.[18]

*          *          *

The international revulsion at the escalation in the bombing was intense. Mass demonstrations occurred across Western Europe, the largest a march of 100,000 in Amsterdam supported by the major Dutch trade unions. Dozens of governments, including many closely allied with the U.S., felt compelled to protest publicly. Swedish Premier Olof Palme, generally cautious in publicly criticizing the U.S. government, declared on December 23:

Things should be called by their proper name. What happens today in

17. Matthew Hallinan, "Problems of the peace movement: Tactical flexibility urged for united antiwar action," *Daily World*, January 20, 1973.
18. "Edited Transcript of Antiwar Report to the Political Committee Meeting, January 26 [1973], by Wendy Reissner," SWP national office mailing to branch organizers and antiwar directors, February 5, 1973. (Copy in author's files.)

Vietnam is a form of torture. . . . What is being done is that a people are being tormented, that a nation is being tormented, to humiliate them to force them to submit to the language of force. That is why the bombings are an outrage.

There are many of this kind in modern history. They are often connected with names—Guernica, Oradour, Babi Yar, Katyn, Lidice, Sharpeville, Treblinka. Violence has triumphed, but the judgment of history has been hard on those who carried the responsibility. Now there is one more to add to the list—Hanoi, Christmas 1972.[19]

On December 29 the Australian Seaman's Union announced that the union's membership had voted to boycott U.S. flagships as long as the bombing of North Vietnam continued. This was supported by other Australian maritime unions. On January 4 representatives of thirty Australian unions handed a statement to the U.S. consulate general in Canberra threatening an intensification of action against U.S. interests in Australia if Nixon did not end the war soon. Until the previous year, Australia had troops fighting on the U.S. side in Vietnam.

In the Italian port of Genoa, dock workers declared a ban on all U.S. shipping. The action was taken independently of the union leadership. By the end of December boycotts were being observed in a half dozen other Italian ports. Dock workers in Denmark proposed a boycott of U.S. shipping throughout Europe and, according to the December 29 *Washington Post*, Thomas Nielson, head of the Danish union federation, announced that he planned to meet with other European labor leaders to coordinate actions.

American reaction was also strong. There were sizable emergency antiwar demonstrations in many places. Congressional doves began to stir again. Much of the major news media expressed shock and despair. The goodwill toward Nixon accompanying his victory evaporated.

Dissent appeared even among the B-52 crews involved in the operation. One factor was the relatively heavy losses of the giant planes, since antiaircraft defense was much better over Hanoi than elsewhere.

Between December 19 and 29 the North Vietnamese claimed as many as thirty-eight B-52s shot down; the Pentagon admitted fifteen. In any case over 10 percent of the operational B-52s in the

19. *Intercontinental Press*, January 15, 1973.

area were downed in less than two weeks, odds bad enough to give any air crew second thoughts, particularly when they felt no moral impulsion to make the sacrifice.

"The flight crews are different now," wrote *New York Times* correspondent Richard Halloran from Guam, where most of the area's B-52s were based. "Before, when they came back, they were always clowning around. Now they're shaken. They just get out of the plane and into the bus and go to the debriefing."[20] According to the *Times* account, some flyers refused to go up.

There are reports here [the dispatch continued] that members of flight crews have deliberately caused some of the complicated electronic machinery aboard a bomber to break down and thus cancel a mission. Some have reportedly neglected to arm the bombs so that they would not explode after they were dropped.

The December 30 *Times* also reported that antiwar activists on Guam had been "harassing" navy trucks carrying the bombs through the island. "A young Navy petty officer in civilian clothes was arrested this week for that," the *Times* reported. "He was asked whether he belonged to an antiwar group. 'No,' he said, 'I just don't like bombs.'"

In face of the world opposition to his move, Nixon backed off a bit. On December 30 the White House announced cessation of the bombing north of the twentieth parallel and said it would resume the secret talks in Paris.

At a press conference later the same day Jerry Gordon declared the January 20 antiwar demonstrations would go ahead as scheduled anyway.

On January 2, the eve of the formal opening of the Ninety-third Congress, congressional doves at last threatened to try to cut off funds for the war if the administration did not quickly obtain a peace settlement. The House Democratic caucus voted 154 to 75 to declare its policy in favor of ending U.S. military operations in Vietnam "immediately," subject only to arrangements for the safe withdrawal of U.S. troops and the return of prisoners of war. Senate Foreign Relations Committee Chairman Fulbright said the members of the committee were determined "that the legislative powers of the Congress should be brought to bear" if peace

20. *New York Times*, December 30, 1972.

had not been negotiated by the inauguration.[21]

In spite of repeated predictions by the administraton that a cease-fire was imminent, the antiwar forces continued to mobilize for the counterinaugural "March Against Death" as it was called. Several dozen members of Congress endorsed the Washington demonstration.

In mid-January the administration made another of its dramatic announcements—this one from Nixon's retreat at Key Biscayne—that the bombing was being further restricted and that an accord would soon be reached. The official Inaugural Committee executive director, Jeb Stuart Magruder, declared at a press conference that three congressional doves had been "actively discussing with these [counterinaugural] groups, seeking to generate from them other than peaceful demonstrations."[22]

NPAC and PCPJ replied that the administration was obviously trying to defuse the antiwar sentiment again and smear the demonstration in an attempt to frighten people away. "Nixon wishes to get past the inauguration without a hitch," said Sid Peck at a joint press conference January 16 with Jerry Gordon.[23]

A service at the National Presbyterian Church, called the "Inauguration of Conscience," was scheduled for Sunday, January 21, by opponents of the war. It received prestigious endorsement. As part of the official inauguration celebrations a concert was scheduled the night before at the Kennedy Center with Eugene Ormandy conducting Tchaikovsky's "1812 Overture." Counterinaugural forces got some musical reinforcement when Leonard Bernstein announced he would do a different concert at the same time at the National Cathedral conducting "Haydn's Mass in Time of War."

Washington columnist Mary McGrory commented:

> Four years ago, when Richard Nixon was first inaugurated, Rennie Davis ran a grubby little counter-encampment and was condemned by one and all for failing to grasp the conventional wisdom that "Nixon knows he's got to end it." Four years, 20,000 U.S. combat losses, two invasions and one savage Christmas bombing later, serious attention is being paid to counter-inaugural activities, even, it would seem, by the recluse in the White House.[24]

21. *New York Times*, January 3, 1973.
22. *Washington Post*, January 17, 1973.
23. Ibid.
24. *New York Post*, January 16, 1973.

(Nixon had made no public appearances since the Christmas bombing began.)

The night of January 19, 15,000 people attended the counter-inaugural concert at the National Cathedral.

The next day the antiwar demonstration drew over 100,000 participants. The inauguration ceremony itself—which was viewed by 20,000—took place at the east face of the capitol and was followed by the official inauguration parade northwestward along Pennsylvania Avenue to the White House. Earlier, a mile or so to the southwest, the antiwar marchers assembled at the Lincoln Memorial and proceeded east along Constitution Avenue to Fifteenth Street where they looped south and doubled back into the Washington Monument area for a huge rally.

Theoretically there was to be no contact between the two events, and, unlike four years before, there was no attempt to disrupt the inaugural parade, no attacks by police or troops, and no trashing. But when Jerry Gordon led the larger gathering in a chant of "Out Now!" it could be heard at the inaugural ceremonies a half mile away. Thousands of antiwar protesters left their own demonstration early to make their way to the sidelines of the inaugural parade, where they stood along the route holding signs and sporting antiwar buttons.

In major cities across the country there were other large demonstrations against the American role in Vietnam, and still others around the world. Nixon's electoral victory had turned sour before his second term in office was a day old.

On January 23, 1973, the American president appeared on television to announce that a cease-fire agreement had been reached. It was essentially the same as the October accords and went into effect with the formal signing on January 27. The American bombing of the NLF areas of South Vietnam continued until the moment of signing. The accords did not provide an immediate cease-fire in Laos and Cambodia, and the American bombing of those countries continued.

# 27

# The End of the War

The January 27, 1973, accords were formally called the Agreement on Ending the War and Restoring Peace in Vietnam. Nevertheless, the civil war in South Vietnam raged for two more years with over 300,000 additional Vietnamese on both sides being killed. In announcing the accords, Nixon declared, "The United States will continue to recognize the Government of the Republic of Vietnam [the Thieu regime] as the sole legitimate government of South Vietnam."[1] Though the U.S. bombing of Vietnam was stopped, and the remaining 23,000 U.S. troops withdrawn on schedule by the end of March 1973, the U.S. continued to support the Thieu regime in its attempts to hold back the revolution.

The U.S. assigned a huge number of military attachés to its embassy in South Vietnam as well as a core of "civilian advisers" and technicians, many of them West Point graduates. These numbered from four to ten thousand men, according to various estimates. In addition, the total of tanks, planes, and other military equipment technically possessed by the Thieu regime as of the signing of the accords was so large that the amount of "replacement" equipment the U.S. could still send to Vietnam under the terms of the agreement was virtually unlimited.

In one sense, then, by April 1973 history had come full circle. Superficially, the U.S. was in very much the same position in South Vietnam it had been in during 1960, providing a few thousand "advisers" and large military and financial aid to the

1. *New York Times*, January 25, 1973.

counterrevolutionary regime. In other respects, of course, the situation had changed. The Saigon regime's armed forces were no more reliable than they had ever been, but they were much larger, now numbering over a million, and much better equipped than in the early 1960s. On the other hand, the NLF forces in South Vietnam were now augmented with main-force units of the North Vietnamese army which stayed in the South under the terms of the accords. Though these together numbered only a fraction of the Saigon regime's troops, the NVA-NLF soldiers were much more highly motivated and had already proved themselves to be among the best fighters in the world.

General Thieu made it clear he expected more direct U.S. military intervention—including U.S. bombing—if he got into serious military trouble. Public statements by the Nixon administration strongly implied this threat, and Thieu would later provide documentation that Nixon had assured him of such backing.

Perhaps the most crucial change in the situation between the early 1960s and the 1973-74 period was within the United States itself, where the accumulated experience of the previous twelve years had produced an overwhelming sentiment against further U.S. intervention.

In the early 1960s the American people were largely ignorant of what was going on in Indochina and naively trusted their government. By 1973, the authority of the national leadership, and particularly of the presidency, was badly tattered. The American people were not willing to trust the government in another venture in Vietnam. To most of them, the United States had pulled out of Vietnam definitively by the summer of 1973, and the very idea of getting back in was anathema.

This made it very dangerous for Washington to re-escalate American involvement. There is no question but that any such move would have had explosive repercussions domestically. By the same token the widespread feeling that the U.S. was definitively out made it unrealistic to expect or attempt massive antiwar mobilizations. The organized antiwar movement was willy-nilly again reduced to a dedicated core which, though it now operated in a highly sympathetic atmosphere, necessarily had its activities reduced to a very modest scale.

As the possibilities for large-scale antiwar activity receded, many individuals who had for years interrupted their regular careers or jobs to participate in its organization returned to their more ordinary pursuits, myself included. We lived, after all, in a workaday world, and neglected families needed attention, not to mention accumulated bills and debts. Others struck out in entirely new directions. For instance, around the time the accords were signed, Rennie Davis dropped rather precipitately out of the movement to take a pilgrimage to India, after which he devoted his talents to organizing mass meetings and collections for a religious sect headed by the fifteen-year-old "Perfect Master," Maharaj-Ji.

NPAC and the SMC maintained skeletal structures to the end of the war, occasionally calling smaller demonstrations or teach-ins. As these groups saw it, their main function was to maintain the potential of renewed mass demonstrations in the event of another intervention by U.S. bombers or troops.

PCPJ, which viewed itself as a multi-issue coalition, attempted to play a role in the building of some sort of new radical populist movement, with little success. Its most significant action was a multi-issue demonstration of several thousand in Washington, D.C., on June 16, 1973, around the theme "Funds for Life, Not Death." NPAC supported this demonstration, emphasizing the demand to halt the bombing of Cambodia.

By then it had become clear that the Nixon regime was in a major crisis over the Watergate affair. One of the speakers in Washington was Anthony Russo, who had recently been acquitted on charges stemming from his part in making public the Pentagon Papers. "We have to realize," declared Russo, "that the antiwar movement brought about Watergate. . . . We didn't realize the power the movement has. We didn't realize that we were driving the government up the wall."[2]

At the time of this demonstration the U.S. was still bombing Cambodia but had stopped bombing Laos, where a tenuous coalition government had been agreed to. By midsummer 1973, Congress was no longer in awe of a weakened presidency and balked at funding continued U.S. bombing anywhere in Indochina. Nixon was forced to accept a compromise that ended the U.S. bombing of Cambodia by August 15, though U.S. pilots semisecretly still flew illegal reconnaissance flights over all three Indochinese countries.

In the fall of 1973 a number of PCPJ leaders participated in an ad hoc American delegation to the World Peace Conference that

2. *Militant,* June 29, 1973.

was held that year in Moscow. (NPAC was not invited, incidentally.) At the conference's commission on social progress and human rights a statement critical of the state of civil liberties in the Soviet Union was read by Paul Mayer of PCPJ over concerted attempts to interrupt him. The statement said in part: "We support the Soviet dissidents in their demands for free speech and assembly." It was signed by PCPJ leaders Mayer, Dave Dellinger, Sid Peck, and Dave McReynolds as well as by Grace Paley, Noam Chomsky, and Daniel Berrigan. (Of the seven signers, only Mayer and Paley attended the conference.) The American CPers who dominated this particular American delegation roundly denounced the statement and pushed through the delegation a vote of 67 to 31 to censure Mayer.[3] Subsequently the divided PCPJ faded away.

Virtually all the local antiwar coalitions also folded up or transformed themselves into something else during this period. The traditional radical and pacifist groups, of course, carried on in their own right, after emphasizing amnesty for those who faced punitive measures for resisting the war, as did the VVAW. Groups such as the Indochina Resource Center carried on their information activity. Probably the most visible antiwar group during 1974 was the Indochina Peace Campaign, which organized a large number of mass meetings on campuses. Usually Jane Fonda and Daniel Ellsberg spoke, and folksinger Holly Near sang. I attended one such meeting at Fisk University near Boston in the fall of 1974. It took place in the gymnasium, which was packed with several thousand people, mostly young, with a large part of the audience sitting on the floor of the basketball court. In the lobby was displayed a sample of the notorious "tiger cages" in which the Thieu regime kept some of its political prisoners.

The speeches were effective, especially Ellsberg's, which held the audience despite its length and unstructured style. Among other things, he emphasized the importance of distrusting the government on foreign policy and pointed out how effective the mass antiwar demonstrations had been in staying the hands of the war-makers.

In the two years following the signing of the accords, then, the American antiwar movement was no longer involved with mass mobilizations. Its organized structures shrank and its activities were mainly informational. They served to undercut any at-

3. *New York Times,* October 30, 1973.

tempts by the government to refurbish its shattered excuses for
another large-scale intervention in Vietnam. And the threat of
renewed mass mobilizations and a domestic explosion in the
event of an attempt to go in again hung like the sword of
Damocles over the head of the American Establishment.

\*        \*        \*

In an article on the situation in Vietnam in the January 1975
issue of *Foreign Affairs,* conservative analyst Maynard Parker
pointed out that "almost from the moment the 1973 agreement
was signed, President Thieu took to the offensive in an attempt to
eradicate the Communists in spots." Maynard cited a speech by
Thieu on January 4, 1974, in which the general ordered his army
to "hit them in their base areas." This signaled a second phase in
which there was a marked increase in large-scale offensive
operations by the Saigon regime and stiff resistance by the other
side. The PRG base areas were strengthened with airfields,
pipelines to supply fuel from the North, and heavy antiaircraft to
protect the installations.

Meanwhile the already impaired authority of the Nixon White
House deteriorated steadily under the impact of the Watergate
scandal. In June 1973 John Dean gave five days of detailed
testimony to the Senate on the attempted coverup of the Watergate conspiracy from his knowledge as counsel to the president.
He implicated not only the White House staff and the Committee
to Reelect the President, but Attorney General Mitchell, the
Justice Department, and the oval office (occupied by the president) itself.

Dean also testified that the sight of a single picket with an
antiwar banner outside the White House had been enough to
disturb the president's peace of mind.

On October 10, 1973, Vice President Spiro T. Agnew—the
champion of "law and order"—was forced to resign in disgrace
for having been caught taking payoffs from businessmen seeking
favors. He confessed to having failed to list as taxable income
some $100,000 of payoff money. After protracted plea bargaining,
Agnew was allowed to plead no contest to the lesser income-tax
charge and received no prison sentence; his resignation and
publication of the facts of the payoffs as part of the court record
were part of the deal. Michigan Congressman Gerald R. Ford, the

House Republican leader, was appointed vice president.

The Watergate scandal continued to unravel and by mid-1974 the initial phases of impeachment proceedings were under way in Congress. On August 9, 1974, Nixon became the only U.S. president in history to resign. Ford took over and former New York Governor Nelson Rockefeller was appointed vice president. Henry Kissinger stayed on as secretary of state.

The Ford administration continued heavy aid to the Saigon and Phnompenh regimes. But in early 1975 the military tide turned against both U.S. client governments.

On January 7, Phuocbinh, capital of Phuoclong province, was taken by the PRG forces. The rest of the province had for years been controlled by the PRG, and militarily Phuocbinh was like an overripe fruit waiting to be plucked. The Pentagon and White House seized on the incident to campaign for increased aid to Thieu. On January 8 it was announced that Ford would ask Congress for an additional $300 million for Saigon on top of the $700 million already appropriated for the fiscal year. An extra $220 million was requested for Lon Nol in Cambodia. In addition, a naval task force headed by the nuclear-powered carrier *Enterprise* set sail from Subic Bay in the Philippines for Vietnamese waters and another headed by the carrier *Midway* sailed from Japan. On January 14 Washington announced that it felt free to openly violate the cease-fire accords, claiming that Hanoi and the PRG had already done so.

While Congress debated the appropriation requests, the military position of the Lon Nol regime in Cambodia began to collapse. By mid-March the American embassy was evacuating most of its personnel in Phnompenh. No longer awed by an all-powerful presidency and reluctant to send good money after bad, Congress voted down the additional military appropriations.

Around the same time heavy fighting developed near the provincial capital of Ban Me Thuot in the central highlands. The PRG-NVA forces took the city and General Thieu ordered it retaken "at any cost." Then he reversed himself and ordered a strategic retreat from the central highlands and some adjacent provinces.

The retreat became a rout. Discipline broke down as the ARVN rushed toward the coastal cities in hopes of evacuation toward the south. ARVN soldiers and officers fought American "advisers" as well as civilians associated with the Thieu regime for places on planes and ships.

Hanoi and the PRG were taken by surprise at the rapidity of the dissolution of the Saigon forces. Their units maintained good order in pursuit of the ARVN, but in many places they couldn't keep up and the PRG underground took over to maintain order as the Saigon forces fled or simply disintegrated. Hue fell, and then the major coastal cities followed one by one, without a fight.

The U.S. puppet regimes in Cambodia and South Vietnam were collapsing at the same time. The Khmer Rouge troops entered Phnompenh on April 17 after Lon Nol fled by air. Meanwhile, as the ARVN retreated in South Vietnam, huge stockpiles of U.S.-supplied weapons fell into PRG-NVA hands. Suddenly, it became clear that without a massive reintroduction of American troops, it was all over for the Thieu regime and for the American effort in South Vietnam. A sustained propaganda campaign was mounted within the United States about an alleged impending bloodbath against several hundred thousand Vietnamese who had cooperated with the Americans. Proposals were bandied about to send in as many as 90,000 U.S. troops, on the pretext that they would be needed to prevent the "bloodbath" while the remaining Americans and a couple of hundred thousand Vietnamese were evacuated.

As it turned out, the Saigon regime melted away too fast for any such plans to be seriously considered. There was no bloodbath as the PRG-NVA forces restored order to the areas they occupied while the Americans and over 100,000 Vietnamese were evacuated.

Part of the U.S. propaganda effort to save face in this situation was a plan called "Operation Babylift" to airlift thousands of Vietnamese "orphans" to the United States for adoption. Most Vietnamese reacted with disgust and anger, including officials of the doomed Saigon regime, especially when it was revealed that some of the "orphans" had living parents.

The PRG described "Operation Babylift" as "kidnapping on a vast scale" and the project was denounced by the International Red Cross and an official of the Vatican's relief organization, Caritas. The airlift itself was conducted in a hasty, callous, and unsafe manner. The first plane carrying the "orphans" crashed on April 4, killing over 100 children; President Ford was left waiting in vain at the airport in the U.S. to greet the plane's arrival. Nevertheless, he had the gall to pursue the project and have himself photographed holding a Vietnamese baby at the door of another plane after it landed in the U.S. Several of the babies died on the long air trip for lack of proper care.

\*            \*            \*

On April 10 President Ford made a speech requesting Congress to grant an additional $1 billion in military and economic aid to Vietnam to be supplied by April 19. There was no technical possibility that this could be done, and no chance that Congress would agree anyway. During the last week in April the PRG forces lobbed a few shells into Saigon's Tansonnhut airport to give the Americans a final nudge.

Meanwhile sporadic demonstrations broke out in the United States demanding total, immediate withdrawal of the U.S. from Vietnam. A demonstration for jobs had already been scheduled for April 26 in Washington by important sections of the labor movement. NPAC and the Washington Area Peace Action Coalition helped build this demonstration and called on antiwar activists and unionists to include demands against any continuation of the war. The demonstration drew 60,000, and several New York unions led a short march from the capitol to the stadium featuring numerous signs demanding "Jobs, Not War."

The very fact that this demonstration was on schedule during the April days provided an obvious potential focus for an emergency outpouring of antiwar outrage if the government had been so foolish as to have attempted to rescue the Saigon regime at the last hour.

By April 27, Thieu himself had fled Vietnam. On April 30, 1975 (April 29 in the U.S.), the last American troops in Vietnam—marines guarding the U.S. embassy—were airlifted off the roof of the building. Less than four hours later the PRG forces marched into downtown Saigon. The American-sponsored bloodbath in Vietnam was finally over.

# Afterword

The Second Indochina War was the first in the epoch of American imperialism in which the United States went down to defeat. After emerging victorious from the Spanish-American War and two world wars, then encountering a stalemate in Korea, the Pentagon's military machine was ignominiously evicted from Vietnam, thanks to the persevering struggle of the Indochinese plus the antiwar resistance of the American people. This was the most sustained and, except for Russia in 1905 and 1917, the most effective antiwar movement within any big power while the shooting was going on.

The official propagandists cooked up various formulas to justify their military intervention. It was depicted as a crusade for democracy and freedom against the threat of communist totalitarianism and for the defense of the independence of the South against invasion from the North. The U.S. was there, it was said, to fulfill treaty obligations to the client Saigon regime and thwart the expansionism of China and the Soviet Union. Toward the end the excuses became exceedingly thin: to assure the return of the POWs; to prevent a bloodbath in the South if the NLF should take over completely; to protect U.S. troops as they were withdrawn. All this was demagogy.

In reality, U.S. intervention had a thoroughly imperialistic character. The colossus of world capitalism hurled its military might without provocation against a small and divided colonial nation thousands of miles away struggling for self-determination and unification. A series of American presidents sought to do what King George III's empire failed to do against the rebel patriots of 1776.

On one side was a state armed to the teeth promoting the strategic aims and material interests of the corporate rich on the global arena; on the other was a worker and peasant uprising heading toward the overthrow of capitalist power and property, despite the limited political program of its leadership.

These underlying anticapitalist and antilandlord tendencies were eventually clearly expressed in the reunification of Vietnam in 1976 and the process of eliminating capitalist property relations in the South. The prolonged civil war in South Vietnam thereby proved to be an integral part of the international confrontation between the upholders of capitalism and the forces moving in a socialist direction that has been unfolding since the October 1917 Bolshevik revolution.

Apart from genocide against the Native Americans, which involved intermittent warfare over four centuries, this was the longest war in America's history. The first U.S. soldier was reported killed in Vietnam in 1959, the last in 1975, a span of sixteen years. (The Revolutionary War lasted eight years and the Spanish-American War only four months.)

According to the U.S. Department of Defense, the total number of American military personnel engaged at one time or another in the Southeast Asian war—including bases in Thailand and elsewhere and on ships at sea—was over eight million. This was more than half the number of Americans engaged in World War II (8,744,000 compared with 16,112,566). Over three million Americans were sent to Vietnam itself. Sixty thousand were killed, 46,000 of these in combat; and 300,000 were wounded. (The ratio of seriously wounded and permanently disabled to killed, incidentally, was much higher among Americans in Vietnam than in previous wars, owing largely to advanced techniques of removing casualties quickly to hospitals.)

The Indochinese were killed in the hundreds of thousands, possibly millions, and their lands devastated. The Pentagon dropped more bomb tonnage on the relatively small area of Indochina than had been dropped anywhere in the world in all previous wars combined.

The direct dollar cost to the U.S. in South Vietnam alone was $141 billion. This was more than $7,000 for each of the area's 20 million inhabitants, whose per capita income was only $157 per year. The collateral expenditures amounted to far more. Economists correctly link the rapid inflation of the late 1960s to the large federal deficits resulting from U.S. spending for the Vietnam War.

Most Americans today regard this as a colossal waste of lives and wealth in a shameful war. But the Pentagon strategists make a different assessment. To be sure, they did not cover themselves with glory or succeed in crushing the Vietnamese revolution and retaining a staging area for U.S. operations in the region. But they did hold back the advancement of the colonial revolution in Vietnam for a decade and a half. That was part of their job of policing the world for American big business, its multinational companies, and its clients in Japan and elsewhere.

In the early sixties the vast majority of Americans ignored the war, or accommodated themselves to it, though without much patriotic fervor. It seemed remote from their immediate concerns, something which they knew little or nothing about and left trustingly to their government. That was still a time of confidence in the wisdom and honesty of the top political leaders and above all in the benevolent intentions of the occupants of the White House. The Washington policy makers took cruel advantage of this naiveté.

Without exaggeration, most Americans were hardly aware that Vietnam existed when the Truman, Eisenhower, and Kennedy administrations were stealthily pulling them step by step into the bloody quagmire. The Democrats and Republicans jointly carried out the "bipartisan foreign policy" in Southeast Asia and rubber-stamped it in Congress while the major media that molded public opinion—and kept it uninformed—gave no warning of what was ahead.

The antiwar movement began with people who were already radicalized: pacifists, socialists, communists, rebellious students, and a scattering of morally outraged individuals. At the start these were a small minority, convinced of the justness of their cause and ready to face unpopularity for their stand. The energy, resoluteness, and fortitude of this vanguard brought the movement into being and remained its prime mover.

The most paradoxical aspect of this profound and unforgettable chapter of American history was the central and decisive role played by the left-wing elements, which included the radical pacifists. When it began, it was almost unthinkable that they could set in motion and head a movement of such vast scope. They themselves did not really expect such a development. They just felt obliged to do whatever they could.

At the beginning of the sixties the American left—old and new—was looked upon as an esoteric fringe with virtually negligible influence. So far as numbers in radical organizations were concerned, this was close to the truth. The cold war and the witch-hunting atmosphere, in conjunction with the prolonged prosperity of the 1950s, had decimated their ranks. Even after their numbers increased manyfold during the sixties and early seventies, the tens of thousands directly supporting the various radical groupings were not very large compared to the entire population.

Yet this unrespectable, "irrelevant," and by no means homogeneous band became "the saving remnant" as it moved into the vacancy left by the established educational, religious, labor union, journalistic, and political institutions. These were tied in with the two-party system and went along with the generals and the State Department, supporting a perfectly obviously illegal and unjust war to one extent or another.

On closer examination this is not so surprising. For only those who were prepared ideologically to defy pervasive, blind conformity could take the risk of overt opposition. If the number of such Americans was so small in the early sixties, this testified less to the irrelevance of the radicals than to the marginal place that deepgoing criticism occupied under the profound corruption and advanced senility of the two-party system.

The movement later made its impact upon that system, as the proliferation of dove Democrats and Republicans showed. But the dove politicians didn't lead, they followed, far behind, stumbling and mumbling all the way. There has since been some deft distorting of the record on this point, but the attempted rehabilitation is belied by the facts.

Only two senators, Morse and Gruening, voted against the Tonkin Gulf resolution which gave Johnson the green light in 1964. A single member of the House, Adam Clayton Powell, registered some sort of dissent by abstaining. Others knew something was wrong. But they were also aware that to avoid "irrelevance" within the two-party system you don't go around offending the powers-that-be and challenging "reasons of state" on grounds of human decency or anything of that sort. Morse, Gruening, and Powell were all knifed by their national party leadership and never won another election. Even after the dramatic switch in the public attitude made dovishness permissible on Capitol Hill, the vast majority in both parties—doves included—consistently voted for the Vietnam military budget up to 1973.

Insofar as the Democratic and Republican doves contributed to the spread of antiwar sentiment—and some of them did by lending their authority occasionally to antiwar activities, publicizing certain facts about the war, and so on—their activities were contradicted by their steering people toward the two parties that supported the war and by their effective votes in Congress.

The issue was not resolved, or even ameliorated, through the two-party electoral process. On the contrary, the election periods were used to precisely the opposite effect. They served to hoodwink the antiwar feelings, defuse antiwar protests, and give the war-makers some extra maneuverability in their pernicious and ill-fated plans. That happened with every congressional and presidential election from 1964, when Johnson ran as a "peace" candidate, to 1972, when the Nixon administration announced that "peace is at hand" and then, after the election, went ahead with another "brutalization" of the Vietnamese population.

Those who retain or preach faith in the reformability of the capitalist two-party system must reckon with the fact that the American movement against the Vietnam War—the greatest moral resurgence in the U.S. since the struggle to abolish slavery—had to arise and maintain itself apart from and in defiance of both parties.

Beyond their agreement in opposing the war, the initiators of the movement held discordant views on many matters and advocated different, and even conflicting, methods. At every point along the road they had to thrash out their principled strategic and tactical differences in order to arrive at unified and concerted action. This was rarely easy and not always possible.

It was necessary to reestablish a tradition of toleration for differences of opinion and a taboo on vitriolic and slanderous polemic. These amenities had been absent for decades in relations between American left-wing groups, ever since the destruction of the old tradition by the Stalinized Communist Party. The tone set by the radical pacifists influenced by A. J. Muste played a salutary role in this respect.

At times some of the latter, however, were uncomfortable with serious polemic itself and downright appalled by the parliamentary maneuvering—however open, aboveboard, and by-the-rules it was—that inevitably attends purposeful debate where disputed questions have to be settled one way or another. But the clash of ideas, and the deliberate efforts to convince people to take sides, was inevitable and essential for practical decision. No amount of "love and trust" would either eliminate or substitute for this contest. The alternative was to leave decisions to prophets and saints, which none of us were.

In the beginning, the movement came to grips with three internal policy problems that were interconnected: red-baiting, nonexclusion, and democratic decision-making.

Red-baiting had to be cleared away so that Marxists and revolutionaries of any persuasion would not be barred from openly participating on an equal footing in all the movement's activities and on its leading bodies. This was a vital part of positioning the movement to stand up to the inevitable barrage of red-baiting from the war-makers and combatting the anticommunist hysteria on which toleration of the war itself was psychologically based. Red-baiting was explicitly rejected and frowned upon early in the movement's development. It had to be so for any concerted efforts to go forward at all. Although this bugaboo cropped up now and then, it never again caught on.

This openness to the left involved a break with the cold-war, anticommunist ideology that had saturated the fabric of American thought since shortly after World War II. The antiwar movement took this head-on with the acknowledgment that every shade of opinion had full citizenship rights within it and none were to be penalized for their political affiliations or views. This percolated through wider and wider circles until eventually the way of thinking in the country was significantly altered.

The setback given to red-baiting was one of the outstanding achievements of the antiwar movement.

This was all the more remarkable considering that "the enemy" was Communist-led and backed by the Soviet Union and China. Under the circumstances it might well have been expected that new waves of anticommunist vehemence would easily have been stirred up. Yet the attempts to do so met with little response and had minimal effect. The same was true of efforts by the jingoistic forces to mount prowar, anticommunist demonstrations. The revulsion against the war proved more powerful than the anticommunist tirades and the pseudopatriotic demagogy.

The policy of nonexclusion came into effect along with the rejection of red-baiting. No "loyalty oaths" were demanded or restrictions imposed on anyone opposed to the war on any grounds. The sole requirement was a readiness to protest and act against the war. This rule had to be enforced on two fronts. Certain skittish moderates tried to bar the left or ultralefts from the coalitions. On the other hand, some sectarian groups clamored for the expulsion of liberal politicians and figures who were willing to join in common action within the framework of the antiwar protests. The movement would not have grown as it did and drawn millions into activity unless it had abided by the principle of nonexclusion.

The procedure of democratic decision-making was best exemplified at the periodic national and regional antiwar conferences, open to all. There the issues were publicly debated and reported. These were also important arenas for the presentation and exchange of ideas on a wide variety of issues. Any group was welcome to set up literature tables, distribute circulars, hold workshops, and so on. There were those—like Dave Dellinger— who disparaged parliamentary debate and large decision-making bodies and preferred small gatherings of selected leaders. Even these were never secret but were open to observers and publicly reported. The mainstream antiwar movement conducted its affairs and arrived at its proposals for action in a goldfish bowl.

By contrast, the Washington war-makers made their decisions behind the backs and without the concurrence of the people. One striking example is cited in the Pentagon Papers as summarized by the *New York Times:*

the Johnson Administration, though the President was reluctant and hesitant to take the final decisions, intensified the covert warfare against North Vietnam and began planning in the spring of 1964 to wage overt war, a full year before it publicly revealed the depth of its involvement and its fear of defeat.[1]

*In the spring of 1964,* that is, while President Johnson was running for reelection as a "peace" candidate.

The conspirators were seated in power in Washington, while the antiwar movement planned its activities in front of the

1. *The Pentagon Papers: As Published by the New York Times* (New York: Bantam, 1971), p. xi.

masses. This did not prevent the government from indicting movement personalities on charges of conspiracy. Though none of the major trials were won by the prosecutors after appeal, they exacted a heavy toll from the individual defendants and taxed the resources of the movement.

In addition, the authorities resorted to the types of repression very inadequately described in the preceding chapters. It would take another volume to outline the victimizations, break-ins, thefts, illegal surveillance, provocations, including violent ones, FBI-fabricated forgeries designed to foment hostility between groups and individuals, arrests, jailings, frame-ups, beatings, kidnappings, shootings, court-martials, bad-conduct discharges, and assorted "dirty tricks" that were used against the antiwar forces—and not just under Nixon. The antiwar movement was "Watergated" from the beginning, and with a vengeance.

In the face of all this, and in light of the entirely justified and extreme anger against the war-makers, the lack of violence on the part of the antiwar movement in the United States is among its noteworthy features. Indeed, its record in this respect is exceptional in the history of social upheavals in the United States. Throughout, the mainstream of the movement rejected violent confrontation as a tactic for the antiwar forces and effectively combatted any tendency along that line.

For differing philosophical and political reasons, the pacifists and Trotskyists were the most consistent supporters of this approach. Brad Lyttle made the following comment on this in 1969:

It may seem odd, but it is true that today the Trotskyists are one of the most powerful forces working to give the anti-war movement a peaceful and orderly character.[2]

That didn't seem odd to me.

For eight of the fifteen years of the war the antiwar movement engaged in continuous street actions one place or another across the country. Yet through the entire fifteen years, while the U.S. government was killing hundreds of thousands in Indochina, not a single person was killed by antiwar demonstrators in the United States.

2. Bradford Lyttle, *Washington Action, Nov. 13-15, 1969* (New York, 1970), p. 15. (Copy in author's files.)

Equally important was the fact that the killings of antiwar activists by the authorities—an ever-present danger—were held to a minimum because of the policy of keeping the onus for violence upon the war-makers and their servitors.

Though the makings for violent clashes were present in every major demonstration, they were consciously counteracted by the organizers and usually fizzled out in minor scuffles and "trashings." Even in the wing of the movement that went in for confrontation, tactical nonviolence was generally adhered to, largely upon the insistence of the pacifists. While such demonstrations were sometimes stormy, the lethal weapons were in the hands of the police, and the injured were almost always protesters.

Even the handfuls who advocated terrorism and excluded themselves from the mainstream antiwar movement over this issue were sufficiently affected by the predominant spirit to confine their bombings to empty buildings or statues. In one case such a group allegedly set off a bomb in an installation connected with military research at the University of Wisconsin that exploded and killed an antiwar graduate student who was unexpectedly in the building. Aside from this incident, members of these groups killed only themselves, in accidental explosions.

Of course, in the war zone itself it was a different story. There the Pentagon had a total monopoly on setting the tone, teaching the methods, and providing the means. Some of the outraged and desperate GIs whom the brass had urged to kill, used the weapons at hand to slay and terrorize their own officers to avoid dying themselves or slaughtering Vietnamese in their own land. No more need be said.

The mass antiwar movement was first of all a generational phenomenon, since the youth were being drafted and doing the fighting and dying. This was its most urgent aspect. The movement competed with the Establishment for the allegiance of the American youth. The government had to conscript them or force their enlistment under the hot breath of the draft. The movement gained their voluntary participation and backing by appealing to their sense of self-preservation, consciences, and deep convictions. It won this contest hands down, and as more and more youth entered the armed forces they carried with them the ferment of antiwar ideas.

Although many were the beneficiaries of draft deferments, college students, and occasionally those from the high schools, formed the core of almost all the mass actions from the SDS sponsored march on Washington in 1965 to the second counter-inaugural in January 1973. The campuses from coast to coast served as the bases and main organizing centers of the movement. College students were able to play such a distinctive role for the first time in American history partly because of the immense expansion of higher education following World War II, when their numbers grew to over eight million by the early seventies.

Writer Susan Jacoby, who graduated from college in 1965, observed in retrospect:

> If my generation had not resisted the war so strongly, I am convinced that the killing in Vietnam—and the neglect of social needs at home—would still be going on.[3]

The movement did not proceed at an even rate but experienced ebbs and flows. Its pace was determined not by the will of the participants, but by the tempo of major political and military events. Activity slackened during national election periods and picked up momentum with each new turn in the military situation and important policy pronouncements in Washington.

The seasonal weather in Indochina—which dictated the timing of military offensives—happened to coincide with the college semesters in this country so that the major military moves in Indochina tended to come when colleges were in full session. Thus the largest mobilizations took place in the spring or in the fall of an off-election year.

The four greatest upsurges occurred around April 15, 1967; October 15–November 15, 1969; early May, 1970; and April 24, 1971. The organizers of the antiwar movement had to take this uneven rhythm of the mass movement into account and were liable to commit bad mistakes if their judgments were wrong, as they sometimes were.

Not a few well-intentioned people kept declaring from 1965 on that the movement was ephemeral and had passed its peak. Susan Jacoby, for instance, testifies:

> Between 1965 and 1967, I had a number of quarrels with friends who

3. *New York Times Magazine,* April 10, 1977.

had become involved in antiwar activities. The Vietnam War, I argued, was a temporary phenomenon; the antiwar movement was diverting energies from the fight for social change in the United States; it was an elitist movement of rich white kids whose parents were able to buy them student deferments.[4]

Such observations did not grasp the necessary designs of the men in power or mistook the inevitable fluctuations in visible mass activity for a general decline in the movement as a whole.

There could be no doubt about the genuine grass-roots character of the movement. The FBI and the CIA were never able to produce a shred of evidence about foreign subsidies or manipulation, for the simple reason that there weren't any. The movement was based on the indignation of millions of Americans against the unjust, immoral, undeclared war and appealed to their sense of justice and decency. It had no official patronage. It had to be built from scratch and was maintained, somewhat haphazardly, by volunteers working for nothing or for bare subsistence. It was skimpily financed by contributions, large and small, from sympathizers and collections at rallies.

The coalitions often teetered on the edge of bankruptcy, warding off bill collectors from day to day. Hundreds and probably thousands of individuals made substantial loans without collateral, knowing they might never be repaid, and often accepted partial or no repayment with good grace for the sake of the cause.

The authorities tried to choke off financial aid by intimidating donors. One recorded example of the undaunted spirit of these supporters was that of Oliver Butterworth, an English professor at Hartford College of Women in Connecticut, who had sent a contribution to NPAC before the April 24, 1971, demonstration in Washington. He was investigated and harassed by agents of the House Committee on Internal Security who subpoenaed his bank records and demanded an explanation from him about the gift. He wrote in his answer:

Since your committee has evidently been recently interested in peace organizations, perhaps you would be good enough to send me the names of peace organizations that you feel are currently the most effective. I feel that such organizations deserve wide public support, because the pro-

4. Ibid.

tracted and unpopular war in Southeast Asia is the single most destructive element in the United States at present.[5]

Whereas the corporations raked in billions in direct profits from military appropriations, no one got anything but poorer out of participating in the opposition. Tens of thousands of activists made heavy sacrifices of time, money, and energy to keep it going. Perhaps it's just as well, for there was no room for careerism or privilege to get a foothold in a movement of this kind.

\*        \*        \*

The task of combatting the Vietnam War was a challenge that tested every tendency competing for a following among the youth. The principal ones can be characterized as follows:

The most sizable, though largely unstructured, amorphous, and erratic layer was made up of student radicals who considered themselves new left and were loosely organized for a time around SDS. On hand from the first were the pacifists, especially the radical pacifists influenced by A. J. Muste. Though no anarchist group existed in the formal sense, an essentially anarchist tendency played a significant role. There were certain religious organizations, among them the American Friends Service Committee and some other Quaker groups.

Then there were the representatives of the three main ideological currents in the international labor and socialist movements: the Moscow-oriented Stalinists around the Communist Party; the Trotskyists in the Socialist Workers Party and the Young Socialist Alliance; and the Social Democrats of the Second International.

Bringing up the rear was an array of tiny sectarian bands, assorted ultralefts, and Maoists, each with its own shibboleths.

SDS was instrumental in launching the mass antiwar drive in early 1965 and calling attention of student activists to the criminal character of the war. It promoted the antidraft and anti-ROTC campaigns in 1966 and helped expose university complicity with the government. But at no time did its shifting corps of leaders grasp the central importance of the antiwar struggle in

5. Letter from Oliver Butterworth to Robert H. Horner, House Committee on Internal Security, August 21, 1971. (Copy in author's files.)

American and world politics. After April 1965 they abstained from organizing and directing it, though they had a wide-open opportunity to do so. Lacking their own leadership, SDS members had to follow the lead that came from others. SDS figures such as Clark Kissinger, Rennie Davis, Carl Davidson, and at times Tom Hayden did play meaningful roles. But SDS as such did not work out or apply any consistent line in the antiwar movement. Except for a few individual stars, SDS did not affect the further development of the antiwar protests after its fragmentation in 1969.

Most of the Social Democrats were shackled to the war policy through their submission to the AFL-CIO bureaucracy, their Democratic Party perspective, and fierce anticommunist ideology. Their conduct has been aptly described by Julius Jacobson, editor of *New Politics*.

[Max] Shachtman, [Bayard] Rustin and their particular followers emerged as hawks on Vietnam in the right of center wing of the Democratic Party. Michael Harrington and Irving Howe and their followers (now organized in the Democratic Socialist Organizing Committee) did not move as far to the right as their recent colleagues turned hawks. But it was far enough to alienate the young anti-war activists, especially when Harrington and Howe made it clear that they were merely *critics* of the "tragic" (their favorite adjective) war, *not real opponents* of an imperialist adventure. They fought bitterly against those who advocated the unilateral withdrawal of American troops from Vietnam which only meant that they favored—"tragically" and shamefacedly—American divisions remaining in Vietnam until Hanoi met Harrington's and Howe's conditions for peace. (In Harrington's book, "Socialism," written when the Vietnam war was at its bloodiest and the anti-war movement at its peak, there is not even a single paragraph in all 400 pages devoted to the war. . . .)[6]

Only a small third segment of Social Democrats, represented in the East by Dave McReynolds and in the West by Charles Curtiss, participated in the organized antiwar movement.

The CP was pulled rather reluctantly into the midst of the antiwar coalitions, which did not conform to the pattern of its traditional manipulated "fronts." It just didn't have the muscle to

6. Julius Jacobson, "Neo-Stalinism: The Achilles Heel of the Peace Movement and the American Left," *New Politics,* vol. XI, no. 3, Summer 1976, emphasis in original.

impose a policy of exclusion against the Trotskyists, Maoists, or anyone else. Its line of conduct was at bottom determined by its ideological centerpiece that all struggles must be subordinated to the diplomacy of the Kremlin vis-à-vis Washington, which at this juncture meant the quest for what came to be called "détente." The CP therefore constantly had its eye on the liberal sector of the U.S. Establishment, and on the elections. (All for naught, as it turned out, for when the ruling class decided the time was opportune, it was Nixon who initiated "détente.") The CP acted as one of the more moderate and restraining factors in the operations of the coalitions.

The CP's participation was important for other reasons and even necessary for the success of some actions. The CP itself was not very large throughout the Vietnam War period, but it had enjoyed hegemony on the left in the United States before 1956 and for years had been ten and sometimes twenty time the size of all the other radical groups combined. It therefore still retained a far larger radius of influence than any other organized component of the movement.

This periphery was made up of ex-members still sympathetic to some degree, social circles of retired members and their children, contacts within the labor and other movements who had worked with the CP on one activity or another in past years, and so on. If the CP wholeheartedly supported an antiwar protest, these people, many of them experienced and influential, could be more readily mobilized to build it. If all of them got behind some project, their weight was multiplied.

On the other hand, if the CP opposed or abstained from an action, though such individuals would not always follow suit, they would have doubts and hesitations that would render it less effective. That is why an important part of the art of building successful actions was encouraging and pressing the CP to participate fully.

A. J. Muste, the respected mentor of the antiwar movement, was a Gandhian pacifist who favored and promoted mass action, thanks in part to his long experience in labor organizing and strike struggles. This veteran, however, died at an early stage and thereafter the pattern for the orientation of the pacifist wing tended to be set by David Dellinger. He was not only a pacifist but an avowed and consistent anarchist. Dellinger insisted that mass action be subordinated to individual resistance and confrontation tactics which were unsuited to the building of the largest possible actions.

The most systematic exponents of the divergent lines of mass action and small-group confrontation were the SWP on the one hand and Dellinger on the other. Dellinger's long record as a war resister, his selflessness, consistency, and hard work gave him prominence in the movement, even though he had no apparatus or organization backing him. His anarchist approach and methods, rather than his pacifism, harmonized with the libertarian moods and impatient impulses of a large stratum of the newly radicalized youth, who—though they did not espouse any particular ideology—were, at least for the time being, anarchistically inclined.

While this same phenomenon was a feature of the youth radicalization around the world, it arose under very special conditions inside the United States. The antiwar movement had to be constituted here after a prolonged period of reaction in a politically backward country without deep-rooted Marxist traditions or any mass socialist, communist, or labor parties. It could not count on support from the conservatized union movement, except for maverick officials and some sympathy from the ranks that grew over time.

Its first legions were recruited from the politically inexperienced student population that remained its backbone throughout. Since many were primed for the most aggressive action, they eagerly embraced the tactic of small-group sallies advocated by Dellinger. Such impatient and reckless militancy was inescapable and certainly had to find room within the totality of the movement. Moreover, it was beneficial for Dellinger and his fellow radical pacifists to win youth in this mood to their nonviolent tactics, which gave a moral weight to their small confrontations and greatly reduced the level of victimization. The harm came from his attempts to subordinate mass mobilizations to these peripheral activities and his insistent efforts to impose such methods on the movement as a whole.

The incorrectness of such an approach had to be patiently explained time and again in order to keep the movement oriented toward the broadest masses and their most decisive sectors, the GIs and the working class. Heated debates went on continually in the leading circles and caucuses between the proponents of these lines. The issues at stake were crucial if the movement was not to be derailed into a blind alley, and they sometimes led to splits.

Dellinger disparaged mobilizations for "immediate withdrawal" as united fronts on the "lowest common denominator." But getting the U.S. out of Vietnam was the antiwar movement's central purpose and the very reason for its existence.

The people around the Communist Party within the coalitions played second fiddle to Dellinger's orchestration in these encounters. As Dellinger saw it:

the Communists, perhaps because they had learned something from the debacle of earlier efforts, more likely because they were too weak and political insecure to stand against a vigorous New Left, did not offer serious resistance to the Mobe's rejection of the lowest common denominator as a guiding principle.[7]

Though the CP disfavored confrontationist tactics, it usually found it expedient to make a bloc with Dellinger against the SWPers, and more seldom and episodically the other way around.

In the long run more and more people caught on to the deficiencies and political dangers of anarchistic confrontationist tactics; the methods of mass mobilization championed by the SWP and others proved effective throughout.

\*        \*        \*

In 1965 and earlier it was not at all evident that Vietnam would bulk so large in American life and become the overriding issue in its politics. The SWP did not foresee this, but it did not commit the mistake of underrating the war's importance. It considered that as a revolutionary socialist organization it had an internationalist obligation to do all it could to combat its own government's attempt to crush a colonial revolution. It was this Leninist guideline that put the SWP on the right track from the beginning. Moreover, in accordance with its orthodox Marxist class-struggle approach the SWP was oriented from the beginning toward winning sympathy for the antiwar movement among workers and GIs.

The SWP was no newcomer. Among its older cadres were individuals who had been in the Socialist Party of Debs's time

7. Dave Dellinger, *More Power Than We Know: The People's Movement Toward Democracy* (Garden City, New York: Anchor/Doubleday, 1975), p. 119.

and in the Industrial Workers of the World and who had been
founders and leaders of the Communist Party until their expulsion for their anti-Stalinist ideas in 1928. SWP members had
experience in opposing the three previous major imperialist wars,
in countless labor struggles, and in party organization. Its
younger cadres were educated in these traditions and in the
revolutionary principles developed and practiced by Marx, En-
gels, Lenin, and Trotsky.

All this was contemptuously dismissed as so much useless
baggage by the new left leaders. However, they could not sweep
aside the antiwar cadres of the SWP and YSA.

While the CP's leadership was made up, with very few exceptions, of people radicalized in the 1930s, the SWP was predominantly led by people of the 1960s generation, who were better
attuned to the new developments and knew how to benefit from
the lessons of the past. I belonged to the "silent generation" in
between, which was sparsely represented in the organized left.

Many on the left attributed the SWP's and YSA's influence
entirely to the organizing abilities, discipline, and hard work of
its members. Such observers failed to notice or understand that
their effectiveness depended at bottom on their Marxist ideas and
working class methods, which were speedily learned, even by
fresh student recruits, from party literature, from more experienced leaders, and from direct practice.

The SWP upheld the autonomy of the antiwar movement as a
mass force. It consistently emphasized the necessity for mass
mobilizations as counterposed to the futility of getting sucked
into two-party politics or embarking on isolating forays by bands
of daring and well-intentioned individuals. This was essentially a
class-struggle approach based on direct action by the masses
against the regime.

The absence of more extensive labor participation did give
greater scope to the projects of the anarchistically inclined, the
ultralefts, and other petty-bourgeois radicals. In face of this it
was a considerable accomplishment that the firm stand of the
SWP and others did prevent the antiwar movement—which was
amorphous in belief and multiclass in composition and
direction—from either being submerged in bourgeois electoral
machinations or setting up barriers to the participation of
ordinary Americans eager to register their opposition to the war.

The SWP was sharply criticized for insisting that the coalitions
center their activities around the single issue of ending the U.S.

presence in Vietnam, formulated most succinctly in "Out Now."
It held fast to this position because that aim was imperative and
important enough *in and of itself* to warrant the utmost concentration upon its fulfillment.

The movement was a united front of a special type, not between
mass organizations of the working class for a concrete set of
demands, but between diverse and multiclass elements whose
sole bond of unity was to oppose the war. It had to confine itself
to implementing actions around that central purpose in order to
hold together. It could not have become a political party, as some
wished, that could develop a program or set about to solve the
fundamental problems of American society, not to mention
bidding for state power. All that was beyond its capacities
because of its class composition and heterogeneous character.
The components of the movement, let alone the average American, were not ready to take unified action on a host of other
questions, no matter how important. Despite repeated attempts
along that line, only the specifically antiwar protests involved
masses of that size.

On only two brief occasions—October 15, 1969, and early May
1970—did the mobilizations attain the level of active participation by several millions, close to a mass force capable of vying for
power. However, those millions were not reaching out for state
power—the vast majority of them still considered themselves
Democrats or Republicans. They were protesting the war.

A social and political revolution in the United States will
necessarily involve a deepgoing break with the two-party system.
It will no less require the active participation on a sustained basis
of tens upon tens of millions of working people, not just challenging one or another government policy but democratically deter-
mining policies in mass organizations of their own while changing the basic structure of society.

No mass socialist movement emerged from the antiwar activity. A number of disappointed people blamed the SWP for this.
(Some at the same time voting for the Democrats.) They expected
too much from the actual state of the movement on the one hand
and underrated its accomplishments on the other. Once the war
in Vietnam was over, the organized movement against it ceased
to exist. This was inevitable.

Numerous unaffiliated radicals made the mistake of treating
the antiwar movement as an embryonic revolutionary party or
trying to convert it into a leftist political formation according to

their specifications. To whatever extent they succeded with any formation, it simply ceased to be an effective antiwar mobilizer. The SWP had no incentive to act that way. It was itself a revolutionary socialist organization with a well-defined program and a serious tradition. It maintained the same kind of relations with the antiwar movement as with any other mass organization with whose particular aims it agreed. That was to have its members and sympathizers loyally build it into the most effective possible instrument to promote its goals. The SWP did not at any time hold organizational hegemony within the movement. It relied on the power of persuasion, seeking to convince others of the correctness of its proposals as these were tested in real life.

Nor was the SWP itself always right. Sometimes we changed our positions in the course of debate or through the necessity for compromise. Quite often, others had better ideas on matters of procedure, cultural style, and publicity. The most revolutionary group can sometimes develop conservative habits and lag in adjusting quickly enough to changing circumstances. By its very nature it cannot be foremost in experimenting with new personal life styles. However, the SWP didn't set itself up as a censor within the movement of these expressions of the counterculture, whether or not it shared them. While it sought to be flexible, it stubbornly refused any compromise on vital issues such as keeping the antiwar movement independent of the capitalist power structure.

The SWP along with others used democratic procedures to full advantage and championed them.

All groupings were encouraged to present their views at antiwar conferences, set up literature tables, distribute their circulars, hold workshops, and have speakers at rallies. The SWP defended everyone's right to get a hearing for their ideas. It did not fear but welcomed the give and take of debate and the clash of ideas. The movement thereby became a great school in which minds were opened and expanded and lasting lessons were learned. The models on such matters as mass mobilizations, nonexclusion, and democratic decision-making provided valuable precedents for the future.

The bitterest foes of the SWP and YSA had to acknowledge that they played a central role in the life of the antiwar movement. Julius Jacobson, an acerbic critic of the Trotskyists, stated: "The one [socialist] organization strengthened by the anti-war movement was the Socialist Workers Party."[8] This is an exaggeration since almost all radical groups except SDS emerged from the antiwar years stronger than they entered them. However, there is no doubt that the SWP gained the most. Its prestige was enhanced, it recruited some of the best militants, and improved its position in comparison with its rivals on the American left. It emerged with a cadre that had absorbed valuable practical lessons not easily learned from books.

Whatever else its work accomplished, the SWP proved that even a small revolutionary party can transmit the experience of past struggles and thereby play an essential role in guiding a seething social and political struggle to victory. That is, after all, the reason for its existence.

\*          \*          \*

It is too early to assess the full consequences of this experience. It is nonetheless clear that the antiwar agitation and mass mobilizations spurred the radicalization of many sectors of the population. "It is no accident," wrote Susan Jacoby for one, "that so many female veterans of the civil-rights movement and the antiwar movement ultimately became involved in the women's liberation movement."[9]

It changed the political face of the United States and motivated a healthy distrust of the rulers in Washington that bore fruit in the Watergate revelations and their sequels.

It broke the fever of the anticommunist hysteria and weakened the efficacy of the "red scares" that have been used as a weapon against any challenge to the status quo.

It challenged and changed the stereotyped image of GIs as obedient pawns of the brass immunized against dissenting currents within the civilian population.

The abhorrence of any further military ventures abroad has restricted the options available to Washington in its imperial designs, as its dilemma over Angola in 1976 indicated.

The American movement against the Vietnam War broke the pattern of large and successful movements for social reform in the United States confining themselves to domestic matters and

8. *New Politics,* Summer 1976.
9. *New York Times Magazine,* April 10, 1977.

accepting uncritically the imperialist foreign policy, aggressive wars, and counterrevolutionary ventures of the American Establishment.

All this cannot but be reflected in future struggles for social progress within the United States and internationally. It is even possible that the antiwar movement will prove to have been in a number of aspects a rehearsal for the coming American socialist revolution.

In any case, the veterans of the antiwar movement have every reason to be proud of their record, part of which is set down in this book. We accomplished what we had set out to do. Our protests did win over public opinion and exert enough pressure— along with that of the Vietnamese—to bring the U.S. forces home. That done, the Vietnamese were finally able to take over their own country.

The American movement against the Vietnam War knocked a gaping hole in the theory that because of its control over the military, the police, the economy, and the tremendously effective modern media, the ruling class could get away with anything so long as there was some degree of prosperity. The antiwar movement started with nothing but leaflets. But it proved that people can think for themselves if the issue touches them deeply enough, technology notwithstanding. In human affairs there is still nothing so powerful as an idea and a movement whose time has come.

# Acknowledgments

This work would not have been possible without the kind cooperation of many people, a number of whom provided documents, source material, and suggestions though they knew the author's interpretations would not necessarily agree with their own in every respect. The author would like to thank the following for assistance of various kinds:

Marc Bedner, Jon Britton, Ken Davey, Leslie Evans, Steve Fuchs, Virginia Garza, Bonnie Gordon, Jerry Gordon, Asher Harer, Patti Iiyama, C. Clark Kissinger, Judy Lansky, Walter Lippmann of SEIU Local 660, Bradford Lyttle, Eleanor McKay and the staff of the State Historical Society of Wisconsin, Pat Quinn, Dave McReynolds, Darlene Moore, George Novack, James Peck, Angie Remedi, Alice Snipper, and Barbara West.

# Abbreviations

AFSC—American Friends Service Committee (Quakers)
ARVN—Army of the Republic of Vietnam (Saigon)
CAPAC—Cleveland Area Peace Action Council
CDC—California Democratic Council
CEWVs—Committees to End the War in Vietnam
CNVA—Committee for Nonviolent Action
Co-Aim—Coalition for an Anti-Imperialist Movement
CORE—Congress of Racial Equality
CP—Communist Party
FOR—Fellowship of Reconciliation
GI-CAP—GI-Civilian Alliance for Peace
GICLDC—GI Civil Liberties Defense Committee
ISC—Independent Socialist Club
LID—League for Industrial Democracy
MPI—Movement for Puerto Rican Independence
M-2-M—May Second Movement
NBAWADU—National Black Antiwar Antidraft Union
NCAWRR—National Coalition Against War, Racism and Repression
NCC—National Coordinating Committee to End the War in Vietnam
New Mobe—New Mobilization Committee to End the War in Vietnam
NLF—National Liberation Front (South Vietnam)
NPAC—National Peace Action Coalition
NVA—North Vietnamese army
PCPJ—People's Coalition for Peace and Justice
PL—Progressive Labor Party
PRG—People's Revolutionary Government (political arm of the South Vietnamese National Liberation Front)
SANE—Committee for a SANE Nuclear Policy

SCLC--Southern Christian Leadership Conference
SDS—Students for a Democratic Society
SL—Spartacist League
SMC—Student Mobilization Committee to End the War in Vietnam
SNCC—Student Nonviolent Coordinating Committee
SP-SDF—Socialist Party-Social Democratic Federation
SWP—Socialist Workers Party
VDC—Vietnam Day Committee
VVAW—Vietnam Veterans Against the War
WILPF—Women's International League for Peace and Freedom
WIN—Workshop in Nonviolence
WRL—War Resisters League
WSP—Women Strike for Peace
YAWF—Youth Against War and Fascism
YPSL—Young People's Socialist League
YSA—Young Socialist Alliance

FRED HALSTEAD was born in Los Angeles in 1927. His mother, an immigrant Jewish garment worker, was a Debs socialist, and his father, of Irish extraction, was a machinist, a member of the Industrial Workers of the World, one of the early American Trotskyists, and a leader of the unemployed movement in Southern California in the early 1930s.

Halstead joined the navy when he was eighteen and was assigned to a ship in the Seventh Fleet in China waters. He participated in the "Going Home Movement" of U.S. GIs at the end of World War II. He planned to be a schoolteacher, and attended UCLA for two years, working as a merchant seaman between semesters. He joined the Socialist Workers Party in 1948, and shortly after was denied clearance as a seaman because the SWP had been placed on the Attorney General's "subversive list," promulgated by President Truman as part of the cold-war witch-hunt. The same list made it virtually impossible to be a schoolteacher, so he went to work in the garment industry at the cutter's trade. He was an active trade unionist and participated in strikes and organizing drives of the National Farm Labor Union, the United Auto Workers, and the International Ladies Garment Workers Union.

In 1953 he moved to Detroit, where he worked in auto plants, cutting upholstery. He also began writing articles for the *Militant*, a socialist weekly newspaper. In early 1956, he visited Montgomery, Alabama, to report on the bus boycott by the Black community there. Back in Detroit, he organized a station-wagon-for-Montgomery committee to help the boycotters. Later in 1956 he went to New York as a staff writer for the *Militant*. For the next nine years he wrote for the *Militant*, supporting himself as a cutter in New York's garment district.

When the movement against the Vietnam War began to grow rapidly in 1965, Halstead represented the SWP in antiwar coalition meetings and was part of the original staff of the Fifth Avenue Vietnam Peace Parade Committee in New York. In 1968 he was the Socialist Workers Party candidate for president of the U.S., and visited Japan, South Vietnam, and Germany to talk to American GIs.

He was on the steering committees of the National Coordinating Committee to End the War in Vietnam, the National Mobilization Committee to End the War in Vietnam, the New Mobilization Committee, and the National Peace Action Coalition. He currently lives in Los Angeles.

# Index